HOW MUCH DO YOU KNOW ABOUT
KEEPING YOUR DOG OR CAT HEALTHY?

Can the same aspirin that can safely relieve a dog's arthritis pain be fatal to a cat?

What conditions may respond better to alternative therapies than to standard prescription medications?

What common over-the-counter medications can be hazardous or fatal to your pet?

What common household products are poisonous to your cat or dog?

How do certain drugs interact with other drugs or with your pet's normal diet?

How can you get rid of fleas and ticks completely, safely, and forever?

What are the best and safest ways to keep your dog or cat free of worms?

The answer to these and all your questions are inside the single most important guide to your pet's health money can buy.

**THE PILL BOOK GUIDE
TO MEDICATION FOR YOUR
DOG AND CAT**

THE
PILL BOOK
GUIDE TO MEDICATION FOR YOUR DOG AND CAT

Production
CMD PUBLISHING
A DIVISION OF
CURRENT MEDICAL DIRECTIONS

KATE A.W. ROBY, V.M.D.
LENNY SOUTHAM, D.V.M.

BANTAM BOOKS
NEW YORK • TORONTO • LONDON • SYDNEY • AUCKLAND

THE PILL BOOK GUIDE TO MEDICATION
FOR YOUR DOG AND CAT
A Bantam Book

PUBLISHING HISTORY
A Bantam Book/October 1998

ISBN 0-553-57989-4

Published simultaneously in the United States and Canada

Bantam Books are published by Bantam Books, a division of Bantam
Doubleday Dell Publishing Group, Inc. Its trademark, consisting of the words
"Bantam Books" and the portrayal of a rooster, is Registered in U.S. Patent
and Trademark Office and in other countries. Marca Registrada. Bantam
Books, 1540 Broadway, New York, New York 10036.

PRINTED IN THE UNITED STATES OF AMERICA

OPM   10 9 8 7 6 5

Contents

About the Authors

Dr. Kate Roby received her veterinary degree from the University of Pennsylvania School of Veterinary Medicine. Her postdoctural training included residencies in large animal medicine and clinical laboratory medicine at the University of Pennsylvania School of Veterinary Medicine and a fellowship in nephrology and metabolism at the Children's Hospital of Philadelphia. After many years of nephrology research at the Hospital of the University of Pennsylvania and many publications, Dr. Roby entered private small animal practice. At present, she combines work in small animal practice with a career as a medical writer.

Dr. Lenny Southam completed an internship in small animal medicine and surgery at the University of Pennsylvania School of Veterinary Medicine, following graduation from the University of Mexico School of Veterinary Medicine. Following her internship, she was a research veterinarian at the Fox Chase Cancer Center in Philadelphia and an adjunct associate professor in the Department of Medicine at the University of Pennsylvania School of Veterinary Medicine and held a fellowship for postdoctoral studies in pathology at the University of Delaware. At present, she has a housecall practice in Pennsylvania where she cares for dogs, cats, horses and a variety of other companion animals. Dr. Southam has published a number of scientific papers as well as articles for pet owners and runs the Vet Care Forum on CompuServe.

Preface

As owners of dogs and cats, you need to know about the medications prescribed for your pets, and your veterinarian should be the primary source of this information. As practicing veterinarians and pet owners, we know that it is often difficult to absorb all the information provided in the short time available during a visit. As veterinarians, we are often faced with trying to explain complex diagnoses and treatments in a relatively short time and under stressful circumstances. We know it is hard to concentrate on what is being said when your pet is sick and some questions may not occur to you until later. The purpose of *The Pill Book Guide to Medication for Your Dog and Cat* is to provide you with a source of easy to understand information about the medications that may be prescribed for your dog or cat. It allows you to look up the information at your leisure without the pressure of trying to take it all in during a hectic veterinary visit. By helping you to learn more about the medications for your dog and cat, we hope that you, your veterinarian, and, most of all, your pets will benefit.

Kate A.W. Roby, V.M.D.
Lenny Southam, D.V.M.

Acknowledgments

Much of the information in this book may be found in the following reference texts. The authors would like to thank all those who contributed to these references as well as to the many other sources we consulted, including journals, books, seminars, and Internet sites.

Adams HR (editor): *Veterinary Pharmacology and Therapeutics.* Seventh Edition. Iowa State University Press, Ames, Iowa, 1995

Birchard SJ, Sherding RG (editors): *Saunders Manual of Small Animal Practice.* WB Saunders, Philadelphia, 1994

Bonagura JD (editor): *Kirk's Current Veterinary Therapy.* Volume XII (and also previous volumes IX, X, and XI)—*Small Animal Practice.* WB Saunders, Philadelphia, 1995

Hardman JG, Limbard LE (editors-in-chief): *Goodman and Gilman's The Pharmacologic Basis of Therapeutics.* Ninth Edition. McGraw-Hill, New York, 1996.

Physicians Desk Reference (PDR). 52nd Edition. Medical Economics, Montvale, New Jersey, 1998

Plumb DC: *Veterinary Drug Handbook.* Second Edition. Iowa State University Press, Ames, Iowa, 1995

Plunkett SJ: *Emergency Procedures for the Small Animal Veterinarian.* WB Saunders, Philadelphia, 1993

Veterinary Pharmaceuticals and Biologicals (VPB). Veterinary Medicine Publishing Group, Lenexa, Kansas, 1997

How to Use This Book

How to Find Your Medication in *The Pill Book Guide to Medication for Your Dog and Cat*

- *The Pill Book Guide to Medication for Your Dog and Cat* lists most medications in alphabetic order by generic name—the common or chemical name—because a medication may have many brand names but only 1 generic name. Most generic medications produce the same therapeutic effects as their brand-name equivalents but are usually less expensive. Drugs that are available generically are indicated by the [G] symbol. The [V] symbol is used to indicate a product marketed and approved for use in animals; the [H] symbol is used to indicate a product marketed and approved for use in people. Many products for people are prescribed by veterinarians for use in animals, and the appropriate uses of these products are described in the individual drug profiles (see *Why There Are So Few FDA Approved Drugs for Dogs and Cats*).

- When a medication has 2 or more active ingredients, it is listed by the most widely known brand name. In a few cases, drugs are listed by type (e.g., Penicillin Antibiotics).

- All brand and generic names are listed in the Index. Brand names are indicated by boldface.

Each medication profile in this book contains the following information:

Generic and Brand Name: The generic name is the common or chemical name of the drug. It is listed along with the current brand names available. In some profiles the heading "Most Common Brand Names" is used, to indicate that other brand names—prescribed less frequently for dogs and cats—are also available in addition to the ones listed; consult your veterinarian in regard to these additional brand names.

Type of Drug: Describes the general pharmacologic class of each drug or how it works in the body: "immunostimulant," "antispasmodic," "smooth muscle stimulant," and so on.

Prescribed for: Lists the conditions for which veterinarians may prescribe the medication.

General Information: Information on how the drug works, how long it takes for it to be effective, or how this drug is similar to or different from other drugs.

Cautions and Warnings: This information alerts you to potential hazards and conditions or diseases in which the drug should be avoided or used with caution. This section includes information on whether the drug is approved by the Food and Drug Administration (FDA) and if not, what is considered acceptable use by the veterinary profession. Also included are Environmental Protection Agency (EPA) warnings. In some profiles this section is divided into separate cautions for owners/handlers and for animals when there are unique warnings regarding human contact with the product. Note that *all* products listed in this book must be kept in a secure container out of sight and out of the reach of children.

Possible Side Effects: Side effects are generally divided into 2 categories—those that are common and rare—to help you better understand what side effects to expect from your pet's medications.

Drug Interactions: Describes what may happen if your pet's medication is given with other drugs and lists what medications should not be given at the same time. Some interactions may be serious. Be sure to inform your veterinarian of any medication your pet is already taking. You may want to keep your own medication records for your pet and discuss it with your veterinarian whenever a new medication is added.

Food Interactions: Provides information on whether to give the medication with meals and other important facts.

Usual Dose: Tells you the largest and smallest doses usually prescribed, what forms the medication is available in, and whether there are any special storage requirements. All medications should be stored in sealed, light-resistant containers to maintain maximum potency, but some products have special storage requirements in regard to refrigeration, humidity, and so on. Most prescription and over-the-counter (OTC) products are sold in more than one strength. Consult your veterinarian regarding the appropriate strength to use for your animal.

Overdosage: Describes signs of overdose, how much of a drug must be given to cause signs of overdose (margin of safety), and what to do if you suspect your dog or cat may have received an overdose.

Special Information: May include information on the condition the drug is prescribed for, alternative treatments, special considerations when using the product, and any special instructions.

Special Populations: Medications are sometimes not suitable for specific breeds, pregnant or lactating pets, puppies and kittens, and/or senior animals. This section includes information on whether medications are suitable to use in these special populations and when they are not.

Safe Use of Medications

The purpose of this book is to provide educational information to the public concerning the most common prescription and over-the-counter medications used by veterinarians to treat dogs and cats. It is not intended to be complete or exhaustive or in any respect a substitute for veterinary care. Only a veterinarian may prescribe these drugs and their exact doses. **NONE of the medications described in this book should be used without first consulting a veterinarian.**

Dose regimens are provided for information only, *not as* guidelines for your use. You should not give any medication to your dog or cat without exact instructions from your veterinarian. This includes medications given orally, topically, by injection, by transdermal patch, or by any other route of administration.

In An Emergency

- In case of accidental ingestion or overdose, contact your veterinarian or the National Animal Poison Control Center (see *Resources for Pet Owners*).
- Keep your veterinarian's and other emergency phone numbers posted near your telephone. When you call for emergency assistance, be prepared to explain

    What substance was consumed and how much.

    Status of the animal (for example, conscious, sleeping, vomiting, or having convulsions).

    The approximate age and weight of the animal.

    Any chronic medical problems your animal has if you know them.

    What medications, if any, your animal is regularly given.

- Do not make the animal vomit unless you have been instructed to do so.

Other Points to Remember for Safe Drug Use

- Store the medicines for your pets in sealed, light-resistant containers to maintain maximum potency. Be sure to follow any special storage instructions listed on the container such as "refrigerate," "do not freeze," or "keep in a cool place." Protect all medicines from excessive humidity.

- Follow the label instructions exactly. If you have any questions, contact your veterinarian.
- If you should miss giving a dose of medication, contact your veterinarian for instructions.
- Let your veterinarian know immediately if you think your pet may be having a reaction to any medication, and keep a record for yourself as well.
- Make sure your veterinarian knows about all medications your pet may be taking, whether over-the-counter or prescription, and keep a record for yourself as well.
- Never keep medicine where children can see it or reach it. Consult your physician immediately if there is ingestion of or exposure to any medication prescribed for your dog or cat.
- Do not use medication prescribed for one pet on any other pet. What is effective and safe for one pet may be harmful or deadly to another.
- Be sure the label stays on the container until the medicine is used or destroyed.
- If you move to another area or change veterinarians for any reason, request that your pet's medical records be copied and sent to your new veterinarian.
- Do not hesitate to discuss the cost of veterinary medical care with your veterinarian. Exercise your right to make decisions about purchasing medicines. Some medications may be less expensive if filled by prescription in a pharmacy than if provided by your veterinarian. Large pharmacy chains can often have lower prices because they purchase large quantities. Do not hesitate to ask your veterinarian or pharmacist about drug costs.

Why There Are So Few FDA Approved Drugs for Dogs and Cats

In order for a medication to be Food and Drug Administration (FDA) approved for use in a particular species of animal, it must undergo testing in that species. That testing must prove efficacy—in other words, that the drug works and for each specific disease at a specific dose. It must also be shown to be safe at the recommended dose. This kind of testing is extremely expensive. The companion animal market may not be large enough for the drug companies to get a cost-effective return on this kind of testing.

As a result, most of the drugs that veterinarians prescribe are used in ways that are not specifically FDA approved in dogs or cats, and the drugs have not been studied in large well-controlled clinical trials. The information for the majority of drugs used in dogs and cats is extrapolated from studies in people or other animals or from very small and/or informal studies in dogs and cats.

Throughout this book you will see in the "Cautions and Warnings" sections of prescription medication profiles, the sentence:

- U.S. federal law restricts the use of this drug by or on the lawful written or oral order of a licensed veterinarian within the context of a valid veterinarian-client-patient relationship.

Or, for nonprescription drugs:

- Use of this drug should be by or on the lawful written or oral order of a licensed veterinarian within the context of a valid veterinarian-client-patient relationship.

Or, for nonprescription insecticides:

- For veterinary use only.

The veterinarian-client-patient relationship is defined by the FDA as the following:

1. The veterinarian has assumed the responsibility for making clinical judgments regarding the health of the animal

and the need for medical treatment, and the client has agreed to follow the veterinarian's instructions.

2. The veterinarian has sufficient knowledge of the animal to initiate at least a general or preliminary diagnosis of the condition of the animal. This means that the veterinarian has recently seen and is personally acquainted with the keeping and care of the animal by virtue of an examination of the animal or by medically appropriate and timely visits to the premises where the animal is kept.

3. The veterinarian is readily available for follow-up evaluation in the event of adverse reactions or failure of the treatment regimen.

These regulations were designed to protect your pet and allow your veterinarian to provide the best possible care for your pet, despite the fact that there are so few FDA approved drugs for dogs and cats. Human drugs that are not FDA approved for use in animals should only be used in the context of a valid veterinarian-client-patient relationship. Conditions of such a relationship include careful medical diagnosis and ongoing evaluation of the patient, current knowledge of the drug and its use in animals, as well as thorough education of the client as to the potential risks and benefits for the patient. These are the veterinarian's responsibilities. Your responsibilities include following your veterinarian's instructions, understanding the possible side effects, and reporting any suspected reactions or lack of response to the drug to your veterinarian immediately. The purpose of this book is to help you understand more about the medications you may be giving to your pet and thereby aid veterinarians in their role as client educators.

How to Choose a Veterinarian

There are many different kinds of veterinary practices and many different styles of practicing veterinary medicine. You not only want the best medical care for your pet, you should also find a practice that suits your interests and the kind of care you want for your pet.

Most veterinarians are general practitioners. Some work on all animals, but many restrict their practice to one or a few species, for example, dogs and cats or just cats. Because of the many medical advances in recent decades, veterinary medicine is moving in the direction of specialization. There are veterinary specialists in cardiology, dermatology, internal medicine, orthopedic surgery, general surgery, ophthalmology, behavior medicine, and other areas. Your veterinarian will refer you to a specialist when your pet needs extra expertise and equipment. In the past, specialists were usually available only at veterinary teaching hospitals. Now there are specialists available in private practice in many parts of the country. Some veterinarians have special training in alternative medicine techniques such as acupuncture, herbal medicine, and chiropractic.

There are still many small practices and solo practitioners who offer outstanding service and personal care. However, there are increasing numbers of large veterinary hospitals, with many veterinarians (including veterinary specialists) and veterinary technicians or nurses on staff. They have sophisticated equipment and often offer 24-hour emergency service. There are also veterinarians who have house-call practices or mobile veterinary hospitals.

With such a variety of services to choose from, the question then becomes, what kind of practice or veterinary service do you want and need?

- If you want a close professional relationship with one veterinarian, a large group practice may not suit your needs, as you will probably see different veterinarians, especially in emergencies.
- Larger practices may offer more services, but they also may be prone to longer waiting room times, as they tend to be very busy.

- Hospital practice hours vary, and you should consider whether the hours the hospital is open will suit your work schedule.
- Some practices encourage children to come along and may even provide play areas.
- If you have a disability, problems with transportation, or for convenience would just prefer having your pet seen at home whenever possible, you should look for a house-call veterinarian or mobile practice.
- Most veterinarians practice conventional medicine. If you are interested in alternative medicine (see *Alternative Medicine* and *Resources for Pet Owners*), you should look for a veterinarian with expertise in these areas.

The yellow pages of your telephone book is a great resource, and most practices list the services they offer, the hours they are open, and other pertinent information. There may be fairly significant differences in what different practices charge, largely due to differences in their own costs of practice. If cost is a major concern, you should call and ask for prices. Be aware that the charges that most price shoppers call to ask for (spay/neuter/vaccinations) are usually fairly standard in any area and may not give you a good gauge of charges overall. In addition, one practice may quote a higher price for a service but include all related items whereas another might quote a lower price but have add-ons that result in a higher price.

Perhaps most important of all is the personality and practice style of the veterinarian you are considering. It is critically important for you to have a good working relationship with your veterinarian. No matter how smart or competent the veterinarian may be, if you cannot work together, it will not help you or your pet. The veterinarian your neighbor raves about may not be a good fit for you. Knowing this, it is still a good idea to talk to pet owners, neighbors, and friends to get an idea of what the veterinarians and the practices in your area are like. Call the ones that you think may suit you and make an appointment to go visit the practice. Ask questions about the services they offer including how they handle emergencies and their normal business hours. Observe and talk with the office and technical staff. They are generally the first people you talk to when you call with questions and are responsible for most of the in-hospital nursing care. Ask about house calls or other services that may be important to you. You should be comfortable with the responses you receive, and if you are not, continue your search. Veterinarians generally know the special interests of other practices in the area and most are happy to refer you to someone who provides those services.

Home Physical Exam

You spend the most time with your pet and know it best. You know what is normal behavior and what is not. With a little extra effort, you can learn to examine your pet in a systematic way. This may help pick up problems early when they are more easily treated. It also lets you provide your veterinarian with information to help determine when something is an emergency, when it can wait for regular office hours, or perhaps be treated at home.

It is important to use all your senses. Look, listen, touch, and smell. Do not forget the most important sense—common sense.

Notice any changes in the way your pet eats and drinks, urinates and defecates, stands, or moves. Listen to the breathing, the heart, and the gurgle of the intestines. You do not need a stethoscope to do this, but if you want to hear better, you can buy an inexpensive stethoscope. Pet your dog or cat all over. You will be able to pick up lumps and bumps, changes in the skin and hair coat, and places that hurt.

Pay attention to anything that smells differently and try to figure out the source of any bad smells. Common sources include the mouth, the folds in the lips, ears, skin, and anal area.

Examination—The Vital Signs

The most important values to help your veterinarian evaluate your pet over the telephone are temperature, pulse, respiration, color of the gums, and capillary refill time (CRT). Practice getting these when your pet is healthy. That way you will be ready in an emergency when you need to be calm and you will know what is normal for comparison.

Take the temperature with a rectal thermometer for humans. You can buy one in any pharmacy. Lubricate the tip with petroleum jelly, a water-soluble lubricant, or water and gently insert it in the rectum. It should go in ½ to 1 inch. If it does not go in immediately, continue to push gently, but do not try to force it. Many pets do not like this procedure at first and you may need help. Most pets will learn to let you take their temperature if you take your time and stay calm. If your pet gets too agitated, it may make sense to skip the temperature and let the veterinarian get it. It is not worth hurting your pet or risk having someone bitten. A warm nose is not a reliable indication of a fever.

The respiratory rate can be measured by counting the breaths either by watching the nostrils or the chest move or by feeling air blow out of the nostrils. Count the number of breaths in 15 seconds, then multiply by 4 to get breaths per minute. If your pet is panting, there is no need to count, just report it as panting. Also notice if the breathing is labored or if your pet had his head stretched forward and elbows rotated away from the body to make breathing easier.

The pulse or heart rate can be measured by feeling the heartbeat with your hand or listening to the heart with a stethoscope over the left side of the chest behind the elbow. If you are listening to the heart, each beat will have two parts that sound like lub-dub. The pulse may also be felt on the inside of a back leg. Put your hand around the upper part of the leg with your thumb on the outside and your fingers on the inside. Slide your fingers toward the back until they fall into the groove in the middle of the inner thigh. Press gently but firmly and you should be able to feel the pulse. Count the number in 15 seconds and multiply by 4 to get the rate per minute. It takes practice, so practice before there is a problem and do not give up.

The color of the gums or mucous membranes in the mouth and CRT give an estimate of how well the heart and lungs are working and if enough oxygen is getting to the cells where it is needed. The gums should be pink except in some breeds such as chows and in animals with dark pigmentation. CRT is determined by pressing on the gums above or behind an upper canine tooth with your finger. Press for a few seconds and then remove your finger. There should be a pale fingerprint for an instant after you remove your finger. The normal pink color should returns within 2 seconds.

Normal Vital Signs for Dogs and Cats

	Dogs	Cats
Temperature (°F)	101.0–102.5	101.0–102.5
Pulse (heartbeats/minute)	80–120	160–180
Respiration (breaths/minute)	20–40	20–40

Call your veterinarian if the temperature is over 103°F. Body temperatures lower than normal are often due to the thermometer not being inserted correctly. They may also be lower

12 to 24 hours before whelping and in the presence of some health problems such as overexposure to cold, shock, and advanced kidney failure.

Pulse rate normally increases with excitement and exercise. It also increases if there is a fever and in some types of heart disease. Decreased pulse rate may occur when your pet is asleep, in some types of heart disease, and with some electrolyte imbalances.

The respiratory rate normally increases when the ambient temperature and humidity are high. Panting is very fast breathing and is a way for dogs and cats to lose excess body heat. Nervous or excited animals may pant even when they are not too hot. The respiratory rate is also elevated if a pet has a fever, in some types of electrolyte imbalances, and if not enough oxygen is being carried to the body. The respiratory rate is decreased in very cold or comatose animals.

Gums become redder with excitement, exercise, certain poisons, or fever. Anemic animals with low levels of red blood cells may have pale or white gums. Animals that do not have enough oxygen due to heart disease or shock may have a bluish tinge to the gums. Yellow gums indicate jaundice and may be a sign of liver disease or anemia due to rapid destruction of red blood cells.

If the CRT is more than 2 seconds, it may indicate a problem with blood circulating to the small blood capillaries. This is a sign of dehydration, shock, and severe heart failure.

Emergency Situations Requiring Immediate Veterinary Care

1. Severe trauma.
2. Heat exhaustion or stroke.
3. Frostbite and exposure to cold.
4. Electric shock.
5. Hemorrhage from the nose, mouth, ears, rectum, urine, or from trauma.
6. Very painful eyes with squinting, dilated, or constricted pupils; pupils of uneven size; conjunctivitis; or protruding eyeball.
7. Frequent vomiting, and/or diarrhea with or without blood.
8. Retching or unproductive vomiting particularly if the stomach area looks bloated.
9. Respiratory distress.
10. Collapse or coma.   (List continues.)

11. Paralysis or severe neck or back pain.
12. Clusters of seizures within a 24-hour period or a seizure that does not stop after a few minutes.
13. Difficulty in delivering or prolonged labor.
14. Suspected poisonings, insect bite reactions, snake bites, scorpion stings, spider bites, toad poisoning (see *Common Household Poisons*).
15. Extreme lethargy.
16. Prolapse of the rectum or uterus.
17. Any other condition that you think might be an emergency.

Medicating and Grooming Tips and Tricks

- *Administering pills to dogs.* The tried and true method of wrapping the pill in some cheese, liverwurst, peanut butter, bread, or other treat is easy and you get credit for giving the treat. If the easy way does not work, stand or squat by your pet's side with the pill in the hand closest to the animal's nose. Put the other hand on the head with the middle finger and thumb positioned just behind the large upper canine teeth. Tilt the head back and nose up by rotating your hand. The mouth opens automatically when the head is tilted back. Use the hand with the pill to help open the mouth and put the pill as far back on the base of the tongue as possible. Remember to take your hand out of the mouth before letting the head tilt forward and the mouth close. You can use the eraser end of a pencil to help push a pill further back. Alternatively, there are pilling syringes available commercially that help get the pill far back in the mouth.

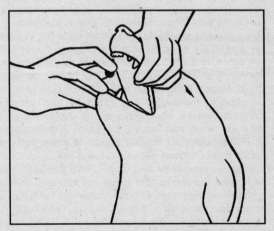

- *Administering pills to cats.* It is often easier to administer pills to cats if you kneel on the floor with the cat between your legs and the head facing out. Cats feel secure in this position and it often makes working with them easier. The same method described for dogs may be used.

- *Administering liquids to cats and dogs.* Use a plastic dropper. Never use glass. Most medications come with droppers or ask your veterinarian for a small plastic syringe without the needle. You can wash and reuse them, since oral medications do not need to be sterile. Fill the dropper with the correct amount of medicine, insert it in the space behind the long upper canine tooth, and squirt in the medication. Hold your pet's mouth closed and keep the head tilted slightly backward for a few seconds until the pet swallows.

- *Administering injections to dogs and cats.* Insulin is the injection pet owners are most likely to give. Use insulin syringes because they have very sharp, thin needles and the animal usually does not mind the injection. Give the injection under the loose skin behind the neck and move the spot around with each shot. Make sure you shake the bottle gently before drawing up insulin so that the drug is evenly distributed in the liquid. Sometimes your veterinarian may teach you to give fluids to your pet. This is most commonly done with cats that have chronic kidney disease. Make sure your veterinarian shows you how and try it while the veterinarian is there to give suggestions.

- *Cleaning and medicating the ear.* Pull the flap upward gently and fill the ear canal with the cleaning solution. Do not be stingy. Rub the base of the ear to help loosen wax and debris, then step back and let the dog or cat shake its head. Repeat until the ear looks clean. Finish with a drying solution or medication suggested by your veterinarian. Vinegar contains about 2.5% acetic acid and is an excellent ear wash that leaves the canal slightly acidic. The acidic environment inhibits growth of many bacteria and yeast that commonly cause ear infections.

- *Using eye ointments and drops.* Have someone help you until your pet learns that it will not hurt and stands still. Hold the eyelids open with the thumb and forefinger of one hand and try to tilt the head slightly. Then apply 1 to 2 drops of liquid with the dropper or a $\frac{1}{4}$ to $\frac{1}{2}$ inch length of ointment. Rest your hand on the animal's head to help steady the tube or bottle and keep ointment tubes parallel to the head to prevent the eye from being poked if the dog or cat moves suddenly.

- *Clipping dog's nails.* Teach your dog to let you hold his paws and play with the nails when he is young. Start clipping off just the tips of the nails. Try not to make it into a fight. Be firm but gentle. Start with the back feet. Most dogs do not mind the back nails clipped as much as the front. This gets the easy part done before your dog gets upset. Use a file. Have a coagulant or quick stop powder to stop bleeding if it occurs. If you clip a little at a time bleeding is less likely because you can tell when you get near the quick. Do not sneak up on your pet when it is asleep.
- *Clipping cat's nails.* Cats nails are formed in layers like onionskin. The cat removes the outer layers by clawing, thus keeping the nails sharp. They are easily clipped using a fingernail clipper for humans. Only take off the points.
- *Stopping bleeding.* Bleeding from a cut should be controlled with direct pressure. Use a thick wad of gauze squares or clean folded cloth or towels. Place it over the cut and maintain pressure with your hand. You may secure bandages on the legs by wrapping them with an elastic bandage or tape. If you use elastic, make sure you do not put it on too tightly. If the wound bleeds through the bandage, put more padding on top. Do not remove the bandage that is already in place.

xxvi   MEDICATING AND GROOMING TIPS AND TRICKS

Home Remedies that Are Safe

Always ask your veterinarian before using over-the-counter (OTC) remedies for your pets. The dose for pets is not necessarily the same as for people and the dose for cats is not the same as for dogs. Many OTC products are not safe and even those that are must be dosed very carefully.

- Cold packs help reduce the inflammation of sprains and other injuries. Ice cubes wrapped in a wet towel work well as do commercially available reusable gel packs.
- Hot packs help infections and abscesses to drain. Towels soaked in hot water and wrung out work well. Make sure the water is not so hot that it may burn the animal.
- Providone-iodine (see *Iodine/Iodide*) surgical scrub and solution or other skin disinfectants are available in pharmacies and may be used to clean superficial skin wounds.
- Antibiotic and antiseptic ointments may be used on superficial skin lesions (see *NeoSporin*).

There are a number of OTC drugs for humans that may be used in dogs and cats. They should NEVER be used without first consulting with your veterinarian and asking about appropriate doses.

- Benadryl (see *Diphenhydramine*) or Chlor-Trimeton (see *Chlorpheniramine*) are useful for allergic reactions and insect stings.
- Pepto-Bismol and Immodium (see *Bismuth Subsalicylate* and *Loperamide*) may be used for a short time to help control diarrhea in dogs.
- Aspirin (see *Aspirin/Acetylsalicylic Acid*) may be used in dogs for pain and inflammation. It may also be used in cats, but the dose must be calculated carefully. Do not use in cats without first talking to your veterinarian.
- Hydrogen peroxide or table salt may be used to induce vomiting (see *Hydrogen Peroxide*).
- Charcoal helps absorb ingested toxins (see *Activated Charcoal*).
- Cough syrup (see *Dextromethophan*) helps control coughing in pets. Pediatric preparations without narcotics should be chosen.
- Mineral oil or petrolatum (see *Lubricant Laxative*) may be used to treat and prevent hairballs in cats and constipation in both dogs and cats.

Preventive Health Care

Prevention is the key to health for your pet just as it is for you. There are many facets to preventive health care, including the day to day care and feeding you provide and regular visits with your veterinarian. The general concepts of health care apply to all animals, but specific measures depend on the species, sex, age, and breed of your pet, what work your pet may do, and the geographic area where you live.

An important part of preventive care is the regularly scheduled visit with your veterinarian. The physical examination may detect health problems while they are still easily treated. The visit gives the veterinarian an opportunity to discuss new health care methods and share ideas and tips with you. It also gives you a chance to discuss your questions and concerns or ask about treatments and products you have heard about from friends or in the press. Routine visits are the best time to administer vaccinations and perform or schedule routine diagnostic testing and treatments.

Vaccines are available to prevent several serious and potentially fatal infectious diseases. Vaccines stimulate the immune system to produce antibodies that target specific viruses, bacteria, or other infectious agents. Most vaccines are injected either into a muscle or under the skin. A few are administered into the nose to stimulate local immunity at the site the infections enter the body. Most vaccines need to be repeated at regular intervals of 2 to 4 weeks when they are first administered to puppies or kittens to assure that the immune system will recognize the infection and respond rapidly if necessary. Your pet is not fully protected until the series is complete, although some protection starts within 7 to 10 days of the first vaccination. Regular boosters after the initial series also help maintain a high level of immunity. The interval may vary depending on the disease, the level of exposure, general health, age, or other variables. Stress, illness, and administration of corticosteroids may decrease the immune response and are reasons to postpone routine vaccination. Some vaccines provide close to 100% protection, but others are not as effective. It is important to avoid exposing your pet to sick animals even after it is vaccinated.

The most common diseases dogs are vaccinated against are canine distemper, canine hepatitis, leptospirosis, parainfluenza, and parvovirus. These vaccines are generally combined into a single injection identified by the first letter of each disease (DHLPP). A vaccine against human measles is sometimes used in young puppies. Measles virus is similar to canine distemper and cross-protects puppies that may still have antibodies from their mother that prevent the distemper vaccine from working. Vaccination against *Bordetella bronchiseptica* (kennel cough) is often recommended for dogs exposed to groups of other dogs, for example in boarding kennels, at training classes, or at dog shows and competitions. It is available as a systemic vaccine or in intranasal form. A vaccine to reduce the risk of Lyme disease is also available and may be useful in areas where this disease is prevalent.

The most common diseases that cats are vaccinated against are panleukopenia (feline distemper) and two respiratory infections caused by the rhinotracheitis herpes virus and calici virus. These are generally combined and referred to as FVRCP (feline viral rhinopneumonitis, calici, panleukopenia). Chlamydia is another organism that causes respiratory disease in cats and is sometimes included in the combination vaccine. The vaccine against feline leukemia virus (FeLV) is often recommended, particularly for cats that go outdoors or are exposed to other cats that may harbor the infection. An intranasal vaccine against a disease called feline infectious peritonitis (FIP) has become available recently. FIP is caused by a complex immune reaction to a viral infection and generally requires exposure very early in life. It is not very common except in catteries and other situations where large numbers of cats are housed together. The usefulness of the vaccine remains controversial.

Rabies is the only vaccine that is given to both dogs and cats. Rabies is a uniformly fatal disease in all mammals, including dogs, cats, and humans, and occurs in every state in the U.S. except Hawaii. The incidence of rabies in humans and pets decreased rapidly after rabies vaccine became available and required by law in many states. The natural reservoir is in wild mammals, and widespread vaccination of pets provides a buffer between the disease in wildlife and humans. Currently, most cases occur in wild animals, but a number of unvaccinated pets die every year and expose their owners or other people. Few people die, but many more undergo postexposure vaccination.

Although vaccines prevent many serious diseases and save the lives of countless pets every year, there are also some risks associated with them. Allergic reactions are rare but may be serious. Listlessness, collapse, diarrhea, vomiting, and swelling or itching of the face within the first day of vaccination should be reported to your veterinarian immediately. There is some evidence that immune-mediated diseases may be more common in the weeks immediately after routine vaccination and may be related to vaccination. Lumps frequently occur at the vaccination site and generally disappear within a month. Lumps that get bigger should be checked. Abscesses are a rare complication and should be drained. Some vaccines, particularly those for rabies and FeLV in cats, are associated with fibrosarcoma, a very aggressive tumor.

Parasite control is another important aspect of preventive health care. Intestinal parasites and heartworm are the most common internal parasites, but lung flukes and kidney worms are occasionally seen. The most common intestinal parasites are roundworm, hookworm, whipworm, and tapeworm. Some may be seen in the stool, but most are too small and must be diagnosed by looking at a sample under the microscope. Routine fecal analysis is a good way to diagnose intestinal worms before they produce clinical signs.

Heartworm is a large parasite that lives in the chambers of the heart. It is most common in dogs but may also infect cats. The signs depend on the number of worms and include respiratory distress and heart failure. A simple diagnostic blood test is used to detect infection. The disease may be treated, but is also easily prevented by either daily (see *Diethylcarbamazine* and *Filaribits Plus*) or monthly medication (see *Ivermectin* and *Milbemycin*). The preventive is often combined with medication for intestinal parasites, offering fairly complete internal parasite control.

The most common external parasite is the flea, and it is responsible for severe allergic skin diseases, hair loss, and tapeworm infection in dogs and cats. There are many flea control products, including the very safe and effective once-a-month products introduced recently (see *Fipronil, Imidacloprid,* and *Lufenuron*). Ticks are common in some areas and transmit a number of diseases, including Lyme disease, Rocky Mountain spotted fever, and tick paralysis. Avoiding areas where ticks are likely, removing ticks, and using insecticides are the major methods of tick control. Fipronil is a very effective preventive when used monthly. Mites are small external parasites related to ticks and are the cause of mange. Intense itching and hair loss are the most common signs. Mange is diagnosed by looking for mites in skin scraping samples using a microscope. Mange may be treated by a number of systemic and topical products.

Gum disease and tartar accumulations are increasingly recognized as causes of chronic discomfort and disease in dogs and cats. They lead to loss of teeth, root abscesses, and may be factors in heart and kidney disease. Routine cleaning by the veterinarian will help prevent these problems, but home care is required, particularly in dogs and cats with severe periodontal disease. Tooth brushes, toothpaste, antiseptic gels, and liquids are available for home care.

Nutrition is also an important aspect of good health. High-quality commercial diets are available for dogs and cats, and nutritional deficiencies are rarely seen except in pets fed unbalanced homemade or fad diets. Overnutrition and obesity are a much greater problem. They are associated with a number of diseases, including hip dysplasia and other developmental bone diseases in dogs, diabetes, and hepatic lipidosis (fatty liver) in cats. Obesity may be prevented by feeding controlled portions or by using diets with lower fat and calorie levels. Specialized diets are available for both dogs and cats to help control some chronic diseases such as heart disease, kidney disease, diabetes, food allergies, and bladder stones.

Diagnostic testing is an important aspect of health care. The FeLV test is used to determine if a cat is infected with FeLV before vaccination or in sick cats to determine if the virus may be the cause. Feline immunodeficiency virus (FIV) is a related virus and the diagnostic test is often combined with that for FeLV. The combination test is used to detect infection on newly acquired cats, particularly in multicat households, as well as to diagnose disease. There is a blood test commonly called the FIP test, but it is not considered very useful. It detects possible exposure to any of a large group of viruses, most of which do not cause disease. It does not indicate if a cat is actually infected. Other tests may be indicated for senior pets or animals intended for breeding and specific types of work. These range from testing for hip dysplasia or congenital eye disease to serum chemistry for early detection of systemic disease, electrocardiograms, and ultrasound.

Although preventive care will not stop your pet from getting sick, it will reduce the risk of many diseases and increase the overall level of health and expected life span. Work with your veterinarian to determine what health care measures are best for your pet.

Alternative Medicine

Alternative medicine is a name used to describe all health care that is not traditional Western medicine. It includes traditional Chinese or Eastern medicine (acupuncture and herbal medicine), naturopathy, osteopathy, chiropractic, reflexology, massage therapy, herbology, and homeopathy.

Holistic medicine is an approach to health care that may involve a variety of techniques (Western and alternative) but focuses on the whole organism, rather than just a diseased part. Holistic health care is a system of comprehensive or total patient care that considers the physical, emotional, social, economic, and spiritual needs of the person (or animal). In veterinary medicine, it also considers the human-animal bond, and the owner must also be considered when formulating a treatment plan. There are growing numbers of health care providers and lay people who are realizing that a holistic approach should be the goal of health care. Many are also realizing that alternative therapies may have a great deal to offer patients, not to the exclusion of Western medicine but as an adjunct.

The following is a brief description of some of the alternative therapies that may be helpful for some veterinary patients. Included are some of the conditions where alternative therapies may be an important adjunct to traditional therapies as well as warnings about potential adverse effects of some of the alternative therapies. None of the alternative therapies should be used as a substitute for appropriate diagnostics and safe, proven conventional therapies, and alternative therapies should be chosen over conventional therapies only when the benefits clearly outweigh the risks. One often forgotten risk is that of omission, or risking a pet's health or life by not using an effective traditional treatment.

Pet owners should be very cautious about having nonveterinarians work on their pets using alternative therapies. Your practitioner should be trained in animal diseases, anatomy, and physiology. Ideally, you should find a veterinarian who is also trained in alternative medicine techniques. This will safeguard you and provide the best possible care for your pet.

Traditional Chinese Medicine

Traditional Chinese medicine is a system of health care that is many thousands of years old and has included treatment of animals as well as people for much of that time. It is a system that is very different from Western medicine and is very difficult for Westerners to understand. As it is practiced in China, it is a holistic approach to health care with a strong emphasis on preventive care. A Chinese doctor considers it a failure if a patient gets sick. Traditional Chinese medicine includes acupuncture and herbal medicine, almost always used together. It is based on a concept called "chi," which can be defined as energy or life force. Disease is considered an imbalance or a block of the normal flow of energy or "chi". The goal of therapy is to return the balance and flow of energy to normal, thereby restoring health, hopefully before overt disease occurs.

Acupuncture is the primary therapy used by veterinarians. It involves the placement of small needles into the skin at specific acupuncture points. Needles are usually left in place for 1 to 10 minutes, and treatments may be repeated 2 to 3 times a week initially, then decreased to once a week or every 2 weeks, or as needed. There is a veterinary certification course that teaches acupuncture techniques and traditional Chinese medicine. See *Resources for Pet Owners* for information on the International Veterinary Acupuncture Society. Acupuncture may be used to treat virtually any disease or condition. It is most commonly used in veterinary practice to relieve chronic pain and may be extremely successful in relieving the pain of chronic arthritis. It has few if any side effects and is well tolerated by animals. Acupuncture is growing in acceptance and is also being used for many other problems besides chronic pain.

Naturopathy

Naturopathy is a system of therapy based on natural foods, light, warmth, massage, fresh air, regular exercise, and the avoidance of medications. Advocates believe that illness can be healed by the natural processes of the body. No one can argue that the body and mind have incredible healing powers or that living a healthy life style is the goal for all of us and our pets, however, if your dog or cat is hit by a car or eats rat poison, do not rely on naturopathy exclusively, and seek conventional medicine for the things it does best.

Osteopathy

Osteopathy is a branch of medicine that uses all of the conventional forms of therapy and diagnosis, but that places a greater emphasis on the influence of the relationship between the organs and the musculoskeletal system. Osteopathic physicians recognize and correct structural problems using manipulation. The process is important in both the diagnosis and the treatment of health problems. Osteopathy is not a well-established branch of veterinary medicine. Contact the Veterinary Institute for Therapeutic Alternatives or the American Holistic Veterinary Medical Association (see *Resources for Pet Owners*) for the latest information on veterinary osteopathy.

Chiropractic

Chiropractic is the manipulation of the spine primarily, but also of limb joints, to correct malalignment (or subluxation) of joints. According to theories of chiropractic, even fairly minor malalignments may cause pressure on surrounding nerves and connective tissue, resulting in pain, irritation, and chronic inflammatory changes. For example, proponents of chiropractic believe that in hip dysplasia, correction of the malalignment by manipulation, especially in young animals, and keeping it properly aligned may result in less hip pain and chronic arthritis than in unadjusted littermates. Chiropractic is most likely to be helpful in animals with problems in the neck (cervical spine), lower back (lumbar spine), and hips/pelvis. Problems with the knee joints may also respond to adjustment of the hips. Animals seem to tolerate chiropractic adjustment well. Some animals will respond dramatically to treatment; others may not respond at all. There are rare but very serious adverse effects (such as brain stem stroke and paralysis) in people and horses who have had chiropractic adjustment, especially of the neck. It is not known if these side effects occur in dogs and cats, but it is a very real possibility. There is an American Veterinary Chiropractic Association and a certification course. See *Resources for Pet Owners* for more information.

Reflexology and Massage Therapy

Reflexology is a system of treating certain disorders by massaging the soles of the feet, using principles similar to those of acupuncture. Massage therapy is the rhythmic movement of muscles to stimulate the flow of blood and lymph, increase relaxation of muscle fibers in spasm, relieve pain, and promote healing. Neither of these therapies is well established in veterinary medicine. Massage therapy has the potential to help animals as much as it does people. It may be especially helpful after surgery or trauma, in animals that have overexerted themselves, and in animals with muscle knots caused by underlying arthritis and chronic minor muscle damage. Reflexology may have the same potential to help animals as does acupuncture, although this has not been proven. Reflexology may not be quite as effective in dogs and cats as it is in people, due to differences in foot structure.

Herbology

Herbs are plants used for medicinal purposes or for their odors or flavors. Herbal medicine is a very ancient tradition in most cultures. Traditional Chinese medicine relies heavily on the use of herbs to promote health and treat illness. Many of the drugs used today in conventional medicine are derived from plants. Quinine and digitalis are two of many examples. Herbalists use naturally occurring chemicals from plants to treat disease. Many of these plant-derived chemicals are biologically active and as potentially toxic as any drugs, whether they are given as herbs or in a purified pill. There are many reports of human poisonings after ingestion of herbs, and herbal remedies should be used as cautiously as any drug—there is essentially no difference. Herbal remedies have not been tested for efficacy or safety in animals. Their production process is not in any way regulated for potency, purity, toxins, or contaminants. You should be aware that herbs may cause drug interactions when used with conventional medicines. They should be used in animals with all the caution that you would use when giving a drug, and perhaps more, because herbs are not regulated as drugs are. Make sure that you find a veterinarian skilled and knowledgeable in herbal medicine and its uses in dogs and cats.

Homeopathy

Homeopathy is a system of medicine in which it is believed that cures are produced by giving minute doses of a chemical, usually derived from plants. This chemical is chosen for the disease, because a large dose of the chemical given to a normal person causes the same signs and symptoms as occur in the disease. Because of the minute doses of chemical in homeopathic remedies, it is highly unlikely that they would cause adverse effects. There are many proponents of homeopathy, and homeopathic remedies have been used by veterinarians to treat dogs and cats for many years. It may well be worth trying homeopathic remedies, especially in those animals where conventional medicine has failed. Relying on homeopathic remedies exclusively, or using them instead of safe and effective conventional treatments, is probably not in the best interest of your pet.

First Aid Guide

Emergencies may be all too common in some veterinary practices. Hopefully your pet will not be one of those involved, but this guide may help you with practical first aid tips for some of the more common emergencies.

The most important step is to get your animal to a veterinary emergency clinic or veterinary hospital as quickly as possible. **Make sure you have the phone number near your phone.** That way you will not need to look for it when you most need it. Also make sure that the pet sitter or boarding kennel knows who to call in an emergency and knows how to reach you. There are several things you can do to safeguard yourself and help your pet before you get to the hospital.

Take a First Aid Course
Courses in first aid for pets are offered in some areas, and courses for people are offered in many places by the Red Cross or other certifying group. Much of what you learn in a course for people is easily adapted to animals.

Severe Trauma
The most common cause of severe trauma in dogs and cats is when an animal is hit by a car. If the dog is conscious, it is likely to be in shock or going into shock and in severe pain. Make sure you muzzle any dog before you try to move it, even if it is your own dog, and you are sure it will not bite you. Any dog may bite when disoriented and in enough pain. Use a necktie or any piece of rope, string, tape, or fabric to temporarily tie around the dog's muzzle while you move it off the road and into a vehicle. Try to use a board or any piece of rigid material for a stretcher, especially for larger dogs. If there is nothing available, use a blanket or clothing to place under the dog and use as a stretcher or sling. Keep the animal as quiet and still as possible, and use clothing or whatever is available to keep the animal as warm as possible during transport.

Bleeding
Severe trauma may cause bleeding externally or internally. Internal bleeding can only be dealt with in a veterinary hospital. External bleeding may be life-threatening, and immediate

placement of pressure bandages to stop or slow the bleeding may save the animal's life during transport to the hospital. Tourniquets are likely to cause more harm than good and are not recommended. Pressure bandages are safer, and they simply require the placement of some soft material such as clothing or towels in a large mass over the area that is bleeding. If possible have someone hold the bandage in place and apply pressure manually. Do not change the bandage if it becomes soaked; apply more material on top. If there is no one to hold the pressure bandage, it may be tied in place with strips of fabric or whatever is available.

Fractured Limbs

Placing a splint on an obviously fractured limb is not a good idea in most cases. It is important to have lots of padding between the splint and the leg or it may cause more damage. A thick bandage with many layers of roll cotton or thick fabric wraps and an outer tight bandage (Robert-Jones bandage) is a good way to stabilize a fractured limb, but it should not be attempted without training.

Coma

If an animal is unconscious, try to get it to veterinary care immediately. If the animal is not breathing, open the mouth wide and check to see if there is anything obstructing the airway (larynx). Try to dislodge or remove anything you see caught in the throat, and immediately transport your animal to veterinary care. If an unconscious animal is vomiting, try to keep the head down to allow the vomit to flow out of the throat and prevent it from being aspirated into the lungs. If necessary, sweep the back of the throat with your fingers to clear the airway.

Seizures

Seizures that last for more than 15 to 20 minutes require immediate veterinary care. The danger for the animal in prolonged seizures (status epilepticus) is hyperthermia, or high body temperature, with subsequent damage to the brain and other tissues. Try to keep the animal cool with water applied to the trunk and limbs and cool air-flow during transport to the hospital.

Heat Stroke

Heat stroke is also a medical emergency requiring immediate

veterinary care (see *Dimethyl Sulfoxide (DMSO)*). Cooling the dog as soon as it is discovered and during transport is a vital first aid measure. Hose the dog off with cool water immediately and keep the dog as cool as possible during transport.

Hypothermia and Frostbite

First aid for hypothermia or low body temperature and frostbite should include moving the animal into a warm room. Cover the animal with warm blankets after you have placed warm water bottles around it. Electric heating pads may cause burns and should be avoided or used with extreme caution. Apply warm compresses to frostbitten areas or soak them in warm water. Do not rub the affected areas. Transport to a veterinary hospital as soon as possible and keep the animal as warm as possible during transport.

Prolapse of the Eye

Prolapse or protrusion of the eyeball out of the socket may occur with severe trauma or in breeds with protuberant eyes and shallow sockets with very little trauma. Try to keep the eye moist with eye wash or saline solution (1 tsp salt in a pint of water if no eye solutions are available), and keep the animal from damaging the eye further during transport to the hospital.

Prolapse of the Rectum or Uterus

Prolapse of the rectum or uterus may occur with prolonged or severe straining. Keep the prolapsed tissue moist with saline (1 tsp salt in a pint of water) or cover with a saline-moistened cloth to keep it clean if necessary, and prevent the animal from licking or damaging the prolapse during transport to the hospital.

Bloat

Bloat of the stomach is frequently accompanied by torsion or twisting of the stomach on its long axis. The main signs are swelling of the belly behind the ribs and retching or vomiting clear fluid frequently. It is a fairly common problem in large dogs. It is life-threatening, and it is extremely important to get emergency veterinary care immediately. There is no effective first aid.

Common Household Poisons

Acetaminophen (Tylenol)

Acetaminophen is a safe and effective pain reliever and fever reducer for people, but it causes serious toxic reactions in dogs and especially in cats (see *Acetylcysteine*). The toxic dose in dogs is 75 mg/lb; the toxic dose in cats is 25 mg/lb. One regular strength Tylenol tablet (325 mg) can easily kill a cat.

Signs of poisoning include depression, vomiting, dark red-brown urine, and death in 2 to 5 days. Cats may have swelling of their face and paws, decreased appetite, salivation, vomiting, depression, brown or purplish gums, and chocolate-colored urine, all within 1 to 2 hours of ingestion, and death in 18 to 36 hours.

The prognosis in cats is guarded to poor; the prognosis in dogs is not as bad, but both depend in part on the dose. Animals suspected of acetaminophen poisoning should be taken to a veterinary hospital immediately. Treatment may include induction of vomiting, charcoal, acetylcysteine, intravenous (IV) fluids, oxygen, and whole blood transfusion. Cats with acetaminophen poisoning should be handled with extreme caution as they may die from stress.

Mouse, Rat, and Snail/Slug Poisons

Warfarin/Brodifacoum/Diphacinone

Most of the mouse and rat poisons marketed today contain long-acting anticoagulants that cause uncontrolled bleeding and death. D-Con, Havoc, Talon, and many other brands contain first-, second- or third-generation warfarin compounds (see *Warfarin*). It is a serious problem when dogs or cats eat the poison, and if you suspect that your pet has eaten mouse or rat poison, you should take it to a veterinarian immediately.

The prognosis depends on the amount and type of poison eaten and how soon the problem is recognized. If it is recognized immediately and vomiting is induced promptly, the prognosis is fairly good. If several days have elapsed and the animal has signs of bleeding, the prognosis is guarded to poor. Signs of poisoning may include depression, weakness, pale gums, bloody stool, and bleeding from the nose, gums, wounds, and urinary tract. Bleeding into the lungs or body cavities is common. Treatment may include induction of vomiting if ingestion was recent and administration of charcoal and saline or sorbitol cathartic, vitamin K_1 (see *Vitamin K_1*), plasma or whole blood transfusions, IV fluids, oxygen, and corticosteroids.

Cholecalciferol/Vitamin D

The other common type of mouse and rat poison contains a form of vitamin D called cholecalciferol (see *Vitamin D/ Calcitriol*). Ortho Mouse-B-Gone, Rampage, Rat-B-Gone, and Quintox are a few brand names that contain cholecalciferol.

The prognosis is poor; ingestion of one packet, one exposure, is lethal. Cholecalciferol causes high blood calcium, kidney failure, and bleeding as a result of calcium deposits in blood vessels.

Treatment may include induction of vomiting if ingestion was recent and administration of charcoal and saline or sorbitol cathartic. If ingestion was not recent, IV fluids, oxygen, corticosteroids, calcitonin to lower blood calcium, and careful monitoring in an intensive care setting are required.

Metaldehyde

Metaldehyde is a poison used in snail, slug, and rat poison. Dogs and cats may be poisoned by eating the bait or by eating poisoned snails, slugs, or rats. Signs start within 1 to 4 hours of ingestion and include anxiety, unsteady gait, muscle tremors, high fever, slow breathing, coma, and death. The toxic dose in dogs is 50 to 500 mg/lb. The prognosis is fair to guarded and depends on the amount ingested and treatment delay. Treatment may include induction of vomiting, giving milk orally to decrease absorption of metaldehyde, and administration of charcoal, muscle relaxants such as methocarbamol and diazepam (see *Methocarbamol* and *Diazepam*), IV fluids, intubation, and oxygen.

Antihistamines and Decongestants

All of the common household antihistamines and decongestants such as diphenhydramine (Benadryl), pseudoephedrine, phenylpropanolamine, and chlorpheniramine may cause severe reactions from overdoses or accidental ingestion. Signs may include depression, breathing difficulty, excitement, muscle tremors, seizures, abnormal heart rhythms, vomiting, and fever. The prognosis is usually good with treatment. Treatment may include induction of vomiting if ingestion was recent and

administration of charcoal, IV fluids, oxygen, diazepam or phenobarbital to control seizures, and propranolol or atropine for
abnormal heart rhythms.

Arsenic

Arsenic may be found in ant and roach poisons, weed killers,
and wood preservatives. The prognosis is poor if treatment is
started when signs of poisoning are already present. Signs
usually start within 30 minutes to a few hours of ingestion and
may include vomiting, bloody vomit and diarrhea, weakness,
and unsteady gait and progress to dehydration, kidney failure,
shock, paralysis, coma, and death. Treatment may include
induction of vomiting if ingestion was recent, administration of
charcoal, dimercaprol, sodium thiosulfate, and penicillamine;
intensive care with IV fluids and blood transfusion; and treatment of kidney failure and liver damage.

Aspirin

Cats are much more susceptible to aspirin toxicity than dogs
(see *Aspirin/Acetylsalicylic Acid*). The toxic dose in dogs is 25
mg/lb/day. The toxic dose in cats is 12 mg/lb/day. Baby aspirin
contains 81 mg; regular aspirin contains 325 mg. Pepto-Bismol
contains 300 mg salicylate per regular strength tablet or 262
mg/tbs regular strength liquid. See *Aspirin/Acetylsalicylic Acid*
for signs of overdose. If treatment is started after the animal is
dehydrated, unconscious, or has bone marrow suppression or
liver damage, the prognosis is poor. Treatment may include
induction of vomiting if ingestion was recent, administration of
charcoal, saline cathartic, IV fluids, oxygen, and stomach pro-
tectants such as misoprostol and sucralfate (see *Misoprostol*
and *Sucralfate*), and dialysis for kidney failure.

Chocolate

Theobromine is the ingredient in chocolate that poisons dogs
and cats. Signs of poisoning occur with theobromine ingestion
of 50 mg/lb body weight. Milk chocolate contains 45 to 61
mg/ounce, and dark or unsweetened chocolate contains over
400 mg/ounce. If a 40-lb dog eats 5 ounces of dark chocolate,
it will become seriously ill. Caffeine is also toxic to dogs and
cats and the toxic dose is 70 mg/lb.

The prognosis is usually good if the animal is hospitalized
promptly and treated aggressively. Death may occur if a large

amount of chocolate is eaten and allowed to be absorbed. Signs may include vomiting, diarrhea, hyperactivity, restlessness, unsteady gait, muscle tremors, abnormal fast or slow heart rhythms, fever, seizures, coma, and death. There is no specific antidote for theobromine or caffeine poisoning in dogs and cats. If ingestion was recent, treatment includes induction of vomiting and administration of charcoal with a cathartic. Supportive care includes IV fluids to promote excretion of theobromine in the urine, urinary catheter to prevent reabsorption of theobromine out of the bladder, oxygen, diazepam or phenobarbital for sedation or to treat seizures (see *Diazepam* and *Phenobarbital*), and atropine or propranolol to treat abnormal heart rhythms (see *Atenolol*). Theobromine takes a long time to be eliminated and treatment may be required for up to 72 hours.

Cocaine

Dogs may become poisoned by eating the tissue of a cocaine user. Signs of poisoning may include salivation, hyperactivity, muscle tremors, depression, seizures, fever, vomiting, coma, and death. The prognosis is guarded and depends on the amount of cocaine ingested. If ingestion was recent, treatment includes induction of vomiting and administration of charcoal with a cathartic. Supportive care includes giving IV fluids, oxygen, and diazepam or phenobarbital for sedation or to treat seizures (see *Diazepam* and *Phenobarbital*), and propranolol to treat abnormal heart rhythms (see *Atenolol*).

Ethylene Glycol (Antifreeze) Toxicity

Ethylene glycol is found in antifreeze, solvents, rust removers, and film processing fluids. The main source of poisoning is from antifreeze. Dogs especially seem to like the taste of antifreeze and become extremely ill after ingestion. The toxic doses are quite small, 2 to 3 ml/lb in dogs and 0.75 ml/lb in cats. The prognosis is poor if the animal is showing any signs of illness. The prognosis is guarded if treatment begins within 1 to 2 hours of ingestion. Mild depression, unsteady gait, decreased appetite, vomiting, low temperature, excessive drinking and urination, seizures, coma, and death may occur 30 minutes to 12 hours after ingestion. Rapid breathing and high heart rate occur 12 to 24 hours after ingestion, and kidney failure with severe depression, vomiting, diarrhea, and decreased urine output occurs 24 to 72 hours after ingestion. If ingestion was recent, treatment includes induction of vomiting and administration of charcoal with a cathartic. Supportive care includes giving IV fluids, B vitamins, and ethanol or fomepizole to prevent metabolism of ethylene glycol to oxalate, and kidney dialysis.

Fleet Enema

Hypertonic sodium phosphate (Fleet) enemas may cause severe toxicity in dogs and especially cats. The toxic dose is 2 ounces in animals less than 25 lbs and 4 ounces in animals over 25 lbs. Signs occur 30 to 60 minutes after the enema was given and may include sleepiness, unsteady gait, rigid muscles, seizures, vomiting and bloody diarrhea, shock, and death. The prognosis is guarded and depends on the dose and the delay in treatment. Treatment includes giving IV fluids, calcium gluconate, potassium chloride, and possibly mannitol if there is brain edema (swelling).

Household Cleaners

Ingestion of detergents, bleaches, disinfectants (phenol and pine oil), window cleaners, and drain and toilet cleaners may all cause severe toxicity and even death. Topical exposures with some products may cause burns and then systemic signs or oral burns if the cleaners are licked off the skin. If your dog or cat ingests or comes in contact with any household cleaners, call your veterinarian immediately or the National Animal Poison Control Center (see *Resources for Pet Owners*).

Ibuprofen

Ibuprofen is a nonsteroidal anti-inflammatory drug (NSAID) with a very narrow margin of safety in dogs and cats. One regular Advil contains 200 mg ibuprofen, and 75 mg/lb causes severe vomiting and stomach ulcers in 1 to 4 hours; 150 mg/lb causes kidney failure in 1 to 3 days. The prognosis depends on the dose and duration of treatment but is usually guarded to poor. If ingestion was recent, treatment includes induction of vomiting and administration of charcoal. Supportive care includes giving IV fluids, sucralfate and misoprostol for stomach ulcers, and dialysis for kidney failure.

Rose Fertilizer (Iron)

The nitrogen, phosphorus, and potash ingredients of rose fertilizer can cause vomiting and diarrhea. The main problem with rose fertilizer is the iron. At a 5% iron concentration, 1 tsp is toxic to a 20-lb dog. Initial signs include vomiting and diarrhea. Kidney and liver failure occur within 12 to 24 hours. The prognosis varies depending on the amount ingested and the delay to treatment. If ingestion was recent, treatment includes induction of vomiting and administration of charcoal and milk of magnesia. The specific antidote for iron is deferoxamine with vitamin C (do not give vitamin C without deferoxamine or it will increase iron absorption). Supportive care includes IV fluids.

Lead Poisoning
Dogs may be poisoned with lead by chewing on or eating lead paint, linoleum, golf balls, batteries, drapery weights, newsprint, and a variety of other common household items. Signs may include decreased appetite, vomiting, diarrhea, seizures, abnormal behavior, unsteady gait, and blindness. The prognosis is generally good with treatment but not if there have been uncontrolled seizures. Treatment includes removal of lead from the gastrointestinal tract with emetics, cathartics, enemas, or surgery. Lead is removed from the body by treating with calcium EDTA, penicillamine, or dimercaprol. Diazepam, phenobarbital, mannitol, and dexamethasone are used to treat seizures. Animals may show signs of lead toxicity before humans do when they are sharing the same environment. You should contact your physician if you have a pet with lead poisoning, especially if you have small children.

Marijuana
Ingestion of marijuana may cause depression, low temperature, aggression, bizarre behavior, salivation, vomiting, muscle tremors, and disorientation. The prognosis is fair. If ingestion was recent, treatment includes induction of vomiting and administration of charcoal. Hospitalization with IV fluids and a quiet environment are recommended.

Organophosphates
Organophosphates are used as insecticides and dewormers. See *Organophosphate Insecticides* for signs of overdose. The prognosis is guarded to poor depending on the severity of signs. If ingestion was recent, treatment includes induction of vomiting and administration of charcoal. If the treatment was

topical, use soap and water baths to remove the material. Atropine, diphenhydramine, pralidoxime (NOT for carbamates), IV fluids, oxygen, and diazepam or phenobarbital for seizures are recommended treatments.

Kerosene, Gasoline
Kerosene may be absorbed through the skin or from the gastrointestinal tract. Signs of toxicity may include salivation, vomiting, diarrhea, unsteady gait, difficulty breathing, tremors, seizures, and coma. Do not induce vomiting. Wash with a mild detergent to remove from the skin. Heart and kidney damage and aspiration pneumonia are possible consequences. Hospitalization and supportive care are recommended.

Pyrethrins
Pyrethrins are used as insecticides. See *Pyrethrins* for signs of overdose. The prognosis is usually fair. Treatment includes bathing with mild detergent to remove topical products and giving charcoal and cathartics (for oral overdose), atropine, and supportive care.

Strychnine
The toxic dose of strychnine is 0.35 mg/lb in dogs and 1 mg/lb in cats. The signs of poisoning include seizures, extreme muscle rigidity, and severe reactions to noise. Stomach contents may contain milo or canary seed with a blue coating. The prognosis is usually poor. Only induce vomiting if the animal is still conscious and not having seizures. Treatment includes giving charcoal and cathartics and sedation or anesthesia to control seizures.

Tricyclic Antidepressants
Amitriptyline and the other tricyclic antidepressants (see *Amitriptyline, Fluoxetine,* and *Clomipramine*) may cause severe reactions if overdoses occur. Seizures, coma, and fatal abnormal heart rhythms are the main signs of overdose. The prognosis is variable and depends on the dose. If ingestion was recent, treatment includes induction of vomiting and charcoal with a cathartic (NOT magnesium sulfate). Heart function should be monitored closely for 5 days, and IV fluids with bicarbonate are recommended. Diazepam or anesthetics are used to control seizures.

Zinc

Zinc toxicity may occur after ingestion of pennies (made after 1983), zinc oxide skin cream, calamine lotion, fertilizer, paint, nails, and shampoos. Signs include decreased appetite, vomiting, diarrhea, depression, pale gums, and red or brown urine due to hemolytic anemia. The prognosis is variable. Treatment includes removing the source of the zinc from the gastrointestinal tract with emetics or surgery. Supportive treatments include giving IV fluids, blood transfusions, and calcium EDTA to remove the zinc in the blood.

Zoonotic Diseases
of Dogs and Cats

Diseases that may be transmitted between animals and humans are called zoonoses. Some specific viruses, bacteria, fungi, and internal or external parasites may cause zoonotic disease.

Dog and cat bites are not, strictly speaking, zoonoses; however, they are the principal mode of transmission for several diseases and frequently result in infection. The number of bites reported annually is staggering and many are not reported. They are a major public health concern. Most bites are due to dogs. Many bites may be avoided by educating people, particularly children, in how to behave around animals, by selecting appropriate species and breeds of animals to be kept as pets, and by proper handling and training of pets. Obedience training classes for dogs are offered in many places. They teach owners how to train their dogs, help socialize dogs with other dogs and people, and are fun for both pets and owners. Well-socialized and trained pets make good pets that are a joy to have. They are much less likely to end up in humane shelters or euthanized for behavior problems.

Streptococcal infections in children are sometimes mistakenly blamed on the family pet. Dogs do get *Streptococcus* infections, but it is a different type than the type that occurs in people. Dogs get Type A and people get Type G.

Pregnant women should avoid handling or ingesting cat feces to avoid toxoplasmosis. However, ownership of cats is not a proven risk factor and there is no risk to pregnant women or their babies from having a pet cat.

Zoonotic diseases are transmitted in different ways. Some are transmitted by direct contact with an animal, including airborne droplets if the animal coughs or sneezes, bites, or scratches. Others are transmitted by contact with a contaminated area. Roundworm and hookworm eggs are passed in the feces of infected animals and contaminate the ground or other surface. Other infections are first passed to an intermediate host, such as a tick, mosquito, or flea, and then into a person when the insect bites a human. Mosquitoes transmit heartworm, ticks transmit Lyme disease and Rocky Mountain spotted fever, and fleas transmit tapeworm.

The danger of zoonoses is magnified in people who have compromised immune systems. The very young and very old, those infected with human immunodeficiency virus (HIV) or who have active acquired immunodeficiency syndrome (AIDS), organ transplant recipients taking immunosuppressive drugs, and cancer patients receiving chemotherapy have an increased risk of acquiring a zoonotic disease.

The list below includes a number of zoonoses seen in the United States. The list is not all-inclusive but includes many of the more common diseases acquired directly from dogs and cats.

- Blastomycosis
- Brucellosis
- Cat scratch disease
- Chlamydiosis
- Dermatophytosis/ringworm
- Giardiasis
- Heartworm
- Hookworm/cutaneous larva migrans
- Leptospirosis
- Mange (*Cheyletiella* and sarcoptic)
- Pasteurellosis
- Plague
- Rabies
- Roundworm/visceral larva migrans
- Sporotrichosis
- Tapeworm/*Echinococcus*
- Toxoplasmosis
- Tularemia

The Most Commonly Recommended Prescription and Nonprescription Drugs in the United States, Generic and Brand Names, with Complete Descriptions of Drugs and Their Efffects

Brand Name

Acemannan (ace-MA-nan) Ⓥ

Generic Ingredient

Aloe-derived mannan polysaccharide

Type of Drug

Immunostimulant.

Prescribed for

Immunosuppression caused by feline leukemia virus (FeLV) and feline immunodeficiency virus (FIV) infections, and cancer.

General Information

Acemannan is derived from the *Aloe barbadensis miller* plant. It stimulates the release of a variety of cytokines, natural substances made by certain cells in the body that communicate with other cells in the body. Several of these cytokines cause death of tumor cells. Acemannan also directly kills some viruses in the laboratory and may help kill viruses in animals. Acemannan is licensed for the treatment of fibrosarcomas in dogs and cats, and it has shown promise in the treatment of FeLV and FIV infections. Other tumors that have responded to Acemannan include squamous cell carcinoma, cutaneous histiocytoma, myxosarcoma, adenocarcinoma, lymphoma, mast cell tumor, and infiltrating lipoma. Acemannan may be given by injection into the abdomen, or directly into a tumor. Oral administration of Acemannan in FeLV- and FIV-infected cats seems to be as effective as injection.

Cautions and Warnings

■ The product license for Acemannan is conditional. Studies to prove efficacy and potency are in progress. It is currently approved for use as an adjunct treatment of fibrosarcoma in dogs and cats (see "Usual Dose").

■ Contact your veterinarian if you think your dog or cat may be having an adverse reaction to Acemannan.

■ U.S. federal law restricts the use of this drug by or on the lawful written or oral order of a licensed veterinarian within the context of a valid veterinarian-client-patient relationship.

Possible Side Effects

▼ Rare: fever, anorexia, depression, diarrhea, fainting, transient slow heart rate, fast heart rate or breathing, collapse, and pain on injection.

Drug Interactions

None known.

Food Interactions

Should probably not be given with food if given orally.

Usual Dose

Dogs and Cats: for fibrosarcoma—0.5 mg/lb injected into the abdomen once a week for a minimum of 6 weeks, with concurrent injection of 2 mg deep into each tumor mass once a week until tumor cell death and delineation is complete (2–4 weeks). Surgical excision is recommended at this point. Once a month injections of 0.5 mg/lb into the abdomen are recommended to prevent recurrence.

Cats: 0.5 mg/lb injected into the abdomen or given orally once a week for FeLV and FIV infections.

Drug Form: powder for reconstitution and injection or oral administration.

Overdosage

There is no information available on overdoses of Acemannan. Effects similar to adverse reactions might be expected (see "Possible Side Effects"). In case of accidental ingestion or overdose, contact your veterinarian or the National Animal Poison Control Center. ALWAYS bring the prescription bottle or container with you if you go for treatment.

Special Populations

Pregnancy/Lactation

There are no safety studies of Acemannan in pregnant or lactating dogs or cats, and it should be avoided unless the benefits outweigh the risks.

Puppies/Kittens

There are no safety studies of Acemannan in puppies or kittens, and it should be avoided unless the benefits outweigh the risks.

Senior Animals

Acemannan should be safe to use in older animals.

Generic Name

Acepromazine (ace-PROE-muh-zeen) G

Most Common Brand Names

Aceproject V   PromAce V
Aceprotabs V

Type of Drug

Phenothiazine tranquilizer.

Prescribed for

Tranquilization, sedation, motion sickness, itching, and scratching.

General Information

Acepromazine maleate is a phenothiazine tranquilizer, similar to chlorpromazine and promazine, but more potent. Acepromazine is one of the most commonly used tranquilizers for cats and dogs. It decreases anxiety and causes central nervous system depression and a drop in blood pressure and heart rate. Acepromazine is occasionally used to prevent motion sickness, and temporarily reduce itching and scratching due to allergies. It may be given by injection with atropine before anesthesia to alleviate anxiety and for some of its beneficial effects in combination with anesthetics. It may be given orally or by injection before euthanasia. It may be prescribed for oral use before veterinary office visits, nail trimming, or grooming appointments if the animal is too fractious to handle safely without sedation.

Acepromazine does not relieve pain, and the tranquilizing effect of the drug may be overcome unexpectedly with enough excitement. It is also usually ineffective if given after excitement has occurred. The side effects of acepromazine are extremely important, and each animal should be evaluated before acepromazine is given. Acepromazine is metabolized in the liver and excreted in the urine.

Information in this profile also applies to chlorpromazine and promazine.

Cautions and Warnings

■ There is a great deal of breed variability and individual variability in the response to acepromazine (see "Special Populations").

■ Acepromazine should be avoided or used with extreme caution in older animals, or those with liver disease, heart disease, injury, or debilitation. If it is used at all in such animals, it should be given in very small doses.

■ In some older animals, a very small dose can have a marked and very prolonged effect.

■ Because acepromazine lowers blood pressure, it should not be used in animals that are dehydrated, anemic, or in shock.

■ Acepromazine should not be used in animals with tetanus or strychnine poisoning.

■ Acepromazine interferes with regulation of body temperature, and care must be taken to ensure that animals given acepromazine do not become too hot or too cold. Because of this adverse effect on temperature regulation, acepromazine should be avoided or used with extreme caution in very young animals.

■ Acepromazine may make animals more likely to have a seizure, so it should not be used in epileptic animals or those prone to seizures.

■ Occasionally, animals may have the opposite response to acepromazine. They may become excited, aggressive, or vicious. This unusual response seems more common in cats.

■ Acepromazine is FDA approved for use in both dogs and cats.

■ U.S. federal law restricts the use of this drug by or on the lawful written or oral order of a licensed veterinarian within the context of a valid veterinarian-client-patient relationship.

Possible Side Effects

▼ Common: droopy, sleepy eyes; the pink inner eyelid is more visible in the inner corner of the eye; animals seem uncoordinated, and have less control of their hind legs; low

> **Possible Side Effects** *(continued)*
>
> blood pressure; slowing of the heart rate; slowing of animal's breathing; and in epileptic animals or animals that have had seizures in the past, increased likelihood of a seizure and sudden collapse.
>
> ▼ Rare: decreased or absent pulse and breathing, pale gums, and unconsciousness; fatal interactions with anesthetics.

Drug Interactions

• Acepromazine should not be used within 1 month of deworming with organophosphate compounds.

• Animals receiving acepromazine require lower doses of barbiturates, narcotics, and other anesthetics, because these combinations increase central nervous system depression.

• Acepromazine should not be used with procaine hydrochloride.

• Quinidine when given with acepromazine causes increased cardiac depression.

• Antidiarrheal mixtures, such as Kaopectate and Pepto-Bismol, or antacids will decrease the absorption of oral acepromazine. Your animal's dose of acepromazine may need to be increased to achieve the desired effect.

• Propranolol increases blood levels of acepromazine. Your animal's dose of acepromazine would need to be decreased in this case.

• Acepromazine may decrease the metabolism of phenytoin. Most animals receiving phenytoin for seizures should not receive acepromazine, because acepromazine lowers the seizure threshold.

• Acepromazine should not be used in animals having a myelogram.

Food Interactions

None described.

Usual Dose

Dogs: 0.25–1.0 mg/lb orally no more than every 6–8 hours for sedation; 0.05 mg/lb to prevent vomiting.

Cats: 0.5–1.0 mg/lb orally.

Drug Form: 5-, 10-, and 25-mg tablets and 10 mg/ml injectable. If you give acepromazine to your animal before veterinary office visits, grooming or nail trimming appointments, or travel, give 30–45 minutes before visit or departure.

Overdosage

Overdose causes excessive sedation, slow breathing and heart rate, pale gums, unsteady gait or inability to stand, and sleepiness. It may also cause sudden collapse, decreased or absent pulse and breathing, unconsciousness, seizures, and death. In case of accidental ingestion or overdose, contact your veterinarian or the National Animal Poison Control Center. ALWAYS bring the prescription bottle or container with you if you go for treatment.

Special Information

Because of all of the potential problems and adverse effects of acepromazine (see "Cautions and Warnings"), many veterinarians are reluctant to prescribe the drug for travel anxiety. The risks of using the drug usually outweigh the benefits when the animal will be away from the owner, or exposed to temperature extremes, as during plane travel, or when there may be limited or no access to veterinary care if problems arise. There are other drugs for travel anxiety and motion sickness that may be effective and much safer than acepromazine, such as diphenhydramine, diazepam, and the motion sickness drugs. Discuss the risks and benefits of acepromazine and its alternatives with your veterinarian. In dogs, there is a great deal of individual variation in the response to acepromazine. Therefore, if you do use acepromazine, it is best to begin with a small dose and give more later if needed. If you do decide to use acepromazine before travel, it is wise to try a test dose at home to judge your animal's reaction to the drug well before you leave.

Special Populations

Special Breeds
Giant breeds and greyhounds may be extremely sensitive to acepromazine, whereas terriers may require higher doses. Breeds with flat faces or short noses, especially boxers, are particularly prone to cardiovascular side effects (drop in blood

pressure and slow heart rate). Acepromazine should be avoided or used with great caution in these breeds. Atropine may be given along with acepromazine to help keep the heart rate and blood pressure up in these breeds.

Pregnancy/Lactation

Acepromazine should be avoided in pregnancy or lactation unless the benefits of using the drug outweigh the risks.

Puppies/Kittens

Acepromazine should be avoided or used with extreme caution in young animals (see "Cautions and Warnings").

Senior Animals

Acepromazine should be avoided or used with extreme caution in older animals (see "Cautions and Warnings").

Generic Name

Acetylcysteine (uh-sete-il-SIS-tene) Ⓖ

Brand Name

Mucosil Ⓗ

Type of Drug

Anticollagenase, mucolytic, antioxidant/antidote for acetaminophen poisoning, and tear film supplement.

Prescribed for

Corneal ulcers, acetaminophen poisoning, keratoconjunctivitis sicca (dry eye), and bronchitis.

General Information

Acetylcysteine breaks down mucus by breaking down the chemical bonds between strands. Because of this it has been used in the eye to treat keratoconjunctivitis sicca (KCS), a disease of decreased tear production where the eye produces large amounts of thick mucus. Acetylcysteine has also been used to break up thick mucus in the airways of animals with allergic bronchitis or infections. It must be inhaled as a fine spray (nebulized) into the airways to be effective. In some infected corneal ulcers there may be large amounts of enzymes from bacteria, dying corneal cells, and inflammatory cells. These enzymes may digest the cornea and cause it to melt. Acetylcysteine inhibits the enzymes that cause melting corneal ulcers, and so protects the cornea from further damage. Acetylcysteine is also an antioxidant, and when used in acetaminophen poisoning, helps reverse the oxidation damage to red blood cells and prevents further liver damage.

Cautions and Warnings

■ Acetylcysteine is not FDA approved for use in dogs or cats. It is commonly used however and considered accepted practice.

■ Acetylcysteine may be irritating to the eye in concentrations greater than 5%. It should be diluted to 5% or less with artificial tears for use in the eye. It may also be irritating to airways and cause airway constriction when nebulized into the lungs.

■ Acetylcysteine may be given orally or intravenously to animals with acetaminophen poisoning. It may cause nausea, vomiting, or allergic reactions when given orally. The taste of acetylcysteine is very bad, and it may need to be given by stomach feeding tube. Allergic reactions may also occur after intravenous use.

■ Contact your veterinarian if you think your dog or cat may be having an adverse reaction to acetylcysteine.

■ U.S. federal law restricts the use of this drug by or on the lawful written or oral order of a licensed veterinarian within the context of a valid veterinarian-client-patient relationship.

Possible Side Effects

▼ Common: nausea and vomiting from the bad taste; eye irritation if greater than 5% solutions are used.

▼ Rare: airway constriction if nebulized into the lungs and allergic or anaphylactic reactions.

Drug Interactions

• Acetylcysteine should not be mixed in solutions with amphotericin B, ampicillin, erythromycin, tetracyclines, hydrogen peroxide, or trypsin.

Food Interactions

None known. The foul taste may need to be disguised by some strong tasting food or liquid when acetylcysteine is given orally.

Usual Dose

Dogs and Cats

Acetaminophen poisoning: 70 mg/lb orally or intravenously, followed by 35 mg/lb every 4 hours for 4–5 doses.

Eye: With artificial tears dilute to 2%–5% and apply every 2 hours for a maximum of 48 hours for melting corneal ulcers. Follow your veterinarian's advice for use of acetylcysteine in KCS.

Respiratory: 50 ml/hr for 30–60 min twice a day by nebulizer.

Drug Form

10% and 20% solutions. Manufacturer gives a shelf-life of 5 days, but it may be used for longer if there is no discoloration and it is kept refrigerated.

Overdosage

Acetylcysteine is considered a fairly safe drug. It takes 5 to 7 times the recommended oral or intravenous dose to cause death in dogs. In case of accidental ingestion or overdose, contact your veterinarian or the National Animal Poison Control Center. ALWAYS bring the prescription bottle or container with you if you go for treatment.

Special Information

Acetaminophen poisoning is a very serious problem, especially in cats. One regular strength Tylenol tablet (325 mg) can kill a cat very quickly. Acetaminophen is less toxic in dogs—75mg/lb is considered a toxic dose. Acetaminophen should never be given to dogs or cats, and any dog or cat with known or suspected acetaminophen ingestion should be taken for emergency veterinary care immediately. Activated charcoal is recommended for treatment of animals with acetaminophen poisoning to prevent further absorption of the drug. The problem is that the activated charcoal may also prevent absorption of acetylcysteine given orally. Activated charcoal should be avoided unless acetylcysteine is given intravenously. It is critically important to give acetylcysteine as soon as possible after acetaminophen ingestion. This is especially important in cats because they develop methemoglobinemia and liver damage so quickly.

Special Populations

Pregnancy/Lactation
Acetylcysteine seems to be safe in pregnant rabbits and rats, but it has not been studied in dogs and cats. It should be avoided unless the benefits outweigh the risks.

Puppies/Kittens
Acetylcysteine should be safe to use in puppies and kittens, but there are no studies to document its safety.

Senior Animals
Acetylcysteine should be safe to use in older animals.

Generic Name

Activated Charcoal [G]

Brand Name

Actidose [H]   SuperChar [V] [H]
Liqui-Char [H]   Toxiban [V] [H]

Type of Drug

Adsorbent/detoxification therapy.

Prescribed for

Poisonings and drug overdoses.

General Information

Activated charcoal is finely ground charcoal, given orally to adsorb or bind toxins in the gastrointestinal (GI) tract. Activated charcoal is not an antidote, but it can decrease the toxic effects of many ingested poisons. Once the toxin is bound to the activated charcoal, it is then less likely to be absorbed from the GI tract, and will pass through to be eliminated in the feces. It is important to give activated charcoal as soon as possible to minimize absorption of the toxin and it may be given repeatedly in the first day.

Charcoal therapy has been effective in the treatment of the following poisons: organophosphates, carbamates, chlorinated hydrocarbons, strychnine, ethylene glycol (antifreeze), and blister beetle. Activated charcoal may reduce the GI absorption of arsenic and mercury compounds, and most polycyclic organic compounds, which includes most pesticides. Activated charcoal may decrease the effects of topical toxins that the animal ingests by grooming such as insecticide dip and crude oil from oil spills. Studies in humans have shown that activated charcoal may decrease blood levels of some systemically administered drugs and anesthetics, probably by binding metabolites excreted in the biliary system.

Activated charcoal is not very effective in adsorbing alcohol, ferrous sulfate, sodium chloride/chlorate, or nitrates. It should not be used to treat ingestion of caustic substances, such as caustic alkalies and mineral acids or petroleum distillates.

It is very important to treat poisonings and drug overdoses promptly. If you suspect that your animal has been poisoned or received a drug overdose, contact your veterinarian or the National Animal Poison Control Center. ALWAYS bring the prescription bottle or container with you if you go for treatment.

Cautions and Warnings

■ Activated charcoal is not a poison antidote. It should be used under veterinary supervision with other more specific therapies and supportive care.

■ Activated charcoal should not be used to treat ingestion of caustic substances.

■ Activated charcoal may make it difficult to see GI damage with endoscopy.

■ Activated charcoal should be given with caution to avoid aspiration during dosing.

Possible Side Effects

Most of the side effects seen during treatment with activated charcoal are related to the toxin. Rapid administration of activated charcoal can cause vomiting.

▼ Common: constipation and diarrhea.

Drug Interactions

• Activated charcoal should not be given within three hours of any other oral drug because it will decrease the absorption of the drug.

• Drugs to induce vomiting such as syrup of ipecac, hydrogen peroxide, or apomorphine should be given before activated charcoal is administered. The activated charcoal should be given after the vomiting has occurred.

Food Interactions

Dairy products and mineral oil decrease the effectiveness of activated charcoal.

Usual Dose

Dogs and Cats: granules: 0.5–2 g/lb orally or by stomach tube every 2–6 hours. Suspension: 3–6 ml/lb orally or by stomach tube every 2–6 hours.

Drug Form: powder, tablets, granules, liquid suspension, and liquid suspension with sorbitol.

Overdosage

None reported when used for acute therapy.

Special Information

Activated charcoal is frequently given with cathartics, such as sorbitol, to move the GI contents more rapidly through the GI tract. This helps to minimize the animal's exposure to the toxin. Activated charcoal is very staining to fabrics and causes your animal's feces to turn black.

Special Populations

Pregnancy/Lactation
Activated charcoal should be safe to use during pregnancy and lactation.

Puppies/Kittens
Activated charcoal should be safe to use in puppies and kittens.

Senior Animals
Activated charcoal should be safe to use in older animals.

Generic Name

Albuterol (al-BUE-tuh-rawl) [G]

Brand Names

Proventil [H]   Ventolin [H]

Type of Drug

Bronchodilator.

Prescribed for

Bronchospasm, asthma, and cough.

General Information

Albuterol sulfate is used in dogs and cats to relax bronchial smooth muscle and open airways. It is sometimes used in the treatment of feline and canine chronic bronchitis or asthma. The primary cause of chronic bronchitis in humans is inhaled tobacco smoke, and inhalation of secondary smoke may be important in dogs and cats as well. It is thought that chronic bronchitis/asthma in cats is caused by allergies to cat litter and household dust, smoke, kapok (a material used as mattress filling and in insulation), talc, and other inhaled allergens. Canine chronic bronchitis may be caused by many different factors, including environmental, inherited, and infectious causes. Albuterol is used in cats in respiratory distress caused by asthma. It is sometimes used in the long-term management of dogs with chronic bronchitis. Albuterol is well absorbed orally and by inhalation.

Cautions and Warnings

■ Albuterol is not FDA approved for use in dogs or cats. It is not commonly used but may be useful in some dogs and cats and is considered accepted practice.

■ Albuterol should be used with caution in animals with diabetes, hyperthyroidism, high blood pressure, seizure disorders, or heart disease or abnormal heart rhythms.

■ Some animals may develop low blood potassium and may need potassium supplementation while on albuterol.

■ Contact your veterinarian it you think your dog or cat may be having an adverse reaction to albuterol.

■ U.S. federal law restricts the use of this drug by or on the lawful written or oral order of a licensed veterinarian within the context of a valid veterinarian-client-patient relationship.

Possible Side Effects

Most side effects are mild and dose related.

▼ Common: increased heart rate, tremors, excitement, restlessness, and nervousness.

Drug Interactions

• Albuterol used in combination with other sympathomimetic drugs such as phenylephrine and ephedrine, increases the risk of cardiovascular side effects.

• Propranolol and other beta-adrenergic blockers decrease the action of drugs similar to albuterol.

• Tricyclic antidepressants and monoamine oxidase inhibitors (MAOIs) increase some of the effects of drugs similar to albuterol.

• Albuterol lowers digoxin levels.

• Gas anesthetic increases the occurrence of abnormal heart rhythms in animals receiving albuterol.

Food Interactions

None known.

Usual Dose

Dogs: 0.01–0.03 mg/lb orally 1–3 times a day. Inhaled—for a 60-lb dog: 0.5 ml of 0.5% solution in 4 ml saline nebulized 4 times a day.

Cats: 0.01–0.03 mg/lb orally 1–3 times a day.

Drug Form: 2- and 4-mg tablets, 2 mg/5 ml syrup, and 0.083% and 0.5% solution for inhalation.

Overdosage

Symptoms of overdose may include abnormal heart rhythms, high blood pressure, fever, vomiting, dilated pupils, excitement, and low blood potassium. In case of accidental ingestion or overdose, contact your veterinarian or the National Animal Poison Control Center. ALWAYS bring the prescription bottle or container with you if you go for treatment.

Special Information

Chronic bronchitis and asthma in dogs and cats are difficult diseases to diagnose and manage. These diseases are not cured but managed for the life of the animal. A small percentage of dogs with chronic bronchitis will respond well to a combination of albuterol and corticosteroids. When these drugs are used together, they can each be used at a lower dose.

Special Populations

Pregnancy/Lactation

Albuterol crosses the placenta, and has been shown to cause birth defects in laboratory animals. It is not known if it is excreted in milk. Albuterol should not be used in pregnant or lactating animals unless the benefits outweigh the risks.

Puppies/Kittens

There is no information on albuterol use in puppies or kittens. Albuterol is used in humans above the age of 2.

Senior Animals

Albuterol should be safe to use in older animals with no other medical conditions (see "Cautions and Warnings").

Generic Name

Allopurinol (al-oe-PURE-in-nol) G

Brand Names

Lopurin H   Zyloprim H

Type of Drug

Enzyme (xanthine oxidase) inhibitor.

Prescribed for

Prevention of urate urinary stones.

General Information

Purines are one of the building blocks of DNA. They come from foods and are also made by the body. They are broken down from hypoxanthine to xanthine to uric acid/urate to allantoin, and allantoin is excreted in the urine of most dogs and cats. Dalmatians have liver and kidney defects that cause decreased conversion of urate to allantoin and excretion of large amounts of urate in the urine and are at risk for urate urinary stones. Dogs and cats with liver shunts also excrete large amounts of uric acid and are at risk for urate stones.

Allopurinol is a synthetic form of hypoxanthine. It binds to the enzyme xanthine oxidase and prevents it from converting hypoxanthine to xanthine and xanthine to uric acid. The result is a reduction in serum and urine uric acid concentrations. Prevention of urate stones is the goal after surgical removal of all stones and confirmation of the diagnosis by stone analysis. Prevention is accomplished by (1) increasing water consumption, (2) feeding a low purine diet, (3) alkalinizing the urine, (4) controlling urinary tract infections, and most importantly, (5) partial blockade of purine degradation by allopurinol (see "Special Information"). Allopurinol is not recommended for animals with liver shunts. They do not have the same metabolic defect as dalmatians, and they are at serious risk of overdosing owing to their liver dysfunction. If surgical correction of the shunt is not possible, steps 1 to 4 listed above are recommended, to decrease urate in the urine.

Cautions and Warnings

■ Allopurinol is not FDA approved for use in dogs or cats. It is commonly used to treat dalmatian dogs with metabolic defects that cause urate stones and is considered accepted practice.

■ Excess allopurinol may cause the formation of xanthine urinary stones.

■ Allopurinol must be used with extreme caution in dogs with decreased liver or kidney function. Dosage reductions and increased monitoring are necessary (see "Special Information").

■ Do not use allopurinol in dogs or cats with urate stones caused by liver shunts.

■ Contact your veterinarian if you think your dog may be having an adverse reaction to allopurinol.

■ U.S. federal law restricts the use of this drug by or on the lawful written or oral order of a licensed veterinarian within the context of a valid veterinarian-client-patient relationship.

Possible Side Effects

Side effects of allopurinol are rare in animals. In humans, gastrointestinal distress, bone marrow suppression, skin rashes, liver damage, and vasculitis are seen.

▼ Common: formation of xanthine urinary stones if excess allopurinol is given (see "Special Information").

▼ Rare: allergic reactions.

Drug Interactions

• Allopurinol and cyclophosphamide together may cause increased bone marrow suppression.

• Probenecid, sulfinpyrazone, and diuretics, such as furosemide and thiazides, may make allopurinol less effective.

• Urine acidifiers, such as methionine and ammonium chloride, reduce the effectiveness of allopurinol.

• Allopurinol inhibits the metabolism of aminophylline, theophylline, azathioprine, warfarin, and mercaptopurine. This causes increased blood levels of these drugs and potential for adverse effects. Doses of these drugs should be reduced 25% to 33%.

• Adverse effects in people are more common when allopurinol is given with amoxicillin and ampicillin (rash), or trimethoprim/sulfamethoxazole (low platelet counts).

Food Interactions

Give with food. Allopurinol should be used with a low purine diet such as Prescription Diet Canine k/d or u/d, Hill's Pet Products for dogs, or Purina Cat Chow dry for cats. DO NOT feed commercial diets designed to acidify the urine, such as Prescription Diet Feline c/d, or Purina CNM-UR formula. Foods that are high in purines include lean meats and organ meats, anchovies and sardines, legumes and poultry. The foods lowest in purines include eggs, cheese, and vegetables other than legumes.

Usual Dose

Dogs: starting dose—5 mg/lb once a day. Maintenance dose—as indicated by 24 hour urine urate excretion (see "Special Information").

Drug Form: 100- and 300-mg tablets.

Overdosage

Chronic overdoses are likely to cause the formation of xanthine urinary stones (see "Special Information"). No reports of massive overdoses were found in the veterinary or human literature. In case of accidental ingestion or overdose, contact your veterinarian or the National Animal Poison Control Center. ALWAYS bring the prescription bottle or container with you if you go for treatment.

Special Information

The four steps that are used to decrease formation of urate stones include:

1. Increase water consumption by giving potassium chloride (KCl/light salt) in capsules. Adjust the dose of KCl to maintain a urine specific gravity of 1.018.
2. Change the diet to a high quality protein, low purine diet (see "Food Interactions").
3. Adjust the fasting urine pH to 7.0–7.5. This should happen with the diet changes outlined in the preceding. If necessary, give oral potassium citrate (see "Potassium Supplements") to achieve the correct urine pH.
4. Control urinary tract infections by running routine urinalyses and by monitoring carefully for signs of increased frequency of urination, straining to urinate, and so on. Contact your veterinarian immediately if you suspect your animal may have a urinary tract infection.

Give allopurinol ONLY to dalmatian dogs. The dose of allopurinol must be adjusted to the needs of each patient to avoid excessive doses of allopurinol, high urine xanthine, and the formation of xanthine stones. The goal is to decrease urine urate excretion to about 300 mg/24 hours. At this rate of urate excretion, neither urate nor xanthine will be able to form stones. A 24-hour urine collection is needed for this test. Spot tests on a single urine sample are not accurate. During the collection period, dogs must drink and eat normally and receive their normal dose of allopurinol. If the urine urate is less than 300 mg/24 hours, reduce the dose of allopurinol; if the urine urate is greater than 300 mg/24 hours, increase the dose of allopurinol. Repeat the collection procedure every 3 to 4 weeks until the desired result is obtained. Therapy must continue for the life of the dog, and the collection procedure should be repeated every year.

Special Populations

Pregnancy/Lactation
There are no studies to document the safety of allopurinol in pregnant or lactating dogs, but it seems to be safe in pregnant rodents. However, it should be avoided in pregnant or lactating dogs unless the benefits outweigh the risks.

Puppies/Kittens
Allopurinol should not be given to puppies or kittens.

Senior Animals
Allopurinol should be safe to use in older animals, unless there is decreased kidney or liver function (see "Cautions and Warnings").

Type of Drug

Aminoglycoside Antibiotics

(uh-MEE-noe-GLIE-koe-side)

Most Common Brand Names

Generic Ingredient: Amikacin Sulfate G
Amiglyde-V V

Generic Ingredients: Bacitracin + Neomycin Sulfate + Polymyxin B Sulfate G
Mycitracin V   TriOptic-P V
Neobacimyx V

Generic Ingredients: Bacitracin + Neomycin Sulfate + Polymyxin B Sulfate + Hydrocortisone Acetate G
Neobacimyx-H V   TriOptic-S V

Generic Ingredients: Flumethasone + Neomycin Sulfate + Polymyxin B Sulfate
Anaprime V

Generic Ingredient: Gentamicin Sulfate G
Garamycin H   Gentocin V

Gentaject V   Tamycin V
GentaVed V

Generic Ingredients: Gentamicin Sulfate + Betamethasone Valerate
Gentocin V   Topagen V

Generic Ingredients: Gentamicin Sulfate + Betamethasone Valerate + Clotrimazole
Otomax V

Generic Ingredient: Kanamycin Sulfate
Amforol V   Kantrim V

Generic Ingredient: Neomycin Sulfate G
Biosol V   Mycifradin H

Generic Ingredients: Neomycin Sulfate + Isoflupredone Acetate
Neo-Predef V

Generic Ingredients: Neomycin Sulfate + Polymyxin B Sulfate
Optiprime V

Generic Ingredients: Nystatin + Neomycin Sulfate + Thiostrepton + Triamcinolone Acetonide
Animax V   Panolog V

Generic Ingredient: Streptomycin Sulfate G
Available as generic injection only H

Generic Ingredients: Thiabendazole + Dexamethasone + Neomycin Sulfate
Tresaderm V

Generic Ingredient: Tobramycin Sulfate G
Nebcin H

Generic Ingredients: Tobramycin + Dexamethasone
Tobradex H

Prescribed for

Susceptible bacterial infections.

General Information

The aminoglycosides are an important group of antibiotics

because of their ability to kill gram-negative bacteria, such as *E. coli* and *Samonella*. However, they are not effective against most gram-positive bacteria, such as streptococcus and staphylococcus, or anaerobic bacteria (bacteria that only grow where there is no oxygen). Gentamicin may be effective against some gram-positive bacteria, including staphylococci. The aminoglycosides must be used with caution because they can damage the kidneys and the inner ear.

The aminoglycosides used in dogs and cats include amikacin, gentamicin, neomycin, kanamycin, streptomycin, and occasionally tobramycin. Aminoglycosides are poorly absorbed from the gastrointestinal (GI) tract after oral dosing, so they must all be given by injection when a systemic effect is needed. All aminoglycosides except neomycin may be given by injection under the skin, in a muscle, or in a vein. Neomycin is too toxic to give by injection, but it is used in many preparations for ears, eyes and skin. Kanamycin, streptomycin, and neomycin may be given orally for a nonsystemic purpose, such as to remove certain bacteria from the GI tract, as in small intestinal bacterial overgrowth, before colon surgery, or as part of treatment of liver failure. Oral neomycin and kanamycin should not be used to treat *Salmonella* infection, as this will cause persistent shedding of the bacteria. The aminoglycosides are often combined with one of the penicillin antibiotics to gain better protection from gram-positive bacteria.

The aminoglycosides have been in use since the 1950s, and many bacterial strains have developed resistance to them. Amikacin is the most recent of the aminoglycosides and has the broadest spectrum. It is often used for bacterial infections that are resistant to tobramycin and gentamicin.

Newer antibiotics like the (fluoro)quinolones may be used instead of the aminoglycosides because they are less toxic and also have a broad spectrum of activity.

Cautions and Warnings

■ The aminoglycosides can cause kidney and inner ear damage even at the recommended dosage. Kidney damage may be reversible if it is discovered soon enough and the medication is discontinued immediately. Ear damage may include both hearing loss and balance problems, and may be irreversible. Risk factors for these side effects include young and old age, severe bacterial infections, dehydration, fever, kidney disease, and larger size (see "Special Populations"). Cats treated with aminoglycosides are very susceptible to inner ear damage, especially balance problems. Aminoglycosides should be avoided in animals with neuromuscular diseases.

■ Contact your veterinarian if you think your dog or cat may be having an adverse reaction to an aminoglycoside.

■ U.S. federal law restricts the use of this drug by or on the lawful written or oral order of a licensed veterinarian within the context of a valid veterinarian-client-patient relationship.

Possible Side Effects

Kidney and inner ear damage with hearing loss and balance problems are more common in animals with one or more risk factors (see "Cautions and Warnings"). With proper precautions such as adjusting the dose, maintaining hydration, and monitoring blood levels of antibiotic, these side effects should be rare.

▼ Rare: neuromuscular blockade; pain and inflammation at the injection site; nerve damage; swelling of the face; allergic reactions; GI symptoms; blood and liver damage; ear, kidney, and GI damage; and severe diarrhea.

Drug Interactions

• Diuretics, including mannitol, will increase the chances of kidney damage from the aminoglycosides.

• Aminoglycosides should be avoided or used with caution with other drugs that have potential toxicity to the ear, kidneys, or nervous system. These include amphotericin B, other aminoglycosides, acyclovir, cisplatin, methoxyflurane, bacitracin, polymyxin B, and vancomycin.

• Use of aminoglycosides with general anesthetics or neuromuscular blocking agents (such as tubocurarine) may enhance the neuromuscular blockade.

Food Interactions

None known.

Usual Dose

Dogs and Cats
    Amikacin: 2.5–5 mg/lb 2–3 times a day by injection.

Gentamicin: 1.1–2.2 mg/lb 2–3 times a day by injection.

Kanamycin: 5 mg/lb orally 3–4 times a day; 2–3 mg/lb 2–4 times a day by injection.

Neomycin: 5–10 mg/lb orally 3–4 times a day. For topical use as directed by your veterinarian.

Streptomycin: 10 mg/lb orally twice a day; 3–10 mg/lb 2 times a day by injection.

Tobramycin: 0.5 mg/lb 3 times a day by injection under the skin. No dose available for cats.

Drug Form

Oral and injectable liquid, powder, tablets, eye and ear ointments and drops, skin ointments, and sprays.

Overdosage

Overdose of the aminoglycosides is likely to cause severe kidney and inner ear damage (see "Possible Side Effects"). In case of accidental ingestion or overdose, contact your veterinarian or the National Animal Poison Control Center. ALWAYS bring the prescription bottle or container with you if you go for treatment.

Special Information

There is some evidence that a higher dose given once a day may reduce the possibility of kidney and ear damage without decreasing the effectiveness of the aminoglycosides. Studies have not confirmed this in dogs or cats, but it is being done by some veterinarians.

Special Populations

Larger Breeds
Animals should be dosed according to size, with larger animals given less on a mg/lb basis.

Working Dogs
Seeing-eye, hunting, or herding dogs, or dogs that work for people who have disabilities should not be given aminoglycosides because of the possibility of inner ear damage with balance or hearing loss.

Pregnancy/Lactation
Aminoglycosides can cause damage to the fetus, and should be avoided during pregnancy and lactation unless the benefits outweigh the risks.

Puppies/Kittens

The aminoglycosides should be avoided or used with extreme caution in very young puppies and kittens as they are more susceptible to the side effects (see "Cautions and Warnings"). Reduced dosage or increased dosage intervals are recommended.

Senior Animals

Aminoglycosides should be avoided or used with extreme caution in older animals or those with kidney dysfunction. Reduced dosage, increased dosage intervals, and monitoring of aminoglycoside levels in the blood are all recommended for older animals.

Generic Name

Aminopentamide (uh-mee-noe-PEN-tuh-mide)

Brand Name

Centrine [V]

Type of Drug

Antispasmodic, smooth muscle relaxant.

Prescribed for

Vomiting, nausea, diarrhea, acute gastrointestinal (GI) spasm, pylorospasm, hypertrophic gastritis, and straining in malabsorption/maldigestion syndromes.

General Information

Aminopentamide hydrogen sulfate decreases the motility and contractions of the GI tract. It can be very effective in stopping vomiting and diarrhea, especially in dogs with persistent acute nausea, vomiting, and diarrhea from dietary indiscretion.

Cautions and Warnings

■ Do not use aminopentamide in dogs or cats with glaucoma or any obstruction of the GI tract. Not for use in puppies, kittens, or older animals. Do not use in animals with heart disease, paralytic ileus, severe ulcerative colitis, urinary obstruction, or myasthenia gravis.

■ Aminopentamide should be used with caution in animals with GI infections, as decreased GI motility may cause retention of the infectious agent or toxins, and prolonged symptoms. Aminopentamide should be used with caution or avoided in animals with liver disease, hyperthyroidism, heart disease, prostate disease, or esophageal reflux.

■ Contact your veterinarian if you think your dog or cat may be having an adverse reaction to aminopentamide.

■ U.S. federal law restricts the use of this drug by or on the lawful written or oral order of a licensed veterinarian within the context of a valid veterinarian-client-patient relationship.

Possible Side Effects

▼ Common: dryness of the mouth and delayed emptying of the stomach.

▼ Rare: dry eyes, blurred vision, and hesitation of urination.

Drug Interactions

• Antihistamines, procainamide, quinidine, meperidine, benzodiazepine tranquilizers, and phenothiazines (for example, acepromazine) may all enhance the effects of aminopentamide.

• Aminopentamide may enhance the effects of nitrofurantoin, thiazide diuretics, and adrenergic agents (for example, phenylpropanolamine).

• Metoclopramide may not work if given with aminopentamide.

Food Interactions

None known.

Usual Dose

Dogs: 10 lbs or less—0.1 mg; 11–20 lbs—0.2 mg; 21–50 lbs—0.3 mg; 51–100 lbs—0.4 mg; over 100 lbs—0.5 mg 2–3 times a day.

Cats: 10 lbs or less—0.1 mg; 11–20 lbs—0.2 mg 2–3 times a day.

Drug Form: 0.2-mg tablets and 0.5 mg/ml injectable.

Overdosage

There is no specific information on aminopentamide overdose, but the symptoms should be the same as those of atropine overdose. Dry eyes and mouth, difficulty swallowing, vomiting, constipation, ileus, urinary retention, stimulation or drowsiness, unsteady gait, seizures, slow breathing, blurred vision, dilated pupils, slow or high heart rate, abnormal heart rhythms, and shock are all possible signs of overdose. In case of accidental ingestion or overdose, contact your veterinarian or the National Animal Poison Control Center. ALWAYS bring the prescription bottle or container with you if you go for treatment.

Special Information

Aminopentamide is a useful drug for certain situations. It should be used with caution and in most cases for one dose to help control relentless vomiting and diarrhea. It should not be used for treatment of any severe infectious gastroenteritis, such as canine parvovirus infection.

Special Populations

Pregnancy/Lactation
Aminopentamide should be avoided in pregnant or lactating animals.

Puppies/Kittens
Aminopentamide should be avoided in puppies and kittens.

Senior Animals
Aminopentamide should be avoided or used with caution in older animals.

Generic Name

Amitraz (AM-ih-traz)

Brand Names

Mitaban Liquid Concentrate [V]
Preventic Tick Collar for Dogs [V]

Type of Drug

Pesticide

Prescribed for

Generalized demodectic mange (demodicosis) in dogs caused

by the mite *Demodex canis* (amitraz liquid); and control of ticks on dogs (tick collar).

General Information

Amitraz kills mites and ticks by interfering with their central nervous system function. Amitraz is a monoamine oxidase inhibitor (MAOI). It also inhibits insulin release, which causes an increase in the blood glucose levels of animals and humans.

Demodex mites, in small numbers, are normal inhabitants of dog skin. Generalized demodicosis occurs when the immune system is not functioning properly, allowing the mites to multiply and cause skin disease. The disease is most likely to occur in puppies or in dogs with an underlying disease such as malnutrition, hypothyroidism, Cushing's disease, diabetes, severe skin infections, and some types of cancer. The diagnosis and treatment of underlying problems may help resolve the skin lesions caused by the mites. Up to 50% of affected puppies will self-cure once they reach 1 year, at which age the immune system is mature. The remaining 50% are probably never cured, and are thought to have an inherited immune defect. These dogs should not be used for breeding, and neutering is recommended.

Cautions and Warnings

For Owners/Handlers

■ Human diabetics should use this product with extreme caution because of the effect on insulin and blood glucose. Humans taking MAOIs, including drugs prescribed for depression, Parkinson's disease, and migraines, should use this product with caution. Nausea and dizziness have been reported in humans after handling this product, particularly in those taking MAOIs. Call your physician or poison control center if you experience side effects or in the case of accidental ingestion.

■ Avoid inhalation of vapors. Use only in well-ventilated area. Wear rubber gloves and avoid direct contact with this product; wash hands and arms thoroughly after handling the solution.

■ The concentrated solution contains alcohol and is flammable until diluted with water. Dispose of unused solution by flushing it down the drain. Rinse bottle and wrap collars in newspaper, then dispose in trash. Do not reuse.

For Animals

■ For external use in dogs only; do not use in dogs younger than 4 months. Do not use in cats.

■ Do not stress dogs for at least 24 hours after treatment with liquid amitraz.

■ Avoid contact with eyes. Use a protective eye ointment before applying liquid amitraz near the eyes.

■ Do not use in dogs with deep severe skin infections until the infection has been treated. Use with caution in diabetic dogs. Do not use in dogs being given other MAOIs.

■ Not recommended for the treatment of localized demodicosis or scabies (sarcoptic mange).

■ U.S. federal law restricts the use of this drug by or on the lawful written or oral order of a licensed veterinarian within the context of a valid veterinarian-client-patient relationship.

Possible Side Effects

▼ Common: sedation (9% of dogs; if a dog cannot be aroused or if sedation persists for longer than 72 hours, contact your veterinarian.) Itching for a short time after treatment (3% of dogs), dry skin and flaking.

▼ Rare: decreased body temperature, elevation of blood glucose, seizures, and sudden death.

Drug Interactions

• Compatibility with other agents has not been determined. Do not mix with other pesticides.

• Risk of side effects is increased when combined with other MAOIs.

• Immunosuppressive drugs, including corticosteroids and some chemotherapeutic agents, should be avoided in dogs that currently have or have previously had generalized demodicosis, because these drugs further suppress an already compromised immune system.

Usual Dose

Dogs

Solution: Long- and medium-haired dogs should be clipped, and all dogs bathed with a mild shampoo before treatment. Shampoos containing benzoyl peroxide are often recommended because they help flush debris from follicles and allow better penetration of the drug.

Mix 1 bottle (10.6 ml) of amitraz with 2 gallons of water to get the recommended dilution of 250 ppm. Fresh solution should be prepared immediately before each use because the solution is very unstable and deteriorates quickly once mixed. The dog should be soaked with the solution by applying it with a sponge over the entire body for about 10 minutes. The feet should be soaked in small bowls of the solution for the entire 10-minute dipping procedure. Treated dogs should be allowed to air dry. Do not rinse or towel dry.

Repeat dipping every 14 days for 3–6 treatments or as recommended by the veterinarian. Skin scrapings are used to monitor the patient and treatments should continue for 3–4 weeks after no mites are seen on the scrapings.

Higher concentrations and more frequent applications have been used successfully in dogs whose infections are not controlled using the usual treatment schedule. The benefit of better control of the disease should be weighed against the increased risk of side effects.

Tick Collars: Place the collar around the dog's neck. It should fit snugly but be loose enough to allow 2 fingers to fit between the collar and the dog's neck. Replace as recommended by the manufacturer.

Cats
Not recommended.

Overdosage

For external use only. Amitraz may be toxic if swallowed or inhaled. Signs include loss of coordination, depression, increased blood glucose levels, decreased pulse rates, and lowered body temperature. Severe toxicity may occur if amitraz-containing collars are ingested.

If side effects are seen or if this product is accidentally ingested, contact your veterinarian or the National Animal Poison Control Center. ALWAYS bring the prescription bottle or container with you if you go for treatment.

Special Information

Alternative treatments for generalized demodicosis include milbemycin oxime and ivermectin. Both of these drugs are FDA approved for use as monthly heartworm preventives and dewormers, but they are not FDA approved for treatment of demodicosis. If your dog does not respond to amitraz, or has an unacceptable level of side effects, consult your veterinarian about these alternatives. Milbemycin and ivermectin are relatively safe and effective treatments for demodicosis, but they should be considered only after discussing the potential benefits and risks with your veterinarian.

Special Populations

Sick/Convalescent Dogs
The amitraz collar should not be used in sick or convalescent dogs. Liquid amitraz should only be used if the potential benefits outweigh the risks.

Toy Dogs
Toy dogs are more likely to show prolonged sedation after application of amitraz liquid.

Pregnancy/Lactation
Reproductive safety has not been established. Use only when benefits outweigh potential risks of therapy in pregnant and lactating dogs. Affected dogs should not be used for breeding since generalized demodicosis is considered a hereditary defect.

Senior Animals
The immune system of older dogs may be impaired due to chronic diseases. The development of demodicosis should trigger a search for underlying causes.

Generic Name

Amitriptyline (ae-mih-TRIP-tuh-lene) G

Most Common Brand Name

Elavil H

Type of Drug

Antianxiety and tricyclic antidepressant.

Prescribed for

Compulsive behaviors, anxiety, and fear.

General Information

Amitriptyline hydrochloride is one of the tricyclic antidepressants (TCAs). TCAs are similar in structure to the phenothiazine tranquilizers (see *Acepromazine*). They work in the central nervous system (CNS) and inhibit the normal function of the neurotransmitters serotonin and norepinephrine by preventing normal reuptake by nerve endings. Different TCAs differ in their potency and in their relative effects on serotonin and norepinephrine. Amitriptyline and imipramine (Tofranil) affect serotonin and norepinephrine equally, and are used primarily as antianxiety drugs. Clomipramine (Anafranil) and fluoxetine (Prozac) affect serotonin primarily and are anticompulsive drugs.

Drugs are used in the treatment of behavior problems because certain undesirable behaviors cannot be managed by behavior modification techniques alone (behavior modification is training based on scientific principles used to alter or change undesirable behaviors). In such cases behavior modification is prevented due to severe anxiety or fear, a strong hormonal component to behavior (as in maternal aggression), or a neurochemical imbalance in the brain (as in compulsive behaviors). All undesirable behaviors have a learned component. Treatment of any undesirable behavior requires behavior modification. Drugs are only useful for certain specific types of behavior problems, and they should *only* be used as an adjunct to behavior modification. When used in this way, they enable behavior modification to be maximally effective.

Drugs should be discontinued *gradually* by reducing the dose over a 2 to 3 week period after the problem has resolved or improved. Dogs with hyperactivity or compulsive behaviors may need continual medication.

Most psychotropic drugs used in veterinary medicine are not licensed for use in animals. There are few controlled studies in animals establishing dose, efficacy, or safety. The long-term effects of these drugs are not known. There may be breed and individual differences in response to these drugs.

Amitriptyline is used in dogs to treat separation anxiety, fear of isolated events such as thunder, fear of everyday events such as vacuum cleaners, and hyperactivity if it is anxiety related. It may be used in cats as an adjunct to treatment of behavior problems caused by anxiety. These may include house-soiling (due to urine spraying or defecation) and excessive grooming.

Cautions and Warnings

For Owners/Handlers

■ KEEP OUT OF REACH OF CHILDREN! Children are very sensitive to the seizure-inducing and cardiotoxic effects of TCAs.

For Animals

■ Amitriptyline should be avoided in animals with liver disease, hyperthyroidism, glaucoma, seizures, heart failure, abnormal heart rhythms, or those on thyroid medication.

■ Most psychotropic drugs cause some degree of CNS depression and are sedatives at higher doses. They may also interfere with learning.

■ Amitriptyline is not FDA approved for use in dogs or cats. It is commonly used to treat anxiety disorders and is considered accepted practice.

■ Contact your veterinarian if you think your dog or cat may be having an adverse reaction to amitriptyline.

■ U.S. federal law restricts the use of this drug by or on the lawful written or oral order of a licensed veterinarian within the context of a valid veterinarian-client-patient relationship.

Possible Side Effects

Amitriptyline may cause drowsiness, but this is usually due to overdosing. It may also cause vomiting and diarrhea and should be given with food to avoid gastrointestinal upset. In people, heart problems, seizures, hallucinations and other CNS signs, gastrointestinal upset, allergic reactions, bone marrow depression, liver disease, hair loss, edema, and lupus-like syndromes have been reported. These signs have are not been reported in animals, but are all potential side effects.

▼ Rare: urine retention and hyperexcitability.

Drug Interactions

• Because of additive effects, amitriptyline should be used cautiously with other anticholinergic and CNS depressant drugs.

• TCAs should not be used with methimazole (see *Methimazole*) because such use increases the risk of bone marrow suppression.

• Cimetidine may decrease TCA metabolism and increase the risk of adverse reactions.

• TCAs should not be given with monoamine oxidase inhibitors.

• Use of TCAs with sympathomimetic agents (such as phenylpropanolamine) may increase the risks of abnormal heart rhythms, high blood pressure, and fever.

Food Interactions

Give with food to avoid GI upset.

Usual Dose

Dogs: 0.5–2.0 mg/lb orally 2–3 times a day.

Cats: 5–10 mg/cat orally, once a day, perhaps best given in the evening.

Drug Form: 10-, 25-, 50-, 75-, 100-, and 150-mg tablets and 10 mg/ml injectable.

Overdosage

Signs of overdose may include depression, abnormal heart rhythms, low blood pressure, convulsions, coma, and death. In case of accidental ingestion or overdose, contact your veterinarian or the National Animal Poison Control Center. ALWAYS bring the prescription bottle or container with you if you go for treatment.

Special Information

See *Fluoxetine* for more information on the use of TCAs for behavior problems.

Special Populations

Pregnancy/Lactation

There are no studies on the safety of amitriptyline in pregnant or lactating dogs or cats. High doses cause birth defects in laboratory animals. It should be avoided unless the potential benefits outweigh the risks.

Puppies/Kittens

Amitriptyline should not be used in puppies or kittens.

Senior Animals

Amitriptyline should be safe to use in older dogs and cats who do not have heart disease, thyroid or liver disease, or seizure disorders (see "Cautions and Warnings").

Generic Name

Ammonium Chloride

(uh-MOE-nee-um KLOR-ide)

Brand Names

MEq-AC V   Uroeze V

Type of Drug

Urine acidifier.

Prescribed for

Cystitis, alkaline urinary stones, feline urologic syndrome (FUS), and urinary tract infections.

General Information

Ammonium chloride is a salt that releases ammonium. When the liver breaks down the ammonium, acid is formed and is excreted in the urine. Acid urine is thought to help treat FUS and prevent the formation of and dissolve the stones that form in alkaline urine (struvite). Acid urine may help clear some urinary tract infections. Acidification of urine may be used to help the kidney excrete certain toxins or drug overdoses.

Cautions and Warnings

■ Ammonium chloride should not be used in dogs or cats with kidney, liver or pancreatic disease, or those with metabolic acidosis (excess acid in blood), as may occur in diabetes mellitus and urinary tract obstruction. Urine pH should be checked routinely to avoid under or overdosing.

■ Contact your veterinarian if you think your dog or cat may be having an adverse reaction to ammonium chloride.

■ U.S. federal law restricts the use of this drug by or on the lawful written or oral order of a licensed veterinarian within the context of a valid veterinarian-client-patient relationship.

Possible Side Effects

▼ Rare: stomach irritation and nausea and vomiting; Metabolic acidosis may develop if the animal is not adequately monitored and the dose is too high (see "Food Interactions").

Drug Interactions

• Ammonium chloride may decrease the effectiveness of quinidine.

• Ammonium chloride decreases the effectiveness of the aminoglycoside antibiotics and erythromycin if they are being used to treat urinary tract infections.

Food Interactions

Ammonium chloride should be given with food to avoid GI upset. Do not use ammonium chloride with diets designed to acidify the urine, unless under the supervision of your veterinarian. Metabolic acidosis may result from excessive acid in the diet.

Usual Dose

Dogs and Cats: 10–20 mg/lb orally twice a day or as needed to lower urine pH to 5.5–6.5.

Drug Form: Uroeze—200- and 400-mg tablets and 200 and 400 mg/tsp powder; MEqAC—357-mg chewable tablets and 535 mg/tsp palatable granules.

Overdosage

Overdose causes metabolic acidosis. Symptoms may include nausea, vomiting, excessive thirst, rapid deep breathing, slow heart rate or other abnormal heart rhythms, weakness, and progressive central nervous system depression. In case of accidental ingestion or overdose, contact your veterinarian or the National Animal Poison Control Center. ALWAYS bring the prescription bottle or container with you if you go for treatment.

Special Information

The cause of FUS is not known, but there is some evidence that acid urine and low dietary magnesium may help prevent recurrence of symptoms. There are a number of commercial diets designed for this purpose, such as Purina CNM-UR For-

mula and Hill's Prescription Diet c/d. Do not use urine acidifiers
with these diets unless under the supervision of your veterinarian. Regular or low magnesium diets may also be used with
added ammonium chloride to acidify the urine. Discuss the
management of FUS with your veterinarian to find the best
treatment for your cat.

Special Populations

Pregnancy/Lactation
Ammonium chloride should be avoided in pregnancy and lactation unless the benefits outweigh the risks.

Puppies/Kittens
Ammonium chloride should not be given to puppies or kittens.

Senior Animals
Ammonium chloride is safe to use in older animals, but should
not be given to those with acidosis, as in poorly controlled diabetes or urinary tract obstruction. It should not be given to
those with kidney or liver dysfunction.

Generic Name

Amphotericin B (am-fuh-TER-ih-sin BEE) G

Brand Names

Abelcet H   Fungizone H
Amphotec H

Type of Drug

Antifungal.

Prescribed for

Susceptible deep (systemic) fungal infections, including those
caused by *Candida* (yeasts), *Cryptococcus, Coccidioides,
Histoplasma, Aspergillus,* and *Blastomyces.*

General Information

Amphotericin B was the original systemic antifungal agent, and
for many years was the only drug other than iodide available
for treating deep fungal infections. It works quickly to fight off

many different kinds of fungi in serious or life-threatening fungal infections. The problem with amphotericin B is that it causes kidney damage in most patients. This has limited its usefulness in many fungal infections. Serious fungal infections may be treated with amphotericin B for a short time at the beginning, followed by the newer antifungals, which are less toxic (see *Fluconazole* and *Itraconazole*). Itraconazole may be equally effective in acute life-threatening fungal infections, but this has not been proven yet.

The only injectable forms of amphotericin B available now are liposome preparations, which reduce the chance of kidney damage. Amphotericin B is not absorbed well when given orally, and may be used to treat fungal infections of the mouth and throat.

Cautions and Warnings

■ Amphotericin B is not FDA approved for use in dogs or cats. It is used occasionally and is considered accepted practice.

■ Amphotericin B should be avoided or used with extreme caution in animals with kidney dysfunction. Kidney function should be monitored throughout the course of treatment.

■ Do not use in animals that are dehydrated or sodium depleted.

■ Contact your veterinarian if you think your dog or cat may be having an adverse reaction to amphotericin B.

■ U.S. federal law restricts the use of this drug by or on the lawful written or oral order of a licensed veterinarian within the context of a valid veterinarian-client-patient relationship.

Possible Side Effects

▼ Common: kidney damage.

▼ Rare: allergic or anaphylactic reactions, liver damage, decreased appetite, vomiting, low blood potassium, and fever.

Drug Interactions

• Amphotericin should not be used with other drugs that may cause kidney damage, such as the aminoglycosides and cyclosporine.

• Amphotericin may cause low blood potassium, and should be used with caution with digoxin, muscle relaxants, or other potassium-depleting drugs such as furosemide, thiazide diuretics, and corticosteroids.

Food Interactions

None known.

Usual Dose

Dogs: The dose will depend on the drug form available. Amphotericin B is given slowly into a vein.

Cats: The dose will depend on the drug form available. Amphotericin B is given slowly into a vein. Cats are more susceptible to the kidney damage, and the cat dose is usually half of the dog dose.

Drug Form: 100 mg/ml oral suspension, and injectable.

Overdosage

There is little specific information available on overdose of amphotericin B. Overdose is likely to cause kidney failure if given in a vein. Amphotericin is poorly absorbed orally so it should be safe if the oral suspension is ingested. In case of accidental ingestion or overdose, contact your veterinarian or the National Animal Poison Control Center. ALWAYS bring the prescription bottle or container with you if you go for treatment.

Special Information

There are many alternatives available now for the treatment of both superficial and deep fungal infections. None of these treatments are FDA approved for use in animals. See *Boric Acid*, *Griseofulvin*, *Miconazole*, and *Clotrimazole* for more information on treatment of superficial fungal infections. See *Fluconazole*, *Itraconazole*, and *Ketoconazole* for more information on treatment of deep fungal infections.

Special Populations

Pregnancy/Lactation

There are no safety studies of amphotericin B in pregnant or lactating dogs or cats. It should be avoided during pregnancy and lactation unless the benefits outweigh the risks.

Puppies/Kittens

Amphotericin B should be avoided in puppies and kittens unless the potential benefits outweigh the risks.

Senior Animals
Amphotericin B should be used with extreme caution in older animals, especially those with decreased liver and kidney function (see "Cautions and Warnings").

Type of Drug
Antacids/Phosphate Binders

Most Common Brand Names*

Generic Ingredient: Aluminum Hydroxide [G]
AlternaGEL [H]
Amphojel [H]

Generic Ingredient: Aluminum Magnesium Hydroxide [G]
Maalox [H]

Generic Ingredient: Calcium Acetate [G]
Phos-Ex [H]
PhosLo [H]

Generic Ingredient: Calcium Carbonate [G]
Tums [H]

*Check package labels carefully to make sure the product does not contain unwanted ingredients.

Prescribed for

Prevention and treatment of stomach ulcers and gastroesophageal reflux (reflux of stomach acid into the esophagus), and high blood phosphate in kidney failure.

General Information

Antacids may be used to treat stomach ulcers and gastroesophageal reflux and prevent them in those at risk. The disadvantage of antacids in dogs and cats is that they must be given every 2 to 4 hours in order to be effective, and they are poorly tolerated because of the taste. For these reasons other medications to block acid production and protect the stomach are often used (see *Cimetidine, Sucralfate, Misoprostol, Omeprazole*).

The main use for antacids in dogs and cats is as an intestinal phosphate binder in those with kidney failure and high blood phosphate. In kidney failure the animal is unable to excrete phosphate in the urine. This causes an increase in blood phosphate and then a variety of metabolic abnormalities that cause animals in kidney failure to feel poorly and deteriorate further. Standard treatment for kidney failure includes reduction of dietary phosphate. If that does not lower blood phosphate, then treatment with intestinal phosphate binders or antacids is used to lower the blood phosphate. Magnesium containing antacids, such as Maalox, should be avoided in kidney failure because they may cause high blood magnesium levels. The aluminum antacids have been used a great deal in dogs and cats and they are powerful and effective phosphate binders. There is some risk that prolonged use of aluminum antacids may cause aluminum toxicity in animals with kidney failure. Dogs and cats better tolerate the tablets and capsules, but they are not as effective as the liquid. Calcium antacids may also be useful as phosphate binders. They are not as potent as the aluminum salts, and there is a risk that they may increase blood calcium, but they are more palatable and fairly well tolerated. All of the antacids may cause a decrease in appetite, as can low-phosphate diets. It is imperative that animals in kidney failure continue to eat, so there may be a balancing act between palatable foods/low phosphate foods and antacids/phosphate binders. The best approach may be to give aluminum salts initially when phosphate levels are high, and then switch to calcium salts as the blood phosphate gets closer to normal. Calcium acetate binds 3 times as much phosphate as calcium carbonate and is less likely to cause high blood calcium. A combination of aluminum antacid with calcium acetate may reduce the risks of aluminum toxicity while promoting maximal intestinal phosphate binding.

Cautions and Warnings

■ Antacids may decrease appetite, especially in animals with kidney failure.

■ Calcium carbonate antacids and calcium acetate may cause high blood calcium in animals with kidney failure.

■ Chronic use of aluminum antacids may cause aluminum toxicity in animals with kidney failure.

■ Aluminum antacids may decrease stomach emptying and should be used with caution in animals with stomach outlet obstruction.

■ Some antacids contain large amounts of sodium or potassium and should be used with caution in those on restricted diets or with high blood sodium or potassium.

■ Contact your veterinarian if you think your dog or cat may be having an adverse reaction to antacids.

■ Use of these drugs should be by or on the lawful written or oral order of a licensed veterinarian within the context of a valid veterinarian-client-patient relationship.

Possible Side Effects

▼ Common: decreased appetite, constipation with aluminum and calcium antacids, and diarrhea with magnesium antacids.

▼ Rare: high blood calcium with calcium carbonate and calcium acetate and aluminum toxicity with chronic use of aluminum antacids.

Drug Interactions

• Antacids may alter the rate and extent of absorption of other drugs and significantly increase or decrease their effects. In general it is best not to give antacids within 1 to 2 hours of other oral medications.

• Calcium carbonate and calcium acetate should not be given to animals on digoxin/digitalis, as high blood calcium may cause abnormal heart rhythms.

Food Interactions

Antacids given as phosphate binders should always be given with food.

Usual Dose

Dogs and Cats: 50 mg/lb/day, divided and given with food 2–3 times a day, when the blood phosphate is greater than 6.0 mg/dl; 15–45 mg/lb/day may be sufficient in early chronic kidney failure when blood phosphate is still normal. The dose of antacid should be adjusted according to blood phosphate levels.

Drug Form: Antacids come in a variety of forms, including liquids, tablets, capsules, and softgels.

Overdosage

Overdose of antacids may cause low blood phosphate. Overdose of calcium antacids may cause high blood calcium. In case of accidental ingestion or overdose, contact your veterinarian or the National Animal Poison Control Center. ALWAYS bring the prescription bottle or container with you if you go for treatment.

Special Information

The management of animals with chronic kidney failure is a complicated and challenging task. Work closely with your veterinarian to establish the most effective treatments and diet for your dog or cat.

Special Populations

Pregnancy/Lactation
There are no studies to document the safety of antacids or phosphate binders in pregnant dogs or cats. They should be avoided unless the benefits outweigh the risks.

Puppies/Kittens
Antacids should be avoided or used with caution in young animals.

Senior Animals
Antacids should be safe to use in older animals if blood calcium and phosphate are monitored (see "Cautions and Warnings").

Generic Name

Apomorphine (ah-po-MOR-fene)

Brand Names

Available in generic form only.

Type of Drug

Emetic.

Prescribed for

Induction of vomiting in dogs and cats.

General Information

Apomorphine induces vomiting in dogs and cats by stimulating dopamine receptors in the brain. It may be used to induce vomiting after an animal has ingested certain toxins or in suspected drug overdose. It is usually given by placing a tablet under the lower eyelid and allowing the drug to be absorbed through the conjunctiva. Many veterinarians consider it as the emetic of choice in dogs. Its use is more controversial in the cat and there are other emetics, such as xylazine, that are more commonly used in the cat.

Emetics are an important part of the treatment of ingested toxins, but they are not appropriate in all cases, or with all toxins (see "Cautions and Warnings"). Emetics usually empty 40% to 60% of the stomach contents.

Cautions and Warnings

■ Apomorphine is not FDA approved for use in dogs and cats. It is commonly used in dogs and considered accepted practice. Experts differ on its use in cats. Narcotics tend to produce excitement in cats and are usually avoided.

■ Emetics should not be used in animals that are in shock, comatose, severely depressed, having difficulty breathing, lacking normal choke reflexes, seizuring, extremely weak, or experiencing other impairments that could lead to aspiration of the vomited material and pneumonia.

■ Emetics should not be used in animals that have vomited repeatedly; they should not be used in animals that have ingested caustic substances because of the risk of further damage to the stomach and esophagus.

■ Apomorphine should not be used in cases of oral opiate or other central nervous system depressant toxicity or in animals hypersensitive to morphine.

■ Emetics should be used with caution in animals that have ingested petroleum distillates because of the risk of aspiration and with caution in animals that have ingested strychnine or other central nervous system stimulants because of the increased risk of seizures.

■ U.S. federal law restricts the use of this drug by or on the lawful written or oral order of a licensed veterinarian within the context of a valid veterinarian-client-patient relationship.

Possible Side Effects

Aspiration pneumonia can occur after an animal vomits if vomit is inhaled into the lungs. This is always a risk, whether the vomiting was spontaneous or induced. Animals that are ill because of eating a toxin are more likely to aspirate vomit than normal animals.

Possible Side Effects *(continued)*

▼ Rare: protracted vomiting; central nervous system stimulation, including excitement and restlessness; and central nervous system and respiratory depression.

Drug Interactions

• Antiemetic drugs, especially those that decrease dopamine may decrease the effect of apomorphine.

• Increased central nervous system and respiratory depression may occur if apomorphine is used with opiates, barbiturates, or other depressant drugs.

Food Interactions

None known.

Usual Dose

Dogs: 1.5–6 mg in conjunctival sac.
Cats: Apomorphine is not commonly used in cats.
Drug Form: 6-mg tablets.

Overdosage

Overdoses of apomorphine may cause respiratory and cardiac depression, central nervous system stimulation (excitement, seizures), or depression and protracted vomiting. In case of accidental ingestion or overdose, contact your veterinarian or the National Animal Poison Control Center. ALWAYS bring the prescription bottle or container with you if you go for treatment.

Special Information

Apomorphine should only be used under direct veterinary supervision. If your animal vomits before arriving at the veterinary hospital, try to save a sample of the vomit for analysis.

Two other methods commonly used to induce vomiting in dogs are the oral administration of hydrogen peroxide and/or table salt. Consult your veterinarian before attempting these methods and use them only under the supervision of a veterinarian.

Special Populations

Pregnancy/Lactation
No safety studies have been performed. Apomorphine should only be used if the benefits outweigh the risks.

Puppies/Kittens
No safety studies have been performed. Apomorphine should not be used in kittens.

Senior Animals
No safety studies have been performed.

Generic Name
Artificial Tears

Most Common Brand Names

Liquifilm Tears [H]	Tears Naturale [H]
Murine Tears Lubricant [H]	Visine Lubricating [H]

Type of Drug

Artificial tears.

Prescribed for

Keratoconjunctivitis sicca (dry eye).

General Information

Artificial tears are used in the management and treatment of keratoconjunctivitis sicca (KCS), in dogs and cats. KCS is a potentially vision-threatening disease, which can be temporary or permanent, and has many different possible causes. KCS is one of the most frequent causes of loss of vision in dogs. The diagnosis of tear deficiency is usually made based on clinical signs and the Schirmer tear test. Tears have cleansing, lubricating, and many protective functions for the eye. Although artificial tears are not as good as natural tears, they are the mainstays for treatment of KCS by providing moisture for the dry outer surface of the eye.

Artificial tears are frequently used with other drugs in the management of KCS. Ophthalmic cyclosporine is successful in about 70% of dogs within 2 to 4 weeks. An additional 10% to 15% respond to long-term treatment (see *Cyclosporine*). Pilocarpine may be given orally to stimulate natural tear production. Ophthalmic steroids, antibiotics, and drugs to decrease mucus accumulation (see *Acetylcysteine*) are also frequently used at the start of treatment. Most animals with KCS require long-term therapy to alleviate the clinical signs and preserve their vision.

Cautions and Warnings

■ Artificial tears are not FDA approved for use in dogs or cats. They are commonly used and considered accepted practice.

■ Contact your veterinarian if you think your dog or cat may be having an adverse reaction to artificial tear products.

■ U.S. federal law restricts the use of this drug by or on the lawful written or oral order of a licensed veterinarian within the context of a valid veterinarian-client-patient relationship.

Possible Side Effects

▼ Common: preservatives found in some tear replacement products can be irritating. Preservative-free artificial tears are preferred.

Drug Interactions

None known.

Usual Dose

Dogs and Cats: as often as possible, 4–12 times a day.
Drug Form: solution and ointment.

Overdosage

No adverse effects have been reported.

Special Information

Tear replacement can require frequent treatments because the solutions drain quickly from the eye. Ointments remain on the eye longer, permitting fewer applications. Petrolatum ophthalmic ointment can be applied after liquid tear solutions to provide longer contact time. Animals with droopy eyelids will need more frequent applications of artificial tears.

Artificial tear solutions are frequently used as the base when compounding custom ophthalmic products.

Special Populations

Pregnancy/Lactation

Artificial tears are safe to use during pregnancy and lactation.

Puppies/Kittens
Artificial tears are safe to use in puppies and kittens.

Senior Animals
Artificial tears are safe to use in older animals.

Generic Name

Aspirin/Acetylsalicylic Acid

(AS-prin/uh-SEE-til-sal-uh-SIL-ik)

Most Common Brand Names G

Aftercare V	Bayer H
Arthricare V	Bufferin H
Ascriptin H	Palaprin V

Type of Drug

Nonsteroidal anti-inflammatory drug (NSAID), pain reliever, and fever reducer.

Prescribed for

Relief of pain and inflammation, especially that associated with arthritis, and anticoagulation (blood thinning) in cats with heart disease.

General Information

Aspirin is a nonsteroidal anti-inflammatory drug (NSAID) of the salicylic acid class. It is not known exactly how NSAIDs work. However, part of their action may be due to their ability to inhibit the body's production of hormones called prostaglandins. NSAIDs also inhibit production of other body chemicals that sensitize pain receptors and stimulate the inflammatory response. Aspirin is quickly absorbed into the bloodstream. Pain and fever relief usually starts within 1 hour and lasts for up to 12 hours in dogs and 3 days in cats. The anti-inflammatory response takes longer to occur. It takes several days to 2 weeks to start and may take 1 month or more to reach maximum effect.

Aspirin, like the other NSAIDs, may cause ulceration of the gastrointestinal (GI) tract. Buffered, enteric coated, or microencapsulated aspirins may lessen the chances of stomach irritation but do not eliminate the risk of GI upset and ulceration. Aspirin is one of the few NSAIDs that is safe to use in both dogs and cats. However, cats metabolize aspirin very slowly and are usually dosed once every 3 days or longer. Other NSAIDs like ibuprofen and acetaminophen (see *Common Household Poisons*) are not safe to use in dogs and cats and may cause severe illness and death. Consult your veterinarian before giving any medications, especially the NSAIDs, as they may reduce pain and fever enough to make evaluation of your pet's condition difficult or impossible.

Aside from its anti-inflammatory and pain relief effects, aspirin also decreases platelet function and therefore reduces clot formation. Aspirin is often prescribed for cats with heart disease that have either had an episode of clotting (thromboembolism) or are at risk of clotting. There is no proof that aspirin works in these cats, and some experts recommend warfarin treatment (see *Warfarin*).

Cautions and Warnings

■ Because aspirin is such an old drug, formal approval by the FDA has not been required for use in any animal species. There are products specifically marketed for dogs. There are no products marketed for cats at present. Aspirin is routinely used in dogs and cats and is considered accepted practice.

■ Do not use aspirin products containing any other unwanted drugs such as caffeine, codeine, or acetaminophen. These drugs may cause severe illness or death.

■ DO NOT use aspirin in cats unless under the supervision of your veterinarian. The dosing interval is 3 days or longer and more frequent dosing may cause severe side effects or death.

■ NSAIDs tend to cause adverse effects in the GI tract and the kidneys. Some individual animals are more sensitive to the adverse effects than others. Those animals at greatest risk for kidney damage are those on diuretics or those with liver, kidney, or heart disease.

■ Aspirin should not be used with other anti-inflammatory drugs that tend to cause GI ulcers, such as corticosteroids (see *Corticosteroids*), and other NSAIDs, unless the patient is being closely monitored.

■ Aspirin should be stopped if possible 1 week before surgery to avoid possible bleeding problems.

■ Aspirin is not recommended for use in dogs with bleeding

disorders such as von Willebrand's disease, as safety has not been established in dogs with these disorders.

■ Contact your veterinarian if you think your dog or cat may be having an adverse reaction to aspirin.

■ U.S. federal law restricts the use of this drug by or on the lawful written or oral order of a licensed veterinarian within the context of a valid veterinarian-client-patient relationship.

Possible Side Effects

GI ulcers and kidney damage are possible side effects. Signs might include decreased appetite, vomiting, black or bloody stool, or increased water consumption and urination.

▼ Rare: allergic reactions, severe anemia, and low blood protein from GI blood loss.

Drug Interactions

• Drugs that alter the pH of urine (acetazolamide, methionine, ammonium chloride, vitamin C) may cause aspirin toxicity.

• Furosemide may increase aspirin blood levels and cause aspirin toxicity in those on higher doses of aspirin.

• Phenobarbital and corticosteroids may decrease the effectiveness of aspirin.

• Aspirin may increase the risks of bleeding when given with heparin or warfarin.

• Give aspirin and tetracyclines at least 1 hour apart.

• Aspirin may increase the blood levels of digoxin and the risks of digoxin toxicity.

• Aspirin may increase the chances of kidney damage from aminoglycoside antibiotics.

• Aspirin may increase the drug effects and potential toxicity of methotrexate, valproic acid, phenytoin, warfarin, penicillins, and sulfonamides.

Food Interactions

Probably best if given with food.

Usual Dose

Dogs: 5–15 mg/lb orally 2–3 times a day.

Cats: 5 mg/lb orally every other day; or one 81-mg "baby" aspirin every 3 days.

Drug Form: Enteric coated aspirin such as Ascriptin, buffered aspirin such as Bufferin, and veterinary chewable and microencapsulated forms are available. Consult your veterinarian for advice on the best form of aspirin for your pet.

Overdosage

An overdose of aspirin may cause depression, decreased appetite, vomiting, fever, and rapid breathing. If untreated, signs could progress to weakness, unsteady gait, edema (excess fluid) of the lungs and brain, seizures, and death. In case of accidental ingestion or overdose, contact your veterinarian or the National Animal Poison Control Center. ALWAYS bring the prescription bottle or container with you if you go for treatment.

Special Information

One in 5 adult dogs has arthritis, according to a recent survey of veterinarians. Many of these are older animals, but arthritis can occur in young dogs as well, especially those with hip dysplasia or knee injuries. It is important for dog owners to recognize the early signs of pain, such as stiffness, lameness, difficulty rising from a resting position, or whimpering, so that a diagnosis can be made and appropriate therapy given. Aspirin may be an effective way to alleviate pain and discomfort from arthritis and is safe in most animals, even when used long-term. Other NSAIDs, such as ibuprofen should not be used in dogs, as they have a very narrow margin of safety and may cause serious side effects.

There are many other alternatives for treatment of arthritis in dogs. These include cartilage protective agents, such as Cosequin (see *Glycosaminoglycan Supplements*) and Adequan (see *Polysulfated Glycosaminoglycan*); other NSAIDs such as carprofen (see *Carprofen*), piroxicam (see *Piroxicam*), and phenylbutazone (see *Phenylbutazone*); anti-inflammatory-analgesic treatments, such as methylsulfonylmethane (see *Dimethyl Sulfoxide (DMSO)*); omega-3 fatty acid supplements (see *Fatty Acids*); acupuncture; weight loss; and controlled exercise or physical therapy. Each dog may respond a little differently to these treatments. Work with your veterinarian to find the safest, most effective treatment or combination of treatments for your dog.

Special Populations

Pregnancy/Lactation

Aspirin causes damage to the fetus, especially late in pregnancy, and should be avoided in pregnant or lactating animals.

Puppies/Kittens

Aspirin should be avoided or used with caution in puppies and kittens.

Senior Animals

Aspirin should be safe to use in older animals with normal kidney function. It should be used with caution in those with dehydration or kidney damage (see "Cautions and Warnings"), and with careful attention to possible drug interactions and monitoring for side effects.

Generic Name

Atenolol (ah-TEN-uh-lol) G

Brand Names

Tenormin H

Type of Drug

Beta-adrenergic blocking agent.

Prescribed for

Dilated cardiomyopathy, hypertrophic cardiomyopathy in cats, high blood pressure, and abnormal heart rhythms.

General Information

Beta-adrenergic blocking agents (beta-blockers) interfere with the actions of the sympathetic nervous system. They block the receptors on the heart and blood vessels where the chemical messengers of the sympathetic nervous system (epinephrine/adrenaline and norepinephrine) bind. Beta-blockers may be used to treat hypertrophic (thickened) and dilated (thinned) cardiomyopathy (heart muscle disease). Atenolol and propranolol are the two beta-blockers used most commonly in dogs and cats. Atenolol works more specifically on the heart and has fewer side effects; propranolol is a nonselective beta-blocker.

They improve breathing and heart function, slow the heart rate, and control abnormal heart rhythms. Studies in people have shown that control of excess sympathetic activity in heart failure leads to improved heart function and prolonged survival. Beta-blockers may also be useful in congenital heart diseases where there is outflow obstruction (sub-aortic and pulmonic stenosis).

Essential hypertension (high blood pressure) is a relatively rare disorder in dogs and cats, although secondary hypertension is quite common in dogs and cats with kidney failure. Diuretics and low salt diets are standard treatments for hypertension. Other adjunct treatments might include atenolol, propranolol, prazosin, or ACE inhibitors (see *Enalapril*) for those resistant to diuretic and dietary therapy.

Beta-blockers may be useful in treating the heart disease and hypertension caused by hyperthyroidism. It is not a substitute for correction of the disorder (see *Methimazole*) and is usually used during the first 2 weeks of methimazole therapy. Beta-blockers may be used topically to treat glaucoma (see *Timolol*). They are also used to treat poisoning with caffeine, chocolate, and cocaine (see *Common Household Poisons*) as well as theophylline overdose.

Beta-blockers affect sympathetic nervous system receptors all over the body. They may cause serious heart problems and other side effects. Some animals are unable to tolerate even small doses, and it is critically important to start with a low dose and increase the dose slowly over 2 to 4 days until the desired effect is achieved.

Cautions and Warnings

■ Beta-blockers should be started and discontinued gradually.

■ Beta-blockers should be avoided or used with extreme caution in animals with overt heart failure, heart block, slow heart rate, or significant kidney dysfunction. They should be avoided in animals with asthma, bronchospasm, or chronic obstructive pulmonary disease. Atenolol has less effect on airways than propranolol, so it is relatively safe in airway disease.

■ Atenolol is not FDA approved for use in dogs or cats. It is commonly used and is considered accepted practice.

■ Contact your veterinarian if you think your dog or cat may be having an adverse reaction to atenolol.

■ U.S. federal law restricts the use of this drug by or on the lawful written or oral order of a licensed veterinarian within the context of a valid veterinarian-client-patient relationship.

Possible Side Effects

Side effects usually result from excessive blockade of sympathetic receptors. Beta-blockers may precipitate congestive heart failure, cause abnormally slow heart rhythms, depression, low blood pressure, spasm of the airways, and low blood glucose. Rarer symptoms of beta-blockade include diarrhea, nausea, stomach pain, or constipation.

Drug Interactions

• Sympathomimetics such as terbutaline, epinephrine, and phenylpropanolamine may be blocked by atenolol and may in turn reduce the effects of beta-blockers.

• Additional heart muscle depression may occur when beta-blockers are used with anesthetics.

• Phenothiazines such as acepromazine and diuretics such as hydralazine and furosemide may enhance the blood-pressure-lowering effects of beta-blockers.

• Beta-blockers may prolong the effects of insulin.

• Beta-blockers should not be used with calcium channel blockers because they both decrease the strength of heart muscle contractions.

Food Interactions

None known.

Usual Dose

Atenolol
   Dogs: 0.12–0.5 mg/lb orally 1–2 times a day. For hypertension—1 mg/lb once a day.
   Cats: 5–6.25 mg/cat orally 1–2 times a day. For hypertension—1 mg/lb once a day.
   Drug Form: 25-, 50-, and 100-mg tablets and 0.5 mg/ml injectable.

Propranolol
   Dogs: 0.1–0.5 mg/lb orally 3 times a day. For hypertension—5–80 (or up to 200) mg/dog 2–3 times a day.

Cats: 0.2–0.6 mg/lb orally 2–3 times a day. For hypertension—2.5–5 mg/cat 2–3 times a day.

Drug Form: 10-, 20-, 40-, 60-, and 80-mg tablets and 1 mg/ml injectable. Inderal comes in a long-acting form (capsule). The doses above *do not* apply to Inderal LA, and this form should not be used unless under the specific instructions of a veterinary cardiologist or internal medicine specialist.

Overdosage

Signs of overdose would include low blood pressure, slow heart rate, airway constriction, heart failure, and low blood glucose. In case of accidental ingestion or overdose, contact your veterinarian or the National Animal Poison Control Center. ALWAYS bring the prescription bottle or container with you if you go for treatment.

Special Information

Atenolol is used more often than propranolol for hypertension because of the once a day dosing and relative lack of side effects. Atenolol may be especially useful when given with digoxin to control heart rate in atrial fibrillation. Atenolol may also be very helpful in cats with asymptomatic or symptomatic hypertrophic cardiomyopathy, particularly those with left ventricular outflow obstruction. Beta-blockade prevents the stress-induced pulmonary edema that occurs in these cats.

Special Populations

Pregnancy/Lactation
Atenolol crosses the placenta and is excreted in concentrated amounts in milk. It should be avoided in pregnant or lactating animals unless the benefits outweigh the risks.

Puppies/Kittens
Atenolol should not be used in puppies or kittens unless under the supervision of a veterinary cardiologist.

Senior Animals
Older animals, especially those with severe heart disease or kidney dysfunction, are more susceptible to the adverse effects of beta-blockers. Beta-blockers should be avoided or used with extreme caution in this group and preferably under the supervision of a veterinary cardiologist.

Generic Name

Azathioprine (AZ-uh-THIGH-oe-prine) G

Brand Names

Imuran H

Type of Drug

Immunosuppressant.

Prescribed for

Autoimmune or immune-mediated diseases, especially those of skin, gastrointestinal tract, and eyes.

General Information

In autoimmune disease, the immune system loses the ability to distinguish between itself and foreign substances, therefore it attacks the body's own tissues. Azathioprine may help stop this attack. It is not known how azathioprine suppresses the immune system. It is used in those immune-mediated disorders that do not respond to corticosteroids alone and is usually combined with corticosteroids. It may be used to treat chronic gastritis, inflammatory bowel disease, eosinophilic gastroenteritis, chronic hepatitis, discoid lupus, pemphigus, systemic lupus erythematosus (SLE), immune-mediated joint disease, intractable uveitis/episcleritis, ocular fibrous histiocytoma of collies, and lung disease secondary to heartworm infection. It may also be used in immune-mediated kidney disease, myasthenia gravis, and immune-mediated hemolytic anemia or thrombocytopenia.

Cautions and Warnings

■ Azathioprine is not FDA approved for use in dogs or cats. It is considered accepted practice to use azathioprine to treat a number of autoimmune or immune-mediated disorders in dogs. Azathioprine may cause bone marrow suppression. Cats are particularly susceptible to this side effect, so azathioprine is not recommended for use in cats.

■ Azathioprine may cause liver damage, pancreatitis, or increased susceptibility to infection.

■ It may take 6 weeks to see a response to azathioprine therapy.

■ Contact your veterinarian if you think your dog may be having an adverse reaction to azathioprine.

■ U.S. federal law restricts the use of this drug by or on the lawful written or oral order of a licensed veterinarian within the context of a valid veterinarian-client-patient relationship.

Possible Side Effects

▼ Common: bone marrow suppression with low platelet and white blood cell counts and anemia. Signs may include bleeding or bruising and increased susceptibility to infection.

▼ Rare: pancreatitis and liver damage and cancer with long-term use.

Drug Interactions

• The dose of azathioprine may need to be reduced if allopurinol is given.

• Azathioprine may reverse or inhibit pancuronium and tubocurarine.

Food Interactions

None known.

Usual Dose

Dogs: 1 mg/lb once a day or every other day.
Drug Form: 50-mg tablets.

Overdosage

There is no specific information available on azathioprine overdose. It could cause severe bone marrow suppression or liver damage. In case of accidental ingestion or overdose, contact your veterinarian or the National Animal Poison Control Center. ALWAYS bring the prescription bottle or container with you if you go for treatment.

Special Information

Dogs receiving azathioprine should have a complete blood count, platelet count, and chemistry panel run every 2 weeks during the beginning of therapy and every 1 to 2 months after the dog is in remission and on maintenance therapy. These tests will pick up bone marrow suppression and pancreatic or liver damage early.

Special Populations

Pregnancy/Lactation
Azathioprine causes damage to the fetus and should be avoided in pregnant or lactating animals.

Puppies/Kittens
Azathioprine should not be used in puppies or kittens.

Senior Animals
Azathioprine should be used with caution in older animals, especially those with bone marrow suppression or liver disease (see "Special Information").

Generic Name

Benzoyl Peroxide (BEN-zoil per-OK-side) [G]

Most Common Brand Names

Allerderm [V]   Pyoban [V]
OxyDex [V]   Sulf/Oxy-Dex [V]

Type of Drug

Topical antibacterial, anti-itch, antiscale, degreasing gel or shampoo.

Prescribed for

Skin problems including superficial and deep bacterial skin infections (pyodermas) and excess scale and/or grease.

General Information

Benzoyl peroxide is a shampoo or topical gel used in a variety of skin problems. It is effective against a broad spectrum of bacteria and has flushing activity in the hair follicles. Benzoyl peroxide is also effective at softening excess scale (keratin) and degreasing skin. It is used in most forms of pyoderma, including impetigo, chin acne, skin fold pyoderma, hotspots, and deeper skin infections. Pyoderma is usually secondary to some other problem and will recur unless the underlying problem is solved. Allergies, breed predisposition, external parasites, hormone problems, keratin disorders, immunodeficiency, poor grooming, anal sac problems, even musculoskeletal problems can be underlying causes of skin infections. Most skin infections are caused by *Staphylococcus,* although other bacteria such as *Pseudomonas, Proteus,* and *E. coli,* may be present in recurrent or deep pyoderma.

Keratinizition defects can present with a variety of symptoms from dry, scaling skin to greasy, smelly skin called seborrhea. There can be hair loss, superficial skin infection, crusting, blackheads, itching and a characteristic seborrheic odor. Most greasy keratinizition disorders will benefit from benzoyl peroxide shampoo. Benzoyl peroxide softens and allows the excess keratin to be mechanically washed away, which is useful in treatment and long-term management of these conditions. It also decreases bacteria on the skin to normal levels for 24 to 48 hours after use.

Benzoyl peroxide shampoo is frequently used in animals with generalized *Demodex* infections prior to dipping with amitraz products (see *Amitraz*). Benzoyl peroxide gel is useful in the spot treatment of localized *Demodex* infections.

In *Malassezia* (yeast) skin infections, benzoyl peroxide shampoo is recommended as a degreasing agent prior to treatment with antifungal shampoo (see *Miconazole* and *Ketoconazole*).

Cautions and Warnings

For Owners/Handlers
- For external use only.
- Avoid contact with eyes, since irritation may result.
- Benzoyl peroxide products may bleach fabric.

For Animals
- Avoid contact with eyes or mucous membranes, since irritation may result.
- Contact your veterinarian if you think your dog or cat may be having an adverse reaction to benzoyl peroxide, or if there is no improvement in 2 weeks.
- U.S. federal law restricts the use of this drug by or on the lawful written or oral order of a licensed veterinarian within the context of a valid veterinarian-client-patient relationship.

Possible Side Effects

▼ Common: drying of skin and hair coat, hair bleaching, and skin irritation.

Drug Interactions

None known.

Usual Dose

Dogs and Cats: Shampoo 2 to 3 times a week or as directed by your veterinarian. Shampoo should be left on the animal for 10 minutes before rinsing. When using the gel, clean affected area with soap and water, and dry thoroughly. Apply a light covering of gel once a day to affected areas and immediate surrounding vicinity. Treatment may involve other procedures, so follow your veterinarian's advice on the use of benzoyl peroxide products.

Drug Form: 2.5% shampoo and 0.5% gel. Stronger concentration human products are not recommended for use in animals.

Overdosage

There is no specific information on overdose of benzoyl peroxide. In case of accidental ingestion or overdose, contact your veterinarian or the National Animal Poison Control Center. ALWAYS bring the prescription bottle or container with you if you go for treatment.

Special Information

Pyoderma and seborrhea can present long-term management challenges. It is important to identify and address the underlying problem in order to control the secondary skin problems. Some breeds are particularly prone to skin infections or seborrhea because of genetic predisposition or skin type.

Benzoyl peroxide products are very drying to the skin. This can be a benefit in some cases, but in other cases a bath oil or coat conditioner may be need to rehydrate the skin. Chlorhexidine products are frequently used when benzoyl peroxide is too drying.

Special Populations

Pregnancy/Lactation
Benzoyl peroxide should be safe to use on pregnant or lactating animals.

Puppies/Kittens
Benzoyl peroxide should be safe to use on puppies and kittens, but there are no studies to confirm safety in this group.

Senior Animals
Benzoyl peroxide should be safe to use on older animals, but there are no studies to confirm safety in this group.

Generic Name

Bethanechol (buh-THAN-uh-kawl) [G]

Most Common Brand Name

Urecholine [H]

Type of Drug

Smooth muscle stimulant.

Prescribed for

Stimulation of bladder contraction.

General Information

Bethanechol chloride causes smooth muscle contractions in many internal organs. These effects are most pronounced in the bladder but may occur in the gastrointestinal (GI) tract as well. Bethanechol may be used in dogs and cats, especially cats, to stimulate bladder contraction. When an animal has had a urinary tract obstruction, most commonly caused by blockage of the urethra by stones or grit, the bladder wall is stretched to the point where the muscle cannot contract. Therefore, even though the obstruction has been relieved, the animal is still unable to empty its bladder. In order for the bladder wall to heal as quickly as possible, it should be kept empty, either by manual compression of the bladder or using bethanecol. Bethanechol should only be used when the urethra is open, as when a catheter is in place, or with urethral relaxants, because bethanecol can cause contraction of urethral smooth muscle as well. Theoretically, the bladder could rupture if bethanecol is given when the urethra is blocked, or in spasm.

Cautions and Warnings

■ Bethanechol is not FDA approved for use in dogs and cats. It is occasionally used to treat bladder problems in cats and dogs and is considered accepted practice.

■ Bethanechol should not be used in animals with known hypersensitivity to this drug. It should not be used in animals that have a mechanical obstruction of the urethra, or in animals where the wall of the bladder may have a structural defect, such as an incision for bladder stone removal.

■ Bethanechol should not be used in animals recovering from surgery to the GI tract, stomach ulcers, or other inflammatory disease of the GI tract, and it should not be used in animals with epilepsy, asthma, hyperthyroidism, or heart disease.

■ Bethanechol should always be used with a urethral relaxant such as phenoxybenzamine, diazepam, or aminopropazine (Jenotone or Peritone), if a urethral catheter is not in place.

■ Bethanechol should be used with caution in animals recovering from urinary tract surgery.

■ U.S. federal law restricts the use of this drug by or on the lawful written or oral order of a licensed veterinarian within the context of a valid veterinarian-client-patient relationship.

Possible Side Effects

Side effects from oral bethanechol are usually mild.

▼ Common: vomiting, diarrhea, increased salivation, and decreased appetite.

Drug Interactions

• Bethanechol should not be used with other cholinergic or anticholinesterase drugs, such as carbachol or neostigmine.

• Quinidine, procainamide, epinephrine, and atropine decrease the effects of bethanechol. Atropine is used to treat bethanechol overdoses.

• Bethanechol should not be used with certain antihypertension medications that lower blood pressure.

Food Interactions

There are usually fewer side effects if given on an empty stomach.

Usual Dose

Contact your veterinarian if salivation or GI upsets are pronounced or persist. Your animal may need a reduced dose.
  Dogs: 5–25 mg orally 3 times a day.
  Cats: 1.25–5 mg orally 3 times a day.
  Drug Form: 5-, 10-, 25-, and 50-mg tablets.

Overdosage

Overdoses of bethanechol can cause GI, cardiovascular, and respiratory symptoms. This is because bethanechol works on smooth muscle throughout the body. In addition to the GI symptoms (see "Possible Side Effects"), other symptoms of overdose may include low blood pressure, irregular heartbeats, and asthma. In case of accidental ingestion or overdose, contact your veterinarian or the National Animal Poison Control Center. ALWAYS bring the prescription bottle or container if you go for treatment.

Special Information

It is common for animals to have difficulty contracting their bladder after a urinary tract obstruction. The bladder wall is stretched to the point where the smooth muscle in the wall does not function normally. Once the obstruction has been relieved, bethanechol may be used to stimulate the bladder to contract and eventually return to normal size, as the bladder wall heals. The time that it takes for the bladder wall to heal depends on the degree of injury. The degree of injury usually depends on how much the bladder was distended and for how long.

Special Populations

Pregnancy/Lactation

There are no studies in humans or in animals on the effects of bethanechol during pregnancy or lactation. It should not be given to pregnant or lactating animals.

Puppies/Kittens

There is no information available on studies in children or young animals, and it should not be given to puppies or kittens.

Senior Animals

There is no information available on studies in senior animals. It is probably safe to use bethanechol in older animals, but it should be avoided if there is heart disease, hyperthyroidism, asthma, or seizures.

Generic Name

Bisacodyl (bis-AK-uh-dil) G

Most Common Brand Names

Dulcolax H   Fleet Bisacodyl H

Type of Drug

Stimulant laxative.

Prescribed for

Constipation and megacolon.

General Information

Laxatives are used to prevent or relieve constipation. They are classified by their action as lubricant, emollient (stool softeners), bulk-forming, osmotic, or stimulant. The choice of laxative, dose, and frequency of administration must be adjusted for each individual to obtain the desired stool consistency and frequency of defecation. Vomiting, straining, and other signs of constipation may be caused by serious problems. Consult your veterinarian before administering laxatives or any other medication to your pet.

Bisacodyl is a stimulant laxative. It stimulates nerves in the colon, causing the muscle to contract and propel stool through the colon. It also increases the amount of water in the stool, making it softer. It may be used to treat mild to moderate cases of constipation. It should not be used if the intestine may be obstructed or weakened, because the intestine may rupture. It may be administered either by mouth or rectally. Results are seen 6 to 10 hours after oral administration or 15 to 60 minutes after rectal administration.

Bisacodyl is used to treat megacolon, a disorder seen most frequently in cats. An enlarged colon with decreased muscle function results in the accumulation of huge amounts of fecal material, making it painful and ultimately impossible to defecate. There is no cure, but the constipation may be managed with individually tailored treatment plans based on the use of the various types of laxatives. Bisacodyl is most useful when administered as needed to supplement other laxatives in mild to moderate episodes of constipation.

Cautions and Warnings

■ DO NOT USE FLEET ENEMA, FLEET ENEMA FOR CHILDREN, OR FLEET PHOSPHO-SODA IN DOGS OR CATS. These Fleet products are saline laxatives. They contain concentrated sodium phosphate, which may cause severe toxic reactions and death, particularly in cats and small-to medium-sized dogs. Do not confuse Fleet Enema, a saline laxative, with Fleet Bisacodyl enema.

■ Do not split, crush, or allow the animal to chew the tablets. Intense cramping may occur. Do not use regularly unless specifically instructed to do so by your veterinarian.

■ Do not use in animals with intestinal obstruction, rectal bleeding, or if intestinal perforation is likely.

■ Contact your veterinarian if you think your dog or cat may be having an adverse reaction to bisacodyl.

■ Bisacodyl is not FDA approved for use in dogs or cats. It is available over-the-counter (OTC) for human use. Extralabel use of the human product is common in dogs and cats and is considered accepted practice when administered under veterinary supervision.

■ U.S. federal law restricts the use of this drug by or on the lawful written or oral order of a licensed veterinarian within the context of a valid veterinarian-client-patient relationship.

Possible Side Effects

▼ Rare: cramping, vomiting, and diarrhea.

Drug Interactions

• Do not administer antacids within 1 hour because the enteric coating may dissolve before it should and increase the risk of side effects.

• Bisacodyl may reduce absorption of other drugs by

increasing the speed of transit through the intestines. Separate doses by 2 hours if possible.

Food Interactions

Do not feed milk within 1 hour of administering bisacodyl.

Usual Dose

Dogs and Cats: tablets—5–20 mg orally once a day as needed. Do not break tablets. Enema—0.5–1 ml/lb up to 1 prepackaged unit once a day as needed. Pediatric suppositories—1–3 once a day as needed.

Drug Form: 5-mg tablets, 5- and 10-mg rectal suppositories, and 10 mg/30 ml enema.

Storage Information: Store at temperatures lower than 86°F.

Overdosage

Overdoses may result in severe cramping, diarrhea, vomiting, and fluid and electrolyte imbalances. In case of accidental ingestion or overdose, contact your veterinarian or the National Animal Poison Control Center. ALWAYS bring the prescription bottle or container with you if you go for treatment.

Special Information

Bisacodyl is available OTC for human use. This and other human OTC products should not be used in dogs or cats unless specifically instructed by your veterinarian. Many OTC products, including some types of laxatives, may cause severe side effects, including death in dogs or cats.

Castor oil is also a stimulant laxative, but it is not very useful for treating animals at home because it is very poorly accepted by most pets. It is more useful in a hospital setting to prepare the bowel for examination by radiographs (X-rays) or endoscope.

Special Populations

Pregnancy/Lactation

No adequate studies are available. It should not be used in pregnant and lactating dogs or cats unless the potential benefits clearly outweigh the risks.

Puppies/Kittens

No adequate studies are available in puppies or kittens. It

should not be used unless the potential benefits clearly outweigh the risks.

Senior Animals

No adequate studies are available in senior dogs or cats. It should be safe, but risks should be weighed against the benefits.

Generic Name

Bismuth Subsalicylate

(BIZ-muth sub-suh-LIS-uh-late)

Most Common Brand Names

BismuKote [V]   Pepto-Bismol [H]

Type of Drug

Antidiarrheal, antimicrobial, general stomach remedy.

Prescribed for

Diarrhea, nausea, indigestion, vomiting, especially caused by dietary indiscretion in dogs, and *Helicobacter* gastritis and duodenitis in dogs.

General Information

Bismuth subsalicylate provides excellent symptomatic relief for dogs that have mild vomiting and/or mild to moderate diarrhea as a result of dietary indiscretion. It makes them feel better by decreasing the nausea and soothing the gastrointestinal tract. It also relieves diarrhea and adsorbs bacterial toxins in the gastrointestinal tract that may be contributing to or causing the diarrhea and illness. Bismuth subsalicylate is also part of the recommended therapy for gastroduodenitis in dogs caused by *Helicobacter* species, because it helps kill the bacteria and also relieves symptoms. Bismuth subsalicylate must be used with caution in cats. Because they metabolize salicylates very slowly, the risks of overdosing and side effects are increased. Cimetidine is substituted for bismuth subsalicylate in treatment for *Helicobacter* in cats.

Cautions and Warnings

■ Bismuth subsalicylate is FDA approved for use in dogs and

cats. Follow your veterinarian's advice on dose and dosing frequency, and be aware that there are a variety of strengths of bismuth subsalicylate in various human and veterinary products.

■ Hospitalization and oral and intravenous hydration may be necessary in cases of diarrhea or gastrointestinal inflammation.

■ Consult your veterinarian if signs of depression, fever, vomiting, diarrhea, or abdominal discomfort persist, or if you think your animal may be having an adverse reaction to bismuth subsalicylate.

■ This medication may cause a harmless temporary darkening of the tongue or stool.

■ Do not use with aspirin or other salicylates. Avoid or use with caution in animals with bleeding disorders.

■ Bismuth subsalicylate may produce severe side effects in cats; avoid or use with caution.

■ Use of this drug should be by or on the lawful written or oral order of a licensed veterinarian within the context of a valid veterinarian-client-patient relationship.

Possible Side Effects

▼ Common: harmless temporary darkening of the tongue or stool.

▼ Rare: constipation (impactions have been reported in human infants and older debilitated people).

Drug Interactions

• Do not give aspirin or any other salicylate at the same time as bismuth subsalicylate. Recommended doses of each can be toxic when combined.

• Bismuth subsalicylate may decrease the absorption of the tetracyclines.

Food Interactions

Do not give with milk.

Usual Dose

Different products contain different concentrations of bismuth subsalicylate, so follow label directions or your veterinarian's advice for veterinary products.

Dogs: Pepto-Bismol, regular strength liquid—0.1–1 ml/lb 3–4

times a day. Regular strength tablets—$1/4$ tablet/20 lbs 3–4
times a day.

    Cats: Pepto-Bismol regular strength liquid—0.5–1 ml/lb 3–4
times a day, for a maximum of 3 days. Follow your veterinarian's advice and instructions carefully on doses for cats.

    Drug Form: liquid, paste, chewable tablets, and caplets.

Overdosage

No information is available on overdoses of bismuth subsalicylate, but the potential for salicylate toxicity exists, especially in
cats (see *Aspirin/Acetylsalicylic Acid*). Blood electrolyte and
acid-base disturbances, fever, bleeding, liver and kidney damage, and convulsions are all possible with salicylate overdose.
In case of accidental ingestion or overdose, contact your veterinarian or the National Animal Poison Control Center.
ALWAYS bring the prescription bottle or container with you if
you go for treatment.

Special Information

Dogs usually hate bismuth subsalicylate liquid; however, the
chewable Pepto-Bismol cherry-flavored tablets may be much
more palatable and can be given as a pill or as a chewable
treat. There is some evidence that Pepto-Bismol may work better than generic and other brand name products and may be
preferable to use.

Special Populations

Pregnancy/Lactation
Bismuth subsalicylate should be avoided during pregnancy and
lactation.

Puppies/Kittens
Use with caution in young animals, and follow your veterinarian's advice on dose.

Senior Animals
Bismuth subsalicylate should be safe to use in older dogs.
Avoid or use with extreme caution in older cats.

Generic Name

Boric Acid

Most Common Brand Names

DermaPet [V]
Interrupt Indoor Carpet Treatment Powder [V]
Solvadry [V]   VetMark [V]

Type of Drug

Topical antiseptic and antifungal, environmental insecticide, and eye and ear wash.

Prescribed for

Ear and skin infections caused by *Malessezia* (yeast), flushing the ear and eye, swimmer's ear, environmental flea control.

General Information

Boric acid is a weak acid that comes as a powder and in a variety of liquid solutions for treatment of ears, eyes, and skin. *Malessezia* ear infections (otitis externa) are a very common and recurrent problem in dogs. Boric acid solution has been shown to be an extremely effective, safe, and inexpensive topical treatment for *Malessezia* infections of the skin and ears. Routine cleaning of the ears with boric acid solution may be an effective way to prevent recurrence of yeast otitis in susceptible animals.

The powder may also be used as an aid in flea control. Treating carpets and upholstered furniture with boric acid powder kills the larval stage of fleas by drying them and acting as an irritant. It also kills other household insects such as ants, roaches, and silverfish. Some commercial environmental flea treatment companies use borate salts.

Boric acid powder is safe if it is used as directed and not ingested or inhaled and may be an effective alternative to insecticides in the house.

Cautions and Warnings

For Owners/Handlers

■ If you are using boric acid powder for environmental flea control, children and pets should be kept out of treatment area until after application is complete.

■ Avoid contamination of food, foodstuffs, and ornamental plants. May be harmful or fatal if swallowed.

■ Avoid eye contact and excessive inhalation. Exposure to the powder causes airway and eye irritation.

For Animals

■ May be harmful or fatal if swallowed. Do not use the powder on animals.

■ If you use the solution to clean or treat skin or ears, make sure the area is dry and the animal does not lick the solution off the skin or haircoat. Do not use the solution on cuts or deep wounds. Exposure to the powder causes airway and eye irritation.

■ Contact your veterinarian if you think your dog or cat may be having an adverse reaction to boric acid solutions or powder.

Possible Side Effects

▼ Rare: irritation; harmful and possibly fatal if ingested or absorbed into the body through wounds or mucous membranes in sufficient quantities (see "Overdosage").

Drug Interactions

None known.

Food Interactions

Boric acid forms a complex with riboflavin (a B vitamin) and promotes its urinary excretion. Boric acid poisoning, therefore, may cause riboflavin deficiency.

Usual Dose

Dogs and Cats: as ear flush and yeast treatment—dissolve 1 tablespoon of boric acid powder in 1 pint of water (1–2 tsp/cup). Use once or twice a day for 7 to 14 days, or as directed by your veterinarian. Dry the area with cotton or paper towels after flushing. DermaPet contains 2% boric acid and 2% acetic acid (vinegar) and has also been shown to be an effective treatment for ear and skin yeast infections.

Drug Form: Boric acid is supplied as a powder in a variety of generic brands. It is inexpensive and easily made into solutions for use as ear and skin treatments. It is probably best to use commercial preparations of boric acid for use in the eye, to ensure sterility and proper concentration.

Overdosage

Boric acid has a fairly wide margin of safety. In dogs fed a single dose of up to 3 g/lb, there were no deaths or serious side effects. Most of the dogs vomited. Chronic low-dose feeding to dogs may cause atrophy of the testicles. In humans, however, systemic symptoms of overdose have been seen with as little as 0.1 g/lb—or about 3 tsp in a normal adult. Repeated small doses tend to be more toxic than a single large dose. The most common symptoms of overdose are vomiting, diarrhea, increased salivation, depression, and loss of appetite. Less common symptoms of overdose are weakness, incoordination, tremors, seizures, retching, and mucus and blood in the stool. Boric acid overdose may cause kidney failure, hyperactivity, agitation, depression, coma, and death.

Continuous long-term use of or exposure to boric acid may cause loss of appetite, mouth ulcers, weight loss, vomiting, diarrhea, rash, loss of hair, anemia, seizures, and death.

In case of accidental ingestion or overdose, contact your veterinarian or the National Animal Poison Control Center. ALWAYS bring the prescription bottle or container with you if you go for treatment.

Special Information

Boric acid is an extremely effective treatment for yeast infections of skin and ears, but it is important for owners to realize that there is usually an underlying cause for chronic and recurrent yeast infections in dogs. The most common underlying problem is allergic skin disease, either from inhaled or ingested allergens. Hair in the ear canal, excessive wax production, long floppy ears, frequent swimming, and polyps or tumors in the ear canal may all predispose the ears to infections as well. If your dog has a yeast infection, it is likely to recur unless the underlying problem is eliminated.

Special Populations

Pregnancy/Lactation

There have been no studies on boric acid in pregnant or lactating animals. It is probably safe to use as an ear flush, but it is best to avoid all use if there is a chance for puppies or kittens to ingest it from nursing or contact with the mother.

Puppies/Kittens

Boric acid should be avoided in puppies and kittens, as they are more susceptible to side effects.

Senior Animals

Boric acid should be safe to use on older animals, but care should be taken to avoid ingestion or absorption through wounds.

Generic Name

Buspirone (bue-SPYE-rone)

Brand Names

BuSpar [H]

Type of Drug

Antianxiety.

Prescribed for

Anxiety disorders, separation anxiety in dogs, urine spraying in cats.

General Information

Buspirone is a member of a relatively new class of drugs (aza-spirodecanediones) that are unrelated to other sedative or anti-anxiety medications. The mechanism of action is unknown, but it probably acts specifically on serotonin receptors (nerve stimulants in the brain). In humans, buspirone decreases anxiety but has no sedative effects.

All undesirable behaviors have a learned component. Treatment of any undesirable behavior requires behavior modification (training based on scientific principles used to alter or change undesirable behaviors). Drugs are used in the treatment of dogs and cats with behavior problems because certain undesirable behaviors cannot be managed by behavior modification techniques alone. In such cases severe anxiety or fear, a strong hormonal component to behavior (as in maternal aggression), or a neurochemical imbalance in the brain (as in compulsive behaviors) prevents effective behavior modification. Drugs are only useful for certain specific types of behavior problems, and they should be ONLY used as an adjunct to behavior modification. When used in this way they enable behavior modification to be maximally effective.

Buspirone has not been very useful in the treatment of fear or anxiety in dogs, but it may be worth trying, especially for separation anxiety, or when other anti-anxiety medications are ineffective or should be avoided (see *Amitriptyline*). Buspirone has been effective in treating some cats that soil the house with urine spraying. It stopped urine spraying in 35% to 40% of female cats, and in 50% to 60% of male cats, less in multicat households. Diazepam works 50% to 60% of the time, and amitriptyline may also be effective. There are no controlled studies comparing the efficacy of the various sedative/anti-anxiety drugs in cats with urine spraying.

Most psychotropic drugs used in veterinary medicine are not licensed for use in animals. There are few controlled studies in animals establishing dose, efficacy, or safety. The long-term effects of these drugs are not known. There may be breed and individual differences in response to these drugs.

Cautions and Warnings

■ Buspirone is not FDA approved for use in dogs or cats. It is used to treat anxiety disorders in dogs and cats and is considered accepted practice.

■ Contact your veterinarian if you think your dog or cat may be having an adverse reaction to buspirone.

■ U.S. federal law restricts the use of this drug by or on the lawful written or oral order of a licensed veterinarian within the context of a valid veterinarian-client-patient relationship.

Possible Side Effects

Little is known about the side effects of buspirone in dogs and cats. One behavior expert reports that there are apparently none, due to its selective action. Dizziness, nausea, headache, nervousness, and excitement are the most common side effects in people.

▼ Rare: in people, allergic reactions, low white blood cell and platelet counts, and increased liver enzymes.

Drug Interactions

• Buspirone should not be given with monoamine oxidase inhibitors.

• Buspirone should be used with caution with other psychotropic drugs, as the interactions have not been studied.

Food Interactions

None known; probably best to give with food.

Usual Dose

Dogs: 2.5–10 mg/dog orally 2–3 times a day.
Cats: 2.5–5 mg/cat orally 2–3 times a day.
Drug Form: 5- and 10-mg tablets.

Overdosage

Overdoses may cause nausea, vomiting, dizziness, drowsiness, and stomach distress in people. There is no specific information on overdoses in dogs and cats. In case of accidental ingestion or overdose, contact your veterinarian or the National Animal Poison Control Center. ALWAYS bring the prescription bottle or container with you if you go for treatment.

Special Information

There are a growing number of veterinary behavior specialists, with effective treatments for most behavior problems. Ask your veterinarian or university referral service for the names of specialists in your area if you are having problems with the behavior of your dog or cat.

Some animal behavior experts consider diazepam the drug of choice for urine spraying in cats. Diazepam decreases anxiety while allowing cats to learn new behaviors through behavior modification. Amitriptyline may also be useful, but it may take longer for the effects to be seen, and it may also decrease learning. Other experts prefer amitriptyline, because of the possible side effects of diazepam—unsteady gait after one hour and prolonged (4 to 5 day) excitement. Buspirone may be effective for urine spraying in about half of treated cats. Discuss the problem with your veterinarian to decide on the best treatment for your cat. Ask for a referral to a veterinary behavior specialist if you need further assistance.

Special Populations

Pregnancy/Lactation
There are no studies on the safety of buspirone in pregnant or lactating dogs and cats. It seems to be safe in pregnant rats and rabbits, but it is excreted in milk and should probably be avoided unless the benefits outweigh the risks.

Puppies/Kittens
Buspirone should not be used in puppies or kittens.

Senior Animals
There are no safety studies in older animals, but buspirone is probably safe to use.

Generic Name

Butorphanol (bue-TOR-fan-awl)

Brand Names

Stadol [H]   Torbugesic-SA [V]
Torbugesic [V]   Torbutrol [V]

Type of Drug

Narcotic pain reliever; cough suppressant.

Prescribed for

Coughing in dogs, pain relief in dogs and cats, nausea and vomiting in dogs and cats receiving chemotherapy.

General Information

Butorphanol tartrate is a pain reliever and powerful cough suppressant. It is marketed and approved as a cough suppressant in dogs, but it is also used for relief of pain and for nausea that occurs with cancer treatment. When treating upper respiratory problems, breaking the cough cycle is an essential part of the treatment. Butorphanol is used to treat kennel cough and other nonproductive coughs caused by inflammation of the upper respiratory tract.

The injectable form of butorphanol is frequently used in veterinary clinics for pain relief after surgery and in some very

painful medical problems, such as burns and pancreatitis.
Butorphanol is also used for sedation before surgery. Butorphanol pills may be dispensed for pain management after
surgery.

This drug may be used to help decrease nausea associated
with cisplatin treatment. Butorphanol has less addictive potential than other narcotic pain relievers.

Cautions and Warnings

■ Injectable butorphanol is FDA approved for use in dogs
and cats. Oral butorphanol is approved for use as a cough suppressant in dogs. Oral butorphanol is used to treat cats and it
is considered accepted practice.

■ Butorphanol, like all narcotics, should be used with caution in animals who are hypothyroid, who have severe kidney
problems, Addison's disease (adrenal insufficiency), or head
trauma, and in older or severely debilitated animals.

■ The manufacturer cautions against its use in dogs with a
history of liver disease and lung conditions where there is a lot
of mucus.

■ Butorphanol should be used with caution in dogs with
heartworm disease.

■ U.S. federal law restricts the use of this drug by or on the
lawful written or oral order of a licensed veterinarian within the
context of a valid veterinarian-client-patient relationship.

Possible Side Effects

▼ Common: mild sedation (animals that are sensitive to
this drug may need to have their dose decreased);
anorexia and vomiting.
▼ Rare: diarrhea.

Drug Interactions

• Butorphanol has an additive effect with other sedatives,
narcotics, antihistamines, and central nervous system depressants.
• Pancuronium should not be used with butorphanol.

Food Interactions

None known.

Usual Dose

Dogs: as cough suppressant—0.25–0.5 mg/lb orally 2–4 times a day. Treatment should not normally be required for more than 7 days. For pain relief—0.1 mg/lb orally twice a day.

Cats: for pain relief—1 mg per cat orally 2 to 4 times a day; 0.2 mg/lb by injection under the skin every 3–6 hours, maximum 4 times a day for up to 2 days.

Drug Form: 1-, 5-, and 10-mg tablets and 2 mg/ml injectable.

Overdosage

Butorphanol has a wide margin of safety before an accidental overdose is life threatening. Symptoms would include profound sedation, central nervous system disturbances, respiratory depression, and coma. In case of accidental ingestion or overdose, contact your veterinarian or the National Animal Poison Control Center. ALWAYS bring the prescription bottle or container with you if you go for treatment.

Special Information

Pain relief in cats treated with butorphanol can be variable. In drug trials, about 75% of treated cats had a satisfactory level of pain relief. The duration of pain relief in cats is also quite variable, from 15 minutes to 8 hours. If your animal is not getting adequate pain relief from butorphanol, it may be worth considering other medications.

Special Populations

Pregnancy/Lactation

Butorphanol crosses the placenta and blood levels in the fetus are approximately the same as maternal blood levels. Butorphanol is also present in milk of lactating patients. There is no indication that the drug causes birth defects, but the manufacturer recommends that it not be used in pregnant animals.

Puppies/Kittens

There are no butorphanol studies in young animals. In humans, butorphanol is not recommended for pediatric use because safety and efficacy have not been established.

Senior Animals

There is no information on studies in senior animals. Butorphanol should be used with caution in older patients and avoided if there is questionable liver or kidney function. In older people and those with liver or kidney disease, the initial recommended dose is half the normal dose, and the interval between doses is increased.

Generic Name

n-Butyl Chloride (BUE-tul-KLOR-ide) Ⓖ

Brand Names

Canine Worm Caps Ⓥ
Happy Jack Worm Capsules Ⓥ
Sergeants Puppy Worm Capsules Ⓥ
Sergeants Sure Shot Worm Capsules Ⓥ

Type of Drug

Anthelmintic/dewormer.

Prescribed for

Roundworm (*Toxocara canis, Toxascaris leonina*) and hookworm (*Ancylostoma caninum, A. braziliense, Uncinaria stenocephala*) in dogs.

General Information

n-Butyl chloride (1–chlorobutane) is a colorless liquid that is packaged in gelatin capsules to make administration easier. It eliminates 90% of roundworms, but only 60% of hookworms at the recommended dosage.

Roundworm and hookworm are contagious and may spread to other animals and to people and therefore are a potential public health risk (see *Zoonotic Diseases of Dogs and Cats*). Roundworm is responsible for visceral larva migrans and hookworm for cutaneous larva migrans.

Roundworms and hookworms live in the intestines, and their eggs pass in the feces to the environment. Animals and humans that come in contact with anything contaminated with feces and parasite eggs are at risk of infection.

n-Butyl chloride is among the few dewormers available over-the-counter (OTC) for use in dogs and is widely available wherever pet supplies are sold (see "Special Information").

Cautions and Warnings

■ Do not use in sick, weak, debilitated, feverish, or under-nourished dogs. Consult your veterinarian for assistance in the diagnosis, treatment, and control of parasitism.

■ Contact your veterinarian if you think your dog may be having an adverse reaction to n-butyl chloride.

■ For veterinary use only.

Possible Side Effects

▼ Common: vomiting, diarrhea, and dehydration.

▼ Rare: hyperactivity, excessive salivation, depression, unsteady gait, fever, anaphylaxis, and death.

Drug Interactions

None known.

Food Interactions

Fasting required.

Usual Dose

Dogs: 0.884 mg (1 ml)/2.5–5 lbs. Do not feed for 18–24 hours before treatment. Dogs may be fed 4–8 hours after treatment. Administration of a mild cathartic such as castor oil 30–60 minutes following treatment may enhance expulsion of worms.

Drug Form: 0.884-g (1 ml), 1.768-g (2 ml), and 4.42-g (5 ml) capsules.

Storage: Store capsules in a dry place at 70–75°F.

Overdosage

Signs of overdose include vomiting, diarrhea, dehydration, excessive salivation, loss of appetite, bloating, fever, depression, weakness, loss of coordination, and death. In case of accidental ingestion or overdose, contact your veterinarian or the National Animal Poison Control Center. ALWAYS bring the prescription bottle or container with you if you go for treatment.

Special Information

The use of OTC drugs to treat parasites without a specific diagnosis may be dangerous and in most cases results in unnecessary or incorrect treatment. Owners sometimes assume that signs such as diarrhea, weight loss, or a pet scooting its bottom on the ground are due to worms and resort to OTC drugs rather than calling their veterinarian. Although these signs may indicate parasites, they may also indicate other health problems. Using OTC products without an accurate diagnosis not only runs the unnecessary risk of side effects but also may delay the diagnosis and treatment of the real problem.

If your pet has parasites, it is important to identify the type. This may be as simple as having your veterinarian do a fecal analysis. An accurate diagnosis of the type of worm allows your veterinarian to prescribe a dewormer that is specific, effective, and safe. Today there are many safer, more effective, and cost effective dewormers than n-butyl chloride.

Special Populations

Pregnancy/Lactation
Studies have not confirmed that this drug is safe during pregnancy and lactation.

Puppies
This drug is considered safe to use in puppies.

Senior Animals
This drug is considered safe to use in healthy older dogs; do not use in debilitated dogs.

Type of Drug
Calcium G

Brand Names

There are many veterinary and human products that contain the calcium salts—calcium acetate, calcium carbonate, calcium chloride, calcium gluconate, calcium lactate. Calcium gluconate injection and generic tablets, and Tums (calcium carbonate) are the products used most frequently in veterinary medicine. Calcium acetate may also be used (see *Antacids/Phosphate Binders*). Consult your veterinarian for advice on the type of calcium and the formulation that is best for your pet.

Prescribed for

Low blood calcium, high blood phosphate, and high blood potassium.

General Information

Calcium is required for normal nerve and muscle functions, as well as cell membrane and enzyme functions in all parts of the body. Hypocalcemia (low blood calcium) may occur in a number of diseases and conditions of dogs and cats. Hypocalcemia may be a severe and life-threatening problem, causing tetany (muscle rigidity) and convulsions. Less severe hypocalcemia may cause unusual behavior, restlessness, unsteady gait, hypersensitivity to light and sound, muscle tremors or twitches, and muscle weakness.

Causes of hypocalcemia may include lactation tetany (eclampsia), dystocia or uterine inertia (difficult delivery), hypoparathyroidism, chronic kidney or liver failure, malabsorption, pancreatitis, nutritional secondary hyperparathyroidism, antifreeze poisoning and administration of Fleet phosphate enemas (see *Common Household Poisons*).

Hypocalcemia does not always require treatment, especially when there are no symptoms. This is often the case in chronic kidney and liver failure and malabsorption. However, animals who have the symptoms of hypocalcemia listed above require immediate evaluation and treatment. This usually means blood tests to diagnose the hypocalcemia and other possible problems. Emergency treatment often includes intravenous calcium gluconate while the animal is carefully monitored for response and adverse effects. Oral calcium supplements may be used after the acute crisis is treated. These include calcium gluconate, calcium lactate, or calcium carbonate tablets. Diluted calcium gluconate may also be given by injection under the skin to maintain calcium levels, especially if oral supplements are not possible.

Lactation tetany can be life-threatening in dogs and cats and should be treated as a medical emergency. Nursing puppies or kittens should be taken from the mother immediately and hand-raised.

Calcium carbonate and calcium acetate may be given orally as intestinal phosphate binders in chronic kidney failure (see *Antacids/Phosphate Binders*). Calcium gluconate may be given intravenously to lower high blood potassium.

Cautions and Warnings

■ Do not give calcium supplements to hypocalcemic animals with no symptoms, especially asymptomatic dogs in kidney failure with high blood phosphate.

■ Do not give calcium supplements to animals with abnormal heart rhythms, or hypercalcemia (high blood calcium).

■ Calcium should be given very cautiously to animals on digoxin or digitalis or those with heart or kidney disease.

■ Calcium chloride should not be used in animals with respiratory failure, respiratory acidosis, or kidney failure, as it may cause acidosis (excess acid in the blood).

■ Do not give oral calcium supplements without the recommendation of your veterinarian.

■ Contact your veterinarian if you think your dog or cat may be having an adverse reaction to calcium.

■ U.S. federal law restricts the use of these drugs by or on the lawful written or oral order of a licensed veterinarian within the context of a valid veterinarian-client-patient relationship.

Possible Side Effects

▼ Common: slow heart rate, nausea, and vomiting if intravenous calcium is given too quickly.

▼ Rare: gastrointestinal (GI) irritation, constipation, and hypercalcemia.

Drug Interactions

• Calcium should be used with caution in patients on digoxin or digitalis, as they are more likely to develop abnormal heart rhythms.

• Calcium may antagonize the effects of verapamil and other calcium channel blockers.

• Thiazide diuretics given with calcium may cause hypercalcemia.

• Intravenous calcium may alter the effects of neuromuscular blocking agents, such as pancuronium and tubocurarine.

• Oral calcium may reduce the absorption of tetracyclines and phenytoin.

• Large doses of vitamin D, vitamin A, or magnesium with calcium may cause hypercalcemia.

Food Interactions

Oral calcium supplements should be given with food if there is evidence of GI irritation, or if the calcium is being given to act as a phosphate binder. More calcium will be absorbed, however, if it is given between meals. Vitamin D should be given with oral calcium supplements to enhance absorption of calcium from the GI tract.

Usual Dose

Dogs and Cats

Oral Calcium: calcium gluconate—250–350 mg/lb/day orally for 3–5 days. Calcium lactate—400–600 mg/day in 3–4 divided doses orally for 3–5 days. Calcium carbonate—50–75 mg/lb/day in 2 divided doses orally for 3–5 days.

Injectable Calcium: calcium gluconate—starting dose—0.25–0.75 ml/lb of 10% calcium gluconate, intravenously, at 1 ml/min, or in 5% dextrose solution slowly IV. Maintenance dose—5–7.5 ml/lb, given over 24 hours or as needed according to blood calcium levels, or calcium gluconate 10% solution diluted 1:1 in saline: 0.5–1 ml/lb, by injection under the skin 3 times a day.

Drug Form

Solutions for injection, oral syrup, tablets, suspensions, and capsules.

Overdosage

Overdoses or administration of other substances that enhance calcium absorption (see "Cautions and Warnings") may cause hypercalcemia. The signs of hypercalcemia include decreased appetite, increased drinking and urination, vomiting, constipation, slow heart rate, weakness, depression, stupor, coma, and seizures. In case of accidental ingestion or overdose, contact your veterinarian or the National Animal Poison Control Center. ALWAYS bring the prescription bottle or container with you if you go for treatment.

Special Information

There is no evidence that calcium supplementation of diets of pregnant dogs prevents eclampsia. It may even make it more likely, as it does in cows. There is no evidence that calcium supplements are helpful for dogs after delivery or for growing puppies, including the large and giant breeds. Calcium supplementation may have been necessary before the advent of current dog food formulations, but it is not recommended now. High calcium diets in large and giant breed puppies cause weakness and bone deformities.

Special Populations

Pregnancy/Lactation
Calcium supplements are not recommended for pregnant or lactating dogs or cats on a good quality commercial diet.

Puppies/Kittens
Calcium supplements are not recommended for puppies or kittens on good quality commercial puppy or kitten chow or milk replacer.

Senior Animals
Calcium should be safe to use in older dogs and cats who do not have kidney or heart disease (see "Cautions and Warnings"). See *Antacids/Phosphate Binders* for more information about the use of calcium as an intestinal phosphate binder in chronic kidney failure.

Type of Drug

Calorie-Vitamin-Mineral Supplements

Most Common Brand Names

Calorie-Vitamin-Mineral Supplements
Nutri-Cal [V]   Pet Nutri-Drops [V]

Vitamin-Mineral Supplements
FaVor [V]   Nutri-Form [V]

Felimins [V]   NutriVed [V]

Felobits [V]   Palamega [V]

Felovite [V]   PalaVite [V]

Hi-Vite [V]   Pet-Tabs [V]

Lixotinic [V]

Prescribed for

Supplementation of the diet and temporary nutritional support.

General Information

Good quality commercial dog and cat foods are carefully formulated to be complete feeds. They contain all of the vitamins, minerals, energy, and protein that are required for your dog or cat. Dogs and cats have different nutritional requirements, and it is not good for dogs to eat cat food or for cats to eat dog food on a regular basis or as a significant part of their diet.

In certain conditions or diseases, dietary supplements may be an important and even critical part of therapy. Many diseases may cause a decrease in appetite at just the time when an animal is most in need of nutritional support and even extra vitamins and minerals. In conditions such as competition, difficult or prolonged delivery of puppies or kittens, and weak puppies or kittens, hypoglycemia (low blood sugar) may occur and these animals may benefit from calorie supplements. Calorie-vitamin-mineral products are excellent ways to provide temporary nutritional support. They should not be used as the sole source of nutrition for any period of time longer than a few days. Animals who are unable or unwilling to eat for prolonged periods need to have a feeding tube placed in order to give one of the specially formulated complete liquid diets now available.

Cats who stop eating when they are sick, especially overweight cats, are at high risk for a disease called fatty liver syndrome. This is a serious and potentially fatal condition where fat is mobilized from body stores and accumulates in the liver, causing liver failure. It is extremely important to provide nutritional support for all sick animals that stop eating, but it is critically important to do so for overweight cats.

Calcium supplements are not recommended for pregnant or lactating animals on good quality commercial diets (see *Calcium*). There is no evidence that calcium supplementation of diets of pregnant dogs prevents eclampsia. It may even make it more likely, as it does in cows. There is no evidence that calcium supplements are helpful for bitches after delivery or for growing puppies, including the large and giant breeds. Calcium supplementation may have been necessary before the advent of current dog food formulations, but it is not recommended now. High calcium diets in large and giant breed puppies cause weakness and bone deformities.

Many vitamin-mineral supplements contain fatty acids as well (see *Fatty Acids*). Consult your veterinarian for advice on the best dietary supplement for your dog or cat.

Cautions and Warnings

■ Calorie-vitamin-mineral supplements are not complete diets and should ONLY be used as a temporary dietary support measure.

■ Do not give calorie-vitamin-mineral supplements to chilled puppies or kittens (see "Special Populations"), or animals that are unconscious or vomiting.

■ Contact your veterinarian if you think your dog or cat may be having an adverse reaction to calorie-vitamin-mineral supplements.

■ For veterinary use only.

Possible Side Effects

▼ Rare: high blood glucose (in poorly regulated diabetic animals because of the sugar content of the supplement).

Food and Drug Interactions

None known.

Usual Dose

Dogs and Cats: Nutri-Cal, as a supplement—1.5 tsp/10 lbs body weight daily. When not eating full feed—3 tsp/10 lbs body weight daily. Follow your veterinarian's advice on the dose and dosing frequency that is best for your dog or cat.

Drug Form: Calorie-vitamin-mineral supplements are supplied as paste and liquid; vitamin-mineral supplements are supplied as chewable tablets, liquid, and paste.

Overdosage

Overdose of calorie-vitamin-mineral dietary supplements may cause high blood glucose. An acute overdose of vitamin-mineral supplements may cause transient gastrointestinal upset. Chronic overdose may cause several diseases associated with excess vitamin and mineral intake (see *Vitamins A, B, C, D, E,* and K_1 and *Calcium*). In case of accidental ingestion or overdose, contact your veterinarian or the National Animal Poison

Control Center. ALWAYS bring the prescription bottle or container with you if you go for treatment.

Special Populations

Hunting/Working Dogs
Performance and working dogs may benefit from calorie-vitamin-mineral supplements during intense or prolonged workouts.

Pregnancy/Lactation
Females that are exhausted from prolonged or difficult deliveries may benefit from calorie-vitamin-mineral supplements. Females with decreased appetite during lactation may also benefit from calorie-vitamin-mineral supplements.

Puppies/Kittens
Do not give oral calorie supplements to chilled puppies or kittens without making sure that body temperature is getting back to normal. Always consult your veterinarian on the care of critically ill or chilled puppies and kittens.

Senior Animals
Calorie-vitamin-mineral supplements are safe and may be very helpful for older animals, especially those with decreased appetite or other illnesses. Calcium supplements should only be used in animals with kidney failure under the supervision of a veterinarian (see *Calcium* and *Antacids/Phosphate Binders*).

Generic Name

Captan (KAP-tan)

Brand Name

Orthocide Garden Fungicide

Type of Drug

Antifungal

Prescribed for

Ringworm (dermatophyte infection).

General Information

Captan is a topical antifungal that is manufactured as a plant fungicide. It is an effective topical dip for animals with dermatophyte infections. Ringworm is usually self-limiting, but treatment may help limit the infection on the affected animal and limit the spread of infection to other animals or people in the household. Ringworm is contagious and may spread to other animals and to people through contact with infected animals or people (see *Zoonotic Diseases of Dogs and Cats* and *Chlorhexidine*).

Captan should probably not be used in cats (see "Cautions and Warnings" and "Possible Side Effects").

Cautions and Warnings

For Owners/Handlers
■ Captan is on the government's Hazardous Substance List, and the Special Health Hazard Substance List. Captan can affect handlers both by breathing in the powder and by absorption through the skin. Captan may cause birth defects, and it should be handled as a possible cancer-causing substance, that is, with extreme care.
■ Captan can cause skin sensitivity. Handlers should wear gloves and protective clothing when using captan. Use in a well-ventilated area.
■ There are other safer topical antifungals that can be used instead of captan. These include chlorhexidine, povidone-iodine, miconazole and ketoconazole.

For Animals
■ For external use only. Consult a veterinarian in case of accidental ingestion.
■ Avoid contact with eyes. Use a protective eye ointment before applying near the eyes.
■ U.S. federal law restricts the use of this drug by or on the lawful written or oral order of a licensed veterinarian within the context of a valid veterinarian-client-patient relationship.

Possible Side Effects
▼ Common: vomiting in cats.

Food and Drug Interactions

None known.

Usual Dose

Dogs and Cats: Dip entire animal in a 2% solution (2 tbs/gal) every 3–5 days. The animal's entire body should be saturated, including the face. Contact with the eyes should be avoided. The solution is not rinsed off, but allowed to dry on the animal.

Drug Form: powder, sold as garden fungicide.

Overdosage

Captan dip should be washed off the animal if an error was made in making the dip solution or if the animal shows any adverse response. In case of accidental ingestion or overdose, contact your veterinarian or the National Animal Poison Control Center. ALWAYS bring the prescription bottle or container with you if you go for treatment.

Special Information

Dermatophyte spores can live in the environment for over a year. In order to prevent reinfection, the entire house should be thoroughly cleaned and vacuumed to remove any infected hairs. All grooming equipment and bedding of infected animals should be discarded or disinfected with Clorox. Any areas where the animal has contact should be cleaned with Clorox if possible.

There is a lot of controversy over topical treatment of cats with ringworm. Some experts have found that bathing infected cats may actually spread the ringworm to new areas. Consult your veterinarian or a veterinary dermatologist for the latest recommendations on the treatment of ringworm.

Special Populations

Pregnancy/Lactation
Captan has been shown to cause birth defects and should not be used in pregnant or lactating animals.

Puppies/Kittens
There are no safety studies on captan in young animals. It should only be used if the benefits outweigh the risks.

Senior Animals
Captan should be safe to use in older animals, but there are no studies to confirm its safety.

Type of Drug

Carbamate Insecticide (KAR-buh-mate)

Brand Names

Generic Ingredient: Carbaryl [G]
Adam's Flea and Tick Dust II [V]
DFT Spray [V]
Dispatch Flea & Tick Spray [V]
Ecto-Soothe Carbaryl Shampoo [V]
Happy Jack's Flea-Tick Powder II [V]
Mycodex Pet Shampoo with Carbaryl [V]
Ritter's Tick and Flea Powder [V]
Vedco Flea and Tick Powder 2.5× [V]
Vet-Kem Flea & Tick Collars for Dogs and Cats [V]
Vet-Kem Flea and Tick Powder [V]

Generic Ingredient: Propoxur [G]
Performer Eliminator Flea & Tick Collars for Cats and
   Dogs [V]
Vet-Kem Ticktrol Tick & Flea Collars for Cats and Dogs [V]

Prescribed for

Flea and tick control on dogs and cats and in the environment.

General Information

Carbamate insecticides were once widely used to control external parasites on animals. Although they are still used, their use has declined due to the introduction of safer compounds such as the pyrethrins (see *Pyrethrins*) and insect growth regulators (see *Insect Growth Regulator*), and, more recently, lufenuron (see *Lufenuron*), fipronil (see *Fipronil*), and imidacloprid (see *Imidacloprid*).

Of the many carbamates developed, only two are used in products for dogs and cats. Carbaryl, a methylcarbamate, is used in flea and tick powders, sprays, collars, and shampoos, and propoxur is used in flea and tick collars. Some of the commercial products combine carbamates with other insecticides to increase the effectiveness.

Carbamates, like organophosphates—see *Organophosphate Insecticides*—kill parasites by inhibiting acetylcholinesterase

(AChE). AChE is an enzyme located at nerve endings that regulates the stimulation of muscles and certain nerves. When AChE is inhibited, the parasite's muscles are overstimulated and cannot relax between contractions. This paralyzes and kills the adult parasite.

Flea control requires that the problem be attacked on several levels. Adult fleas on the animal must be killed. Flea shampoos, powders, sprays, and dips work at this level. Mechanical removal by frequent grooming and keeping your pet away from other animals and places where new fleas may be acquired also helps. However, addressing the infestation on the animal is rarely enough because fleas remaining in the environment continue to reproduce very rapidly. Environmental treatment with bombs or sprays kills many fleas. A major limitation is that bombs and sprays do not reach all of the flea's hiding places, which leaves live fleas to continue the infestation. Residual action products help extend the action, but still fall short of giving good control and may result in increased levels of toxic insecticides in the home and environment. In addition, most insecticides do not kill flea eggs, which hatch into new adult fleas within a few days. The use of insect growth regulators, which prevent eggs from hatching, dramatically increases the effectiveness of flea control on animals and in the environment. Very good flea control is possible by combining insecticides and insect growth regulators in a multilevel approach. The drawback is that it demands a great deal of motivation on the part of the owner.

Because of the potential for affecting the environment, insecticide use is primarily regulated by the Environmental Protection Agency (EPA). Label instructions should be carefully read and followed.

Cautions and Warnings

■ Do not use carbamate insecticides in animals that are stressed, debilitated or sick, have diarrhea, are constipated, or that may have an intestinal impaction. Do not use in dogs or cats with heartworm infection, heart or liver disease, or other infections.

■ Do not use within a few days of giving other drugs that inhibit AChE, including other insecticides and dewormers.

■ Do not use with tranquilizers, muscle relaxants, or modified live-virus vaccines. Acepromazine or other phenothiazine drugs should not be used within a month of administering carbamates.

■ Contact your veterinarian if you think your dog or cat may be having an adverse reaction to carbamate insecticides.

■ It is a violation of federal law to use these products in a manner inconsistant with their labeling. Use only on animal species indicated on specific product's label.

■ EPA approved for indicated uses in dogs, cats, and the environment.

Possible Side Effects

▼ Common: loss of appetite, vomiting, loose stools, and diarrhea.

▼ Rare: muscle twitching, pupil contraction, tearing, and labored breathing.

Drug Interactions

• Neuromuscular blocking drugs, including phenothiazine drugs, procaine, magnesium ion, inhaled anesthetics, and other AChE inhibitors such as organophosphates, morphine, neostigmine, physostigmine, and pyridostigmine may increase the risk of side effects.

• Antibiotics, including the aminoglycosides (streptomycin, neomycin, kanamycin, and gentamicin); polypeptides (polymyxin and colistin); lincomycin; and clindamycin may have activity at the neuromuscular level and may increase the risk of side effects.

• Central nervous system depressants, including phenothiazine tranquilizers (acepromazine), benzodiazepines, reserpine, meprobamate, ethanol, and barbiturates (phenobarbital) may increase the severity of side effects.

• Muscle relaxants such as succinylcholine may increase the risk of side effects.

• Cimetidine may inhibit liver detoxification of carbamates and increase the risk of side effects.

• Dimethyl sulfide (DMSO) may increase the risk of side effects of carbamates.

• Pyrantel dewormers act at the same level as carbamates and may increase the risk of side effects.

Usual Dose

Dogs and Cats: Read and follow label directions carefully.
Drug Form: collars, dips, and shampoos.

Overdosage

The major signs of overdose include abdominal cramping, vomiting, diarrhea, increased frequency of urination and defecation, increased salivation, constriction of the pupils, muscle tremors, respiratory distress, hyperexcitability, seizures, and death. In case of accidental ingestion or overdose, contact your veterinarian or the National Animal Poison Control Center. ALWAYS bring the prescription bottle or container with you if you go for treatment.

Special Information

See *Fipronil* for more information about fleas and ticks.

Special Populations

Pregnancy/Lactation
The risk of side effects in pregnant animals has not been established. Carbamates should not be used unless the benefits outweigh the risks. Do not use in lactating animals.

Puppies/Kittens
Follow label instructions. In general, carbamates should not be used in puppies or kittens under 3 months of age.

Senior Animals
There are no specific contraindications for the use of carbamates in healthy senior animals.

Type of Drug

Carbonic-Anhydrase Inhibitors (CAIs)

Brand Names

Generic Ingredient: Acetazolamide G
Dazamide H   Diamox H

Generic Ingredient: Dichlorphenamide
Daranide H

Generic Ingredient: Methazolamide G
Neptazane

Prescribed for

Glaucoma.

General Information

Acetazolamide, dichlophenamide, and methazolamide inhibit an enzyme called carbonic anhydrase, which produces intraocular fluid. This fluid fills the globe of the eye and maintains the normal shape and pressure. In glaucoma, the amount of fluid and pressure increases. This damages the delicate structures of the eye causing redness, clouding of the cornea, pain, and eventually blindness. The pupil is characteristically dilated and the globe enlarged in chronic cases. CAIs reduce the amount of fluid produced; therefore, the intraocular pressure decreases and the clinical signs improve. CAIs may become less effective after long-term use and regular monitoring of the patient is indicated.

These CAIs are well absorbed after oral administration. The maximum effect is seen in 2 to 4 hours and lasts for 4 to 6 hours. They are excreted by the kidneys where they increase secretion of some electrolytes and have a mild diuretic effect. This may cause electrolyte imbalances in some animals.

Acetazolamide is available as an injectable product that is often used for the initial treatment in severe cases of glaucoma because it acts more rapidly than the other preparations. Methazolamide and dichlorphenamide produce fewer side effects than acetazolamide and are preferred oral treatments. Dorzalamide is a topical CAI available as eye drops that may be useful in some animals.

Cautions and Warnings

■ Do not use CAIs in animals with significant respiratory, liver, or kidney disease; Addison's disease; electrolyte imbalances; or preexisting blood disorders.

■ Use CAIs cautiously in animals with a history of reactions to sulfonamides because cross sensitivity may occur.

■ Contact your veterinarian if you think your dog or cat may be having an adverse reaction to a CAI.

■ Acetazolamide is FDA approved for use in dogs; however, the veterinary product is not currently available. The other CAIs are not FDA approved but are used. Extralabel use of the human product in dogs and cats is considered accepted practice.

■ U.S. federal law restricts the use of these drugs by or on the lawful written or oral order of a licensed veterinarian within the context of a valid veterinarian-client-patient relationship.

Possible Side Effects

▼ Common: vomiting, diarrhea, loss of appetite, and increased urination.

▼ Rare: abnormal bleeding or bruising, sedation, depression, and allergic reactions.

Drug Interactions

• CAIs may interfere with primidone absorption.

• CAIs may alter the excretion rates of drugs that are excreted in the urine, including quinidine, procainamide, phenobarbital, and methotrexate.

• CAIs may increase potassium excretion causing low potassium blood levels when given with corticosteroids, amphotericin B, or other diuretics. The low blood levels of potassium increase the risk of digitalis toxicity.

• Aspirin may increase the risk of side effects with CAIs.

• Rarely, CAIs may reduce the effects of insulin, and higher doses may be needed to control diabetes.

Food Interactions

None known. Administering with food may reduce the risk of intestinal upset.

Usual Dose

Acetazolamide
    Dogs: 5–13 mg/lb 2–3 times a day.
    Cats: 3 mg/lb 3 times a day.
    Drug Form: 125- and 250-mg tablets, 500-mg extended-release capsules, and injectable.

Dichlorphenamide
    Dogs: 1–2.3 mg/lb 2–3 times a day.
    Cats: 0.5 mg/lb 2–3 times a day.
    Drug Form: 50-mg tablets.

Methazolamide
    Dogs and Cats: 0.5–2.0 mg/lb 3 times a day.
    Drug Form: 25- and 50-mg tablets.

Overdosage

Signs of overdose may include loss of appetite, vomiting, depression, weakness, and/or tremors. In case of accidental ingestion or overdose, contact your veterinarian or the National Animal Poison Control Center. ALWAYS bring the prescription bottle or container with you if you go for treatment.

Special Information

Glaucoma is a common cause of blindness in dogs. It also occurs in cats but is less common. Acute glaucoma is considered a medical emergency. Rapid, effective treatment is required to save vision and control pain. It is treated using a number of different types of drugs and each must be administered based on the individual animal's response. Even in the best of circumstances, medical treatment is complicated and frequently not successful at preserving vision or controlling the pain. Surgery is the best option in most cases both to preserve vision if possible and deal with the pain. For more information on glaucoma in dogs and cats, call your veterinarian or a veterinary ophthalmologist.

Special Populations

Pregnancy/Lactation

CAIs cross the placenta and may cause birth defects in some species. It is also found in milk and may affect nursing animals. It should not be used in pregnant or lactating animals unless the benefits outweigh the risks. If used in lactating animals, the offspring should be switched to milk replacer.

Puppies/Kittens

Safety has not been established in puppies or kittens. CAIs should not be administered unless the benefits clearly outweigh the risks.

Senior Animals

Well-controlled studies have not been done in senior animals, but these drugs are frequently used and senior animals do not appear to be at an increased risk of side effects.

Generic Name

Carnitine (KAR-nih-tene) Ⓖ

Brand Name

Carnitor Ⓗ

Type of Drug

Amino acid nutritional supplement.

Prescribed for

Dilated cardiomyopathy and cardiomyopathy caused by doxorubicin and valproic acid toxicity in dogs, and hepatic lipidosis in cats.

General Information

Carnitine (levocarnitine, L-carnitine) is an amino acid that is important in fat and energy metabolism. The heart muscle gets most of the energy it needs to beat from this carnitine driven energy production. If there is not enough carnitine available to produce the required energy, the heart does not function properly and eventually fails. This type of heart failure is called dilated cardiomyopathy because it is caused by a heart (cardio-) muscle (-myo-) disease (-pathy) that causes the muscle to stretch and the heart chambers to enlarge (dilate). Other signs of carnitine deficiency include low blood sugar, enlarged liver, neurologic signs, weakness, and lethargy.

Carnitine is normally found in meat and dairy products and is also synthesized in the body. Dietary deficiencies are rare unless total nutrition and protein consumption is very low. The major cause of carnitine deficiency is probably due to a genetic defect that prevents carnitine from getting into the cells where it is needed.

Dilated cardiomyopathy is a common cause of heart failure particularly in some of the large breeds of dogs, and carnitine may be a factor in up to 90% of them. Some dogs have decreased carnitine blood levels, but many have normal levels. Dogs with normal blood levels, however, often have severely decreased levels in the heart muscle. This supports the idea that the transport system that moves carnitine into the cells is defective. Administration of carnitine increases blood levels above normal and increases the amount that gets into the muscle cells. Heart failure caused by cardiomyopathy should be treated with appropriate cardiac drugs as well as carnitine. The doses of cardiac drugs may generally be reduced if heart function improves after carnitine supplementation.

Carnitine may also be beneficial in cardiomyopathy caused by the toxic effects of doxorubicin, a chemotherapeutic drug, and valproic acid, an antiseizure drug. It is sometimes used as a dietary supplement in cats with hepatic lipidosis, although there is no proof that it actually helps.

Only about 15% of supplemental carnitine is absorbed in humans and it is eliminated in both urine and feces. Since the kidneys excrete carnitine, blood levels may be increased in animals with kidney disease. Data for dogs and cats is not available, but they are probably similar to humans.

There are two forms of carnitine, levocarnitine (L-carnitine) and dextrocarnitine (D-carnitine). Some preparations may be a mixture and others are purified so that they contain only the levo form. Levocarnitine is the active form and mixtures of levocarnitine and dextrocarnitine may reduce the amount of the active form absorbed; therefore, only purified levocarnitine preparations should be used.

Cautions and Warnings

■ Dilated cardiomyopathy is a serious disease. If you think your cat or dog may have signs of heart disease or other nutritional deficiency, see your veterinarian so the problem may be diagnosed. Treating with supplements may delay proper treatment and put your pet's health and life in danger.

■ Use products that contain only the levo form of carnitine (see "General Information").

■ Contact your veterinarian if you think your dog or cat may be having an adverse reaction to carnitine.

Possible Side Effects

Side effects are uncommon and generally mild. Loose stool and diarrhea are the most common. Nausea and vomiting occur less frequently. Increased body odor is reported in humans and may occur in animals.

Drug Interactions

• Valproic acid may increase the dosage of carnitine required.
• Dextro form of carnitine interferes with absorption of the levocarnitine form.

Food Interactions

Administering with food decreases the risk of gastrointestinal upset.

Usual Dose

Dogs: 23–45 mg/lb 3 times a day.
Cats: Need for supplementation in hepatic lipidosis is controversial and there is no consensus on an appropriate dosage.
Drug Form: 250- and 330-mg tablets, 100 mg/ml oral solution, and 200 mg/ml injectable.

Overdosage

Signs of overdosage include diarrhea and other signs of gastrointestinal upset. In case of accidental ingestion or overdose, contact your veterinarian or the National Animal Poison Control Center. ALWAYS bring the prescription bottle or container with you if you go for treatment.

Special Information

A recent study on American cocker spaniels with dilated cardiomyopathy found decreased taurine blood levels and normal carnitine blood levels. Heart muscle levels of carnitine, which is a much better indication of deficiency, were not measured in this study. The majority of these dogs improved significantly with a combination of taurine (see *Taurine*) and carnitine supplementation. Although none improved enough to stop treatment with cardiac drugs, the doses needed were reduced. This study suggests that taurine deficiency, as well as carnitine, may be a factor in heart failure in some breeds of dogs.

Special Populations

Breeds

Doberman pinschers have a high risk of developing dilated cardiomyopathy and heart failure. Other large breeds also have an increased risk. The tendency for this disease to affect certain breeds indicates that there is probably a genetic cause. Impaired carnitine transport into heart muscle cells may be involved. Close monitoring of susceptible breeds and early supplementation may be beneficial.

Pregnancy/Lactation

Controlled studies in pregnant dogs and cats have not been done, but studies in other animals indicate that it is safe. Carnitine is excreted in milk. It is believed that use of carnitine during pregnancy and lactation is safe, but the potential benefits should be weighed against the risks.

Puppies/Kittens

Controlled studies in puppies and kittens have not been done. Administration is generally considered safe, but the benefits and risks should be considered before use.

Senior Animals

Controlled studies in senior animals have not been done. Carnitine should be safe, but benefits and risks should be considered before use.

Generic Name

Carprofen (Kar-PROE-fen)

Brand Name

Rimadyl [V]

Type of Drug

Nonsteroidal anti-inflammatory drug, pain reliever, and fever reducer.

Prescribed for

Relief of pain and inflammation in dogs, especially that associated with arthritis.

General Information

Carprofen is a nonsteroidal anti-inflammatory drug (NSAID) of the propionic acid class that includes ibuprofen, naproxen, and ketoprofen. It has recently been approved by the FDA for use in dogs. It is not known exactly how NSAIDs work. However, part of their action may be owing to their ability to inhibit the body's production of hormones called prostaglandins. NSAIDs also inhibit production of other body chemicals that sensitize pain receptors and stimulate the inflammatory response. NSAIDs are quickly absorbed into the blood stream. Pain and fever relief usually starts within 1 hour and lasts for up to 12 hours in the case of carprofen. The anti-inflammatory response to these agents usually takes longer to work (several days to 2 weeks) and may take 1 month or more to reach maximum effect.

Other NSAIDs in this class, especially ibuprofen, have a narrow margin of safety in dogs and tend to cause serious side effects, such as gastrointestinal (GI) ulcers and kidney damage. Carprofen was not associated with kidney toxicity or GI ulcers in safety studies of up to 10 times the recommended dose.

Carprofen has been shown in clinical trials to be effective for the relief of signs of arthritis in dogs, and should be used in dogs only.

Cautions and Warnings

■ Carprofen should not be used in dogs exhibiting previous hypersensitivity to this drug.

■ As a class, the cyclo-oxygenase inhibitory NSAIDs tend to cause adverse effects in the GI tract and the kidneys. Carprofen seems to have much less potential for causing ulcers or kidney damage than the other drugs in its class.

■ Some individual dogs are more sensitive to the adverse effects than others. Those dogs at greatest risk for kidney damage are those on diuretics or those with liver, kidney, or heart disease.

■ Carprofen should not be used with other anti-inflammatory drugs that tend to cause GI ulcers, such as corticosteroids and other NSAIDs, unless the dog is being closely monitored.

■ Carprofen is not recommended for use in dogs with bleeding disorders such as von Willebrand's disease, as safety has not been established in dogs with these disorders.

■ Contact your veterinarian if you think your dog may be having an adverse reaction to carprofen.

■ For use in dogs only. Do not use in cats.

■ U.S. federal law restricts the use of this drug by or on the lawful written or oral order of a licensed veterinarian within the context of a valid veterinarian-client-patient relationship.

Possible Side Effects

There were no adverse reactions seen during carprofen studies in dogs. There were rare reports of vomiting, diarrhea, changes in appetite, lethargy, behavior changes, and constipation, but the incidence of these side effects was the same for the vehicle as for carprofen. GI ulcers and kidney damage are remote possibilities. Signs might include decreased appetite, black or bloody stool, or increased water consumption and urination.

Since the release of carprofen on the market and its widespread use, there have been rare reports of liver damage in dogs. The manufacturer estimates the incidence is 0.01%, or 1 in 10,000 dogs receiving carprofen. The problem seems to be more common in Labrador retrievers, but this may not be a true breed association. Signs of this adverse reaction include decreased appetite, vomiting and diarrhea, and increased blood levels of liver enzymes. Apparently, dogs that are affected will recover with supportive care after the carprofen has been discontinued. Some veterinarians are recommending that dogs on carprofen be checked routinely for evidence of liver damage. This may be a wise precaution while we are waiting for more information about this rare adverse reaction.

Contact your veterinarian if you think your dog may be having an adverse reaction to carprofen. To report possible adverse reactions of your dog to Rimadyl, call: 1-800-366-5288.

Drug Interactions

• Drug interactions with carprofen have not been studied in dogs. Caution should be used if other drugs are being given at the same time as carprofen.

Food Interactions

None are known. Probably best if given with food.

Usual Dose

Dogs: 1 mg/lb twice a day. It is probably safe to use long-term for arthritis in dogs.

Drug Form: 25-, 75-, and 100-mg caplets.

Overdosage

Dogs given 10 times the recommended dose for 14 days tolerated the dose, but some had evidence of GI ulceration—black
or bloody stool and low albumin. In case of accidental ingestion
or overdose, contact your veterinarian or the National Animal
Poison Control Center. ALWAYS bring the prescription bottle or
container with you if you go for treatment.

Special Information

See *Aspirin/Acetylsalicylic Acid* for more information on treatment for arthritis.

Special Populations

Pregnancy/Lactation
There are no safety studies for carprofen in pregnant or lactating dogs. The drug should be avoided in these animals.

Puppies/Kittens
Carprofen should not be given to puppies or kittens.

Senior Animals
Carprofen may be used in older dogs. However, if there is
heart, liver or kidney disease, carprofen should be used with
caution, or avoided.

Type of Drug

Cephalosporin Antibiotics

(CEF-uh-loe-SPOR-in)

Brand Names

First Generation Cephalosporins

Generic Ingredient: Cefadroxil [G]
Cefa-Drops [V]   Cefa-Tabs [V]   DuriCef [H]

Generic Ingredient: Cefazolin [G]
Ancef [H]   Kefzol [H]

Generic Ingredient: Cephalexin [G]
Keflex [H]

Generic Ingredient: Cephradine G
Velosef H

Second Generation Cephalosporins

Generic Ingredient: Cefaclor G
Ceclor H

Generic Ingredient: Cefoxitin
Mefoxin H

Third Generation Cephalosporins

Generic Ingredient: Cefixime
Suprax H

Generic Ingredient: Ceftiofur
Naxcel V

Prescribed for

Infections caused by microorganisms sensitive to these drugs.

General Information

Cephalosporins are antibiotics that kill bacteria by disrupting construction of the bacterial cell wall. Cephalosporins primarily kill bacteria that are growing and should not be used with antibiotics that are bacteriostatic (drugs that inhibit bacterial growth). There are over 20 cephalosporins available for use in animals and people, including oral and injectable forms.

Cephalosporins are classified as first, second, and third generation. First-generation cephalosporins are effective against most gram-positive bacteria (such as streptococcus and staphylococcus) and many anaerobic bacteria (bacteria that grow only where there is no oxygen). They have limited activity against gram-negative bacteria (such as *E. coli* and *Salmonella*). Oral first-generation cephalosporins include cephradine, cephalexin, and cephadroxil. Cefazolin is an injectible first-generation cephalosporin. Second-generation cephalosporins generally are effective against the same bacteria as first-generation and are more effective against gram-negative bacteria. Cefaclor is an oral second-generation cephalosporin. Cefoxitin is an injectable second-generation cephalosporin. Third-generation cephalosporins retain the gram-positive activity of the first and second generations but also have much expanded gram-negative activity. Cefixime is the only oral third-generation cephalosporin currently used in veterinary medicine. Ceftiofur is an injectable third-generation cephalosporin approved for use in dogs.

Cephalosporins may be used to treat bacterial infections of skin, respiratory tract, urinary tract, and bone and joints, as well as peritonitis (infection of the abdominal cavity) and septicemia (blood infection). Because of their safety and broad spectrum of activity, they are often used as first-line therapy for critically ill animals. Cephalosporins are excreted by the kidney, which makes them excellent antibiotics for kidney and urinary tract infections. They are less toxic than many other antibiotics, which, along with the broad range of bacteria they kill, makes them a good choice for debilitated animals or as initial therapy while awaiting results of bacterial culture.

Cautions and Warnings

For Owners/Handlers

■ Cephalosporins and penicillins can cause allergic reactions in certain individuals. People who are allergic to penicillin may have a similar reaction to cephalosporins. Persons with known hypersensitivity to either of these drugs should avoid exposure to these products.

For Animals

■ Many cephalosporins are not FDA approved for use in dogs or cats. They are commonly used and considered accepted practice.

■ Cephalosporins and penicillins can cause allergic reactions in certain individuals. Animals who are allergic to penicillin may have a similar reaction to cephalosporins. Animals with known hypersensitivity to either of these drugs should not be treated with these products.

■ Contact your veterinarian if you think your dog or cat may be having an adverse reaction to these antibiotics.

■ U.S. federal law restricts the use of this drug by or on the lawful written or oral order of a licensed veterinarian within the context of a valid veterinarian-client-patient relationship.

Possible Side Effects

Cephalosporins are generally very safe antibiotics. Side effects are rare at normal doses. Oral cephalosporins may cause gastrointestinal upsets, including nausea, vomiting, loss of appetite, and diarrhea.

Possible Side Effects (continued)

▼ Rare: allergic reactions, such as rash, itching, difficulty breathing, changes in blood cells, or, in extreme cases, an anaphylactic reaction. Cephalexin can cause salivation, rapid breathing, and excitability in dogs, and fever and vomiting in cats.

Drug Interactions

• Probenicid blocks kidney excretion of cephalosporins and may increase blood levels of the antibiotic.

• Cephalosporins should be used with caution with oral anticoagulants and drugs such as the aminoglycosides that may cause kidney damage.

• Cephalosporins are usually not recommended with bacteriostatic antibiotics such as chloramphenicol.

Food Interactions

Oral cephalosporins are tolerated better if given with a small meal.

Usual Dose

Cefaclor
  Dogs and Cats: 3.6–7 mg/lb orally 3 times a day.
  Drug Form: 250- and 500-mg tablets and 125, 187, 250, and 375 mg/5 ml suspension.

Cefadroxil
  Dogs and Cats: 10 mg/lb twice a day.
  Drug Form: 50-mg, 100-mg, 200-mg, 500-mg, and 1-g tablets or capsules and 125, 250, and 500 mg/5 ml suspension.

Cefazolin
  Dogs and Cats: 5–15 mg/lb by injection into a muscle (IM) or vein (IV) 3 times a day.
  Drug Form: injectable.

Cefixime
  Dogs and Cats: 5.5 mg/lb orally twice a day.
  Drug Form: 200- and 400-mg tablets and 100 mg/5 ml oral suspension.

Cefoxitin
   Dogs and Cats: 11–20 mg/lb by IM or IV injection 3 times a day.
   Drug Form: injectable.

Ceftiofur
   Dogs: 1 mg/lb once a day by injection under the skin.
   Drug Form: Sterile powder in 1-g vials for reconstitution with sterile water.

Cephalexin
   Dogs and Cats: 4.5–14 mg/lb 2–4 times a day.
   Drug Form: 250-mg, 500-mg, and 1-g tablets or capsules and 25, 50, and 100 mg/ml suspension.

Cephradine
   Dogs and Cats: 5.5–14 mg/lb 3–4 times a day.
   Drug Form: 250- and 500-mg capsules.

Overdosage

A single overdose is unlikely to cause problems. Oral overdoses may cause gastrointestinal distress. High doses or prolonged use may cause neurologic problems, hepatitis, kidney damage, and damage to the bone marrow. In case of accidental ingestion or overdose, contact your veterinarian or the National Animal Poison Control Center. ALWAYS bring the prescription bottle or container with you if you go for treatment.

Special Information

Like any medication, cephalosporins should only be given when prescribed by a veterinarian for a specific illness. Always give the antibiotic exactly as directed, including the number of pills and length of time. If you stop too early, the infection is likely to recur even if the animal appeared better after only a few days. Cephalosporins are also available as injectable antibiotics. Veterinarians may choose injectable drugs for life-threatening infections or when the animal is vomiting, unable to take oral medication, or is not eating.

Special Populations

Pregnancy/Lactation
Cephalosporins cross the placenta and are found in milk. They

should be avoided in pregnant or lactating animals unless the benefits outweigh the potential risks.

Puppies/Kittens

There are no safety studies on cephalosporin use in puppies or kittens. Many cephalosporins are used safely in children. They are also commonly used in puppies and kittens and considered reasonably safe.

Senior Animals

Cephalosporins are considered safe to use in older animals. They should be used with caution in animals with kidney disease or blood clotting disorders.

Generic Name

Chlorambucil (klor-AM-bue-sil)

Brand Name

Leukeran [H]

Type of Drug

Immunosuppressant and anticancer drug.

Prescribed for

Immune-mediated skin diseases, glomerulonephritis (kidney disease), and cancers of the lymph system.

General Information

Chlorambucil is an alkylating agent similar to cyclophosphamide. It alters DNA synthesis and inhibits the growth of rapidly dividing cells. It has been used to treat diseases in which immune cells attack the animal's own tissue. Chlorambucil has been very successful in treating pemphigus foliaceous and severe eosinophilic granuloma complex in cats, where there is serious skin damage because of immune attack. It has also been used to treat canine glomerulonephritis, where immune cells attack the glomerulus (filtering unit of the kidney). Chlorambucil has also been used successfully to treat chronic lymphocytic leukemia, macroglobulinemia, and polycythemia vera. It has the potential to be useful in other immune-mediated diseases and cancers.

Cautions and Warnings

■ Chlorambucil is not FDA approved for use in dogs or cats, but it is commonly used to treat certain disorders and is considered accepted practice.

■ Bone marrow suppression is the most likely problem with chlorambucil use. Owners should watch closely for signs of bleeding or bruising, increased urination, depression, decreased appetite, or infection.

■ Contact your veterinarian if you think your dog or cat may be having an adverse reaction to chlorambucil.

■ U.S. federal law restricts the use of this drug by or on the lawful written or oral order of a licensed veterinarian within the context of a valid veterinarian-client-patient relationship.

Possible Side Effects

▼ Rare: mild, gradual, and rapidly reversible bone marrow suppression (complete blood and platelet counts should be done every 2 to 3 weeks during chlorambucil therapy to monitor for decreased white blood cell and platelet counts); decreased appetite, vomiting, and diarrhea in cats (usually resolved when daily doses are decreased to every other day); fever, liver damage, skin hypersensitivity, peripheral nerve damage, lung fibrosis, sterile cystitis, leukemia, and cancer in people with long-term use (possible in animals also, but not been reported); and delayed regrowth of shaved fur in dogs (poodles and Kerry blues are the most susceptible breeds).

Drug Interactions

• Chlorambucil should be used with caution with other drugs that may cause bone marrow suppression, such as chloramphenicol, amphotericin B, and many anticancer drugs. Bone marrow suppression may be additive.

• When chlorambucil is used with azathioprine, cyclophosphamide, or corticosteroids, there may be increased risk of infection.

Food Interactions

None known.

Usual Dose

Dogs: for pemphigus or glomerulonephritis—0.05–0.1 mg/lb orally once a day or every other day with corticosteroids. For adjunct therapy of cancer, macroglobulinemia, or polycythemia—2–6 mg/m^2 once a day or every other day. For chronic lymphocytic leukemia—20 mg/m^2 every 1–2 weeks, or 6 mg/m^2 once a day.

Cats: for pemphigus—0.1 mg/lb orally once a day or every other day with corticosteroids. For SLE (systemic lupus erythematosus)—0.1–0.25 mg/lb every 2–3 days. For chronic lymphocytic leukemia—2 mg/m^2 every other day or 20 mg/m^2 every other week.

Drug Form: 2-mg tablet.

Overdosage

High doses may damage the cerebellum, the part of the brain that controls coordination. Seizures, vomiting, diarrhea, and bone marrow suppression are also possible. In case of accidental ingestion or overdose, contact your veterinarian or the National Animal Poison Control Center. ALWAYS bring the prescription bottle or container with you if you go for treatment.

Special Information

Chlorambucil is well tolerated by most cats and seems to be a particularly effective treatment for immune-mediated diseases, such as pemphigus and eosinophilic granuloma complex, that often do not respond to steroids alone. Once the cat is in remission, it is important to taper both the steroids and the chlorambucil slowly, over months, to the lowest dose that will control the disease. Most cats will not need to stay on chlorambucil long-term but can be controlled with low-dose or alternate-day corticosteroids alone, after chlorambucil therapy has gotten the disease under greater control. Follow your veterinarian's instructions carefully, and watch your cat closely. It may be more difficult to get some cats back in remission with chlorambucil after relapses.

Special Populations

Pregnancy/Lactation
Chlorambucil should be avoided during pregnancy or lactation.

Puppies/Kittens
Chlorambucil should be avoided in puppies and kittens.

Senior Animals
Chlorambucil should be safe to use in older animals, but it must be used with caution in animals with infections or previous bone marrow suppression.

Generic Name

Chlorhexidine (klor-HEKS-ih-dene) [G]

Most Common Brand Names

ChlorhexiDerm [V]	Nolvasan [V]
Hexadene [V]	Solvahex [V]

Combination Product

Generic Ingredients: Chlorhexidine + Nicotinamide
Stomadhex Bioadhesive Tablets [V]

Type of Drug

Antiseptic, antibacterial, antifungal.

Prescribed for

Bacterial and fungal skin infections.

General Information

Chlorhexidine is the active ingredient in shampoos, surgical soaps, solution, and ointments used on animals to treat bacterial or fungal skin infections. It may be used as an antiseptic for minor wounds or abrasions. It is used in the treatment of some bacterial skin infections (pyoderma). The majority of pyodermas are caused by the bacteria *Staphylococcus.* They can be superficial or deep, localized as hot spots or found in skin folds. Some animals have recurrent skin infections that present long-term management challenges. Skin infections can be very painful and your veterinarian may need to sedate or even anesthetize your animal to initially clip, clean, and treat the infected areas. Chlorhexidine is not usually used in animals with deeper skin infections that affect the subcutaneous tissues. Povidone-iodine soaps are more commonly used in these deeper pyodermas.

Chlorhexidine is also used as a shampoo or dip solution in animals with ringworm or fungal skin infections. It is the most commonly recommended topical treatment for ringworm in cats (see *Griseofulvin*). Ringworm is contagious and may spread to other animals and to people through contact with infected animals or people (see *Zoonotic Diseases of Dogs and Cats*).

Dogs and cats are most commonly infected with *Microsporum canis* or *Trichophyton*. Hair loss, scaling, crusting and redness are common symptoms but some infected animals, especially cats, have no symptoms. In such cases, the ringworm is only discovered when it develops in a human or animal contact. Ringworm usually does not cause itching, although some cats may be moderately or intensely itchy. Ringworm infection in cats is usually generalized even if skin lesions appear localized.

Localized ringworm may be treated with topical antifungals such as chlorhexidine, captan dip, povidone-iodine, thiabendazole, clotrimazole, or miconazole. Affected areas should be clipped and treatment continued for 2 weeks beyond negative cultures. Dogs with a few local areas of hair loss can be treated with spot treatments depending on the number and severity of the lesions. Standard treatment for generalized ringworm involves long-term treatment with both topical antifungals such as chlorhexidine and systemic antifungal drugs (see *Griseofulvin*) after a total body clip.

Chlorhexidine is also found in medicated oral cleansing solution and in antiseptic ear cleaning treatments. Chlorhexidine should only be used in ears when the eardrum is intact. If the eardrum has ruptured, chlorhexidine may cause loss of hearing and equilibrium.

Cautions and Warnings

■ For external use only. Consult a veterinarian in case of accidental ingestion.

■ Avoid contact with eyes and mucous membranes. Use a protective eye ointment before applying near the eyes.

■ DO NOT flush the ears with chlorhexidine if the eardrum is ruptured.

■ U.S. federal law restricts the use of this drug by or on the lawful written or oral order of a licensed veterinarian within the context of a valid veterinarian-client-patient relationship.

Possible Side Effects

▼ Common: hearing and equilibrium loss if chlorhexidine penetrates the eardrum into the middle ear.

▼ Rare: local irritation and ulcers on the surface of the eye after eye contact.

Food and Drug Interactions

None known.

Usual Dose

Dogs and Cats: Shampoo 2 to 3 times a week or as directed by your veterinarian. Shampoo should be left on the animal for 10 minutes before rinsing. When using the ointment, clean affected area with soap and water, and dry thoroughly. Apply a light covering of ointment once a day to affected areas and immediate surrounding vicinity. Treatment may involve other procedures, as in ear cleaning and tooth brushing, so follow your veterinarian's advice on the use of chlorhexidine products.

Drug Form: 1% and 2% shampoo and surgical scrub, 2% solution, 1% ointment, 1% oral solution, and ear solution. Bioadhesive tablets for use in the mouth.

Overdosage

In case of accidental ingestion or overdose, contact your veterinarian or the National Animal Poison Control Center. ALWAYS bring the prescription bottle or container with you if you go for treatment.

Special Information

Chlorhexidine shampoo can be used regularly on dogs that are prone to recurrent pyoderma. Benzoyl peroxide shampoo is more effective than chlorhexidine shampoo in reducing the number of bacteria on the skin, but it can dry the skin, bleach the hair coat, and be irritating to some animals. Chlorhexidine is not quite as effective as benzoyl peroxide, but it is better tolerated. Sometimes a 0.5% chlorhexidine rinse is recommended after bathing for increased residual activity.

Stomadhex is a bioadhesive tablet that is applied to the gums for residual antibacterial action in the mouth. Your veterinarian

may recommend them if your dog or cat has problems with gin-
givitis or as a routine after teethcleaning in the hospital.

Fungal spores can live in the environment for over a year. In
order to prevent continued reinfection, the entire house should
be thoroughly cleaned and vacuumed to remove any infected
hairs. All grooming equipment and bedding of infected animals
should be discarded or disinfected with Clorox. Any areas
where the animal has contact should be cleaned with Clorox
if possible.

There is a lot of controversy over topical treatment of cats
with ringworm. Some experts have found that bathing infected
cats may actually spread the ringworm to new areas. Consult
your veterinarian or a veterinary dermatologist for the latest
recommendations on the treatment of ringworm.

Special Populations

Pregnancy/Lactation
Chlorhexidine should be safe to use on pregnant or lactating
animals.

Puppies/Kittens
Chlorhexidine should be safe to use on puppies and kittens.

Senior Animals
Chlorhexidine should be safe to use on older animals.

Generic Name

Chlorpheniramine (KLOR-fen-ERE-uh-mene) G

Most Common Brand Names

Allergy Relief H   Chlor-Trimeton H

Type of Drug

Antihistamine.

Prescribed for

Itching caused by allergies in dogs and cats, miliary dermatitis
in cats.

General Information

Chlorpheniramine maleate and other antihistamines competitively block histamine at the H_1 histamine receptor site. They are used to control itching and allergic symptoms in dogs and cats. Antihistamines alone may control itching in about 40% of dogs. Chlorpheniramine may control itching in about 70% of cats. If antihistamines are unable to control all the signs, they may allow a lower dose of corticosteroids to be used. Chlorpheniramine is the antihistamine of choice for most cats.

Cautions and Warnings

■ There are no FDA approved products containing chlorpheniramine for use in dogs or cats, but these products are commonly used in dogs and cats and considered accepted practice.

■ DO NOT give over-the-counter chlorpheniramine products containing alcohol, caffeine, acetaminophen, or other medications to animals. These other medications may cause severe side effects or death.

■ Chlorpheniramine should be used with caution in animals with prostatic enlargement, bladder neck obstruction, severe heart failure, some forms of glaucoma, or pyeloduodenal obstruction (obstruction at the junction of the stomach and small intestine), allergic lung disease, hyperthyroidism, and high blood pressure.

■ Contact your veterinarian it you think your dog or cat may be having an adverse reaction to chlorpheniramine.

■ U.S. federal law restricts the use of this drug by or on the lawful written or oral order of a licensed veterinarian within the context of a valid veterinarian-client-patient relationship.

Possible Side Effects

▼ Common: sedation, diarrhea, vomiting, and loss of appetite.
▼ Rare: dry mucous membranes and urinary retention.

Drug Interactions

• Chlorpheniramine may have an additive effect when combined with other central nervous system depressant drugs, such as barbiturates and tranquilizers.

• Chlorpheniramine may have an additive effect when combined with other anticholinergic agents, such as atropine.

• Chlorpheniramine should not be used with monoamine oxidase inhibitors (MAOIs).

• Antihistamines may counteract warfarin and heparin.

Food Interactions

None known.

Usual Dose

Dogs: 2–4 mg orally 2–3 times a day (0.1 mg/lb 3 times a day).

Cats: 1–2 mg orally 2–3 times a day (0.1–0.2 mg/lb twice a day).

Drug Form: available over the counter in tablet and liquid form. Many over-ther-counter products are combination products. Do not give products containing alcohol, acetaminophen, or caffeine to animals. Use only the specific product prescribed by your veterinarian.

Overdosage

An overdose may cause excitement or excessive sedation. A massive overdose may cause seizure, respiratory depression, coma, and death. In case of accidental ingestion or overdose, contact your veterinarian or the National Animal Poison Control Center. ALWAYS bring the prescription bottle or container with you if you go for treatment.

Special Information

Allergies, such as flea allergy dermatitis, and atopy (a tendency toward multiple allergies) are challenging management problems for pet owners and veterinarians. Medications such as antihistamines and corticosteroids may be useful for symptomatic relief but are not cures for the underlying allergy. Some animals respond better to one antihistamine than another. The only way to determine which works best for your animal is to give each one a trial until you find the one that is most effective. You need to work with your veterinarian to determine the causes of your animal's allergy and develop a management program to relieve the symptoms.

Special Populations

Pregnancy/Lactation

Chlorpheniramine has not been studied in pregnant dogs and

cats. It does not cause birth defects in laboratory animals but is excreted in milk. It should only be used in pregnant or lactating animals if the benefits outweigh the risks.

Puppies/Kittens

There are no studies on chlorpheniramine use in puppies or kittens. It should only be used if the benefits outweigh the risks.

Senior Animals

There are no studies in dogs and cats, but older humans are more sensitive to side effects from antihistamines. In most cases, it is better to start with a reduced dose.

Generic Name

Cimetidine (sih-MET-ih-dene) [G]

Brand Names

Tagamet [H]   Tagamet HB [H]

The information in this profile also applies to the following drugs:

Generic Ingredient: Famotidine
Pepcid [H]   Pepcid AC [H]

Generic Ingredient: Ranitidine [G]
Zantac [H]

Type of Drug

Histamine H_2 receptor antagonist.

Prescribed for

Ulcers of the gastrointestinal tract and esophagus caused by kidney failure, NSAIDs, corticosteroids, or stress; mast cell tumors; *Helicobacter* gastritis/duodenitis in cats; acetaminophen overdose; modulation of immune response; and pancreatic insufficiency.

General Information

Cimetidine, famotidine, and ranitidine are a group of anti-ulcer medications called histamine H_2 antagonists. These drugs all prevent the stomach from producing acid. They are effective in treating the symptoms of ulcers and preventing ulcers from occurring in those at risk.

All the histamine H_2 antagonists work in the same way; they differ only in their potency. Cimetidine is the least potent, with 1000 mg roughly equal to 300 mg of nizatidine or ranitidine or 40 mg of famotidine. The ulcer healing rate and chance of side effects with all of these drugs are about the same.

These drugs may be given to decrease stomach acid in order to protect the replacement enzymes to dogs with pancreatic insufficiency, and they are used in animals in acute kidney failure to prevent gastrointestinal ulcers. Cimetidine is used as an immune modulator in some recurrent deep skin infections in dogs and as an adjunct cancer therapy. Treatment of *Helicobacter* in cats includes histamine H_2 receptor antagonist, with doxycycline and metronidazole.

Histamine H_2 receptor antagonists are frequently used with other drugs such as sucralfate (see *Sucralfate*) to hasten ulcer healing. They are metabolized in the liver and excreted in the urine.

Cautions and Warnings

■ Cimetidine, famotidine, and ranitidine are not FDA approved for use in dogs or cats. They are routinely used and considered accepted practice.

■ Histamine H_2 receptor antagonists are considered very safe drugs with few side effects.

■ Because cimetidine affects the metabolism of many other drugs, the drug interactions are numerous and important (see "Drug Interactions"). Famotidine and ranitidine have fewer drug interactions than cimetidine.

■ Histamine H_2 receptor antagonist metabolism is decreased in elderly human patients, especially those with kidney or liver disease. They should be used with caution in older animals, and the dose usually needs to be decreased.

■ There may be a temporary increase in stomach acid after these drugs are discontinued. Cimetidine will cause the most marked acid rebound.

■ Contact your veterinarian it you think your dog or cat may be having an adverse reaction to these drugs.

■ U.S. federal law restricts the use of these drugs by or on the lawful written or oral order of a licensed veterinarian within the context of a valid veterinarian-client-patient relationship.

Possible Side Effects

Side effects in animals are very rare. The side effects listed here occur in humans.

▼ Rare: mild diarrhea, nausea, vomiting, mental confusion especially in seniors, headache, breast swelling, and white blood cell and platelet changes; abnormal heart rhythms can occur with rapid intravenous administration.

Drug Interactions

• Separate oral doses of histamine H_2 receptor antagonists from antacids, metoclopramide, sucralfate, digoxin, and ketoconazole; separate by 2 hours if possible.

• Cimetidine may increase the effects of a variety of drugs by preventing their breakdown or elimination from the body, possibly leading to drug toxicity. These drugs include aminophylline, oral antidiabetes drugs, benzodiazepine tranquilizers (except lorazepam, oxazepam, and temazepam), calcium channel blocking drugs, fluorouracil, lidocaine, metoprolol, metronidazole, mexiletine, narcotic pain-relieving drugs, ondansetron, pentoxifylline, phenytoin, procainamide, propranolol, quinidine, theophylline drugs, triamterene, tricyclic antidepressants, valproic acid, and warfarin.

• Drugs whose absorption may be decreased by cimetidine are iron, indomethacin, fluconazole, ketoconazole, and the tetracycline antibiotics.

• Enteric coated tablets should not be given with cimetidine because the change in stomach acidity will cause the tablets to disintegrate prematurely in the stomach.

• The effects of digoxin and tocainide may decrease when given with cimetidine.

• Famotidine may make low white blood cell counts worse if given with other bone marrow suppressing drugs.

• Propantheline bromide delays the absorption but increases the blood levels of ranitidine.

• Ranitidine may increase blood levels of procainamide.

• Ranitidine may change blood clotting in animals on warfarin.

Food Interactions

Food may delay or slightly decrease absorption of cimetidine, but it is generally given with meals. There is no information on food interactions with famotidine and ranitidine.

Usual Dose

Cimetidine

   Dogs: 5 mg/lb orally or by injection into a vein (IV) or muscle 3–4 times a day; for kidney failure—1–2.5 mg/lb orally or IV twice a day.

   Cats: 5 mg/lb orally 3–4 times a day.

   Drug Form: 200-, 300-, 400-, and 800-mg prescription tablets; 100-mg over-the-counter tablets; 60 mg/ml oral solution; and 150 mg/ml injectable.

Famotidine

   Dogs: 0.25 mg/lb orally once or twice a day.

   Cats: 0.25 mg/lb orally once a day.

   Drug Form: film coated tablets, oral powder for suspension, injectable liquid.

Ranitidine

   Dogs: 0.5–1.0 mg/lb orally 2–3 times a day.

   Cats: 0.25–2.0 mg/lb orally twice a day.

   Drug Form: 150- and 300-mg tablets and capsules and 15 mg/lb syrup.

Overdosage

Overdoses of cimetidine are associated with breathing difficulties and heart rhythm disturbances, but little else is known. Massive overdoses of famotidine may cause vomiting, restlessness, pale gums, redness of mouth and ears, low blood pressure, high heart rate, and collapse. Clinical experience with ranitidine overdosage is very limited, but there appears to be a wide margin of safety in laboratory animals. In case of accidental ingestion or overdose, contact your veterinarian or the National Animal Poison Control Center. ALWAYS bring the prescription bottle or container with you if you go for treatment.

Special Information

Histamine H_2 antagonists are frequently used with nonsteroidal anti-inflammatory drugs, corticosteroids, and other drugs that are likely to cause stomach ulcers. Some research suggests that misoprostol is more effective for this purpose. One disadvantage to histamine H_2 antagonists is a temporary rebound increase in stomach acid after the drug is discontinued. Cimetidine seems to be most likely histamine H_2 antagonist to cause this rebound effect. In most cases, the choice of H_2 antagonist is made based on expense and frequency of administration. In some instances, ranitidine is preferred over cimetidine because it has fewer drug interactions and it is metabolized differently in the liver. It may be prescribed in animals with gastrointestinal ulceration due to liver disease or in animals taking medication that is incompatible with cimetidine.

Special Populations

Pregnancy/Lactation
There are no safety studies in pregnant dogs and cats. These drugs should be avoided unless the benefits outweigh the potential risks.

Puppies/Kittens
There is no information on histamine H_2 antagonist use in young animals. There is some pediatric use of cimetidine in humans, but it is generally not recommended.

Senior Animals
Histamine H_2 antagonists should be safe in older animals if kidney and liver function are adequate. Usually a lower dose is recommended. In humans, the side effect of disorientation occurs more commonly in older patients.

Generic Name

Cisapride (CIS-uh-pride)

Brand Name

Propulsid Ⓗ

Type of Drug

Gastrointestinal stimulant.

Prescribed for

Gastroesophageal reflux and delayed emptying of the stomach, chronic constipation, and megacolon in cats.

General Information

Cisapride is classified as a gastrointestinal stimulant. It is a relatively new drug but shows promise in the treatment of esophageal reflux and inadequate stomach emptying. It is thought to stimulate nerve networks in the gastrointestinal tract. It increases muscle tone and peristalsis (rhythmic contractions) at the lower end of the esophagus. This prevents stomach contents from flowing back into the esophagus. It also accelerates emptying of the stomach and propulsion through the intestines by increasing peristalsis. It does not increase gastric acid secretion.

Cisapride is metabolized in the liver. Giving other drugs that are metabolized by the same enzymes has caused serious and potentially fatal irregular heart rhythms in humans. The risk in dogs and cats is not known (see "Cautions and Warnings").

Cautions and Warnings

■ Do not use cisapride with ketoconazole, itraconazole, miconazole, troleandomycin, erythromycin, fluconazole, clarithromycin, or other drugs that inhibit cytochrome enzymes in the liver (see "General Information").

■ Do not use in animals with intestinal obstruction or impaction, bleeding, perforation, or other conditions where increased motility may be harmful.

■ The dose may need to be decreased in animals with liver disease.

■ Contact your veterinarian if you think your dog or cat may be having an adverse reaction to cisapride.

■ Cisapride is not FDA approved for use in dogs or cats, but it seems to be useful and is considered accepted practice.

■ U.S. federal law restricts the use of this drug by or on the lawful written or oral order of a licensed veterinarian within the context of a valid veterinarian-client-patient relationship.

Possible Side Effects

▼ Rare: diarrhea and abdominal pain.

Drug Interactions

• Ketoconazole, itraconazole, miconazole, troleandomycin,

erythromycin, fluconazole, and clarithromycin may interact with cisapride, resulting in potentially fatal heart irregularities.

• Cisapride may affect absorption of other drugs given orally because it increases gastrointestinal motility, and the dose of some drugs may need to be changed.

• Anticholinergic drugs may decrease the effect of cisapride.

• Cisapride may increase the effects of anticoagulants and coagulation times should be monitored.

• Cisapride may enhance the sedative effects of alcohol or benzodiazepines.

Food Interactions

None known.

Usual Dose

Dogs: 0.05–0.23 mg/lb 2–3 times a day, administered at least 30 minutes before feeding.

Cats: 2.5–5 mg/cat 2–3 times a day.

Drug Form: 10- and 20-mg tablets and 1 mg/ml oral suspension.

Storage: Store at room temperature in tightly closed containers and protect from light.

Overdosage

There is a wide margin of safety for cisapride. Diarrhea, difficulty breathing, drooping of the upper eyelid, tremors, convulsions, and other central nervous system signs have been reported. Doses over 1000 times the recommended dose caused death in dogs. In case of accidental ingestion or overdose, contact your veterinarian or the National Animal Poison Control Center. ALWAYS bring the prescription bottle or container with you if you go for treatment.

Special Information

Cisapride may be useful in chronic constipation and megacolon in cats when combined with a stool softener and diet with increased fiber.

Special Populations

Pregnancy/Lactation

Studies show that high doses of cisapride decrease fertility and cause birth defects in rats and rabbits. Use in pregnant animals should be avoided unless the potential benefits clearly outweigh the risks. Cisapride is excreted in milk and should be avoided or used with caution in lactating dogs and cats.

Puppies/Kittens

Specific information on use in puppies and kittens is not available. Use should be avoided unless the benefits clearly outweigh the risks.

Senior Animals

There are no controlled studies in senior dogs or cats; however, it is probably safe.

Generic Name

Clemastine (KLEH-mas-tene) G

Brand Name

Tavist H

Type of Drug

Antihistamine.

Prescribed for

Itching caused by allergies in dogs.

General Information

Clemastine fumarate and other antihistamines competitively block histamine from binding at the H_1 histamine receptor site. They are used to control itching in dogs with allergies. Antihistamines alone will control itching in about 40% of these dogs. If an antihistamine is unable to control all allergic symptoms, it may allow a lower dose of corticosteroid to be used. Studies have shown that clemastine and corticosteroids combined have enhanced activity, allowing for lower drug doses. Clemastine may cause less sedation than many antihistamines.

Cautions and Warnings

■ Clemastine is not FDA approved for use in dogs or cats. It is commonly used in dogs and considered accepted practice. Other antihistamines are more commonly used to treat cats.

■ Clemastine should be used with caution in animals with prostatic enlargement, bladder neck obstruction, severe heart failure, some forms of glaucoma, or pyeloduodenal obstruction (obstruction at the junction of the stomach and small intestine).

■ Contact your veterinarian if you think your dog or cat may be having an adverse reaction to clemastine.

■ U.S. federal law restricts the use of this drug by or on the lawful written or oral order of a licensed veterinarian within the context of a valid veterinarian-client-patient relationship.

Possible Side Effects

▼ Common: sedation and dry mucous membranes.

Drug Interactions

• Clemastine may have an additive effect when combined with other central nervous system depressant drugs, such as barbiturates and tranquilizers.

• Clemastine may have an additive effect when combined with other anticholinergic agents.

• Clemastine should not be used with monoamine oxidase inhibitors (MAOIs).

• Clemastine may decrease the effects of heparin and warfarin.

Food Interactions

None known.

Usual Dose

Dogs: 0.025–0.05 mg/lb orally twice a day.

Drug Form: 1.34- and 2.68-mg tablets, available over-the-counter.

Overdosage

Overdoses may cause increased sedation, anticholinergic effects, and low blood pressure. In case of accidental ingestion or overdose, contact your veterinarian or the National Animal Poison Control Center. ALWAYS bring the prescription bottle or container with you if you go for treatment.

Special Information

Allergies, such as flea allergy dermatitis, and atopy (a tendancy toward multiple allergies) are challenging management problems for pet owners and veterinarians. Medications like antihistamines and corticosteroids may be useful for symptomatic relief but are not a cure for the underlying allergy. Some animals respond better to one antihistamine than another. The only way to determine which works best for your animal is to give each one a trial until you find the one that is most effective. You need to work with your veterinarian to determine the causes of your animal's allergy and develop a management program to relieve the symptoms.

Special Populations

Pregnancy/Lactation

Clemastine has not been studied in pregnant dogs. It does not cause birth defects in laboratory animals but is excreted in milk. It should only be used in pregnant or lactating animals if the benefits outweigh the risks.

Puppies

There are no studies on clemastine use in puppies. It should only be used if the benefits outweigh the risks.

Senior Animals

There are no studies in dogs, but older humans are more sensitive to side effects from antihistamines.

Generic Name

Clindamycin (klin-duh-MYE-sin) G

Brand Names

Antirobe V   Clinda-Derm H
Cleocin H

Type of Drug

Antibiotic and antiprotozoal.

Prescribed for

Susceptible bacterial infections and infections caused by the protozoa *Toxoplasma, Coccidia,* and *Babesia.*

General Information

Clindamycin is a derivative of lincomycin. It is a newer antibiotic effective in treating a variety of bacterial infections, including those caused by anaerobic bacteria (bacteria that grow in the absence of oxygen). Anaerobes are fairly common in infections of teeth, bone, joints, and lining of the lung (pleura), or in blood infections. Clindamycin is one of the antibiotics of choice for deep pyodermas (skin infections) and abscesses, and chronic prostatitis (infection of the prostate gland) in dogs. Clindamycin is also the treatment of choice for *Toxoplasma* infection (toxoplasmosis), including the ocular form, in dogs and cats. During the initial few days of treatment, clindamycin only prevents coccidia from growing; after that it kills them. It has been used to treat *Babesia* infection in people and may be effective for this purpose in dogs and cats as well. Clindamycin may be combined with cephalosporins or enrofloxacin for serious mixed infections or blood infections and may be combined with pyrimethamine for *Toxoplasma* brain infections.

Cautions and Warnings

■ Clindamycin is FDA approved for use in dogs but not cats. It is commonly used in cats, however, and is considered accepted practice. Clindamycin should be used with caution in animals with allergic skin disease, liver, or kidney disease. It should also be used with caution in cats with toxoplasmosis involving the lung. Some experimentally infected cats died after clindamycin injections.

■ Clindamycin may cause elevations in liver enzymes. The manufacturer recommends that during prolonged therapy of 1 month or greater, periodic liver and kidney function tests and blood counts be performed.

■ Clindamycin should not be used in animals that have had an allergic reaction to lincomycin. Contact your veterinarian if you think your dog or cat may be having an adverse reaction to clindamycin.

■ U.S. federal law restricts the use of this drug by or on the lawful written or oral order of a licensed veterinarian within the context of a valid veterinarian-client-patient relationship.

Possible Side Effects

▼ Rare: allergic reactions, vomiting, and bloody diarrhea.

Drug Interactions

• Clindamycin should not be used with chloramphenicol or erythromycin, due to possible antagonism.

• Clindamycin should not be used with other neuromuscular blocking agents.

Food Interactions

None known.

Usual Dose

Dogs and Cats: 2.5–12.5 mg/lb orally twice a day. The lower doses may be used for abscesses and tooth infections, the middle range for bone infections, and the highest doses for toxoplasmosis.

Drug Form: 25-, 75- and 150-mg Antirobe capsules and 25 mg/ml Antirobe Aquadrops. Human products are available as injectable, capsules, flavored granules, topical gel, lotion, cream, and solution.

Overdosage

There is little information on overdoses. In dogs, oral doses at 10 times the recommended dose for 1 year did not cause any toxicity. Higher doses caused decreased appetite, vomiting, and weight loss. In case of accidental ingestion or overdose, contact your veterinarian or the National Animal Poison Control Center. ALWAYS bring the prescription bottle or container with you if you go for treatment.

Special Populations

Pregnancy/Lactation
There are no safety studies for clindamycin in pregnant or lactating dogs and cats. It should be avoided unless the benefits outweigh the risks. Clindamycin is excreted in milk and may cause diarrhea in nursing puppies or kittens.

Puppies/Kittens
There are no safety studies for clindamycin in puppies or kittens. It should be avoided unless the benefits outweigh the risks.

Senior Animals
Clindamycin should be safe to use in older animals but should be used with caution in those with kidney or liver dysfunction.

Generic Name

Clomipramine (kloe-MIP-ruh-mene) [G]

Brand Name

Anafranil [H]

Type of Drug

Psychotropic, antianxiety, tricyclic antidepressant.

Prescribed for

Compulsive behaviors, anxiety, fear, and dominance aggression.

General Information

Clomipramine is one of the tricyclic antidepressants (TCAs). TCAs are similar in structure to the phenothiazine tranquilizers (see *Acepromazine*). These chemicals block the movement of certain stimulant chemicals in and out of nerve endings, have a sedative effect, and counteract the effects of the nerve chemical acetylcholine. They work in the central nervous system (CNS) to inhibit serotonin and norepinephrine reuptake by nerve endings. Different TCAs differ in their potency and in their relative effects on serotonin and norepinephrine. Amitriptyline (see *Amitriptyline*) and imipramine (Tofranil) affect serotonin and norepinephrine equally and are used primarily as antianxiety drugs. Clomipramine (Anafranil) and fluoxetine (Prozac) affect serotonin primarily and are anti-compulsive drugs.

All undesirable behaviors have a learned component. Treatment of any undesirable behavior requires behavior modification (training based on scientific principles used to alter or change undesirable behaviors). Drugs are used in the treatment of dogs and cats with behavior problems because certain undesirable behaviors cannot be managed by behavior modification techniques alone. In such cases severe anxiety or fear, a strong hormonal component to behavior (as in maternal aggression), or a neurochemical imbalance in the brain (as in compulsive behaviors) prevents effective behavior modification. Drugs are only useful for certain specific types of behavior problems, and they should ONLY be used as an adjunct to behavior modification. When used in this way they enable behavior modification to be maximally effective.

Most psychotropic drugs used in veterinary medicine are not licensed for use in animals. There are few controlled studies in animals establishing dose, efficacy, or safety. The TCAs may interfere with learning. The long-term effects of these drugs are not known. There may be breed and individual differences in response to these drugs.

Clomipramine is used in dogs and cats to treat compulsive behaviors, now recognized to be conflict behaviors. These are behaviors that are related to normal behaviors, such as grooming, but are out of context, repetitive, exaggerated, and have no purpose. These behaviors include chewing the feet, licking one spot (lick granuloma), scratching, fly-snapping, circling and whirling, tail-chasing, pacing, rhythmic barking, flank-sucking, and self-mutilation in dogs, and wool-sucking and excessive grooming or self-mutilation in cats. Conflict behaviors occur when an animal is motivated to do something but is physically prevented from doing so or has 2 equally strong conflicting motivations. Once compulsive behavior is well established, the chemical changes in the brain are almost irreversible. At this point, environmental changes and behavior modification alone usually are not sufficient to treat compulsive disorder.

Clomipramine may also be used to treat aggression related to dominance or aggression toward owners, although drug therapy is usually not recommended for dominance aggression. Clomipramine may be used to treat anxiety disorders, but amitriptyline (see *Amitriptyline*) is usually the drug of choice.

Cautions and Warning

For Owners/Handlers

■ KEEP OUT OF REACH OF CHILDREN! Children are very sensitive to the seizure-inducing and cardiotoxic effects of TCAs.

For Animals

■ Clomipramine should be avoided in animals with liver disease, kidney failure, hyperthyroidism, glaucoma, seizures, heart failure, abnormal heart rhythms or those on thyroid medication.

■ Most psychotropic drugs cause some degree of CNS depression and are sedative at higher doses. They may also interfere with learning.

■ Clomipramine is not FDA approved for use in dogs or cats. It is commonly used to treat compulsive disorders and is considered accepted practice.

■ Contact your veterinarian if you think your dog or cat may be having an adverse reaction to clomipramine.

■ U.S. federal law restricts the use of this drug by or on the lawful written or oral order of a licensed veterinarian within the context of a valid veterinarian-client-patient relationship.

Possible Side Effects

Clomipramine may cause drowsiness, but this is usually due to overdosing. It may also cause vomiting and diarrhea and should be given with food to avoid gastrointestinal upset. A variety of adverse reactions to clomipramine have been reported in people, including heart problems, seizures, hallucinations and other CNS signs, gastrointestinal upset, allergic reactions, bone marrow depression, liver disease, hair loss, edema, and lupus-like syndromes. These signs have not been reported in animals but are all potential side effects.

▼ Rare: urine retention and hyperexcitability.

Drug Interactions

• Because of additive effects, clomipramine should be used cautiously with other anticholinergic and CNS depressant drugs.

• TCAs should not be used with methimazole as the risk of bone marrow suppression is increased.

• Cimetidine may decrease TCA metabolism and increase the risk of adverse reactions.

• TCAs should not be given with monoamine oxidase inhibitors (MAOIs).

• Use of TCAs with sympathomimetic agents (such as phenylpropanolamine) may increase the risks of abnormal heart rhythms, high blood pressure, and fever.

Food Interactions

Give with food to avoid gastrointestinal upset.

Usual Dose

Dogs: 0.5–1.5 mg/lb orally once or twice a day.

Cats: 0.5 mg/lb orally once a day.
Drug Form: 25-, 50-, and 75-mg capsules.

Overdosage

Signs of overdose may include depression, abnormal heart rhythms, low blood pressure, convulsions, coma, and death. In case of accidental ingestion or overdose, contact your veterinarian or the National Animal Poison Control Center. ALWAYS bring the prescription bottle or container with you if you go for treatment.

Special Information

See *Fluoxetine* for more information on the use of TCAs to treat behavior problems.

Special Populations

Pregnancy/Lactation
There are no studies on the safety of clomipramine in pregnant or lactating dogs or cats. High doses cause birth defects in laboratory animals. It should be avoided unless the potential benefits outweigh the risks.

Puppies/Kittens
Clomipramine should not be used in puppies or kittens.

Senior Animals
Clomipramine should be safe to use in older dogs and cats who do not have heart, thyroid, kidney, or liver disease, or seizure disorders (see "Cautions and Warnings").

Generic Name

Clotrimazole (kloe-TRIM-uh-zole) G

Most Common Brand Names

Gyne-Lotrimin H
Veltrim Dermatologic 1% Cream V

Combination Products

Generic Ingredients: Gentamicin Sulfate + Betamethasone Valerate + Clotrimazole
Otomax V

Type of Drug

Antifungal.

Prescribed for

Susceptible superficial fungal infections, *Malassezia* or *Candida* ear infections and dermatitis, *Aspergillus* infection of the nose, and ringworm topical treatment.

General Information

Clotrimazole and miconazole are imidazole antifungals that cannot be given orally or by injection (see *Ketoconazole*), but are very effective as topical treatment of superficial fungal infections, especially those caused by the yeasts, *Malassezia* and *Candida*. *Malassezia* ear infection is an extremely common and recurrent problem in dogs (see "Special Information"). Clotrimazole is also effective in treating *Aspergillus* infections of the nasal passages and sinuses. It is infused into the nasal passages and sinuses for an hour while the dog is under anesthesia. Clotrimazole may also be used for topical treatment of ringworm (see *Griseofulvin*). Many antifungals are now available over the counter. You should consult with your veterinarian for advice on the best treatment for your animal.

Cautions and Warnings

For Owners/Handlers
■ Avoid contact with eyes, since irritation may result.
■ Wash hands after use to prevent spread of fungal infections.

For Animals
■ Avoid contact with eyes or mucous membranes, since irritation may result.
■ Contact your veterinarian if you think your dog or cat may be having an adverse reaction to clotrimazole, or if there is no improvement in 2 weeks.
■ U.S. federal law restricts the use of this drug by or on the lawful written or oral order of a licensed veterinarian within the context of a valid veterinarian-client-patient relationship.

Possible Side Effects

▼ Rare: mild skin irritation (redness, swelling, itching, and oozing) and allergic reactions.

Drug Interactions

• Amphotericin B and clotrimazole inhibit each other; they should not be used together.

Usual Dose

Dogs and Cats: Clean affected area with soap and water and dry thoroughly, apply a light covering of ointment once a day to affected areas and immediate surrounding vicinity. Treatment may involve other procedures, as in ear cleaning, so follow your veterinarian's advice on the use of clotrimazole products.

Drug Form: ointment and cream.

Overdosage

There is no specific information on overdose of clotrimazole. Clotrimazole is poorly absorbed after oral administration, so signs from oral overdose are unlikely. In case of accidental ingestion or overdose, contact your veterinarian or the National Animal Poison Control Center. ALWAYS bring the prescription bottle or container with you if you go for treatment.

Special Information

Clotrimazole is an extremely effective treatment for yeast infections of skin and ears, but there is usually an underlying cause for chronic and recurrent yeast infections in dogs. You should expect that if your dog has a yeast infection, it is likely to recur unless the underlying problem is eliminated. The most common underlying problem is allergic skin disease, either from inhaled or ingested allergens. Hair in the ear canal, excessive wax production, long floppy ears, frequent swimming, and polyps or tumors in the ear canal may all predispose the ears to infections as well. There are other effective topical treatments for chronic yeast infections, including boric acid, miconazole, and amphotericin B. Newer antifungals such as tioconazole (Vagistat) are now available over the counter. Consult your veterinarian for advice on the most effective topical antifungal for your pet.

Special Populations

Pregnancy/Lactation

There are no studies to confirm the safety of clotrimazole in pregnant or lactating dogs or cats. Clotrimazole should be avoided unless the potential benefits outweigh the risks.

Puppies/Kittens
There are no studies to confirm the safety of clotrimazole in puppies or kittens. Clotrimazole should be avoided unless the potential benefits outweigh the risks.

Senior Animals
Clotrimazole should be safe to use in older animals, but there are no studies to confirm this.

Type of Drug

Corticosteroids (Glucocorticosteroids, Glucocorticoids)

(kor-tih-koe-STER-oids)

Most Common Brand Names

Generic Ingredient: Betamethasone
Betasone [V]   Celestone Soluspan [H]

Generic Ingredient: Cortisone Acetate [G]
Cortone [H]

Generic Ingredient: Dexamethasone [G]
Azium [V]   Pet-Derm III [V]
Decadron [H]   Voren [V]

Generic Ingredient: Flumethasone
Flucort [V]

Generic Ingredient: Hydrocortisone [G]
Cortef [H]   Hydrocortone [H]

Generic Ingredient: Methylprednisolone [G]
Medrol [V]

Generic Ingredients: Methylprednisolone + Aspirin
Cortaba [V]

Generic Ingredient: Methylprednisolone Acetate [G]
Depo-Medrol [V]

Generic Ingredient: Prednisolone [G]
Cortisate-20 [V]   Prelone [H]
Pediapred [H]   Sterisol–20 [V]

Predate 50 [V]   Solu-Delta-Cortef [V]
Prednis [V]

Generic Ingredients: Prednisolone + Tetracycline Hydrochloride + Novobiocin Sodium
Delta Albaplex [V]

Generic Ingredients: Prednisolone + Trimeprazine
Temaril-P [V]

Generic Ingredient: Prednisone [G]
Meticorten [V]   Sterapred [H]

Generic Ingredient: Triamcinolone Acetonide [G]
Aristocort [H]   Vetalog [V]
Cortalone [V]

Prescribed for

Itching, inflammation, immune-mediated diseases (allergy, including anaphylactic reactions, rheumatoid arthritis, systemic lupus, asthma, pemphigus, and immune-mediated thrombocytopenia or hemolytic anemia), adrenal insufficiency (Addison's disease), some neurologic disorders including spinal cord injuries, arthritis, inflammatory bowel disease, shock, and certain types of cancer, including mast cell tumors and lymphosarcoma.

General Information

Corticosteroids are hormones normally produced by the adrenal gland. They are essential for life and affect every level of metabolism and function of all cells and organ systems. There are 2 major types of adrenal cortical hormones distinguished by their major effect. The mineralocorticoids primarily control salt and water balance in the body (see *Desoxycortisterone Pivalate* and *Fludrocortisone*). The corticosteroids, also called glucocorticosteroids, glucocorticoids, or simply steroids, are referred to in this book as corticosteroids. They are important in normal protein, carbohydrate, and fat metabolism.

Understanding the normal function and regulation of these extremely powerful hormones is important in using them successfully as drugs and minimizing their side effects. This fascinating and very complex topic is well beyond the scope of this book, but a few examples may be useful. Corticosteroids stabilize cell membranes, which is the basis for their use in treating animals with anaphylactic reactions (serious, systematic allergic reactions). They reduce nonspecific immune responses, such as inflammation, and specific cell-mediated and antibody immunity. This makes the hormones useful in treating allergic reactions such as asthma and itching; inflammatory diseases such as arthritis, inflammatory bowel disease, and some nervous system diseases; immune-mediated diseases such as rheumatoid arthritis, systemic lupus, asthma, pemphigus, hemolytic anemia, and thrombocytopenia; as well as certain types of cancer, including mast cell tumors and lymphosarcoma. On the negative side, suppressing the immune response may make an animal more susceptible to infection. Another side effect is ulcers caused by increased secretion of gastric acid.

Cushing's disease or hyperadrenocorticism is caused by excess corticosteroid. Too little mineralocorticoid and corticosteroid cause Addison's disease or hypoadrenocorticism. Both of these diseases may occur naturally and are potentially fatal. Using corticosteroids to treat other diseases may also cause Cushing's or Addison's diseases. Signs of Cushing's occur when a high dose of the hormones is administered (see "Possible Side Effects"). A high dose of corticosteroids suppresses the adrenal glands' natural production of hormones. Abruptly stopping their administration results in insufficient corticosteroid levels and signs of Addison's disease until the adrenal gland starts to produce the required hormones again.

The basic rule in prescribing corticosteroids is to use the preparation with the shortest duration of action, at the lowest dose level and for the shortest period of time possible. They may be given by injection or orally. Often, the veterinarian gives an initial injection and pills are dispensed to continue the treatment at home. Corticosteroids may be injected directly into a joint or injected into a specific lesion in some cases. They are also used topically to treat certain conditions of the skin, ears, and eyes. Some preparations may include other active ingredients such as antibiotics, antifungals, or miticides for topical use (see *Corticosteroids, Topical*). Most combination products for internal use have been discontinued because it is better to select the appropriate drugs and doses rather than settling for what is available premixed. Combinations of corticosteroids and non-steroidal anti-inflammatory drugs (NSAIDs) such as aspirin may increase the risk of ulcers and other side effects. They should be used very cautiously.

Prolonged high-dose therapy may be needed to treat diseases such as immune-mediated diseases and cancer. If high-dose treatment is needed, it is very important to taper the dosage slowly in order to avoid causing signs of Addison's disease. Since the corticosteroids play a major role in coping with stress, the dosage may need to be increased in animals on long-term treatment before stressful situations such as surgery.

Allergy and chronic arthritis are often controlled with low doses of short-acting preparations and tapered down from daily administration to every 2–3 days. This allows the adrenal gland to continue functioning and may be used safely for prolonged periods.

There are many different corticosteroids available. A major goal in developing new corticosteroids is to reduce their crossover effect on salt and water balance. In addition, they differ in potency and duration of action.

Prednisolone and prednisone are short-acting and useful for long-term alternate day use, dexamethasone and flumethasone are more potent and longer acting, and methylprednisolone acetate injectable is a long-acting repository form that often lasts for 3–4 weeks or more.

Cautions and Warnings

■ Do not inject into muscle when treating bleeding disorders such as immune-mediated thrombocytopenia since the trauma of the injection may cause bleeding and/or infection.

■ The long-acting corticosteroids should not be used for long-term treatment if it can be avoided. Alternate day therapy with short-acting preparations such as prednisolone is preferred. Animals who have received long-term therapy should be taken off slowly by tapering the dosage and prolonging the interval between doses. Animals on long-term corticosteroid therapy may need additional corticosteroids to cope with the stress of surgery, trauma, or illness.

■ Do not use corticosteroids and aspirin or other NSAIDs at the same time without carefully weighing the benefit against the increased risk of ulcers.

■ Do not use in dogs or cats with bacterial, viral, or fungal infections; animals with a history of generalized demodectic mange, stomach ulcer, corneal (eye) ulcer, Cushing's disease, diabetes, high blood pressure, kidney disease, or congestive heart failure; or during pregnancy unless the benefits outweigh the risks.

■ Contact your veterinarian if you think your dog or cat may be having an adverse reaction to corticosteroids.

■ U.S. federal law restricts the use of this drug by or on the lawful written or oral order of a licensed veterinarian within the context of a valid veterinarian-client-patient relationship.

Possible Side Effects

Side effects are generally dose-dependent. Serious side effects with low dose and alternate day therapy are rare. Cats are more resistant than dogs to side effects even at the higher dosages often needed in this species.

▼ Common: increased appetite, thirst, urination, and weight gain.

▼ Rare at low dosages, more common at higher dosages: Cushing's disease, dull haircoat, panting, vomiting, diarrhea, pancreatitis, gastrointestinal ulcers, diabetes, muscle wasting, and behavioral changes. Some long-acting corticosteroids may affect male fertility.

Drug Interactions

• The risk of digitalis toxicity is increased if corticosteroids are given with drugs that lower potassium including amphotericin B, furosemide, and thiazide.

• Insulin requirements may increase because corticosteroids increase glucose levels.

• Phenytoine, phenobarbital, and rifampin may increase the dose of corticosteroids required.

• Cyclosporine, cyclophosphamide, estrogens, erythromycin, and mitotane may reduce the required dose of corticosteroids.

• Modified live virus vaccine should not be used in animals on high dose immunosuppressive steroid therapy. The immune response to any vaccination may be reduced when corticosteroids are given at the same time.

• The risk of gastrointestinal ulcers may be increased if steroids and other drugs prone to causing ulcers, such as NSAIDs, are given at the same time.

• Use of corticosteroids and anticholinesterase agents, such as neostigmine, in patients with myasthenia gravis may cause severe muscle weakness.

Food Interactions

None known.

Usual Dose

Dosage and dosing schedules vary over a large range depending on the condition being treated and the response. The following are typical dosages. If you have questions about the dosage prescribed for your pet, discuss them with your veterinarian.

Betamethasone
  Dogs and Cats: 0.05–0.1 mg/lb 1–2 times a day. As anti-inflammatory—0.01–0.02 mg/lb once every 1–3 days.
  Drug Form: 6 and 7 mg/ml injectable.

Cortisone Acetate
  Dogs and Cats: for adrenal insufficiency—1.1 mg/lb taper down to 0.2 mg/lb.
  Drug Form: 25-mg tablets and 50 mg/ml injectable.

Dexamethasone
  Dogs and Cats: as anti-inflammatory—0.05–0.1 mg/lb 1–2 times a day. For shock—1–2 mg/lb injected into a vein (IV) or dexamethasone sodium phosphate 2–7 mg/lb IV.
  Drug Form: 0.5 mg/5 ml oral liquid; 0.25-, 0.5-, 0.75-, 1-, 1.5-, 4-, and 6-mg tablets; and 2, 3, 4, 10, 16, and 24 mg/ml injectable.

Flumethasone
  Dogs: 0.07–0.15 mg/lb 1–2 times a day.
  Cats: 0.07–0.15 mg/lb 1–2 times a day.
  Drug Form: 0.5 mg/ml injectable.

Hydrocortisone
  Dogs and Cats: for replacement therapy—0.1–0.5 mg/lb 1–2 times a day. As anti-inflammatory—1.1–2.2 mg/kg twice a day.
  Drug Form: 10-mg tablets and 50 mg/ml injectable.

Methylprednisolone
  Dogs and Cats: 0.5 mg/lb 3 times a day.
  Drug Form: 1- and 4-mg tablets.

Methylprednisolone Acetate
  Dogs: 0.5 mg/lb, by injection under the skin or in a muscle, every 1–3 weeks or less often. Usually lasts 3–4 weeks.

Cats: 2.5 mg/lb by injection under the skin or in a muscle (average sized cat = 20 mg) may last for 1 week to 6 months. Usually lasts 3–4 weeks.

Drug Form: 20 and 40 mg/ml injectable.

Methylprednisolone Sodium Succinate

Dogs and Cats: for emergency treatment of spinal trauma — starting dose 10 mg/lb IV repeated as indicated by careful monitoring of effect over 24–48 hours.

Prednisolone and Prednisone

Prednisone is rapidly converted by the liver to prednisolone. Unless an animal is in severe liver failure, the two drugs are interchangeable.

Dogs: as anti-inflammatory—0.22–0.5 mg/lb 1–2 times a day then taper to every other day. For immunosuppression—1–3 mg/lb once a day then taper to 1–2 mg/lb every other day.

Cats: as anti-inflammatory—1 mg/lb 1–2 times a day then taper to every other day. For immunosuppression—1–3 mg/lb once a day then taper to 1–2 mg/lb every other day.

Drug Form: 1-, 2.5-, 5-, 10-, 20-, and 50-mg tablets; 5 and 15 mg/5 ml oral syrup; 10, 20, 40, and 50 mg/ml injectable.

Triamcinolone

Dogs and Cats: 0.05 mg/lb initially once a day, may increase to 0.1 mg/lb once a day if initial response is unsatisfactory. As soon as possible, but not later than 2 weeks, reduce dose gradually to 0.01–0.025 mg/lb once a day.

Drug Form: 0.5- and 1.5-mg tablets and 2 and 6 mg/ml injectable.

Overdosage

Short-term administration even at massive dosages is unlikely to cause serious harmful effects. Supportive treatment is indicated for any signs that may occur. Chronic high dose therapy can result in serious side effects associated with Cushing's disease (see "Possible Side Effects"). Abruptly stopping treatment without tapering the dose may cause signs of hypoadrenocorticism or Addison's disease.

In case of accidental ingestion or overdose, contact your veterinarian or the National Animal Poison Control Center. ALWAYS bring the prescription bottle or container with you if you go for treatment.

Special Information

Corticosteroids are commonly used in emergency situations to treat shock and inflammation caused by trauma. In these situations the time frame for treatment, the selection of drugs, and the procedures used are complex and critical. Treatment must be started as soon as possible. Minutes, not hours, may determine life or death, or the degree of recovery after an animal is hit by a car or suffers spinal injury. Sufficient quantities of the proper drugs must be readily available and must be administered at specific intervals. Constant careful monitoring of the patient's vital signs is critical to determine the effectiveness of treatment and tailor it to the individual's response. Not only are the drugs and equipment very expensive, but the treatment and monitoring require the constant presence of specially trained veterinary and nursing staff. This level of emergency care is increasingly available to pet owners. It is expensive, but many consider it worth the cost.

Special Populations

Pregnancy/Lactation

Corticosteroids should be avoided during pregnancy and lactation unless the benefits outweigh the risks. Excessive levels may cause birth defects. Corticosteroids are found in milk and high doses or prolonged administration may affect nursing puppies or kittens.

Puppies/Kittens

Corticosteriods may be used in puppies and kittens. It is important to minimize the dose and duration of treatment to reduce the chance of side effects. High doses have been shown to retard growth.

Senior Animals

There are no specific restrictions for use in senior animals.

Type of Drug

Corticosteroids, Topical

(kor-tih-koe-STER-oids) G

Most Common Brand Names

Generic Ingredients: Dexamethasone + Neomycin Sulfate + Thiabendazole
Tresaderm V

Generic Ingredients: Fluocinolone Acetonide + Dimethyl Sulfoxide
Synotic Otic V

Generic Ingredient: Hydrocortisone

Bur-O-Cort 2:1 V	CortiSpray V
Bur-Otic-HC V	Derma Cool-HC V
Burrow's H V	Hydro-10 V
Clearx Ear V	Hydro-Plus V
CortiCalm V	PTD-HC V
Cortisoothe V	

Generic Ingredients: Oxytetracycline + Hydrocortisone
Terra-Cortril V

Generic Ingredient: Triamcinolone Acetonide G
Vetalog V

Generic Ingredients: Triamcinolone Acetonide + Nystatin + Neomycin Sulfate + Thiostrepton
Panolog V

Prescribed for

Temporary relief of inflammation and itching of the skin and ears.

General Information

Topical corticosteroids are applied to the skin or in the ears to relieve inflammation and itching. Corticosteroids alone do not treat the underlying cause of the itching. For this reason, many topical preparations are combined with antibiotics, antifungals, and/or other ingredients to help treat superficial infections and/or ear mites (see *Tresaderm* and *Panolog*).

Topical corticosteroids relieve itching by interfering with the natural body mechanisms that produce inflammation and itching. You should not treat your pet with topical corticosteroids without your veterinarian's recommendation. It could hide important signs that would allow your veterinarian to diagnose and treat the underlying problem. It could also make some problems worse, such as mange and fungal or bacterial infections.

It is often difficult to use topical preparations effectively on the skin because the haircoat prevents easy application without first shaving the area and the ointments make the haircoat oily and messy. Another drawback to using topical preparations is that dogs and cats lick themselves and ingest most or all of topically applied products. They may ingest enough of the drug to get systemic side effects. Oral medication should be used if extensive areas of skin need treating or the condition does not respond adequately to topical treatment.

Topical corticosteroids alone or combined with antibiotics are extensively used to treat itchy, inflamed, and infected ears. They work best if the ears are cleaned first to remove excessive pus and other debris, which prevents the drug from contacting the surface of the ear canal and prevents it from working. Thickened skin from longstanding irritation reduces the effectiveness of topical corticosteroid also. The fluocinolone and dimethyl sulfoxide (DMSO) combination product is useful in these situations because the DMSO (see *Dimethyl Sulfoxide*) helps penetrate the thickened skin.

There are many topical corticosteroid preparations, both brand names and generics. Similar preparations may contain different concentrations of ingredients or combinations of ingredients, and this may be important in which product is prescribed. The carrier may also affect the action. Ointments stay in contact with the affected area for longer than solutions; therefore, the corticosteroid is able to have a greater effect. Solutions are easier to apply to ears and may make better contact with the entire ear canal.

Cautions and Warnings

■ Do not use topical corticosteroids in dogs or cats with bacterial, viral, or fungal infections; animals with a history of generalized demodectic mange, corneal ulcer, Cushing's disease, or diabetes.

■ Contact your veterinarian if you think your dog or cat may be having an adverse reaction to topical corticosteroids.

■ Many products are FDA approved for use in dogs and cats. Products for human use are commonly used on animals, and it is considered accepted practice.

■ U.S. federal law restricts the use of these drugs by or on the lawful written or oral order of a licensed veterinarian within the context of a valid veterinarian-client-patient relationship.

Possible Side Effects

Side effects generally depend on how much the animal ingests by licking and the total amount applied. Serious side effects with topical use are rare. The most common include increased appetite, thirst, urination, and weight gain (see *Corticosteroids*).

Drug Interactions

• The risk of drug interactions with topical corticosteroids is low. See *Corticosteroids* for possible interactions after ingestion.

Usual Dose

Dogs and Cats: Clean first and then apply a thin coat on area to be treated 2–3 times a day or as directed by your veterinarian. For ears—apply enough to coat entire ear canal and massage in well.

Drug Form: ointments, creams, lotions, sprays, and liquids.

Storage: Check the label. Some products require refrigeration.

Overdosage

The risk of overdosage with topical corticosteroids is low. See *Corticosteroids* for more information on overdosage if topical products are ingested. In case of accidental ingestion or overdose, contact your veterinarian or the National Animal Poison Control Center. ALWAYS bring the prescription bottle or container with you if you go for treatment.

Special Populations

Pregnancy/Lactation

Even though the amount of corticosteroid that is absorbed after topical application is much lower than when given orally, many animals will ingest some by licking. Excessive levels may cause birth defects, and corticosteroids are excreted in milk. Topical corticosteroids should be avoided or used sparingly during pregnancy and lactation and only if the benefits outweigh the risks.

Puppies/Kittens

Topical corticosteroids may be used in puppies and kittens. It is important to minimize the dose and duration of treatment to reduce the chances of side effects.

Senior Animals

There are no specific restrictions for use in senior animals.

Generic Name

Cyclophosphamide (SYE-cloe-FAHS-fah-mide)

Brand Name

Cytoxan [H]

Type of Drug

Immunosuppressant and anticancer.

Prescribed for

Immune-mediated diseases such as pemphigus (a chronic, severe skin disease), autoimmune hemolytic anemia (AIHA), immune-mediated thrombocytopenia (ITP), rheumatoid arthritis, kidney disease (glomerulonephritis), severe irritable bowel syndrome, systemic lupus erthematosus (lupus), multiple myeloma, and cancer.

General Information

Cyclophosphamide is an alkylating agent used to treat cancer. It works as an immunosuppressant and anticancer agent by preventing cells from dividing. It is used in dogs and cats to treat immune-mediated diseases that do not respond to corticosteroids alone. It is usually used with corticosteroids. Cyclophosphamide may also be used to treat certain types of cancer, such as lymphoma/lymphosarcoma, mammary cancer, mast cell tumors, and hemangiosarcoma. It is usually used in combination with other chemotherapy agents such as vincristine, L-asparaginase, doxorubicin, methotrexate, and chlorambucil, along with corticosteroids.

Cautions and Warnings

■ Cyclophosphamide is not FDA approved for use in dogs or cats. It is used to treat certain types of cancer and immune-mediated diseases and is considered accepted practice.

■ Cyclophosphamide is a powerful immune-suppressive drug and may increase susceptibility to infection, delay wound healing, and cause a variety of serious side effects (see "Possible Side Effects"). Complete blood counts should be done on a regular basis during therapy to monitor for bone marrow suppression.

■ Cyclophosphamide should be used with extreme caution and in reduced doses in animals with decreased kidney or liver function.

■ Contact your veterinarian if you think your dog or cat may be having an adverse reaction to cyclophosphamide.

■ U.S. federal law restricts the use of this drug by or on the lawful written or oral order of a licensed veterinarian within the context of a valid veterinarian-client-patient relationship.

Possible Side Effects

▼ Common: hemorrhagic cystitis (bladder inflammation with bleeding), bone marrow suppression, increased susceptibility to infection, low white blood cell count, nausea, vomiting, diarrhea, and hair loss.

▼ Rare: allergic or anaphylactic (serious systemic allergic) reactions, induction of transitional cell carcinoma of the bladder, bladder fibrosis, anemia, low platelet counts, lung damage, low blood sodium, and leukemia.

Drug Interactions

• Phenobarbital and other barbiturates may increase the likelihood of cyclophosphamide toxicity.

• Allopurinol and thiazide diuretics may increase the bone marrow suppression caused by cyclophosphamide.

• The dose of digoxin may need to be increased if cyclophosphamide is given.

• Chloramphenicol may decrease the effectiveness of cyclophosphamide.

• Doxorubicin may increase the risks of heart damage when used with cyclophosphamide.

Food Interactions

None known.

Usual Dose

Dogs and Cats: 1 mg/lb (50 mg/m^2) orally once a day, or every 48 hours, or 4 consecutive days in each week, for a maximum of 3 weeks. Alternate dose: 150–300 mg/m^2 orally or by intravenous injection; repeat in 21 days.

Drug Form: 25- and 50-mg tablets and powder for injection.

Overdosage

There is little information on overdose of cyclophosphamide. The lethal intravenous dose in dogs is 20 mg/lb. An oral overdose could be expected to produce all of the side effects listed above (see "Possible Side Effects"). In case of accidental ingestion or overdose, contact your veterinarian or the National Animal Poison Control Center. ALWAYS bring the prescription bottle or container with you if you go for treatment.

Special Information

The sterile hemorrhagic cystitis that occurs as a side effect of cyclophosphamide is common in dogs but quite rare in cats. The risks can be lessened if cyclophosphamide tablets are given in the morning, urine flow is increased, and frequent urination is encouraged. Salting the food or giving a diuretic like furosemide are effective ways to increase urine flow. If corticosteroids are part of therapy, giving them at the same time as cyclophosphamide may decrease the chances of hemorrhagic cystitis. The urine should always be cultured to make sure that there is not an infection as a result of the immunosuppression.

Special Populations

Breeding Animals
Cyclophosphamide may cause sterility in males and females.

Pregnancy/Lactation
Cyclophosphamide causes birth defects and fetal death, and it is excreted in milk. It should not be used in pregnant or lactating animals.

Puppies/Kittens
Cyclophosphamide should not be used in puppies or kittens.

Senior Animals

Cyclophosphamide should be safe to use in older animals, but should be used with caution and at reduced doses in animals with decreased liver or kidney function (see "Cautions and Warnings").

Generic Name

Cyclosporine (sye-kloe-SPOR-in)

Brand Names

Neoral Ⓗ   Sandimmune Ⓗ

Optimmune Ⓥ

Type of Drug

Immunosuppressant.

Prescribed for

Preventing the rejection of a transplanted kidney, dry eye (keratoconjunctivitis sicca, KCS) in dogs, chronic superficial keratitis (CSK, or pannus) in dogs, perianal fistulas (deep infections around the anus) in dogs, asthma in cats, sebaceous adenitis, and other autoimmune or immune-mediated diseases.

General Information

Cyclosporine is a relatively new drug that has revolutionized organ transplantation in people over the past 15 years and has also been used extensively in immune-mediated diseases. It helps prevent the immune system from attacking foreign tissue. In autoimmune disease, when the immune system loses the ability to distinguish between itself and foreign substances, cyclosporine may help prevent immune system attack on the body's own tissues. It may also help in control of severe allergy, where the immune system reacts in an exaggerated fashion to substances in the environment. It has been used successfully to prevent rejection of transplanted kidneys in cats and to treat immune-mediated eye diseases, such as KCS and CSK. It is just starting to be used in veterinary medicine for the treatment of a variety of autoimmune or immune-mediated diseases, such as asthma, perianal fistulas, and immune-mediated skin disorders.

Cautions and Warnings

■ The only form of cyclosporine that is FDA approved for use in dogs is the eye ointment, Optimmune. Because of the low concentration of cyclosporine (0.2%) in the standard eye preparations, very little is absorbed from the eye into the bloodstream. Therefore, there should be no side effects with the use of standard eye preparations of cyclosporine. Oral, intravenous, or high-dose eye forms are used with care in dogs and cats and are accepted practice for certain diseases.

■ Because the margin of safety for cyclosporine is very narrow and there is much variability in its absorption, target blood levels of the drug may be exceeded and kidney and liver damage are likely to occur. The newer microemulsion oral form of cyclosporine—Neoral—should make it easier to achieve the correct therapeutic levels in the blood, but it is still necessary to moniter blood levels.

■ Because cyclosporine is an immunosuppressant, it may make the animal more susceptible to infections.

■ Cyclosporine interacts with a variety of other drugs and should be used with caution in combination with other medications (see "Drug Interactions").

■ Contact your veterinarian if you think your dog or cat may be having an adverse reaction to cyclosporine.

■ U.S. federal law restricts the use of this drug by or on the lawful written or oral order of a licensed veterinarian within the context of a valid veterinarian-client-patient relationship.

Possible Side Effects

▼ Common: excessive shedding; if the blood levels go above the therapeutic range, there may be decreased appetite, nausea, vomiting, diarrhea, weight loss, gingival hyperplasia (overgrown gums), warts, increased hair growth, involuntary shaking, decreased insulin release and insulin resistance, and kidney and/or liver damage.

▼ Rare: infections, cancer, seizures in cats, and lameness in some dogs.

Drug Interactions

Note that there should be no drug interactions with the standard eye preparations.

• Drugs that may increase cyclosporine concentrations in

the blood are bromocriptine, danazol, diltiazem, doxycycline, erythromycin, fluconazole, itraconazole, ketoconazole, methylprednisolone, nicardipine, and verapamil.

• Drugs that may decrease cyclosporine concentrations in the blood are carbamazepine, phenobarbital, phenytoin, rifampin, and trimethoprim-sulfamethoxazole (IV only).

• Drugs that may make kidney damage more likely are aminoglycoside antibiotics (e.g., gentamicin, amikacin), amphotericin B, cimetidine, erythromycin, ketoconazole, melphalan, ranitidine, and vancomycin.

• Cyclosporine and corticosteroids given together may increase the risk of infection.

Food Interactions

Cyclosporine absorption may be increased if given with a fatty meal. Follow your veterinarian's instructions exactly and be consistent when and how you give the drug. It is best to give with the same food each time.

Usual Dose

Dogs: starting dose—5 mg/lb orally once a day.

Cats: starting dose—5 mg/lb orally twice a day; or 2.5 mg/lb in both eyes 4 times a day.

Eyes: Optimmune (0.2% cyclosporine) should be applied to the affected eye(s) twice a day as a $1/4$ in. strip of ointment.

Drug Form: The drug is supplied both as an emulsion (Sandimmune) and a microemulsion (Neoral) for oral use; an eye ointment (Optimmune); and in an intravenous form. Cyclosporine powder is also mixed with olive oil for use in the eye.

Overdosage

An overdose of cyclosporine is likely to produce severe liver and kidney damage. It is also likely to cause the signs listed above (see "Possible Side Effects"). In case of accidental ingestion or overdose, contact your veterinarian or the National Animal Poison Control Center. ALWAYS bring the prescription bottle or container with you if you go for treatment.

Special Information

Because of the narrow margin of safety for cyclosporine—too little does not work, too much causes kidney and liver damage and other side effects—it is very important to measure blood levels when cyclosporine is being given. During the first months of treatment, blood cyclosporine concentrations should be measured 2 to 4 times a month.

If cyclosporine ointment is being used topically to treat a local problem, such as gum disease in cats or eye disease in dogs, there is not enough absorbed into the bloodstream to cause problems.

It may be possible to decrease the frequency of use of the eye preparations as the diseases KCS and CSK respond. Use as directed by your veterinarian.

Cyclosporine may also be given in higher concentrations via the eyes (1% to 4% solution of cyclosporine in olive oil) to achieve therapeutic blood levels. This may be especially useful in cats that do not tolerate the oral dose because of its taste.

Special Populations

Pregnancy/Lactation
Cyclosporine has not been studied in animals that are pregnant or lactating, and it should be avoided.

Puppies/Kittens
Cyclosporine has not been studied in puppies or kittens, and it should be avoided.

Senior Animals
The standard eye preparations of cyclosporine should be safe to use in older animals, because the concentration of cyclosporine is low and relatively little of the drug is absorbed into the bloodstream. Cyclosporine given orally, or in higher concentrations via the eyes to achieve therapeutic blood levels, should be used with caution in older dogs and cats, and it should be avoided or used with extreme caution in animals with liver or kidney disease.

Generic Name

Cyproheptadine (sye-proe-HEP-tuh-dene) G

Brand Name
Periactin H

Type of Drug
Antihistamine, serotonin antagonist.

Prescribed for

Feline asthma, decreased appetite in cats, allergy, Cushing's disease.

General Information

Histamine is one of the substances released by the tissues of the body during an allergic reaction. A variety of symptoms are produced by histamine, including itching, swelling, and sneezing. A massive release of histamine can produce anaphylactic shock, a serious systemic allergic reaction leading to circulatory collapse.

Histamine is only one of many mediators of allergic reactions, so cyproheptadine hydrochloride, which only blocks histamine, is only partially effective in relieving allergy symptoms. Because of its anti-serotonin effects in the brain, cyproheptadine may be used to stimulate appetite, especially in cats that are not eating well because of illness. In a small percentage of dogs with Cushing's disease, there is a defect in brain serotonin activity. Cyproheptadine is one of the anti-serotonin drugs (see *Selegiline*) that may be helpful in relieving symptoms of Cushing's disease. Cyproheptadine is one of the recommended treatments for feline asthma, usually as an adjunct to corticosteroid therapy.

Cautions and Warnings

■ Cyproheptadine is not FDA approved for use in dogs or cats. It is considered accepted practice to use it in a number of conditions in dogs and cats (see "Prescribed for").

■ Avoid cyproheptadine in animals with glaucoma, prostate disease, pyloric obstruction, or urinary obstruction.

■ Cyproheptadine may cause increased appetite, and weight gain is likely if more food is given.

■ Cyproheptadine should be used with caution or in reduced doses in animals with liver or kidney disease.

■ Cyproheptadine should be discontinued 3–7 days before allergy skin testing.

■ Contact your veterinarian if you think your dog or cat may be having an adverse reaction to cyproheptadine.

■ U.S. federal law restricts the use of this drug by or on the lawful written or oral order of a licensed veterinarian within the context of a valid veterinarian-client-patient relationship.

Possible Side Effects
- ▼ Common: increased appetite.
- ▼ Rare: sedation and dry eyes and mouth.

Drug Interactions

• If cyproheptadine is given with other central nervous system (CNS) depressants, such as barbiturates and tranquilizers, there may be additive CNS depression.

• Monoamine oxidase inhibitors (MAOIs) including furazolidone may increase the side effects of cyproheptadine.

Food Interactions

None known.

Usual Dose

Dogs: 0.1–1 mg/lb orally 2–3 times a day.

Cats: 1–2 mg orally twice a day for appetite stimulation. Taper the dose after 1 week. For side effects of cancer chemotherapy: 4–8 mg 2–3 times a day.

Drug Form: 4-mg tablets and 2 mg/5 ml oral solution.

Overdosage

Overdoses may cause CNS depression or excitement, severe drying of mouth and eyes, high heart rate, urine retention, fever and low blood pressure. In case of accidental ingestion or overdose, contact your veterinarian or the National Animal Poison Control Center. ALWAYS bring the prescription bottle or container with you if you go for treatment.

Special Populations

Pregnancy/Lactation

There are no safety studies of cyproheptadine in pregnant dogs or cats, so it should be avoided in pregnant or lactating animals unless the benefits outweigh the risks.

Puppies/Kittens

Cyproheptadine should probably be avoided in puppies and kittens.

Senior Animals

Cyproheptadine should be safe to use in older animals, but it should be used with caution and in reduced doses in those with kidney or liver disease.

Generic Name

Danazol (DAN-uh-zole)

Brand Name

Danocrine [H]

Type of Drug

Androgenic steroid (synthetic male hormone), immune modulator.

Prescribed for

Immune-mediated or autoimmune hemolytic anemia (AIHA), immune-mediated thrombocytopenia/thrombocytopenic purpura (ITP).

General Information

Danazol is used to treat two difficult disorders of the immune system, ITP and AIHA. In these disorders the body attacks and destroys its own red blood cells (RBCs) and/or platelets. The cause of these disorders is not known. They can occur in any breed or sex but seem to occur more commonly in middle-aged spayed female dogs, especially cocker spaniels. Danazol is a weak male hormone that prevents the immune system from attacking and destroying RBCs and platelets. When danazol is used with corticosteroids to treat ITP and AIHA, lower doses of corticosteroids may be used for shorter periods of time. This decreases the side effects from long-term corticosteroid use (see *Corticosteroids*). Treatment usually begins with high-dose corticosteroids and danazol. Once the anemia or thrombocytopenia (low platelet count) improves, corticosteroids are gradually tapered off and discontinued. When remission has been maintained with danazol alone, the danazol dose is lowered and then tapered off after 2 to 3 months. Some human patients have had longer periods of remission with danazol than with other drugs. Danazol has not been well studied in dogs or cats, but it seems to be extremely helpful in many animals with these difficult diseases.

Cautions and Warnings

■ Danazol is not FDA approved for use in dogs or cats. It is more frequently used in dogs and is considered accepted practice.

■ Danazol should be used with caution in animals with heart, liver, or kidney disease.

■ Danazol may cause liver damage. Thyroid hormone (T4) blood levels may be decreased and liver enzymes may be increased during treatment with danazol.

■ Danazol is a weak androgen and may cause masculinization of females or atrophy of the testicles in males.

■ Contact your veterinarian if you think your dog or cat may be having an adverse reaction to danazol.

■ U.S. federal law restricts the use of this drug by or on the lawful written or oral order of a licensed veterinarian within the context of a valid veterinarian-client-patient relationship.

Possible Side Effects

▼ Rare: weight gain, lethargy, masculinization, and mild liver enzyme elevations.

Drug Interactions

• Danazol may enhance the effects of anticoagulants.
• Danazol may decrease the effects of insulin.

Food Interactions

None known.

Usual Dose

Dogs: 2.5–5 mg/lb orally twice a day.
Cats: 2.5 mg/lb orally twice a day.
Drug Form: 50-, 100-, and 200-mg capsules.

Overdosage

There is no information on overdoses of danazol. In case of accidental ingestion or overdose, contact your veterinarian or the National Animal Poison Control Center. ALWAYS bring the prescription bottle or container with you if you go for treatment.

Special Information

Combining danazol with corticosteroids is probably advantageous for most cases of ITP and AIHA. Some animals will be resistant to corticosteroids alone, and there is evidence that getting the disease under control quickly is important in preventing complications. There are the added benefits of using less corticosteroid and potentially prolonging remission.

Special Populations

Pregnancy/Lactation
Danazol causes damage to the fetus. It should not be used during pregnancy or lactation.

Puppies/Kittens
Danazol should be avoided in young animals.

Senior Animals
Danazol should be safe to use in older animals, as long as there is no significant heart, liver, or kidney impairment.

Generic Name

Desmopressin (dez-moe-PRES-in) Ⓖ

Most Common Brand Name

DDAVP Ⓗ

Type of Drug

Antidiuretic hormone.

Prescribed for

Diabetes insipidus and von Willebrand's disease.

General Information

Desmopressin is a synthetic antidiuretic hormone (ADH). ADH, also known as vasopressin, is released by the pituitary gland and causes the kidney to retain water. Diabetes insipidus (DI) is a disease where there is either a lack of ADH (central DI), or the kidney does not respond to ADH (nephrogenic DI). Nephrogenic DI is a rare inherited disorder in dogs.

Central DI may be either a birth defect or the result of a pituitary/hypothalamic tumor or trauma. In both cases the signs are excessive thirst and urination with an inability to concentrate the urine. Desmopressin is used to diagnose and treat central DI; it has no effect on animals with nephrogenic DI. Eyedrops are commonly used in dogs, both as the diagnostic test for central DI, as well as treatment.

Desmopressin is also used to treat von Willebrand's disease. Von Willebrand's disease is an inherited bleeding disorder where there is a lack of von Willebrand's factor (vWF), or the factor is present but nonfunctional. The treatment of choice is transfusion of clotting factors or fresh frozen plasma, both of which contain vWF. Desmopressin may cause vWF to be released from cell stores and cause a transient (3–4 hour) improvement. This effect is not as pronounced in dogs as it is in people, and it does not work in all dogs. The effectiveness of desmopressin depends on the dog's ability to produce any functional vWF. If desmopressin is planned for use before surgery to treat a dog with von Willebrand's disease, it should be tested first to see if it will be effective.

Cautions and Warnings

■ Desmopressin is not FDA approved for use in dogs or cats. It is used to diagnose and treat central DI and for temporary treatment of von Willebrand's disease and is considered accepted practice. Desmopressin should be used with caution in dogs with Type IIB vWD and those at risk for clotting, as it may enhance platelet aggregation resulting in low platelet counts and an increased risk of bleeding.

■ Water overload and low blood sodium (hyponatremia) may occur if desmopressin is given to diagnose or treat central DI, and water consumption continues at a high rate. Hyponatremia may cause seizures, coma and death. Water intake should be restricted according to your veterinarian's instructions after desmopressin is given. Desmopressin should not be used in animals with kidney disease.

■ Contact your veterinarian if you think your dog or cat may be having an adverse reaction to desmopressin.

■ U.S. federal law restricts the use of this drug by or on the lawful written or oral order of a licensed veterinarian within the context of a valid veterinarian-client-patient relationship.

Possible Side Effects

▼ Rare: water overload and hyponatremia (possible if an animal given desmopressin continues to drink excessively), eye irritation, allergic reactions, clotting, and low platelet counts.

Drug Interactions

• Chlorpropamide, carbamazepine, clofibrate, fludrocortisone, and urea may increase the antidiuretic effects of desmopressin.

• Lithium, epinephrine, demeclocycline, heparin, and alcohol may decrease the effects of desmopressin.

Food Interactions

None known.

Usual Dose

Dogs: for central DI—1–4 drops of nasal spray once or twice a day in the nose or in the eyes; adjust the dose as needed to control drinking and urination. For von Willebrand's disease—0.5 mcg/lb injected under the skin.

Cats: to diagnose central DI—1 drop of nasal spray in the eye twice a day for 2–3 days. For treatment of central DI—1–2 drops in the eye once or twice a day; adjust the dose as needed to control drinking and urination.

Drug Form: 0.1 mg/ml nasal spray, 0.1- and 0.2-mg tablets, and 4 and 15 mcg/ml injectable. Doses for the oral tablets have not been reported in dogs or cats.

Overdosage

Overdoses may cause nausea, cramps, defecation, pale gums, hyponatremia, seizures, coma, loss of circulation in the extremities, and gangrene. In case of accidental ingestion or overdose, contact your veterinarian or the National Animal Poison Control Center. ALWAYS bring the prescription bottle or container with you if you go for treatment.

Special Information

Both nephrogenic and central DI patients may benefit from thiazide diuretic and dietary sodium restriction therapy. Chlorpropamide, one of the sulfonylureas, may also be useful. It stimulates release of ADH, and sensitizes the kidney to ADH. Discuss management of these diseases with your veterinarian to determine the best treatment for your pet.

Special Populations

German Shorthair Pointers
Type IIB von Willebrand's disease has been reported in German shorthair pointers. It may occur in other breeds as well. Humans with this type of vWD are at increased risk of complications from abnormal clotting. It is not clear whether this is also true for affected dogs, but it is prudent to avoid desmopressin pending further information unless the potential benefit clearly outweighs the risk.

Pregnancy/Lactation
There are no safety studies of desmopressin in pregnant dogs or cats. It does seem to be safe in pregnant rabbits, but it should probably be avoided unless the benefits outweigh the risks.

Puppies/Kittens
Desmopressin should not be used in puppies or kittens. It should be used with caution in adolescent animals, with careful water restriction and under the supervision of your veterinarian.

Senior Animals
Desmopressin should be safe to use in older animals (see "Cautions and Warnings"), but should be avoided in those with kidney disease.

Generic Name

Desoxycorticosterone Pivalate (DOCP)

(des-OK-see-KOR-tih-ko-stuhr-one PIV-uh-late)

Brand Name

Experimental drug available from Novartis.

Type of Drug

Mineralocorticosteroid.

Prescribed for

Adrenocortical insufficiency (hypoadrenocorticism, Addison's disease).

General Information

Corticosteroids are hormones normally produced by the adrenal gland. They are essential for life and affect every level of metabolism and function of all cells and organ systems. There are two major types of adrenal cortical hormones distinguished by their major effect. The glucocorticoids are also called glucocorticosteroids, corticosteroids, or simply steroids (see *Corticosteroids*). They are important in normal protein, carbohydrate, and fat metabolism. The mineralocorticoids primarily control salt and water balance in the body. They act on the kidney causing it to retain sodium and excrete potassium. Normal mineralocorticoid activity requires functional kidneys.

DOCP is a mineralocorticoid used to treat primary adrenal insufficiency (Addison's disease). Decreased mineralocorticoid and/or glucocorticoid production may result from adrenal tumors, infection, immune-mediated disease, or intentional destruction of the adrenal gland during treatment for the overproduction of adrenal hormones—Cushing's disease (see *Mitotane*). Affected animals are weak; depressed; and often have a history of vomiting, diarrhea, loss of appetite, and collapse that responded to treatment with fluids and corticosteroids in the past. Addison's disease generally responds well to hormone replacement. DOCP has very little glucocorticoid activity, and therefore, a glucocorticoid should also be administered initially. The dose of glucocorticoids should be reduced to the minimum that will control signs. It may be eliminated in about half the animals, but the owner should always have some glucocorticoid on hand in case it is needed in times of increased stress, surgery, or illness.

Adrenal insufficiency may also be caused by abruptly stopping long-term glucocorticoid administration; however, mineralocorticoid therapy is generally not needed in these cases.

DOCP is currently awaiting FDA approval for use in dogs but is available as an experimental drug. Veterinarians may obtain it by contacting the manufacturer. It is a long-acting preparation that is administered by intramuscular (IM) injection. Another drug, fludrocortisone (see *Fludrocortisone*) is also used to treat Addison's disease in dogs and cats. It is FDA approved for use in humans but not in animals.

Electrolytes and kidney function should be checked regularly during treatment. Potassium may need to be supplemented if blood levels get too low. Owners should monitor their pet for signs of adrenal insufficiency and overdosage (see "Overdosage"), including a sudden weight gain or loss, and consult their veterinarian immediately if any are seen. This allows the treatment to be modified before major complications occur.

Cautions and Warnings

■ Use DOCP cautiously in dogs or cats with kidney or heart failure or those that develop edema (swelling).

■ For IM administration only. Do not administer intravenously.

■ Contact your veterinarian if you think your dog or cat may be having an adverse reaction to DOCP.

■ This is an experimental drug and is not yet FDA approved. However, the information available indicates that it is a good option for treatment of mineralocorticoid insufficiency.

■ U.S. federal law restricts the use of this drug by or on the lawful written or oral order of a licensed veterinarian within the context of a valid veterinarian-client-patient relationship.

Possible Side Effects

Side effects are usually caused by overdosage (see "Overdosage"). The most common is irritation at the site of injection.

Drug Interactions

• The risk of low potassium levels is increased if DOCP is administered with other potassium lowering drugs such as amphotericin B and furosemide.

• DOCP may increase the risk of digitalis toxicity.

• Diuretics increase excretion of sodium and may counteract the effect of DOCP.

• DOCP may increase the required insulin dose in diabetics, and it may reduce salicylate blood levels in animals receiving salicylate-containing drugs. The clinical significance of these interactions has not been determined.

Food Interactions

None known. Adding salt to the diet may help animals with Addison's disease.

Usual Dose

Dose must be individually determined based on regular monitoring of blood potassium and sodium.

Dogs: 0.5–1 mg/lb injected in a muscle once every 21–30 days.

Cats: 12.5 mg/cat once a month adjusted as needed based on serial electrolyte monitoring.

Drug Form: a multiple dose injectable product containing 25 mg/ml is being proposed to the FDA for use in dogs.

Storage: Store at room temperature and protect from light.

Overdosage

Overdosage may cause increased thirst and urination, high blood pressure, edema, low blood potassium, weakness, and weight gain. Heart enlargement may occur with prolonged overdose. In case of accidental ingestion or overdose, contact your veterinarian or the National Animal Poison Control Center. ALWAYS bring the prescription bottle or container with you if you go for treatment.

Special Populations

Pregnancy/Lactation
Safety in pregnant animals has not been established; use only if the potential benefits outweigh the risks.

Puppies/Kittens
Safety in puppies and kittens has not been established; use only if the potential benefits outweigh the risks.

Senior Animals
Safety has not been established, but senior animals should not be at increased risk. DOCP is a reasonable option in senior animals with Addison's disease provided they have adequate kidney function.

Generic Name

Dextromethorphan (dex-TROE-meh-thor-fan) [G]

Most Common Brand Names

Babee Cof [H]	Hold [H]
Benylin* [H]	Robitussen* [H]
St. Joseph Cough Suppressant for Children [H]	
Vicks Formula 44 Soothing Cough Relief [H]	

Not all products in this brand group contain dextromethorphan.

Combination Products

Generic Ingredients: Dextromethorphan + Guiafenesin
Life Science Cough Tablets [V]   Safe Tussin [H]

Type of Drug

Cough suppressant.

Prescribed for

Dry nonproductive coughs and chronic bronchitis.

General Information

Dextromethorphan is used primarily as a cough suppressant in dogs with collapsing trachea, chronic bronchitis, and upper respiratory infections, including kennel cough. It can also be used in cats with chronic bronchitis. It is not recommended when there is a moist cough or increased respiratory secretions. Dextromethorphan works by suppressing the cough reflex in the brain and is well absorbed orally. It is not a narcotic and does not produce sedation.

Cautions and Warnings

■ Do not use cough suppressants without the advice and consent of your veterinarian.

■ Dextromethorphan should not be given within 14 days of monoamine oxidase inhibitors (MAOIs).

■ Most dextromethorphan products are manufactured as combination products with other drugs. DO NOT give combination products containing acetaminophen, caffeine, alcohol, or

other medication to animals. These other medications may
cause severe side effects or death. Use only the dextromethorphan product specified by your veterinarian.

■ In humans, dextromethorphan may be associated with histamine release; consequently, it is used with caution in allergic
children.

■ U.S. federal law restricts the use of this drug by or on the
lawful written or oral order of a licensed veterinarian within the
context of a valid veterinarian-client-patient relationship.

Possible Side Effects

▼ Rare: gastrointestinal disturbances, including nausea, dizziness, and occasional drowsiness.

Drug Interactions

• Dextromethorphan has an additive effect with other sedatives, narcotics, antihistamines, and central nervous system
depressants.

Food Interactions

None known.

Usual Dose

Dogs and Cats: 0.25–1 mg/lb 3–4 times a day.
Drug Form: available over the counter in tablet or liquid form.
DO NOT give products containing alcohol, acetaminophen, or
caffeine to animals.

Overdosage

Overdoses of dextromethorphan may cause excitement and
mental confusion. Very high overdoses may cause respiratory
depression. In case of accidental ingestion or overdose, contact your veterinarian or the National Animal Poison Control
Center. ALWAYS bring the prescription bottle or container with
you if you go for treatment.

Special Information

Chronic coughing is irritating to the respiratory tract. Cough
suppressants are used to break this cough cycle so that the
respiratory tract may become less inflamed. Many dextrometh-

orphan products are in combination with guaifenesin, which is an expectorant. This combination is safe to use in dogs and cats under veterinary supervision. Although dextromethorphan may not be as effective as some of the narcotic cough suppressants, it is available over the counter and may be used in cats. Pediatric Robitussin is a convenient dosing form, especially for small dogs and cats. It contains 1.5 mg/ml syrup, so the dose is 3 to 7 ml per 10 lbs body weight.

Special Populations

Pregnancy/Lactation
Safety studies have not been performed on pregnant animals, and it is not known if dextromethorphan is excreted in breast milk. Dextromethorphan should only be used in pregnant or lactating dogs if the benefits outweigh the risks.

Puppies/Kittens
No safety studies have been performed in puppies or kittens, but dextromethorphan is considered safe in children age 2 and up. It is not recommended for use in infants.

Senior Animals
No safety studies have been performed in older animals, but it is probably safe to use.

Generic Name

Diazepam (dye-AZ-uh-pam) G

Most Common Brand Names

Diastat H   Valium H

Type of Drug

Benzodiazepine tranquilizer.

Prescribed for

Sedation, seizures, status epilepticus, muscle relaxation, and anxiety in dogs and cats. Appetite stimulation in cats.

General Information

Diazepam is classified as a benzodiazepine tranquilizer and

acts directly on specific nerves in the brain. It is rapidly absorbed after ingestion and distributed throughout the body, including the brain. The maximum effect occurs between $1/2$ and 2 hours after administration. The drug is metabolized by the liver to nordiazepam, which is also an active benzodiazepine. Both diazepam and nordiazepam are eventually excreted in the urine. Diazepam is metabolized and excreted within several hours in dogs and cats. Nordiazepam, however, is active longer and may account for both desirable actions and undesirable side effects, particularly as it accumulates after multiple doses over several days.

At low doses, diazepam acts as a sedative; at moderate doses, it has more antianxiety activity; and at high doses, it produces deeper sedation and sleep. Diazepam also decreases muscle tone causing relaxation. This action is independent of the sedative effects. Some of the antianxiety effects may, in fact, result from muscle relaxation, since tension is a factor in anxiety.

Diazepam is commonly used as a sedative before anesthesia. The muscle relaxation and antianxiety effects calm the animal, making the procedure easier and reducing the amount of other drugs needed. Some minor procedures may be performed using diazepam combined with other sedative drugs.

The antianxiety activity makes diazepam suitable for treating a number of behavioral problems. It often helps calm dogs that react to thunderstorms or other loud noises. It is used to treat cats that urinate or spray inappropriately because of frustration or social stress. Territorial and social aggression between cats may be reduced. Hair loss caused by excessive grooming, and some stereotypic behaviors respond well to treatment with diazepam. Other behavior-modifying drugs may also help with these problems (see *Amitriptyline* and *Buspirone*). Benzodiazepines generally interfere with conscious learning and training, but reduced anxiety levels in nervous animals may facilitate learning. Some aggressive animals may become easier to handle after treatment with diazepam, but paradoxically, others may become more aggressive. If diazepam is used in potentially aggressive animals, owners and handlers should take appropriate precautions to protect themselves from injury.

Diazepam, either alone or in combination with other drugs, is used to relax muscle spasms. A spasm is a reaction to pain and also perpetuates pain in muscle and skeletal injury. Reducing the spasm and pain is an important part of the treatment of conditions such as intervertebral disk disease, urethral obstruction in lower urinary tract disease, muscle cramping and tremors, and tetanus.

Diazepam is an excellent antiseizure drug. It may be used for the long-term treatment of cats either alone or in addition to phenobarbital. It is not suitable for long-term treatment of epilepsy in dogs since it loses effectiveness within a few weeks. Phenobarbital (see *Phenobarbital*) and/or potassium bromide (see *Potassium Bromide*) are the first choice drugs for long-term treatment of epilepsy in dogs. Diazepam, however, is the first choice drug for treating ongoing clusters of seizures occurring within a 24-hour period and status epilepticus with continuous seizures lasting for more than 30 minutes. These are potentially life-threatening emergencies and you should call your veterinarian or emergency clinic immediately. In-hospital treatment consists of diazepam and/or other antiseizure drugs administered directly into a vein (IV). Recently, studies in humans and dogs have shown that administration of diazepam through the rectum by enema is effective and suitable for at-home use. It shortens the duration and intensity of cluster seizures, reduces the aftereffects, reduces hospitalization time, and consequently, reduces the cost. A diazepam-containing enema is commercially available.

Benzodiazepines, particularly diazepam, is a powerful appetite stimulant in cats. Cats often start eating within seconds of a small IV dose or minutes of an oral dose. It is used to stimulate the appetite of cats that are refusing food because of fatty liver syndrome, cancer, and other diseases.

Diazepam is relatively free of side effects (see "Possible Side Effects"). Even in high doses, it does not depress breathing or heart function. A rare, but very serious side effect in cats is liver failure that may be fatal. The reason for this reaction is unknown. It is not due to overdosing and affected cats do not have a history of liver disease or increased liver enzyme levels. It typically occurs within several days after treatment with diazepam is started. Monitoring liver enzymes in cats about 1 week after starting diazepam treatment has been suggested and may detect some cases.

Cautions and Warnings

For Owners/Handlers
■ This drug is classified by the Drug Enforcement Agency as a controlled substance. It may be addictive. Keep out of reach of children.

For Animals
■ Diazepam should be used with caution in animals that have liver problems or kidney problems or are severely debilitated.
■ Diazepam may be addictive. It must be discontinued slowly. Discuss drug withdrawal with your veterinarian before stopping treatment if your animal is on long-term therapy.
■ Diazepam can impair the abilities of working animals, including seeing eye and working companion dogs. It should not be used unless the risks to both the dog and owner are first considered.
■ Unexpected behavior, such as excitement and aggression, may occur after diazepam administration in some animals. Alternative drugs should be considered in these animals.
■ Contact your veterinarian if you think your dog or cat may be having an adverse reaction to diazepam.
■ Diazepam is not FDA approved for use in dogs or cats. It is commonly used and is considered accepted practice.
■ U.S. federal law restricts the use of this drug by or on the lawful written or oral order of a licensed veterinarian within the context of a valid veterinarian-client-patient relationship.

Possible Side Effects

▼ Common: drowsiness, mild lack of coordination, and in cats, increased appetite.
▼ Rare: excitement, aggression, bizarre behavior, and in cats, liver failure.

Drug Interactions

• Diazepam may increase depression or sedation if administered with other tranquilizers, narcotics, barbiturates, monoamine oxidase inhibitors (MAOIs), antihistamines, and antidepressants.
• The effects of diazepam may be increased if taken with

cimetidine, erythromycin, isoniazid, ketoconazole, propranolol, and valproic acid.

• Antacids may slow the absorption of diazepam; administer 2 hours apart to avoid any interaction.

• Diazepam may increase blood levels and toxic effects of digoxin and phenytoin.

• Rifampin may decrease the effectiveness of diazepam.

Food Interactions

Diazepam should be given on an empty stomach unless it causes stomach upset and vomiting. In that case it may be given with food.

Usual Dose

Dogs: for sedation and anxiety related disorders—0.5–1 mg/lb orally 3 times a day; for cluster seizures—0.25 mg/lb administered as an enema at home.

Cats: for sedation and anxiety related disorders—0.1–0.2 mg/lb 2–3 times a day; as an appetite stimulant—0.025–0.2 mg/lb or 1mg orally once daily; for epilepsy—0.25–0.5 mg/lb once a day or divided into 2–3 doses a day.

Drug Form: 2-, 5-, and 10-mg tablets; 1 mg/ml oral solution; 5 mg/ml rectal gel; and 5 mg/ml injectable.

Storage: Store at room temperature, in tight containers, and protected from light. It is important to store liquid diazepam in the original container and not transfer it to plastic syringes or other plastic containers. Diazepam adheres to some types of plastic, decreasing the effectiveness of the solution.

Overdosage

Signs of overdosage are generally limited to sleepiness, disorientation, depression, and decreased reflexes. More serious signs including coma and death may occur particularly when diazepam is combined with other sedative drugs. In case of accidental ingestion or overdose, contact your veterinarian or the National Animal Poison Control Center. ALWAYS bring the prescription bottle or container with you if you go for treatment.

Special Information

There are a number of benzodiazepines that are used in humans and may prove useful in animals. They are all similar in structure and work by facilitating the gamma-aminobutyric acid

(GABA) neurotransmitters. However, they vary in how long they take to work, how long they last, and what effects predominate. The advantage is that the drug selected may target the specific problems better. Using a drug that both acts and is eliminated quickly would be beneficial in treating anxiety related to loud noises such as thunder. Longer acting drugs would be better for controlling anxiety or seizures.

Special Populations

Pregnancy/Lactation
Diazepam may cause birth defects and is excreted into milk. It should not be used in pregnant or lactating animals unless the benefits outweigh the risks.

Puppies/Kittens
Diazepam may be used to control cluster seizures or status epilepticus in puppies and kittens. It is generally considered a safe sedative, however, careful dosing is important. Young animals lose body heat rapidly, and this must be prevented during sedation and anesthesia.

Senior Animals
Diazepam is generally safe to use in senior animals. Those with liver or kidney disease may require smaller doses.

Generic Name

Dichlorophene (dye-KLOR-oe-fene) [G]

Brand Names

Happy Jack Tapeworm Tablets [V]

Combination Products

Generic Ingredients: Dichlorophene+Toluene [G]
Multipurpose Worm Caps [V]   Trivermicide [V]
Pet Worm Caps [V]   Tri–Wormer [V]

Type of Drug

Anthelmintic/dewormer.

Prescribed for

Roundworm (*Toxocara canis, Toxascaris leonina*), hookworm

(*Ancylostoma caninum, Uncinaria stenocephala*), and tapeworm (*Taenia pisiformis, Dipylidium caninum, Echinococcus granulosus*) in dogs and cats.

General Information

Dichlorophene and toluene have been used as dewormers for many years. They are often combined to provide a broad spectrum of activity against the most common dog and cat parasites. Toluene has activity against roundworm and hookworm, and dichlorophene against tapeworm.

Roundworm, hookworm, and some tapeworm species are contagious and may spread to other animals and to people and are therefore a potential public health risk. Roundworm causes visceral larva migrans, hookworm causes cutaneous larva migrans, and *E. granulosus* causes alveolar hydatid disease. *D. caninum* occasionally infects children who accidentally ingest infected fleas (see *Zoonotic Diseases of Dogs and Cats*).

Roundworms and hookworms live in the intestine and their eggs pass in the feces to the environment. Animals and humans that come in contact with anything contaminated with feces and parasite eggs may become infected.

Tapeworms have distinctive larval and adult forms. The larva infects an intermediate host. Fleas are the intermediate host for *D. caninum*. Rodents and rabbits are intermediate hosts for *Taenia* species. *Echinococcus* larvae are found in a variety of domestic and wild ruminants, pigs, rodents, and humans.

Dogs and cats become infected after eating the intermediate host and reinfection is likely unless contact with the intermediate host is prevented. *D. caninum* is the most common tapeworm in the United States. Effective flea control greatly reduces, and may eliminate, the incidence of reinfection and the need for retreatment.

Dichlorophene is a phenol derivative. It is poorly absorbed from the intestinal tract, which may account for the relative lack of side effects. It kills tapeworms by interfering with their energy metabolism. Dead tapeworms are digested; therefore, recognizable segments are not seen in the feces. Dichlorophene is 72% effective against *Taenia* species and 85% effective against *D. caninum*. The efficacy against *Echinococcus* is variable and dichlorophene is not a good choice to remove this parasite.

Toluene is a liquid derivative of coal tar and is used primarily as an industrial solvent. It is the ingredient in airplane glue that makes it popular among "glue sniffers." Toluene is irritating to mucous membranes and causes profuse salivation if it comes in contact with the inside of the mouth. Gelatin capsules are used to prevent irritation, but they are bulky and easily bitten into by dogs that resist being medicated. Toluene is 95% to 98% effective against adult roundworm and 82% to 96% effective against adult hookworm.

Dichlorophene and toluene are among the few dewormers available over the counter (OTC) for use in dogs and cats. They are widely available wherever pet supplies are sold (see "Special Information").

Cautions and Warnings

■ For veterinary use only. Contact your physician or poison control center in case of accidental ingestion or inhalation by humans.

■ Do not use in sick, feverish, physically weak, or undernourished animals. Consult your veterinarian for assistance in the diagnosis, treatment, and control of parasitism.

■ Contact your veterinarian if you think your dog or cat may be having an adverse reaction to a dichlorophene and/or toluene dewormer.

Possible Side Effects

▼ Common: profuse salivation, vomiting, and diarrhea; loss of coordination, tremors, abnormal behavior, depression, and dilation of the pupils.

▼ Rare: seizures and death.

Drug Interactions

None known.

Food Interactions

Fasting required (see "Usual Dose").

Usual Dose

Dogs and Cats: dichlorophene 100 mg/lb, toluene 120 mg/lb. Withhold solid food and milk for 12 hours before and 4 hours after administration. Broth may be given.

Drug Form: capsules for 1-, 2.5-, 5-, 10-, 25-, and 40-lb body weight.

Storage: Store in dry place at 70–75°F. Protect from freezing.

Overdosage

Side effects of dichlorophene + toluene dewormers are common even at recommended doses. Neurologic signs may occur at 1½ times the recommended dose, which is a very narrow margin of safety. The median lethal oral dose (the dose at which 50% of animals will die, or the LD50) for dichlorophene in dogs is only 9 times the recommended dose.

Signs of overdose include vomiting, profuse salivation, loss of coordination, aberrant behavior, dilated pupils, depression, tremors, weakness, and seizures. These signs appear within 6 hours of ingestion. Most animals recover within 24 hours and death is rare.

In case of accidental ingestion or overdose, contact your veterinarian or the National Animal Poison Control Center. Do not induce vomiting. ALWAYS bring the prescription bottle or container with you if you go for treatment.

Special Information

The use of OTC drugs to treat parasites without a specific diagnosis may be dangerous, and in most cases results in unnecessary or incorrect treatment. Owners sometimes assume that signs such as diarrhea, weight loss, or a pet scooting its bottom on the ground are due to worms and resort to OTC drugs rather than calling their veterinarian. Although these signs may indicate parasites, they may also indicate other health problems. Using OTC products without an accurate diagnosis not only runs the unnecessary risk of side effects but also may delay the diagnosis and treatment of the real problem.

If your pet has parasites, it is important to identify the type. This may be as simple as having your veterinarian do a fecal analysis. An accurate diagnosis of the type of worm allows your veterinarian to prescribe a dewormer that is specific, effective, and safe. Today there are many safer, more effective, and cost effective dewormers than dichlorophene or toluene.

Special Populations

Pregnancy/Lactation

Chronic exposure to toluene is associated with birth defects in humans. Studies have not confirmed toluene's safety for dogs and cats. Without specific information confirming safety, these drugs should not be used during pregnancy and lactation.

Puppies/Kittens
This product is labeled for use in puppies and kittens, but adverse side effects are more likely to occur in this age group than in healthy adults.

Senior Animals
Studies have not confirmed the existence of side effects of toluene and dichlorophene in older animals. This age group is more likely to have chronic diseases that would increase the risk of using this dewormer.

Generic Name

Dichlorvos (dye-KLOR-vose)

Brand Name
Task [V]

Type of Drug
Organophosphate insecticide and anthelmintic/dewormer.

Prescribed for
Roundworms (*Toxocara canis, Toxocara cati, Toxascaris leonina*) and hookworms (*Ancylostoma caninum, Ancylostoma tubaeforme, Uncinaria stenocephala*) in dogs and cats.

General Information
Dichlorvos is an organophosphate also known as 2,2-dichlorovinyl dimethyl phosphate or DDVP. It is rapidly absorbed from the intestines and detoxified in the liver. It can reach toxic levels quickly if more is absorbed than the liver can metabolize rapidly. The metabolites are not toxic and are excreted in urine and feces. Only traces are found in the milk of lactating animals.

Organophosphates kill parasites by inhibiting acetylcholinesterase (AChE). AChE is an enzyme located at nerve endings that regulates the stimulation of muscles and certain nerves. When AChE is inhibited, the parasite's muscles are overstimulated and cannot relax between contractions. This paralyzes and kills the parasite. Organophosphates have been widely used to control parasites and insects on animals and in the environment. AChE plays a major role in regulating nerve and muscle function in all animal species, including dogs, cats, and humans. Consequently, they are potentially very toxic to the animal being treated, humans who handle the products, and other animals that are exposed through environmental contamination.

Dichlorvos can be incorporated into polyvinyl chloride resin pellets. Dichlorvos is released slowly from the pellets as they pass through the intestines. This results in prolonged anthelmintic activity along the entire length of the intestinal tract. It also decreases the toxicity and risk of side effects because the dose is absorbed slowly enough for the liver to detoxify quickly before the dichlorvos can reach toxic levels. The pelleted formulation is 6 to 20 times safer than straight dichlorvos.

Dichlorvos is close to 100% effective against roundworm and hookworm infections. It is over 90% effective against moderate whipworm infections. The effectiveness is reduced in heavy whipworm infections and re-treatment is required.

Roundworm and hookworm are contagious and may spread to other animals and to people and are therefore a potential public health risk. Roundworm is responsible for visceral larva migrans and hookworm for cutaneous larva migrans (see *Zoonotic Diseases of Dogs and Cats*).

Cautions and Warnings

For Owners/Handlers

■ For use in animals only. Avoid contact with skin while handling the pelleted formulation and wash hands with soap and water afterward. Contact your physician, hospital emergency room, or poison control center in case of accidental ingestion by humans.

For Animals

■ Do not use in puppies or kittens under the age of 10 days or less than 1 lb body weight. Do not use oral pellets in puppies or cats. Use only tablets labeled for use in puppies and cats.

■ The resin pellets used to carry the drug are not digestible and may be seen in the feces after treatment.

■ Do not use within a few days of giving other drugs that inhibit AChE, including some flea and tick treatments. Do not use with tranquilizers, muscle relaxants, or modified live-virus vaccines. Acepromazine or other phenothiazine drugs should not be used within 1 month of administering dichlorvos.

■ Do not use with any other dewormer with the exception of diethylcarbamazine (DEC) if DEC is being used as a daily heartworm preventive.

■ Do not use in animals that are stressed, debilitated or sick, have diarrhea, are constipated, or that may have an intestinal impaction. Do not use in dogs or cats with heartworm infection, heart or liver disease, or other infections.

■ Contact your veterinarian if you think your dog or cat may be having an adverse reaction to dichlorvos.

■ U.S. federal law restricts the use of this drug by or on the lawful written or oral order of a licensed veterinarian within the context of a valid veterinarian-client-patient relationship.

Possible Side Effects

▼ Common: Diarrhea (in 4% of dogs and cats) and vomiting (in 8% of puppies and 3% of kittens).

▼ Rare: muscle twitching, pupil contraction, tearing, and labored breathing (see "Overdosage").

Drug Interactions

• Neuromuscular blocking drugs, including phenothiazine drugs, procaine, magnesium ion, inhaled anesthetics, and other AChE inhibitors such as other organophosphates, carbamates, morphine, neostigmine, physostigmine, and pyridostigmine, act in the same way as dichlorvos and may increase the risk of side effects.

• Antibiotics, including the aminoglycosides (streptomycin, neomycin, kanamycin, and gentamicin); polypeptides (polymyxin and colistin), lincomycin; and clindamycin, may have activity at the neuromuscular level and increase the risk of side effects.

• Central nervous system depressants, including phenothiazine tranquilizers (acepromazine), benzodiazepines, reserpine, meprobamate, ethanol, and barbiturates (phenobarbital), may increase the severity of side effects.

• Muscle relaxants such as succinylcholine may increase the risk of side effects.

• Cimetidine may inhibit liver detoxification of organophosphates and increase the risk of side effects.

• Dimethyl sulfoxide (DMSO) may increase the risk of side effects of organophosphates.

• Pyrantel dewormers act at the same level as organophosphates and may increase the risk of side effects.

Food Interactions

Diets low in protein and malnutrition decrease organophosphate metabolism in some species and may increase the risk of side effects.

Usual Dose

Dogs: 12–15 mg/lb.

Puppies/Cats/Kittens: 5 mg/lb.

Drug Form: 10- and 20-mg tablets; 68-, 136-, and 204-mg capsules; and 136-, 204-, and 544-mg pellets.

Storage: Dichlorvos is easily inactivated if exposed to moisture or oxidizing agents. Store in closed container and protect from light. Keep refrigerated.

Overdosage

Signs of overdose may include increased frequency of urination and defecation, diarrhea, increased salivation, vomiting, retching, constriction of the pupils, tearing, muscle tremors, decreased heart rate, respiratory distress, hyperexcitability, seizures, and death. Doses as low as 5 to 6 times the recommended dose may cause death in dogs and cats. In case of accidental ingestion or overdose, contact your veterinarian or the National Animal Poison Control Center. ALWAYS bring the prescription bottle or container with you if you go for treatment.

Special Information

The development of new drugs that are less toxic to humans, animals, and the environment has reduced the use of organophosphates. Although dichlorvos is a relatively safe organophosphate dewormer, there are now many safer and more effective drugs available.

Special Populations

Pregnancy/Lactation

The risk of side effects in pregnant and nursing animals is the same as for healthy adult dogs and cats.

Puppies/Kittens

Young animals are more susceptible to side effects. Dichlorvos should not be used in young kittens or puppies under age 10 days.

Senior Animals

There are no specific contraindications for the use of dichlorvos in healthy senior animals. Dichlorvos should not be used in senior animals that are debilitated, sick, or have chronic kidney or liver disease.

Generic Name

Diethylcarbamazine

(dye-eth-ul-kar-BAM-uh-zene) [G]

Brand Names

Carbam [V]	Hetrazan [H]
Caricide [V]	Nemacide [V]
Difil [V]	Paltone CHWP [V]
Dirocide [V]	PET-DEC [V]
Filaribits [V]	

Combination Product

Generic Ingredients: Diethylcarbamazine + Oxibendazole
Filaribits Plus [V] (see Filaribits Plus)

Type of Drug

Heartworm preventive and dewormer.

Prescribed for

Prevention of heartworm disease (Dirofilaria immitis) in dogs, treatment and prevention of roundworm (Toxocara canis, T. leonina) in dogs and cats, and treatment of Filaroides osleri in dogs.

General Information

Diethylcarbamazine citrate (DEC) works by paralyzing susceptible parasites. It also alters the structure of the parasite, making it more susceptible to destruction by the immune system of the host animal.

Prevention of heartworm disease is the major use of this drug. Heartworm disease is caused by the filarial parasite *D. immitis*. Infective *D. immmitis* larvae are transmitted from mosquitoes to dogs. The infective larva migrates to the heart and develops into an adult heartworm. Adult heartworms mate, producing microfilariae that circulate in the blood. The cycle is completed when a mosquito feeds on the blood of an infected dog and acquires microfilarial larvae that may infect the next dog from which the mosquito feeds. DEC prevents heartworm disease by killing infective larvae after infection; therefore, the drug must be given daily to prevent infection.

DEC also kills the microfilarial stage of *D. immitis*; however, it is not used for this purpose because it may cause severe and sometimes fatal reaction. For this reason, it is very important to be sure that a dog is not already infected when preventive treatment is started.

DEC may be used to treat *Oslerus* (*Filaroides*) *osleri*, a filarial parasite that may infect the trachea and lower airways of dogs.

DEC is effective against adult roundworm, but it is seldom prescribed for this because there are a number of alternatives that cause fewer side effects. However, it prevents roundworm infection when given daily at the same low dose used to prevent heartworm disease.

Cautions and Warnings

■ Test dogs for heartworm and microfilaria *before* using DEC to treat roundworms or as a heartworm preventive! Dogs on year-round daily heartworm preventive treatment should be tested for heartworm or microfilaria every 6 months. Do not use in dogs or cats with adult heartworm or microfilaria until they have been treated for both adults and microfilaria, and rechecked to confirm that the microfilariae have been cleared.

■ Contact your veterinarian if you think your dog or cat may be having an adverse reaction to DEC.

■ U.S. federal law restricts the use of this drug by or on the

lawful written or oral order of a licensed veterinarian within the context of a valid veterinarian-client-patient relationship.

Possible Side Effects

Side effects are most common at the higher dosages used to treat roundworm and are rare at the low daily dose used to prevent heartworm disease.

▼ Common: diarrhea and vomiting.

▼ Rare: anaphylactic-like reaction (salivation, diarrhea, vomiting, depression, loss of coordination, collapse, lethargy, pale mucous membranes, weak pulses, increased pulse, labored breathing, and death).

Drug Interactions

None known.

Food Interactions

Giving with food or soon after eating may prevent vomiting.

Usual Dose

Dogs: for heartworm prevention—3 mg/lb once a day starting before mosquito season begins and continuing for 60 days after exposure to mosquitoes ends. Should be given year-round in areas where mosquitoes are active throughout the year. For roundworm treatment—25–50 mg/lb; repeat in 10 to 20 days. For roundworm prevention—3 mg/lb once a day. For *O. osleri*—10 mg/lb once a day for 4 days.

Cats: for roundworm treatment—25–50 mg/lb.

Drug Form: 60-, 120-, and 180-mg chewable tablets; 50-, 100-, 200-, 300-, and 400-mg tablets; and 60 mg/lb syrup.

Storage: DEC should be stored in tight containers at room temperature and protected from light.

Overdosage

In dogs, large overdoses may cause vomiting, diarrhea, and depression. In case of accidental ingestion or overdose, contact your veterinarian or the National Animal Poison Control Center. ALWAYS bring the prescription bottle or container with you if you go for treatment.

Special Information

Newer heartworm preventive drugs, such as ivermectin and milbemycin oxime, which are given only once-a-month, have largely replaced DEC. The main advantage of the once-a-month drugs is a lower risk of serious side effects from accidentally treating a dog with active heartworm disease. Many owners also prefer the convenience of only medicating once a month. Some of the once-a-month products remove the most common intestinal parasites in addition to preventing heartworm disease. The same advantage is available in the DEC + oxibendazole combination for owners who prefer a once-a-day product. Overall, DEC remains a safe and effective alternative as long as treatment is administered daily without fail. Missing more than 1 daily dose in a row increases the risk of developing heartworm disease.

Special Populations

Pregnancy/Lactation
DEC is safe to use throughout pregnancy and lactation in heartworm-free dogs as a daily heartworm preventive.

Puppies/Kittens
DEC is safe to use in puppies and kittens. It may be used daily in nursing puppies for heartworm prevention.

Senior Animals
DEC is safe to use in older heartworm-free dogs and cats.

Generic Name

Digoxin (dih-JOK-sin) [G]

Brand Names

Cardoxin [V]   Lanoxin [H]

Type of Drug

Digitalis glycoside.

Prescribed for

Congestive heart failure, dilated cardiomyopathy, abnormal heart rhythms.

General Information

Digoxin has a direct effect on heart muscle, causing it to contract with greater strength. This allows a failing heart to pump blood more effectively and relieves many of the symptoms of heart failure. The sympathetic nervous system is stimulated during heart failure. This is a normal response that increases heart rate and the amount of blood pumped. As heart failure progresses, this activity is counterproductive and results in many adverse effects, including inefficient pumping and decreased blood circulation. Digoxin counteracts sympathetic stimulation. It decreases the heart rate so that there is enough time for the heart to fill between beats, and thereby increases the amount of blood that is actually pumped and circulated. By improving circulation, it reduces the back pressure on blood vessels and reduces swelling in the body and fluid build-up in the lungs. Digoxin also helps correct certain abnormal heart rhythms where there is a rapid heart rate driven by input from above the ventricles (main pumping chambers).

Digoxin has been used for many years in dogs and cats with heart failure. It may be useful in treating heart failure caused by valve disease, congenital heart disease, nutritional deficiency (see *Taurine* and *Carnitine*), and endocrine disease, as well as heart damage caused by infections, lack of blood flow, and toxins.

Digoxin improves the quality of life and probably prolongs the life of heart failure patients. Because of its effects on the sympathetic nervous system, it may even be helpful for animals that have heart disease but are not yet in heart failure. There is still a lot of controversy over when to start digoxin therapy and which patients to treat, because the necessary studies have not been done to fully answer those questions.

The current recommendations for treatment of congestive heart failure include salt and exercise restriction, and administration of diuretics (see *Furosemide* and *Thiazide Diuretics*), digoxin, and enalapril (see *Enalapril*). Discuss the treatments with your veterinarian or veterinary cardiologist to decide the best time to begin therapy and the best medications to use for your pet.

The margin of safety of digoxin is very small, so the effective dose and the toxic dose are very close. It is usually necessary to measure digoxin blood levels to make sure the dose is not too high or too low, especially in the beginning of treatment, or if there are any signs of toxicity (see "Possible Side Effects"). Digoxin toxicity is estimated to occur in up to 25% of dogs undergoing treatment. If signs of toxicity occur, blood digoxin levels should be measured and digoxin discontinued until the results are known. Digoxin is excreted by the kidneys, and the dose may need to be lowered for animals with kidney disease. Digitoxin, another digitalis glycoside, is removed mostly by the liver and may be used for dogs in kidney failure. Digitoxin is not recommended for use in cats or in dogs with liver disease.

Cautions and Warnings

■ Digoxin is FDA approved for use in dogs only. It is used in cats as well and is considered accepted practice.

■ Cats are more susceptible to the adverse effects of digoxin and should be treated with caution.

■ The veterinary elixir is available in two different concentrations. Do not confuse the two.

■ Animals with low blood potassium should not be given digoxin, as abnormal heart rhythms are likely.

■ Animals with hypothyroidism, hyperthyroidism, abnormal blood electrolyte levels, or kidney disease should be given lower doses of digoxin and monitored carefully.

■ There are many possible drug interactions with digoxin, and they may be significant in the management of patients on digoxin (see "Drug Interactions").

■ Contact your veterinarian IMMEDIATELY if you think your dog or cat may be having an adverse reaction to digoxin.

■ U.S. federal law restricts the use of this drug by or on the lawful written or oral order of a licensed veterinarian within the context of a valid veterinarian-client-patient relationship.

Possible Side Effects

▼ Common: decreased appetite, vomiting, diarrhea, depression, unsteady gait, weakness, and abnormal heart rhythms.

▼ Rare: central nervous system and visual disturbances are rare side effects in people that may occur in animals.

Drug Interactions

• Antacids, cimetidine, metoclopramide, oral neomycin, penicillamine, and chemotherapy agents such as cyclophosphamide and doxorubicin may decrease the amount of digoxin absorbed from the gastrointestinal tract.

• Diuretics (furosemide and thiazides), amphotericin B, corticosteroids, laxatives, diazepam, quinidine, anticholinergics, succinylcholine, verapamil, tetracycline, and erythromycin may all increase digoxin toxicity.

Food Interactions

Do not give digoxin with food. Absorption of digoxin may be decreased by 50% if there is food in the stomach.

Usual Dose

Dogs: 0.0025–0.005 mg/lb orally twice a day.
Cats: 0.0015–0.002 mg/lb orally twice a day.
Drug Form: elixirs, capsules, tablets, and injectables. The veterinary elixir (Cardoxin) comes in two strengths: 0.15 mg/ml and 0.05 mg/ml. Do not confuse the two.

Overdosage

Overdose will cause the side effects noted above (see "Possible Side Effects"). In case of accidental ingestion or overdose, contact your veterinarian or the National Animal Poison Control Center. ALWAYS bring the prescription bottle or container with you if you go for treatment.

Special Information

Digoxin is better absorbed from elixirs and capsules than from tablets. There are also differences in the amount of digoxin absorbed from different brands. Do not change the type or brand of digoxin given when your animal is on an effective dose regimen.

Special Populations

Pregnancy/Lactation
There are no safety studies on digoxin in pregnant or lactating dogs or cats. Digoxin should be avoided unless the benefits outweigh the risks.

Puppies/Kittens
Digoxin should be used with caution in puppies and kittens, and the supervision of a veterinary cardiologist is strongly recommended.

Senior Animals

Digoxin should be used with caution in older animals, and the supervision of a veterinary cardiologist is strongly recommended.

Generic Name

Diltiazem (dil-TYE-uh-zem) G

Brand Names

Cardizem H   Tiazac H
Dilacor XR H

Type of Drug

Calcium channel blocker

Prescribed for

Heart failure, hypertrophic cardiomyopathy in cats, and abnormal heart rhythms.

General Information

Diltiazem is one of a class of drugs called calcium channel blockers, which also includes verapamil and nifedipine. They work by slowing the passage of calcium into muscle cells. This causes smooth muscle in the blood vessels that supply the heart to relax; as a result, the blood vessels open wider and more blood reaches the heart tissues. Diltiazem also reduces the speed at which electrical impulses are carried through the heart and is effective for certain abnormal heart rhythms; these include atrial fibrillation and flutter, and supraventricular tachycardias (abnormal heart rhythms arising from the atria).

Diltiazem appears to be a safe and effective treatment for cats with hypertrophic cardiomyopathy (thickened heart muscle disease). Adverse effects are extremely rare at recommended doses (see "Usual Dose"), and studies have shown that diltiazem is more effective than propranolol or verapamil in relieving symptoms and prolonging survival (see *Atenolol*). It improves the heart's ability to pump and may even reverse some of the damage when used long-term. Diltiazem is recommended for cats with hypertrophic cardiomyopathy even when they have no obvious heart failure symptoms. Cats with hypertrophic cardiomyopathy often present with life-threatening breathing difficulty due to fluid in the lungs (pulmonary edema) or fluid around the lungs (pleural effusion). Emergency treatment includes oxygen, furosemide injections, and nitroglycerin. After the cat is stabilized and the diagnosis is confirmed, oral treatment with diltiazem is started and usually causes improvement within 72 hours.

Diltiazem may be used to treat hypertension (high blood pressure) because it causes peripheral blood vessels to dilate. Calcium channel blockers have not been used yet to any extent for the treatment of hypertension in dogs or cats. Essential hypertension is a relatively rare disorder in dogs and cats, although secondary hypertension is quite common in those with kidney failure. Diuretics and low salt diets are standard treatments for hypertension. Other adjunct treatments might include atenolol, prazosin, or ACE inhibitors for those resistant to diuretic and dietary therapy.

Cautions and Warnings

■ Calcium channel blockers should be avoided or used with extreme caution in animals with overt heart failure, heart block, or slow heart rate, or significant kidney or liver dysfunction.

■ Diltiazem is not FDA approved for use in dogs or cats. It is commonly used and is considered accepted practice.

■ Contact your veterinarian if you think your dog or cat may be having an adverse reaction to diltiazem.

■ U.S. federal law restricts the use of this drug by or on the lawful written or oral order of a licensed veterinarian within the context of a valid veterinarian-client-patient relationship.

Possible Side Effects

Side effects at recommended doses are extremely rare.

▼ Rare: abnormal heart rhythms, low blood pressure, collapse, and sudden death; in people, increased liver enzymes, gastrointestinal distress, and rashes.

Drug Interactions

• ACE inhibitors (enalapril) and calcium channel blockers

such as diltiazem should not be used together or should be used with extreme caution.

• Digoxin, epinephrine, and hydralazine may produce severe low blood pressure when given with diltiazem.

• Beta-blockers (atenolol) and diltiazem may be used together but should be used with extreme caution and careful monitoring.

• Theophylline, quinidine, cyclosporine, and propranolol doses may need to be adjusted if they are given with diltiazem.

• Cimetidine and other H2 blockers may increase the blood levels of diltiazem.

• Diltiazem may increase blood levels of digoxin and the likelihood of digoxin toxicity.

Food Interactions

None known.

Usual Dose

Dogs: 0.25–0.75 mg/lb orally 3 times a day. For abnormal heart rhythms, start at 0.12 mg/lb and adjust as needed to desired heart rate over a number of days.

Cats: 0.9–1.2 mg/lb orally 2–3 times a day.

Drug Form: 30-, 60-, 90- and 120-mg tablets; 60-, 90-, and 120-mg sustained-release capsules; and 5 mg/ml injectable. Doses listed above are for regular diltiazem tablets. *Do not* use sustained release forms unless under the specific directions of a veterinary cardiologist.

Overdosage

Signs of overdose could include low blood pressure, slow heart rate, abnormal rhythms, heart failure, collapse, and sudden death. In case of accidental ingestion or overdose, contact your veterinarian or the National Animal Poison Control Center. ALWAYS bring the prescription bottle or container with you if you go for treatment.

Special Populations

Pregnancy/Lactation

Diltiazem crosses the placenta, causes damage to the fetus in rodents, and is excreted in milk. It should be avoided in pregnant or lactating animals unless the benefits outweigh the risks.

Puppies/Kittens
Diltiazem should not be used in puppies or kittens unless under the supervision of a veterinary cardiologist.

Senior Animals
Older animals are more susceptible to the adverse effects of calcium channel blockers, especially those with severe heart disease, or liver or kidney dysfunction. Diltiazem should be avoided or used with extreme caution in this group, and preferably under the supervision of a veterinary cardiologist.

Generic Name

Dimenhydrinate (dye-men-HYE-drih-nate) G

Most Common Brand Names

Dramamine H   Nico-Vert H
Dimetabs H

Type of Drug

Antihistamine and antiemetic.

Prescribed for

Motion sickness in dogs and cats.

General Information

Dimenhydrinate is an antihistamine that is frequently used for motion sickness in dogs. It can be used for motion sickness in cats, but there are other drugs that are thought to be more effective, such as chlorpromazine. Antihistamines are thought to block input from the vestibular system (inner ear and balance system), although it is not known exactly how this works. Dimenhydrinate will cause some central nervous system (CNS) depression and sedation. The sedative effects of antihistamines may diminish with time. This drug's effectiveness for motion sickness may decrease with prolonged use. Dimenhydrinate is available over the counter.

Cautions and Warnings

■ Dimenhydrinate is not FDA approved for use in dogs or cats. It is commonly used and is considered accepted practice.

■ Dimenhydrinate should be used with caution in animals with prostatic enlargement, bladder neck obstruction, severe heart failure, some forms of glaucoma, pyelo-duodenal obstruction (obstruction at the junction of the stomach and small intestine), hyperthyroidism, seizure disorders, high blood pressure, or allergic lung disease.

■ Dimenhydrinate may mask symptoms of ear problems.

■ Contact your veterinarian if you think your dog or cat may be having an adverse reaction to dimenhydrinate.

■ U.S. federal law restricts the use of this drug by or on the lawful written or oral order of a licensed veterinarian within the context of a valid veterinarian-client-patient relationship.

Possible Side Effects

▼ Common: sedation, dry mouth, and urinary retention.
▼ Rare: diarrhea, vomiting, and decreased appetite.

Drug Interactions

• Dimenhydrinate may have an additive effect when combined with other CNS depressant drugs, such as barbiturates and tranquilizers.

• Dimenhydrinate may have an additive effect when combined with atropine-like drugs.

• Dimenhydrinate may enhance the effects of epinephrine.

• Dimenhydrinate may decrease the effects of heparin and warfarin.

Food Interactions

Dimenhydrinate may be better tolerated if given with food.

Usual Dose

Dogs: 2–4 mg/lb orally 3 times a day.
Cats: 12.5 mg orally 3 times a day.
Drug Form: 50-mg tablets and 12.5 mg/4 ml liquid.

Overdosage

The usual signs of overdose are sedation and clumsiness. Convulsions, coma, and difficulty breathing can develop after a massive overdose. In case of accidental overdose, contact your veterinarian or the National Animal Poison Control Center.

ALWAYS bring the prescription bottle or container with you if you go for treatment.

Special Information

When using dimenhydrinate for motion sickness, give 30 to 60 minutes before traveling. Dimenhydrinate should not be used within 1 week of skin testing for allergies.

Special Populations

Pregnancy/Lactation
Antihistamine use in pregnant humans is controversial because some antihistamines have been shown to cause birth defects in laboratory animals. Dimenhydrinate is excreted in breast milk. It should only be used in pregnant or lactating animals if the benefits outweigh the risks.

Puppies/Kittens
There are no safety studies in puppies or kittens, but dimenhydrinate is used in young children.

Senior Animals
There are no studies in dogs, but older humans are more sensitive to side effects from antihistamines. In most cases, it is better to start with a reduced dose.

Generic Name

Dimethyl Sulfoxide (DMSO)

(dye-METH-ul sul-FOK-side) [G]

Brand Names

Domoso [V]   Rimso-50 [H]
Kemsol [H]

Combination Product
Generic Ingredients: DMSO + Fluocinolone Acetonide
Synotic Otic [V]

The information in this profile also applies to the following drug:

Generic Ingredient: Methylsulfonyl Methane (MSM) [G]
Flex-a-gan [V]   Vita-Flex MSM [V]

Type of Drug

DMSO: Anti-inflammatory, analgesic, oxygen free-radical scavenger, vehicle to enhance penetration of other drugs. MSM: Anti-inflammmatory and analgesic.

Prescribed for

Central nervous system and spinal cord trauma and disorders, heat stroke, pain and inflammation, reduction of swelling from acute trauma, arthritis, amyloidosis (kidney disease due to amyloid), cystitis, resuscitation after cardiac arrest, and acute kidney failure (DMSO). Arthritis and inflammatory bowel disease (MSM).

General Information

DMSO is a liquid solvent that is extremely hygroscopic (absorbs water) and is able to penetrate skin and other tissues, often carrying other drugs with it. Most people think it has a sickening foul odor like sweet garlic. DMSO is an effective oxygen free-radical scavenger. It is anti-inflammatory, relieves pain, protects against clots, and can protect against ischemia (loss of blood flow to tissues) and radiation damage. DMSO also penetrates skin and all the tissues of the body and may carry other drugs with it. Synotic may be useful in treatment of chronic inflammatory conditions of the ear. It is also used with enrofloxacin (Baytril injectable) added—see *Quinolone (Fluoroquinolone) Antibiotics*—to treat resistant bacterial infections of the ear. Synotic may also be used topically for severe inflammatory skin diseases, such as pemphigus.

  MSM is a metabolite of DMSO that seems to have some of the anti-inflammatory and analgesic properties of DMSO. It is a white odorless powder or tablet that is given orally. Although there are no well-designed and controlled studies to prove its efficacy, it does seem to reduce the pain and inflammation of arthritis in some animals and has also been used as an anti-inflammatory in other chronic conditions, such as inflammatory bowel disease.

Cautions and Warnings

For Owners/Handlers

  ■ Contact of DMSO with skin should be avoided. Rubber gloves should be worn while applying this drug. DMSO may penetrate some kinds of rubber and plastic, so it should be kept in its original container, tightly capped. If absorbed through the skin, DMSO will cause odorous breath and unpleasant mouth taste.

■ Mild sedation or drowsiness, sensations of warmth, burning, irritation, itching, and skin redness have been reported in some persons following exposure to DMSO.

■ DMSO causes histamine release, so it may cause an allergic type reaction when applied to the skin.

■ Do not use if you are pregnant or if there is any chance you may be pregnant. Consult a physician in case of accidental ingestion by humans, or adverse reactions to DMSO skin contact.

For Animals

■ DMSO may cause skin irritation if applied topically. This irritation is usually mild and resolves quickly.

■ DMSO causes some hemolysis (breakdown of red blood cells) when given intravenously.

■ DMSO is approved for topical use in the pain and swelling of trauma, but it may mask the pain and swelling of fractures.

■ Because DMSO causes mast cell degranulation/histamine release, it could potentially cause a significant and possibly fatal release of histamine if given to an animal with an undetected mast cell tumor.

■ Contact your veterinarian if you think your dog or cat may be having an adverse reaction to DMSO or MSM.

■ U.S. federal law restricts the use of these drugs by or on the lawful written or oral order of a licensed veterinarian within the context of a valid veterinarian-client-patient relationship.

Possible Side Effects

▼ Common: unpleasant smell and taste after DMSO use, skin irritation after topical application of DMSO, hemolysis after intravenous use and subsequent red urine from hemoglobin, decreased appetite, nausea and decreased water consumption owing to the odor/taste of DMSO, and possible toxicity of other drugs given with DMSO.

▼ Rare: diarrhea with oral MSM use and lens changes with DMSO use.

Drug Interactions

• DMSO should be used with extreme caution when other medications are being used. If DMSO is used topically, it may carry other topical medications with it and cause systemic effects. It may also transport or translocate medications across tissue membrane barriers they would not normally cross, altering the effects of certain drugs.

• DMSO enhances the effect of insulin, barbiturates, local anesthetics, aspirin, tetracyclines, corticosteroids, organophosphates, and others.

• MSM is extremely safe and may be used in combination with NSAIDs, other anti-inflammatory agents, or arthritis medications.

• DMSO reduces the effect of digoxin and digitalis compounds.

Food Interactions

None known.

Usual Dose

Dogs: DMSO—apply topically as directed by your veterinarian; for injection into a vein (IV)—175–1000 mg/lb in a 10% to 45% solution, administered slowly. *MSM*—Follow package directions, purity varies, and therefore amount of powder administered varies. Vita-Flex dose is 1 heaping scoop—10-g scoop—once or twice a day; Flex-a-gan dose is ½ tablet twice a day for small dogs, 1 tablet twice a day for large dogs.

Cats: DMSO—apply topically as directed by your veterinarian; (IV) dose—175–500 mg/lb in a 10% to 45% solution, administered slowly. *MSM:* Follow package directions, purity varies, and therefore amount of powder administered varies. Approximately ⅛ tsp powder, once or twice a day, or ¼ tablet Flex-a-gan twice a day.

Drug Form: DMSO liquid, 90% or 50% and DMSO gel; MSM powder and tablets.

Overdosage

DMSO is considered to have a low toxicity. It has been shown to cause severe myopia (near-sightedness) in toxicity studies of dogs, rabbits, and pigs, because of refractive changes in the lens. MSM is also thought to have low toxicity. In case of accidental ingestion or overdose, contact your veterinarian or the National Animal Poison Control Center. ALWAYS bring the prescription bottle or container with you if you go for treatment.

Special Information

Reperfusion injury is the injury that occurs in tissues after blood supply has been shut off for any reason. This injury occurs after cardiac arrest, application of a tourniquet, injury to the brain or spinal cord, and so on. DMSO may prevent reperfusion injury because it scavenges the oxygen free-radicals that form in ischemic tissue and helps prevent clots. Because of its penetration abilities, DMSO is able to reach ischemic tissues and therefore may be extremely useful in situations where there would be reperfusion injury. Heat stroke is a fairly common problem in dogs and has a guarded to poor prognosis even with standard recommended therapy—shock-doses of IV fluids and corticosteroids, slow cooling, antibiotics, heparin, intensive care. DMSO, given intravenously, seems to dramatically improve the recovery rate of dogs with heat stroke.

DMSO dissolves the amyloid fibrils that cause amyloidosis and may be useful in some early cases of amyloidosis, but its usefulness is limited in most cats because of the nausea and decreased appetite and water consumption that the bad odor causes.

DMSO has been used in people to treat interstitial cystitis (chronic bladder wall inflammation). It may be useful in cats with severe hemorrhagic cystitis, especially those not responding to corticosteroids. It is also recommended for treatment of hemorrhagic cystitis caused by cyclophosphamide, a cancer chemotherapy agent. Diluted DMSO is infused into the bladder through a catheter, so treatment does require anesthesia. DMSO has been used to treat a variety of problems and in combination with many other drugs. Its therapeutic potential has not been studied thoroughly. Owners should be wary of exaggerated claims and be wary of toxic potential when other drugs are used in combination with DMSO.

Special Populations

Pregnancy/Lactation
DMSO has caused birth defects in laboratory animals, so it should be avoided in pregnant or lactating animals.

Puppies/Kittens

There are no safety studies in young animals, so DMSO should probably be avoided unless the benefits outweigh the potential risks.

Senior Animals

DMSO and MSM should be safe to use in older animals (see "Drug Interactions").

Generic Name

Diphenhydramine (dye-fen-HYE-druh-mene) G

Most Common Brand Names

Benadryl H   Histacalm V

Type of Drug

Antihistamine, antitussive (cough suppressant), antiemetic (alleviates nausea), and sedative.

Prescribed for

Allergies, motion sickness, insect bites or stings, travel anxiety, nausea, coughing, reverse-sneeze.

General Information

Histamine is one of the substances released by the tissues of the body during an allergic reaction. A variety of symptoms are produced by histamine, including itching, swelling and sneezing. A massive release of histamine can produce anaphylactic shock (severe, systemic allergic reaction leading to circulatory collapse). Histamine is only one of many mediators of allergic reactions, so diphenhydramine, which only blocks histamine, is only partially effective in relieving allergy symptoms. Diphenhydramine also causes drowsiness and combats motion sickness, so it can be very helpful for animals with travel anxiety and motion sickness. It is often used with corticosteroids to treat severe allergic reactions to venomous insect bites, such as bee stings and spider bites. It may also be useful as an aid in the treatment and management of allergic skin disease, although it is unlikely to help significantly when used alone. It is also used as an anti-itch ingredient of shampoos, sprays, or other medications for external use. Diphenhydramine is available in generic and brand name in tablet, caplet, softgel, liquid, powder, spray, shampoo, gel, cream, and ointment forms both alone and in combination products in many products for human use.

Cautions and Warnings

■ Diphenhydramine is FDA approved for external use only in dogs or cats. Injectable and oral forms are commonly used, however, and it is considered accepted practice.

■ Avoid diphenhydramine use in animals with glaucoma, prostate disease, pyloric obstruction, urinary obstruction, or allergic lung disease.

■ Contact your veterinarian if you think your dog or cat may be having an adverse reaction to diphenhydramine.

■ U.S. federal law restricts the use of this drug by or on the lawful written or oral order of a licensed veterinarian within the context of a valid veterinarian-client-patient relationship.

Possible Side Effects

▼ Common: drowsiness, dry mouth, and urine retention.
▼ Rare: decreased appetite, vomiting, and diarrhea.

Drug Interactions

• Increased sedation may occur if diphenhydramine is used with other central nervous system depressant drugs.
• Diphenhydramine may counteract the effects of anticoagulants.
• Diphenhydramine may enhance the effects of epinephrine.

Food Interactions

None known.

Usual Dose

Dogs: 1–2 mg/lb 3–4 times a day.
Cats: 1–2 mg/lb 2–3 times a day.
Drug Form: Diphenhydramine comes in a variety of forms for internal and external use (see "General Information"). The pediatric elixir or syrup (12.5 mg/ml) may be the easiest form to administer orally to dogs and cats. It is also available in 25- and 50-mg tablets and capsules and injectable.

Overdosage

Overdose may cause excitement, seizures, lethargy, coma, decreased breathing, and death. In case of accidental ingestion or overdose, contact your veterinarian or the National Animal Poison Control Center. ALWAYS bring the prescription bottle or container with you if you go for treatment.

Special Information

Antihistamines should be discontinued at least 4 days before allergy skin testing. Diphenhydramine is given before surgical removal of mast cell tumors in case of massive histamine release from the tumor. It is also used to treat nervous system side effects from metoclopramide and poisoning by organophosphates, carbamates, and phenothiazines.

Special Populations

Pregnancy/Lactation
Diphenhydramine has not been studied in dogs or cats, but it does cross the placenta and enter the milk of rats, so it should probably be avoided in pregnant or lactating animals.

Puppies/Kittens
Because of the lack of studies, it is not known if diphenhydramine is safe to use in puppies or kittens.

Senior Animals
Diphenhydramine should be safe to use in older animals. Doses may need to be reduced for those with kidney or liver disease.

Generic Name

Docusate (DOK-yew-sate) G

Most Common Brand Names

Colace H   Duco-Soft V

Type of Drug

Emollient laxative and surfactant.

Prescribed for

Constipation, megacolon, and removal of ear wax.

General Information

Laxatives are used to prevent or relieve constipation. They are classified by their action as lubricant, emollient (stool softeners), bulk-forming, osmotic, or stimulant. The choice of laxative, dose, and frequency of administration must be adjusted for each individual to obtain the desired stool consistency and frequency of defecation. Vomiting, straining, and other signs of constipation may be caused by serious problems. Consult your veterinarian before administering laxatives or any medication to your pet.

Docusate is available as the salt of sodium, calcium, or potassium. The sodium salt was formerly called dioctyl sodium succinate and some products may still be referred to as DSS. Docusate is a surface-active agent or surfactant. It reduces surface tension and allows water and fat to penetrate and mix with the intestinal contents, resulting in a softer mass. It may also increase secretion of water from the body into the colon.

Docusate is used as a laxative in dogs and cats to soften hard, dry feces and facilitate their passage. It is useful either orally or rectally in the treatment of megacolon. Megacolon is a disorder seen most frequently in cats. An enlarged colon with decreased muscle function results in the accumulation of huge amounts of fecal material, making it painful and ultimately impossible to defecate. There is no cure, but the constipation may be managed with individually tailored treatment plans based on the use of various types of laxatives.

Docusate may be used to clean ears. The surface-active properties help dissolve excessive ear wax.

Cautions and Warnings

■ Use with caution in animals with fluid or electrolyte abnormalities. Do not use in animals that are dehydrated.

■ Docusate is FDA approved for over-the-counter (OTC) use in dogs and cats.

■ Contact your veterinarian if you think your dog or cat may be having an adverse reaction to docusate.

Possible Side Effects

Side effects are rare when used as directed. Liquid preparations are bitter and may cause irritation of the esophagus and excessive salivation if administered orally.

Possible Side Effects *(continued)*

▼ Rare: Cramping, diarrhea, and irritation of the intestinal mucosa.

Drug Interactions

• Do not give with mineral oil (see *Lubricant Laxative*), because it may increase the systemic absorption of the mineral oil.

• Do not use with other laxatives unless directed by your veterinarian.

Food Interactions

Give on an empty stomach unless otherwise directed by your veterinarian.

Usual Dose

Dogs: tablets—50–200 mg orally 1–2 times a day. Enema—5–12 ml of ready-to-use products or as directed by your veterinarian.

Cats: tablets—50–100 mg/cat once a day. Enema—5–12 ml of ready-to-use products or as directed by your veterinarian.

Drug Form: 50- and 100-mg capsules, 1% solution liquid or syrup, and enema—5% solution that must be diluted as directed before using, ready-to-use enema syringe containing 240 mg docusate in 12-ml glycerin (veterinary product), and 200-mg docusate in 5 ml (human product).

Overdosage

Side effects from overdosing are rare. Fluid and electrolyte abnormalities are possible. In case of accidental ingestion or overdose, contact your veterinarian or the National Animal Poison Control Center. ALWAYS bring the prescription bottle or container with you if you go for treatment.

Special Populations

Pregnancy/Lactation

Docusate is considered safe to use in pregnant and lactating dogs and cats.

Puppies/Kittens
Docusate is considered safe to use in puppies and kittens.

Senior Animals
Docusate is considered safe to use in senior dogs and cats.

Generic Name
Electrolyte Solutions Ⓖ

Most Common Brand Names

Multisol-R Ⓥ   Pedialyte Ⓗ

Normosol-M Ⓗ   Re-Sorb Ⓥ

Normosol-R Ⓗ

Type of Drug

Solutions of water, electrolytes (salts), and/or dextrose.

Prescribed for

Dehydration, vomiting, diarrhea, shock, kidney failure, diabetes with ketoacidosis, pancreatitis, peritonitis, liver disease, Addison's disease, and urinary obstruction.

General Information

Many illnesses and problems are treated with fluids (water, electrolytes, and/or glucose). Body fluids are composed mostly of water, salts, or electrolytes, such as sodium, potassium, chloride, bicarbonate, phosphate, magnesium, and glucose. Water, electrolytes, and glucose may be needed in varying amounts depending on the illness. Animals may become dehydrated either because they do not feel well and therefore do not drink as much as they should, or because they lose fluids— water and electrolytes—from vomiting, diarrhea, or urination. Elecrolyte solutions include lactated Ringer's solution, 0.9% (normal) saline, 0.45% (half-strength) saline with 2.5% dextrose (a form of sugar), 5% dextrose, and 7.5% saline.

Animals may go into shock (circulatory collapse) for a variety of reasons, including severe trauma, blood loss, bacterial infections, low blood glucose, heat stroke, complications of diabetes, Addison's disease, kidney failure, urinary obstruction, poisoning, and many others. In all of these conditions, fluids are the mainstay of therapy.

Fluids may be given in a variety of ways, depending on the illness or problem. For mild dehydration or as an adjunct to other fluid therapy, oral fluids may be given. Oral fluids, such as Pedialyte or Re-Sorb, may be very effective therapy for diarrhea. If the animal cannot be given oral fluids because of vomiting or for other reasons, fluids are given by injection, either into a vein (intravenously), under the skin (subcutaneously), into the bone marrow cavity, or into the abdomen. The route of injection depends on the illness and other issues, such as type and amount of fluid needed. If fluids are needed rapidly or in large volumes, as in shock, they are given intravenously, usually through one or more intravenous catheters. Fluids may be given under the skin if the dehydration is mild or moderate and the animal is well enough to absorb the fluids from under the skin. Bone marrow or abdominal injections may be used if access to veins is a problem and the animal is too ill for injections under the skin.

Animals needing fluid therapy, but not intensive care, may do better at home than in the hospital. Your veterinarian may teach you to administer fluids under the skin, so your pet is able to stay at home while receiving the fluid therapy it needs.

Cautions and Warnings

■ Do not give oral or injectable fluid and electrolyte solutions without consulting your veterinarian. Volume overload is possible if kidney or heart failure is present. Oral rehydration may not be adequate if the dehydration is severe, and a veterinarian should see any animal with persistent vomiting and/or diarrhea. Potassium-containing fluids may cause severe potassium overload in animals with acute kidney failure. Contact your veterinarian if it appears that fluids given subcutaneously are not being absorbed promptly or completely. Do not give glucose/dextrose-containing fluids subcutaneously, unless directed by your veterinarian.

■ Contact your veterinarian if you think your dog or cat may be having an adverse reaction to oral or injectable fluid therapy.

■ U.S. federal law restricts the use of these drugs by or on the lawful written or oral order of a licensed veterinarian within the context of a valid veterinarian-client-patient relationship.

Possible Side Effects

▼ Common: accumulation under the chest and abdomen because of the effect of gravity on fluids given subcutaneously, and leakage from the injection site.

▼ Rare: infections at the injection site.

Food and Drug Interactions

None known.

Usual Dose

Dogs: Offer free-choice water and oral electrolyte solutions to dogs with diarrhea. Dogs that have been vomiting are usually offered electrolyte solutions as the first trial after withholding food and water. Follow your veterinarian's instructions carefully for giving subcutaneous fluids. The dose range may be 5–20 ml/lb, 1–4 times a day depending on the degree of dehydration or the underlying problem. Maintenance fluid requirement is 20–30 ml/lb/day. Estimated ongoing losses from vomiting, diarrhea, and polyuria (passage of a large amount of urine) are added on to maintenance amounts.

Cats: Offer free-choice water and oral electrolyte solutions to cats with diarrhea, respiratory infections, or other medical problems where water consumption decreases. Cats often prefer the electrolyte solution, especially if they are dehydrated. Follow your veterinarian's instructions carefully for giving subcutaneous fluids. The dose range may be 5–20 ml/lb, 1–4 times a day, depending on the degree of dehydration or the underlying problem. Maintenance fluid requirement is 20–30 ml/lb/day. Estimated ongoing losses from vomiting, diarrhea, and polyuria are added on to maintenance amounts.

Drug Form: Oral electrolytes may come ready to use—for example, Pedialyte—or as a powder to be mixed with water—for example, Re-Sorb. Follow label directions for mixing with water and keep solutions refrigerated. Fluids for subcutaneous use should be in a sterile 500-ml or 1-L fluid bag, with a sterile administration set, or in a sterile syringe for very small animals, puppies, or kittens.

Overdosage

Fluid overdose is likely only in animals in acute kidney failure/kidney shutdown or heart failure. Potassium overdose may be a serious problem for animals in acute kidney failure. In case of accidental ingestion or overdose, contact your veterinarian or the National Animal Poison Control Center. ALWAYS bring the prescription bottle or container with you if you go for treatment.

Special Information

Lactated Ringer's solution probably stings less than the other fluids when given under the skin. Dextrose should be avoided in fluids given under the skin. If glucose is needed, it is best to give orally or intravenously. Gator-Aid may be used for oral rehydration if other solutions are not available.

Special Populations

Pregnancy/Lactation
Fluid and electrolyte solutions should be safe to use in pregnant and lactating animals.

Puppies/Kittens
Fluid and electrolyte solutions should be safe to use in puppies and kittens, but their small size can make volume overload more likely.

Senior Animals
Oral and subcutaneous fluids should be safe to use in older animals. Avoid volume and potassium overload, especially in those with heart or kidney failure, and avoid lactate in those with liver failure.

Generic Name

Enalapril (uh-NAL-uh-pril)

Brand Names

Enacard [V]   Vasotec [H]

Type of Drug

Angiotensin-converting-enzyme (ACE) inhibitor.

Prescribed for

Heart failure, dilated cardiomyopathy, and high blood pressure (hypertension).

General Information

Enalapril belongs to a class of drugs known as angiotensin-converting-enzyme (ACE) inhibitors that includes lisinopril and captopril. ACE inhibitors work by preventing the conversion of a hormone called angiotensin I to another hormone called angiotensin II, a potent blood vessel constrictor. Preventing this conversion relaxes blood vessels, helps to lower blood pressure, and relieves the symptoms of heart failure by making it easier for a failing heart to pump blood through the body. Enalapril also affects other hormones and enzymes that control blood vessels, which is probably important in the effectiveness of this medicine. Captopril was the first of the ACE inhibitors to become available and was used extensively in the 1980s in dogs and cats. Lisinopril is one of the newer ACE inhibitors, and it is longer acting than either enalapril or captopril.

Enalapril is the only ACE inhibitor that has been studied extensively in dogs with heart disease. These studies have shown that dogs with heart failure that are treated with enalapril live longer and have a significantly improved quality of life. It is not known exactly how enalapril works in dogs. It slows the heart rate, decreases pulmonary edema, reduces coughing, and improves breathing, appetite, and exercise tolerance. Surprisingly, despite all of these improvements in clinical signs, there is no measurable effect on systemic vascular resistance or cardiac output. In the past, dogs in heart failure were usually treated with a combination of digoxin to improve contraction of the heart, and diuretics, to reduce excess fluid in the lungs and vascular space. It is clearly beneficial to add enalapril to this older therapy early in heart disease that is caused by mitral insufficiency (leaky valve) or dilated cardiomyopathy (heart muscle disease). Enalapril seems to be better tolerated by dogs than other ACE inhibitors like captopril or lisinopril. Low blood pressure is more likely if other vasodilators or diuretics are being given, if the recommended dose of enalapril is exceeded, or if the animal is dehydrated.

There is some controversy about when in the course of mitral regurgitation to start enalapril therapy. Some advocate starting enalapril before heart failure is obvious; others advise waiting until there are clinical signs and x-ray or echocardiogram evidence of heart failure. Consult your veterinarian or veterinary cardiologist about the best management for your dog or cat with heart disease.

Primary hypertension is a relatively rare disorder in dogs and cats, but it is quite common secondary to kidney failure. Diuretics and low salt diets are standard treatments for hypertension. Other adjustments might include atenolol, prazosin, or ACE inhibitors for those resistant to diuretic and dietary therapy. The dose of ACE inhibitors for hypertension is higher than the dose for heart failure. This may lead to an increased risk of kidney damage, but some dogs tolerate high doses of ACE inhibitor with no adverse effects.

Cautions and Warnings

■ Although enalapril is FDA approved for use in dogs only, it is used to treat cats as well and is considered accepted practice. Your dog or cat should have a complete cardiac evaluation before starting enalapril therapy to determine whether enalapril is the appropriate drug.

■ Dogs and cats should be observed closely for weakness or depression for 48 hours after starting therapy or increasing the dose. Low blood pressure may occur but is rare with recommended doses of enalapril (see "Overdosage"). Enalapril may decrease blood flow to the kidneys and cause a decrease in kidney function or exacerbate a kidney problem that already exists. Kidney function should be tested before starting therapy and 2 to 7 days after therapy is begun. Enalapril may cause decreased appetite, vomiting, or diarrhea.

■ Contact your veterinarian if you think your dog or cat may be having an adverse reaction to enalapril.

■ U.S. federal law restricts the use of this drug by or on the lawful written or oral order of a licensed veterinarian within the context of a valid veterinarian-client-patient relationship.

Possible Side Effects

▼ Rare: low blood pressure, kidney dysfunction, decreased appetite, vomiting, and diarrhea.

Drug Interactions

• Diuretics or other vasodilators given with enalapril may

cause low blood pressure. The dose of furosemide should probably be reduced 25% to 50% when adding enalapril to heart failure therapy.

• High blood potassium may develop if enalapril is given with potassium supplements or potassium sparing diuretics like spironolactone.

• Nonsteroidal anti-inflammatory drugs (NSAIDs) may reduce the effectiveness of enalapril.

Food Interactions

None known.

Usual Dose

Enalapril
    Dogs: 0.25 mg/lb once or twice a day. Starting dose is once a day; if no response is seen in 2 weeks, dose may be increased to twice a day.
    Cats: 0.1–0.25 mg/lb once or twice a day. Starting dose is once a day; if no response is seen in 2 weeks, dose may be increased to twice a day.
    Drug Form: Enacard—1-, 2.5-, 5-, 10-, and 20-mg tablets. Vasotec—2.5-, 5-, 10-, 20-mg tablets and 1.25 mg/ml injectable.

Captopril
    Dogs: for heart disease—0.25–1 mg/lb orally 2–3 times a day. For hypertension—0.5–5 mg/lb orally 2–3 times a day.
    Cats: for heart disease—3–6 mg/cat orally 2–3 times a day. For hypertension—6.25–12.5 mg/cat 2–3 times a day.
    Drug Form: 12.5-, 25-, 50- and 100-mg tablets.

Lisinopril
    Dogs: for heart disease—0.12–0.25 mg/lb orally once a day. For hypertension—0.2–1 mg/lb orally, once a day.
    Cats: for heart disease—0.12–0.25 mg/lb orally once a day.
    Drug Form: 2.5-, 5-, 10-, 20-, and 40-mg tablets.

Overdosage

Overdoses may cause severe low blood pressure and kidney failure. Early symptoms may include weakness, lethargy, and depression. In case of accidental ingestion or overdose, contact your veterinarian or the National Animal Poison Control

Center. ALWAYS bring the prescription bottle or container with you if you go for treatment.

Special Information

The human enalapril (Vasotec) may be available from the pharmacy at a lower cost than the veterinary product (Enacard). Consult your veterinarian about the advantages of the smaller Enacard pill size, if your dog is small or if you are treating a cat.

Special Populations

Pregnancy/Lactation

The safety of enalapril has not been established in pregnant or lactating dogs or cats. It causes problems in pregnant laboratory animals and people and does enter the milk, so it is not recommended.

Puppies/Kittens

Enalapril should not be used in puppies or kittens unless under the supervision of a veterinary cardiologist.

Senior Animals

Enalapril is safe to use in older animals but should be used with caution in those with kidney disease (see "Cautions and Warnings").

Generic Name

Epsiprantel (EP-sih-pran-tel)

Brand Name

Cestex [V]

Type of Drug

Anthelmintic/dewormer

Prescribed for

Dipylidium caninum and *Taenia pisiformis* tapeworm in dogs and *D. caninum* and *T. taeniaeformis* tapeworm in cats.

General Information

Epsiprantel paralyzes the tapeworm, causing it to detach from the intestinal wall of the host animal. The host digests the detached worm, and worm fragments are seldom seen in the feces. Very little of the drug is absorbed systemically and most is excreted unchanged in the feces.

Tapeworms have distinctive larval and adult forms. The larva generally infects an intermediate host. Fleas are the intermediate hosts for *D. caninum*. Rodents and rabbits are intermediate hosts for *Taenia* species. Dogs and cats become infected after eating the intermediate host and reinfection is likely unless this is prevented. *D. caninum* is the most common tapeworm in the U.S. *D. caninum* infection is contagious and may spread to other animals and people (see *Zoonotic Diseases of Dogs and Cats*). It may infect children who accidentally ingest infected fleas. Effective flea control greatly reduces, and may eliminate, the incidence of reinfection, the need for retreatment, and the risk of human infection (see *Fipronil*).

Cautions and Warnings

■ For use in dogs and cats only. Not labeled for use in puppies or kittens under 7 weeks (see "Special Populations").

■ Contact your veterinarian if you think your dog or cat may be having an adverse reaction to epsiprantel.

■ U.S. federal law restricts the use of this drug by or on the lawful written or oral order of a licensed veterinarian within the context of a valid veterinarian-client-patient relationship.

Possible Side Effects

▼ Rare: vomiting and diarrhea.

Food and Drug Interactions

None known.

Usual Dose

A single dose is usually effective in dogs and cats, but measures should be taken to prevent reinfection (see "General Information").

Dogs: 2.5 mg/lb.
Cats: 1.25 mg/lb.
Drug Form: 12.5-, 25-, 50-, and 100-mg film-coated tablets.

Overdosage

Signs of overdose are not likely. None were reported in dogs given 36 times the recommended dose. Occasional vomiting may be seen in kittens given massive overdoses. In case of accidental ingestion or overdose, contact your veterinarian or the National Animal Poison Control Center. ALWAYS bring the prescription bottle or container with you if you go for treatment.

Special Populations

Pregnancy/Lactation

Studies have not confirmed that epsiprantel is safe to use in pregnant or breeding animals; however, adverse effects on the fetus are unlikely because the drug is not absorbed systemically.

Puppies/Kittens

The manufacturer suggests that epsiprantel not be used in puppies or kittens under 7 weeks old. However, there are no reports of adverse effects at this age.

Senior Animals

This drug is safe to use in senior animals.

Generic Name

Erythromycin (eh-rith-roe-MYE-sin) [G]

Most Common Brand Names

E.E.S. [H]

E-Mycin [H]

Eramycin [H]

EryPed [H]

Ery-Tab [H]

Erythrocin Stearate [H]

Erythromycin Base Film Tabs [H]

Type of Drug

Macrolide antibiotic.

Prescribed for

Infections susceptible to this antibiotic.

General Information

Erythromycin is an antibiotic that can either kill bacteria or inhibit bacterial growth depending on the bacterial organism and the dose. It is often used in animals allergic to penicillin. It is the antibiotic of choice for *Campylobacter* infections. *Campylobacter* can cause acute diarrhea in dogs and cats. In dogs, it is also prescribed for skin infections caused by *Staphylococcus intermedius* and for bacterial prostatitis caused by *Staphylococcus* and *Streptococcus.* At low doses erythromycin stimulates gastric motility and can be used as an anti-emetic.

There are different forms of the drug—erythromycin, erythromycin estolate, and erythromycin ethylsuccinate—which are based on slight differences in their chemistry.

Cautions and Warnings

■ Erythromycin is FDA approved for use in cats and dogs.

■ Erythromycin is excreted by the liver. It should be used with caution in animals with preexisting liver problems.

■ U.S. federal law restricts the use of this drug by or on the lawful written or oral order of a licensed veterinarian within the context of a valid veterinarian-client-patient relationship.

Possible Side Effects

▼ Common: diarrhea, vomiting, and decreased appetite.

Drug Interactions

• Erythromycin may slow the clearance of theophylline, causing increased theophylline levels and possible toxicity.

• Erythromycin may increase blood levels of terfenadine. This drug interaction may lead to serious cardiac toxicity.

• Erythromycin may increase the anticoagulant effects of warfarin. Your animal's warfarin dose may need to be decreased.

• Erythromycin may inhibit the metabolism of methylprednisolone.

• Erythromycin should not be used with lincomycin, clindamycin, chloramphenicol, or penicillin.

• Erythromycin may increase digoxin levels. Your animal's digoxin dose may need to be decreased.

• Erythromycin levels may be increased in animals taking phenytoin.

Food Interactions

Food will decrease the absorption of erythromycin. However, if erythromycin upsets your animal's stomach, it may be better tolerated if given with food.

Usual Dose

Dogs: 5–11 mg/lb orally 2–3 times a day. Antiemetic—0.3–0.5 mg/lb orally 3 times a day.

Cats: 5–11 mg/lb orally 2–3 times a day.

Drug Form: 125-, 200-, 250-, 333-, 400-, and 500-mg tablets and capsules and 20, 25, 40, 50, 80, and 100 mg/ml oral suspensions.

Overdosage

Erythromycin is generally a very safe drug. Oral overdose may cause exaggerated side effects, vomiting, diarrhea, and stomach discomfort. In case of accidental ingestion or overdose, contact your veterinarian or the National Animal Poison Control Center. ALWAYS bring the prescription bottle or container with you if you go for treatment.

Special Information

Like any medication, erythromycin should only be given when prescribed by a veterinarian for a specific illness. Always give the antibiotic exactly as directed, including the number of pills and length of time. If you stop too early, the infection is likely to recur even if the animal appeared better after only a few days.

Special Populations

Pregnancy/Lactation

Erythromycin crosses the placenta and is present in breast milk. It should only be used when the benefits outweigh the risks.

Puppies/Kittens

No studies have been performed in puppies or kittens, but erythromycin is used in infants and children.

Senior Animals

Erythromycin should be safe to use in senior animals with normal liver function.

Generic Name

Erythropoietin (uh-RITH-roe-poi-ET-in)

Most Common Brand Names

Epogen [H]   Marogen [H]

Type of Drug

Hormone that stimulates red blood cell production by the bone marrow.

Prescribed for

Anemia caused by kidney failure.

General Information

Erythropoietin is a hormone produced by the kidneys that stimulates the bone marrow to produce red blood cells (RBCs). In chronic kidney failure, the kidneys can no longer produce erythropoietin. Because of the lack of erythropoietin and other factors in chronic disease, anemia is almost always a complication of kidney failure. Anemia may significantly interfere with quality of life by causing weakness and exercise intolerance. Animals will often improve significantly if the anemia can be reversed. Improvements in appetite, energy, weight gain, alertness, strength, and playfulness are seen in most patients. Epogen and Marogen are genetically engineered recombinant human erythropoietins made for use in people. They have replaced transfusions and androgens (male hormones) for treatment of anemia in people with chronic kidney failure. They are proving useful in the treatment and supportive care of animals with chronic kidney failure.

Cautions and Warnings

■ Erythropoietin is not FDA approved for use in dogs or cats, but there have been promising results from clinical trials, and it is considered accepted practice to use erythropoietin for the treatment of anemia in chronic kidney failure.

■ Animals may develop antibodies to human erythropoietin after repeated injections. This makes the treatment ineffective. Treatment should be discontinued if the animal develops antibodies to erythropoietin, as allergic reactions are possible.

■ Erythropoietin should be avoided in animals with iron deficiency or high blood pressure. Oral or injectable iron supplements should be used during treatment.

■ Contact your veterinarian if you think your dog or cat may be having an adverse reaction to erythropoietin.

■ U.S. federal law restricts the use of this drug by or on the lawful written or oral order of a licensed veterinarian within the context of a valid veterinarian-client-patient relationship.

Possible Side Effects

▼ Common: 25% to 30% of animals will develop antibodies to recombinant human erythropoietin, making the therapy ineffective.

▼ Rare: seizures, high blood pressure and iron depletion (see "Overdosage").

Drug Interactions

None known.

Food Interactions

Oral iron supplements should be given to animals receiving erythropoietin.

Usual Dose

Dogs and Cats: starting dose—100-200 U/lb 3 times a week until the animal is no longer anemic. Maintenance dose—150–200 U/lb once or twice a week. Maintenance dose depends on each individual's response to treatment.

Drug Form: liquid for injection under the skin.

Overdosage

Overdoses will cause the hematocrit or packed cell volume (PCV)—measures of the number of red blood cells—to go too high. The PCV should be checked once or twice a week after the start of treatment to monitor response to treatment and prevent overshooting the target PCV range. Seizures and high blood pressure could result from overdosing and a high PCV. In case of accidental overdose, contact your veterinarian or the National Animal Poison Control Center. ALWAYS bring the prescription bottle or container with you if you go for treatment.

Special Information

Erythropoietin should probably be reserved for those animals with a PCV less than 25%. Clinical signs usually start when the PCV falls below 30%, but the risks and expense of treatment may outweigh the benefits for those with moderate anemia and minimal disability.

Special Populations

Pregnancy/Lactation
Not applicable—animals with chronic kidney failure would not be bred.

Puppies/Kittens
Not applicable—chronic kidney failure cannot occur in animals this young.

Senior Animals
Erythropoietin should be safe to use in older animals—the most likely age group for chronic kidney failure. It should be avoided or used with caution in animals with seizures, high blood pressure, or iron deficiency, as it may make all of these problems worse.

Type of Drug

Estrogens (ES-troe-jens)

Brand Names

Generic Ingredient: Diethylstilbestrol (DES)
Stilphostrol [H]

Generic Ingredient: Estradiol Cypionate [G]
ECP [V]

Generic Ingredient: Conjugated Estrogens
Premarin [H]

Prescribed for

Estrogen-responsive urinary incontinence in spayed female dogs, prevention of pregnancy after mismating in female dogs and cats, and treatment of certain estrogen-responsive cancer.

General Information

Estrogens are steroid hormones produced by the ovary in females. They interact with many other hormones to regulate all aspects of reproduction. Estrogens are needed for the normal development and maintenance of female sex organs and secondary sex characteristics. In general, they oppose the effect of progesterone (see *Progestins*), the other major ovarian hormone. Estrogens inhibit ovulation, interfere with implantation of embryos in the uterus, and inhibit lactation.

DES and estradiol cypionate are the most commonly used estrogens in small animal veterinary practice. Estradiol is a naturally occurring estrogen and estradiol cypionate is a long-acting injectable formulation marketed for use in livestock. DES is a synthetic nonsteroidal compound with estrogenic activity marketed for human use. It is currently off the market due to adverse side effects in humans, but existing stocks may still be available.

Estradiol cypionate and DES have been used to prevent pregnancy in cats and dogs. This use is out of favor. DES is not very effective. Estradiol cypionate is effective, but serious side effects are fairly common and there are safer alternatives available.

Estrogens are commonly used to treat urinary incontinence in spayed females. This type of incontinence is caused by decreased urethral muscle tone. It is a common problem in spayed females and causes dribbling when the dog is resting or sleeping. Estrogens increase the urethral tone and prevent the urine from leaking. Estradiol cypionate is effective, but not recommended because of the risk of serious side effects with long-acting preparations. DES is effective and the risk of side effects is low at the dose normally used. Conjugated estrogen products available for humans are also effective and their use is increasing as DES becomes harder to obtain.

Estrogens have been used to treat some tumors. They interfere with growth stimulated by other hormones such as progesterone and testosterone. The risk of side effects needs to be weighed carefully against the projected benefits.

Cautions and Warnings

■ Estrogen is contraindicated during pregnancy. It may cause birth defects and bone marrow suppression in the fetus.

■ Contact your veterinarian if you think your dog or cat may be having an adverse reaction to estrogen.

■ There are no FDA approved estrogen products on the market for dogs or cats, but it is accepted practice to use some of the available human label products.

■ U.S. federal law restricts the use of this drug by or on the lawful written or oral order of a licensed veterinarian within the context of a valid veterinarian-client-patient relationship.

Possible Side Effects

The incidence of side effects depends on the preparation and dosage. The long-acting products are more likely to produce severe side effects. Side effects include signs of estrus, lethargy, diarrhea, vomiting, vaginal discharge, pyometra (serious uterine infection with pus accumulating in the uterus), excessive water consumption, excessive urination, aplastic anemia, and bleeding; feminization may be seen in males on long-term treatment.

Drug Interactions

• Rifampin, phenobarbital, and phenylbutazone and other drugs known to induce liver enzymes may interfere with the activity of estrogen. Whether this is clinically significant is not clear.

• Estrogens may enhance corticosteroid activity and suppression of the adrenal glands.

• Estrogens may decrease the activity of anticoagulants.

Food Interactions

None known.

Usual Dose

Dogs
   DES: for urinary incontinence—0.1–1 mg/dog once a day for 1–5 days, then once a week. For mismating—0.1–1 mg/dog once a day for 5 days. For tumors—0.1–1 mg once every 1–2 days.

Estradiol Cypionate: for mismating—0.01–0.02 mg/lb injected into a muscle (IM) once within 72 hours of mating. Total dose should not exceed 1 mg/dog. *Conjugated estrogens:* For urinary incontinence—0.3–0.625 mg/dog once every 4 days.

Cats
DES: for tumors—0.05–0.1 mg total dose once a day.
Estradiol Cypionate: for mismating—0.125–0.25 mg total dose IM within 3–5 days of mating.

Drug Form
DES—0.1-, 0.25-, 0.5-, 1-, and 5-mg tablets.
Estradiol Injection—2 mg/ml in 50-ml vials.

Overdosage

Bone marrow suppression with decreased red and white cells, and platelet counts may progress to bleeding and fatal aplastic anemia in dogs and cats. High doses of DES given for prolonged periods may cause ovarian tumor in dogs. Side effects in cats given 1 mg/lb of DES once a day may cause heart, liver, and pancreatic lesions and death secondary to bone marrow suppression. In case of accidental ingestion or overdose, contact your veterinarian or the National Animal Poison Control Center. ALWAYS bring the prescription bottle or container with you if you go for treatment.

Special Information

Estrogens have serious and sometimes fatal side effects. Discuss the risks of estrogen use with your veterinarian, and ask about alternatives such as phenylpropanolamine (see *Phenylpropanolamine*) for urinary incontinence and prostaglandins (see *Prostaglandins*) or spaying for mismating. Cancer treatment is improving constantly. The best way to find out the current state of the art is to consult a veterinary oncologist. Increasing numbers of specialists are working in private practice. Ask your veterinarian or the nearest veterinary school for a referral.

Special Populations

Pregnancy/Lactation
Estrogens may cause abortion and birth defects. Not recommended for use in pregnant or lactating dogs or cats.

Puppies/Kittens
Estrogens are not recommended for use in puppies or kittens.

Senior Animals
Severe side effects such as bone marrow suppression are more common in senior animals particularly with high doses. The lowest effective dose should be used in senior animals and other treatments considered either in place of or combined with estrogens.

Type of Drug
Fatty Acids

Brand Names

3V Caps Ⓥ	Efa-Z Plus Ⓥ
Aftercare Ⓥ	F.A. Caps Ⓥ
Arthricare Ⓥ	F.A. Caps ES Ⓥ
DermCaps Ⓥ	Omega EFA Ⓥ
Efa-Caps Ⓥ	Palamega Ⓥ
Efavite Ⓥ	Pet-Derm Ⓥ

Prescribed for

Allergy, inflammation, dermatitis, itching, arthritis, improvement in skin and haircoat, eosinophilic granuloma complex and miliary dermatitis in cats, and cancer.

General Information

Fatty acids are one type of lipid, the term used for a variety of fatty materials such as fat, oil, and wax. A molecule or one chemical unit of fat is made of three fatty acids (carbon chains) attached to a glycerol, hence the name triglyceride. Fats are called saturated or unsaturated, depending on the number of carbon double bonds along the fatty acid chain. Saturated means "saturated" with hydrogen ions and therefore fewer double bonds. Less saturated or unsaturated means less hydrogen and more double bonds. Omega-3 and omega-6 refer to the position of the first double bond along the fatty acid chain.

Essential fatty acids are those fatty acids that cannot be made by the body, but must be obtained through food. They include the omega-6 and omega-3 fatty acids. The essential fatty acids, linoleic and linolenic, are necessary for normal skin and haircoat. Fatty acids are the building blocks of all of the cell walls in the body. Fatty acids are also the building blocks of prostaglandins (PGs), which control inflammation, and of many other substances that control blood pressure, blood clotting, and other body functions. There has been much research recently on the fats that are rich in omega-3 fatty acids (such as fish oils), and in linolenic acid, which is found in large amounts in evening primrose oil and borage seed oil. There is a lot of interest in these oils because there is growing evidence that these fatty acids play an important role in inflammation, heart and vascular disease, and even cancer. It may be possible to modulate the inflammatory response in a number of conditions by altering the dietary fatty acid ratios, thereby pushing prostaglandin production down the path to the anti-inflammatory PGs, instead of the inflammatory PGs. Dietary fatty acids and oils may be given as supplements. There are also a number of dog and cat foods now made with adjusted ratios of fatty acids, more omega-3 and less omega-6.

Cautions and Warnings

■ Increased bleeding times and decreased platelet function have been seen in human patients given fish oils. Fish oils should be used with caution in animals with bleeding or clotting disorders.

■ Rarely, some animals may become more itchy or lethargic on fatty acid supplements.

■ Contact your veterinarian if you think your dog or cat may be having an adverse reaction to fatty acid supplements.

■ Use of these supplements should be by or on the lawful written or oral order of a licensed veterinarian within the context of a valid veterinarian-client-patient relationship.

Possible Side Effects

▼ Rare: increased itching, lethargy.

Drug Interactions

• Fatty acid supplements should be used with caution in animals receiving anticoagulants such as aspirin, warfarin, or heparin.

Food Interactions

None known.

Usual Dose

Because of the unique nature of each commercially available product, follow label directions. Consult your veterinarian for advice on which product or type of fatty acid supplement is best for your dog or cat.

Drug Form: capsules, liquids, and tablets.

Overdosage

Vomiting and diarrhea may occur with high doses of fatty acid supplements. In case of accidental ingestion or overdose, contact your veterinarian or the National Animal Poison Control Center. ALWAYS bring the prescription bottle or container with you if you go for treatment.

Special Information

There are a variety of fatty acid supplements available over the counter for human use. The exact effects of many of these supplements on various disease states are not known. Evening primrose oil has been shown to help the majority of dogs with allergic skin disease. Derm Caps have been shown to improve symptoms of arthritis in dogs. Omega-3 fatty acid supplements may be helpful in those animals with increased risks of clotting, such as cats with cardiomyopathy; or dogs with Cushing's disease, heartworm disease, or chronic kidney failure. Consult your veterinarian about the benefits of fatty acid supplements for your animal.

Special Populations

Pregnancy/Lactation

There are no safety studies for fatty acid supplements in pregnant dogs or cats. They should be avoided in pregnant and lactating animals unless the benefits outweigh the risks.

Puppies/Kittens

Fatty acid supplements should be avoided in puppies and kittens as their safety has not been established.

Senior Animals

Fatty acid supplements should be safe to use in older animals.

Generic Name

Febantel (FEB-un-tul)

Brand Names

Combination Products

Generic Ingredients: Febantel + Praziquantel
RM Parasiticide-10 V

*Generic Ingredients: Febantel + Praziquantel + Pyrantel
Pamoate*
Drontal Plus for Dogs V

Type of Drug

Anthelmintic/dewormer.

Prescribed for

Dogs: roundworm (*Toxocara canis, Toxascaris leonina*), hookworm (*Ancylostoma caninum, Uncinaria stenocephala*), and whipworm (*Trichuris vulpis*).

Cats: roundworm (*Toxocara cati*) and hookworm (*Ancylostoma tubaeforme*).

General Information

Febantel is classified as a probenzimidazole. It is rapidly absorbed and converted to the active metabolites, fenbendazole and oxfendazole, which belong to the benzimidazole group. Thiabendazole, the first benzimidazole, was developed around 1960 and is credited with being the first modern dewormer. Since then, a number of related drugs have been developed in the search for safe and effective dewormers for all species of animals and humans. This group of drugs kills the parasite by blocking its energy metabolism.

Febantel is a broad-spectrum dewormer that is very effective against roundworm, hookworm, and whipworm. Roundworm and hookworm are contagious and may spread to other animals and to people and are therefore a potential public health risk. Roundworm is responsible for visceral larva migrans and hookworm for cutaneous larva migrans (see *Zoonotic Diseases of Dogs and Cats*).

Roundworm and hookworm live in the intestine and their eggs pass in the feces to the environment. Animals and humans that come in contact with anything contaminated with feces and parasite eggs are at risk of infection.

There are no products currently on the U.S. market that contain only febantel; however, it is available in combination products.

Cautions and Warnings

■ Contact your veterinarian if you think your dog or cat may be having an adverse reaction to febantel.

■ U.S. federal law restricts the use of this drug by or on the lawful written or oral order of a licensed veterinarian within the context of a valid veterinarian-client-patient relationship.

Possible Side Effects

Side effects at the recommended dose are rare and generally mild.

▼ Rare: salivation, vomiting or gagging, diarrhea, loss of appetite, and, in cats only, depression.

Drug Interactions

None known.

Food Interactions

Efficacy is increased when given with food.

Usual Dose

Febantel

Puppies and Kittens (younger than 6 months): 6.8 mg/lb once a day for 3 days.

Dogs and Cats: 4.5 mg/lb once a day for 3 days or 16.3 mg/lb once.

Drug Form: Currently not available for use in dogs and cats except as combination products.

Drontal Plus for Dogs

Dogs: tablets for small dogs (less than 26 lbs): 2–4 lbs—0.5 tablets; 5–7 lbs—1.0 tablets; 8–12 lbs—1.5 tablets; 13–18 lbs—2.0 tablets; 19–25 lbs—2.5 tablets. Tablets for medium and large dogs (over 26 lbs): 26–30 lbs—1 tablet.

Drug Form: tablets for small dogs—113.4 mg febantel + 22.7 mg praziquantel + 22.7 mg pyrantel pamoate. Tablets for medium and large dogs—340.2 mg febantel + 68.0 mg praziquantel + 68.0 mg pyrantel pamoate.

RM Parasiticide-10
Puppies and Kittens: 1 ml/5 lb once a day for 3 days.
Dogs and Cats: 1 ml/7.5 lb once a day for 3 days.
Drug Form: Paste contains 34 mg febantel + 3.4 mg praziquantel/ml.

Overdosage

Transient salivation, diarrhea, vomiting, and loss of appetite occur in dogs and cats given 15 times the recommended dose and in puppies and kittens given 10 times the recommended dose. The median lethal dose (the dose at which 50% of animals will die, or LD50) is 1,000 times the recommended dose. In case of accidental ingestion or overdose, contact your veterinarian or the National Animal Poison Control Center. ALWAYS bring the prescription bottle or container with you if you go for treatment.

Special Populations

Pregnancy/Lactation
Febantel, by itself, is considered safe when used as directed in pregnant animals; however, the combination products containing febantel and praziquantel may cause an increase in early abortion and should not be used in pregnant dogs and cats. There are no specific contraindications for use in lactating dogs and cats.

Puppies/Kittens
These medications are safe when used as directed in puppies and kittens.

Senior Animals
These medications are safe when used as directed in senior dogs and cats.

Generic Name

Fenbendazole (fen-BEN-duh-zole)

Brand Name

Panacur [V]

Type of Drug

Anthelmintic/dewormer.

Prescribed for

Dogs: roundworm (*Toxocara canis, Toxascaris leonina*), hookworm (*Ancylostoma caninum, Uncinaria stenocephala*), whipworm (*Trichuris vulpis*), tapeworm (*Taenia pisiformis*), lungworm (*Capillaria aerophilia, Filaroides hirthi*), and lung fluke (*Paragonimus kellicoti*).

Cats: roundworm (*Toxocara cati, T. leonina*), hookworm (*Ancylostoma tubaeforme, A. braziliense, Uncinaria steno-cephala*), tapeworm (*Taenia taeniaformis*), lungworm (*Aelurostrongylus abstrusus, Capillaria aerophilia*), and lung fluke (*Paragonimus kellicoti*).

General Information

Fenbendazole is classified as a benzimidazole. The parent drug, thiabendazole, was developed around 1960 and is credited with being the first modern dewormer. Since then, extensive research has developed a number of related drugs that are safe and effective against a broad spectrum of parasites in all species of animals and humans. This group of drugs kills the parasite by disrupting its energy metabolism.

Fenbendazole is FDA approved for use in dogs and a number of other species, including a number of wild cat species. It is not labeled for use in domestic cats, but is widely prescribed and appears to be one of the most effective and safe dewormers currently on the market.

It is labeled for use against roundworm, hookworm, and whipworm, the major intestinal parasites of dogs. It removes *Taenia* tapeworm but not the very common *Dipylidium caninum*. It is often used for parasitic infections that are not listed on the package label, including lungworm, lung fluke, *Strongyloides,* and *Giardia*.

Fenbendazole is used to treat a number of zoonotic para-sites. Roundworm is responsible for visceral larva migrans and hookworm for cutaneous larva migrans. Giardia causes diar-rhea in animals and humans. These parasites may be transmit-ted through contaminated food, water, or other material (See *Zoonotic Diseases in Dogs and Cats*).

Cautions and Warnings

■ Contact your veterinarian if you think your dog or cat may be having an adverse reaction to fenbendazole.

■ U.S. federal law restricts the use of this drug by or on the lawful written or oral order of a licensed veterinarian within the context of a valid veterinarian-client-patient relationship.

Possible Side Effects

▼ Rare: vomiting.

Drug Interactions

None known.

Food Interactions

Efficacy is increased when given with food.

Usual Dose

Single doses (even at high dosages) are not effective in dogs and cats. At least 3 consecutive daily doses must be given.

Dogs and Cats: 23 mg/lb for 3 consecutive days. Other dosage schedules may be indicated for some parasitic infec-tions.

Drug Form: 222 mg/g (22.2%) granules. Liquid and paste for-mulations marketed for large animals are also used in dogs and cats.

Overdosage

Doses up to 100 times the recommended dose are tolerated without serious side effects. An accidental overdose may cause minor vomiting and diarrhea. Hypersensitivity reactions to dying parasites have been seen, particularly at high dosages. In case of accidental ingestion or overdose, contact your veterinarian or the National Animal Poison Control Center.

ALWAYS bring the prescription bottle or container with you if
you go for treatment.

Special Populations

Pregnancy/Lactation
Febendazole is considered safe to use in pregnant and lactating animals. It greatly reduces transmission of roundworm and hookworm from mother to puppies when given at the normal dose from the 40th day of pregnancy through the 14th day after whelping.

Puppies/Kittens
Febendazole is considered safe to use in puppies and kittens.

Senior Animals
Febendazole is considered safe to use in older animals.

Generic Name

Fentanyl (FEN-tuh-nil) [G]

Brand Names

Duragesic (transdermal) [H]   Sublimaze (injection) [H]

Type of Drug

Opioid (narcotic) analgesic.

Prescribed for

Relief of chronic or postoperative pain in cats and dogs.

General Information

Fentanyl is a powerful pain-relieving narcotic. It has been difficult in the past to adequately control severe pain in cats. Aspirin and other NSAIDs only relieve mild to moderate pain, and narcotics have limited use in cats, as they tend to produce excitement. Butorphanol may be used in cats, but is not very practical because it does not last very long and must be injected frequently (see *Butorphanol*). Fentanyl has recently been marketed in a transdermal patch for use in people. It provides slow and continuous delivery of fentanyl through the skin. These patches have been used in cats and dogs. They are well tolerated and seem to provide reasonable pain relief that is appropriate for treatment of chronic or postoperative pain.

Cautions and Warnings

For Owners/Handlers

■ Fentanyl is a controlled substance that is regulated by the Drug Enforcement Agency. It is a violation of federal law for fentanyl to be administered to animals except by a veterinarian registered with the DEA. Fentanyl can produce drug dependence similar to that produced by morphine; therefore, it has the potential for abuse.

■ Wash with copious amounts of water if the gel from the patch comes in contact with skin.

■ Keep both used and unused patches out of the reach of children. Used patches should be folded so that the adhesive side of the system adheres to itself and flushed down the toilet immediately on removal.

For Animals

■ The fentanyl patch is not FDA approved for use in dogs or cats. It is used in both species, however, and is considered accepted practice.

■ Fentanyl should be used with caution in patients with impaired liver or kidney function or those with heart disease and slow heart rates.

■ Fentanyl uptake from the patch may be greater if the patient has a fever or is in contact with an external heat source. Increased monitoring for side effects is indicated.

■ Contact your veterinarian if you think your dog or cat may be having an adverse reaction to fentanyl.

■ U.S. federal law restricts the use of this drug by or on the lawful written or oral order of a licensed veterinarian within the context of a valid veterinarian-client-patient relationship.

Possible Side Effects

▼ Rare: respiratory depression and slow heart rate (both usually dose related).

Drug Interactions

• There may be additive central nervous system or respiratory depression when fentanyl is used with other central nervous system depressants, such as anesthetics, antihistamines, phenothiazines (acepromazine), barbiturates (phenobarbital), or other tranquilizers. Fentanyl should not be used for 14 days after use of monoamine oxidase inhibitors (MAOIs; amitraz).

Food Interactions

None known.

Usual Dose

Dogs: 1 fentanyl patch (2.5 mg) applied to a shaved patch of skin on the chest or back. Pain relief may last up to 3 days. Patches should only be applied by your veterinarian to ensure proper placement and delivery of the drug. Fentanyl—0.01–0.02 mg/lb by injection under the skin, in the muscle, or in a vein.

Cats: 1 fentanyl patch (2.5 mg) applied to a shaved patch of skin on the chest. Pain relief may last up to 3 days. Patches should only be applied by your veterinarian to ensure proper placement and delivery of the drug.

Drug Form: 2.5-, 5-, 7.5- and 10-mg patches and 0.05 mg/ml injectable.

Overdosage

Fentanyl overdose may cause slow respiration and heart rate. If you notice slow breathing, remove the patch and contact your veterinarian immediately. In case of accidental ingestion or overdose, contact your veterinarian or the National Animal Poison Control Center. ALWAYS bring the prescription bottle or container with you if you go for treatment.

Special Populations

Pregnancy/Lactation
Fentanyl damages the fetus in rodents and should not be used during pregnancy or lactation unless the benefits outweigh the risks.

Puppies/Kittens
Fentanyl should not be used in puppies or kittens.

Senior Animals
Fentanyl should be safe to use in senior animals with normal kidney and liver function (see "Cautions and Warnings").

Brand Name

Filaribits Plus ⊽

Generic Ingredients

Diethylcarbamazine (DEC) + Oxibendazole

Type of Drug

Heartworm preventive, anthelmintic/dewormer.

Prescribed for

Heartworm (*Dirofilaria immitis*) and hookworm (*Anclylostoma caninum*) prevention, and whipworm (*Trichuris vulpis*) and roundworm (*Toxocara canis*) removal in dogs.

General Information

Daily low dose DEC prevents heartworm disease by killing infective larvae after they are transmitted from the mosquito and before they reach the heart. DEC also kills the microfilarial stage of *D. immitis*. However, it is not used for this purpose because it may cause severe, and sometimes fatal, systemic reactions (see *Diethylcarbamazine*).

Oxibendazole belongs to the benzimidazole family of dewormers and acts by blocking energy metabolism of sensitive parasites. Oxibendazole is the cause of liver damage occasionally associated with the use of this drug combination. The liver damage is not related to dose and there is no reliable way to identify whether an individual dog is at risk.

The combination of DEC and oxibendazole prevents heartworm disease and hookworm infection. Preexisting hookworm infections should be treated before starting this medication. This product also removes existing whipworm and roundworm infections, and prevents reinfection as long as the dog continues to be dosed daily.

Cautions and Warnings

■ Test dogs for heartworm and microfilaria before using Filaribits Plus. Do not use in dogs with adult heartworm or microfilaria until they have been treated. Dogs must be free of microfilaria before giving this drug combination. Dogs on year-round daily heartworm preventive treatment should be retested for microfilaria every 6 months.

■ Treat existing hookworm infection before starting this combination.

■ This product may cause liver damage. Avoid or use with caution in dogs with a history of liver damage or disease. Dogs with a history of liver disease, or those receiving other drugs that may cause liver damage, may be at increased risk and should be carefully monitored. Most dogs recover once the drug is discontinued, but fatalities may occur. Contact your veterinarian if you think your dog or cat may be having an adverse reaction to Filaribits Plus.

■ U.S. federal law restricts the use of this drug by or on the lawful written or oral order of a licensed veterinarian within the context of a valid veterinarian-client-patient relationship.

Possible Side Effects

▼ Rare: liver damage (loss of appetite, vomiting, depression, yellow gums and eyes, weight loss, increased drinking and urination, loss of coordination, and dark colored urine).

Drug Interactions

• There are no specific drug interactions reported. Because of the risk of liver damage, it seems prudent to avoid using Filaribits Plus with other drugs that may cause liver damage. These include carprofen, phenylbutazone, phenobarbital and some of the other anticonvulsants, ketoconazole and related antifungal drugs, mibolerone, mebendazole, sulfonamides, sulfa/trimethoprim combinations, tetracycline, pennyroyal oil, azathioprine, and some antineoplastics, including methotrexate.

Food Interactions

None known.

Usual Dose

Dogs: 3 mg/lb DEC and 2.3 mg oxibendazole. Read label to determine the number of tablets for your dog.

Drug Form: chewable tablets containing 60-mg DEC and 45-

mg oxibendazole, 121-mg DEC and 91-mg oxibendazole, or 180-mg DEC and 136-mg oxibendazole.

Storage: Store at room temperature and protect from freezing.

Overdosage

Large overdoses may cause vomiting, diarrhea, and depression in dogs. In case of accidental ingestion or overdose, contact your veterinarian or the National Animal Poison Control Center. ALWAYS bring the prescription bottle or container with you if you go for treatment.

Special Information

Newer heartworm preventive drugs that are given only once-a-month, such as ivermectin and milbemycin oxime, have largely replaced DEC. The main advantage of the once-a-month drugs is a lower risk of serious side effects from accidentally treating a dog with active heartworm disease. Many owners also prefer the convenience of only medicating once a month. Some of the once-a-month products remove the most common intestinal parasites in addition to preventing heartworm. The same advantage is available in Filaribits Plus for owners who prefer a once-a-day product. Overall, Filaribits Plus remains a safe and effective alternative as long as treatment is administered daily without fail. Missing more than 1 daily dose in a row increases the risk of developing heartworm disease.

Special Populations

Specific Breeds
Doberman pinschers have an increased risk of liver disease, including that associated with DEC + oxibendazole.

Pregnancy/Lactation
Filaribits Plus is considered safe to use in pregnant and lactating dogs.

Puppies
This medication is considered safe to use in puppies of all ages.

Senior Animals
This medication is considered safe to use in senior animals.

Generic Name

Fipronil (FIH-proe-nil)

Brand Names

Frontline Spray Treatment [V]
Frontline Top Spot for Cats [V]
Frontline Top Spot for Dogs [V]

Type of Drug

Gamma aminobutyric acid (GABA) inhibitor, insecticide, and acaricide (kills ticks and mites).

Prescribed for

Killing fleas and all stages of the brown dog tick, American dog tick, lone star tick, and deer tick on dogs, puppies, cats, and kittens.

General Information

Fipronil is a new type of insecticide with a different action than any of the conventional flea and tick products including carbamates (see *Carbamates*), organophosphates (see *Organophosphate Insecticides*), and pyrethrins (see *Pyrethrins*). It acts on the GABA receptors in the parasite's central nervous system, causing paralysis and death. GABA is a chemical that transmits signals between nerves and is present in mammals only in the brain. Fipronil is unable to pass through the blood-brain barrier and therefore does not reach the brain. It is extremely safe and the cautionary statements on the package are limited to common sense precautions such as avoiding excessive contact and wearing gloves, which are required by the Environmental Protection Agency (EPA) for even the safest insecticides.

Fipronil is available as a spray and as a spot treatment to apply directly to the pet's skin (see "Usual Dose"). Fipronil is oil soluble and spreads over the entire body with the natural skin oils. It also accumulates in the sebaceous or oil glands. This acts as a reservoir that continues to be slowly released onto the skin and hair, giving long-term protection even after bathing, swimming, or being exposed to rain. Fipronil kills 100% of fleas and ticks within 24 to 48 hours, and continues to kill new fleas and ticks for a minimum of 30 days. Fleas and ticks do not need to bite before being killed and ticks are generally killed before they attach. This greatly reduces the risk of transmission of several diseases (see "Special Information"). Fipronil also kills larval and adult fleas in the environment because it remains active on fur that is shed. This greatly reduces or eliminates the need to use insecticides to treat the environment.

Fipronil is being tested or is already in use to control a number of parasites on other animal species, humans, and crop plants both in the U.S. and worldwide. It effectively kills a number of mite species, including the ear mite (*Otodectes cynotis*), scabies (*Sarcoptes scabiei* and *Notoedres cati*), and demodex (*Demodex canis*) mites of dogs and cats. These uses are not currently listed on the label or approved by the EPA. Fipronil is not soluble in water and does not enter the ground water. It has a very low impact on the environment and has been shown to be safe in a number of wild bird species, water animals, and mammals.

Cautions and Warnings

For Owners/Handlers

■ Not for human use. May be harmful if swallowed or absorbed through the skin. May cause eye irritation. Avoid breathing spray mist. Avoid contact with the area of application until dry. Wear household latex gloves. Wash hands with soap and water after handling this product. Contact your physician or poison control center in case of accidental ingestion by humans.

■ Flammable. Keep away from open flames, cigarettes, and high heat. Do not contaminate water, food, or feed by storage or disposal. Wrap original container in newspaper and discard in trash.

For Animals

■ For external use only. Do not get in eyes or mouth.

■ Avoid application for 48 hours before and after bathing because bathing temporarily removes the natural skin oils that help distribute the drug. Fipronil must be applied directly to the skin. It is not effective if applied on the fur.

■ Consult your veterinarian before using fipronil on animals receiving other treatments, insecticides, or drugs; or on animals that are sick, debilitated, or convalescing.

■ Contact your veterinarian if you think your dog or cat may be having an adverse reaction to fipronil.

■ It is a violation of federal law to use this product in a manner inconsistent with its labeling. For veterinary use only.

■ Call 1-800-660-1842 for 24-hour assistance.

Possible Side Effects

▼ Common: a greasy spot for about 24 hours after using the spot treatment and salivation after applying the spray due to the alcohol used to carry the fipronil.

▼ Rare: temporary irritation or hair loss at site of application.

Drug Interactions

None reported.

Usual Dose

Fipronil should be applied once a month for optimal control of fleas and ticks.

Dogs

Top Spot: 9.7% fipronil in premeasured pipettes. Part the fur and deposit entire contents of the pipette on the skin between the shoulder blades. Do not rub in.

Spray: 1–2 pumps/lb of the 250-ml bottle, or 3–6 pumps/lb of the 100-ml bottle. Ruffle the coat against the grain and spray. Dog should be damp to wet. Cover entire body. Spray onto gloved hand to apply on head and face. Apply outside or in a well-ventilated area, as the alcohol used in the spray may be irritating.

Cats

Top Spot: 9.7% fipronil in premeasured pipettes. Part the fur at the back of the neck and deposit entire contents of the pipette on the skin. Make sure the application is located so that the cat cannot ingest it while grooming. Do not rub in.

Spray: 1–2 pumps/lb of the 250-ml bottle or 3–6 pumps/lb of the 100-ml bottle. Apply in the same manner as for dogs.

Drug Form

Dogs: 0.67-ml, 1.34-ml, 2.68-ml pipettes for spot application.

Cats: 0.5-ml pipettes for spot application.
Spray: 0.29% 100-ml, 250-ml metered spray bottles.

Overdosage

Serious side effects from accidental ingestion of fipronil are unlikely. Dogs and cats dosed orally with over 70 and 25 times the recommended topical dose, respectively, showed no significant side effects. No side effects were reported in animals treated topically at 5 times the maximum recommended dose for 6 months. In case of accidental ingestion or overdose, contact your veterinarian or the National Animal Poison Control Center. ALWAYS bring the prescription bottle or container with you if you go for treatment.

Special Information

Flea control is very important and very much underrated by many pet owners. There is a tendency to consider fleas unavoidable and to ignore infestations. However, there are several new, extremely safe and effective flea control products available now that make elimination of fleas possible. Fleas are the number one cause of skin disease in dogs and cats. Heavy infestations cause itching that is often severe and that may cause loss of hair, weeping infected lesions commonly called hot spots, and weight loss. They are very annoying to both pets and owners. Many dogs and cats develop allergies to the saliva of biting fleas. These animals may have severe reactions to very low-level flea infestations. Fleas also transmit a number of diseases. They are the major transmitters of tapeworm (*Dipylidium caninum*) to dogs and cats. In some areas, they carry plague (*Yersinia pestis*), which may be transmitted to dogs, cats, and humans (see *Zoonotic Diseases of Dogs and Cats*).

Ticks transmit several very important diseases, including Lyme disease, Rocky Mountain spotted fever, ehrlichiosis, and babesiosis. All of these are potential zoonoses and significant public health concerns (see *Zoonotic Diseases of Dogs and Cats*). Keeping ticks from biting is the only way to prevent these serious and potentially fatal diseases, and fipronil is the safest and most effective tick control available to date. In areas where ticks are a severe problem, the manufacturer suggests that the spray may provide better coverage and control. The spray may also be used on the legs and belly in addition to the spot treatment. This is particularly useful for large dogs.

Special Populations

Pregnancy/Lactation
Fipronil is considered safe to use in pregnant and lactating cats and dogs.

Puppies/Kittens
The spray is approved for puppies and kittens from 2 days of age. The spot product is approved for use on puppies over age 8 weeks and kittens over age 12 weeks.

Senior Animals
Fipronil is considered safe to use on senior dogs and cats.

Generic Name

Fluconazole (flue-KON-uh-zole)

Brand Name
Diflucan [H]

Type of Drug
Antifungal.

Prescribed for
Susceptible superficial and deep (systemic) fungal infections, including those caused by *Dermatophytes* (ringworm), *Malassezia* and *Candida* (yeasts), *Cryptococcus, Coccidioides, Histoplasma, Aspergillus,* and *Blastomyces.*

General Information
Fluconazole was the first of the new triazole antifungals (see *Itraconazole*). It has a spectrum of action equal to or greater than amphotericin B or ketoconazole, and it is safer to use than either of these older antifungals. Because it may take 1 to 2 weeks to see a response to fluconazole, serious fungal infections may be treated with amphotericin B (see *Amphotericin B*) for a short time, followed by fluconazole. Fluconazole may be used to treat fungal infections of the skin and life-threatening systemic infections of bone, lung, gastrointestinal tract, urinary tract, and central nervous system. It is probably the drug of choice for cryptococcosis in cats. Cures were achieved in 28 of

29 cats with *Cryptococcus* infections of the nasal passages and skin of the head, and it was even effective in cats with feline immunodeficiency virus (FIV) infection. Long-term treatment (2 to 4 months) is often required for many of these infections, and some may never be completely cured. Most deep fungal infections should be treated for at least a month after symptoms are gone, and care should be taken because infection in people can occur from contact with infected animals (see *Zoonotic Diseases of Dogs and Cats*).

Cautions and Warnings

■ Fluconazole is not FDA approved for use in dogs or cats. It is commonly used and is considered accepted practice.

■ Clinical response to fluconazole may take 10 days to 2 weeks.

■ Fluconazole should be avoided in animals with liver disease.

■ The kidneys excrete fluconazole and the dose should be reduced in animals with decreased kidney function.

■ Contact your veterinarian if you think your dog or cat may be having an adverse reaction to fluconazole.

■ U.S. federal law restricts the use of this drug by or on the lawful written or oral order of a licensed veterinarian within the context of a valid veterinarian-client-patient relationship.

Possible Side Effects

▼ Common: mild decrease in appetite and increase in liver enzymes.

▼ Rare: allergic or anaphylactic reactions, liver damage, vomiting, and diarrhea.

Drug Interactions

• Fluconazole should not be given with terfenadine, astemizole, or cisapride, as fatal abnormal heart rhythms may occur.

• Antacids and H_2 blockers such as cimetidine decrease absorption of fluconazole. These drugs should be given 2 hours after the dose of fluconazole.

• The dose of warfarin may need to be decreased if fluconazole is given.

• Phenytoin or phenobarbital and fluconazole may alter each

other's metabolism, and animals receiving both should be monitored carefully for side effects.

• Fluconazole may prolong the effect of methylprednisolone.

• Cyclosporine, digoxin, and quinidine blood levels may be increased by fluconazole.

• Rifampin may decrease the blood levels of fluconazole.

• Fluconazole may cause severe hypoglycemia (low blood glucose) when used with oral hypoglycemic agents such as glipizide.

• Theophylline blood levels may be increased by fluconazole. Measurement of theophylline blood levels is recommended.

Food Interactions

Fluconazole should be given with meals to avoid gastrointestinal side effects.

Usual Dose

Dogs: 1.75–2.5 mg/lb orally twice a day.

Cats: 1.75-5 mg/lb orally twice a day.

Drug Form: 50-, 100-, 150- and 200-mg tablets; 10- and 40-mg/ml oral suspension; and 2 mg/ml injectable.

Overdosage

There is little specific information available on overdose of fluconazole. Symptoms of overdose in rodents included slow respiration, salivation, tearing, urine leaking, and purple mucous membranes (see "Possible Side Effects"). In case of accidental ingestion or overdose, contact your veterinarian or the National Animal Poison Control Center. ALWAYS bring the prescription bottle or container with you if you go for treatment.

Special Information

There are many alternatives available now for the treatment of both superficial and deep fungal infections. None of these treatments are FDA approved for use in animals. See *Boric Acid, Griseofulvin, Miconazole* and *Clotrimazole* for more information on treatment of superficial fungal infections. See *Amphotericin B, Itraconazole,* and *Ketoconazole* for more information on treatment of deep fungal infections. Fluconazole is very effective and safe antifungal therapy, but it is also expensive.

Special Populations

Pregnancy/Lactation
Fluconazole causes damage to the fetus and is excreted in milk; it should be avoided during pregnancy and lactation unless the benefits outweigh the risks.

Puppies/Kittens
Fluconazole should be avoided in puppies and kittens unless the potential benefits outweigh the risks.

Senior Animals
Fluconazole should be safe to use in older animals with normal liver and kidney function (see "Cautions and Warnings").

Generic Name

Fludrocortisone (floo-droe-KOR-tih-sone)

Brand Name
Florinef [H]

Type of Drug
Synthetic adrenal corticosteroid and mineralocorticoid.

Prescribed for
Adrenocortical insufficiency (hypoadrenocorticism, Addison's disease).

General Information
Corticosteroids are hormones normally produced by the adrenal gland. They are essential for life and affect every level of metabolism and function of all cells and organ systems. There are two major types of adrenal cortical hormones distinguished by their major effect. The glucocorticoids are also called glucocorticosteroids, corticosteroids, or simply steroids (see *Corticosteroids*). They are important in normal protein, carbohydrate, and fat metabolism. The mineralocorticoids primarily control salt and water balance in the body. They act on the kidney, causing it to retain sodium and excrete potassium. Normal mineralocorticoid activity requires functional kidneys.

Fludrocortisone acetate is a synthetic glucocorticoid that has significant mineralocorticoid activity. It is used to treat animals that have primary adrenal insufficiency (Addison's disease). Decreased mineralocorticoid and/or glucocorticoid production may result from adrenal tumors, infection, immune-mediated disease, or intentional destruction of the adrenal gland during treatment for overproduction of adrenal hormones—Cushing's disease (see *Mitotane*). Affected animals are weak; depressed; and often have a history of vomiting, diarrhea, loss of appetite, and collapse that responded to treatment with fluids and corticosteroids in the past. Addison's disease generally responds well to hormone replacement. Since fludrocortisone has both mineralocorticoid and glucocorticoid activity, additional glucocorticoids may not be needed. However, all patients should receive them during times of increased stress, surgery, or illness.

Adrenal insufficiency may also be caused by abruptly stopping long-term glucocorticoid administration; however, mineralocorticoid therapy is generally not needed in those cases.

Fludrocortisone is currently the only drug approved for mineralocorticoid replacement therapy and is FDA approved only for humans. Another drug, desoxycorticosterone pivalate (see *Desoxycorticosterone Pivalate (DOCP)*), is awaiting approval for use in dogs, but is currently available only as an experimental drug.

Electrolytes and kidney function should be checked regularly during treatment. Potassium may need to be supplemented if blood levels get too low. Owners should monitor their pet for signs of adrenal insufficiency and overdosage (see "Overdosage"), including a sudden weight gain or loss, and consult their veterinarian immediately if any are seen. This allows the treatment to be modified before major complications occur.

Cautions and Warnings

■ Fludrocortisone should not be used in animals with fungal infections because the glucocorticoid activity may depress the immune system.

■ Fludrocortisone is not FDA approved for use in dogs or cats, but its use to treat Addison's disease is accepted practice.

■ Contact your veterinarian if you think your dog or cat may be having an adverse reaction to fludrocortisone.

■ U.S. federal law restricts the use of this drug by or on the lawful written or oral order of a licensed veterinarian within the context of a valid veterinarian-client-patient relationship.

Possible Side Effects

Serious side effects are usually due to overdosage (see "Overdosage") or discontinuing treatment abruptly. Because fludrocortisone has glucocorticoid activity, it may produce side effects associated with those drugs (see *Corticosteroids*).

▼ Common: increased thirst and urination; relative resistance requiring increasing doses.

Drug Interactions

• The risk of low potassium levels is increased if fludrocortisone is administered with other potassium lowering drugs such as amphotericin B and furosemide.

• Fludrocortisone increases the risk of digitalis toxicity.

• Diuretics increase excretion of sodium and may counteract the effect of fludrocortisone.

• Fludrocortisone may increase the effects of anticoagulants such as warfarin or coumadin.

• Fludrocortisone may increase the required insulin dose in diabetics and it may reduce salicylate blood levels in animals receiving salicylate-containing drugs. The clinical significance of these interactions has not been determined.

• Barbiturates, phenytoin, or rifampin may increase metabolism of fludrocortisone and the dose may need to be increased.

• Anabolic steroids (stanozolol) increase the risk of edema (swelling).

Food Interactions

None known.

Usual Dose

Dogs: 0.009 mg/lb (0.1–1.0 mg total dose) orally once a day. Adjust based on blood electrolyte levels. These should be measured every 1–2 weeks initially and every 3–4 months during maintenance therapy.

Cats: 0.1 mg total dose orally once a day and adjust based on blood electrolyte levels. These should be measured every 1–2 weeks initially and every 3–4 months during maintenance therapy.

Drug Form 0.1-mg tablets.

Overdosage

Overdosage may cause increased thirst and urination, high blood pressure, edema, low blood potassium, weakness, and weight gain. Heart enlargement may occur with prolonged overdose. In case of accidental ingestion or overdose, contact your veterinarian or the National Animal Poison Control Center. ALWAYS bring the prescription bottle or container with you if you go for treatment.

Special Information

Increasing doses of fludrocortisone are often needed to control the signs of adrenal insufficiency. Adding salt to the diet may help stabilize these animals. Alternatively, DOCP may provide better control.

Special Populations

Pregnancy/Lactation
Adequate studies are not available, but corticosteroids may affect the fetus and are excreted in milk. Pregnant or nursing animals should not receive fludrocortisone unless the benefit clearly outweighs the risk.

Puppies/Kittens
Safety and effectiveness of this medication has not been established; use only if the benefit clearly outweighs the risk.

Senior Animals
There is no specific contraindication to use in senior animals provided they have adequate kidney function.

Generic Name

Fluoxetine (flue-OX-eh-tene)

Brand Name

Prozac [H]

Type of Drug

Psychotropic, antianxiety, tricyclic antidepressant.

Prescribed for

Compulsive behaviors, anxiety, and fear.

General Information

Fluoxetine is one of the tricyclic antidepressants (TCAs). TCAs are similar in structure to the phenothiazine tranquilizers (see *Acepromazine*). These chemicals block the movement of certain stimulant chemicals in and out of nerve endings, have a sedative effect, and counteract the effects of acetylcholine (a chemical of the parasympathetic nervous system). They work in the central nervous system (CNS) to inhibit serotonin and norepinephrine reuptake by nerve endings. Different TCAs differ in their potency and in their relative effects on serotonin and norepinephrine. Amitriptyline and imipramine (Tofranil) affect serotonin and norepinephrine equally, and are used primarily as antianxiety drugs. Clomipramine (Anafranil) and fluoxetine (Prozac) affect serotonin primarily and are anticompulsive drugs.

All undesirable behaviors have a learned component. Treatment of any undesirable behavior requires behavior modification (training based on scientific principles used to alter or change undesirable behaviors). Drugs are used in the treatment of dogs and cats with behavior problems because certain undesirable behaviors cannot be managed by behavior modification techniques alone. In such cases severe anxiety or fear, a strong hormonal component to behavior (as in maternal aggression), or a neurochemical imbalance in the brain (as in compulsive behaviors) prevents effective behavior modification. Drugs are only useful for certain specific types of behavior problems, and they should ONLY be used as an adjunct to behavior modification. When used in this way they enable behavior modification to be maximally effective.

Most psychotropic drugs used in veterinary medicine are not licensed for use in animals. There are few controlled studies in animals establishing dose, efficacy, or safety. The TCAs may inhibit learning. The long-term effects of these drugs are not known. There may be breed and individual differences in response to these drugs.

Fluoxetine is used in dogs to treat compulsive behaviors, now recognized to be conflict behaviors. These are behaviors that are related to normal behaviors, such as grooming, but are out of context, repetitive, exaggerated, and have no purpose. These behaviors include chewing the feet, licking one spot (lick granuloma), scratching, fly-snapping, circling and whirling, tail-chasing, pacing, rhythmic barking, flank-sucking, and self-mutilation in dogs, and wool-sucking and excessive grooming or self-mutilation in cats. Conflict behaviors occur when an animal is motivated to do something, but is physically prevented from doing so, or has two equally strong conflicting motivations. Once compulsive behavior is well established, the chemical changes in the brain are almost irreversible. At this point, environmental changes and behavior modification alone usually are not sufficient to treat compulsive disorder.

Fluoxetine may also be used to treat severe scratching related to allergic skin disease. This treatment is usually a last resort in those animals where corticosteroids, antihistamines, and hyposensitization have failed, or in whom there is suspicion that the scratching has become a compulsive behavior. It may be used in cats as an adjunct to treatment of compulsive behaviors, such as wool-sucking, and excessive grooming. Fluoxetine may be used to treat anxiety disorders, but amitriptyline (see *Amitriptyline*) is usually the drug of choice.

Cautions and Warning

For Owners/Handlers

■ KEEP OUT OF REACH OF CHILDREN! Children are very sensitive to the seizure-inducing and cardiotoxic effects of TCAs.

For Animals

■ Fluoxetine should be avoided in animals with liver disease, kidney failure, hyperthyroidism, glaucoma, seizures, heart failure, abnormal heart rhythms, or those on thyroid medication.

■ Most psychotropic drugs cause some degree of CNS depression and are sedative at higher doses. They may also interfere with learning.

■ Fluoxetine is not FDA approved for use in dogs or cats. It is used to treat compulsive disorders, and is considered accepted practice.

■ Contact your veterinarian if you think your dog or cat may be having an adverse reaction to fluoxetine.

■ U.S. federal law restricts the use of this drug by or on the lawful written or oral order of a licensed veterinarian within the context of a valid veterinarian-client-patient relationship.

Possible Side Effects

Fluoxetine may cause drowsiness, but this is usually due to overdosing. It may also cause vomiting and diarrhea, and should be given with food to avoid gastrointestinal (GI) upset. Urine retention may be a common side effect in cats on fluoxetine. A variety of adverse reactions to fluoxetine have been reported in people, including heart problems, seizures, hallucinations and other CNS signs, GI upset, allergic reactions, bone marrow depression, liver disease, hair loss, edema and lupus-like syndromes. These signs have not been reported in animals but are all potential side effects.

▼ Rare: urine retention and hyperexcitability.

Drug Interactions

• Because of additive effects, fluoxetine should be used cautiously with other anticholinergic (drugs that inhibit acetylcholine) and CNS depressant drugs.

• TCAs should not be used with methimazole because the risk of bone marrow suppression is increased.

• Cimetidine may decrease TCA metabolism and increase the risk of adverse reactions.

• TCAs should not be given with monoamine oxidase inhibitors (MAOIs).

• Use of TCAs with sympathomimetic agents (such as phenylpropanolamine and epinephrine) may increase the risks of abnormal heart rhythms, high blood pressure, and fever.

Food Interactions

Give with food to avoid GI upset.

Usual Dose

Dogs and Cats: 0.25-0.5 mg/lb orally once a day.
Drug Form: 10- and 20-mg pulvules (capsules) and 20 mg/5 ml oral liquid.

Overdosage

Signs of overdose may include depression, abnormal heart rhythms, low blood pressure, convulsions, coma, and death. In case of accidental ingestion or overdose, contact your veterinarian or the National Animal Poison Control Center. ALWAYS bring the prescription bottle or container with you if you go for treatment.

Special Information

There are a growing number of veterinary behavior specialists with effective treatments for most behavior problems. Ask your veterinarian or university referral service for the names of specialists in your area if you are having problems with the behavior of your dog or cat.

If there is no response to TCA drug treatment, consider the following. There may be additional behavior or other problems, the behavior modification technique may not be appropriate, may not be adequately explained or carried out by the owner, the drug may not be the best choice for the problem, or the dose and dosing interval may need to be modified. In some cases it may take 2 to 3 weeks for an effect to be seen. Discuss using a different drug with your veterinarian, if all of the preceding concerns have been attended to and the behavior is still not improving. Ask for a referral to a veterinary behavior specialist if you need further assistance.

Drugs should be discontinued *gradually* 2 to 3 weeks after the problem has resolved or improved. Reduce the dose but not the frequency of administration over a 3-week period. If owners cannot comply with behavior modification, most behavior experts suggest that drug therapy should be discontinued, as it will not be optimally effective, the problem is not likely to be corrected, and the continued use of TCAs is potentially risky. If there are adverse side effects, the drug should be discontinued. Dogs with hyperactivity or compulsive behaviors may need continual medication.

Special Populations

Pregnancy/Lactation
There are no studies on the safety of fluoxetine in pregnant or lactating dogs or cats. High doses cause birth defects in laboratory animals. Fluoxetine should be avoided unless the potential benefits outweigh the risks.

Puppies/Kittens
Fluoxetine should not be used in puppies or kittens.

Senior Animals
Fluoxetine should be safe to use in older dogs and cats who do not have heart, thyroid, kidney, or liver disease, or seizure disorders (see "Cautions and Warnings").

Generic Name

Furosemide (fue-ROE-seh-mide) [G]

Brand Names

Disal [V]   Furoject [V]
Diuride [V]   Lasix [H] [V]

Type of Drug

Diuretic.

Prescribed for

Pulmonary edema, congestive heart failure, hypertrophic and restrictive cardiomyopathy (heart muscle diseases) in cats, acute noninflammatory tissue edema, fluid in the abdomen due to liver failure, and other conditions where it may be desirable to rid the body of excess fluid.

General Information

Furosemide is one of the loop diuretics. They act on a part of the kidney called the loop of Henle and are much more potent than the thiazide diuretics (see *Thiazide Diuretics*) in their ability to promote salt and water excretion.

Diuretics are the foundation of therapy for congestive heart failure. In heart failure the kidneys retain fluid to compensate for the failing heart. This attempt to compensate goes too far and ultimately causes too much fluid to be retained. Diuretics reverse this by promoting sodium and water loss through the kidneys. Thiazides are useful in mild to moderate, but not severe congestive heart failure or severe pulmonary edema. Furosemide is a more potent diuretic and is the drug of choice for these conditions. Hydrochlorothiazide may be useful combined with furosemide to treat refractory right-sided congestive heart failure in cats. Cats with restrictive and hypertrophic cardiomyopathy often have severe and life-threatening accumulations of fluid in the lungs (pulmonary edema) and around the lungs (pleural effusion). Furosemide may be life-saving emergency treatment for these cats because it can rapidly relieve their breathing difficulties, and allow therapy for the heart disease to be started.

Laryngeal paralysis in dogs may be accompanied by severe pulmonary edema (fluid in the lungs), and furosemide may be a valuable part of therapy for this syndrome. Furosemide may also help eliminate fluid in the abdomen due to liver failure, or edema (fluid accumulation) in other parts of the body.

Diuretics are not recommended for the treatment of most kidney disease. Furosemide may cause a transient increase in blood flow to the kidneys, but it does not improve kidney function. Furosemide makes dehydration and electrolyte imbalances more likely, and both of these cause a decrease in kidney function. Furosemide is occasionally used at a very specific stage of treatment for acute kidney failure when other treatments, such as fluid loading, mannitol, and dopamine are not effective. If it helps, the animal should be carefully monitored for adverse effects.

Potent diuretics like furosemide should always be used with caution, because they can rapidly produce severe dehydration and electrolyte imbalances, even in healthy animals. Diuretics will do little to relieve fluid accumulation and edema caused by low blood protein or vasculitis (inflammed, leaking blood vessels) and may even worsen the animal's overall condition.

Cautions and Warnings

- Furosemide should not be given to animals in kidney failure or to those that are dehydrated or likely to become dehydrated, as with vomiting or diarrhea. It should be used with extreme caution in animals with electrolyte abnormalities, liver disease, or diabetes mellitus.

■ Furosemide should not be given as the sole therapy for congestive heart failure, but should be used with enalapril and/or digoxin.

■ Furosemide may cause damage to hearing and balance, especially in cats given high-dose intravenous therapy.

■ Contact your veterinarian if you think your dog or cat may be having an adverse reaction to furosemide.

■ U.S. federal law restricts the use of this drug by or on the lawful written or oral order of a licensed veterinarian within the context of a valid veterinarian-client-patient relationship.

Possible Side Effects

▼ Common: dehydration and low levels of blood sodium, potassium, chloride, calcium, and magnesium. Low blood magnesium may contribute to abnormal heart rhythms and is associated with poor prognosis or outcome in critically ill patients.

▼ Rare: allergic reactions, increased blood glucose, ear damage, anemia, low white blood cell counts, and gastrointestinal disturbances.

Drug Interactions

• Furosemide increases the risk of kidney and ear damage from gentamicin and the aminoglycosides.

• Digitalis toxicity is more likely in animals with low blood potassium from furosemide.

• The dose of theophylline may need to be reduced in animals given furosemide.

• There is a greater risk of low blood potassium when furosemide is given with corticosteroids or amphotericin B.

• Furosemide may inhibit the effects of probenecid and sulfinpyrazone.

• Furosemide may alter the requirement for insulin in diabetic animals.

• The dose of aspirin may need to be reduced in animals given furosemide.

• Quinidine and neuromuscular blocking agents may be altered by the use of furosemide.

Food Interactions

None known.

Usual Dose

Dogs and Cats: 1–2 mg/lb, orally or by injection in a vein, in a muscle, or under the skin. The dosing interval may vary from once every 2–3 days, to every hour for emergency intravenous therapy. Oral doses are usually given 2–3 times a day.

Drug Form: 12.5-, 20-, 40-, 50-, and 80-mg tablets; 8 and 10 mg/ml oral solution; and 10 and 50 mg/ml injectable.

Overdosage

Overdose may cause dehydration and electrolyte imbalances. Signs of overdose may include increased or decreased thirst and urination, lethargy, increased heart rate, gastrointestinal distress, collapse, coma, and seizures. Chronic overdose may cause kidney damage. In case of accidental ingestion or overdose, contact your veterinarian or the National Animal Poison Control Center. ALWAYS bring the prescription bottle or container with you if you go for treatment.

Special Populations

Pregnancy/Lactation
Furosemide should be avoided in pregnant or lactating animals unless the potential benefits outweigh the risks.

Puppies/Kittens
Furosemide should be avoided in puppies and kittens unless the potential benefits outweigh the risks.

Senior Animals
Furosemide should be safe to use in senior animals with normal kidney and liver function (see "Cautions and Warnings").

Generic Name

Glipizide (GLIP-ih-zide)

Brand Name

Glucotrol [H]

Type of Drug

Antidiabetic.

Prescribed for

Diabetes mellitus.

General Information

Diabetes mellitus is a disease in which there is a lack of insulin production and/or tissues do not respond to insulin (see *Insulin*), and high blood glucose is the result. Glipizide is an oral medication that lowers blood sugar (glucose) levels in both diabetics and nondiabetics. It is not known exactly how glipizide works, but it may stimulate the pancreas to release more insulin, increase the peripheral tissue sensitivity to insulin, and decrease liver production of glucose. Glipizide has not been very effective in treating diabetic dogs, probably because they have little if any insulin production, and are more like humans with true insulin-dependent diabetes mellitus (IDDM). As many as 30% to 50% of cats may have a disease like non–insulin-dependent diabetes mellitus (NIDDM) in people. In this type of diabetes, the pancreas can make some insulin, but probably less than normal, and there is resistance to the effects of insulin in peripheral tissues. Some diabetic cats have an excellent response to glipizide, others have a partial response, and some have no response at all. It is probably worthwhile to try glipizide in diabetic cats that are healthy otherwise, do not have ketoacidosis (ketones and excess acid in the blood), and are suspected of having NIDDM. Glipizide should not be used to replace insulin in cats whose diabetes has been well regulated. Glipizide does not seem to help those cats that have been on insulin and developed insulin resistance.

Cautions and Warnings

■ Glipizide is not FDA approved for use in dogs or cats. It is considered accepted practice to use glipizide as an adjunct to treatment of diabetes in cats suspected of having NIDDM. Glipizide is not a substitute for insulin, and you should work closely with your veterinarian to find the best treatment for your diabetic cat. Glipizide should be discontinued if the diabetes worsens during the first weeks of therapy, or if there is evidence of liver damage. It may take 1 to 2 months of treatment with glipizide for a beneficial effect to be seen.

■ Glipizide should be avoided in cats with thyroid, liver, or kidney disease, or in any sick or debilitated animal.

■ Glipizide should not be used in diabetic cats with ketoacidosis/ketosis, in cats who are well regulated on insulin, or in cats who have developed insulin resistance after being well regulated on insulin.

■ Contact your veterinarian if you think your cat may be having an adverse reaction to glipizide.

■ U.S. federal law restricts the use of this drug by or on the lawful written or oral order of a licensed veterinarian within the context of a valid veterinarian-client-patient relationship.

Possible Side Effects

There are no common side effects with glipizide. Low blood glucose may occur, especially if the dose is not given with food. Vomiting may occur immediately after dosing. Liver damage may occur, and usually resolves after the glipizide is discontinued. Side effects occur in less than 15% of cats.

▼ Rare: allergic reactions.

Drug Interactions

• Chloramphenicol, furazolidone, nonsteroidal anti-inflammatory drugs, salicylates, sulfonamides, warfarin, probenecid, monoamine oxidase inhibitors (MAOIs), and cimetidine may enhance the effects of glipizide.

• Glipizide may prolong the effects of barbiturates (such as phenobarbital).

Food Interactions

Glipizide should always be given with food.

Usual Dose

Cats: starting dose—0.25 mg/lb twice a day. If no improvement after 2 weeks, the dose may be increased to 0.5 mg/lb twice a day.

Drug Form: 5- and 10-mg tablets.

Overdosage

Severe low blood glucose is the most serious concern after an overdose. Signs could include weakness, incoordination, trembling, lethargy, or abnormal behavior. Severe hypoglycemia may cause seizures, hypoglycemic shock, coma, and death. In case of accidental ingestion or overdose, contact your veterinarian or the National Animal Poison Control Center. ALWAYS bring the prescription bottle or container with you if you go for treatment.

Special Information

There is no reliable test to determine which diabetic cats have NIDDM and are likely to respond to glipizide. Thus, a therapeutic trial is necessary to see if your cat will respond to glipizide. Obese diabetic cats may be more likely to respond to glipizide. Even those cats who do respond to glipizide initially are likely to have progression of their disease, and require insulin eventually. This may happen in a few weeks or after a year or more.

Special Populations

Pregnancy/Lactation
Glipizide should not be used in pregnant or lactating animals.

Kittens
Glipizide should not be used in kittens.

Senior Animals
Glipizide should be safe to use in older animals whose diabetes is not complicated by other diseases. It should be avoided in cats with hyperthyroidism, liver or kidney disease, and in those who are ill or debilitated.

Generic Name

Glycosaminoglycan Supplements

(glie-kose-uh-mee-noe-GLIE-kan) [G]

Most Common Brand Names

Acetylator [V]	Glucosamine Multi-Source [V]
CartiVet [V]	Glucosamine Single-Source [V]
Cosequin [V]	Glyco-Flex [V]
Flex Free [V]	Vetri-Disc [V]

Type of Drug

Oral chondroprotective nutraceutical, disease-modifying osteo-arthritis agent, nutritional supplement.

Prescribed for

Noninfectious, degenerative, and/or traumatic arthritis.

General Information

Oral glycosaminoglycans (GAGs) are nutritional supplements that are administered to promote healing of injured or arthritic joints. The term *nutraceutical* has been coined to describe this type of dietary supplement that has medicinal properties. GAGs are available from many outlets, including your veterinarian, health food stores, pharmacies, and catalogs.

Oral GAGs are indicated for the same type of problems as the prescription polysulfated GAG Adequan (see *Polysulfated Glycosaminoglycan*). They are used in dogs and cats with signs of degenerative joint disease (DJD), or osteoarthritis, and joint pain resulting from injury. Normal joints have pads of cartilage protecting the ends of the bones that form the joint, and lubricating joint fluid that helps to reduce friction and wear. GAGs are the major natural building blocks of both cartilage and joint fluid. Joint injury initiates a self-perpetuating cycle of inflammation, cartilage damage, and poor quality joint fluid that ultimately leads to irreversible degeneration and DJD. The use of GAGs is based on the premise that injured joints will heal more rapidly if high concentrations of the building blocks are available.

GAGs are derived from a number of natural sources. Cartilage from cattle or sharks is the most common source. The green-lipped mussel *Perna canaliculus* is used in another popular product. All of these products contain glycosamine, chondroitin and/or hyaluronic acid, or its salt, hyaluronate. Most also contain additional minerals and/or vitamins.

There is extensive anecdotal and clinical evidence that oral GAGs may be useful, but the well-controlled studies needed to confirm these observations are lacking. As with injectable GAGs, these supplements are not a substitute for accurate diagnosis, medical treatment of infected joints, or surgery and joint stabilization when indicated.

Oral GAGs are widely used by pet owners with or without veterinary supervision. Veterinarians also commonly prescribe them. They are used together with injectable GAGs and when clinical signs are mild. They are often prescribed for cats instead of injectable products because cats may tolerate oral medication better than injections.

Cautions and Warnings

■ Do not use in place of accurate diagnosis, professional treatment, or in infected joints. Treating with supplements instead of seeking professional advice may delay proper treatment and put your pet's health and life in danger.

■ Contact your veterinarian if you think your dog or cat may be having an adverse reaction to oral GAGs.

Possible Side Effects

▼ Rare: diarrhea.

Food and Drug Interactions

None known.

Usual Dose

Dogs and Cats: Read the label and follow your veterinarian's instructions.

Drug Form: powders, capsules, and liquids.

Overdosage

Signs of overdose are unlikely. Diarrhea is the most likely side effect of overdosage. In case of accidental ingestion or overdose, contact your veterinarian or the National Animal Poison Control Center. ALWAYS bring the prescription bottle or container with you if you go for treatment.

Special Populations

Pregnancy/Lactation
Oral GAGs are probably safe, but there are no well-controlled studies in pregnant or lactating animals. As with any medication, they should be used only if the potential benefits outweigh the risks.

Puppies/Kittens
There are no well-controlled studies in puppies and kittens. Oversupplementation of nutrients, minerals, and vitamins may increase the risk of developmental diseases in growing puppies and kittens. Use only if the benefits outweigh the risks.

Senior Animals
Oral GAGs are probably safe, but there are no well-controlled studies in senior animals. The major risk is that owners may use GAGs instead of seeking veterinary advice and could delay accurate diagnosis and treatment of serious problems.

Type of Drug

Gold Compounds

Brand Names

Generic Ingredient: Auranofin (Triethylphosphine Gold)
Ridaura [H]

Generic Ingredient: Aurothioglucose
Solganal [H]

Generic Ingredient: Gold Sodium Thiomalate
Myochrysine [H]

Prescribed for

Immune-mediated arthritis, rheumatoid arthritis, and pemphigus.

General Information

The main use for gold compounds is in rheumatoid arthritis. Rheumatoid arthritis is one of the autoimmune or immune-mediated diseases. These are diseases in which the immune system can no longer distinguish between self and nonself and begins to attack the body's own tissues. In rheumatoid arthritis there are usually autoantibodies or antibodies against self (positive rheumatoid factor), antigen-antibody complexes in joints, and swollen painful joints, usually multiple and symmetrical joints, with damage to the cartilage and bone of the joint surfaces. Gold compounds are the treatment of choice for rheumatoid arthritis, and should always be tried first in this disease. The mechanism of action of gold is not known. It does cause immunosuppression, inhibits the tissue enzymes that may help damage joints, and has anti-inflammatory effects (protection against oxygen free-radicals).

Gold can be given as injectable aurothiomalate or orally as auranofin. It is usually combined with low-dose corticosteroids. There is some controversy about whether the oral or injectable forms are more effective. Diarrhea is the most troublesome side effect of the oral form. Reducing the dose may be helpful. The oral preparation should be used for at least 1 month to induce remission. Some experts indicate that it may take 6 to 12 weeks to see a response. It can then be used for relapses if they occur or as low-dose maintenance therapy (see "Usual Dose"). Complete remission is not likely but many animals improve significantly with gold therapy.

Gold has been used to treat pemphigus in dogs and cats. Pemphigus is another autoimmune disease. In this disease the immune system attacks the animal's skin. When the disease does not respond to corticosteroids alone, gold therapy may be tried. There are other possible therapies as well that are usually tried first (see *Azathioprine* and *Chlorambucil*).

Cautions and Warnings

■ Gold compounds are not FDA approved for use in dogs or cats. They are used occasionally and are considered accepted practice.

■ Routine complete blood counts and urinalyses should be done to check for evidence of bone marrow suppression or kidney damage before each injection or during oral therapy.

■ Gold therapy should not be used in animals with lupus, severe debilitation, previous heavy metal exposure, significant kidney, liver, bone marrow, or blood disease.

■ A small test dose may be given to make sure there are no

sensitivities to the drug. A response to therapy may not be seen for 6 to 12 weeks.

■ Contact your veterinarian if you think your dog or cat may be having an adverse reaction to gold compounds.

■ U.S. federal law restricts the use of this drug by or on the lawful written or oral order of a licensed veterinarian within the context of a valid veterinarian-client-patient relationship.

Possible Side Effects

▼ Common: pain at the site of injection.

▼ Rare: allergic reactions, diarrhea, inflammation and ulceration of the mouth or skin, low platelet counts, low white blood cell counts, severe enterocolitis (inflammation of the intestines) and kidney damage.

Drug Interactions

• Gold compounds should not be used with penicillamine, hydroxychloroquine, or immunosuppressants (cyclophosphamide, azathioprine) other than corticosteroids.

• Gold therapy should not be used immediately after azathioprine, as it may cause a fatal skin disease called toxic epidermal necrolysis.

Food Interactions

None known.

Usual Dose

Dogs: Auranofin— 0.05–0.1 mg/lb orally twice a day. Aurothioglucose and gold sodium thiomalate— dogs less than 20 lbs: 1 mg by injection into a muscle (IM) first week, 2 mg second week, and 0.5 mg/lb once a week for maintenance. Dogs greater than 20 lbs: 2–5 mg by IM injection first week, 5–10 mg second week, and 0.5 mg/lb once a week for maintenance.

Cats: Auranofin— 0.05–0.1 mg/lb orally twice a day. Aurothioglucose—0.5–1 mg/cat, by IM injection once a week.

Drug Form: 3-mg capsules and 50 mg/ml injectable.

Overdosage

Overdose is likely to cause nausea, vomiting, diarrhea, skin lesions, fever, kidney damage, and bone marrow suppression.

In case of accidental ingestion or overdose, contact your veterinarian or the National Animal Poison Control Center. ALWAYS bring the prescription bottle or container with you if you go for treatment.

Special Information

Gold injections are likely to be painful, and it is possible to reduce the pain by adding a local anesthetic such as lidocaine to the injection.

Special Populations

Pregnancy/Lactation
Gold therapy damages the fetus, and should be avoided in pregnant or lactating animals.

Puppies/Kittens
Gold therapy should not be used in puppies or kittens.

Senior Animals
Gold therapy should be used with caution in older animals (see "Cautions and Warnings").

Generic Name

Griseofulvin (gris-ee-oe-FUL-vin) G

Brand Names

Griseofulvin Microsize
Fulvicin U/F V   Grisactin H
Grifulvin V H

Griseofulvin Ultramicrosize
Fulvicin P/G H   Grisactin Ultra H
Gris-PEG H

Type of Drug

Antifungal.

Prescribed for

Ringworm (dermatophyte infection).

General Information

Griseofulvin is an antibiotic that is effective against the fungi that cause ringworm or dermatophyte infections of the skin, hair, and claws. It is effective against species of *Tinea, Trichophyton, Microsporum,* and *Epidermophyton.* It is not effective against bacteria or other fungi. Griseofulvin is taken orally, absorbed, and then concentrated in skin, hair, and claw. It is only effective in new growth, and will not kill dermatophytes in existing or old skin, hair, and claw.

Dogs and cats are infected with *Microsporum canis* or *Trichophyton* most commonly. Hair loss, scaling, crusting, and redness are common symptoms but some infected animals have no symptoms. Ringworm is highly contagious and may easily be spread to other animals and to people through contact with infected animals or people (see *Zoonotic Diseases of Dogs and Cats*). Most cats with ringworm are asymptomatic carriers, and are only discovered when ringworm develops in a human or animal contact. Ringworm usually does not cause itching, but some cats may be moderately or intensely itchy. In cats, infections are usually generalized even if skin lesions appear localized. The infection is usually diagnosed by culturing hair from suspect areas, or by Wood's lamp examination. Half of *M. canis* will glow yellow-green (fluoresce) under a Wood's lamp, but other species never fluoresce and iodine treatment may eliminate the fluorescence.

Localized ringworm may be treated with topical antifungals such as chlorhexidine, povidone-iodine, thiabendazole, clotrimazole, or miconazole. Affected areas should be clipped and treatment continued for 2 weeks beyond negative cultures. Standard treatment for generalized ringworm involves long-term treatment with both topical antifungals and griseofulvin after a total body clip. Griseofulvin must be given daily for a minimum of 4 weeks, or until cultures are negative. Griseofulvin comes in two forms, microsize and ultramicrosize. The ultramicrosize is better absorbed and is therefore given in a lower dose.

Cautions and Warnings

For Owners/Handlers

■ Consult your physician if you think you may have ringworm. In people, ringworm is usually a crusty, scaly patch or

patches on the skin surrounded by a red ring—ringworm cannot live in inflamed skin, so it moves out in a circle away from
the area of inflammation.

For Animals

■ Griseofulvin is not FDA approved for use in dogs or cats. It
is commonly used to treat generalized dermatophyte infections
and is considered accepted practice.

■ Griseofulvin may cause liver damage and should not be
given to animals with liver disease.

■ Griseofulvin may cause severe bone marrow suppression,
especially in cats.

■ Kittens are more sensitive to griseofulvin and should be
monitored carefully (see "Possible Side Effects").

■ Contact your veterinarian if you think your dog or cat may
be having an adverse reaction to griseofulvin.

■ U.S. federal law restricts the use of this drug by or on the
lawful written or oral order of a licensed veterinarian within the
context of a valid veterinarian-client-patient relationship.

Possible Side Effects

▼ Common: decreased appetite, vomiting, and diarrhea.

▼ Rare: allergic reactions, anemia and low white blood
cell counts from bone marrow suppression, depression,
unsteady gait, liver damage, and skin inflammation (sensitivity to the sun).

Drug Interactions

• If griseofulvin and phenobarbital are given together, the
dose of griseofulvin may need to be increased.

• Griseofulvin may reduce the effectiveness of coumarin/
warfarin anticoagulants.

Food Interactions

Griseofulvin must be given with fatty meals for adequate
absorption.

Usual Dose

Dogs and Cats
   Griseofulvin Microsize: starting dose—25 mg/lb once a day.

Increase to 50 mg/lb if no response is seen in 2 weeks. Dose may be divided into 2–3 treatments a day.

   Griseofulvin Ultramicrosize: starting dose—15 mg/lb once a day. Increase to 30 mg/lb if no response is seen in 2 weeks. Dose may be divided into 2–3 treatments a day.

Drug Form

   Griseofulvin Microsize: 250- and 500-mg tablets, 125 mg/5 ml pediatric oral suspension (may be best drug form for kittens), and powder containing 2.5-g griseofulvin in 15-g packets (for horses).

   Griseofulvin Ultramicrosize: 125-, 165-, 250-, and 330-mg tablets and capsules.

Overdosage

There is little information available on griseofulvin overdose. It may be expected to cause the symptoms known to be adverse effects (see "Possible Side Effects"). In case of accidental ingestion or overdose, contact your veterinarian or the National Animal Poison Control Center. ALWAYS bring the prescription bottle or container with you if you go for treatment.

Special Information

All grooming equipment and bedding of infected animals should be discarded or disinfected with Clorox. Any areas where the animal has contact should be cleaned with Clorox if possible.

   There is a lot of controversy over topical treatment of cats with ringworm. Some experts have found that bathing infected cats may actually spread the ringworm to new areas. Consult your veterinarian or a veterinary dermatologist for the latest recommendations on the treatment of ringworm.

   Itraconazole and ketoconazole are also effective systemic treatments for ringworm. They should probably be reserved for those animals that cannot tolerate or are resistant to griseofulvin.

Special Populations

Pregnancy/Lactation

Griseofulvin is known to cause birth defects in cats and probably does so in all species. It should not be used during pregnancy or lactation.

Puppies/Kittens

Griseofulvin should be avoided or used with extreme caution in puppies and kittens, as they are more susceptible to adverse effects (see "Possible Side Effects").

Senior Animals

Griseofulvin should be safe to use in senior animals, but should be avoided in those with liver disease or previous liver damage.

Generic Name

Heparin (HEP-uh-rin)

Type of Drug

Anticoagulant.

Prescribed for

Diseases and conditions where there is excessive clotting or increased risk of clotting, such as disseminated intravascular coagulation (DIC), thromboembolism (clotting) secondary to cardiomyopathy in cats, pancreatitis, burns, heat stroke, and pulmonary thromboembolism.

General Information

Heparin sodium is a naturally occurring anticoagulant. The drug form is derived from pig intestine or cow lung. It may be used to treat or prevent clotting in a number of diseases where excessive clotting has already occurred and is likely to spread, or where there is an increased risk of clotting. Heparin can only be given by injection under the skin or in a vein. Normally heparin is given to hospitalized animals, but there may be situations where your veterinarian will teach you to give heparin under the skin, as you would insulin, so that treatment can be continued while your pet recuperates at home. Heparin may be the initial treatment for diseases where there is increased clotting risk, followed by oral warfarin/coumarin for longer-term anticoagulation (see *Warfarin*).

The dose of heparin may vary widely depending on the condition being treated. There are no good studies to prove the effectiveness of any dose, and individual animals vary in their response. In some conditions, such as DIC, low-dose heparin may be used along with supportive care such as fluids, whole blood or clotting factors, and aspirin (see *Aspirin/Acetylsalicylic Acid*). It is also important to treat the actual cause of DIC. It is critically important to measure prothrombin time (PT) and partial thromboplastin time (PTT), blood tests that measure clotting ability, whenever anticoagulants are used. This will prevent excessive bleeding from overdose or changes in the animal's own clotting function.

Cautions and Warnings

■ Follow your veterinarian's instructions precisely and make sure you understand the dose and dosing frequency if you are giving your pet heparin at home.

■ Monitor clotting function tests frequently to determine effectiveness of anticoagulant therapy.

■ Do not use heparin in animals with low platelet counts or uncontrolled bleeding.

■ Contact your veterinarian if you think your dog or cat may be having an adverse reaction to heparin.

■ U.S. federal law restricts the use of this drug by or on the lawful written or oral order of a licensed veterinarian within the context of a valid veterinarian-client-patient relationship.

Possible Side Effects

Bleeding and low platelet counts may occur with overuse of anticoagulants or with a change in the animal's own clotting functions during heparin therapy. Hematomas (blood accumulations), pain, and inflammation may occur after deep subcutaneous or intramuscular injections.

▼ Rare: allergic reactions.

Drug Interactions

• Heparin should be used with caution when other anticoagulants such as aspirin, warfarin, dipyridamole, or phenylbutazone are given. Increased monitoring is recommended.

• Heparin may reduce the effects of corticosteroids or insulin.

• Heparin may increase the effects of diazepam.

• Antihistamines, nitroglycerin, digoxin, and tetracyclines may decrease the effects of heparin.

Food Interactions

None known.

Usual Dose

Initial doses may need to be 2–3 times higher than recommended doses to prevent clotting.

Dogs: low-dose heparin—30–40 units/lb, by injection under the skin, 2–3 times a day. For thromboembolism—50–100 units/lb, intravenous loading dose, followed by 50–150 units/lb by injection under the skin, 3–4 times a day.

Cats: for thromboembolism—75–100 units/lb, by injection under the skin, 3 times a day.

Drug Form: 1,000, 2,500, 5,000, 7,500, 10,000, 15,000, and 20,000 USP units/ml injectable.

Overdosage

Overdose of anticoagulants may cause bleeding into the urine, body cavities, or gastrointestinal tract, from the gums, or respiratory tract, or excessive bruising/bleeding at sites of trauma. In case of accidental overdose, contact your veterinarian or the National Animal Poison Control Center. ALWAYS bring the prescription bottle or container with you if you go for treatment.

Special Information

Pulmonary thromboembolism (clotting in the lungs) is an important, potentially life-threatening, and underdiagnosed problem in animals, as it is in people. It may occur as a result of heartworm disease (see *Melarsomine* and *Thiacetarsamide*), hypothyroidism, pancreatitis, kidney disease, DIC, antithrombin III deficiency, hyperadrenocorticism/Cushing's disease, and immune-mediated hemolytic anemia (AIHA). The most common sign is sudden onset of rapid or difficult breathing.

Some experts recommend heparin for all cases of AIHA, and severe cases of pancreatitis. Clinical studies are needed to determine which animals will benefit from heparin therapy.

Special Populations

Pregnancy/Lactation

Heparin does not cross the placenta and is probably safe to

use during pregnancy, but there are no safety studies in pregnant or lactating dogs or cats. Heparin should be used only when the benefits outweigh the risks.

Puppies/Kittens

Heparin should be avoided or used with caution in puppies and kittens. Their small size usually makes monitoring of clotting function impossible.

Senior Animals

Heparin should be safe to use in older animals with proper monitoring.

Generic Name

Hydrocodone (hye-droe-COE-done) [G]

Brand Name

Hycodan [H]

Type of Drug

Narcotic cough suppressant.

Prescribed for

Dry nonproductive cough in dogs.

General Information

Hydrocodone bitartrate is used primarily as a cough suppressant in dogs with collapsing trachea, bronchitis, and upper respiratory infection, including kennel cough. It is not recommended when there is a moist cough or increased respiratory secretions. Hydrocodone works by suppressing the cough reflex in the brain. It is well absorbed orally and generally is effective for 6 to 12 hours. The hydrocodone products used in small animals are combinations with homatropine, an anticholinergic drug used to decrease secretions.

Cautions and Warnings

For Owners/Handlers

■ Hydrocodone is a Class III controlled drug, and has the potential for abuse in people.

For Animals

■ Hydrocodone is not FDA approved for use in dogs, but it is commonly used in dogs and considered accepted practice. Narcotics are not recommended for use in cats.

■ Hydrocodone should not be used in animals sensitive to narcotics or animals taking monoamine oxidase inhibitors (MAOIs).

■ Hydrocodone, like all narcotics, should be used with caution in patients who are hypothyroid, have severe kidney problems, Addison's disease (adrenal insufficiency), head trauma patients, and older or severely debilitated animals.

■ Hydrocodone should be used with caution in patients with acute abdominal problems.

■ Hydrocodone should not be used in respiratory diseases with increased mucus or secretions.

■ Most hydrocodone products are manufactured as combination products with other drugs. DO NOT give combination products containing acetaminophen or other medication to animals. These other medications may cause severe side effects or death.

■ U.S. federal law restricts the use of this drug by or on the lawful written or oral order of a licensed veterinarian within the context of a valid veterinarian-client-patient relationship.

Possible Side Effects

▼ Common: sedation, constipation, vomiting, and other gastrointestinal disturbance.

Drug Interactions

• Hydrocodone has an additive effect with other sedatives, narcotics, antihistamines, and central nervous system depressants.

Food Interactions

None known.

Usual Dose

Dogs: 0.12 mg/lb orally 2–4 times a day.
Cats: Narcotics are not recommended in cats.
Drug Form: 5-mg hydrocodone with 1.5-mg homatropine tablet, or in 5 ml of syrup.

Overdosage

Signs of overdose may include profound sedation, central nervous system disturbances, respiratory depression, and coma. In case of accidental ingestion or overdose, contact your veterinarian or the National Poison Control Center. ALWAYS bring the prescription bottle or container if you go for treatment.

Special Information

Chronic coughing is irritating to the respiratory tract. Cough suppressants are used to break this cough cycle. For many veterinarians, hydrocodone is the preferred cough suppressant. The side effect of drowsiness may be a benefit when hydrocodone is given at night so that both the dog and the owner are able to sleep.

Special Populations

Pregnancy/Lactation

Safety studies have not been performed on pregnant animals, and it is unknown if hydrocodone is excreted in breast milk. Hydrocodone should only be used in pregnant or lactating dogs if the benefits outweigh the risks.

Puppies/Kittens

Safety studies have not been performed in young animals. Hydrocodone should not be used in kittens.

Senior Animals

Older animals may be more sensitive to side effects from this drug, and should be treated with the smallest effective dose.

Generic Name

Hydrogen Peroxide

(HYE-droe-jen Per-OKS-ide) G

Brand Name

Peroxyl H

Type of Drug

Topical antiseptic and emetic.

Prescribed for

Induction of vomiting and first aid for superficial wounds and abrasions.

General Information

Hydrogen peroxide is an antibacterial and cleansing chemical used as a disinfectant for minor wounds and mouth irritations. It works best on surface conditions rather than deep wounds. The bubbling action that occurs when hydrogen peroxide contacts tissue and mucous membranes helps remove debris.

Oral hydrogen peroxide is also used to induce vomiting in dogs that have eaten certain foreign bodies, drug overdoses, or toxic materials (see *Apomorphine*). Emetics are an important part of the treatment of ingested toxins, but they are not appropriate in all cases, or with all toxins (see "Cautions and Warnings"). Emetics will usually empty 40% to 60% of the stomach contents.

Cautions and Warnings

■ DO NOT administer an emetic to your dog or cat without the advice of your veterinarian.

■ DO NOT use hydrogen peroxide solutions more concentrated than 3% on wounds or as an emetic, as they may cause severe irritation or internal injury.

■ Do not exceed the recommended dose of hydrogen peroxide as an emetic without specific instructions from your veterinarian.

■ Emetics should not be used in animals that are in shock, comatose, severely depressed, having difficulty breathing, lacking normal choke reflexes, seizuring, extremely weak, or with other impairments that may lead to aspiration of the vomited material and pneumonia.

■ Emetics should not be used in animals that have vomited repeatedly.

■ Emetics should not be used in animals that have ingested caustic substances because of the risk of further damage to the stomach and esophagus.

■ Emetics should be used with caution in animals that have ingested petroleum distillates because of the risk of aspiration.

■ Emetics should be used with caution in animals that have ingested strychnine or other central nervous system stimulants because of the increased risk of seizures.

■ Contact your veterinarian if you think your dog or cat may be having an adverse reaction to hydrogen peroxide.

■ Use of this drug should be by or on the lawful written or oral order of a licensed veterinarian within the context of a valid veterinarian-client-patient relationship.

Possible Side Effects

There are no common side effects to the use of hydrogen peroxide. Wound edges may become white as a result of the actions of hydrogen peroxide. This is expected and is not harmful. If minor wounds or irritation do not respond to treatment, consult your veterinarian immediately. Aspiration of stomach contents is always a risk when an animal vomits. This may produce severe or fatal aspiration pneumonia.

Food and Drug Interactions

None known.

Usual Dose

Dogs and Cats: as an emetic—5 ml/10 lbs, orally, maximum dose 30 ml, repeat the dose once if no vomiting occurs in 15 minutes. Apply liberally to superficial wounds or abrasions as first aid treatment. See your veterinarian as soon as possible and continue to use only on the advice of your veterinarian.

Drug Form: 3% solution of hydrogen peroxide is the only strength recommended for use in animals.

Storage Instructions: The strength of hydrogen peroxide deteriorates when exposed to light, repeated shaking, and heat.

Overdosage

In case of accidental ingestion or overdose, contact your veterinarian or the National Animal Poison Control Center. ALWAYS bring the prescription bottle or container with you if you go for treatment.

Special Information

Other recommended methods of inducing vomiting include 1 to 2 teaspoons table salt (sodium chloride) placed in the back of the throat. Your veterinarian may use apomorphine in dogs or xylazine in cats to induce vomiting in the hospital. Ipecac is occasionally used in dogs, but it is not recommended as an emetic in dogs or cats because of its irritant properties.

Special Populations

Pregnancy/Lactation
Hydrogen peroxide should be safe to use topically in pregnancy and lactation. Induce vomiting only under the supervision of your veterinarian.

Puppies/Kittens
Hydrogen peroxide should be safe to use topically in puppies and kittens. Induce vomiting only under the supervision of your veterinarian.

Senior Animals
Hydrogen peroxide should be safe to use topically in senior animals. Induce vomiting only under the supervision of your veterinarian.

Generic Name

Hydroxyzine (hye-DROK-suh-zene) G

Most Common Brand Names

Atarax H   Vistaril H

Type of Drug

Antihistamine.

Prescribed for

Itching caused by allergies in dogs.

General Information

Hydroxyzine hydrochloride and hydroxyzine pamoate are antihistamines. Hydroxyzine is primarily used to alleviate itching in dogs with allergies. In addition, hydroxyzine relaxes muscle, alleviates nausea, opens airways, and relieves pain. Antihistamines alone will control itching in about 40% of allergic dogs. If antihistamines alone are unable to control all the signs, it may allow a lower dose of corticosteroids to be used.

Cautions and Warnings

■ Hydroxyzine is not FDA approved for use in dogs or cats. It is commonly used in dogs and is considered accepted practice. The safe dosage has not been established for cats. There are published reports of hydroxyzine use in cats for miliary dermatitis and eosinophilic granuloma complex. Other antihistamines may be preferred in cats because of sedation and other side effects.

■ Hydroxyzine should be used with caution in animals with prostatic enlargement, bladder neck obstruction, severe heart failure, some forms of glaucoma, or pylelo-duodenal obstruction (obstruction at the junction of the stomach and small intestine).

■ U.S. federal law restricts the use of this drug by or on the lawful written or oral order of a licensed veterinarian within the context of a valid veterinarian-client-patient relationship.

Possible Side Effects

▼ Common: sedation.
▼ Rare: excitement, fine tremors, whole body tremors, and seizures.

Drug Interactions

• Hydroxyzine may have an additive effect when combined with other central nervous system depressant drugs, such as barbiturates and tranquilizers.
• Hydroxyzine may have an additive effect when combined with other anticholinergic agents such as atropine.
• Hydroxyzine may inhibit the effects of epinephrine.

Food Interactions

None known.

Usual Dose

Dogs: 1 mg/lb orally 3–4 times a day.
Cats: 10-mg orally twice a day has been used (safe dosage has not been established).
Drug Form: 10-, 15-, 50-, and 100-mg tablets and 10 and 25 mg/5 ml syrup.

Overdosage

Overdoses may cause increased sedation and possibly low blood pressure. In case of accidental ingestion or overdose, contact your veterinarian or the National Animal Poison Control Center. ALWAYS bring the prescription bottle or container with you if you go for treatment.

Special Information

Allergies, such as flea allergy dermatitis, and atopy (a tendency toward multiple allergies) are challenging management problems for pet owners and veterinarians. Medications such as antihistamines and corticosteroids are only one part of the program necessary to make an animal comfortable and control signs of allergy. Some animals respond better to one antihistamine than another. The only way to determine which works best for your animal is to give each one a trial until you find the one that is most effective. You need to work with your veterinarian to determine the causes of your animal's allergy and develop a management program to relieve the signs.

Special Populations

Pregnancy/Lactation
High doses of antihistamines have been shown to cause birth defects in laboratory animals. It is not known if hydroxyzine is excreted in milk. Hydroxyzine should only be used in pregnant or lactating animals if the benefits outweigh the risks.

Puppies/Kittens
There are no studies in puppies or kittens. Hydroxyzine is used on occasion in children.

Senior Animals
There are no studies in dogs, but older humans are more sensitive to side effects from antihistamines.

Generic Name

Imidacloprid (ih-mid-uh-KLOE-prid)

Brand Name

Advantage [V]

Type of Drug

Insecticide.

Prescribed for

Prevention and treatment of flea infestations on dogs and cats.

General Information

Imidacloprid is a new type of insecticide with a different action than the conventional flea products, including carbamates, organophosphates, and pyrethrins. It interferes with nicotinic receptors in the central nervous system, causing paralysis and death. Imidacloprid kills 98% to 100% of existing larval and adult fleas within 12 to 24 hours of treatment, but has no activity against mites or ticks. It continues to protect dogs and cats from fleas for up to 4 weeks, even after bathing, swimming, or exposure to sun or rain. Occasionally, retreatment may be necessary in less than a month, particularly in animals that are bathed or that swim frequently, but it should not be used more frequently than once a week.

Imidacloprid is available as a spot treatment that is applied directly to the pet's skin (see "Usual Dose") and continues to kill new fleas for a minimum of 30 days. Fleas do not need to bite before being killed. This greatly reduces the irritation from bites and the risk of transmission of several diseases (see "Special Information").

Cautions and Warnings

For Owners/Handlers
■ Not for human use. Harmful if swallowed. Causes eye irritation. Do not get in eyes, on skin, or on clothing. Wash hands thoroughly with soap and water after handling. Contact your physician or poison control center in case of accidental ingestion by humans.

■ Do not contaminate water, food, or feed by storage or disposal. Wrap container in several layers of newspaper and discard in trash. Do not reuse empty container.

For Animals

■ For external use only. Avoid getting in mouth or eyes.

■ Do not use in kittens under 8 weeks of age or puppies under 7 weeks of age. Consult your veterinarian before using on debilitated, pregnant, or nursing animals, or if your pet is on other medication.

■ Contact your veterinarian if you think your dog or cat may be having an adverse reaction to imidacloprid.

■ It is a violation of federal law to use this product in a manner inconsistent with its labeling.

■ For veterinary use only.

Possible Side Effects

Side effects are rare when used as directed. The product is bitter and cats may salivate for a short time if imidacloprid gets into the mouth.

Food and Drug Interactions

None known.

Usual Dose

Dogs and Cats: 10 mg/lb. Apply solution directly to skin by parting the hair and using pipette to place solution on the skin. It may be applied to several spots along the back, particularly in large dogs. In cats, it should be placed on the back of the neck where the cat is not able to lick it.

Drug Form: 9.1% solution in individual doses based on body weight. For cats and kittens: under 9 lbs—0.4 ml; over 9 lbs—0.8 ml. For dogs and puppies: under 10 lbs—0.4 ml; 11–20 lbs—1.0 ml; 21–55 lbs—2.5 ml; over 55 lbs—5.0 ml.

Storage: Store in a cool dry place.

Overdosage

Imidacloprid has extremely low toxicity when used on the skin as directed. The ingestion of high doses may produce twitching and muscle weakness. In case of accidental ingestion or overdose, contact your veterinarian or the National Animal Poison Control Center. ALWAYS bring the prescription bottle or container with you if you go for treatment.

Special Information

See *Fipronil* for more information on fleas and ticks.

Special Populations

Pregnancy/Lactation
Imidacloprid is considered safe to use in pregnant dogs and cats.

Puppies/Kittens
Imidacloprid is considered safe to use in puppies over age 7 weeks and kittens over age 8 weeks.

Senior Animals
Imidacloprid is considered safe when used as directed in healthy senior dogs and cats.

Type of Drug

Insect Growth Regulator

Brand Names

Generic Ingredient: Methoprene [G]
Precor [V]

Methoprene Combination Products
Ovitrol Flea Egg Collar (for Dogs) and Flea Egg-Control Collar (for Cats & Kittens) [V]
Ovitrol Plus [V]
Ovitrol Plus Complete Flea Collar (for Dogs & Puppies) [V]
Ovitrol Plus Flea & Tick Dip/Mousse/Water-Based Flea Spray [V]
Siphotrol Biorational Yard Spray Concentrate [V]
Siphotrol Plus II House Treatment/Plus Area Treatment/Plus Fogger [V]

Generic Ingredient: Pyridine G
Biolar V   BioSpot V
Nylar V

Pyridine Combination Products
Breakthru! Carpet Spray and Fogger V
Breakthru! With Nylar Spot-On for Dogs V
Happy Jack Flea Flogger Plus V

Prescribed for

Flea control on dogs and cats and in the environment.

General Information

Insect growth regulators (IGRs) prevent the larva or egg from developing into an adult parasite. They mimic the effect of the natural insect growth hormone and prevent metamorphosis into the adult. They are available as collars, sprays, dips, and premise treatments either alone or in combination with insecticides that kill adult fleas and/or ticks.

Flea control requires that the problem be attacked on several levels. Adult fleas on the animal must be killed. Flea shampoos, powders, sprays, spot-ons, and dips work at this level. Mechanical removal by frequent grooming and keeping your pet away from other animals and places where new fleas may be acquired also helps. However, addressing the infestation on the animal is rarely enough because fleas remaining in the environment continue to reproduce very rapidly. Environmental treatment with bombs or sprays kills many fleas. A major limitation is that bombs and sprays do not reach all of the flea's hiding places, which leaves live fleas to continue the infestation. Residual action products help extend the action, but still fall short of giving good control and may result in increased levels of toxic insecticides in the home and environment. In addition, most insecticides do not kill flea eggs, which hatch into new adult fleas within a few days. The use of IGRs, which prevent eggs from hatching, dramatically increases the effectiveness of flea control on animals and in the environment. Very good flea control is possible by combining insecticides and IGRs in a multilevel approach. The drawback is that it demands a great deal of motivation on the part of the owner.

Because of the potential for affecting the environment, insecticide use is primarily regulated by the Environmental Protection Agency (EPA). Label instructions should be carefully read and followed.

Cautions and Warnings

■ Contact your veterinarian if you think your dog or cat may be having an adverse reaction to an IGR.

■ It is a violation of federal law to use these products in a manner inconsistent with their labeling.

Possible Side Effects

Side effects are rare and appear to be limited to individual sensitivity.

Food and Drug Interactions

None known.

Usual Dose

Dogs and Cats: Read and follow label instructions on individual products.

Drug Form: collars, sprays, dips, and premise treatments.

Overdosage

IGRs are extremely safe and signs of overdosage are unlikely. In case of accidental ingestion or overdose, contact your veterinarian or the National Animal Poison Control Center. ALWAYS bring the prescription bottle or container with you if you go for treatment.

Special Information

See *Fipronil* for more information on fleas and ticks.

Special Populations

Pregnancy/Lactation
IGRs are considered safe to use in pregnant and lactating dogs and cats.

Puppies/Kittens
IGRs are considered safe to use in puppies and kittens.

Senior Animals
IGRs are considered safe to use in senior animals.

Generic Name

Insulin (IN-suh-lin)

Most Common Brand Names

Humulin [H]   Lente Iletin [H]
Iletin [H]   NPH [H]

Type of Drug

Antidiabetic (hormone that regulates blood glucose).

Prescribed for

Diabetes mellitus.

General Information

Insulin is a hormone normally produced by the pancreas. Diabetes mellitus is a disease in which there is a lack of insulin or a lack of response to insulin. Insulin allows sugar (glucose) to pass from the blood into cells where it is used for fuel. When glucose is unable to enter cells, blood levels may become extremely high. When blood glucose levels are high, glucose "spills" into the urine. This makes diabetics drink a lot of water, urinate excessively, eat a lot, lose weight, and, if untreated, can result in severe metabolic complications (diabetic ketoacidosis—ketones and excess acid in the blood). Diabetes is treated by giving insulin injections to replace insulin that is lacking, or to overcome insulin resistance.

There are over 30 insulin preparations available. They are either human insulins, which are genetically engineered by recombinant DNA techniques, or they are purified from beef or pork pancreas. Human insulin works better in people, and the manufacturers are discontinuing some of the beef/pork insulins. Protamine zinc insulin (PZI), a long-acting beef/pork insulin that works especially well in cats, was discontinued in 1991. Human insulin has not worked as well in cats because it is structurally different from cat insulin, and cats may rapidly develop antibodies and resistance to it. Beef/pork insulin is almost identical to dog and cat insulin. PZI is only available now on a "compassionate use" or "investigational" basis. It is awaiting FDA approval for dogs and cats.

Insulin is available in short-, intermediate-, and long-acting preparations. All human and beef/pork regular insulins are short-acting, NPH and Lente insulins are intermediate-acting, and Ultralente and PZI insulins are long-acting.

Cautions and Warnings

■ There are no insulins that are FDA approved for use in dogs or cats. PZI is the insulin of choice for most dogs and cats, but until it becomes readily available, other beef/pork or human insulins such as Ultralente must be used.

■ Make sure you give the exact dose of insulin that was prescribed. Too much insulin excessively lowers blood glucose (see "Overdosage") and too little does not control the diabetes. Make sure you have the correct insulin syringes. U-100 (100 units/ml) insulin must be given with U-100 syringes, and U-40 (40 units/ml) insulin must be given with U-40 syringes.

■ Do not change insulin brands or types unless under the supervision of your veterinarian.

■ Do not give insulin at the same site every time.

■ Do not give the normal insulin dose if your animal refuses to eat a meal (see "Food Interactions").

■ Avoid diet changes or changes in exercise routine, and try to keep feeding, exercise, and insulin dosing on a regular schedule.

■ Improper doses of insulin and poorly controlled diabetes with persistent high blood glucose results in damage to a variety of organs, especially the eyes, kidneys, and liver, and makes the animals more susceptible to infections and ketoacidosis.

■ Contact your veterinarian if you think your dog or cat may be having an adverse reaction to insulin.

■ U.S. federal law restricts the use of this drug by or on the lawful written or oral order of a licensed veterinarian within the context of a valid veterinarian-client-patient relationship.

Possible Side Effects

▼ Common: low blood glucose, high blood glucose, development of antibodies and resistance to a particular product or type of insulin (up to 35% of cats may not respond to human insulin), and reaction under the skin if the same injection site is used repeatedly.

▼ Rare: allergic reactions.

Drug Interactions

• Your animal's insulin dose may need to be raised if you are giving another drug that increases blood glucose levels. These drugs include corticosteroids, dextrothyroxine, dobutamine, epinephrine, estrogen/progesterone combinations, and furosemide and thiazide diuretics.

• Other medicines may lower blood glucose and may require a reduced insulin dose. These drugs include anabolic steroids, beta-blockers (such as propranolol), phenylbutazone, sulfinpyrazone, tetracyclines, aspirin and other salicylates, monoamine oxidase inhibitors (MAOIs), glipizide, and chromium picolinate.

• Animals receiving digoxin and/or thiazide diuretics should be monitored carefully for low potassium.

Food Interactions

Follow your veterinarian's advice on when to feed your dog or cat in relation to insulin dosing. The best feeding schedule may be frequent small meals during the day for once a day insulin dosing. Twice a day feeding may be best for twice a day dosing. The goal is to make sure there is insulin in the animal when food is given. Do not give the regular dose of insulin if your dog or cat vomits or does not eat a meal. Consult your veterinarian for instructions, or give no insulin or a smaller than usual dose. Try to get on a regular schedule of insulin dosing, eating, and exercise. Too much exercise or too little food may cause low blood glucose. If your dog or cat is showing mild symptoms (see "Overdosage"), try feeding its regular food. Keep Karo syrup on hand for emergencies. Place some in your animal's mouth and seek veterinary care as soon as possible if your dog or cat is showing any signs of insulin overdose or low blood glucose.

Usual Dose

The dose of insulin depends on the type and brand of insulin used, as well as each individual animal's requirement for a particular type or brand. If you change brands you will probably need to adjust the dose. Short-acting insulins are usually used in the hospital for emergencies. NPH or Lente insulins usually need to be given 2 to 3 times a day. Ultralente is usually given once a day but may need to be given twice a day. Regulation of blood glucose in diabetics is a process that may take weeks, as doses are slowly increased to find the dose that keeps blood glucose as close to normal as possible.

Dogs: starting dose of Ultralente is 0.25–0.5 U/lb once a day; maintenance dose is modified as needed. Insulin resistance is likely if the dose is over 0.75 U/lb twice a day.

Cats: starting dose of Ultralente is 1–3 Units once a day; maintenance dose is modified as needed. Insulin resistance is likely if the dose is over 6 U twice a day.

Drug Form: injectable suspensions or liquids. Keep refrigerated and mix well but do not shake before use.

Overdosage

Insulin overdose causes low blood glucose. This may be fairly mild and cause weakness, incoordination, trembling, lethargy, or abnormal behavior. Severe hypoglycemia may cause seizures, hypoglycemic shock, coma, and death. A relative insulin overdose may occur if a diabetic receives its normal dose of insulin but does not eat, or exercises strenuously.

Sometimes insulin overdose may cause paradoxical high blood glucose after an initial lowering. This may be mistaken as insulin resistance, when in fact it results from insulin overdose and the dose of insulin should be reduced. Contact your veterinarian if blood or urine glucose levels are high despite normal or increased doses of insulin. Your veterinarian can determine if this is a result of insulin resistance or insulin overdose. In case of accidental overdose, contact your veterinarian or the National Animal Poison Control Center. ALWAYS bring the prescription bottle or container with you if you go for treatment.

Special Information

Animals with uncomplicated diabetes may safely begin insulin therapy at home. Insulin requirements are greatly affected by diet, activity level, and stress; therefore, home is the ideal place to figure out the proper dose. However, most owners are unable to check blood glucose levels, the ideal way to monitor response to insulin. Urine glucose may be a reasonable way to monitor response to treatment, but it is much less accurate than blood glucose. If the animal has complications of diabetes, or is difficult to regulate, hospitalization is probably necessary.

Some diabetic cats may be extremely difficult to manage. Their diabetes may come and go in an erratic and unpredictable fashion, which means they may need insulin one week or month and not the next. Some cats seem to recover completely. Discuss management carefully with your veterinarian, and monitor urine or blood glucose levels as often as possible so that you can give your animal the proper amount of insulin.

Chromium picolinate and glipizide (see *Glipizide*) are two agents that help lower blood glucose. They may be useful adjuncts to insulin therapy. Do not give either of these to your diabetic animal without the supervision of your veterinarian.

Special Populations

Pregnancy/Lactation
Insulin should be safe to use in pregnant or lactating animals; however, diabetic animals should be neutered and not bred. Heat cycles and pregnancy make diabetic management far more difficult, and diabetes may be partly inherited.

Puppies/Kittens
Juvenile onset diabetes may occur rarely in puppies 2 to 6 months of age, and they should be treated with insulin. Diabetes does not occur in kittens.

Senior Animals
Diabetes is likely to occur in older animals and may occur along with other diseases of older animals. Heart, liver, or kidney disease, Cushing's disease (in dogs), infections (especially of the mouth or urinary tract), hypothyroidism (in dogs), chronic pancreatitis, pancreatic insufficiency, and hyperthyroidism (in cats) are all known to cause insulin ineffectiveness or resistance. It is important for you to work closely with your veterinarian in treating animals with diabetes and other complications, as management of these animals can be challenging.

Generic Name

Interferon (Recombinant Human Interferon-Alpha) (in-ter-FEER-on)

Brand Names

Intron A H   Roferon-A H

Type of Drug

Cytokine, antiviral, immune-modulator, and anticancer.

Prescribed for

Viral infections, especially feline leukemia virus (FeLV), feline immunodeficiency virus (FIV), and feline herpes virus corneal (eye) disease, and cancer.

General Information

Interferons are cytokines, natural substances made by certain cells in the body that communicate with other cells in the body. Interferon-alpha is produced by cells in response to viral infections, and it turns on a cascade of other cytokines that kill viruses, and potentially tumor cells, throughout the body. Recent reports have shown that FeLV-infected cats treated with low-dose oral interferon-alpha had one or more of the following: improved activity and appetite, resolved blood abnormalities, clearance of virus from the blood, and prolonged survival. Interferon-alpha has been used successfully in human medicine to treat a variety of viral infections and cancers, and has shown promise so far in animal studies. It is not known exactly how interferon works, but it seems that the best responses are seen when very low doses are given orally. The interferon seems to be acting on immune/lymphoid cells in the throat, which are activated, and move throughout the body, turning on other immune cells to fight viruses and cancer cells.

Cautions and Warnings

■ Interferon is not FDA approved for use in dogs or cats. It is commonly used, however, and is considered accepted practice.

■ Contact your veterinarian if you think your dog or cat may be having an adverse reaction to interferon.

■ U.S. federal law restricts the use of this drug by or on the lawful written or oral order of a licensed veterinarian within the context of a valid veterinarian-client-patient relationship.

Possible Side Effects

No side effects have been reported so far in animals. Larger doses given by injection usually cause flu-like symptoms (fever, chills, headache, muscle and joint pain, nausea, vomiting, and diarrhea) in people. Large doses may also cause bone marrow suppression in people. The same side effects could be expected in animals given large doses by injection.

Drug Interactions

None known.

Food Interactions

Do not mix with food or give while the animal is eating.

Usual Dose

Dogs and Cats: Low-dose oral interferon-alpha—30–40 IU in 1 ml saline orally once a day or as directed by your veterinarian. Injectable interferon-alpha—10,000 IU given by injection under the skin twice a day.

Drug Form: Interferon is supplied as a concentrated liquid for injection. Your veterinarian will dilute the concentrated solution in saline so that you can easily give the low-dose interferon orally to your animal. Keep the solution in the refrigerator.

Overdosage

Overdoses may cause flu-like symptoms and bone marrow suppression (see "Possible Side Effects"). In case of accidental ingestion or overdose, contact your veterinarian or the National Animal Poison Control Center. ALWAYS bring the prescription bottle or container if you go for treatment.

Special Information

Interferon has shown promise when it has been used alone as a treatment for FeLV, and as a treatment for FeLV-FIV (feline AIDS complex) in combination with interleukin-2 and zidovudine (AZT). It has also been used with tumor necrosis factor-alpha to treat solid tumors, as a single agent in T-cell lymphomas, and in combination with etretinate or chlorambucil to treat non-Hodgkin's lymphoma in humans. It is being used to treat eosinophilic granuloma complex, cutaneous T-cell lymphoma in animals, and chronic or recurrent corneal disease in cats caused by herpes virus (feline rhinotracheitis virus). Preliminary results are promising.

Low-dose oral interferon therapy is showing promise in a number of disorders. It is inexpensive, safe, easy to administer, and well worth trying in viral infections and cancers.

There are other promising new treatments for FeLV/FIV infected cats as well. Acemannan Immunostimulant, derived from aloe, has prolonged the survival and improved the quality of life of infected cats, and seems to work as well orally as by injection. It is also effective against a variety of cancers when injected into the tumor, and is licensed by the FDA for use in dogs and cats. Staphylococcal protein A (SPA) and Immunoregulin (*Propionibacterium acnes*) have also shown promise in treating FeLV infected cats (see *Propionibacterium acnes*).

Special Populations

Pregnancy/Lactation
Low-dose interferon should be safe to use during pregnancy and lactation.

Puppies/Kittens
Low-dose interferon should be safe to use in puppies and kittens.

Senior Animals
High-dose interferon should be used with caution in older animals or those with bone marrow suppression.

Generic Name

Iodine/Iodide (EYE-oe-dine/EYE-oe-dide) G

Most Common Brand Names

Betadine H V   Xenodine V
Efodine H

Type of Drug

Disinfectant, antiseptic, antibacterial, antifungal, antiviral, required nutrient.

Prescribed for

Ringworm; bacterial skin infections; care of wounds, burns, and superficial abrasions; and hyperthyroidism in cats.

General Information

Iodine is a trace mineral that is a required nutrient. It is a part of the thyroid hormone and is necessary for normal thyroid function. Commercial dog and cat foods contain iodine in required amounts. Iodine may be provided in home-made diets by adding iodized salt.

Iodine has been used since the early 1800s as a disinfectant. It was initially used as tincture of iodine (alcohol base). Tincture of iodine is irritating, painful, and damaging to tissue when applied to open wounds, and can delay healing. It is also allergenic, corrosive to metal, and stains skin and clothing. For these reasons it has fallen out of favor. Tamed iodine or povidone-iodine retains the antiseptic properties of the tincture but has none of its adverse effects.

Radioactive iodine is used to treat hyperthyroidism in cats (see *Methimazole*). In cats with hyperthyroidism, the radioactive iodine is concentrated in the abnormal thyroid nodules and destroys those tissues. The normal thyroid tissue is not affected because it has been suppressed by the excess activity of the abnormal tissue and does not take up the radioactive iodine. This is the treatment of choice for most cats with hyperthyroidism because it is safe and effective and does not require lifetime medication. Most cats are cured with a single dose, but 5% to 10% may remain hyperthyroid. A few cats (less than 5%) will develop permanent hypothyroidism a few months after treatment. These cats then require lifelong thyroid supplementation. Relapses are also rare (less than 5%), and usually occur 3 or more years after treatment. There are limited sites licensed to perform this treatment and it is expensive due to the strict radiation safety precautions and procedures that must be followed after treatment. Consult your veterinarian for more information about the treatments for hyperthyroidism, and advice on the best treatment for your cat.

Iodide has been used in the past as a systemic antifungal treatment. It is rarely used since the newer antifungals such as ketoconazole (see *Ketoconazole*), fluconazole (see *Fluconazole*), and itraconazole (see *Itraconazole*) have become available. Povidone iodine is an effective topical antifungal and may be used in the treatment of ringworm (see *Griseofulvin*), and yeast (*Malassezia*) infections of skin and ears. There are many other antifungals available; consult your veterinarian for advice on the best product for your pet.

Potassium iodide given orally causes increased bronchial secretions as well as loosening of secretions. Expectorants such as potassium iodide may be useful in removing the cause of coughing, and may be one of the ingredients in cough preparations.

Cautions and Warnings

For Owners/Handlers
■ Avoid contact with eyes. Iodine can be absorbed through the skin when povidone iodine is used, and may cause hyperthyroidism when used excessively.

For Animals
■ Excessive use of topical povidone-iodine may lead to iodine absorption through the skin, high blood levels, and hyperthyroidism, especially if kidney function is impaired and excess iodine cannot be rapidly excreted.
■ Avoid contact with eyes.
■ Contact your veterinarian if you think your dog or cat may be having an adverse reaction to iodine.
■ U.S. federal law restricts the use of this drug by or on the lawful written or oral order of a licensed veterinarian within the context of a valid veterinarian-client-patient relationship.

Possible Side Effects

▼ Rare: allergy or sensitivity to iodine after repeated contact, excess iodine absorption through the skin and hyperthyroidism, and mild transient pain of the thyroid gland (with radioactive iodine treatment for hyperthyroidism).

Food and Drug Interactions

None known.

Usual Dose

Dogs and Cats: Follow your veterinarian's advice on the use of povidone iodine products in the care of wounds or skin infections.
Drug Form: Povidone-iodine is available in solution, shampoo, surgical scrub, spray, and ointment.
Storage: Avoid storage in excessive heat.

Overdosage

There is no specific information on overdose of povidone-iodine. Chronic excessive topical use in animals with decreased kidney function may be expected to produce signs of hyperthyroidism such as increased or decreased appetite, weight loss, hyperactivity, and increased heart rate. In case of accidental ingestion or overdose, contact your veterinarian or the National Animal Poison Control Center. ALWAYS bring the prescription bottle or container with you if you go for treatment.

Special Information

Povidone-iodine solution may be added to a warm water solution of Epsom salts and used as an effective antiseptic and soothing soak for cuts, abrasions, and skin infections of the feet and limbs. Add povidone-iodine liquid concentrate to the Epsom salt solution to make it the color of weak tea. Soak for 5 to 10 minutes twice a day or as directed by your veterinarian.

Special Populations

Pregnancy/Lactation
Povidone-iodine should be safe to use topically in pregnant or lactating animals if it is not used in large wounds or used excessively (see "Cautions and Warnings").

Puppies/Kittens
Use povidone-iodine with caution in puppies and kittens. Do not use for longer than a few days except on the advice of your veterinarian.

Senior Animals
Povidone-iodine should be safe to use in older animals with normal kidney function.

Generic Name

Ipecac Syrup (IP-uh-kak)

Brand Names

Available in generic form over-the-counter.

Type of Drug

Emetic.

Prescribed for

Induction of vomiting in dogs and cats.

General Information

Ipecac may be used to induce vomiting in dogs and cats after ingestion of certain toxic compounds or in suspected drug overdose. It works by irritating the gastric lining and stimulating the chemoreceptor trigger zone in the central nervous system. Ipecac causes emptying of the stomach and a portion of the upper intestine. Vomiting empties between 40% and 60% of the stomach contents and usually occurs within 10 to 30 minutes. Some animals need a second dose to induce vomiting, but if the second dose is not productive, gastric lavage or other therapy should be considered because ipecac can be toxic to the heart.

Cautions and Warnings

■ Ipecac is not FDA approved for use in dogs or cats. It may be used in dogs and cats, but other methods are preferred.

■ Emetics should not be used in animals that are in shock, comatose, severely depressed, having difficulty breathing, lacking normal choke reflexes, seizuring, extremely weak, or with other impairments that may lead to aspiration of the vomited material or pneumonia.

■ Emetics should not be used in animals that have vomited repeatedly.

■ Emetics should not be used in animals that have ingested caustic substances because of the risk of further damage to the stomach and esophagus.

■ Emetics should be used with caution in animals that have ingested petroleum distillates because of the risk of aspiration.

■ Emetics should be used with caution in animals who have ingested strychnine or other central nervous system stimulants because of the increased risk of seizures.

■ Ipecac should be used with caution in animals with heart problems.

■ Use of this drug should be by or on the lawful written or oral order of a licensed veterinarian within the context of a valid veterinarian-client-patient relationship.

Possible Side Effects

Aspiration pneumonia can occur after an animal vomits if vomit is inhaled into the lungs. This is always a risk,

---

Possible Side Effects *(continued)*

whether the vomiting was spontaneous or induced. Animals that are ill because of eating a toxin are more likely to aspirate vomit than normal animals.

▼ Common: salivation, tearing, and increased bronchial secretions.

▼ Rare: prolonged vomiting, diarrhea, and depression.

Drug Interactions

• Ipecac should be used before activated charcoal, because the charcoal binds the ipecac and decreases its effectiveness.

Food Interactions

Milk, dairy products, or carbonated beverages decrease the effectiveness of ipecac.

Usual Dose

Dogs: 0.5–1.0 ml/lb orally.

Cats: 1–1.8 ml/lb orally (diluted to 50% with water) via stomach tube. (Most veterinary experts do not recommend the use of ipecac in cats.)

Drug Form: 15- and 30-ml and pint containers of oral syrup.

Overdosage

Overdoses of ipecac can be very toxic to the heart, causing abnormal heart rhythms, low blood pressure, and myocarditis (heart muscle damage). In case of accidental ingestion or overdose, contact your veterinarian or the National Animal Poison Control Center. ALWAYS bring the prescription bottle or container with you if you go for treatment.

Special Information

All suspected poisonings and drug overdoses should be treated under veterinary supervision. Because speed is so important when treating poisonings and overdoses, your veterinarian may instruct you to give ipecac at home or before bringing your animal in for further treatment. If your animal vomits before arriving at the veterinary hospital, try to save the vomit for analysis.

Other recommended and more commonly used emetics in dogs include orally administered hydrogen peroxide and/or table salt. Consult your veterinarian before attempting these methods and use them only under the supervision of a veterinarian. Apomorphine is also commonly used in the hospital to induce vomiting in dogs (see *Apomorphine*). Injectable xylazine is the recommended emetic for cats.

Special Populations

Pregnancy/Lactation
There are no safety studies on the use of ipecac in pregnant and lactating animals. It should be avoided and other emetics, such as hydrogen peroxide and/or table salt, used instead. Use emetics *only* under direct veterinary supervision.

Puppies/Kittens
There are no safety studies on the use of ipecac in puppies or kittens. It should not be used in kittens. It should be avoided in puppies and other emetics, such as hydrogen peroxide and/or table salt, used instead. Use emetics *only* under direct veterinary supervision.

Senior Animals
There are no safety studies on the use of ipecac in older animals. It should be avoided and other emetics, such as hydrogen peroxide and/or table salt, used instead. Use emetics *only* under direct veterinary supervision. DO NOT use ipecac in older animals with pre-existing heart problems.

Generic Name

Itraconazole (ih-trah-KON-uh-zole)

Brand Name
Sporanox [H]

Type of Drug
Antifungal.

Prescribed for
Susceptible superficial and deep (systemic) fungal infections,

including those caused by Dermatophytes (ringworm), *Malassezia* and *Candida* (yeasts), *Cryptococcus, Coccidioides, Histoplasma, Aspergillus,* and *Blastomyces;* and sporotrichosis, protothecosis, and pheaohyphomycosis.

General Information

Itraconazole is the newest of the triazole antifungals (see *Fluconazole*). It has a spectrum of action equal to or greater than amphotericin B or ketoconazole, and is safer to use than either of these older antifungals. Because it may take 1 to 2 weeks to see a response to itraconazole, serious fungal infections may initially be treated with amphotericin B (see *Amphotericin B),* followed by itraconazole. Itraconazole may be used to treat fungal infections of the skin and life-threatening systemic infections of bone, lung, and gastrointestinal tract. It is probably the drug of choice for fungal infections of the central nervous system. Itraconazole has been very effective in treating some of the rarer fungal infections. Long-term treatment is often required for many of these infections, and some may never be completely cured. Sporotrichosis should be treated for at least a month after symptoms are gone, and care should be taken because human infection can occur from contact with infected animals (see *Zoonotic Diseases of Dogs and Cats).*

Cautions and Warnings

■ Itraconazole is not FDA approved for use in dogs or cats. It is commonly used and is considered accepted practice.

■ Clinical response to itraconazole may take 10 days to 2 weeks.

■ Itraconazole should be avoided in animals with liver disease.

■ Contact your veterinarian if you think your dog or cat may be having an adverse reaction to itraconazole.

■ U.S. federal law restricts the use of this drug by or on the lawful written or oral order of a licensed veterinarian within the context of a valid veterinarian-client-patient relationship.

Possible Side Effects

▼ Common: liver damage and decreased appetite.

▼ Rare: vasculitis with skin ulcers and swellings of the legs.

Drug Interactions

• Itraconazole should not be given with terfenadine, astemizole, or cisapride, as fatal abnormal heart rhythms may occur.

• Antacids and H$_2$ blockers such as cimetidine decrease absorption of itraconazole. These drugs should be given 2 hours after the dose of itraconazole.

• The dose of warfarin may need to be decreased if itraconazole is given.

• Phenytoin or phenobarbital and itraconazole may alter each other's metabolism, and animals receiving both should be monitored carefully for side effects.

• Itraconazole may prolong the effect of methylprednisolone.

• Cyclosporine, digoxin, and quinidine blood levels may be increased by itraconazole.

• Rifampin may decrease the blood levels of itraconazole.

• Itraconazole may cause severe hypoglycemia (low blood glucose) when used with oral hypoglycemic agents such as glipizide.

Food Interactions

Itraconazole should be given with meals.

Usual Dose

Dogs and Cats: 2.5 mg/lb orally twice a day.
Drug Form: 100-mg capsules and 10 mg/ml oral solution.

Overdosage

There is little specific information available on overdose of itraconazole. There were no signs of toxicity seen in dogs given 10 times the recommended dose for 3 months. Signs of overdose should be similar to the side effects (see "Possible Side Effects"). In case of accidental ingestion or overdose, contact your veterinarian or the National Animal Poison Control Center. ALWAYS bring the prescription bottle or container with you if you go for treatment.

Special Information

There are many alternatives available now for the treatment of both superficial and deep fungal infections. None of these treatments are FDA approved for use in animals. See *Boric Acid, Griseofulvin, Miconazole,* and *Clotrimazole* for more information on treatment of superficial fungal infections. See

Amphotericin B, Fluconazole and *Ketoconazole* for more information on treatment of deep fungal infections.

About 10% of dogs on itraconazole develop liver damage. This usually occurs in the second month of treatment and is marked by loss of appetite. Appetite usually returns 3 to 4 days after discontinuing itraconazole. Treatment may then be restarted at half the original dose. Most dogs that develop liver damage have high itraconazole blood levels and will still benefit from therapy at a reduced dose. Vasculitis with skin ulcers and swelling of the legs has been seen as a less common complication; this occurs in dogs on the higher itraconazole dose and does not recur when the drug is restarted at half the original dose. Cats tolerate itraconazole better than ketoconazole, but they may also develop liver damage and decreased appetite.

Sporanox capsules contain small pellets that can be put into food. This is especially useful in treating cats. Cats will readily eat the food containing itraconazole. Itraconazole is probably the safest and the best of the antifungals developed to date, but it is fairly expensive.

Special Populations

Pregnancy/Lactation
Itraconazole causes damage to the fetus and is excreted in milk. It should be avoided during pregnancy and lactation unless the benefits outweigh the risks.

Puppies/Kittens
Itraconazole should be avoided in puppies and kittens unless the potential benefits outweigh the risks.

Senior Animals
Itraconazole should be safe to use in older animals with normal liver function (see "Cautions and Warnings").

Generic Name

Ivermectin (EYE-ver-MEK-tin)

Most Common Brand Names

Eqvalan [V]	Heartgard for Cats [V]
Heartgard-30 [V]	Ivomec [V]

Combination Product

Generic Ingredients: Ivermectin + Pyrantel Pamoate
Heartgard-30 Plus Ⓥ

Type of Drug

Heartworm preventive, anthelmintic/dewormer, microfilaricide, and miticide.

Prescribed for

Prevention of heartworm disease (*Dirofilaria immitis*) and removal of heartworm microfilaria (*D. immitis*), roundworm (*Toxocara canis, Toxascaris leonina*), hookworm (*Ancylostoma caninum, A. braziliense, Uncinaria stenocephala*), whipworm (*Trichuris vulpis*) *Strongyloides stercoralis*, lungworm (*Capillaria aerophilia, Oslerus osleri*), and mites (*Otodectes cynotis, Sarcoptes scabiei, Cheyletiella* spp., *Notoedres cati, Demodex canis, Pneumonyssus caninum*) in dogs and cats.

General Information

The soil-living bacteria *Streptomyces avermitilis* produce ivermectin. It is in the same group of macrolide drugs and acts against the same parasites as milbemycin oxime, another popular once-a-month heartworm preventive (see *Milbemycin Oxime*).

Ivermectin interferes with parasite nerve function. This results in paralysis and death of susceptible parasites. Mammalian muscles are controlled by a different type of nerve and are not affected by ivermectin. Mammals do have similar nerve types in the brain and central nervous system, but ivermectin does not pass through the blood-brain barrier and therefore does not affect the central nervous system. For this reason, ivermectin has very few side effects in dogs and cats.

Prevention of heartworm disease is the major and only FDA approved use of this drug in dogs and cats. Heartworm disease is caused by the filarial parasite *D. immitis*. Infective heartworm larvae are transmitted from mosquitoes to dogs. The infective larva migrates to the heart and develops into an adult heartworm. Adult heartworm mate, producing microfilariae that circulate in the blood. The cycle is completed when a mosquito feeds on the blood of an infected dog and acquires microfilarial larvae that may infect the next dog from which the mosquito feeds. Ivermectin is 100% effective against heartworm larvae transmitted from infected mosquitoes within 45 days before treatment.

One way to diagnose heartworm infection is to use a microscope to look for microfilaria in a blood sample. Using ivermectin at the heartworm preventive dose in dogs with heartworm disease may reduce the number of microfilaria and make this test falsely negative. For this reason, an alternative test that detects antigen from adult heartworm is recommended.

Ivermectin may be used at a higher dose to kill microfilariae. Large numbers of dying microfilaria may cause an allergic, shock-like reaction. This treatment should be done only under direct veterinary supervision.

Ivermectin at dosages higher than those approved by the FDA for heartworm prevention may be used to remove a number of other parasites. These include the common intestinal parasites—roundworm (*Toxocara canis, Toxascaris leonina*), hookworm (*Ancylostoma caninum, A. braziliense, Uncinaria stenocephala*), and whipworm (*Trichuris vulpis*)—and filarial lungworm (*Capillaria aerophilia, Oslerus osleri*). It also kills mites, including skin mites (*Sarcoptes scabiei, Notoedres cati, Cheyletiella* spp., *Demodex canis*), ear mites (*Otodectes cynotis*), and nasal mites (*Pneumonyssus caninum*). It has no activity against tapeworms, flukes, or protozoa.

Heartworm, roundworm, hookworm, and some mites are contagious and may spread to other animals and to people (see *Zoonotic Diseases of Dogs and Cats*).

Cautions and Warnings

■ Ivermectin may be toxic to fish and other animals that are accidentally exposed by contamination of the environment and water. Dispose of unused ivermectin and containers by incineration or in an approved landfill.

■ All adult animals that have been off heartworm preventive for 6 months or longer should be tested for heartworm infection before starting preventive treatment (see "General Information"). Animals off heartworm preventive for 2 to 6 months should restart heartworm preventive and be tested 6 months from the last date of exposure. It takes 6 months from the time of infection for the tests to become positive. Start ivermectin within 30 days of discontinuing diethylcarbamazine when switching from daily heartworm preventive or any of the once-a-month preventives.

■ Do not use in collies and other herding breeds or cross-bred dogs at doses higher than those recommended for heartworm prevention (see "Special Populations"). Be aware that the use of high doses of ivermectin may increase the risk of side effects even for dogs that are not in a high-risk breed.

■ Contact your veterinarian if you think your dog or cat may be having an adverse reaction to ivermectin.

■ FDA approved only for prevention of heartworm in dogs and cats. Extralabel use is common and accepted practice but should be done only under veterinary supervision and after considering the potential risks and benefits.

■ U.S. federal law restricts the use of this drug by or on the lawful written or oral order of a licensed veterinarian within the context of a valid veterinarian-client-patient relationship.

Possible Side Effects

Side effects are rare at recommended doses for heartworm prevention. The occurrence of side effects is increased when ivermectin is used at higher dosages to remove other parasites (see "General Information").

▼ Rare: tremors, loss of coordination, dilated pupils, decreased body weight, and death in dogs; agitation, vocalization, loss of appetite, dilation of the pupil, loss of coordination, tremors, blindness, head-pressing, wall-climbing, and disorientation in cats (see also "Overdosage" and "Special Populations").

Food and Drug Interactions

None known.

Usual Dose

Ivermectin
Dogs
   Heartworm prevention—0.003–0.0066 mg/lb once a month. Do not use in collies or other herding dogs except for heartworm prevention.
   Microfilaricide—0.023–0.09 mg/lb single dose
   Roundworm—0.09 mg/lb.
   Hookworm—0.023 mg/lb.

Whipworm—0.045 mg/lb.

Parasitic lung disease—0.09 mg/lb orally once.

Miticide—*Sarcoptes scabiei, Cheyletiella* spp., or *Otodectes cynotis*—0.14 mg/lb repeat in 14 days.

Demodex canis—0.27 mg/lb once a day for at least 90 days depending on response. The effective dose is not firmly established. Dose, dosing interval, and duration may vary.

Cats

Heartworm prevention—0.011–0.033 mg/lb

Miticide—*Notoedres cati* and *Otodectes cynotis*—0.14 mg/lb

Drug Form

Tablets—0.68-, 0.136-, and 0.272-mg for dogs; 0.055- and 0.165-mg for cats. Oral and injectable formulations for large animals are also used in dogs and cats.

Heartgard-30 Plus

Dogs: Less than 25 lbs—68 mcg ivermectin + 57 mg pyrantel, 26–50 lbs—136 mcg ivermectin + 114 mg pyrantel; 50–100 lbs— 272 mcg ivermectin + 227 mg pyrantel; over 100 lbs— appropriate combination of above.

Drug Form: Chewable tablets in 3 sizes as listed above.

Overdosage

Dilation of the pupil, incoordination, vomiting, diarrhea, depression, and shock are the principal signs of overdose.

There is a wide margin of safety for ivermectin in most dogs. The following information comes from tests on beagles. It does not apply to collies or other herding breeds, which may have severe side effects at much lower dosages, and individual animals of any breed may be more sensitive.

Side effects rarely occur in dogs given a single dose of less than 0.9 mg/lb, which is 150 times the dose used to prevent heartworm, 10 times the dose for intestinal parasites, and 3 times the dose used for demodicosis. Severe side effects, including tremors and loss of coordination, are seen at doses of 4.5 mg/lb, and death may occur at doses greater than 18.2 mg/lb. The median lethal dose (the dose at which 50% of animals will die, or LD50) is 36.4 mg/lb. Dogs given 0.23 mg/lb daily for 14 weeks developed no side effects. At 2 to 3 times this dose, the only side effects were dilated pupils and decreased body weight. At 4 times that dose, half of the dogs treated had significant side effects.

Side effects due to overdose in cats are seen within 10 hours of treatment; they are primarily neurologic and include agitation, vocalization, loss of appetite, dilation of the pupil, loss of coordination, tremors, blindness, head-pressing, wall-climbing, and disorientation. Most cats recover within 2 to 4 weeks.

In case of accidental ingestion or overdose, contact your veterinarian or the National Animal Poison Control Center. ALWAYS bring the prescription bottle or container with you if you go for treatment.

Special Populations

Herding Breeds

About 25% of collie dogs are more sensitive to the toxic effects of ivermectin than dogs of other breeds. This may be due to a more permeable blood-brain barrier or drug accumulation in the central nervous system of this breed. Other herding breeds, including Shetland sheepdogs, Old English sheepdogs, Australian sheepdogs, and crosses of these are also at increased risk of side effects. Other breeds may be added to the list as the use of high dose ivermectin becomes more common. Ivermectin is considered safe at the heartworm preventive dose in these breeds. The dose for removal of microfilaria is also less than the dose at which severe side effects generally occur. However, treated dogs should be observed for 8 to 12 hours after treatment and any side effects should be reported to your veterinarian.

Pregnancy/Lactation

Ivermectin is considered safe to use in dogs and cats during pregnancy and lactation. Transplacental and mammary transmission of roundworms and hookworms can be prevented by treating the mother dog 10 days before and after delivery with 0.23 mg/lb. This should be done only after considering the risks and benefits and only under your veterinarian's direct supervision.

Puppies/Kittens

Ivermectin is considered safe to use in puppies and kittens over age 6 weeks at the dosage recommended for heartworm prevention.

Senior Animals

Ivermectin is considered safe to use in senior dogs and cats at the dosage recommended for heartworm prevention.

Generic Name

Ketoconazole (kee-toe-KON-uh-zole)

Brand Name

Nizoral [H]

Type of Drug

Antifungal.

Prescribed for

Susceptible superficial and deep (systemic) fungal infections, including those caused by dermatophytes (ringworm), *Malassezia* (yeast), *Cryptococcus, Coccidioides, Histoplasma,* and *Blastomyces*; hyperadrenocorticism (Cushing's disease), canine Chagas' myocarditis, and epidermal dysplasia of West Highland white terriers.

General Information

Ketoconazole was the first of the antifungal imidazoles (see *Clotrimazole* and *Miconazole*) that could be given orally for the treatment of deep fungal infections. Because it takes 1 to 2 weeks to see a response to ketoconazole, serious fungal infections may be initially treated with amphotericin B (see *Amphotericin B*), followed by ketoconazole. Ketoconazole may be used to treat fungal infections of the skin and life-threatening systemic infections of bone, lung, and gastrointestinal tract. Oral ketoconazole may be useful in treating superficial fungal infections of the skin caused by *Malassezia*. The reason for this beneficial effect is not known.

Ketoconazole may not be a good choice for fungal infections of the central nervous system because it does not penetrate the blood-brain barrier well. *Aspergillus* is often resistant to ketoconazole at doses that are safe. Ketoconazole may cause decreased appetite, vomiting, and liver damage, and is poorly tolerated by most cats. Fluconazole and itraconazole are newer antifungals that are better tolerated by cats, but are fairly expensive (see *Itraconazole*).

Ketoconazole also inhibits the body's production of steroid hormones (see "Special Populations" and "Cautions and Warnings"), and it has been used to treat Cushing's disease, where there is excess steroid production by the adrenal glands.

Chagas' myocarditis is a heart disease caused by the proto-
zoan parasite *Trypanosoma cruzi*. Although the mechanism of
action is not known, ketoconazole appears to be an effective
treatment for the early stages of this disease.

West Highland White terriers may have an inherited skin disease (epidermal dysplasia) that predisposes them to almost
constant *Malassezia* infections of the skin. Oral ketoconazole
may be needed to control the infection when topical therapy is
not effective.

Cautions and Warnings

■ Ketoconazole is not FDA approved for use in dogs or cats.
It is commonly used and is considered accepted practice.

■ Clinical response to ketoconazole may take 10 days to 2
weeks.

■ Ketoconazole should be avoided in animals with liver disease or low platelet counts.

■ Dogs undergoing high-dose ketoconazole therapy may
need support with oral corticosteroids.

■ Contact your veterinarian if you think your dog or cat may
be having an adverse reaction to ketoconazole.

■ U.S. federal law restricts the use of this drug by or on the
lawful written or oral order of a licensed veterinarian within the
context of a valid veterinarian-client-patient relationship.

Possible Side Effects

Cats are more susceptible than dogs to liver damage and
other side effects of ketoconazole.

▼ Common: decreased appetite, vomiting, and diarrhea.

▼ Rare: allergic or anaphylactic reactions, liver damage, low platelet counts, and reversible lightening of the
haircoat.

Drug Interactions

• Antacids and H_2 blockers such as cimetidine will decrease
the absorption of ketoconazole. Give these drugs 2 hours after
the ketoconazole dose.

• Mitotane and ketoconazole should not be given together.

• The dose of warfarin may need to be decreased if ketoconazole is given at the same time.

• Phenytoin or phenobarbital and ketoconazole may alter
each other's metabolism, and animals receiving both should be
monitored carefully for side effects.

• Ketoconazole may prolong the effect of methylprednisolone.

• Cyclosporine blood levels may be increased by ketoconazole.

• Theophylline blood levels may be decreased by ketoconazole in some animals. Measurement of theophylline blood levels is recommended.

• Rifampin may decrease the blood levels of ketoconazole.

• Cisapride, astemizole, and terfenadine should not be given
with ketoconazole as they may cause serious heart problems.

• Ketoconazole may cause severe hypoglycemia (low blood
glucose) when used with oral hypoglycemic agents such as
glipizide.

Food Interactions

Side effects are less likely if the dose is given with food.

Usual Dose

Dogs: 2.5–7.5 mg/lb orally, twice a day, for 21-45 days. Clean
affected areas with soap and water, dry, and apply cream once
a day to affected areas and immediately adjacent skin and
haircoat, or as directed by your veterinarian. Cleaning of some
areas such as ears may vary; follow the advice of your veterinarian. Apply shampoo to wet haircoat after using a degreasing shampoo such as benzoyl peroxide or selenium sulfide.
Leave ketoconazole shampoo on for 10–15 minutes before
rinsing.
Cats: 2.5-5 mg/lb orally 2–3 times a day.
Drug Form: 200-mg tablets, 2% cream, and 2% shampoo.

Overdosage

There is no specific information available on overdose of ketoconazole. The lethal dose is approximately 250 mg/lb, or
almost 100 times the recommended dose. Symptoms of overdose should be similar to the side effects (see "Possible Side
Effects"). In case of accidental ingestion or overdose, contact
your veterinarian or the National Animal Poison Control Center.

ALWAYS bring the prescription bottle or container with you if you go for treatment.

Special Information

There are many alternatives available now for the treatment of both superficial and deep fungal infections. None of these treatments are FDA approved for use in animals. See *Boric Acid, Griseofulvin, Miconazole,* and *Clotrimazole* for more information on treatment of superficial fungal infections. See *Amphotericin B, Fluconazole,* and *Itraconazole* for more information on treatment of deep fungal infections.

Special Populations

Breeding Animals
Ketoconazole may cause reversible infertility in male dogs by decreasing testosterone synthesis.

Pregnancy/Lactation
Ketoconazole causes damage to the fetus and is excreted in milk; it should be avoided during pregnancy and lactation unless the benefits outweigh the risks.

Puppies/Kittens
Ketoconazole should be avoided in puppies and kittens unless the potential benefits outweigh the risks.

Senior Animals
Ketoconazole should be safe to use in older animals with normal liver function (see "Cautions and Warnings").

Generic Name

Lactulose (LAK-tue-lose) [G]

Most Common Brand Names

Constilac [H]   Duphalac [H]
Cholac [H]

Type of Drug

Osmotic laxative.

Prescribed for

Constipation, megacolon, and hepatic encephalopathy in dogs and cats.

General Information

Laxatives are used to prevent or relieve constipation. They are classified by their action as lubricant, emollient (stool softeners), bulk-forming, osmotic, or stimulant. The choice of laxative, dose, and frequency of administration must be adjusted for each individual to obtain the desired stool consistency and frequency of defecation. Vomiting, straining, and other signs of constipation may be caused by serious problems. Consult your veterinarian before administering laxatives or any medication to your pet.

Lactulose is a safe and effective osmotic laxative for use in dogs and cats. It is a synthetic disaccharide (2 simple sugar molecules linked together) derived from lactose, the primary sugar in milk. Disaccharides must be split into 2 simple sugars before they can be absorbed into the body and metabolized. The enzymes in the intestines of mammals cannot split lactulose; therefore, it is not absorbed and passes through the intestines to the colon unchanged. The normal bacteria in the colon have the enzymes needed to split lactulose and break it down into organic acids. These increase the concentration of these substances in the colon and result in more water entering the colon. The increased water content softens the stool and increases the fecal mass, which helps stimulate evacuation, usually within 3 to 12 hours.

Megacolon is a disorder seen most frequently in cats. An enlarged colon with decreased muscle function results in the accumulation of huge amounts of fecal material, making it painful and ultimately impossible to defecate. There is no cure, but the constipation may be managed with individually tailored treatment plans based on the use of various types of laxatives. Lactulose is frequently used to facilitate passage of the fecal mass by making it softer.

Lactulose is also used to treat neurologic signs associated with liver failure. The liver normally detoxifies ammonia. In liver failure, ammonia accumulates in the blood and causes the neurologic signs characteristic of liver failure. The organic acids formed by the metabolism of lactulose acidify the colon.

This pulls toxic ammonia from the blood into the colon and it is excreted with the stool.

Cautions and Warnings

■ Lactulose syrup contains some free lactose and galactose. Absorption of these sugars may increase the insulin requirement in diabetic patients.

■ Do not use other laxatives when administering lactulose to treat hepatic encephalopathy because it may be difficult to monitor the effect of lactulose and adjust the dose.

■ Do not use in dehydrated patients. Use with caution in those patients with pre-existing fluid and electrolyte imbalances and monitor carefully. Treated animals must have free access to drinking water.

■ Contact your veterinarian if less than 2 to 3 soft stools a day are produced, if neurologic signs worsen when treating hepatic encephalopathy, or if you think your dog or cat may be having an adverse reaction to lactulose.

■ Lactulose is not FDA approved for use in dogs or cats, but it is routinely used and is considered accepted practice.

■ U.S. federal law restricts the use of this drug by or on the lawful written or oral order of a licensed veterinarian within the context of a valid veterinarian-client-patient relationship.

Possible Side Effects

▼ Common: flatulence, gastric distention, cramping, and diarrhea, particularly early in treatment.

Drug Interactions

• Oral antibiotics, including neomycin and others that affect intestinal bacteria, may increase the effectiveness of lactulose in reducing blood ammonia levels.

• Oral antacids may reduce the acidity of the colon and consequently the efficacy of lactulose.

• Insulin requirements may increase due to the presence of free sugar in the lactulose preparation (see "Cautions and Warnings").

Food Interactions

None known.

Usual Dose

Dogs: for hepatic encephalopathy—0.23 ml/lb 3–4 times a day. Adjust dosage so that 2–3 soft stools are produced a day. Reduce dose if diarrhea occurs. For constipation—1 ml/10 lb 3 times a day, then adjust as needed.

Cats: for hepatic encephalopathy—0.25–5 ml/cat and adjust until soft stools are produced. For constipation—1 ml/10 lb 3 times a day, then adjust as needed.

Drug Form: liquid containing 667 mg/ml.

Storage: Store in tight containers at room temperature. Do not freeze. The solution may turn dark or cloudy if exposed to heat or light. This does not affect the effectiveness of the drug.

Overdosage

Diarrhea, flatulence, abdominal pain, and dehydration are reported in mild to moderate overdose. Metabolic acidosis (excess acid in the blood) may occur with large overdoses. In case of accidental ingestion or overdose, contact your veterinarian or the National Animal Poison Control Center. ALWAYS bring the prescription bottle or container with you if you go for treatment.

Special Information

The available lactulose solutions are sweet liquids that many cats and dogs do not like, making administration difficult. Milk may be a readily accepted alternative in some cases. Lactase, the enzyme needed to metabolize lactose in milk, is present in young mammals, but the levels decrease as the animal matures if it stops drinking milk. If enough milk is consumed to exceed the capacity of the lactase present, lactose acts as an osmotic laxative in the same fashion as lactulose.

Special Populations

Pregnancy/Lactation

Studies in rodents and rabbits using 3 to 6 times the human dose did not reveal side effects during pregnancy or lactation. However, there are no adequate studies in dogs or cats. Lactulose is probably safe, but the potential benefits and risks should be considered.

Puppies/Kittens
Studies are not available, but lactulose is probably safe to use in puppies and kittens.

Senior Animals
Lactulose is considered safe to use in senior dogs and cats.

Generic Name

Lidocaine (LYE-doe-kane) [G]

Brand Names

Anthocaine [V]	Xylocaine [H]
Lidoject [V]	

*Combination Products**

Allerspray with Bittran II [V]
Butler Otic Clear [V]
Chlor-A-Clens-L [V]
Derma Cool [V]
Hexaseptic Flush Plus [V]
VetMark Anti-Itch Gel and Spray [V]

Topical combination products may contain a variety of other topical ingredients that have soothing and antiseptic properties.

Type of Drug

Local anesthetic and antiarrhythmic.

Prescribed for

Local and topical anesthesia, relief of pain and itching from minor burns, allergies, insect bites, skin irritations, and ventricular arrhythmias (abnormal heart rhythms arising from the main pumping chambers).

General Information

Topical anesthetics work by blocking pain and itch signals in the skin and keeping them from traveling up the nerves to the brain. The duration of anesthesia is usually short, lasting only

15 to 45 minutes. Lidocaine hydrochloride should not be used more than 3 to 4 times a day, so it is not likely to provide around the clock relief.

Your veterinarian may use lidocaine to produce local anesthesia for a variety of minor surgical or other procedures in which general anesthesia may be unnecessary or risky. Such procedures may include skin biopsies, suturing wounds, giving painful injections (e.g., gold compounds), or passing urinary catheters. Lidocaine with epinephrine may be used for local infiltration to keep the lidocaine from being absorbed and moving away from the site rapidly.

Lidocaine is also used to treat abnormal heart rhythms, such as ventricular tachycardia and ventricular premature beats. These are serious and potentially life-threatening arrhythmias that usually only occur in very sick animals. Lidocaine should only be used for this purpose in an intensive care setting where there is adequate patient monitoring.

Cautions and Warnings

■ Lidocaine is FDA approved for use in dogs and cats as a local and topical anesthetic. It is not approved for use as an antiarrhythmic, but it is commonly used to treat dogs and is considered accepted practice. Some experts suggest that it should not be used in cats as an antiarrhythmic, because of their sensitivity to the drug.

■ Do not use in patients with heart block, atrial fibrillation, or slow heart rate.

■ Use with caution in patients with liver disease, congestive heart failure, shock, dehydration, respiratory depression, or low blood oxygen.

■ Topical anesthetics should not be used for serious burns, allergies, or puncture wounds. Seek veterinary care for such problems.

■ Cats are very sensitive to the effects of lidocaine, and it should be used with caution in cats to avoid skin absorption of small but potentially harmful amounts of lidocaine.

■ Contact your veterinarian if you think your dog or cat may be having an adverse reaction to lidocaine.

■ U.S. federal law restricts the use of this drug by or on the lawful written or oral order of a licensed veterinarian within the context of a valid veterinarian-client-patient relationship.

Possible Side Effects

There are no common side effects from the use of lido-caine. Higher doses may cause drowsiness, depression, unsteady gait, muscle tremors, abnormal heart rhythms, transient nausea and vomiting, and seizures in cats.

▼ Rare: allergic reactions.

Drug Interactions

• Cimetidine, propranolol, procainamide, quinidine, or pheny-toin may increase lidocaine levels or effects.

• Lidocaine with epinephrine should not be used with monoamine oxidase inhibitors (MAOIs; amitraz), as it may produce severe hypotension (low blood pressure).

Food Interactions

None known.

Usual Dose

Dogs: Follow package directions for the use of topical combination products. Usual applications are 3–4 times a day. The maximum recommended infiltration dose of lidocaine in people is 2 mg/lb (1 ml/10 lbs, of 2% solution), lidocaine with epinephrine is 3.5 mg/lb (1.75 ml/10 lbs, of 2% solution). Treatment of arrhythmias involves an initial intravenous dose followed by a constant infusion that may be required for 1–3 days. Constant monitoring is required to avoid under- or over-dosing.

Cats: Follow package directions for the use of topical combination products. Usual applications are 3–4 times a day. Other antiarrhythmic drugs are usually recommended for cats.

Drug Form: topical gels, sprays, creams, and ointments; 1% and 2% injectable.

Overdosage

Overdoses may cause drowsiness, depression, unsteady gait, muscle tremors, abnormal heart rhythms, and transient nausea and vomiting (and seizures in cats). Ingested overdoses are unlikely to be a problem because lidocaine is so poorly absorbed when taken orally. In case of accidental ingestion or overdose, contact your veterinarian or the National Animal Poison Control Center. ALWAYS bring the prescription bottle or container with you if you go for treatment.

Special Populations

Pregnancy/Lactation

There are no safety studies for lidocaine in pregnant or lactating dogs or cats. It may be safe to use topically, but it should be avoided unless the benefits outweigh the risks.

Puppies/Kittens

Lidocaine should be avoided or used with extreme caution in puppies, and should not be used in kittens.

Senior Animals

Lidocaine should be safe to use in older animals with normal heart and liver function (see "Cautions and Warnings").

Generic Name

Lime Sulfur/Sulfonated Lime Solution

Brand Name

LymDyp [V]

Type of Drug

Antiseptic, keratolytic (removal of scale), antifungal, and miticidal dip.

Prescribed for

Ringworm, scaly/oily skin, bacterial or fungal skin infections, and *Sarcoptes* and *Cheyletiella* infestations.

General Information

Lime sulfur is one of the earlier treatments used for skin problems. It is used less frequently now with the advent of other agents specific for fungi, bacteria, and mites. The odor is quite offensive, but it is still considered an effective treatment. The mechanism of action of lime sulfur is not known. It is considered safe if used at the appropriate concentration (2% to 5%). Higher concentrations can cause severe irritation and scalding of the skin.

Lime sulfur is one of many effective topical treatments for ringworm or dermatophyte infections (see *Miconazole, Clotrimazole, Chlorhexidine, Captan, Ketoconazole,* and *Griseofulvin*). It may also be useful for dogs with seborrhea (scaly/oily skin) and secondary bacterial or yeast infections. Infestations with the mites *Sarcoptes scabiei* (scabies) and *Cheyletiella* cause intense itching and scaling skin disease. They may be treated effectively with lime sulfur dips. Both scabies and *Cheyletiella* are contagious and can spread through contact with infested animals to other animals and people (see *Zoonotic Diseases of Dogs and Cats*). There are other effective treatments (see *Ivermectin*), and control measures that may be needed to eliminate an infestation and prevent recurrence. See your veterinarian immediately if your animal has a skin problem, so that a diagnosis can be made and appropriate treatments and recommendations given.

Cautions and Warnings

■ Lime sulfur may cause severe skin irritation or scalding if used in concentrations greater than 2% to 5%.

■ Contact your veterinarian if you think your dog or cat may be having an adverse reaction to lime sulfur. Discontinue use or use less frequently if irritation occurs.

■ Use of this drug should be by or on the lawful written or oral order of a licensed veterinarian within the context of a valid veterinarian-client-patient relationship.

Possible Side Effects

▼ Common: stains fabrics and light-colored haircoats and tarnishes jewelry.
▼ Rare: skin irritation.

Food and Drug Interactions

None known.

Usual Dose

Dogs and Cats: Dilute 4 oz LymDyp in 1 gallon of warm water (25 ml/L); apply as a rinse or dip at 5–7 day intervals, for 8 weeks. Do not rinse. Allow pet to air dry or use a blow dryer.

Drug Form: concentrated lime sulfur solution; must be diluted before use.

Overdosage

Topical overdoses, or using lime sulfur in concentrations greater than 2% to 5%, or more frequently than every 5 to 7 days, may cause severe skin irritation and scalding. No information is available on overdose by accidental ingestion. Accidental ingestion of lime sulfur is unlikely due to its foul odor. In case of accidental ingestion or overdose, contact your veterinarian or the National Animal Poison Control Center. ALWAYS bring the prescription bottle or container with you if you go for treatment.

Special Populations

Pregnancy/Lactation
There are no safety studies on the use of lime sulfur in pregnant or lactating animals. It is the recommended treatment for scabies in pregnant or nursing animals, but it should probably be avoided unless the benefits outweigh the risks.

Puppies/Kittens
Lime sulfur is the recommended treatment for scabies in puppies less than 12 weeks of age. It should be safe if used according to recommended doses (see "Cautions and Warnings" and "Usual Dose").

Senior Animals
Lime sulfur should be safe to use in older, and even debilitated animals, if used according to recommended doses (see "Cautions and Warnings" and "Usual Dose").

Generic Name

Limonene (LIM-oe-nene)

Brand Names

Back to Nature Shampoo [V]   VIP Flea Control Shampoo [V]
D'Limonene Pet Shampoo [V]   VIP Flea Dip [V]

Combination Product

Generic Ingredients: Limonene + Linalool [G]
Interrupt Pet Spray [V]

Type of Drug

Citrus oil insecticide.

Prescribed for

Flea control on dogs and cats.

General Information

The insecticidal properties of the oil from citrus fruit have been recognized for many years. Several commercial products that contain limonene (d-limonene), linolool, or crude citrus oil extracts are marketed for control of fleas on dogs and cats. They are in shampoos, sprays, dips, and premise treatments.

Limonene (d-limonene) and linalool are derived from the volatile oils in the peels of citrus fruit. Exposure to the vapors paralyzes and kills insects very quickly. Direct contact with the oil is not required. Flea eggs and larva are also killed. The oil evaporates rapidly, leaving the animal's coat free from residue and with a citrus smell. It is generally safe, but some cases of toxicity and death in cats have been reported after use of crude citrus oil extracts.

The insecticidal activity of citrus extracts is enhanced when combined with synergists such as piperonyl butoxide and N-octyl-bicycloheptene dicarboximide (MGK264). These increase the activity of the insecticide by inhibiting the flea's enzymes, which normally degrade the insecticide. Their use also reduces the amount of insecticide that must be used to be effective. In general, the toxicity of synergists is low. However, caution is indicated when using products containing piperonyl butoxide on cats. It may increase the risk of neurologic side effects such as tremors, incoordination, and lethargy even at the concentration found in many commercial products.

Flea control requires that the problem be attacked on several levels. Adult fleas on the animal must be killed. Flea shampoos, powders, sprays, and dips work at this level. Mechanical removal by frequent grooming and keeping your pet away from other animals and places where new fleas may be acquired also helps. However, addressing the infestation on the animal is rarely enough because fleas remaining in the environment continue to reproduce very rapidly. Environmental treatment with bombs or sprays kills many fleas. A major limitation is that bombs and sprays do not reach all of the flea's hiding places, which leaves live fleas to continue the infestation. Residual action products help extend the action, but still fall short of giving good control and may result in increased levels of toxic insecticides in the home and environment. In addition, most insecticides do not kill flea eggs, which hatch into new adult fleas within a few days. The use of IGRs, which prevent eggs from hatching, dramatically increases the effectiveness of flea control on animals and in the environment. Very good flea control is possible by combining insecticides and IGRs in a multi-level approach. The drawback is that it demands a great deal of motivation on the part of the owner.

Because of the potential for affecting the environment, insecticide use is primarily regulated by the Environmental Protection Agency (EPA). Label instructions should be carefully read and followed.

Cautions and Warnings

- Do not get in eyes or on irritated skin.
- Contact your veterinarian if you think your dog or cat may be having an adverse reaction to limonene or linolool.
- It is a violation of federal law to use these products in a manner inconsistent with their labeling.

Possible Side Effects

▼ Rare: skin irritation and excessive salivation.

Food and Drug Interactions

None known.

Usual Dose

Dogs and Cats: Read and follow label directions for individual products.

Drug Form: shampoos, sprays, and dips.

Storage: Store in a cool, dark area.

Overdosage

Excessive salivation, muscle tremors, loss of coordination, decreased body temperature, and death in cats have been reported after use of products containing crude citrus oil extracts. In case of accidental ingestion or overdose, contact your veterinarian or the National Animal Poison Control Center. ALWAYS bring the prescription bottle or container with you if you go for treatment.

Special Information

See *Fipronil* for more information on fleas and ticks.

Special Populations

Pregnancy/Lactation

Limonene is generally considered safe to use in pregnant animals. Use with care on lactating animals and do not apply on or near mammary glands. Allow to dry before returning mother to puppies or kittens.

Puppies/Kittens

Limonene is generally considered safe to use in puppies and kittens over 4 weeks old.

Senior Animals

Limonene is generally considered safe to use in senior animals.

Generic Name

Lincomycin (lin-koe-MYE-sin)

Brand Names

Lincocin [V] [H]

Type of Drug

Antibiotic.

Prescribed for

Susceptible bacterial infections.

General Information

Lincomycin hydrochloride is one of the macrolide antibiotics, a group that includes erythromycin and clindamycin. It is an older antibiotic effective in treating infections caused by gram-positive bacteria (such as streptococcus and staphylococcus) and anaerobic bacteria (bacteria that grow only where there is no oxygen). Anaerobic bacteria are fairly common in infections of teeth, bone, joints, and lining of the lung and in septicemia (blood infections). Lincomycin is used to treat infections resistant to penicillins and cephalosporins, and infections in those animals allergic to penicillins and cephalosporins. Lincomycin is one of the antibiotics of choice for deep skin infections and abscesses, and upper respiratory tract infections in dogs.

Cautions and Warnings

■ Lincomycin is FDA approved for use in dogs and cats. Lincomycin should be used with caution in animals with liver or kidney disease.

■ It should not be used in animals that have had an allergic reaction to clindamycin, and it should be avoided in animals with yeast infections.

■ Contact your veterinarian if you think your dog or cat may be having an adverse reaction to lincomycin.

■ U.S. federal law restricts the use of this drug by or on the lawful written or oral order of a licensed veterinarian within the context of a valid veterinarian-client-patient relationship.

Possible Side Effects

▼ Rare: vomiting in cats, diarrhea in dogs, allergic reactions.

Drug Interactions

• Lincomycin should not be used with chloramphenicol, clindamycin, or erythromycin, due to possible antagonism.

• Lincomycin should not be used with other neuromuscular blocking agents.

• When used together, lincomycin and spectinomycin work better than either one alone.

• Lincomycin should not be given at the same time as antidiarrheal medications containing kaolin, as kaolin prevents absorption of lincomycin. Separate doses by at least 2 hours.

Food Interactions

None known.

Usual Dose

Dogs: 7–16 mg/lb orally twice a day.
Cats: 7–16 mg/lb orally twice a day.
Drug Form: 100-, 200- and 500-mg Lincocin tablets, Lincocin Aquadrops (50 mg/ml) for oral use, and 100 mg/ml injectable.

Overdosage

There is little information on overdoses. In dogs, oral doses at 10 times the recommended dose for one year did not cause any signs of overdose. In case of accidental ingestion or overdose, contact your veterinarian or the National Animal Poison Control Center. ALWAYS bring the prescription bottle or container with you if you go for treatment.

Special Information

Clindamycin has largely replaced lincomycin use in dogs and cats because of its greater spectrum of activity. Lincomycin is less expensive, however, and is still a useful and safe antibiotic used by many veterinarians.

Special Populations

Pregnancy/Lactation

Lincomycin did not cause any damage to the fetus in pregnant dogs that were given twice the recommended dose. There are no reports of studies in pregnant cats and its use should be avoided unless the benefits outweigh the risks. Lincomycin is excreted in milk and may cause diarrhea in nursing puppies or kittens. Again, the benefits should be weighed against the risks before using it in lactating dogs and cats.

Puppies/Kittens

There are no safety studies for lincomycin in puppies or kittens. It should be avoided unless the benefits outweigh the risks.

Senior Animals

Lincomycin is safe to use in older animals but should be used with caution in those with kidney or liver dysfunction.

Brand Name

Lomotil (LOE-moe-til) [H]

Generic Ingredients

Diphenoxylate Hydrochloride + Atropine [G]

Type of Drug

Antidiarrheal.

Prescribed for

Diarrhea, irritable bowel syndrome, and fecal incontinence.

General Information

Diphenoxylate hydrochloride is a narcotic antidiarrheal drug that is usually combined with atropine. This combination works by modifying motility in the gastrointestinal (GI) tract, decreasing secretions, and increasing fluid absorption in the GI tract. It also increases anal sphincter tone. Lomotil is used for many types of diarrhea in dogs to improve stool consistency, decrease volume of stool, and decrease abdominal pain and urgency. In most cases, the drug is only prescribed for a short time. There are some infectious diarrheas where your veterinarian may choose not to use Lomotil, because slowing the GI tract keeps the infectious agent and its toxins in the GI tract longer.

Lomotil is sometimes prescribed as a part of an overall management program for dogs with irritable bowel syndrome, along with dietary management, stress management, and other drugs. Lomotil is also used in the management of dogs with fecal incontinence because of the decrease in stool volume and increased anal sphincter tone.

Cautions and Warnings

■ Lomotil is not FDA approved for use in dogs or cats. It is commonly used in dogs and is considered accepted practice.

■ The use of narcotic antidiarrheal drugs is controversial in cats because of side effects (see "Possible Side Effects"). These drugs should only be used in cats after consultation with your veterinarian.

■ Lomotil should be used with caution in animals with head injuries, hypothyroidism, severe kidney or liver problems, Addison's disease (decreased adrenal function), or severe debilitation.

■ Lomotil should not be used in animals known to be hypersensitive to narcotic painkillers.

Possible Side Effects

In dogs, side effects are uncommon at normal doses and are more likely to occur with long-term therapy. Lomotil is not commonly used in cats because it may cause excitement or agitation.

▼ Rare: constipation, bloat, sedation, paralytic ileus (paralysis of the intestines), toxic megacolon, pancreatitis (inflammation of the pancreas), and, central nervous system (CNS) depression.

Drug Interactions

• Lomotil has an additive effect with other CNS depressants, such as antihistamines, tranquilizers, barbiturates, and alcohol.

• Lomotil should not be given with or within 14 days of monoamine oxidase inhibitors (MAOIs).

Food Interactions

None known.

Usual Dose

Dogs: 0.03–0.1 mg/lb 2–3 times a day.

Drug Form: 2.5 mg diphenoxylate and 0.025 mg atropine in each tablet or in 5 ml of liquid.

Overdosage

Overdoses of Lomotil cause constipation, CNS depression, cardiovascular depression, and GI and respiratory toxicity. In human medicine, Lomotil overdose patients are kept under close observation for 48 hours. Respiratory depression may occur as late as 30 hours after an overdose. In case of accidental ingestion or overdose, contact your veterinarian or the National Animal Poison Control Center. ALWAYS bring the prescription bottle or container with you if you go for treatment.

Special Information

It is easy for animals to become dehydrated when they have diarrhea. It is important that your dog continues to drink water, electrolyte solutions such as Pedialyte or Re-Sorb, or clear liquids such as beef or chicken broth. Your veterinarian can help you assess your animal's fluid needs. Any animal with persistent diarrhea should be seen by a veterinarian.

Special Populations

Pregnancy/Lactation
Lomotil has not been found to cause birth defects in humans. It is excreted in milk. This drug should only be used during pregnancy and lactation if the benefits outweigh the risks.

Puppies/Kittens
Lomotil has not been studied in puppies. It should only be used in puppies if the benefits outweigh the risks and particular care should be used to establish the correct weight and dose. Do not use in kittens.

Senior Animals
Lomotil can be used with caution in older dogs provided liver and kidney function are not impaired.

Generic Name

Loperamide (loe-PER-uh-mide) Ⓖ

Brand Names

Imodium-AD Ⓗ

Type of Drug

Antidiarrheal.

Prescribed for

Diarrhea, inflammatory bowel disease (IBD), and fecal incontinence.

General Information

Loperamide hydrochloride is a narcotic antidiarrheal drug. It works by modifying motility, decreasing secretions, and increasing fluid absorption in the gastrointestinal (GI) tract. It also increases anal sphincter tone. Loperamide is used for many types of diarrhea in dogs to improve stool consistency, decrease volume of stool, and decrease abdominal pain and urgency. There are some infectious diarrheas where your veterinarian may choose not to use drugs such as loperamide because slowing the GI tract may keep the infectious agent and its toxins in the GI tract longer.

Loperamide is frequently prescribed as a part of an overall management program for dogs with IBD, along with dietary management, stress management, and other drugs. Loperamide is also useful in the management of dogs with fecal incontinence because of the decrease in stool volume and increased anal sphincter tone.

The use of narcotic antidiarrheal drugs is controversial in cats because of side effects. Although loperamide is a narcotic, it is not thought to be addictive. Loperamide can be purchased without a prescription under a variety of brand names.

Cautions and Warnings

■ Loperamide is not FDA approved for use in dogs or cats. It is commonly used in dogs and is considered accepted practice. The use of narcotic antidiarrheal drugs is controversial in cats because of side effects (see "Possible Side Effects"). These drugs should only be used in cats after consultation with your veterinarian.

■ Loperamide should be used with caution in animals with hypothyroidism, severe kidney or liver problems, Addison's disease (decreased adrenal function), or severe debilitation. Loperamide should not be used in animals known to be hypersensitive to narcotic painkillers.

Possible Side Effects

In dogs, side effects are uncommon at normal doses and are more likely to occur with long-term therapy. Loperamide is not commonly used in cats because it may cause excitement or agitation.

Possible Side Effects *(Continued)*

▼ Rare: constipation, bloat, sedation, paralytic ileus (paralysis of the intestines), toxic megacolon, pancreatitis (inflammation of the pancreas), and central nervous system (CNS) depression.

Drug Interactions

• Loperamide has an additive effect with other CNS depressants, such as antihistamines, tranquilizers, barbiturates, and alcohol.

• Loperamide should not be given with or within 14 days of monoamine oxidase inhibitors (MAOIs).

Food Interactions

None known.

Usual Dose

Dogs: 0.05–0.1 mg/lb orally 3–4 times a day.
Cats: 0.005–0.05 mg/lb twice a day.
Drug Form: 2-mg caplet or capsule, and liquid containing 1 mg/5 ml.

Overdosage

Overdoses of loperamide cause constipation, CNS depression, cardiovascular depression, and GI and respiratory toxicity. In case of accidental ingestion or overdose, contact your veterinarian or the National Animal Poison Control Center. ALWAYS bring the prescription bottle or container with you if you go for treatment.

Special Information

It is easy for animals to become dehydrated when they have diarrhea. It is important that your animal continues to drink water, electrolyte solutions such as Pedialyte or Re-Sorb, or clear liquids such as beef or chicken broth. Your veterinarian can help you assess your animal's fluid needs. Any animal with persistent diarrhea should be seen by a veterinarian.

Special Populations

Pregnancy/Lactation
This drug has not been found to cause birth defects in humans,

and it is unknown if it is excreted in milk. Loperamide should only be used during pregnancy and lactation if the benefits outweigh the risks.

Puppies/Kittens

Loperamide has not been studied in puppies. In humans, children are more prone to CNS side effects than adults. Loperamide should only be used in puppies if the benefits outweigh the risks and particular care should be used to establish the correct weight and dose. Do not use in kittens.

Senior Animals

Loperamide should be used with caution in older dogs with normal liver function.

Type of Drug

Lubricant Laxative

Brand Names

Generic Ingredient: Mineral Oil G
Fleet Mineral Oil Enema H

Generic Ingredient: Petrolatum (Petroleum Jelly) G

Felaxin V	Laxanip V
Laxatone V	Petrotone V
Lax'aire V	Vaseline Pure Petroleum Jelly H

Prescribed for

Constipation, fecal impactions, megacolon, and hair balls in dogs and cats.

General Information

Laxatives are used to prevent or relieve constipation. They are classified by their action as lubricant, emollient (stool softener), bulk-forming, osmotic, or stimulant. The choice of laxative, dose, and frequency of administration must be adjusted for each individual to obtain the desired stool consistency and frequency of defecation. Vomiting, straining, and other signs of constipation may be caused by serious problems. Consult your veterinarian before administering laxatives or any medication to your pet.

Mineral oil and petrolatum are lubricant laxatives. Both are tasteless, colorless to yellow, oily products distilled from crude petroleum. Mineral oil is liquid and petrolatum is solidified into a gel. Unlike digestible fats and oils (see "Special Information"), they are very poorly absorbed from the intestines and work by coating the intestinal lining and contents. The amount of water retained in the intestine is increased, making the contents bulkier and softer. It moves through the intestines faster and is easier to pass.

Lubricant laxatives are frequently prescribed for simple constipation and impactions in dogs and cats. They are usually administered orally and many commercial products are available often with added flavoring, vitamins, or other nutrients added. Mineral oil may also be used as an enema.

Lubricant laxatives are the most commonly prescribed remedies for ingested hair because of self-grooming (hair balls) and mild signs of megacolon in cats. Megacolon is a disorder seen most frequently in cats. An enlarged colon with decreased muscle function results in the accumulation of huge amounts of fecal material, making it painful and ultimately impossible to defecate. There is no cure, but constipation may be managed with individually tailored treatment plans based on the use of various types of laxatives. Lubricant laxatives, either orally or as an enema, promote softer feces and defecation.

Lubricant laxatives are generally very safe. The most common side effect is leakage of oil from the rectum. This may interfere with healing of open wounds around the anus but is otherwise not a danger to the health of the pet. A major concern is that it may stain clothes, upholstery, and other furnishings. The most serious side effect from orally administered mineral oil is aspiration into the trachea and lungs causing pneumonia. Using semisolid petrolatum products reduces this risk. Long-term use of these laxatives may interfere with absorption of fat-soluble vitamins and drugs. Administering the laxative between meals or at least 2 hours before or after meals minimizes this problem. Rarely, enough mineral oil may be absorbed if it is used long term to cause inflammatory lesions of the liver or other internal organ. This effect has not been reported in cats receiving petrolatum long term.

In addition to being used as laxatives, mineral oil and petrolatum are used to provide a mechanical barrier and to preserve moisture when applied to the skin, ears, or eyes. Mineral oil and petrolatum are often used in topical preparations to carry drugs such as antibiotics and corticosteroids and to increase the amount of time these drugs stay in contact with the affected area.

Cautions and Warnings

■ Avoid aspiration. Do not administer to animals that are comatose, debilitated, asleep, struggling, vomiting, very young, or have swallowing difficulty, megaesophagus, gastric motility problems, or bloat.

■ Do not use with docusate (see *Docusate*).

■ Do not use long term unless instructed by your veterinarian.

■ Contact your veterinarian if you think your dog or cat may be having an adverse reaction to mineral oil or petrolatum.

■ Mineral oil and petrolatum, when used orally, are FDA approved for over-the-counter (OTC) use in dogs and cats.

Possible Side Effects

▼ Common: mineral oil leakage from the anus with high doses.

▼ Rare: aspiration pneumonia; decreased absorption of fat-soluble vitamins (A, D, E, and K), fatty acids, other fat-soluble nutrients, and some drugs; inflammatory lesions of the liver or other internal organs after long-term use.

Drug Interactions

• Docusate may increase absorption of mineral oil and the risk of internal inflammatory lesions.

• Mineral oil and petrolatum may decrease the absorption of some drugs.

Food Interactions

Lubricant laxatives may decrease absorption of fat-soluble vitamins, essential fatty acids, and other fat-soluble nutrients.

Usual Dose

Dogs: 2–60 ml.

Cats: 2–10 ml.
Drug Form: mineral oil—liquid in various size containers, and enemas. Petrolatum—bulk containers, and tubes.
Storage: Store at temperatures lower than 86°F.

Overdosage

Overdoses may cause leakage of mineral oil from the anus, and diarrhea. In case of accidental ingestion or overdose, contact your veterinarian or the National Animal Poison Control Center. ALWAYS bring the prescription bottle or container with you if you go for treatment.

Special Information

Mineral oil is available OTC as an enema for human use. This and other human OTC products should not be used in dogs or cats unless specifically instructed by your veterinarian. Many OTC products, including some types of enemas, may cause severe side effects, including death in dogs or cats.

Sometimes pet owners mistakenly administer vegetable oil or other digestible fats or oils as laxatives. These are not effective lubricant laxatives because they do not remain in the intestinal tract. Rather, they are digested and used by the body as a source of energy and nutrients. Mineral oil, on the other hand, is not absorbed and has no nutritional or energy value.

Special Populations

Pregnancy/Lactation
Lubricant laxatives are considered safe to use in pregnant and lactating animals.

Puppies/Kittens
Lubricant laxatives are considered safe to use in puppies and kittens.

Senior Animals
Lubricant laxatives are considered safe to use in senior animals.

Generic Name

Lufenuron (lue-FEN-ure-on)

Brand Names

Program [V]

Combination Product

Generic Ingredients: Lufenuron + Milbemycin Oxime
Sentinel [V]

Type of Drug

Insect development inhibitor.

Prescribed for

Control of flea infestations.

General Information

Lufenuron is an oral medication that acts like flea birth control. It prevents the development of flea eggs by interfering with the production of chitin. Chitin is the material that forms the hard outer covering of fleas and the mouthparts of larval fleas. Without chitin, the larva is not able to hatch from the egg. It dies and the flea life cycle is interrupted. The recommended dose of lufenuron provides over 96% control of egg development on cats and over 99% on dogs for at least 32 days following treatment. Mammals do not make chitin, so lufenuron is very safe to use in dogs and cats.

An adult flea must bite a lufenuron-treated animal before its eggs become infertile. For this reason, all dogs and cats in the household must be treated for this type of flea control to be effective. Fleas on animals that are not treated will continue to lay eggs that hatch and develop into adult fleas. Lufenuron does not kill adult fleas. The adult fleas on lufenuron-treated animals and in the environment die eventually, but it may take several months and they will continue to bite the host animals in the meantime. For this reason, lufenuron works best when started before the beginning of flea season when the number of adult fleas is low, or it can be administered year round. New fleas may enter the environment if pets go outside or are exposed to other animals with fleas. These fleas will be infertile once they bite a treated animal, but they are not killed. Flea control is improved when lufenuron is used together with insecticides that kill adult fleas on the animal and in the environment.

Lufenuron is inadequate as the sole treatment for animals with flea allergy dermatitis (a skin disease caused by an allergic reaction to flea bites; see "Special Information"), because adult fleas are still able to bite the allergic animal. Lufenuron is also inadequate if it is not possible to prevent exposure to untreated animals or infested environments.

Cautions and Warnings

■ Contact your veterinarian if you think your dog or cat may be having an adverse reaction to lufenuron.

■ This product is available over the counter without a prescription.

■ For veterinary use only.

Possible Side Effects

▼ Rare: vomiting, depression, loss of appetite, diarrhea, and itching.

Drug Interactions

None known.

Food Interactions

MUST be given with food to ensure adequate absorption.

Usual Dose

Lufenuron

If the full dose is not consumed, re-dose once as soon as possible. Treat each pet in the household separately to ensure that each gets its full dose.

Dogs: minimum dose—4.5 mg/lb given once a month with food.

Cats: minimum dose—13.6 mg/lb given once a month with food.

Drug Form: dogs—45.0-, 90.0-, 204.9-, and 409.8-mg tablets; cats—liquid-containing packets with sizes up to 10 lbs and 11–20 lbs, and injectable.

Sentinel

Dogs: 0.23 mg/lb milbemycin + 4.55 mg/lb lufenuron minimum. Use appropriate size tablet or combination of tablets once a month.

Drug Form: tablets with 2.3 mg milbemycin + 46 mg lufenuron for 2–10 lb dogs; 5.75 milbemycin + 115 mg lufenuron for 11–25 lb dogs; 11.5 mg milbemycin + 230 mg lufenuron for 26–50 lb dogs; and 23.0 mg milbemycin + 460 mg lufenuron for 51–100 lb dogs.

Overdosage

No signs of overdose were seen in adult dogs given up to 20 times the recommended dose. At this dose, puppies less than 8 weeks of age had decreased appetite and activity. No signs of overdose were seen in cats with doses up to 17 times the recommended dose. In case of accidental ingestion or overdose, contact your veterinarian or the National Animal Poison Control Center. ALWAYS bring the prescription bottle or container with you if you go for treatment.

Special Information

See *Fipronil* for more information on fleas and ticks.

Special Populations

Pregnancy/Lactation
Lufenuron is considered safe to use in pregnant and lactating dogs and cats. Lufenuron is found in the milk of treated animals, but no side effects have been seen even after administering 10 times the normal dose to the mother.

Puppies/Kittens
Lufenuron is considered safe when used as directed in puppies and kittens over age 6 weeks.

Senior Animals
Lufenuron is considered safe when used as directed in senior dogs and cats.

Generic Name

Meclizine (MEK-lih-zene) G

Most Common Brand Names

Antivert H   Bonine H

Type of Drug

Antihistamine, and antiemetic.

Prescribed for

Motion sickness in dogs and cats.

General Information

Meclizine hydrochloride is an antihistamine that is primarily used to control vomiting and motion sickness in dogs and cats. Meclizine will cause some central nervous system depression and sedation. The sedative effects of antihistamines may diminish with time.

Cautions and Warnings

■ Meclizine is not FDA approved for use in dogs or cats. It is commonly used and is considered accepted practice.

■ Meclizine should be used with caution in animals with prostatic enlargement, bladder neck obstruction, severe heart failure, some forms of glaucoma, and pyeloduodenal obstruction (obstruction at the junction of the stomach and small intestine).

■ Meclizine may mask symptoms of ear problems.

■ U.S. federal law restricts the use of this drug by or on the lawful written or oral order of a licensed veterinarian within the context of a valid veterinarian-client-patient relationship.

Possible Side Effects

▼ Common: sedation, dry mouth, and increased heart rate.

▼ Rare: excitement.

Drug Interactions

• Meclizine may have an additive effect when combined with

other central nervous system depressant drugs, such as barbiturates and tranquilizers.

• Meclizine may have an additive effect when combined with other anticholinergic agents such as atropine.

Food Interactions

Meclizine may be better tolerated if given with food.

Usual Dose

Dogs: 12.5–25 mg orally once a day.
Cats: 12.5 mg (1–2 mg/lb) orally once a day.
Drug Form: 12.5-, 15-, 25-, 30-, and 50-mg tablets and capsules.

Overdosage

The usual signs of overdose are sedation and clumsiness. Hyperexcitability, convulsions, coma, and difficulty breathing can develop after a massive overdose. In case of accidental ingestion or overdose, contact your veterinarian or the National Animal Poison Control Center. ALWAYS bring the prescription bottle or container with you if you go for treatment.

Special Information

When using meclizine for motion sickness, give 30 to 60 minutes before traveling. Meclizine should not be used within 1 week of skin testing for allergies.

Special Populations

Pregnancy/Lactation
Meclizine has been shown to cause birth defects in laboratory animals. It is not known if meclizine is excreted in breast milk. It should only be used in pregnant or lactating animals if the benefits outweigh the risks.

Puppies/Kittens
There are no safety studies in puppies or kittens.

Senior Animals
There are no studies in dogs, but older humans are more sensitive to side effects from antihistamines. In most cases, it is better to start with a reduced dose.

Generic Name

Meclofenamic Acid

(MEK-loe-fen-ah-mik AS-id) G

Brand Name

Arquel V

Type of Drug

Nonsteroidal anti-inflammatory drug (NSAID), pain reliever, fever reducer.

Prescribed for

Relief of pain and inflammation in dogs, especially that associated with arthritis.

General Information

Meclofenamic acid is a nonsteroidal anti-inflammatory drug (NSAID) of the anthranilic acid class. It is not known exactly how NSAIDs work. Part of their action may be due to their ability to inhibit the body's production of hormones called prostaglandins. NSAIDs also inhibit production of other body chemicals that sensitize pain receptors and stimulate the inflammatory response. NSAIDs are quickly absorbed into the blood stream. Pain relief is usually noted in 3 to 4 days with meclofenamic acid. The anti-inflammatory response to these agents usually takes longer to work (several days to 2 weeks) and may take 1 month or more to reach maximum effect. Because of the narrow margin of safety and common side effects, the manufacturer recommends that meclofenamic acid be given for only 5 to 7 days. Dogs treated for longer should be given the lowest possible dose and monitored carefully for side effects.

Cautions and Warnings

■ Meclofenamic acid is FDA approved for use in dogs only. It should not be used in cats.

■ Gastrointestinal (GI) side effects are common, and most dogs should not be treated for longer than 5 to 7 days.

■ Meclofenamic acid should not be used with other anti-inflammatory drugs that tend to cause GI ulcers, such as corticosteroids and other NSAIDs, unless the dog is being closely monitored.

■ Meclofenamic acid should be avoided in dogs with kidney disease, congestive heart failure, liver disease, or those that are dehydrated or on diuretics.

■ Meclofenamic acid should not be given to dogs about to undergo surgery, because of the risks of kidney damage and bleeding, the latter caused by decreased platelet function.

■ Meclofenamic acid is not recommended for use in dogs with bleeding disorders such as von Willebrand's disease, as safety has not been established in dogs with these disorders.

■ Contact your veterinarian if you think your dog may be having an adverse reaction to meclofenamic acid.

■ U.S. federal law restricts the use of this drug by or on the lawful written or oral order of a licensed veterinarian within the context of a valid veterinarian-client-patient relationship.

Possible Side Effects

▼ Common: decreased appetite, vomiting, bloody diarrhea, diarrhea, tarry stools, and ulcers of the small intestine.

▼ Rare: fatigue, depression, personality change, fever, rapid breathing, edema, urinary incontinence, and irreversible aplastic anemia.

Drug Interactions

• Meclofenamic acid may increase the blood levels or prolong the effects of phenytoin, valproic acid, oral anticoagulants (warfarin), NSAIDs, sulfonamides, and glipizide.

• Aspirin should not be given with meclofenamic acid because of decreased blood levels of meclofenamic acid and increased risks of side effects.

Food Interactions

Give with food, preferably a full meal.

Usual Dose

Dogs: 0.5 mg/lb once a day for 5–7 days. Stop until signs recur and then give 0.5 mg/lb every third day for 7 days, then every fourth day, then every fifth day, and so on, until signs recur. Use the longest dosing interval that provides pain relief.

Cats: Meclofenamic acid is not recommended for use in cats.

Drug Form: 10- and 20-mg tablets; granules for horses, 500 mg/10 g packet (¼ tsp granules contains approximately 55 mg of meclofenamic acid).

Overdosage

Overdoses would be expected to cause severe GI ulceration and kidney damage. In case of accidental ingestion or overdose, contact your veterinarian or the National Animal Poison Control Center. ALWAYS bring the prescription bottle or container with you if you go for treatment.

Special Information

See *Aspirin/Acetylsalicylic Acid* for more information on treatments for arthritis.

Special Populations

Pregnancy/Lactation
There are no safety studies for meclofenamic acid in pregnant or lactating bitches. The drug should be avoided in these animals unless the benefits outweigh the risks.

Puppies/Kittens
Safety has not been established in dogs younger than age 8 months, and meclofenamic acid should be avoided in this group unless the benefits outweigh the risks. It should not be given to kittens.

Senior Animals
Meclofenamic acid should be avoided in older animals with decreased heart, liver, or kidney function, or those with active GI tract disease.

Generic Name

Melarsomine (muh-LAR-soe-mene)

Brand Name

Immiticide [V]

Type of Drug

Antiheartworm/anthelmintic.

Prescribed for

Removal of adult heartworms.

General Information

Melarsomine hydrochloride is an arsenic compound used to kill adult heartworms (*Dirofilaria immitis*) in dogs. Heartworm disease is serious and potentially fatal. Melarsomine is recommended for treatment of dogs with stabilized Class 1, 2, or 3 heartworm disease. Class 1 is mild or asymptomatic disease. Class 2 is moderate disease with anemia, heart enlargement, and abnormal lungs on x-ray; exercise intolerance, poor condition, and occasional cough. Class 3 is severe disease with right heart failure, constant fatigue and cough, difficulty breathing, anemia, and signs of clots in blood vessels of the lung (pulmonary thromboembolism) on x-rays. Dogs with large numbers of adult heartworms but few or no signs of disease are also Class 3. The prognosis for dogs with Class 3 heartworm disease is guarded, and they should be stabilized prior to treatment and given a modified dose of melarsomine (see "Usual Dose"). Class 4 heartworm disease (Caval syndrome) is very severe, with heartworms in the vena cava (vessel to the right heart) and right atrium.

Cautions and Warnings

For Owners/Handlers
- Wash hands thoroughly after use or wear gloves.
- May cause eye irritation. Flush eyes with copious amounts of water if exposed.
- Consult a physician in case of accidental exposure by any route; ingestion, exposure to skin or eyes, or injection.

For Animals
- Melarsomine is FDA approved for use in dogs only.
- All dogs with heartworm disease are at risk for pulmonary thromboembolism, as dead and dying worms pass from the right heart and pulmonary arteries into the lungs. Death of worms may cause fever, weakness, and cough.
- Dogs with severe damage to pulmonary arteries from heartworm disease may have difficulty breathing, coughing up blood, right heart failure, and death after treatment with melarsomine.
- Dogs should be monitored carefully during treatment and should be restricted from exercise.

■ Class 3 dogs should be hospitalized during and after treatment with severe exercise restriction. Expect 10% to 20% of Class 3 dogs to die after melarsomine treatment.

■ Melarsomine should not be used in dogs with Class 4 heartworm disease.

■ Pain and swelling and other injection site reactions are possible, especially if the injections are not given exactly as specified by the manufacturer.

■ Recommended treatment with one round of melarsomine may not kill 100% of adult heartworms. Follow-up heartworm antigen testing at 4 months is advised to determine if treatment was completely successful.

■ Contact your veterinarian if you think your dog may be having an adverse reaction to melarsomine.

■ U.S. federal law restricts the use of this drug by or on the awful written or oral order of a licensed veterinarian within the context of a valid veterinarian-client-patient relationship.

Possible Side Effects

▼ Common: mild to moderate inflammation at the injection site with pain, swelling, and reluctance to move (30% of treated dogs). Coughing, gagging, depression, lethargy, decreased appetite, fever, lung congestion, and vomiting are the most common side effects.

▼ Rare: severe injection site reactions in less than 1% of dogs, persistent lump or abscess at the injection site, severe drooling and panting 30 minutes after injection, diarrhea, coughing up blood, abnormal heart rhythms, and death.

Food and Drug Interactions

None known.

Usual Dose

Dogs: Class 1 and 2—1.1 mg/lb by injection, twice, 24 hours apart. Class 3—1.1 mg/lb by injection once, followed by 1.1 mg/lb, twice, 24 hours apart, 1 month later.

Drug Form: powder for reconstitution and injection deep in the lumbar muscle, exactly as specified by the manufacturer.

Overdosage

Melarsomine has a low margin of safety. A single dose of 3 times the recommended amount may cause lung damage and death. Prolonged overdose causes kidney damage. Tremors, lethargy, restlessness, unsteady gait, panting, difficulty breathing, severe drooling, and vomiting may progress to collapse, coma, and death. In case of accidental ingestion or overdose, contact your veterinarian or the National Animal Poison Control Center. ALWAYS bring the prescription bottle or container with you if you go for treatment.

Special Information

There are only two treatments for removal of adult heartworms. Melarsomine is usually the preferred treatment. Thiacetarsemide (see *Thiacetarsemide*) is more difficult to administer, and it causes severe local reactions if even the tiniest amount goes outside of the vein. It is not as effective as melarsomine and it may cause severe liver damage at the recommended dose. Thiacetarsamide cannot be given as a graded dose to dogs with severe heartworm disease, as melarsomine can. Dogs with Class 4 heartworm disease should have worms surgically removed from the vena cava and right atrium before treatment with melarsomine. The prognosis for these dogs is guarded to poor.

Special Populations

Cats
Cats with heartworms may be treated with the arsenic compounds, but they are more likely to have fatal reactions and it is usually not recommended. The life span of heartworms is shorter in cats and there are usually fewer worms, so cats are often treated with corticosteroids to alleviate symptoms, as the disease is allowed to run its course.

Pregnancy/Lactation
Studies have not confirmed the safety of melarsomine in pregnant or lactating dogs, and it should not be given.

Senior Animals
Dogs 8 years and older treated with melarsomine had significantly more depression, lethargy, decreased appetite, and vomiting than younger dogs. Light heartworm infections (few

worms) may cause few if any symptoms. In some older animals the risks of treatment may outweigh the benefits. In older dogs with mild infections it may be best to treat with milbemycin or ivermectin to kill microfilaria and prevent reinfection, and allow the adult worms to eventually die on their own.

Generic Name

Methimazole (meh-THIM-uh-zole)

Brand Name

Tapazole [H]

Type of Drug

Antithyroid.

Prescribed for

Hyperthyroidism in cats.

General Information

Hyperthyroidism is common in middle-aged and older cats, and it is usually caused by benign nodules in one or both thyroid glands. These nodules make too much thyroid hormone. Only 1% to 2% of hyperthyroid cats have a malignant thyroid tumor. Untreated hyperthyroidism is eventually fatal, however, because of the metabolic effects of hyperthyroidism.

Methimazole is one of a group of compounds called thionamides that have antithyroid activity. These compounds inhibit the synthesis of thyroid hormones by the thyroid gland. Propylthiouracil (PTU) was the first drug used to treat hyperthyroidism in cats, but it is no longer recommended, because of the high incidence of mild to severe complications (decreased appetite, vomiting, lethargy, immune-mediated hemolytic anemia, low platelet counts, and development of serum antinuclear antibodies).

Side effects with methimazole tend to occur within the first 3 months of therapy. Adverse reactions may occur at any time but are much less likely if there were no problems in the first 3 months. The most common clinical signs—decreased appetite, vomiting, and lethargy—occur in approximately 15% of cats and usually within the first 2 weeks of therapy. These signs are usually mild and transient and only rarely necessitate discontinuing the drug. A few cats may scratch their face and neck in the first few weeks of therapy. If the scratching is severe enough to produce wounds, the drug should be discontinued and corticosteroids given. Many cats will develop serum antinuclear antibodies (positive ANA). The higher the dose and the longer the treatment, the more likely this is to occur. So far there have been no reports of clinical signs of autoimmune or lupus-like disease in those cats with positive ANA. There are several mild blood abnormalities that may occur with methimazole, including increased blood eosinophils and lymphocytes or decreased white blood cell count. Serious blood reactions (low platelets and/or very low white blood cells) may occur in approximately 4% of cats and can be life threatening. Low platelets may cause bleeding, usually from the nose or mouth. Very low white blood cell counts usually lead to serious infections. White blood cell and platelet counts should be done every 2 to 3 weeks for the first 3 months of therapy to monitor for these adverse reactions. Liver failure within the first 2 months of therapy is a rare complication. Signs include decreased appetite, depression, vomiting, and jaundice (yellow gums, skin, and eyes). Recovery usually begins within a week, once the drug is discontinued.

Cautions and Warnings

■ Methimazole is not FDA approved for use in dogs or cats. It is commonly used to treat hyperthyroidism in cats and is considered accepted practice.

■ Each cat is different in its response to methimazole, so it is necessary to monitor the blood thyroid hormone level (T4) at least every few weeks in the beginning of therapy to adjust the dose to the smallest amount of methimazole that will keep the T4 normal. The blood T4 should be checked every 6 months to 1 year thereafter, to make sure you still have the best dose for your cat. Remember that the lowest possible dose that will keep the T4 in the normal range is the goal, and your cat's dose requirement may change over time.

■ U.S. federal law restricts the use of this drug by or on the lawful written or oral order of a licensed veterinarian within the context of a valid veterinarian-client-patient relationship.

Possible Side Effects

▼ Common: decreased appetite, vomiting, and lethargy.

▼ Rare: scratching of face and neck, development of ANA, decreased white blood cell and platelet counts, and liver failure.

Drug Interactions

None known.

Food Interactions

Probably best if given with food.

Usual Dose

Cats: starting dose—2.5–7.5 mg twice a day, depending on the size of the cat and the severity of the hyperthyroidism. The drug should be given twice a day, but some cats have been effectively managed with once a day dosing. Because the drug only suppresses thyroid hormone production, it must be continued for the life of the cat for medical management to be effective.

Overdosage

Overdosing will make your cat hypothyroid and increase the risk of the adverse reactions noted above. Because the response of each cat to methimazole varies, it is fairly easy to give too much and lower the T4 too much. Signs of hypothyroidism could include weakness, lethargy, low heart rate, low temperature, and increased or decreased appetite. Blood T4 levels should be checked at least every 2 to 3 weeks in the beginning of therapy and every 6 months to 1 year thereafter to avoid overdosing. In case of accidental ingestion or overdose, contact your veterinarian or the National Animal Poison Control Center. ALWAYS bring the prescription bottle or container with you if you go for treatment.

Special Information

There are three accepted treatments at this time for feline hyperthyroidism. One is surgical removal of the thyroid nodule. This therapy may cure the cat, but because of the risks of surgery and the possibility of recurrence, this approach is not used often. Recurrence is likely after surgery because of other smaller nodules that were missed at surgery or that grow after surgery. The best treatment is probably radioactive iodine (see *Iodine/Iodide*). This is a single treatment that destroys the abnormal thyroid tissue but spares the normal thyroid and is considered a cure. The major disadvantage of this therapy is the expense. Methimazole may be the best alternative for most cat owners. It does mean a commitment to giving medication for the life of the cat, monitoring for adverse effects of the drug, and regular blood tests to ensure proper dosing. If you and your veterinarian decide on surgery or radioactive iodine treatment, methimazole will still be used before either procedure, to make sure that your cat's thyroid function is normal before proceeding. If it is difficult to administer pills to your cat, there are liquid formulations of methimazole that may be very palatable and easier for you to give to your cat. Consult your veterinarian for information on compounding pharmacies.

Special Populations

Pregnancy/Lactation
The effects on reproduction have not been studied, but methimazole should probably not be used in cats that are pregnant or lactating. It is not known whether there are adverse effects on male fertility.

Puppies/Kittens
Methimazole should not be used in puppies or kittens.

Senior Animals
Most of the cats who have hyperthyroidism are older and therefore more likely to have the kidney diseases that are common in older cats. Hyperthyroidism may be "protective" of kidney function in a sense, because it causes higher blood flow to the kidneys. When the hyperthyroidism is corrected, with methimazole or any other therapy, an underlying kidney problem may be "unmasked." It is best to monitor kidney function during the start of treatment.

Generic Name

Methionine (muh-THYE-oe-nene) [G]

Brand Names

Ammonil [V]	Methio-Form [V]
Bio-Meth [V]	Methio-Tabs [V]
Methigel [V]	

Type of Drug

Urine acidifier.

Prescribed for

Cystitis, alkaline urinary stones, feline urologic syndrome (FUS), urinary tract infections.

General Information

Methionine (DL-methionine) is a sulfur-containing amino acid, one of the building blocks of proteins. After methionine is metabolized by the liver, sulfate is excreted in the urine as sulfuric acid, thereby acidifying the urine.

Acid urine is thought to help treat FUS and prevent the formation of and dissolve the struvite stones that form in alkaline urine (see *Ammonium Chloride*). Acid urine may help clear some urinary tract infections. Acidification of urine may be used to help the kidney excrete certain toxins or drug overdoses.

Cautions and Warnings

■ Methionine should not be used in patients with kidney or pancreatic disease, or metabolic acidosis (excess acid in the blood), as may occur in diabetes mellitus and urinary tract obstruction. Urine pH should be checked routinely to avoid under- or over-dosing.

■ Do not use methionine or supplements containing methionine in patients with liver disease, as it may cause hepatic encephalopathy (neurologic signs due to liver failure) and coma.

■ Do not give methionine to animals with urate stones (see *Allopurinol*).

■ Contact your veterinarian if you think your dog or cat may be having an adverse reaction to methionine.

■ U.S. federal law restricts the use of this drug by or on the

lawful written or oral order of a licensed veterinarian within the context of a valid veterinarian-client-patient relationship.

Possible Side Effects

▼ Common: gastrointestinal distress (e.g., stomach irritation, nausea, and vomiting) and metabolic acidosis (if the animal is not adequately monitored and the dose is too high).

▼ Rare: Heinz body hemolytic anemia, methemoglobinemia (damaged hemoglobin and red blood cells), unsteady gait, and blue-purple gums.

Drug Interactions

• Methionine may decrease the effectiveness of quinidine.
• Methionine decreases the effectiveness of the aminoglycoside antibiotics and erythromycin if they are being used to treat urinary tract infections.

Food Interactions

Give with food in divided doses to avoid gastrointestinal distress. Do not use methionine with diets designed to acidify the urine (Purina CNM-UR Formula, Hill's Science Diet cd), unless under the supervision of your veterinarian. Metabolic acidosis may result from excessive acid in the diet.

Usual Dose

The daily dose varies, depending on the diet. The goal of therapy is to lower urine pH to 5.5–6.5 and keep it there consistently.

Dogs: 0.2–1 g/dog orally 3 times a day.

Cats: 0.2–1 g/cat orally once a day. May be given in divided doses.

Drug Form: gel, tablet, and powder. Methionine is also an ingredient in some veterinary vitamin-mineral supplements.

Overdosage

Overdose causes metabolic acidosis. Symptoms may include nausea, vomiting, excessive thirst, rapid deep breathing, slow heart rate or other abnormal heart rhythms, weakness, and progressive central nervous system depression. Doses of only two times the recommended dose in cats may cause decreased appetite, Heinz body hemolytic anemia, methemoglobinemia, unsteady gait, and blue-purple gums. In case of accidental ingestion or overdose, contact your veterinarian or the National Animal Poison Control Center. ALWAYS bring the prescription bottle or container with you if you go for treatment.

Special Information

The cause of FUS is not known, but there is some evidence that acid urine and low dietary magnesium may help prevent recurrence. There are a number of commercial diets designed for this purpose. Regular or low magnesium diets may also be used with methionine added to acidify the urine. Ammonium chloride is an alternate and probably safer urine acidifier in cats. Discuss the management of FUS with your veterinarian to find the best treatment for your cat.

Special Populations

Pregnancy/Lactation
Methionine should be avoided during pregnancy or lactation unless the benefits outweigh the risks.

Puppies/Kittens
Methionine should not be given to puppies or kittens. Kittens that consume adult cat food to which methionine has been added may become severely ill (see "Overdosage").

Senior Animals
Methionine is safe to use in older animals but should not be given to those with acidosis, as in poorly controlled diabetes or urinary tract obstruction. It should not be given to those with kidney, pancreas, or liver dysfunction.

Generic Name

Methocarbamol (meth-oe-KAR-buh-mol) [G]

Brand Names

Robaxin [V] [H]

Combination Product

Generic Ingredients: Methocarbamol + Aspirin
Robaxisol [H]

Type of Drug

Muscle relaxant.

Prescribed for

The reduction of muscle spasms due to acute inflammation or traumatic conditions.

General Information

Methocarbamol is a centrally acting muscle relaxant. It does not work on the muscle directly, but is thought to work as a central nervous system (CNS) depressant and sedative. In humans, it is absorbed quickly after oral administration and peak levels occur about 2 hours after dosing.

Methocarbamol is used to treat muscle spasms associated with back problems, traumatic sprains, bursitis, and muscle spasms related to surgery. It is safe to use with corticosteroids and other medications used for the treatment of muscle spasm.

Cautions and Warnings

■ Methocarbamol is FDA approved for use in cats and dogs. Methocarbamol is a CNS depressant. At normal doses, it is considered a safe and relatively nontoxic drug.

■ Injectable methocarbamol contains polyethylene glycol and should not be used in animals with decreased kidney function. Human studies suggest that injectable methocarbamol should be avoided in patients with epilepsy.

■ Contact your veterinarian if you think your dog or cat is having an adverse reaction to methocarbamol.

■ U.S. federal law restricts the use of this drug by or on the lawful written or oral order of a licensed veterinarian within the context of a valid veterinarian-client-patient relationship.

Possible Side Effects

▼ Common: sedation.

▼ Rare: excessive salivation, vomiting, loss of balance, weakness, and staggering; usually these reactions accompany intravenous injection of a large dose or rapid injection.

Drug Interactions

• Methocarbamol causes additive CNS depression if given with other CNS depressants.

Food Interactions

None known.

Usual Dose

Dogs and Cats: starting dose—20 mg/lb orally 3 times a day. Maintenance dose—10–20 mg/lb orally 3 times a day.

Drug Form: 500- and 750-mg tablets and 100 mg/ml injectable. Methocarbamol + aspirin combination—400-mg methocarbamol and 325-mg aspirin.

Overdosage

Overdoses usually cause CNS depression, excessive sedation, staggering, and prostration; nausea, salivation, and vomiting are sometimes seen with intravenous administration. In case of accidental ingestion or overdose, contact your veterinarian or the National Animal Poison Control Center. ALWAYS bring the prescription bottle or container with you if you go for treatment.

Special Information

Methocarbamol may be used to treat convulsions caused by strychnine poisoning. The sale of strychnine is illegal in the United States, but occasional accidental poisonings still occur when stockpiles are used to kill wild animals.

Special Populations

Pregnancy/Lactation
Studies show no adverse reactions from methocarbamol in the pregnant rat or fetus. No other animal studies have been performed. Methocarbamol should not be used in pregnant animals unless the benefits outweigh the possible risks. It is not known if methocarbamol is excreted in milk. It should be avoided in lactating animals.

Puppies/Kittens
There are no safety studies in young animals or in children. Methocarbamol should be avoided in puppies and kittens unless the benefits outweigh the possible risks.

Senior Animals

Methocarbamol should be safe to use in older animals. Injectable methocarbamol should be avoided in animals with decreased kidney function.

Generic Name

Metoclopramide (met-oe-KLOE-pruh-mide) [G]

Most Common Brand Name

Reglan [H]

Type of Drug

Antiemetic and gastrointestinal stimulant.

Prescribed for

Nausea, vomiting, delayed emptying of the stomach, and esophageal reflux.

General Information

Metoclopramide hydrochloride stimulates movement of the upper gastrointestinal (GI) tract, but does not stimulate excess stomach acid or other secretions. Its effect against nausea and vomiting may be caused by the drug's direct effect on dopamine receptors in the brain. Metoclopramide is frequently used in animals that have kidney failure to decrease the nausea and vomiting caused by uremia (toxins in the blood) from kidney failure.

In the GI tract, metoclopramide works by tightening the sphincter between the esophagus and the stomach. This helps prevent esophageal reflux. Metoclopramide increases contractions in the stomach and relaxes the adjacent part of the small intestine, enabling the stomach to empty faster. Conditions that would cause delayed emptying of the stomach include gastritis, and metabolic or postoperative slowing of the bowel (ileus).

Cautions and Warnings

■ Metoclopramide is not FDA approved for use in dogs or cats. It is commonly used, however, and is considered accepted practice.

■ Metoclopramide should not be used in animals with GI bleeding, obstruction, or perforation, or in those hypersensitive to it.

■ Metoclopramide should be used with caution in animals prone to seizures, as it may lower the seizure threshold.

■ Metoclopramide should not be used in animals with pheochromocytoma, a tumor of the adrenal gland.

Possible Side Effects

Side effects are not common at normal doses. The most common side effect is sedation.

▼ Rare: disorientation, behavior changes, and constipation.

Drug Interactions

• Metoclopramide may affect the absorption of other medications.

• Digoxin absorption is decreased. This is not true for Lanoxin, a brand of digoxin.

• Metoclopramide increases the absorption of cimetidine, tetracycline, aspirin, and diazepam from the GI tract, so the doses of these drugs may need to be decreased.

• Metoclopramide may change insulin requirements.

• Phenothiazine tranquilizers, sedatives, and narcotics may increase the likelihood of central nervous system disturbances.

• Metoclopramide should be used with caution or avoided in animals taking monoamine oxidase inhibitors (MAOIs).

• Atropine, anticholinergic drugs, and narcotic pain relievers may negate the GI motility effects of metoclopramide.

Food Interactions

Metoclopramide may accelerate food absorption.

Usual Dose

Dogs and Cats: 0.1–0.2 mg/lb orally 3–4 times a day.

Drug Form: 5- and 10-mg tablets, 5 mg/5 ml oral syrup, and 5 mg/ml injectable.

Overdosage

There is a wide margin of safety for oral metoclopramide. Symptoms of overdose include sedation, staggering, nausea, vomiting, and constipation. In case of accidental ingestion or overdose, contact your veterinarian or the National Animal Poison Control Center. ALWAYS bring the prescription bottle or container with you if you go for treatment.

Special Information

Drugs to prevent vomiting are not always appropriate. Some circumstances where drugs such as metoclopramide may not be appropriate include GI infections, GI obstructions, and toxins in the GI tract.

Metoclopramide is frequently used to treat nausea and vomiting in animals in kidney failure. Because the drug is metabolized in the kidney, the dose may need to be decreased in animals with decreased kidney function. Metoclopramide is used to decrease nausea and vomiting associated with chemotherapy in humans, but it is not particularly effective for this purpose in animals.

Special Populations

Pregnancy/Lactation
Studies in laboratory animals have showed no harmful effects on pregnancy or fertility. Metoclopramide is excreted in human milk. Safety studies have not been performed in dogs and cats. Metoclopramide should only be used when the benefits outweigh the risks.

Puppies/Kittens
Safety studies have not been performed in puppies and kittens. Metoclopramide should only be used when the benefits outweigh the risks.

Senior Animals
There are no studies in older dogs or cats. Metoclopramide is probably safe to use in older animals, although the dose may need to be reduced, especially if kidney function is decreased. In humans, side effects are more common in older patients.

Generic Name

Metronidazole (met-roe-NYE-duh-zole) G

Brand Name

Flagyl H

Metizol H

Metrogel H

MetroCream H

Protostat H

Type of Drug

Antiprotozoal, antibiotic, and anti-inflammatory in the bowel.

Prescribed for

Protozoal infections in cats and dogs (commonly *Giardia* or *Entamoeba*) and bacterial infections in cats and dogs. Metronidazole may also be prescribed for inflammatory bowel disease, colitis caused by other antibiotics, periodontal (gum) disease, especially in cats, *Clostridium perfringens* enterotoxemia, tetanus, diarrhea of undetermined cause, pancreatic insufficiency (with small intestinal bacterial overgrowth), and complications of severe liver disease. Metronidazole gel may be applied to the skin to treat certain skin infections, like chin acne in cats. Metronidazole may be given intravenously by your veterinarian before, during, and after bowel surgery to prevent infection.

General Information

Metronidazole is used to treat protozoal infections and bacterial infections where anaerobic bacteria (bacteria that grow only where there is no oxygen) are present. Metronidazole also has anti-inflammatory effects in the bowel and may be helpful in certain kinds of diarrhea and in inflammatory bowel disease of unknown cause. The mechanism of this anti-inflammatory effect is not well understood. Metronidazole kills microorganisms by disrupting their DNA. This drug is rapidly absorbed from the gastrointestinal tract into the bloodstream. It is metabolized by the liver and excreted in the urine and the feces.

Cautions and Warnings

■ This drug is not FDA approved for use in cats or dogs. It is commonly used to treat protozoal and some types of bacterial infections, and it is considered accepted practice.

■ Metronidazole should be avoided or used with caution at reduced doses in animals with kidney or liver disease.

■ U.S. federal law restricts the use of this drug by or on the lawful written or oral order of a licensed veterinarian within the context of a valid veterinarian-client-patient relationship.

Possible Side Effects

Neurologic signs may be seen after accidental overdose or more commonly with long-term moderate to high-dose therapy as in the treatment of difficult bacterial infections. These signs often begin 7 to 12 days following the start of treatment. (See "Overdosage").

▼ Common: clinical signs related to the bad taste, or gastrointestinal upset. Excessive salivation, gagging, regurgitation, pawing at the mouth, nausea, vomiting, and decreased appetite are the most frequent complaints. The pills are extremely bitter, so the method of giving these pills can be a factor in how well your animal tolerates the drug.

▼ Rare: diarrhea, depression, lethargy, weakness, low white blood cell count, liver failure, and blood in the urine, or dark urine due to pigment changes.

Drug Interactions

• Animals taking oral anticoagulant (blood thinning) drugs such as warfarin should have their dose of anticoagulant reduced because metronidazole increases the effect of anticoagulants.

• Cimetidine can interfere with the liver's ability to break down metronidazole, causing increased levels of metronidazole in your animal's blood. The metronidazole dose may have to be reduced if your animal is taking cimetidine.

• Phenobarbital may increase the metabolism of metronidazole, and make it less effective.

• Metronidazole may increase blood levels of phenytoin by interfering with its breakdown in the liver. This could increase the risk of phenytoin side effects and might result in the need to adjust your animal's phenytoin dosage.

Food interactions

Probably tolerated better if given with food.

Usual Dose

There are very wide ranges in doses, frequency of dosing, and duration of treatment, because metronidazole is used for such a wide variety of conditions.

Dogs

For Giardia and Entamoeba infections: 7–14 mg/lb orally 1–2 times a day for 5–7 days.

For anaerobic infections: 11–23 mg/lb orally 2–4 times a day (dosing intervals and duration of treatment can vary depending on the animal's condition and which other antibiotics are being used concurrently).

For hepatic encephalopathy: 3.5 mg/lb orally twice a day.

For periodontal disease: 9 mg/lb orally once a day for 10–20 days.

For inflammatory bowel disease: 5–7 mg/lb orally 2–3 times a day.

Cats

For Giardia and Entamoeba infection: 5–11 mg/lb orally 1–2 times a day for 5–10 days (maximum dose: 23 mg/lb in a 24-hour period).

For gingivitis/stomatitis/pharyngitis complex: 23 mg/lb orally once a day.

For anaerobic infections: 11–14 mg/lb orally 1–2 times a day (dosing intervals and duration of treatment can vary depending on the animal's condition and which other antibiotics are being used concurrently).

Drug Form
Flagyl: 375-mg capsule.
Protostat: 250- and 500-mg tablets (this dosage also available as generic).
Metrogel: 7.5 mg/g topical gel.

Overdosage

Signs of overdose of metronidazole include gastrointestinal signs (see "Possible Side Effects"). High doses of metronidazole can cause problems with the animal's nervous system. Most of the neurologic signs are seen in animals that are on long-term moderate or high doses (oral doses greater than 66 mg/kg/day), and often begin 7 to 12 days following the start of treatment. Signs could include loss of coordination, staggering, tremors, head tilt, disorientation, seizures, slow heart rate, rigidity, and stiffness. Call your veterinarian immediately if you think your pet may be having an adverse reaction to metronidazole. After the drug is discontinued, it may be several days to 2 weeks before the neurologic signs begin to diminish. In case of accidental ingestion or overdose, contact your veterinarian or the National Animal Poison Control Center. ALWAYS bring the prescription bottle or container with you if you go for treatment.

Special Information

When metronidazole is used to treat bacterial infections, it is frequently used with other antibiotics. This is because metronidazole is only effective against anaerobic bacteria; it is not at all effective against other types of bacteria. Many infections have more than one kind of bacteria and so the antibiotic therapy will sometimes require more than one drug to kill all the different types of bacteria. This drug is compatible for use with many other antibiotics.

Metronidazole may be used with corticosteroids (or other medications) in the treatment of inflammatory bowel disease or gum disease (gingivitis/stomatitis) in cats.

Because of metronidazole's bad taste, you may have difficulty giving it to your dog or cat. Ask your veterinarian for advice on how best to give the drug to your pet. Using a "pet piller" (plastic plunger used to place pills in the throats of dogs and cats) or wrapping the pill in food and placing it far into the back of the mouth are two methods that may be helpful. Crushing the pills and placing the dose in empty gelatin capsules is another alternative. Furazolidone may be a better drug for *Giardia* infection in cats, because it does not taste bad and therefore is better tolerated.

Special Populations

Pregnancy/Lactation

Metronidazole causes birth defects in laboratory animals. It should be avoided in pregnant animals, especially in the first trimester. Some metronidazole is excreted in breast milk, and it should not be used in lactating animals.

Puppies/Kittens

Metronidazole should not be used in young puppies and kittens.

Senior Animals

Metronidazole is safe to use in older animals if kidney and liver function are normal. If kidney and liver function are impaired, metronidazole should be avoided, or the dose should be decreased.

Generic Name

Mibolerone (mye-BOLE-er-one)

Brand Name

Cheque Drops ☑V

Type of Drug

Androgenic, anabolic, antigonadotropic steroid.

Prescribed for

Prevention of estrus (heat), infertility due to abnormally short estrus cycles, and signs of false pregnancy in adult female dogs.

General Information

Mibolerone is an androgenic steroid. It opposes the effects of estrogen and blocks the release of luteinizing hormone (LH) from the pituitary gland. LH is the hormone that causes ovulation and stimulates the production of progesterone by the ovary. The estrus cycle is suppressed by blocking the hormones that control the reproductive cycle and ovulation. Like other androgenic hormones, mibolerone has anabolic actions and stimulates metabolism; however, it is not used solely for this purpose.

The drug must be started at least 30 days before proestrus starts to prevent estrus. It is effective in 90% of treated dogs. It is not recommended in dogs primarily used for breeding because post-treatment estrus is not predictable. The average time of recurrence is 70 days, but ranges from 7 to 200 days after the drug is discontinued.

Short estrus cycles are a cause of infertility because they do not allow the uterus enough time to develop and prepare for implantation of the fertilized egg. Mibolerone may be used to suppress the cycle allowing the uterus to undergo the necessary changes. The female should be bred on the cycle following termination of treatment.

Mibolerone is sometimes used to reduce signs of false pregnancy. It is effective, but the signs may recur after treatment is stopped. In general, signs of false pregnancy resolve without treatment, which is the preferred option in most cases.

Mibolerone has been used in cats, but it is not recommended because the risk of serious side effects is very high (see "Overdosage").

Cautions and Warnings

■ Do not use in Bedlington terriers or other breeds with a predisposition to kidney or liver disease (see "Special Populations"). Do not use in individuals with a history of liver or kidney disease.

■ Do not use in dogs with perianal adenoma, perianal adenocarcinoma (tumors around the anus), or other androgen-dependent cancer.

■ Do not use before the first estrus cycle, or to shorten the estrus cycle. Do not use in pregnant dogs, during lactation, or for more than 24 months.

■ DO NOT USE IN CATS.

■ Contact your veterinarian if you think your dog or cat may be having an adverse reaction to mibolerone.

■ FDA approved for prevention of estrus in adult female dogs. All other uses are extralabel.

■ U.S. federal law restricts the use of this drug by or on the lawful written or oral order of a licensed veterinarian within the context of a valid veterinarian-client-patient relationship.

Possible Side Effects

▼ Common: increased size of the clitoris, vaginal discharge, mounting or aggressive behavior, change in voice, oily skin, reproductive tract lesions, and tearing.

▼ Rare: musky body odor, liver disease, and death.

Drug Interactions

• Do not use with progestins or estrogens.
• May reduce effectiveness of phenytoin in controlling seizures.

Food Interactions

None known.

Usual Dose

Dogs: for suppression of estrus (treatment must begin at least 30 days prior to proestrus). 1–24 lbs—30 mcg (0.3 ml) once a day; 25–49 lbs—60 mcg (0.6 ml) once a day; 50–99 lbs—120 mcg (1.2 ml) once a day; over 100 lbs—180 mcg (1.8 ml) once a day. German shepherds or German shepherd crosses—180 mcg (1.8 ml) once a day, regardless of weight. For false pregnancy—use 10 times the normal dose once a day for 5 days.

Drug Form: 100 mcg/ml oral drops.

Overdosage

The drug did not cause death when over 5000 times the recommended dose was administered to female dogs for 1 month. Side effects reported at this dose include excessive tearing, depression, loss of appetite, weight loss, muscle pain and liver changes. Chronic liver disease is common in dogs receiving therapeutic or increased doses for a period of several years. In cats, a daily dose of 60 mcg may cause liver disease and 120 mcg may cause death. This is very close to the 50 mcg dose that suppresses estrus. This margin of safety is very low and the risk of using this drug in cats is unacceptable. Other side effects are enlargement of the clitoris, and thyroid and pancreatic dysfunction. In case of accidental ingestion or overdose, contact your veterinarian or the National Animal Poison Control Center. ALWAYS bring the prescription bottle or container with you if you go for treatment.

Special Information

Suppression of estrus with hormone therapy is effective; however, the incidence of side effects is high. Surgical removal of the ovaries and uterus is safer and the preferred method for prevention of pregnancy in pets.

Special Populations

Specific Breeds

Mibolerone should not be administered to Bedlington terriers according to the manufacturer. Although not specifically contraindicated, it may be prudent to avoid administering this product to dogs of other breeds predisposed to liver disease. The Doberman pinscher has a hereditary predisposition to liver disease. West Highland white and Skye terriers are genetically predisposed to liver disease associated with increased copper accumulation. There are a number of other breeds with an increased incidence of copper-associated liver disease, although a genetic link has not been proven.

Pregnancy/Lactation

Mibolerone should not be used during pregnancy or lactation. It causes masculinization of female fetuses and may inhibit lactation.

Puppies

Immature dogs are at an increased risk of side effects. Mibolerone should not be used in puppies or before the first estrus cycle.

Senior Animals

There are no specific contraindications for healthy senior dogs.

Generic Name

Miconazole (mye-KON-uh-zole) [G]

Most Common Brand Names

Conofite [V]   Micatin [H]

Dermazole [V]   Monistat [H]

Type of Drug

Antifungal.

Prescribed for

Susceptible superficial fungal infections, *Malassezia* infections of the skin and ears, fungal infections of the cornea, and ringworm topical treatment.

General Information

Clotrimazole and miconazole nitrate are imidazole antifungals that cannot be given orally or by injection (see *Clotrimazole* and *Ketoconazole*) but are very effective as topical treatments for superficial fungal infections, especially those caused by the yeasts *Malassezia* and *Candida*. *Malassezia* otitis externa (ear infection) is an extremely common and recurrent problem in dogs (see "Special Information").

Malassezia is being recognized more commonly as a cause of skin infections secondary to underlying skin disease. It is especially common in dogs with severe greasy scaling (seborrhea), inflammation and itching associated with allergies, superficial bacterial infections (pyoderma), and primary seborrhea. Some veterinary experts have had greater success treating *Malassezia* dermatitis using ketoconazole 2% shampoo (see *Ketoconazole*) than miconazole shampoo (Dermazole). Some animals with superficial fungal infections may also benefit from treatment with oral antifungals (see *Ketoconazole*).

Miconazole may also be used for topical treatment of ringworm (see *Griseofulvin*). Many antifungals are now available over the counter. Consult your veterinarian for advice on the best treatment for your animal.

Cautions and Warnings

For Owners/Handlers

■ Avoid contact with eyes, since irritation may result.

■ Wash hands after use to prevent spread of fungal infections.

For Animals

■ Avoid contact with eyes or mucous membranes, since irritation may result.

■ Contact your veterinarian if you think your dog or cat may be having an adverse reaction to miconazole or if there is no improvement in 2 weeks.

■ U.S. federal law restricts the use of this drug by or on the lawful written or oral order of a licensed veterinarian within the context of a valid veterinarian-client-patient relationship.

Possible Side Effects

▼ Rare: mild skin irritation (redness, swelling, itching, and oozing) and allergic reactions.

Drug Interactions

• Amphotericin B and miconazole inhibit each other and should not be used together.

Usual Dose

Dogs and Cats: Clean affected area with soap and water and dry thoroughly. Apply a light covering of ointment, spray, or lotion once a day to affected areas and immediate surrounding vicinity. Treatment may involve other procedures, as in ear cleaning, so follow your veterinarian's advice on the use of miconazole products. Shampoo: apply to a wet coat, work into skin and hair, and lather freely. Leave on for 5–10 minutes. May be used once a day or as directed by your veterinarian. Experts often recommend shampooing with a degreasing agent such as benzoyl peroxide (see *Benzoyl Peroxide*) before using antifungal shampoos.

Drug Form: ointment, spray, lotion, and shampoo.

Overdosage

There is no specific information on overdose of miconazole. Miconazole is poorly absorbed after oral administration, so signs from oral overdose are unlikely. In case of accidental ingestion or overdose, contact your veterinarian or the National Animal Poison Control Center. ALWAYS bring the prescription bottle or container with you if you go for treatment.

Special Information

Miconazole is an extremely effective treatment for yeast infections of skin and ears, but there is usually an underlying cause for chronic and recurrent yeast infections in dogs. You should expect that if your dog has a yeast infection, it is likely to recur unless the underlying problem is eliminated. The most common underlying problem is allergic skin disease, either from inhaled or ingested allergens. Hair in the ear canal, excessive wax production, long floppy ears, frequent swimming, and polyps or tumors in the ear canal may all predispose the ears to infections as well. There are other effective topical treatments for chronic yeast infections, including boric acid, clotrimazole, and amphotericin B. Selenium sulfide and chlorhexidine are also effective antifungal shampoos. Newer antifungals such as tioconazole (Vagistat) are now available over the counter. Consult your veterinarian for advice on the most effective topical antifungal for your pet.

Special Populations

Pregnancy/Lactation
There are no studies to confirm the safety of miconazole in pregnant or lactating dogs or cats. Miconazole should be avoided unless the potential benefits outweigh the risks.

Puppies/Kittens
There are no studies to confirm the safety of miconazole in puppies or kittens. Miconazole should be avoided unless the potential benefits outweigh the risks.

Senior Animals
Miconazole should be safe to use in older animals.

Generic Name

Milbemycin Oxime (MIL-buh-MYE-sin OK-seme)

Brand Name

Interceptor Flavor Tabs V

Combination Product

Generic Ingredients: Milbemycin Oxime + Lufenuron
Sentinel V

Type of Drug

Heartworm preventive, anthelmintic/dewormer, microfilaricide, and miticide.

Prescribed for

Prevention of heartworm (*Dirofilaria immitis*), control of hookworm (*Ancylostoma caninum, A. braziliense, Uncinaria stenocephal*), removal of heartworm microfilaria (*D. immitis*), roundworm (*Toxocara canis, Toxascaris leonina*), whipworm (*Trichuris vulpis, Strongyloides stercoralis*), lungworm (*Capillaria aerophilia, Oslerus osleri*), and mites (*Otodectes cyanotes, Sarcoptes scabiei, Cheyletiella* spp., *Notoedres cati, Demodex canis, Pneumonyssus caninum*) in dogs and cats.

General Information

The soil-living bacteria *Streptomyces hygroscopicus aureolacrimosus* produce milbemycin oxime. It is in the same group of macrolide drugs and acts against the same parasites as ivermectin, another popular once-a-month heartworm preventive (see *Ivermectin*).

Milbemycin interferes with parasite nerve function. This results in paralysis and death of susceptible parasites. Mammalian muscles are controlled by a different type of nerve and are not affected by milbemycin. Mammals do have similar nerve types in the brain and central nervous system, but milbemycin does not pass through the blood-brain barrier. For this reason, milbemycin has very few side effects in dogs and cats. Prevention of heartworm disease is the major use of this drug.

Milbemycin is 100% effective against heartworm larvae transmitted from infected mosquitoes within 45 days before treatment. It also kills the microfilarial stage of heartworm at the same dose. This may result in false negative results on diagnostic tests based on the detection of microfilaria. In addition, large numbers of dying microfilaria may cause an anaphylactic-like (serious systemic allergic) reaction. For these reasons, all potentially infected animals should be tested for heartworm infection before starting on a heartworm preventive and the use of milbemycin to remove microfilaria should be done under direct veterinary supervision. An alternative test that detects antigen from adult heartworm instead of microfilaria is recommended for heartworm diagnosis in animals receiving milbemycin as a preventive.

Milbemycin is approved by the FDA to prevent heartworm disease, control adult hookworm (*Ancylostoma caninum, A. braziliense, Uncinaria stenocephala*), and remove and control adult roundworm (*Toxocara canis, Toxascaris leonina*) and whipworm (*Trichuris vulpis*) infections in dogs. It is also effective against the filarial lungworms (*Capillaria aerophilia, Oslerus osleri*) that infect the lower airways of dogs and cats and several species of mites including the skin mites (*Sarcoptes scabiei, Notoedres cati, Cheyletiella* spp., *Demodex canis*), ear mites (*Otodectes cynotis*), and nasal mites (*Pneumonyssus caninum*). It has no activity against tapeworms, flukes, or protozoa.

Heartworm, roundworm, hookworm, and some mites are

contagious and may spread to other animals and to people (see *Zoonotic Diseases of Dogs and Cats*).

Cautions and Warnings

■ Milbemycin may be toxic to fish and other animals that are accidentally exposed by contamination of the environment and water. Dispose of unused milbemycin and containers by incineration or in an approved landfill.

■ All adult animals that have been off heartworm preventive for 6 months or longer should be tested for heartworm infection before starting preventive treatment (see "General Information"). Animals off heartworm preventive for 2 to 6 months should restart heartworm preventive and be tested 6 months from the last date of exposure. It takes 6 months from the time of infection for the tests to become positive. Start milbemycin within 30 days of discontinuing diethylcarbamazine when switching from daily heartworm preventive.

■ Contact your veterinarian if you think your dog or cat may be having an adverse reaction to milbemycin.

■ Milbemycin is approved by the FDA for the prevention of heartworm, the control of hookworm, and the removal and control of roundworm and whipworm in dogs. Extralabel use in cats and dogs is common and is considered accepted practice, but should be done only under veterinary supervision and after considering the potential risks and benefits.

■ U.S. federal law restricts the use of this drug by or on the lawful written or oral order of a licensed veterinarian within the context of a valid veterinarian-client-patient relationship.

Possible Side Effects

▼ Rare: depression, lethargy, vomiting, loss of coordination, loss of appetite, diarrhea, convulsions, weakness, and excessive salivation.

Food and Drug Interactions

None known.

Usual Dose

Milbemycin Oxime

Dogs: for heartworm prevention microfilaricide, control of whipworm, control and prevention of roundworm and hookworm—0.23–0.45 mg/lb once a month. For demodicosis—0.45–0.9 mg/lb/day for at least 90 days.

Cats: for heartworm prevention—0.23–0.45 mg/lb once a month.

Drug Form: 2.3-, 5.75-, 11.5-, and 23.0-mg chewable tablets.

Sentinel

Dogs: 0.23 mg/lb milbemycin + 4.55 mg/lb lufenuron minimum. Use appropriate size tablet or combination of tablets once a month.

Drug Form: tablets with 2.3 mg milbemycin + 46 mg lufenuron for 2–10 lb dogs; 5.75 milbemycin + 115 mg lufenuron for 11–25 lb dogs; 11.5 mg milbemycin + 230 mg lufenuron for 26–50 lb dogs; and 23.0 mg milbemycin + 460 mg lufenuron for 51–100 lb dogs.

Overdosage

No signs of overdose were seen in dogs given 200 times the recommended dose. Collies given 10 times the upper end of the recommended dose had no signs of overdose, but fever and loss of coordination were seen in some collies given 12.5 times the recommended dose (5.7 mg/lb). In case of accidental ingestion or overdose, contact your veterinarian or the National Animal Poison Control Center. ALWAYS bring the prescription bottle or container with you if you go for treatment.

Special Populations

Collies/Herding Breeds

Collies and other herding breeds are more likely to have side effects to milbemycin than other breeds (see "Overdosage"). This is similar to the increased sensitivity to ivermectin seen in these breeds. In spite of this, milbemycin is considered safe in these breeds because side effects are not seen until over 10 times the recommended dose is given and generally resolve rapidly once treatment is stopped.

Pregnancy/Lactation

Milbemycin is considered safe to use in pregnant dogs. Milbemycin is excreted in milk, but this does not cause side effects in either the mother or puppies.

Puppies/Kittens

Milbemycin is considered safe to use at recommended doses in puppies. It is labeled for use in puppies and kittens over age 8 weeks, but is considered safe and is commonly used in younger animals.

Senior Animals

Milbemycin is considered safe to use in senior dogs.

Generic Name

Misoprostol (mee-soe-PROS-tol)

Brand Name

Cytotec [H]

Type of Drug

Antiulcer.

Prescribed for

Protection from injury to the stomach and duodenum caused by nonsteroidal anti-inflammatory drugs (NSAIDs).

General Information

Prostaglandins are hormones produced by cells in the body that mediate inflammation. Many of the prostaglandins cause inflammation, but some have anti-inflammatory effects. One type of prostaglandin, PGE_1, protects the stomach lining at low doses, and decreases stomach acid secretion at higher doses. The protection of the stomach at lower doses is probably due to an increased protective mucus layer that lines the stomach, increased blood flow to the stomach lining, increased healing rate of stomach lining, and increased production of bicarbonate, a natural antacid found in the stomach. Misoprostol is a synthetic analog of PGE_1. It is especially effective in preventing stomach and duodenal injury for those animals on chronic NSAID therapy for arthritis or other conditions.

Cautions and Warnings

For Owners/Handlers
■ Pregnant women should handle the drug with caution.

For Animals
■ Misoprostol is not FDA approved for use in dogs or cats. It has been shown to protect the stomach against NSAID-induced damage in dogs, and it is considered accepted practice to use misoprostol for protection of the stomach and duodenum in those animals at risk. A dose has not been established for cats.
■ Higher doses may cause diarrhea, cramping, and nausea; misoprostol may cause abortion in pregnant females.
■ Animals with kidney disease may need a lower dose.
■ Contact your veterinarian if you think your dog or cat may be having an adverse reaction to misoprostol.
■ U.S. federal law restricts the use of this drug by or on the lawful written or oral order of a licensed veterinarian within the context of a valid veterinarian-client-patient relationship.

Possible Side Effects

Side effects with misoprostol are usually not severe and resolve on their own in a few days, or with dose reduction, or by giving the dose with food.

▼ Common: diarrhea, nausea, and cramping, especially at higher doses, may occur in up to 30% of people taking misoprostol; side effects seem to be less frequent in dogs but are dose-related; misoprostol may also cause abortion in pregnant females.

Drug Interactions

None known.

Food Interactions

None known. Probably best to give with food to avoid gastrointestinal upset.

Usual Dose

Dogs: 1–2.5 mcg/lb orally 3 times a day. The high dose—5

mcg/lb—decreases acid secretion as well as protecting the stomach lining.

Cats: The dose in cats has not been established.

Drug Form: 100-mcg tablets.

Overdosage

Overdoses in laboratory animals caused diarrhea, vomiting, tremors, seizures, and low blood pressure. Overdoses may cause damage to liver, kidney, and gastrointestinal tract. In case of accidental ingestion or overdose, contact your veterinarian or the National Animal Poison Control Center. ALWAYS bring the prescription bottle or container with you if you go for treatment.

Special Information

There are some data to suggest that misoprostol may be more effective than the histamine H_2 blocker antacids, such as cimetidine, and/or sucralfate. The cost of misoprostol may be prohibitive for long-term use, and the cimetidine-sucralfate option is still a reasonable and effective alternative. Misoprostol may protect against kidney damage caused by cyclosporine.

Special Populations

Pregnancy/Lactation
Misoprostol should be avoided in pregnant animals because it may cause abortion. It should be avoided in nursing animals because it may cause diarrhea in nursing puppies or kittens.

Puppies/Kittens
Misoprostol has not been studied in young animals and should probably be avoided.

Senior Animals
Misoprostol should be safe to use in older animals, but should be used with caution in those with decreased kidney function.

Generic Name

Mitotane (MYE-toe-tane)

Brand Name

Lysodren [H]

Type of Drug

Chemotherapeutic and adrenal function inhibitor.

Prescribed for

Cushing's disease caused by pituitary-dependent hyperadrenocorticism (PDH) or adrenal tumors, and congenital adrenal hyperplasia-like syndrome in dogs.

General Information

Mitotane, also known as o,p′–DDD, is structurally related to the insecticide DDT. It was identified in the late 1940s when severe adrenal destruction was reported in dogs treated with DDT.

Mitotane is cytotoxic and destroys the adrenal gland cells that produce corticosteroids (see *Corticosteroids*). It primarily affects the cells that produce the glucocorticoids but may also destroy some of the cells that produce mineralocorticoids (see *Desoxycorticosterone Pivalate (DOCP)* and *Fludrocortisone*). Mitotane is absorbed from the intestine and distributed to all parts of the body, including the adrenals. It is changed into the active metabolite in adrenal cells and in the process destroys those cells. Ultimately, it is detoxified and eliminated by the liver.

Mitotane is used to treat Cushing's disease caused by either PDH or adrenal tumors. The pituitary is a gland located at the base of the brain, which produces a hormone that stimulates the adrenal gland to produce corticosteroids. Pituitary tumors are responsible for 85% of the cases of spontaneous Cushing's disease. The other 15% are caused by adrenal gland tumors.

Mitotane is also used to treat congenital adrenal hyperplasia-like syndrome. This is a hereditary disease caused by abnormal production of sex steroid hormones by the adrenal gland. The primary sign is generalized hair loss, except on the lower legs and head, which remain hairy.

The effect of mitotane is rapid and results in an abrupt

decrease in corticosteroid levels as well as signs of Cushing's disease. The decrease in corticosteroids commonly results in signs of hypoadrenocorticism, or Addison's disease, including loss of appetite, vomiting, diarrhea, weakness, and depression. If severe side effects occur, decreasing the dosage or temporarily stopping the mitotane usually corrects the problem. Supplemental corticosteroids may be administered in severe cases while the animal adapts to the change in corticosteroid level. All dogs receiving mitotane therapy should receive additional glucocorticoid supplementation if subject to high stress, such as surgery, trauma, or illness.

Most dogs need to continue on long-term maintenance mitotane therapy. Regular monitoring is needed to fine-tune the dosage. Monitoring at home is also important, and changes in food consumption are useful for this. Rarely, mitotane permanently destroys adrenal function and long-term corticosteroid replacement is required.

Cautions and Warnings

For Owners/Handlers
■ Mitotane is a very toxic drug. Wash hands after handling.

For Animals
■ Use with caution in dogs with kidney or liver disease, and monitor carefully.

■ Insulin requirements may change rapidly particularly during the initial phase of treatment. Diabetics should be monitored very closely and the insulin dosage adjusted as needed.

■ Contact your veterinarian if you think your dog may be having an adverse reaction to mitotane.

■ Mitotane is not FDA approved for use in dogs, but it is routinely used and is considered accepted practice.

■ U.S. federal law restricts the use of this drug by or on the lawful written or oral order of a licensed veterinarian within the context of a valid veterinarian-client-patient relationship.

Possible Side Effects

▼ Common: loss of appetite, vomiting, diarrhea, weakness, lethargy, loss of coordination, and depression.

▼ Rare: increased liver enzymes, liver disease, neurologic signs (see "Overdosage"), and Addison's disease (see "General Information").

Drug Interactions

• Mitotane may decrease the insulin requirement of diabetic dogs.

• The diuretic spironolactone may block the action of mitotane.

• Mitotane may increase the required dose of barbiturates, warfarin, and other drugs that are metabolized in the liver. Conversely, these drugs may increase the dose of mitotane needed.

• Mitotane may increase the depressant effects of sedatives and other drugs that cause central nervous system depression.

Food Interactions

Administering with food, particularly fatty food, increases absorption.

Usual Dose

Dogs: starting—22.7 mg/lb once a day or divided into 2 doses a day for 5–10 days. Maintenance—11.3 mg/lb once or twice a week. Dose and dosing schedule vary depending on response to treatment.

Cats: Mitotane is not recommended for use in cats.

Drug Form: 500-mg tablets.

Storage: Store at room temperature in tightly closed, light resistant containers.

Overdosage

The primary signs of overdosage include loss of appetite, vomiting, diarrhea, weakness, lethargy, loss of coordination, and depression. Liver and central nervous system damage may result from long-term administration of high doses. In case of accidental ingestion or overdose, contact your veterinarian or the National Animal Poison Control Center. ALWAYS bring the prescription bottle or container with you if you go for treatment.

Special Information

Ketoconazole (see *Ketoconazole*) inhibits adrenal hormone production and is an alternative treatment for dogs that do not respond well to mitotane. Surgical removal of one or both adrenal glands is another option. In cases where there is a tumor on only one of the adrenal glands, removing that gland cures the disease and eliminates the need for medical management. Removal of both adrenals is an option if a tumor is present on both glands and in dogs with PDH that do not respond well to medical management.

Surgery is the best treatment option for both PDH and adrenal tumors in cats. Mitotane and ketoconazole are not recommended. Neither is very effective and the risk of side effects is unacceptably high with mitotane.

Special Populations

Pregnancy/Lactation
It is unknown if the drug crosses the placenta or is distributed into milk. However, it is a toxic drug and should be avoided in pregnant dogs. If used in lactating animals, puppies should be given milk replacer and not allowed to nurse.

Puppies/Kittens
This drug is not likely to be indicated in puppies because the diseases it treats rarely occur in young animals. It should not be used at all in kittens.

Senior Animals
Senior dogs should not be at increased risk of side effects from mitotane as long as liver and kidney function are normal.

Generic Name

Moxidectin (MOK-see-DEK-tin)

Brand Name

ProHeart [V]

Type of Drug

Heartworm preventive.

Prescribed for

Prevention of heartworm (*Dirofilaria immitis*).

General Information

Moxidectin is in the same group of macrolide drugs as ivermectin and milbemycin oxime, other commonly prescribed once-a-month heartworm preventives (see *Ivermectin* and *Milbemycin Oxime*), and is also derived from a *Streptomyces* soil-living bacteria. It became available in mid-1997. Although it is recently approved and relatively little clinical information is available, it is similar enough to the other drugs in this class to make it likely that they share many properties.

Moxidectin interferes with parasite nerve function. This results in paralysis and death of susceptible parasites. Mammalian muscles are controlled by a different type of nerve and are not affected by moxidectin. Mammals do have similar nerve types in the brain and central nervous system, but moxidectin does not pass through the blood-brain barrier. For this reason moxidectin has very few side effects in dogs. Prevention of heartworm disease is currently the only approved use of this drug.

Moxidectin at the recommended dose is 100% effective against heartworm larvae transmitted from infected mosquitoes within 30 to 60 days before treatment. It does not kill the microfilarial stage of heartworm at the recommended dose but does at higher doses. This may result in false negative results on diagnostic tests based on the detection of microfilaria. In the clinical trials done for drug approval, no adverse effects were seen when moxidectin was administered to dogs with active heartworm infections and microfilaria. Anaphylactic-like (severe systemic) reactions to large numbers of dying microfilaria have been noted with the other two macrolide drugs and are likely to occur with moxidectin at higher doses also. For these reasons, all potentially infected animals should be tested for heartworm infection before starting on a heartworm preventive. An alternative test that detects antigen from adult heartworms instead of microfilaria is recommended for heartworm diagnosis in animals receiving moxidectin as a preventive.

Heartworm is contagious and may spread to other animals and people via infected mosquitoes (see *Zoonotic Diseases of Dogs and Cats*).

Cautions and Warnings

■ Moxidectin is FDA approved for dogs and puppies only. All adult animals that have been off heartworm preventive for 6 months or longer should be tested for heartworm infection before starting preventive treatment. Animals off heartworm preventive for 2 to 6 months should restart heartworm preventive and be tested 6 months from the last date of exposure. It takes 6 months from the time of infection for the tests to become positive. Start moxidectin within 30 days of discontinuing other heartworm preventive when switching from either daily diethylcarbamazine or other once-a-month macrolide drugs.

■ Contact your veterinarian if you think your dog or cat may be having an adverse reaction to moxidectin.

■ U.S. federal law restricts the use of this drug by or on the lawful witten or oral order of a licensed veterinarian within the context of a valid veterinarian-client-patient relationship.

Possible Side Effects

▼ Rare: lethargy, vomiting, loss of coordination, loss of appetite, diarrhea, nervousness, weakness, increased thirst, and itching.

Food and Drug Interactions

None known.

Usual Dose

Dogs: minimum 1.36 mcg/lb once a month. Use the appropriate sized tablet or combination of tablets based on the body weight range stated on the box.

Drug Form: 30-, 68-, and 136-mcg tablets.

Storage: Protect from moisture and light. Store at room temperature.

Overdosage

Moxidectin did not produce serious signs of overdose when given at 300 times the recommended dose for a year. Three times the recommended dose was administered to male and female breeding dogs without causing serious side effects or effects on reproduction. Five times the recommended dose was administered to collies, a number of other breeds, and dogs with heartworm infection without causing serious signs of overdose. At 30 times the recommended dose, mild signs of depression, loss of coordination, and salivation were reported in a collie. Loss of appetite, lethargy, and increased respiratory rates were noted in heartworm-infected dogs at 10 times the recommended dose. In case of accidental ingestion or overdose, contact your veterinarian or the National Animal Poison Control Center. ALWAYS bring the prescription bottle or container with you if you go for treatment.

Special Information

The manufacturer recommends observing the dog for several minutes after administering moxidectin. If you think the entire dose was not swallowed, redose at the recommended dose.

Special Populations

Collies/Herding Breeds

Collies and other herding breeds are more likely to have side effects to the once-a-month macrolide drugs, including moxidectin. In spite of this, moxidectin is considered safe in these breeds because side effects are not seen until well over the recommended dose is given and generally resolve rapidly once treatment is stopped (see "Overdosage").

Pregnancy/Lactation

Moxidectin is considered safe to use in pregnant and lactating dogs.

Puppies

Moxidectin is considered safe to use in puppies over 8 weeks. No side effects were seen when given at 10 times the recommended dose in puppies over 8 weeks. Starting once-a-month preventive treatment in puppies at age 2 months will protect them even if they were exposed shortly after birth.

Senior Animals

Moxidectin is considered safe to use in senior dogs.

Generic Name

Mupirocin (mue-PERE-roe-sin)

Brand Names

Bactoderm [V]
Bactroban [H]

Type of Drug

Antibiotic.

Prescribed for

Susceptible bacterial skin infections.

General Information

Mupirocin is a new antibiotic effective against a wide variety of
bacteria. Many bacteria have developed resistance to the
antibiotics that have been in use for years. Bacteria that are
resistant to chloramphenicol, erythromycin, gentamicin, lincomycin, neomycin, novobiocin, penicillin, streptomycin, and
tetracycline, should still be sensitive to mupirocin, as there is
no cross-resistance. Mupirocin is especially useful in skin
infections involving antibiotic-resistant bacteria. It should probably be reserved for those types of infections.

Cautions and Warnings

■ Mupirocin is FDA approved for use in dogs only. It should
be used in cats with caution.

■ Mupirocin should not be used in deep or extensive skin
lesions because the polyethylene glycol base may be absorbed
and cause kidney damage.

■ Do not use in eyes.

■ Contact your veterinarian if you think your dog or cat may
be having an adverse reaction to mupirocin.

■ U.S. federal law restricts the use of this drug by or on
the lawful written or oral order of a licensed veterinarian
within the context of a valid veterinarian-client-patient relationship.

Possible Side Effects

No adverse reactions to mupirocin have been reported.
Allergic reactions are possible with any medication.

Drug Interactions

None known.

Usual Dose

Dogs: Apply twice a day to affected area after cleaning and
removing any crusts or exudate.
Cats: Use according to your veterinarian's instructions.
Drug Form: Ointment for use on skin.

Overdosage

Polyethylene glycol may cause kidney damage if large
amounts are ingested or absorbed through wounds. The toxic
dose in cats would be about half a tube of ointment; in
dogs it would be 1 to 2 tubes per 10 lbs body weight. In case
of accidental ingestion or overdose, contact your veterinarian or the National Animal Poison Control Center. ALWAYS
bring the prescription bottle or container with you if you go for
treatment.

Special Populations

Pregnancy/Lactation
Safety has not been established in pregnant dogs or cats.
Although it appears to be safe in laboratory animals, its use
should probably be avoided in pregnant and lactating animals
unless the benefits outweigh the risks.

Puppies/Kittens
Mupirocin should be safe to use in puppies. There is no data on
safety in kittens.

Senior Animals
Mupirocin is safe to use in older dogs. Avoid ingestion or
excessive absorption of ointment through wounds.

Generic Name

Mycobacterium bovis/Bacillus Calmette-Guérin (BCG)

(MYE-koe-bak-tere-ee-um BOE-vis/buh-SIL-us kal-MET gay-RAH)

Brand Names

Regressin-V [V]   Tice BCG vaccine [H]
TheraCys BCG Live [H]

Type of Drug

Mycobacterial immunostimulant.

Prescribed for

Cancer.

General Information

There are a number of biologic products that nonspecifically
stimulate the immune system. Bacteria have been the most
consistent immunostimulants. The two most commonly used
bacteria are *Mycobacteria* and *Propionibacteria* (see *Propionibacterium acnes*). BCG is a live attenuated strain (unlikely to
cause infection) of *Mycobacterium bovis* that has been useful
in treating some human and animal cancers. Sometimes
pieces of the bacteria (extracts) are used instead of live bacteria (Regressin-V). When injected into the body or into a tumor,
BCG may boost the immune system's attack on the tumor cells.
In some tumors, such as equine sarcoid, BCG is considered a
cure in most cases. In humans it may be injected into the bladder to treat bladder cancer. BCG has been used to treat a variety of tumors in dogs, with varying success. It may be injected
into the tumor or given intravenously (into a vein). Intravenous
BCG delays the spread of osteosarcoma (bone cancer) and
mammary tumors to the lungs but is not a cure. BCG is *not* a
vaccine for the prevention of cancer.

Cautions and Warnings

For Owners/Handlers
■ BCG contains viable attenuated *M. bovis*. Handle as infectious material.

■ If injected into a tumor, and the tumor breaks open and drains, consider the drainage potentially infectious. Keep draining tumors covered and dispose of contaminated bandage material as infectious waste.

■ Keep treated animals away from children.

■ BCG should *not* be handled by persons with a known immunologic deficiency.

■ Use gloves and wash hands thoroughly after contact.

For Animals

■ BCG is not FDA approved for use in dogs or cats, but it is considered accepted practice to use as adjunct therapy for certain cancers. Regressin-V is approved for use in animals.

■ BCG may cause severe allergic reactions with repeated injections.

■ Contact your veterinarian if you think your dog or cat may be having an adverse reaction to BCG.

■ U.S. federal law restricts the use of this drug by or on the lawful written or oral order of a licensed veterinarian within the context of a valid veterinarian-client-patient relationship.

Possible Side Effects

▼ Common: allergic or anaphylactic (severe systemic allergic) reactions (after repeated injections); fever, chills, decreased appetite, inflammation, and swelling; and drainage in and around injected tumors.

▼ Rare: In people, systemic infection with *M. bovis* and death. These effects have not been reported in animals but are theoretically possible as very rare side effects.

Drug Interactions

• Corticosteroids will blunt or negate the effects of BCG. Corticosteroids or other immunosuppressive drugs should be discontinued at least 7 days before starting treatment.

• Antibiotics effective against *M. bovis* may negate the effects of BCG.

Food Interactions

None known.

Usual Dose

Dogs and Cats: The dose and dosing interval depend on the type of tumor and the route of administration. Usually $\frac{1}{3}$ of a vial of BCG is injected into the tumors once every 10 days to 2 weeks. Your veterinarian will discuss the protocol with you. Regressin-V should be given by injection into tumors only, and the dose is a minimum of 1 ml, maximum 30 ml (average 10-ml cumulative dose), repeated every 1–3 weeks.

Drug Form: BCG—freeze-dried bacteria for reconstitution in water, saline, or adjuvant for injection. Regressin-V—emulsion for injection.

Storage: BCG—keep refrigerated and use immediately after reconstitution. Regressin-V—keep refrigerated.

Overdosage

Overdose may cause fever, chills, decreased appetite, nausea, vomiting, severe anaphylactic reactions, collapse and death, especially if the animal has received BCG previously. In case of accidental ingestion or overdose, contact your veterinarian or the National Animal Poison Control Center. ALWAYS bring the prescription bottle or container with you if you go for treatment.

Special Information

Regressin-V is a *Mycobacterium* cell wall fraction that is FDA approved for animal use. It contains a local anesthetic and a green tracking dye that helps indicate infiltrated areas of the tumor. The cell wall fraction should have less toxic and allergic potential than the live bacteria but may not have the antitumor activity of BCG. Decreased appetite, mild fever and drowsiness are still common side effects for 1 to 2 days following injection and are expected results of immune stimulation. Tumors are also likely to open and drain for several weeks after injection. Dogs whose mammary tumors are treated with Regressin-V prior to surgery have significantly longer periods of remission.

Special Populations

Pregnancy/Lactation
Do not use in pregnant or lactating animals unless the benefits outweigh the risks.

Puppies/Kittens
Do not use in puppies or kittens unless the benefits outweigh the risks.

Senior Animals
BCG should be safe to use in older animals and even those with chronic heart or kidney disease that are poor surgical risks. Owners should be aware of the risks of possible allergic or anaphylactic reactions. These reactions may have more serious consequences in older or debilitated animals.

Brand Name

NeoSporin [H]

Generic Ingredients

Neomycin Sulfate + Bacitracin + Polymyxin B Sulfate [G]

Other Brand Names

NeoSporin [H]   Neobacimyx [V]
Mycitracin [V]   TriOptic-P [V]

Type of Drug

Topical antibiotic combination.

Prescribed for

Superficial infections caused by microorganisms sensitive to these drugs.

General Information

Neomycin sulfate, bacitracin, and polymyxin B sulfate are topical antibiotics frequently combined in ointments for topical use. They are used to treat or prevent infections of the skin caused by bacteria that grow in superficial wounds and cause inflammation, itching, and oozing. They are also used in ophthalmic ointments used to treat conjunctivitis and other infections of the eye and surrounding tissue (see *Ophthalmic (Eye) Preparations*).

NeoSporin provides a broad spectrum of activity against the most common bacteria that cause superficial infections.

Neomycin is an aminoglycoside (see *Aminoglycoside Antibiotics*). It is effective against some gram-positive bacteria (including staphylococci) and gram-negative bacteria (such as *E. coli* and *Salmonella*) and many strains of *Pseudomonas* and *Proteus*. Polymyxin B is a bactericidal antibiotic active against gram-negative bacteria, including *Pseudomonas*. Bacitracin enhances the activity of the combination against gram-positive bacteria, including many streptococci and staphylococci. None of these antibiotics are used systemically in dogs or cats because they are too toxic, but they are safe when applied topically because they are not absorbed through the skin.

Topical antibiotics must be applied directly to the skin. This may require clipping or shaving the area. Gentle cleansing helps remove accumulations of pus and exudate that inhibit antibiotic activity.

Dogs and cats generally try to remove ointments by licking. This reduces the usefulness of these preparations. The licking not only removes the ointment but also may make the skin irritation worse. Ingesting limited amounts of NeoSporin is not dangerous because none of the ingredients are absorbed from the intestines. Ointments should only be used to treat small wounds and for only a few days. They should not be used on large areas or in deep wounds. They are not effective and should not be used in puncture wounds because they do not penetrate into the damaged tissue.

Cautions and Warnings

■ For external use only.

■ Do not use over large areas or in deep or puncture wounds.

■ Do not use triple antibiotics in the eyes unless the preparation is specifically labeled for ophthalmic use.

■ Contact your veterinarian if you think your dog or cat may be having an adverse reaction to NeoSporin, if the infection does not seem to be responding, or if the animal appears sick.

■ NeoSporin is FDA approved for topical use in animals.

■ U.S. federal law restricts the use of this drug by or on the lawful written or oral order of a licensed veterinarian within the context of a valid veterinarian-client-patient relationship.

Possible Side Effects

▼ Rare: hypersensitivity (itching, burning, and/or inflammation), and overgrowth of nonsusceptible bacteria and fungi.

Drug Interactions

None known.

Usual Dose

Dogs and Cats: Apply a thin film on affected area 3–4 times a day or as directed by your veterinarian.

Drug Form: ointment for topical use on skin. Ophthalmic ointment for use in eyes (see *Ophthalmic (Eye) Preparations*).

Overdosage

Overdosage from NeoSporin is not likely because it is not absorbed from skin or intestines if accidentally ingested. Oral neomycin rarely causes diarrhea, deafness, or kidney damage, but the amount needed to cause overdosage is not likely to be ingested from either licking or chewing a tube of ointment. In case of accidental ingestion or overdose, contact your veterinarian or the National Animal Poison Control Center. ALWAYS bring the prescription bottle or container with you if you go for treatment.

Special Populations

Pregnancy/Lactation
NeoSporin is considered safe to use in pregnant animals. Do not use on or around nipples of lactating animals because nursing puppies and kittens may ingest it (see "Overdosage").

Puppies/Kittens
NeoSporin is considered safe to use in puppies and kittens when used in small amounts.

Senior Animals
NeoSporin is considered safe to use in senior animals.

Type of Drug

Nitrofuran Antibacterials

Most Common Brand Names

Generic Ingredient: Nitrofurantoin
Furadantin [H]   Macrodantin [H]

Generic Ingredient: Nitrofurazone [G]
Fura Ointment [V]   KV Wound Powder [V]
Fura-Zone [V]

Prescribed for

Urinary tract infections (nitrofurantoin), superficial bacterial infections of skin wounds, burns, ulcers, and abrasions (nitrofurazone).

General Information

Nitrofurantoin is an antibacterial agent. It is not known exactly how it works, but it is effective against several gram-negative and some gram-positive bacteria, including some strains of *E. coli, Klebsiella, Enterobacter, Enterococci, Staphylococci, Salmonella,* and *Shigella.* It is used as a urinary tract antiseptic because most of the drug is excreted and concentrated in the urine. It is not used to treat other bacterial infections because the doses needed to treat infections elsewhere are too toxic.

Nitrofurazone is a related compound that is used topically in animals to prevent and treat bacterial infections of skin wounds, burns, ulcers, and abrasions.

Cautions and Warnings

For Owners/Handlers
■ Some people may be hypersensitive to nitrofurazone. Use gloves when applying or wash hands afterward.
■ Nitrofurazone has been shown to produce mammary tumors in rats and ovarian tumors in mice.

For Animals
■ Nitrofurantoin is not FDA approved for use in dogs or cats. It is used occasionally to prevent and treat urinary tract infections and is considered accepted practice.
■ Do not use nitrofurazone on deep wounds, puncture

wounds, or serious burns unless under the direction of your veterinarian.

■ Do not use nitrofurantoin in animals with decreased kidney function or liver damage.

■ Contact your veterinarian if you think your dog or cat may be having an adverse reaction to the nitrofurans.

■ U.S. federal law restricts the use of these drugs by or on the lawful written or oral order of a licensed veterinarian within the context of a valid veterinarian-client-patient relationship.

Possible Side Effects

• Rare: allergic reactions; carcinogenic with long-term or frequent use; vomiting, diarrhea, and liver damage; in people, liver, lung, and nerve damage and hemolytic anemia.

Drug Interactions

• Nitrofurantoin interferes with the action of the quinolone antibiotics (enrofloxacin, orbifloxacin, and difloxacin), and they should not be used together.

• Sulfinpyrazone and probenecid may decrease the excretion of nitrofurantoin and increase the risk of side effects.

Food Interactions

Nitrofurantoin should be given with food.

Usual Dose

Dogs and Cats

Nitrofurantoin—2 mg/lb orally 3 times a day; may be used to prevent urinary tract infections—1.5–2 mg/lb orally once a day before bedtime.

Nitrofurazone—follow label directions or your veterinarian's instructions. Usually wounds are gently cleansed with warm water and dried. Nitrofurazone is applied directly to the affected area once a day. Bandaging is optional.

Drug Form

Nitrofurantoin: 5 mg/ml oral suspension and 25-, 50- and 100-mg capsules.

Nitrofurazone: 0.2% in ointment, gel, soluble dressing, solution, and powder.

Overdosage

Overdose may cause decreased appetite, vomiting, diarrhea, and liver damage (see "Possible Side Effects"). In case of accidental ingestion or overdose, contact your veterinarian or call the National Animal Poison Control Center. ALWAYS bring the prescription bottle or container with you if you go for treatment.

Special Populations

Breeding Males
Nitrofurans may cause infertility in male dogs.

Pregnancy/Lactation
Nitrofurans are known to cause damage to the fetus. They should be avoided in pregnant or lactating animals unless the benefits outweigh the risks.

Puppies/Kittens
Nitrofurans may cause hemolytic anemia and are potential cancer risks; they should be avoided or used with caution in puppies and kittens.

Senior Animals
Nitrofurans should be safe to use in healthy senior animals (see "Cautions and Warnings").

Generic Name

Nitroglycerin (nye-troe-GLIH-ser-in) G

Most Common Brand Name

Nitro-Bid Ointment H

Type of Drug

Vasodilator.

Prescribed for

Acute heart failure, severe edema secondary to hypertrophic cardiomyopathy (heart muscle disease) in cats, and myocardial infarction.

General Information

Nitroglycerin relaxes smooth muscle in the walls of blood ves-

sels. It is used in the initial emergency treatment of heart failure even though it has not been proven effective in either people or animals. It improves heart and lung function by lowering
blood pressure, opening up the arteries that supply the heart
muscle (as well as the rest of the body), and opening the veins
to decrease back pressure and edema formation. Emergencies in which nitroglycerin may be used include acute congestive heart failure, myocardial infarction, and hypertrophic
cardiomyopathy with respiratory distress.

Other emergency treatments for acute heart failure include
furosemide and oxygen. Nitroglycerin tolerance develops
quickly so there is no benefit to prolonged administration.

Cautions and Warnings

For Owners/Handlers
■ Nitroglycerin is readily absorbed through the skin. Do not
touch areas where nitroglycerin has been applied. Use gloves
to apply.

For Animals
■ Do not use nitroglycerin in patients with severe anemia,
low blood pressure, or head trauma.

■ Contact your veterinarian if you think your dog or cat may
be having an adverse reaction to nitroglycerin.

■ U.S. federal law restricts the use of this drug by or on the
lawful written or oral order of a licensed veterinarian within the
context of a valid veterinarian-client-patient relationship.

Possible Side Effects

▼ Rare: low blood pressure, increased heart rate, rash
at the skin site where applied, and allergic reactions.

Drug Interactions

• Use of nitroglycerin with other blood-pressure-lowering
drugs such as diuretics (furosemide and thiazides), beta-blockers (propranolol and atenolol), prazosin, or ACE inhibitors (captopril, enalapril, and lisinopril) may increase the risks of low
blood pressure.

Food Interactions

None known.

Usual Dose

Dogs: 1/4–1 inch of 2% ointment applied to the inside of the ear or groin every 4–6 hours for the first 2–4 days of treatment. Some experts recommend treatment for the first 7 days after acute congestive heart failure.

Cats: 1/4 inch of 2% ointment applied to the inside of the ear every 4–6 hours during the first 24 hours of treatment for severe respiratory distress due to hypertrophic cardiomyopathy.

Drug Form: 2% ointment for administration across the skin. Oral spray and tablets, transdermal patches, and intravenous forms are available for use in people but are rarely if ever used in animals.

Overdosage

Overdose of nitroglycerin may cause severe low blood pressure. In case of accidental ingestion or overdose, contact your veterinarian or the National Animal Poison Control Center. ALWAYS bring the prescription bottle or container with you if you go for treatment.

Special Populations

Pregnancy/Lactation

There are no safety studies for nitroglycerin in pregnant or lactating dogs or cats. It should be avoided unless the potential benefits outweigh the risks.

Puppies/Kittens

Nitroglycerin should be avoided or used with extreme caution in puppies and kittens.

Senior Animals

Nitroglycerin should be safe to use in older animals (see "Cautions and Warnings").

Generic Name

Nystatin (nye-STAH-tin) G

Most Common Brand Names

Mycostatin H   Nystop H

Combination Products

Generic Ingredients: Nystatin + Neomycin Sulfate + Thiostrepton + Triamcinolone Acetonide

Animax V   Quadritop V

Panolog V

Type of Drug

Antifungal.

Prescribed for

Superficial fungal infections due to yeasts (*Malassezia* and *Candida*).

General Information

Nystatin is structurally similar to amphotericin B (see *Amphotericin B*). It is primarily used in topical preparations to treat superficial skin and ear infections caused by yeasts (*Malassezia* and *Candida*). When given by injection, nystatin causes severe kidney damage, so it is not used for systemic fungal infections. It may be used to eliminate yeast from the gastrointestinal tract, oral cavity, and vagina in people. It rarely if ever has such applications in dogs or cats. Nystatin is not absorbed from the gastrointestinal tract if taken orally, is poorly absorbed through the skin, and is considered safe enough to use during pregnancy in people. Other newer and more effective antifungals are used to treat ringworm, a fungal infection caused by dermatophytes (see *Griseofulvin, Miconazole, Clotrimazole,* and *Ketoconazole*).

Cautions and Warnings

■ These topical products are not intended for internal use, and although accidental ingestion is generally not harmful, you should minimize the amount of ointment or cream that is licked off.

■ Contact your veterinarian if you think your dog or cat may be having an adverse reaction to nystatin.

■ U.S. federal law restricts the use of this drug by or on the lawful written or oral order of a licensed veterinarian within the context of a valid veterinarian-client-patient relationship.

Possible Side Effects

▼ Rare: vomiting and diarrhea (with large oral doses) and allergic reactions.

Food and Drug Interactions

None known.

Usual Dose

Dogs and Cats: Apply to affected area 2–3 times a day, usually after cleaning to remove any crusts or exudate, or as directed by your veterinarian.

Drug Form: ointment, cream, solution, powder, oral tablets, and pastilles.

Overdosage

Large oral doses may cause gastrointestinal upset. In case of accidental ingestion or overdose, contact your veterinarian or the National Animal Poison Control Center. ALWAYS bring the prescription bottle or container with you if you go for treatment.

Special Populations

Pregnancy/Lactation
Nystatin is safe to use during pregnancy and lactation.

Puppies/Kittens
Nystatin is safe to use on puppies and kittens.

Senior Animals
Nystatin is safe to use in senior animals.

Generic Name

Omeprazole (oe-MEP-ruh-zole)

Brand Name

Prilosec Ⓗ

Type of Drug

Antiulcer.

Prescribed for

Ulcers of the gastrointestinal tract and esophagus.

General Information

Omeprazole is one of a group of antiulcer medications that prevent the secretion of acid in the stomach. It is effective in treating the symptoms of ulcers and preventing ulcers from occurring in those at risk. Omeprazole is from a new class of drugs called gastric acid (proton) pump inhibitors. Omeprazole stops the production of stomach acid by a mechanism that is different from cimetidine or ranitidine or the other H_2 antagonists. It is sometimes effective in the treatment of ulcers that are not responsive to H_2 blockers or sucralfate. There is limited veterinary experience with these drugs because they are new and expensive.

Cautions and Warnings

■ Omeprazole is not FDA approved for use in dogs or cats. Although it is a new drug, its use is considered accepted practice.

■ Omeprazole should be used with caution in animals with decreased liver function. The omeprazole dose may need to be decreased in these animals.

■ Contact your veterinarian if you think your dog or cat may be having an adverse reaction to omeprazole.

■ U.S. federal law restricts the use of this drug by or on the lawful written or oral order of a licensed veterinarian within the context of a valid veterinarian-client-patient relationship.

Possible Side Effects

▼ Rare: gastrointestinal distress, including loss of appetite, gastrointestinal pain, nausea, vomiting, excess gas, diarrhea; blood abnormalities; urinary tract problems; and central nervous system disturbances.

Drug Interactions

• Omeprazole may increase the effects of diazepam, phenytoin, and warfarin by slowing their breakdown and elimination.
• Omeprazole may decrease the absorption of ketoconazole, ampicillin, and iron salts.
• Omeprazole should not be used with drugs that cause bone marrow suppression.

Food Interactions

Give before meals, preferably in the morning.

Usual Dose

Dogs: 0.1–0.4 mg/lb orally once or twice a day.
Cats: 0.1–0.4 mg/lb twice a day (see "Special Information").
Drug Form: 20-mg capsules.

Overdosage

Clinical experience with omeprazole overdosage is very limited. There appears to be a very wide margin of safety in laboratory animals. In case of accidental ingestion or overdose, contact your veterinarian or the National Animal Poison Control Center. ALWAYS bring the prescription bottle or container with you if you go for treatment.

Special Information

Omeprazole has also been used in humans for the treatment of *Helicobacter*-related gastric disease. *Helicobacter* is also thought to be a cause of gastric disease in dogs and cats and omeprazole may potentially be used in its treatment.

Because of the expense, omeprazole use has been somewhat limited in veterinary medicine. It appears to be a safe and effective drug and may be useful in instances where other antiulcer medications have not been successful. Some experts do not recommend omeprazole in cats.

Special Populations

Pregnancy/Lactation
Omeprazole has not been studied in pregnant cats or dogs. It is unknown if omeprazole is excreted in milk. Its use should be avoided unless the benefits outweigh the potential risks.

Puppies/Kittens
There is no information on omeprazole use in young animals.

Senior Animals
Omeprazole should be safe in older animals if liver function is adequate. Usually a lower dose is recommended.

Type of Drug

Ophthalmic (Eye) Preparations

Brand Names

Antibiotic Preparations

Generic Ingredient: Chloramphenicol [G]

Bemacol [V]   Chlorbiotic [V]

Generic Ingredient: Gentamicin Sulfate

Gentocin [V]

Generic Ingredients: Neomycin Sulfate + Bacitracin + Polymyxin B Sulfate [G]

Mycitracin [V]   TriOptic-P [V]

Neobacimyx [V]

Generic Ingredients: Oxytetracycline HCl + Polymyxin B Sulfate

Terramycin [V]

Corticosteroid Preparations

Generic Ingredient: Dexamethasone [G]

AK-Dex [H]   Maxidex [H]

Decadron Phosphate [H]

Generic Ingredient: Prednisolone Acetate [G]

Econopred Plus [H]

Generic Ingredients: Prednisolone + Atropine
Pred Forte [H]

Antibiotic-Corticosteroid Preparations

Generic Ingredients: Chloramphenicol + Prednisolone Acetate
Chlorasone [V]

Generic Ingredients: Gentamicin Sulfate + Betamethasone
Gentocin Durafilm [V]

Generic Ingredients: Neomycin Sulfate + Bacitracin + Polymyxin B Sulfate + Hydrocortisone Acetate [G]
Neobacimyx-H [V]   TriOptic-S [V]

Generic Ingredients: Neomycin Sulfate + Polymyxin B Sulfate + Hydrocortisone
Cortisporin [H]

Generic Ingredients: Neomycin Sulfate + Polymyxin B Sulfate + Flumethasone
Anaprime [V]

Generic Ingredients: Neomycin Sulfate + Dexamethasone
NeoDecadron [H]

Generic Ingredients: Neomycin Sulfate + Isoflupredone Acetate
Neo-Predef [V]

Prescribed for

Infections, itching, inflammation, and immune-mediated syndromes of the eye and surrounding tissue that are responsive to topical antibiotics and/or corticosteroids.

General Information

Antibiotics and/or corticosteroids are the main types of topical ophthalmic preparations used to treat the eyes of dogs and cats. All of these preparations are applied directly to the surface of the eye or the underside of the eyelid. The drugs are distributed across the surface of the eye by blinking. This brings the medicine into contact with the clear cornea and white sclera of the eyeball and with the conjunctiva that covers the inside of the eyelids. Most of the effect is from direct contact on these superficial surfaces. Small amounts diffuse into

the eyeball itself and are absorbed into the systemic circulation. Systemic effects are rare because so little is absorbed.
The preparations are formulated either as ointments or as
drops. The ointments form a protective film and adhere to the
surface of the eye. Drops are generally water-soluble and are
quickly diluted by normal tears. Some drops contain methylcel-
lulose or artificial tears, which have more of a lubricating effect
than water. Drugs in ointment work for a longer time than
drops, but drops deliver a higher concentration more quickly.
Ointments may be applied less frequently than drops because
of the longer contact time.

Antibiotic preparations are used to treat bacterial infections
of the cornea and conjunctiva. Broad-spectrum and combinations of antibiotics are often prescribed for minor infections or
pending a specific diagnosis. Single antibiotic preparations are
used when it is likely that the infecting organism is sensitive or
based on an actual culture of the bacteria. Antibiotic ointments
are also used to prevent infection and protect the cornea after
superficial injury or scratches. The antibiotics most commonly
found in ophthalmic preparations include bacitracin, neomycin,
and polymyxin B combinations (see *NeoSporin*); chloramphenicol; and gentamicin (see *Aminoglycoside Antibiotics*).

Corticosteroids (see *Corticosteroids*) are used to treat
inflammation and itching. They are indicated for inflammatory,
allergic, and immune-mediated conditions involving the eye.
Hydrocortisone is relatively weak and reduces itching and
inflammation from minor irritation or infection. It does not penetrate the eyeball well and is not effective for inflammation
inside the eye. Dexamethasone and other long-acting corticosteroids are more potent and therefore useful in immune-mediated inflammation. They should not be used if the cornea is
ulcerated or weakened because they increase the risk of perforation and rupture of the eye. There are only a few products
available containing only corticosteroids; therefore, combination products with antibiotics and corticosteroids are sometimes used even though the antibiotic is not a necessary part
of the treatment.

Antibiotics combined with a mild corticosteroid such as
hydrocortisone may be indicated to reduce the inflammation
and itching associated with superficial infections. Combinations with more powerful corticosteroids such as flumethasone

and dexamethasone may increase the risk of uncontrolled infection and corneal ulcers. Antibiotic-steroid combinations should be avoided when treating conjunctivitis in cats. This condition may be caused by feline herpes virus infections and corticosteroids may increase the reproduction of the virus and increase the risk of serious signs of infection. Tetracycline and erythromycin eye ointments are generally preferred in cats. It does not treat the virus infection but does help control myco-plasma and chlamydia, which are bacteria that are frequently present.

Cautions and Warnings

■ Do not use corticosteroid ophthalmic products on corneal ulcers or in severe infections.

■ Do not use ophthalmic preparations without consulting your veterinarian.

■ Contact your veterinarian if you think your dog or cat may be having an adverse reaction to any ophthalmic preparation.

■ Many products are FDA approved for use in dogs and cats and the use of products for humans is common and accepted practice.

■ U.S. federal law restricts the use of these drugs by or on the lawful written or oral order of a licensed veterinarian within the context of a valid veterinarian-client-patient relationship.

Possible Side Effects

Side effects are rare. The most common is stinging as the drops are applied.

▼ Rare: hypersensitivity reactions to the drugs or inert ingredients.

Food and Drug Interactions

None known.

Usual Dose

Dogs and Cats: ointment—$\frac{1}{4}$–$\frac{1}{2}$ inch worm 3–4 times a day or as directed. Drops—1–2 drops every 2–4 hours or as directed.

Drug Form: 3- and 5-g tubes of ointment and 5-ml dropper bottles.

Overdosage

Overdosage is not likely when used topically. The amount of drug contained in each tube or bottle is usually not enough to cause serious problems even if ingested. In case of accidental ingestion or overdose, contact your veterinarian or the National Animal Poison Control Center. ALWAYS bring the prescription bottle or container with you if you go for treatment.

Special Populations

Pregnancy/Lactation
These products are generally safe to use in pregnant and lactating animals but should be used only as instructed by your veterinarian.

Puppies/Kittens
Most products are safe to use in puppies and kittens. Preparations with corticosteroids should be avoided in kittens (see "General Information").

Senior Animals
There are no specific restrictions for use of these products in senior animals.

Type of Drug

Organophosphate Insecticides

Most Common Brand Names

Generic Ingredient: Chlorpyrifos [G]

3X Flea, Tick, and Mange Collar [V]

Adams Automatic Room Fogger with Dursban

Adams Flea & Tick Dip with Dursban [V]

Ban-Guard Dip for Dogs [V]

Carpet Mist [V]

Davis Dursban Dip for Dogs [V]

Defend Premise Spray/Yard and Kennel Spray [V]

DuoCide Flea and Tick Collar [V]

Enduracide Dip for Dogs [V]

Mycodex Environmental Control Lawn & Kennel Spray [V]

Vet-Kem Dursban Flea & Tick Collar for Dogs [V]

Generic Ingredient: Diazinon
Escort Flea and Tick Collar [V]
Preventef Flea and Tick Collars with EFA [V]

Generic Ingredient: Fenthion
ProSpot [V]

Generic Ingredient: N-(Mercaptomethyl) phthalimide S-(O,O-dimethyl phosphorodithioate)
Paramite [V]

Prescribed for

Flea, tick, and mite control on dogs and cats and in the environment.

General Information

Organophosphates were once widely used to control internal and external parasites on animals and in the environment. Their use has declined due to the introduction of safer compounds such as the pyrethrins (see *Pyrethrins*) and insect growth regulators, or IGRs (see *Insect Growth Regulator*), and, more recently, lufenuron (see *Lufenuron*), fipronil (see *Fipronil*), and imidacloprid (see *Imidacloprid*).

Chlorpyrifos, diazinon, fenthion, and phthalimide are the organophosphates currently available commercially for use in dogs and cats. They are used primarily in flea and tick collars and in dips. One product is applied to one or more spots on a dog's back. It is not very effective and is much more toxic than the recently introduced products for topical application. Organophosphates are also in some insecticides used to treat the home and yard. Organophosphates kill parasites by inhibiting acetylcholinesterase (AChE). AChE is an enzyme located at nerve endings that regulates the stimulation of muscles and certain nerves. When AChE is inhibited, the parasite's muscles are overstimulated and cannot relax between contractions. This paralyzes and kills the parasite. Organophosphates have been used widely to control parasites and insects on animals and in the environment.

Flea control requires that the problem be attacked on several levels. Adult fleas on the animal must be killed. Flea shampoos, powders, sprays, and dips work at this level. Mechanical removal by frequent grooming and keeping your pet away from other animals and places where new fleas may be acquired also helps. However, addressing the infestation on the animal is rarely enough because fleas remaining in the environment continue to reproduce very rapidly. Environmental treatment with bombs or sprays kills many fleas. A major limitation is that bombs and sprays do not reach all of the flea's hiding places, which leaves live fleas to continue the infestation. Residual action products help extend the action but still fall short of giving good control and may result in increased levels of toxic insecticides in the home and environment. In addition, most insecticides do not kill flea eggs, which hatch into new adult fleas within a few days. The use of IGRs, which prevent eggs from hatching, dramatically increases the effectiveness of flea control on animals and in the environment. Very good flea control is possible by combining insecticides and IGRs in a multi-level approach. The drawback is that it demands a great deal of motivation on the part of the owner.

Because of the potential for affecting the environment, insecticide use is primarily regulated by the Environmental Protection Agency (EPA). Label instructions should be carefully read and followed.

Cautions and Warnings

■ Do not use in animals that are stressed, debilitated or sick, have diarrhea, are constipated, or in animals that may have an intestinal impaction. Do not use in dogs or cats with heartworm infection, heart or liver disease, or other infections.

■ Do not use within a few days of giving other drugs that inhibit AChE, including other insecticides and dewormers.

■ Do not use with tranquilizers, muscle relaxants, or modified live-virus vaccines. Acepromazine or other phenothiazine drugs should not be used within 1 month of administering organophosphates.

■ Contact your veterinarian if you think your dog or cat may be having an adverse reaction to organophosphate insecticides.

■ EPA approved for indicated uses in dogs, cats, and the environment.

Possible Side Effects

▼ Common: loss of appetite, vomiting, loose stools, and diarrhea.

Possible Side Effects *(continued)*

▼ Rare: muscle twitching, pupil contraction, tearing, and labored breathing.

Drug Interactions

• Neuromuscular-blocking drugs including phenothiazine drugs, procaine, magnesium ion, inhaled anesthetics, and other AChE inhibitors, including other organophosphates, carbamates, morphine, neostigmine, physostigmine, and pyridostigmine may increase the risk of side effects.

• Antibiotics (including the aminoglycosides—streptomycin, neomycin, kanamycin, and gentamicin), polypeptides (polymyxin and colistin), lincomycin, and clindamycin may have activity at the neuromuscular level and may increase the risk of side effects.

• Central nervous system depressants, including phenothiazine tranquilizers (acepromazine), benzodiazepines, reserpine, meprobamate, ethanol, and barbiturates (phenobarbital) may increase the severity of side effects.

• Muscle relaxants such as succinylcholine may increase the risk of side effects.

• Cimetidine may inhibit liver detoxification of organophosphates and increase the risk of side effects.

• Dimethyl sulfoxide (DMSO) may increase the risk of side effects.

• Pyrantel dewormers act at the same level as organophosphates and may increase the risk of side effects.

Food Interactions

Diets low in protein and malnutrition may decrease organophosphate metabolism and increase the risk of side effects.

Usual Dose

Dogs and Cats: Read and follow label directions carefully.
Drug Form: collars, dips, topical spot treatment, and environmental treatment.

Overdosage

Signs of overdose may include increased frequency of urination and defecation, diarrhea, increased salivation, vomiting, retching, constriction of the pupils, tearing, muscle tremors, decreased heart rate, respiratory distress, hyperexcitability, seizures, and death. In case of accidental ingestion or overdose, contact your veterinarian or the National Animal Poison Control Center. ALWAYS bring the prescription bottle or container with you if you go for treatment.

Special Information

See *Fipronil* for more information on fleas and ticks.

Special Populations

Pregnancy/Lactation
The risk of side effects in pregnant animals has not been established. Organophosphates should not be used unless the benefits outweigh the risks. Do not use in lactating animals.

Puppies/Kittens
Follow label instructions. In general, organophosphates should not be used in puppies or kittens under 3 months of age.

Senior Animals
There are no specific contraindications for the use of organophosphates in healthy senior animals.

Generic Name

Oxymetazoline (OKS-ee-met-AZE-oe-lene) Ⓖ

Most Common Brand Names

Afrin Ⓗ   Nostrilla Ⓗ
Neo-Synephrine 12-Hour Ⓗ

Type of Drug

Nasal decongestant.

Prescribed for

Clearing up the stuffy nose that occurs in kittens and cats with viral upper respiratory tract infections.

General Information

Decongestants work by constricting blood vessels in the nose, which then decreases swelling in mucous membranes. Oxymetazoline hydrochloride may be used in cats and especially kittens with severe upper respiratory tract infections caused by feline rhinotracheitis (herpesvirus), calicivirus, and chlamydia. Young kittens with severe nasal congestion are unable to nurse properly, and older kittens that are eating solid food seem to eat very poorly when they are unable to breathe through their nose. It is critically important that these animals begin to eat again as soon as possible, so relieving their nasal congestion is an important part of supportive therapy. Other therapy may include fluids to correct and prevent dehydration, antibiotics to prevent or treat secondary bacterial infections, keeping the animal warm, assisted feeding, or even tube feeding for those animals with severe and prolonged decrease in appetite.

Oxymetazoline may also be used as a nasal decongestant in dogs and puppies. Do not use nasal decongestants without the recommendation of your veterinarian. Nasal congestion may be caused by serious bacterial or fungal infections or by tumors. These conditions need to be diagnosed promptly for effective treatment to be given.

Cautions and Warnings

■ A common problem to all topical nasal decongestants is rebound nasal congestion, especially when decongestant is used for more than 3 days. This side effect will disappear 3 to 7 days after the decongestant is discontinued.

■ DO NOT use full strength oxymetazoline on cats or kittens (see "Usual Dose"). Use extreme caution when treating kittens and do not apply excessive amounts; do not drop or spray into the nose.

■ Contact your veterinarian if you think your dog or cat may be having an adverse reaction to oxymetazoline.

■ Use of this drug should be by or on the lawful written or oral order of a licensed veterinarian within the context of a valid veterinarian-client-patient relationship.

Possible Side Effects

▼ Common: rebound nasal congestion (see "Cautions and Warnings") if used for more than a few days, temporary stinging and sneezing, and head shaking and saliva-

Possible Side Effects *(continued)*

tion if cats or kittens immediately lick oxymetazoline off the nose.

▼ Rare: high blood pressure, agitation, nausea, and slow heart rate (reported in people).

Drug Interactions

• Oxymetazoline should not be used with monoamine oxidase inhibitors (amitraz).

Food Interactions

None known.

Usual Dose

Dogs: Moisten the tip of the nose or place one drop of 0.025 % oxymetazoline in each nostril twice a day.

Cats and Kittens: Moisten the tip of your finger with diluted oxymetazoline (see "Drug Form") and touch the moistened finger to the tip of the cat's or kitten's nose while the head is held back. Use no more than twice a day.

Drug Form: 0.025% and 0.05% nasal drops and spray. Oxymetazoline 0.05% should be diluted in water in a 1:1 or 1:2 solution before using in kittens.

Overdosage

Overdose of oxymetazoline may cause central nervous system depression, low blood pressure, shock, and coma. In case of accidental ingestion or overdose, contact your veterinarian or the National Animal Poison Control Center. ALWAYS bring the prescription bottle or container with you if you go for treatment.

Special Information

Have your veterinarian show you how to apply oxymetazoline to avoid overdosing. Feline respiratory viruses are highly contagious, and infected cats or kittens should be nursed at home if possible and kept away from uninfected or unvaccinated cats. Do not contaminate the oxymetazoline container or allow contaminated materials to come in contact with other cats.

Special Populations

Pregnancy/Lactation
Normally very little oxymetazoline is absorbed from the nose
and it may be safe to use in pregnant or lactating animals.
There are no safety studies for oxymetazoline in animals, however, and it should probably be avoided unless the benefits outweigh the risks.

Puppies/Kittens
Oxymetazoline should be safe to use in puppies and kittens if
extreme care is taken to avoid overdosing (see "Usual Dose").

Senior Animals
Oxymetazoline should be safe to use in senior animals if
extreme care is taken to avoid overdosing (see "Usual Dose").

Generic Name

Oxytocin (ok-sih-TOE-sin) G

Brand Name

Pitocin H

Type of Drug

Hormone.

Prescribed for

Stimulation of uterine contractions and milk letdown.

General Information

Oxytocin is a hormone produced in a part of the brain called
the hypothalamus and stored in the anterior pituitary gland of
the brain. It is released by the pituitary during delivery and
causes contraction of the uterus and during lactation causes
milk letdown.

It is used by veterinarians to induce labor, to increase contractions of the uterus during a difficult labor, on completion of
a cesarean section, or after normal delivery of puppies or kittens. In a difficult labor, oxytocin may be used by a veterinarian
after physical examination, x-rays, and/or ultrasound exam
have been done to determine the cause. It may be used to

stimulate uterine contractions in the treatment of uterine infections after delivery, retained placenta or bleeding after delivery, and after replacement of a uterine prolapse.

Oxytocin may be given to help promote milk letdown. It will not increase milk production but will stimulate the mammary glands to eject milk. Some animals, especially those who have had a cesarean delivery, may have difficulty with milk letdown.

Cautions and Warnings

■ Oxytocin is FDA approved for use in dogs and cats.

■ Oxytocin should only be used when the animal's cervix is dilated so that uterine contents can be pushed out. It should not be used when the fetus is unable to be delivered because of an abnormal position or because it is too large to pass through the birth canal.

■ Inappropriate use of oxytocin can cause the uterus to rupture.

■ Some animals are hypersensitive to oxytocin, and an otherwise normal dose can cause extreme contractions or uterine rupture.

■ Oxytocin should not be used in pyometra (uterine infection with pus accumulation), because it may cause rupture of the uterus.

■ Oxytocin increases the reabsorption of water by the kidneys. Water-intoxication (low sodium) may occur if electrolyte-free intravenous solution is used with oxytocin during a long labor.

■ U.S. federal law restricts the use of this drug by or on the lawful written or oral order of a licensed veterinarian within the context of a valid veterinarian-client-patient relationship.

Possible Side Effects

▼ Common: uterine cramping and discomfort.
▼ Rare: uterine rupture.

Drug Interactions

• Oxytocin should be used with caution with cyclopropane general anesthesia owing to maternal low blood pressure and other cardiovascular changes.

Usual Dose

Dogs: 5–20 units by injection in the muscle or intravenously, every 15–45 min for uterine inertia, or once after delivery.
Cats: 0.5–3 units by injection in the muscle or intravenously.
Drug Form: 10 and 20 USP units/ml injectable.

Overdosage

Overdoses of oxytocin will cause violent uterine contractions. This may cause uterine rupture and damage to the fetuses.

Special Information

Almost all oxytocin use will occur in a hospital setting, except for the management of lactation problems. Discuss labor and delivery with your veterinarian when your animal becomes pregnant. It is much easier to have an emergency plan in place rather than wait for the emergency to happen.

Special Populations

Pregnancy/Lactation
Oxytocin is a hormone specifically used to treat problems of parturition (labor) and lactation.

Senior Animals
Oxytocin is not commonly used in senior animals.

Generic Name

Pancreatic Enzymes (pan-kree-AT-ik)

Brand Names

Pancrezyme [V]   Viokase-V [V]

Type of Drug

Replacement pancreatic digestive enzymes.

Prescribed for

Exocrine pancreatic insufficiency (EPI).

General Information

The pancreas has two functions. One function (endocrine) is to produce hormones, such as insulin. The other function (exocrine) is to produce the digestive enzymes protease, lipase, and amylase. Protease breaks down protein, lipase breaks down fat, and amylase breaks down starch. These enzymes are secreted into the first part of the small intestine where they break down fat, protein, and starch into smaller units that can be absorbed. When the pancreas is damaged or there is an inherited pancreatic defect, enzyme production is impaired, and food cannot be digested or absorbed properly. Lack of pancreatic enzymes usually causes weight loss despite a voracious appetite, flatulence, large volumes of foul-smelling stool, and/or diarrhea. Supplementing an affected animal with replacement enzymes usually returns its digestive functions to normal (see "Special Information"). Treatment is required throughout the life of the animal. The veterinary products are recommended for dogs and cats. Both of these are whole raw pork pancreas products, not extracts, and not enteric-coated.

Cautions and Warnings

For Owners/Handlers
■ Wash hands if powder is spilled on skin; pancreatic enzymes may cause irritation.
■ Avoid inhaling powder; pancreatic enzymes may cause mucous membrane irritation and allergic reactions in susceptible individuals.

For Animals
■ Do not use in animals allergic to pork.
■ Contact your veterinarian if you think your dog or cat may be having an adverse reaction to pancreatic enzymes.
■ U.S. federal law restricts the use of this drug by or on the lawful written or oral order of a licensed veterinarian within the context of a valid veterinarian-client-patient relationship.

Possible Side Effects

▼ Rare: allergic reactions.

Drug Interactions

• Antacids may decrease the effectiveness of pancreatic enzymes.

• Cimetidine or other H$_2$ antagonists may increase the amount of enzyme that reaches the intestine.

Food Interactions

Most dogs with EPI can be fed regular dog food. However, if the response to enzyme replacement is incomplete, low fat, low fiber, highly digestible diets may be needed. It may be necessary to supplement the diet with medium chain triglycerides (MCT oil). These fats do not require enzymes for absorption. Multivitamin supplements may be needed, especially the fat-soluble vitamins A, D, E, and K.

Usual Dose

Dogs: 1–2 tsp veterinary powder mixed with food just prior to feeding. Premixing is not necessary. Give 2–3 meals a day. After diarrhea is in remission and the animal is gaining weight, reduce the dose to the smallest effective amount; 1 tsp twice a day is usually enough for most dogs.

Cats: ¼–¾ tsp veterinary powder with each meal.

Drug Form: tablets, capsules, powders, granules, and enteric-coated preparations.

Overdosage

Overdoses may cause nausea, cramping, and diarrhea. In case of accidental ingestion or overdose, contact your veterinarian or the National Animal Poison Control Center. ALWAYS bring the prescription bottle or container with you if you go for treatment.

Special Information

The most common form of EPI is a disease of unknown cause that is probably inherited and causes atrophy (loss of tissue) of the pancreas in young dogs. Many breeds may be affected, especially large breeds. German shepherds are most commonly affected. Onset of signs is usually before 2 years of age. The disorder is diagnosed or confirmed by a blood test called TLI (trypsin-like immunoreactivity).

EPI may also occur as result of chronic inflammatory damage to the pancreas. This usually occurs in middle-aged to older dogs. EPI is very rare in cats.

There are many pancreatic enzyme products available for people, but only the two veterinary products, Viokase-V and

Pancrezyme powders, are recommended for dogs and cats. If the animal does not respond to enzyme replacement, antibiotics for small intestinal bacterial overgrowth are recommended. If there is still no response, give an H_2 blocker, such as cimetidine or ranitidine, to decrease stomach acid destruction of enzymes.

Special Populations

Pregnancy/Lactation
There is no information available on the safety of these products in pregnant or lactating dogs or cats. Animals with juvenile onset EPI should be neutered, as the disease is inherited.

Puppies/Kittens
There is no information available on the safety of these products in puppies or kittens.

Senior Animals
Pancreatic enzyme replacement is safe for use in older animals.

Brand Name

Panolog [V]

Generic Ingredients

Nystatin + Neomycin Sulfate + Thiostrepton + Triamcinolone Acetonide

Other Brand Names
Animax [V]　　　　Dermavet [V]
Derma 4 [V]　　　Quadritop [V]
Dermagen [V]

Type of Drug

A combination antifungal (nystatin), antibiotic (neomycin and thiostrepton), and corticosteroid (triamcinolone) in an ointment or cream base for topical use.

Prescribed for

Superficial bacterial or fungal infections, itching, and minor irritation of skin and ears. It is particularly useful in the treatment of acute and chronic otitis (ear infections/inflammation), anal gland infections and acute moist dermatitis (early hot spots).

General Information

Panolog ointment or cream and other brands have been used for many years in animals. The information in this monograph applies to all of these brands, with a few distinctions made between ointment and cream. Panolog is effective in a variety of conditions because its ingredients include an anti-inflammatory and anti-itch steroid, two powerful topical antibiotics, and an antifungal. For more information about the individual ingredients triamcinolone, nystatin, and neomycin, see *Corticosteroids, Nystatin,* and *Aminoglycoside Antibiotics.* Thiostrepton is a polypeptide antibiotic from *Streptomyces aureus* that is effective against many gram-positive bacteria, such as streptococcus and staphylococcus, as well as some gram-negative bacteria, such as *E. coli* and *Salmonella.* It is primarily used for topical therapy.

Panolog is an excellent first-line drug for ear infections caused by bacteria or yeasts that are susceptible to neomycin, thiostrepton, or nystatin. It is not effective against infections caused by resistant organisms or in the presence of large amounts of exudate (pus and other debris) typical of severe chronic ear infections. The polyethylene and mineral oil gel base of the ointment is usually quite effective against ear mites because it "drowns" them, but it is not a specific remedy.

Panolog cream is a more recent form of the product. It has a water-soluble vanishing cream base, which is more pleasant to use on skin than the more oily ointment. The ointment is still the most effective form for treating ears and anal glands.

Cautions and Warnings

■ For external use only in dogs and cats.

■ Panolog is not intended for the treatment of deep abscesses (infection pockets), deep-seated skin infections, puncture wounds, or serious burns.

■ Contact your veterinarian if you think your dog or cat may be having an adverse reaction to Panolog.

■ U.S. federal law restricts the use of this drug by or on the

lawful written or oral order of a licensed veterinarian within the context of a valid veterinarian-client-patient relationship.

Possible Side Effects

The most common side effects of Panolog are allergic reactions to one or more of the ingredients. Contact your veterinarian if you see increased irritation, think your dog or cat may be having a reaction, or think the condition is not responding to treatment. This product is not intended for internal use, and although accidental ingestion is generally not harmful, you should minimize the amount of ointment or cream that is licked off. If Panolog is applied inside an ear with a ruptured eardrum, it may cause damage to the middle ear and temporary hearing loss. Discontinue use of Panolog and contact your veterinarian if you notice hearing loss.

▼ Rare: increased thirst, appetite, or urination or weight gain, caused by absorption through the skin or through accidental ingestion by pets licking themselves. For more information, see *Corticosteroids*.

Drug Interactions

None known.

Usual Dose

Dogs and Cats: Apply to affected area 2 to 3 times a day, usually after cleaning to remove any crusts or exudate, or as directed by your veterinarian.

Drug Form: ointment and cream.

Overdosage

In case of accidental ingestion or overdose, contact your veterinarian or the National Animal Poison Control Center. ALWAYS bring the prescription bottle or container with you if you go for treatment.

Special Information

Remember that the antibiotics and antifungal in this combination product have been in use for a long time. There are many resistant strains of bacteria and fungi now that may no longer respond to this medication.

Special Populations

Pregnancy/Lactation
Panolog should probably be avoided in pregnant animals because of the risks of abortion or damage to the fetus from steroids. Do not use Panolog on the teats or mammary glands of lactating females, as ingestion by nursing puppies and kittens should be avoided.

Puppies/Kittens
Panolog is safe to use in puppies and kittens.

Senior Animals
These preparations are safe to use in older animals.

Type of Drug

Penicillin Antibiotics (pen-ih-SIL-in)

Brand Names

Generic Ingredient: Amoxicillin [G]

Amoxil [H]	Polymox [H]
Amoxi-Drop [V]	Robamox-V [V]
Amoxi-Inject [V]	Trimox [H]
Amoxi-Tabs [V]	Wymox [H]
Biomox [V]	

Generic Ingredients: Amoxicillin + Clavulanate Potassium

Augmentin [H]	Clavamox [V]

Generic Ingredient: Ampicillin [G]

Amcill [H]	Polyflex [V]
Amp-Equine [V]	Princillin [V]
D-Amp [H]	Principen [H]
Omnipen [H]	Totacillin [H]
Polycillin [H]	

Generic Ingredient: Carbenicillin Indanyl Sodium

Geocillin [H]

Generic Ingredient: Cloxacillin Sodium G
Cloxapen H   Tegopen H

Generic Ingredient: Dicloxacillin Sodium G
Dycill H   Pathocil H
Dynapen H

Generic Ingredient: Nafcillin
Unipen H

Generic Ingredient: Oxacillin G
Bactocill H   Prostaphlin H

Generic Ingredient: Penicillin G G
Penicillin G Potassium V   Pentids H
Penicillin G Procaine V

Generic Ingredient: Penicillin V G
Beepen-VK H   Pen-Vee K H
Betapen-VK H   Phenoxymethyl Penicillin H
Ledercillin VK H   Robicillin VK H
Penicillin VK H   V-Cillin K H
Pen-V H   Veetids H

Prescribed for

Infections caused by microorganisms sensitive to this drug.

General Information

The penicillin antibiotics are bactericidal. They kill bacteria by destroying the cell wall and are most effective against actively reproducing bacteria. The penicillins should not be used at the same time as bacteriostatic antibiotics (drugs that inhibit bacterial growth) because the latter reduce the effectiveness of the penicillins.

There are four groups of penicillins distinguished by their effectiveness against different types of bacteria. The natural penicillins, which include penicillin G and V, work against *Streptococcus* and other gram-positive bacteria as well as some gram-negative bacteria. Some bacteria, including many species of *Staphylococcus,* produce an enzyme called penicillinase or beta-lactamase that inactivates penicillin. Penicillinase-resistant penicillins such as cloxacillin, dicloxacillin, oxacillin, and nafcillin work against these bacteria as well.

The aminopenicillin group of penicillins is effective against a much broader spectrum of bacteria, including both gram-positive and a number of gram-negative ones, but not against those that produce penicillinase. Antibiotics in this group include ampicillin, amoxicillin, and hetacillin. Ampicillin and amoxicillin are widely used as the first choice antibiotic in infections when the cause is unknown or pending the results of bacterial culture because they have a broad spectrum of activity. Oral amoxicillin is often preferred over ampicillin because of greater absorption from the intestinal tract, particularly when given with food.

Extended-spectrum penicillins include carbenicillin, ticarcillin, and piperacillin. These are active against a broad spectrum of bacteria, including *Pseudomonas*, which is often resistant to other antibiotics. However, they are inactive against the penicillinase-producing bacteria. Many of these are only available in injectable form, which is less convenient than oral dosing but may be the only option in resistant infections.

Potentiated penicillins include amoxicillin-potassium clavulanate, ampicillin-sulbactam, and ticarcillin-potassium clavulanate. The clavulanate and sulbactam inactivate bacterial penicillinase, allowing the antibiotic to kill otherwise insensitive bacteria, including some *E. coli, Pasturella, Staphylococcus,* and *Proteus,* which are common causes of infections in animals.

Penicillins are widely distributed throughout most organs and tissues of the body shortly after administration. Penetration into the central nervous system and eye occurs only when there is inflammation, which limits their usefulness for infections of these organs. Excretion occurs primarily through the kidney and urine, making them effective for susceptible infections of the lower urinary tract.

Cautions and Warnings

For Owners/Handlers

■ Cephalosporins and penicillins can cause allergic reactions in certain individuals. Persons with known hypersensitivity to either of these drugs should avoid exposure to these products.

For Animals

■ Penicillins should not be used in animals that have had an allergic reaction to any antibiotic in this group or to cephalosporin antibiotics due to the possibility of cross-reactivity.

■ Systemic antibiotics should be given by injection rather than orally in extremely sick animals because antibiotics may be poorly absorbed from the intestinal tract of these animals.

■ Contact your veterinarian if you think your dog or cat may be having an adverse reaction to penicillin.

■ U.S. federal law restricts the use of these drugs by or on the lawful written or oral order of a licensed veterinarian within the context of a valid veterinarian-client-patient relationship.

Possible Side Effects

▼ Rare: vomiting, diarrhea, and loss of appetite; diarrhea caused by alterations in the normal intestinal bacteria, particularly when penicillin is used for prolonged periods; hypersensitivity; fever; swollen glands; depression; rapid or labored breathing; increased heart rate; swelling of the face or limbs; tendency to bleed; and anemia.

Drug Interactions

• Penicillin should not be combined with bacteriostatic antibiotics such as erythromycin, tetracycline, or neomycin.

• In low concentrations, certain penicillins, including ampicillin, oxacillin, and nafcillin, may be synergistic with rifampin. Higher concentrations of the same antibiotics have the opposite effect and inhibit the activity of rifampin.

• Penicillin may be combined with the aminoglycoside or cephalosporin antibiotics.

• Probenecid blocks the kidney excretion of most penicillins, thereby increasing serum level. This effect is used to prolong the activity of penicillin.

• Ampicillin may reduce the effectiveness of atenolol.

• Large doses of certain penicillins, including ticarcillin and carbenicillin, have been associated with bleeding. They should be used cautiously in patients receiving oral anticoagulants or heparin.

• Ampicillin may cause false-positive urine glucose determinations with some tests. This is important when using urine glucose to monitor diabetics.

Food Interactions

Food in the stomach reduces absorption of most penicillins. They should be given on an empty stomach at least 1 hour before or 2 hours after feeding.

Amoxicillin may be given with food.

The potentiated penicillins should be given just before feeding to reduce the risk of digestive upset.

Usual Dose

Amoxicillin

Dogs: 5–10 mg/lb twice a day.

Cats: 5–10 mg/lb once or twice a day.

Drug Form: 50-, 100-, 150-, 200-, 300-, and 400-mg tablets and powder for oral suspension 50 mg/ml after reconstitution with water. Additional human formulations available.

Amoxicillin and Potassium Clavulanate

Dogs and Cats: 6.25 mg/lb twice a day. Do not exceed 30 days of therapy.

Drug Form: 62.5-, 125-, 250-, and 375-mg tablets and powder for oral suspension 62.5 mg/ml after reconstitution with water. Additional human formulations available.

Ampicillin

Dogs and Cats: 10–15 mg/lb 3 times a day.

Drug Form: 250- and 500-mg tablets and 25 and 250 mg/5ml oral suspension.

Carbenicillin Indanyl Sodium

Dogs and Cats: 5 mg/lb 3 times a day for urinary tract infections.

Drug Form: 382-mg tablets.

Cloxacillin Sodium

Dogs and Cats: 10–20 mg/lb 3 times a day.

Drug Form: 250- and 500-mg capsules and 125 mg/5ml oral suspension.

Dicloxacillin Sodium

Dogs and Cats: 5–25 mg/lb 3 times a day.

Drug Form: 250- and 500-mg capsules and 62.5 mg/5ml oral suspension.

Nafcillin
   Dogs and Cats: 5 mg/lb 4 times a day.
   Drug Form: 250-mg capsules.

Oxacillin
   Dogs and Cats: 10–20 mg/lb 3 times a day.
   Drug Form: 250- and 500-mg capsules and 125 mg/5ml oral suspension.

Penicillin G
   Dogs and Cats: 20,000 IU/lb 4 times a day on an empty stomach.
   Drug Form: 200,000-, 250,000- and 400,000-unit tablets.

Penicillin V
   Dogs and Cats: 2.5–5 mg/lb 3–4 times a day.
   Drug Form: 250- and 500-mg tablets and 125 and 250 mg/5ml oral suspension.

Storage Information
   Tablets should be stored in tight containers and kept at room temperature.
   Oral liquid penicillins should be refrigerated and must be thrown out after 14 days in the refrigerator or 7 days at room temperature.

Overdosage

Penicillin overdose is unlikely, but if it occurs, diarrhea and vomiting are the primary signs. Loss of coordination may occur in dogs after high doses or prolonged use. In case of accidental ingestion or overdose, contact your veterinarian or the National Animal Poison Control Center. ALWAYS bring the prescription bottle or container with you if you go for treatment.

Special Information

Like any medication, penicillin should only be given when prescribed by a veterinarian for a specific illness. Always give the antibiotic exactly as directed, including the number of pills and the length of time. It takes 7-10 days for penicillin to eradicate most susceptible organisms. If you stop before that, the infection is likely to recur even if the animal appeared better after only a few days.

Special Populations

Toy Breeds and Cats
The sodium or potassium in some preparations of penicillin may cause electrolyte imbalances, particularly in very small animals with preexisting electrolyte abnormalities, kidney, or heart disease.

Pregnancy/Lactation
Penicillins cross the placenta into fetal blood circulation. Birth defects and other adverse effects have not been reported, but safety has not been absolutely established either. They should be used only when potential benefits outweigh the possible risk.

Puppies/Kittens
The penicillins are generally safe to use in puppies and kittens.

Senior Animals
The penicillins are among the safest drugs to use in senior animals. Dogs and cats with decreased kidney function may need a lower dose than normal, but because of the wide margin of safety, normal doses will still be safe.

Generic Name

Phenobarbital (FEEN-oe-BAR-bih-tol) Ⓖ

Brand Name
Solfoton Ⓗ

Type of Drug
Barbiturate and antiseizure.

Prescribed for
Epilepsy in dogs and cats.

General Information
Phenobarbital is the first choice drug for the treatment of epilepsy in dogs and cats. It belongs to a group of drugs called barbiturates that depress the central nervous system (CNS). Barbiturates are used to treat and prevent seizures, as seda-

tives, as anesthetics, and for euthanasia. The specific effect depends on which barbiturate is used and the dosage. Although barbiturates cause CNS depression, they may paradoxically produce excitement, particularly early in the course of treatment.

Epilepsy is a chronic disease characterized by recurring seizures. Episodes occur at variable intervals separated by days, weeks, or even months. Seizures are also called convulsions or fits. Grand mal or generalized convulsive seizures are the most common type seen in dogs and cats. They are characterized by loss of consciousness and spasmodic contractions of the major muscles of the legs and body. Seizures may occur singly or in clusters of two or more very close together. Seizure activity that is continuous for 30 minutes or more is called status epilepticus. Status is a life-threatening emergency and requires immediate veterinary attention.

There are many causes of seizures and epilepsy, including infections, such as distemper, encephalitis, rabies, and abscesses; metabolic disorders, such as low blood glucose or calcium levels, liver failure, and lack of oxygen; poisons, such as lead, ethylene glycol, organophosphates, and carbamate insecticides; brain tumors; and head trauma. When the primary cause is identified, it should be treated. Often the cause is not known (idiopathic).

It is estimated that 2% to 3% of dogs and 0.5% of cats are epileptic. Most cases of epilepsy that start in young adult dogs and cats are idiopathic. Seizures and epilepsy that start in puppies and kittens are more likely to be caused by infections or poisonings. Those that start in older animals are generally caused by infections or tumors. Underlying causes should always be looked for and treated when identified.

There are a number of conditions that do not cause seizures, but may affect seizure activity in animals that are epileptic. Phenothiazine tranquilizers, such as acepromazine (see *Acepromazine*) and the female hormone estrogen (see *Estrogens*) may increase the incidence of seizures. Progestin (see *Progestins*), another female hormone, decreases the incidence of seizures.

Regardless of the cause, antiseizure medication is indicated in animals with moderate to severe epilepsy. The aim of antiseizure therapy is to decrease the duration and severity of individual seizures, increase the interval between seizures, and avoid drug toxicity. In most cases, medication must be given for the entire life of the animal once it is started. Animals that have only 1 seizure or infrequent seizures of short duration are not treated because the risk of side effects of antiseizure medication is greater than the risk of an occasional seizure.

Phenobarbital is a long-acting barbiturate. It is particularly good for long-term control of epilepsy because it blocks seizure and muscle activity without producing significant sedation. It is also relatively safe, effective, and inexpensive.

Phenobarbital is rapidly absorbed after oral administration and peak levels occur in 4 to 8 hours. It is widely distributed throughout the body, including the brain. About 25% is eliminated by the kidneys and the remainder is metabolized by the liver. It takes about 2 days for half of an oral dose to be eliminated. This results in fairly constant blood levels with long-term administration. It also means that it takes about 1 week after a dosage change for blood levels to stabilize, and blood levels are best checked at least 1 week after any dose changes. With long-term administration, the rate of phenobarbital metabolism is increased because the liver is stimulated to produce more of the enzymes needed to break down the drug. Therefore, the dose may need to be increased periodically.

Primidone is another antiseizure drug sometimes used in dogs. Its activity is primarily due to phenobarbital. After oral administration, it is rapidly converted to phenylethamalonamide (PEMA) and phenobarbital. All three compounds have antiseizure activity with primidone being most active followed by phenobarbital and then PEMA. However, primidone is metabolized very rapidly in dogs and contributes very little to the overall antiseizure activity. Phenobarbital, which is metabolized slowly, accounts for about 90% of the overall activity and is the metabolite that should be used to monitor and adjust dosage.

Primidone, possibly due to the phenobarbital component, also stimulates the liver enzymes that increase its rate of metabolism, and the dosage may need to be increased periodically. Primidone has a higher risk of liver toxicity than phenobarbital alone, which is a disadvantage for long-term use. Whether there are any advantages to using primidone instead of phenobarbital alone is questionable. However, some think that it may provide better seizure control in some animals.

Primidone is more toxic in cats than dogs. It should be used very cautiously, if at all.

Cautions and Warnings

For Owners/Handlers

■ The potential for serious and possibly fatal side effects by accidental ingestion and overdosage in humans is high. Store in child-resistant packaging and out of reach of children.

■ Phenobarbital is a strictly controlled drug with abuse potential. It is available by prescription only.

For Animals

■ Use cautiously in animals that are dehydrated, anemic, have decreased adrenal function, or heart disease.

■ Do not use high doses in animals with kidney disease or severe respiratory problems.

■ Barbiturates should not be administered to animals with severe liver disease.

■ Physical drug dependence is common with long-term use. If barbiturates are discontinued, reduce the dose gradually over a period of several weeks.

■ Contact your veterinarian if you think your dog or cat may be having an adverse reaction to phenobarbital.

■ Phenobarbital is not FDA approved for use in dog or cats, but it is the first choice treatment for epilepsy and its use is accepted practice.

■ U.S. federal law restricts the use of this drug by or on the lawful written or oral order of a licensed veterinarian within the context of a valid veterinarian-client-patient relationship.

Possible Side Effects

▼ Common: increased appetite, weight gain, increased thirst, increased urination, sedation and/or anxiety, and agitation.

▼ Rare: liver failure, anemia, loss of coordination, and profound depression.

Drug Interactions

• Depression is increased if phenobarbital is administered with other CNS depressants (narcotics, antihistamines, and phenothiazine), and valproic acid.

• Monoamine oxidase inhibitors (MAOIs; amitraz) prolong the effects of phenobarbital.

• Phenobarbital may decrease the effect of oral anti-coagulants (warfarin), steroids (corticosteroids and estrogens), doxycycline, griseofulvin, metronidazole, beta-blockers (propranolol), quinidine, and theophylline.

• Phenobarbital may either increase or decrease the metabolism of phenytoin, and which of these effects occurs in an individual animal is unpredictable.

• Rifampin may reduce the effect of phenobarbital.

Food Interactions

None known.

Usual Dose

Low doses are used initially and increased as needed based on effect and blood levels of the drug.

Dogs: 0.5–4.0 mg/lb twice a day.

Cats: 0.5–1.0 mg/lb twice a day.

Drug Form: 15-, 30-, 60-, and 100-mg tablets and 4 mg/ml elixir.

Overdosage

Signs of overdosage include those listed under "Possible Side Effects," as well as loss of appetite, vomiting, jerky eye movement, depression, coma, and death. Chronic overdosage may cause kidney and liver failure. Signs include pale or yellow gums. In case of accidental ingestion or overdose, contact your veterinarian or the National Animal Poison Control Center. ALWAYS bring the prescription bottle or container with you if you go for treatment.

Special Information

Successful control of epilepsy requires that medication be given precisely as instructed by your veterinarian. Even animals on antiseizure medication may have occasional seizures. Immediate treatment is not necessary or indicated provided the seizure ends within a few minutes. Keep a record of when seizures occur, including date, time of day, and anything else that you think may be different or have contributed. Missed dosages, changes in exercise routines, and changes of food or treats should be noted. Changes in appetite, thirst, weight, urination, activity level, and gum color are other things that are easy for you to monitor at home. Changes should be reported to your veterinarian as soon as practical. Your veterinarian may want to re-examine your pet regularly and take blood for a complete blood count, serum chemistry including liver and kidney function, and to check serum levels of phenobarbital to be sure they are neither too low nor too high.

If seizure control with phenobarbital alone is not adequate, discuss other treatment options with your veterinarian. A consult with a veterinary neurologist may be advisable if the usual drugs are not controlling the seizures adequately. Other drugs used to treat epilepsy include potassium bromide (see *Potassium Bromide*), phenytoin (see *Phenytoin*), and diazepam (see *Diazepam*). Acupuncture has been used to treat some cases of epilepsy. There are a number of new drugs entering the market for use in humans. There is very little information on whether these have potential benefit for dogs and cats.

Special Populations

Pregnancy/Lactation
Barbiturates cross the placenta and may cause birth defects, drug dependency, and signs of withdrawal in newborns. Small amounts are secreted in milk. Phenobarbital should not be used in pregnant or lactating animals unless the benefits clearly outweigh the risks.

Puppies/Kittens
Newborn puppies and kittens from mothers receiving phenobarbital may be drug-dependent and show signs of dependency including depression, hyperexcitability, and seizures. Treatment may be required for these newborns. Phenobarbital is the drug of choice in puppies and kittens for long-term control of recurrent seizures.

Senior Animals
The same indications, precautions, and risks apply to senior animals as to the general population.

Generic Name

Phenoxybenzamine

(fuh-nok-see-BEN-zuh-mene)

Brand Name

Dibenzyline [H]

Type of Drug

Smooth muscle relaxant (alpha-adrenergic blocker).

Prescribed for

Urethral relaxation, and high blood pressure from pheochromo-cytoma (a tumor of the adrenal gland).

General Information

Phenoxybenzamine is used in dogs and cats that have diffi-culty urinating because of urethral spasm. Phenoxybenzamine relaxes the smooth muscle of the urethral sphincter. This drug is frequently used in cats after a mechanical obstruction of the urethra has been relieved. Phenoxybenzamine may lower blood pressure by opening and relaxing small peripheral blood vessels.

Cautions and Warnings

■ Phenoxybenzamine is not FDA approved for use in dogs or cats. It is commonly used and is considered accepted prac-tice.

■ Phenoxybenzamine should not be used in animals with glaucoma or diabetes mellitus.

■ Phenoxybenzamine should be used with caution in ani-mals with heart disease, kidney damage, or arteriosclerosis.

■ U.S. federal law restricts the use of this drug by or on the lawful written or oral order of a licensed veterinarian within the context of a valid veterinarian-client-patient relationship.

Possible Side Effects

▼ Common: low or high blood pressure, contracted pupils, increased pressure within the eye, increased heart

---

Possible Side Effects *(continued)*

rate, inhibition of ejaculation, nasal congestion, nausea, and vomiting.

Drug Interactions

• Phenoxybenzamine blocks the activity of alpha-adrenergic drugs, such as phenylephrine.

• Phenoxybenzamine combined with epinephrine causes increased low blood pressure, vasodilation, and increased heart rate.

Food Interactions

Phenoxybenzamine should be given with food.

Usual Dose

Dogs: 0.14–0.25 mg/lb orally 2–3 times a day.
Cats: 0.25 mg/lb once a day, or 0.12 mg/lb twice a day.
Drug Form: 10-mg capsules.

Overdosage

Overdose of phenoxybenzamine will cause low blood pressure, increased heart rate, vomiting, lethargy, and shock. In case of accidental ingestion or overdose, contact your veterinarian or the National Animal Poison Control Center. ALWAYS bring the prescription bottle or container with you if you go for treatment.

Special Information

Urination disorders in cats and dogs have many different causes. In rare cases they are caused by problems in the central nervous system, but usually urethral spasm is caused by damage to the penile urethra from obstruction. Accurate diagnosis is important because different medications can be very specific for individual disorders.

Special Populations

Pregnancy/Lactation
It is not known if phenoxybenzamine crosses the placenta or is excreted in milk.

Puppies/Kittens

There are no studies on phenoxybenzamine in puppies or kittens.

Senior Animals

Phenoxybenzamine should be safe to use in older animals if there are no medical contraindications (see "Cautions and Warnings").

Generic Name

Phenylbutazone (fen-ul-BUE-tuh-zone) Ⓖ

Brand Names

Bizolin-200 Ⓥ	Phen-Buta Ⓥ
Butatabs D Ⓥ	Pro-Bute Ⓥ

Type of Drug

Nonsteroidal anti-inflammatory drug (NSAID), pain reliever, and fever reducer.

Prescribed for

Relief of pain and inflammation in dogs, especially that associated with osteoarthritis.

General Information

Phenylbutazone is a nonsteroidal anti-inflammatory drug (NSAID) of the pyrazolone class. It is not known exactly how NSAIDs work. However, part of their action may be due to their ability to inhibit the body's production of hormones called prostaglandins. NSAIDs also inhibit production of other body chemicals that sensitize pain receptors and stimulate the inflammatory response. NSAIDs are quickly absorbed into the blood stream. Pain and fever relief usually starts within 1 hour and lasts for up to 8 hours in the case of phenylbutazone. The anti-inflammatory response to these agents usually takes longer to work (several days to 2 weeks) and may take 1 month or more to reach maximum effect.

Phenylbutazone has a narrow margin of safety in dogs and tends to cause serious side effects like gastrointestinal (GI) ulcers and kidney damage.

Cautions and Warnings

■ Phenylbutazone is FDA approved for use in dogs only, and it should not be used in cats.

■ NSAIDs tend to cause adverse effects in the GI tract and the kidneys. Some individual dogs are more sensitive to the adverse effects than others. Those dogs at greatest risk for kidney damage are those on diuretics or those with liver, kidney, or heart disease.

■ Phenylbutazone should not be used with other anti-inflammatory drugs that tend to cause GI ulcers, such as corticosteroids and other NSAIDs, unless the dog is being closely monitored.

■ Phenylbutazone is not recommended for use in dogs with bleeding disorders such as von Willebrand's disease, as safety has not been established in dogs with these disorders.

■ Phenylbutazone should not be used in dogs with a history of blood or bone marrow problems.

■ Contact your veterinarian if you think your dog may be having an adverse reaction to phenylbutazone.

■ U.S. federal law restricts the use of this drug by or on the lawful written or oral order of a licensed veterinarian within the context of a valid veterinarian-client-patient relationship.

Possible Side Effects

▼ Common: GI ulcers and kidney toxicity [signs include decreased appetite, black or bloody stool, increased water consumption, increased urination, and edema (swelling)].

▼ Rare: allergic reactions, low white blood cell counts, and low platelet counts.

Drug Interactions

• Phenylbutazone may increase blood levels or prolong the duration of action of penicillin, phenytoin, valproic acid, warfarin, NSAIDs, sulfonamides, and glipizide.

• With chronic use, phenylbutazone may decrease the effectiveness of phenytoin and digoxin.

• Barbiturates (phenobarbital), rifampin, corticosteroids, chlorpheniramine, and diphenhydramine may decrease the effectiveness of phenylbutazone.

• Phenylbutazone may increase the chances of liver damage when given with other liver damaging drugs.

Food Interactions

None known. Probably best if given with food.

Usual Dose

Dogs: starting dose—1.5–7 mg/lb orally 3 times a day. Do not exceed a maximum of 800 mg/day regardless of weight. Taper to the lowest effective dose after 3 days.

Drug Form: 100- and 200-mg tablets. Other forms (paste, gel, 1-g tablets, and injectable) are marketed for horses. These are not recommended for dogs, as the chance of inaccurate dosing is greater.

Overdosage

An overdose of phenylbutazone is likely to cause kidney failure, liver damage, bone marrow depression, and GI ulceration and/or perforation. A large overdose may cause rapid breathing, low blood pressure, seizures, and coma. In case of accidental overdose, contact your veterinarian or the National Animal Poison Control Center. ALWAYS bring the prescription bottle or container with you if you go for treatment.

Special Information

See *Aspirin/Acetylsalicylic Acid* for more information on treatment of arthritis.

Special Populations

Pregnancy/Lactation

There are no safety studies of phenylbutazone in pregnant or lactating bitches. It causes damage to the fetus in rodents, and should be avoided unless the benefits outweigh the risks.

Puppies/Kittens

Phenylbutazone should not be used in puppies or kittens.

Senior Animals

Phenylbutazone may be used in older dogs. However, if there is heart, liver, blood, bone marrow or kidney disease, phenylbutazone should be avoided (see "Cautions and Warnings").

Generic Name

Phenylpropanolamine

(FEN-il-PROE-pah-NOLE-ah-mene) Ⓖ

Most Common Brand Names

Dexatrim Ⓗ
Propagest Ⓗ

Type of Drug

Alpha-adrenergic agonist and sympathetic nervous system stimulant.

Prescribed for

Incontinence because of decreased urethral sphincter tone.

General Information

Phenylpropanolamine (PPA) is also called norephedrine. It mimics epinephrine (adrenaline), a neurotransmitter of a branch of the central nervous system called the sympathetic or adrenergic branch. Receptors are located in all parts of the body; therefore, PPA has the potential to affect many systems and functions, which accounts for both its desired effects and unwanted side effects.

The primary use of PPA in veterinary medicine is to increase muscle tone in the urethra and prevent urinary incontinence caused by urine leaking out of the bladder. Urinary incontinence is caused by decreased tone in the sphincter muscle of the urethra, which is the tube that carries urine out of the bladder during urination.

PPA is an effective nasal decongestant and appetite suppressant in people, but it is not useful for these purposes in dogs and cats.

PPA may be used illegally to produce methamphetamine. Because of this, purchase of large quantities is strictly controlled.

Cautions and Warnings

■ Use PPA with caution in animals with glaucoma, enlarged

prostate, hyperthyroidism, diabetes mellitus, heart problems, or high blood pressure.

■ Contact your veterinarian if you think your dog or cat may be having an adverse reaction to PPA.

■ PPA is FDA approved for over-the-counter (OTC) sale but not for use in dogs or cats; however, it is accepted practice to prescribe it for the treatment of urinary incontinence.

■ U.S. federal law restricts the use of this drug by or on the lawful written or oral order of a licensed veterinarian within the context of a valid veterinarian-client-patient relationship.

Possible Side Effects

Side effects in dogs and cats are uncommon and generally mild when they occur. The most common side effect is restlessness.

▼ Rare: increased heart rate, increased blood pressure, vasoconstriction, and loss of appetite.

Drug Interactions

• The risk of side effects is increased if PPA is administered with other drugs that stimulate the adrenergic branch of the central nervous system such as ephedrine and epinephrine.

• PPA should not be given within 2 weeks of treatment with monoamine oxidase inhibitors (MAOIs), such as amitraz (see *Amitraz*).

• The risk of high blood pressure is increased if PPA is administered with certain nonsteroidal anti-inflammatory drugs (NSAIDs), including aspirin or tricyclic antidepressants.

• An increased risk of irregular heart rhythms may occur if PPA is administered with digitalis.

• PPA administered with beta-blockers may reduce the effect of both drugs.

Food Interactions

None known.

Usual Dose

Dogs: 0.5–1 mg/lb orally 2–3 times a day or one 75-mg sustained-release capsule 1–2 times a day.

Cats: 0.5–1 mg/lb orally 2–3 times a day.

Drug Form: 25- and 37.5-mg tablets.

Storage: Store at room temperature in light-resistant, tight containers.

Overdosage

Signs of overdosage include those listed under "Side Effects", increased blood pressure, increased heart rate followed by decreased heart rate and heart failure, and nervous system signs ranging from over stimulation to coma. In case of accidental ingestion or overdose, contact your veterinarian or the National Animal Poison Control Center. ALWAYS bring the prescription bottle or container with you if you go for treatment.

Special Information

Development of urinary incontinence due to decreased sphincter muscle tone is associated with a number of risk factors. It is more likely to occur in dogs than cats, in females than males, and in spayed females than in intact ones. Large and giant breeds have a higher risk than smaller breeds. Old English sheepdogs, rottweilers, Doberman pinschers, weimaraners, and Irish setters have a higher incidence and Labrador retrievers have a relatively low risk. Obese animals and those with bob or docked tails may also be prone to incontinence. The problem is seen most frequently when an affected animal is tired, relaxed, or sleeping.

Estrogens (see *Estrogens*) are also used to treat this problem. Surgery is an option, but is not always successful and should be done by a veterinarian experienced with the techniques.

Special Populations

Pregnancy/Lactation

It is unknown if PPA crosses the placenta or enters the milk. There is some evidence that it may decrease implantation of the fertilized egg; however, this has not been a recognized side effect in clinical practice. This drug should not be used in pregnant or lactating animals unless the benefits outweigh the risks.

Puppies/Kittens

No controlled studies in puppies or kittens were found. There should be little use for this drug in puppies and kittens and it should be used only if the benefits outweigh the risks.

Senior Animals
PPA is considered safe to use in healthy senior dogs and cats.

Generic Name

Phenytoin (FEN-ih-toin) G

Brand Name
Dilantin H

Type of Drug
Antiseizure.

Prescribed for
Epilepsy and digitalis toxicity.

General Information
Phenytoin is an antiseizure drug used primarily to treat epilepsy. Epilepsy is a chronic disease characterized by recurring seizures. Episodes occur at variable intervals separated by days, weeks, or even months. Seizures are also called convulsions or fits. Grand mal or generalized convulsive seizures are the most common type seen in dogs and cats. They are characterized by loss of consciousness and spasmodic contractions of the major muscles of the legs and body. Seizures may occur singly or in clusters of 2 or more very close together. Seizure activity that is continuous for 30 minutes or more is called status epilepticus. Status is a life-threatening emergency and requires immediate veterinary attention.

There are many causes of seizures and epilepsy, including infections such as distemper, encephalitis, rabies, and abscesses. Metabolic disorders such as low blood glucose or calcium levels, liver failure, and lack of oxygen; poisons such as lead, ethylene glycol, organophosphates, and carbamate insecticides; brain tumors; and head trauma are other causes. When the primary cause is identified, it should be treated. Often the cause is not known (idiopathic).

It is estimated that 2% to 3% of dogs and 0.5% of cats are

epileptic. Most cases of epilepsy that start in young adult dogs and cats are idiopathic. Seizures and epilepsy that start in puppies and kittens are more likely to be due to infections or poisonings. Those that start in older animals are generally due to infections or tumors. Underlying causes should always be looked for and treated when identified.

There are a number of conditions that do not cause seizures but may affect seizures activity in animals that are epileptic. Phenothiazine tranquilizers such as acepromazine (see *Acepromazine*) and the female hormone estrogen (see *Estrogens*) may increase the incidence of seizures. Progestin (see *Progestins*), another female hormone, decreases the incidence of seizures.

Regardless of the cause, antiseizure medication is indicated in animals with moderate to severe epilepsy. The aim of antiseizure therapy is to decrease the duration and severity of individual seizures, increase the interval between seizures, and avoid drug toxicity. In most cases, medication must be given for the entire life of the animal once it is started. Animals that have only 1 seizure or infrequent seizures of short duration are not treated because the risk of side effects of antiseizure medication is greater than the risk of an occasional seizure.

Phenytoin inhibits the spread of seizure activity in the brain by inhibiting the activity of the nerves that initiate it. Phenytoin is poorly absorbed in dogs with less than half of an oral dose entering the body. Once absorbed, it is distributed throughout the entire body but is rapidly metabolized in the liver and excreted by the kidneys. It takes only 2 to 8 hours for half of an oral dose to be eliminated in dogs. In contrast, the half-life in cats is long at 42 to 108 hours.

Phenytoin has a similar stabilizing effect on the conduction system of the heart and is sometimes used to treat some irregular rhythms particularly those due to digitalis toxicity (see *Digoxin*).

The use of phenytoin to treat epilepsy in dogs and cats has declined in recent years. It is now hardly ever used because there are more effective and safer alternatives for most animals.

Cautions and Warnings

■ Some data suggest that the potential for liver damage is increased if phenytoin is used with either primidone or phenobarbital. Weigh the potential risks versus the benefits before combining these drugs.

■ Contact your veterinarian if you think your dog or cat may be having an adverse reaction to phenytoin.

■ FDA approved for use in dogs, but the veterinary preparation is not currently on the market. It is not approved for use in cats.

■ U.S. federal law restricts the use of this drug by or on the lawful written or oral order of a licensed veterinarian within the context of a valid veterinarian-client-patient relationship.

Possible Side Effects

In dogs, loss of appetite, vomiting, loss of coordination, sedation, abnormal or excessive growth of the gums, and liver failure has been seen. In cats, loss of appetite, loss of coordination, sedation, and thinning of the skin has been seen.

Drug Interactions

• Chloramphenicol, allopurinol, cimetidine, diazepam, alcohol, isoniazid, phenylbutazone, sulfonamides, trimethoprim, valproic acid, salicylates, and chlorpheniramine may increase the effects of phenytoin.

• Barbiturates, diazoxide, folic acid, pyridoxine, theophylline, antacids, anticancer drugs, calcium, and nitrofurantoin may decrease the activity of phenytoin.

• Phenytoin may decrease the activity of corticosteroids, disopyramide, doxycycline, estrogens, quinidine, dopamine, and furosemide.

• Phenytoin may increase the toxicity of primidone, phenobarbital, meperidine, and lithium.

Food Interactions

Phenytoin should be given with food because it increases absorption and reduces the risk of vomiting.

Usual Dose

Dogs: for epilepsy—9–16 mg/lb 3 times a day. For abnormal heart rhythm—13–14 mg/lb 3 times a day.

Cats: The use of phenytoin is not generally recommended. If prescribed, discuss the benefits and risks with your veterinarian. When used, the dose for treatment of abnormal heart rhythm or epilepsy is generally in the range of 1 mg/lb once a day and monitor very carefully.

Drug Form: 50-mg tablets, 30- and 100-mg slow release capsules, and 25 mg/ml oral suspension.

Storage: Store at room temperature and protect from light and moisture.

Overdosage

Signs of overdosage include those listed under "Possible Side Effects", as well as liver failure, low blood pressure, respiratory depression, coma, and death. In case of accidental ingestion or overdose, contact your veterinarian or the National Animal Poison Control Center. ALWAYS bring the prescription bottle or container with you if you go for treatment.

Special Information

Successful control of epilepsy requires that medication be given precisely as instructed by your veterinarian. Even animals on antiseizure medication may have occasional seizures. Immediate treatment is not necessary or indicated provided the seizure ends within a few minutes. Keep a record of when seizures occur, including date, time of day, and anything else that you think may be different or have contributed to the occurance. Missed dosages, changes in exercise routines, and changes of food or treats should be noted. Changes in appetite, thirst, weight, urination, activity level, and gum color are other things that are easy for the owner to monitor at home. Changes should be reported to your veterinarian as soon as practical. Your veterinarian may want to re-examine your pet regularly and take blood for a complete blood count, serum chemistry including liver and kidney function, and to check serum levels of phenobarbital to be sure they are neither too low nor too high.

If seizure control with phenytoin alone is not adequate, discuss other treatment options with your veterinarian. A consult with a veterinary neurologist may be advisable if the usual drugs are not controlling the seizures adequately. Other drugs used to treat epilepsy include potassium bromide (see *Potassium Bromide*), phenobarbital and primidone (see *Phenobarbital*), and diazepam (see *Diazepam*). Acupuncture has been used to treat some cases of epilepsy. There are a number of new drugs entering the market for use in humans. There is very little information on whether these have potential benefit for dogs and cats.

Special Populations

Pregnancy/Lactation
Small amounts of phenytoin may be excreted into the milk and it readily crosses the placenta. Safe use of this drug has not been established during pregnancy or lactation. Use this drug only if the benefits outweigh the risks.

Puppies/Kittens
The safety of this drug in puppies and kittens has not been established. Do not use in kittens and use only if the benefits outweigh the risks in puppies.

Senior Animals
Healthy senior animals should be at the same risk as the general population.

Generic Name

Piperazine (PIP-pur-uh-zene) G

Brand Names

Anchor Piperazine Water Wormer V
Happy Jack Kennel Wormer V
Happy Jack Puppy Paste V
Pipa-Tabs V
Pipfuge V
Purina Liquid Wormer V
Sergeants Worm Away V

Type of Drug

Anthelmintic/dewormer.

Prescribed for

Roundworm (*Toxocara canis, T. cati,* and *Toxascaris leonina*) in dogs and cats.

General Information

Many dewormers contain salts of piperazine because these are more stable than the base form. The activity of the different salts depends entirely on the amount of the base and must be dosed accordingly. This makes it important to follow the directions on the label of the specific product.

Piperazine paralyzes but does not kill roundworms. Worms are expelled alive in the feces. Diarrhea or purgative laxatives increase intestinal motility and reduce the time the drug is in contact with the parasites. This reduces the effectiveness of the drug by allowing the parasites to recover before they are expelled.

Roundworms are contagious and may be spread to people, causing visceral larva migrans (see *Zoonotic Diseases of Dogs and Cats*). Appropriate precautions should be taken when handling feces from infected dogs and cats. You should dispose of feces in a manner that prevents pet and human exposure and wash your hands with soap and water after possible contact with feces.

Piperazine is among the few dewormers available over the counter (OTC) for use in dogs and cats. It is widely available wherever pet supplies are sold (see "Special Information").

Cautions and Warnings

■ Do not use in sick and debilitated animals or in those with liver or kidney disease.

■ Contact your veterinarian if you think your dog or cat may be having an adverse reaction to piperazine.

■ For veterinary use only.

Possible Side Effects

▼ Rare: vomiting, diarrhea, loss of coordination, head pressing, and in animals with large numbers of worms, intestinal obstruction and rupture.

Drug Interactions

• Do not use with laxatives.

Food Interactions

None known.

Usual Dose

Follow package directions for specific products.

Dogs and Cats: 45–65 mg/kg of piperazine base. Retreat in 2 weeks.

Drug Form: 50- and 250-mg tablets, 140-mg capsules, 17% and 34% solutions, powder, and paste.

Storage: Keep in tightly closed container and protected from exposure to light.

Overdosage

Piperazine has a wide margin of safety. Signs of overdose include vomiting; weakness; difficulty breathing; twitching of ears, whiskers, tail, and eyes; loss of coordination; excessive salivation; depression; dehydration; head-pressing; paralysis; and death. In case of accidental ingestion or overdose, contact your veterinarian or the National Animal Poison Control Center. ALWAYS bring the prescription bottle or container with you if you go for treatment.

Special Information

The use of OTC drugs to treat parasites without a specific diagnosis may be dangerous, and in most cases results in unnecessary or incorrect treatment. Owners sometimes assume that signs such as diarrhea, weight loss, or a pet scooting its bottom on the ground are due to worms and may resort to OTC drugs rather than calling their veterinarian. Although these signs may indicate parasites, they may also indicate other health problems. Using OTC products without an accurate diagnosis not only runs the unnecessary risk of side effects but also may delay the diagnosis and treatment of the real problem.

If your pet has parasites, it is important to identify the type. This may be as simple as having your veterinarian do a fecal analysis. An accurate diagnosis of the type of worm allows your veterinarian to prescribe a dewormer that is specific, effective, and safe.

Special Populations

Pregnancy/Lactation

Piperazine is considered safe to use during pregnancy and lactation, but other dewormers are preferred.

Puppies/Kittens

Piperazine is considered safe to use in puppies and kittens of all ages.

Senior Animals

Piperazine is considered safe to use in older dogs and cats.

Generic Name

Piroxicam (pih-ROX-ih-kam) G

Brand Name

Feldene H

Type of Drug

Nonsteroidal anti-inflammatory drug (NSAID), pain reliever, fever reducer, and antitumor agent.

Prescribed for

Arthritis, pain and inflammation, and cancer.

General Information

Piroxicam is an NSAID and cyclo-oxygenase inhibitor that has also been shown to have antitumor activity in dogs and cats. It is not known exactly how NSAIDs work. However, part of their action may be due to their ability to inhibit the body's production of hormones called prostaglandins. NSAIDs also inhibit production of other body chemicals that sensitize pain receptors and stimulate the inflammatory response. NSAIDs are quickly absorbed into the bloodstream. Pain and fever relief usually starts within 1 hour and lasts for 24 to 48 hours in the case of piroxicam. The anti-inflammatory response to these agents usually takes longer to work (several days to 2 weeks) and may take 1 month or more to reach maximum effect.

The antitumor activity of piroxicam is not well understood. It does not kill tumor cells directly but probably prevents them from producing some of the prostaglandins and cytokines that protect them from the host's immune attack. Piroxicam has been especially effective in the treatment of bladder tumors in dogs, but it has also shown great promise in treating a variety of other tumors.

Cautions and Warnings

■ Piroxicam is not FDA approved for use in dogs or cats. It is used with caution and close monitoring and is considered accepted practice.

■ Like many NSAIDs, piroxicam can produce gastrointestinal (GI) ulceration and kidney damage. It is one of the more potentially dangerous NSAIDs to use in dogs and should probably only be given with some other drug to protect the GI tract, such as sucralfate (see *Sucralfate*), an H_2 blocker, such as cimetidine (see *Cimetidine*), or misoprostol (see *Misoprostol*). Cats may not be as susceptible to this adverse reaction as dogs, but they should be monitored very closely when on long-term piroxicam therapy.

■ Piroxicam should not be used in animals with bleeding disorders. It should be avoided in animals with a history of GI ulceration, unless precautions are taken to protect the GI tract. It should also be avoided in animals with kidney disease or dehydration, as it may produce kidney damage.

■ Do not use in animals with a history of severe allergy to aspirin or other NSAIDs.

■ Contact your veterinarian if you think your dog or cat may be having an adverse reaction to piroxicam.

■ U.S. federal law restricts the use of this drug by or on the lawful written or oral order of a licensed veterinarian within the context of a valid veterinarian-client-patient relationship.

Possible Side Effects

▼ Common: ulceration of the GI tract, especially the stomach and duodenum, causing decreased appetite, vomiting, black or bloody stool, and kidney damage (papillary necrosis).

▼ Rare: peritonitis (inflammation of the lining of the abdominal cavity); reported in humans: headache, dizziness, ringing of the ears, increased liver enzymes, itching and rash, and edema (swelling).

Drug Interactions

• Piroxicam should not be used with other anti-inflammatory drugs that tend to cause GI ulcers, such as corticosteroids and other NSAIDs, especially aspirin.

• Piroxicam may reduce the excretion of methotrexate and cause toxicity.

Food Interactions

It is best to give piroxicam with food.

Usual Dose

Dogs: 0.15 mg/lb orally once a day for antitumor effects; or every other day for anti-inflammatory effects.

Cats: 0.06 mg/lb orally once a day for antitumor effects.

Drug Form: 10- and 20-mg capsules.

Overdosage

An overdose of piroxicam is likely to cause severe GI ulceration and kidney damage. In case of accidental ingestion or overdose, contact your veterinarian or the National Animal Poison Control Center. ALWAYS bring the prescription bottle or container with you if you go for treatment.

Special Information

Piroxicam has been used to treat a variety of different cancers, often with extraordinary success. The best studied has been bladder cancer (transitional cell carcinoma) in dogs. Of 34 dogs in the study, more than two-thirds had complete or partial remission—their tumors disappeared or shrank significantly— and 10 had an increase in tumor size or appearance of new tumors. Other types of cancer, even some with metastasis (spread to distant sites), have also been treated with piroxicam with success. So far these are only scattered reports, and the studies to prove the success in larger numbers of animals are still to be done. This is a very promising cancer therapy, especially for inoperable tumors, and is probably worth trying in many dogs and cats as long as precautions to prevent GI ulcers are taken.

Special Populations

Pregnancy/Lactation

Studies of piroxicam in pregnant or lactating animals are incomplete, and it should probably be avoided, unless the benefits outweigh the potential risks.

Puppies/Kittens

There are no studies of piroxicam in puppies or kittens, and it should probably be avoided, unless the benefits outweigh the potential risks.

Senior Animals

Piroxicam is probably safe to use in older animals, but it should be avoided or used with great care in animals with liver or kidney disease or animals susceptible to GI ulcers (see "Cautions and Warnings").

Generic Name

Polysulfated Glycosaminoglycan (PSGAG)

(POL-ee-SUL-fay-tid GLYE-kose-uh-MEE-noe-GLYE-kan)

Brand Name

Adequan [V]

Type of Drug

Disease-modifying arthritis agent and chondroprotective agent.

Prescribed for

Noninfectious, degenerative and/or traumatic arthritis.

General Information

Polysulfated glycosaminoglycan (PSGAG) is classified as a disease-modifying osteoarthritis and chondroprotective agent. It was recently FDA approved for use in dogs. It is indicated for the treatment of arthritis due to injury, arthritis, or degenerative joint disease (DJD).

Normal joints have pads of cartilage protecting the ends of the bones that form the joint, and lubricating joint fluid that helps to reduce friction and wear. Glycosaminoglycans (GAGs) are the major building blocks of both cartilage and joint fluid. Joint injury initiates a self-perpetuating cycle of inflammation, cartilage damage, and poor quality joint fluid that ultimately leads to irreversible degeneration and DJD. The use of PSGAG is based on the premise that injured joints will heal more rapidly if high concentrations of the building blocks are available.

PSGAG is frequently prescribed in older dogs for DJD of the hips. The results of one study indicate that it may actually reduce the signs of hip dysplasia when given to young dogs during their major growth period. It is also commonly used after stifle (knee) surgery to reduce the risk of developing arthritis and shorten recovery time. One study showed that the cartilage in injured stifle joints of dogs did not deteriorate as rapidly if they were treated with PSGAG. This product shows a great deal of promise in treating joint disease, but it is not a substitute for accurate diagnosis, or surgery and joint stabilization when indicated. It should not be used to treat infected joints.

PSGAG is a semisynthetic GAG extracted from tracheal cartilage of cattle and modified by adding sulfate groups to form chondroitin sulfate. PSGAG inhibits the enzymes that cause inflammation, and stimulates the production of cartilage and the lubricating joint fluid. Chemically, it is also related to the anticoagulant heparin and in high doses, it may prolong the time it takes for blood to clot.

PSGAG is distributed throughout the body after injection in muscle. It is found in all tissues and joints within 2 hours with the highest levels occurring in inflamed joints. It reaches maximal levels 48 hours after injection and lasts for 72 hours. PSGAG that is not incorporated into other tissues is excreted unchanged by the kidneys.

Cautions and Warnings

■ Do not use PSGAG in animals with infected joints.

■ Do not use PSGAG in animals with known or suspected bleeding disorders such as hemophilia, von Willebrand's disease, or low platelet counts.

■ Use PSGAG with caution in animals with kidney or liver disease.

■ Contact your veterinarian if you think your dog or cat may be having an adverse reaction to PSGAG.

■ PSGAG is FDA approved for use in dogs. Although not approved for use in cats, it is used and is considered accepted practice.

■ U.S. federal law restricts the use of this drug by or on the

lawful written or oral order of a licensed veterinarian within the context of a valid veterinarian-client-patient relationship.

Possible Side Effects

Side effects are reported in less than 2% of cases. The most common side effect is pain at the injection site.
▼ Rare: diarrhea and bleeding.

Drug Interactions

• Use with caution with drugs that may inhibit coagulation, including aspirin and other nonsteroidal anti-inflammatory drugs (NSAID), warfarin, or heparin.

Food Interactions

None known.

Usual Dose

Dogs: 2 mg/lb by injection in a muscle (IM) twice a week for 4 weeks. It is often used for longer periods, although the FDA approval specifies 4 weeks.

Cats: 1 mg/lb by IM injection every 3–5 days for 4 or more weeks.

Drug Form: 100 and 250 mg/ml injectable.

Overdosage

Side effects are uncommon even when high doses are given. Hemorrhage at the injection site has been reported. Microscopic changes of the liver, kidneys, lymph nodes, and at the injection site were seen in dogs dosed at 3 and 10 times the recommended dose for 3 times the recommended duration. The median lethal dose (the dose at which 50% of animals will die or LD50) is over 225 times the recommended dose. In case of accidental ingestion or overdose, contact your veterinarian or the National Animal Poison Control Center. ALWAYS bring the prescription bottle or container with you if you go for treatment.

Special Information

The use of antiarthritic agents that protect and promote repair of cartilage in joints rather than only controlling pain and inflammation is very desirable. PSGAG is the first product licensed by the FDA for use in dogs that may do this. DJD is not as severe a problem in cats as it is in dogs and treatment has not received the same level of attention. Although PSGAG is not labeled for use in cats, it has been used with favorable results.

Hyaluronic acid or its salt, sodium hyaluronate, is another GAG product and it is licensed for intravenous and intra-articular use in horses. Available information suggests that it may also be useful in other species including dogs and cats.

There are a number of related substances and precursors for GAG designed for oral administration (see *Glycosaminoglycan Supplements*).

Special Populations

Pregnancy/Lactation
Reproductive studies in dogs and cats have not been done. Use this drug with caution during pregnancy or lactation and only if the benefits outweigh the risks.

Puppies/Kittens
This product is not approved for use in kittens and safety studies have not been done. There are no specific contraindications to using this product in young animals.

Senior Animals
PSGAG is considered safe to use in senior animals provided they do not have other risk factors (see "Cautions and Warnings").

Generic Name

Potassium Bromide

(poe-TAS-ee-um BROE-mide) G

Brand Names

None. Potassium bromide is obtained either from a chemical supply company or a specialty compounding pharmacy.

Type of Drug

Antiseizure.

Prescribed for

Epilepsy.

General Information

Potassium bromide (KBr) is an antiseizure drug used to treat epilepsy. It is the current drug of choice for seizures that are not controlled with phenobarbital alone (see *Phenobarbital*). It is generally used in addition to phenobarbital, but it may also be used alone particularly in dogs that should not take phenobarbital because of liver damage.

Epilepsy is a chronic disease characterized by recurring seizures. Episodes occur at variable intervals separated by days, weeks, or even months. Seizures are also called convulsions or fits. Grand mal or generalized convulsive seizures are the most common type seen in dogs and cats. They are characterized by loss of consciousness and spasmodic contractions of the major muscles of the legs and body. Seizures may occur singly or in clusters of 2 or more very close together. Seizure activity that is continuous for 30 minutes or more is called status epilepticus. Status is a life-threatening emergency and requires immediate veterinary attention.

There are many causes of seizures and epilepsy including infections such as distemper, encephalitis, rabies, and abscesses. Metabolic disorders such as low blood glucose or calcium levels, liver failure, and lack of oxygen; poisons such as lead, ethylene glycol, organophosphates, and carbamate insecticides; brain tumors; and head trauma are other causes. When the primary cause is identified, it should be treated. Often the cause is not known (idiopathic).

It is estimated that 2% to 3% of dogs and 0.5% of cats are epileptic. Most cases of epilepsy that start in young adult dogs and cats are idiopathic. Seizures and epilepsy that start in puppies and kittens are more likely to be caused by infections or poisonings. Those that start in older animals are generally caused by infections or tumors. Underlying causes should always be looked for and treated when identified.

There are a number of conditions that do not cause seizures but may affect seizure activity in animals that are epileptic. Phenothiazine tranquilizers such as acepromazine (see *Acepromazine*) and the female hormone estrogen (see *Estrogens*) may increase the incidence of seizures. Progestin (see *Prog-*

estins), another female hormone, decreases the incidence of seizures.

Regardless of the cause, antiseizure medication is indicated in animals with moderate to severe epilepsy. The aim of antiseizure therapy is to decrease the duration and severity of individual seizures, increase the interval between seizures, and avoid drug toxicity. In most cases, medication must be given for the entire life of the animal once it is started. Animals that have only 1 seizure or infrequent seizures of short duration are not treated because the risk of side effects of antiseizure medication is greater than the risk of an occasional seizure.

KBr is a salt that dissociates into potassium (K) and bromide (Br) when it is dissolved in water. Br is the element that has antiseizure activity. It works by inhibiting excitability of nerve cells in the brain where seizures start.

KBr is completely absorbed and distributed in the body, central nervous system, and brain. It is excreted very slowly and takes 4 to 5 months for blood levels to stabilize. This means that it may take months for the full effect of a dosage change to occur. Occasionally, an initial loading dose is administered to reduce this lag time. Most of the time this is not necessary because antiseizure activity occurs before blood levels are completely stable.

Cautions and Warnings

■ Contact your veterinarian if you think your dog or cat may be having an adverse reaction to KBr.

■ KBr is not FDA approved for use in dogs or cats, but it is used to treat seizures in dogs and is considered accepted practice.

■ U.S. federal law restricts the use of this drug by or on the lawful written or oral order of a licensed veterinarian within the context of a valid veterinarian-client-patient relationship.

Possible Side Effects

▼ Common: transient sedation (for several weeks after initiating treatment when combined with phenobarbital), loss of appetite, vomiting, and constipation.

▼ Rare: pancreatitis (in dogs receiving combined treatment with phenobarbital or primidone).

Drug Interactions

• Increased sedation may occur if KBr is used with other sedative drugs.

• Low salt diets may reduce available chloride and increase the risk of side effects.

• Increased salt (NaCl) in the diet may decrease the effects of KBr.

Food Interactions

None known.

Usual Dose

Dogs: initial (not always used)—180–270 mg/lb for 2–3 days. Maintenance—10–20 mg/lb once a day if used with phenobarbital or primidone, or 28–35 mg/lb if used alone. Dosage must be adjusted individually based on effect and blood levels.

Cats: KBr is not recommended for use in cats.

Drug Form: reagent and USP grade bulk form.

Storage: Store in tight containers and do not put in contact with any metal.

Overdosage

Chronic overdosage is more likely to produce adverse effects than a single large dose. The signs include those listed under "Possible Side Effects," muscle pain, loss of coordination, decreased reflexes and pupils of unequal size. Toxicity generally presents as profound sedation to stupor, unsteady gait, tremors, or other central nervous system signs. In case of accidental ingestion or overdose, contact your veterinarian or the National Animal Poison Control Center. ALWAYS bring the prescription bottle or container with you if you go for treatment.

Special Information

Successful control of epilepsy requires that medication be given precisely as instructed by your veterinarian. Even animals on antiseizure medication may have occasional seizures. Immediate treatment is not necessary or indicated provided the seizure ends within a few minutes. Keep a record of when seizures occur including date, time of day, and anything else that you think may be different or have contributed. Missed dosages, changes in exercise routines, and changes of food or treats should be noted. Changes in appetite, thirst, weight, urination, activity level, and gum color are other things that are easy for the owner to monitor at home. Changes should be reported to your veterinarian as soon as practical. Your veterinarian may want to re-examine your pet regularly and take blood for a complete blood count, serum chemistry, including liver and kidney function, and to check serum levels of phenobarbital to be sure they are neither too low nor too high.

If seizure control with KBr either alone or in combination with other antiseizure drugs is not adequate, discuss other treatment options with your veterinarian. A consultation with a veterinary neurologist may be advisable if the usual drugs are not controlling the seizures adequately. Other drugs used to treat epilepsy include phenobarbital and primidone (see *Phenobarbital*), phenytoin (see *Phenytoin*), and diazepam (see *Diazepam*). Acupuncture has been used to treat some cases of epilepsy. There are a number of new drugs entering the market for use in humans. There is very little information on whether these have potential benefit for dogs and cats.

Special Populations

Pregnancy/Lactation
Safety during pregnancy and lactation has not been established in dogs or cats. Toxicity has been reported in human infants from mothers who have ingested KBr during pregnancy or lactation. KBr should be administered to pregnant or nursing dogs or cats only if the benefits outweigh the risks.

Puppies/Kittens
Safety in puppies and kittens has not been established. Use only if the benefits outweigh the risks.

Senior Animals
Senior animals are more likely to have side effects and not tolerate KBr.

Type of Drug

Potassium Supplements

Most Common Brand Names

Generic Ingredient: Potassium Chloride G
K-Dur H   Klor-Con H

Generic Ingredient: Potassium Citrate G
Citrolith H   Urocit-K H
Polycitra-K H   VetLife Potassium Citrate Granules V

Generic Ingredient: Potassium Gluconate G
Kaon H   Tumil-K V

Prescribed for

Prevention and treatment of potassium deficits, kidney failure in cats, calcium oxalate urinary stones.

General Information

Potassium is one of the main salts (electrolytes) of the body. It is important for the maintenance of all cell functions and especially kidney, nervous tissue, and heart function. In animals with kidney failure, especially cats, there may be potassium deficiency. This occurs because of potassium loss in the urine, and lack of potassium in the diet, especially with diets that acidify the urine, and low magnesium/low ash diets. Potassium gluconate is used to supplement the diet, return total body or blood potassium to normal, and prevent progression of kidney failure (see "Special Information").

Metabolic acidosis (excess acid in the blood) occurs in two-thirds to three-fourths of dogs and cats with kidney failure. Potassium citrate is probably the best way to treat acidosis and may be used to treat low potassium as well. Potassium citrate is also the treatment of choice for calcium oxalate urinary stones.

Potassium chloride is not recommended for oral use in dogs and cats because it may contribute to metabolic acidosis, and it is poorly tolerated because of its taste. It may be used intravenously in the hospital to treat low potassium.

Cautions and Warnings

■ Potassium supplements should be avoided in animals with high blood potassium, heart disease, acute kidney failure or decreased/absent urine output, or Addison's disease.

■ Contact your veterinarian if you think your dog or cat may be having an adverse reaction to potassium supplements.

■ U.S. federal law restricts the use of this drug by or on the lawful written or oral order of a licensed veterinarian within the context of a valid veterinarian-client-patient relationship.

Possible Side Effects

▼ Rare: high potassium levels, vomiting, and gastrointestinal distress; potassium given intravenously too quickly can cause abnormal heart rhythms and death. Metabolic alkalosis (excess bicarbonate in the blood) may occur with potassium citrate.

Drug Interactions

• Potassium supplements should be avoided or used with caution in animals on digoxin/digitalis.

• Angiotensin converting enzyme inhibitors, such as captopril and enalapril, and potassium sparing diuretics, such as spironolactone, may all cause high potassium when given with potassium supplements.

Food Interactions

Potassium supplements should be given with food to avoid gastrointestinal upset. Potassium citrate should not be given with diets that are meant to acidify the urine, such as Purina CNM UR-Formula and Hill's Prescription Diet cd.

Usual Dose

Dogs and Cats
Potassium citrate: for metabolic acidosis, starting dose—0.15–0.25 mEq/lb twice a day. Maintenance dose is adjusted according to response to therapy. Blood bicarbonate levels measured before dosing are used to assess response. For calcium oxalate stones, 20–30 mg/lb twice a day, or 10–20 mg/lb 3 times a day.

Potassium gluconate: Tumil-K, $\frac{1}{4}$ level teaspoon powder, or one tablet, or $\frac{1}{2}$ tsp gel per 10 lbs twice a day. Adjust dose as needed.

Drug Form: liquids, powders, granules, and gel.

Overdosage

Overdoses may cause muscle weakness, vomiting, diarrhea, and abnormal heart rhythms. These signs are worsened if there is also low blood calcium or sodium, or acidosis. In case of accidental ingestion or overdose, contact your veterinarian or the National Animal Poison Control Center. ALWAYS bring the prescription bottle or container with you if you go for treatment.

Special Information

Studies in cats with chronic kidney disease indicate that potassium supplements, even in those that have normal blood potassium levels, may help cats preserve their remaining kidney function and halt the progression of the disease. Potassium gluconate should be given to all cats with kidney failure and low or normal blood potassium levels. Potassium citrate should be used in those with metabolic acidosis, to treat both the acidosis and potassium depletion.

Special Populations

Pregnancy/Lactation
Potassium supplements should be safe to use in pregnant or lactating animals but should be used with caution and under the supervision of your veterinarian to avoid high potassium.

Puppies/Kittens
Potassium supplements should be safe to use in puppies or kittens but should be used with caution and under the supervision of your veterinarian to avoid high potassium.

Senior Animals
Potassium supplements should be safe to use in older animals. Use only under the supervision of your veterinarian, and avoid in animals with high blood potassium, heart disease (see "Drug Interactions"), acute kidney failure, decreased/absent urine output, or Addison's disease.

Generic Name

Praziquantel (prah-zee-KWAN-tul)

Brand Name

Biltricide [H]   Droncit [V]

Combination Products

Generic Ingredients: Praziquantel + Febantel
RM Parasiticide-10 [V]

Generic Ingredients: Praziquantel + Pyrantel Pamoate
Drontal for Cats and Kittens [V]

Generic Ingredients: Praziquantel + Pyrantel Pamoate + Febantel
Drontal Plus for Dogs [V]

Type of Drug

Anthelmintic/dewormer.

Prescribed for

Tapeworm (*Dipylidium caninum, Taenia pisiformis, T. taeniae-formis, Echinococcus granulosus, E. multilocularis, Diphyllobothrium latum, Spirometra mansonoides*) and lung fluke (*Paragonimus kellicotti*) in dogs and cats.

General Information

Praziquantel is absorbed from the intestine and metabolized in the liver. It then reenters the intestine in bile and kills the tapeworm. The exact mechanism of action against tapeworm has not been determined. It appears to interfere with the motility and function of the suckers that attach the parasite to the intestinal wall. It also causes the integument (the outer protective covering of the worm) to disintegrate, which kills the worm. Dead worms are digested and are not seen in the stool after treatment. Praziquantel is effective against larval and adult stages, but not against eggs.

Tapeworms have distinctive larval and adult forms. The larva infects an intermediate host. Fleas are the intermediate host for *D. caninum*. Rodents and rabbits are intermediate hosts for *Taenia* species. Larval *Diphyllobothrium* infect snails and fish.

Echinococcus larvae are found in a variety of domestic and wild ruminants, pigs, rodents, and humans. *Paragonimus* requires both snail and crayfish as intermediate hosts.

Dogs and cats become infected after eating the intermediate host and reinfection is likely unless this is prevented. *D. caninum* is the most common tapeworm in the U.S. Effective flea control greatly reduces, and may eliminate, the incidence of reinfection and the need for retreatment.

D. caninum and *E. multilocularis* are contagious and may spread to other animals and to people (see *Zoonotic Diseases of Dogs and Cats*). The *D. caninum* tapeworm may infect children who accidentally ingest infected fleas. Humans are an intermediate host for *E. multilocularis*. Contact with the feces of dogs harboring the adult tapeworm is the cause of alveolar hydatid disease (see *Zoonotic Diseases of Dogs and Cats*). Dogs at risk of infection should be retreated every 21 to 26 days to control excretion of tapeworm eggs.

Cautions and Warnings

■ The manufacturer of praziquantel does not recommend using it in puppies less than 4 weeks old or kittens less than 6 weeks old. However, the combination product containing praziquantel and febantel is approved for use in dogs, cats, puppies, and kittens of all ages. This apparent disparity is an artifact of the drug approval process rather than an actual difference in the products.

■ Do not use in sick animals, or those with liver or kidney disease. Contact your veterinarian if you think your dog or cat may be having an adverse reaction to praziquantel.

■ U.S. federal law restricts the use of this drug by or on the lawful written or oral order of a licensed veterinarian within the context of a valid veterinarian-client-patient relationship.

Possible Side Effects

Side effects with oral tablets are generally rare and mild. Side effects are more common with the injectable form, but are still seen in less than 10% of animals.

▼ Common: pain in the area injected; vomiting, diarrhea, weakness, and excessive salivation (dogs and cats); staggering (dogs only); and sleepiness and loss of appetite (cats only).

Possible Side Effects *(Continued)*

▼ Rare: loss of appetite and lethargy (dogs only).

Drug Interactions

None known.

Food Interactions

Fasting before giving this drug is not recommended; it should be given with food.

Usual Dose

Praziquantel
   Dogs and Cats: for removal of *Dipylidium, Taenia,* and *Echinococcus*—2.3–4.5 mg/lb; for removal of *Diphyllobothrium* or *Spirometra*—3.4 mg/lb once a day for 2 days; for removal of *Paragonimus*—11.4 mg/lb twice a day for 2 days.
   Drug Form: 34-mg canine tabs, 23-mg feline tabs, and 56.8 mg/ml injectable.
   Storage: Store at room temperature in tight containers; protect from exposure to light.

Drontal for Cats and Kittens
   See *Pyrantel* for usual dose.

Drontal Plus for Dogs
   See *Febantel* for usual dose.

RM Parasiticide-10
   See *Febantel* for usual dose.

Overdosage

Praziquantel has a wide margin of safety. Over 20 times the recommended dose was administered orally without producing severe side effects or death. Signs of massive oral overdose include vomiting, diarrhea, salivation, and depression. Cats had muscle tremors and loss of coordination and died when 20 times the recommended dose was injected. In case of accidental ingestion or overdose, contact your veterinarian or the National Animal Poison Control Center. ALWAYS bring the prescription bottle or container with you if you go for treatment.

Special Populations

Pregnancy/Lactation
No adverse effects have been reported.

Puppies/Kittens
Praziquantel is safe to use in puppies and kittens, although some products recommend against using it in very young animals.

Senior Animals
Praziquantel is considered safe to use in older dogs and cats.

Brand Name

Primor [V]

Generic Ingredients

Ormetoprim + Sulfadimethoxine

Type of Drug

Antibiotic combination.

Prescribed for

Susceptible bacterial infections, coccidiosis.

General Information

Ormetoprim and sulfadimethoxine (available as Primor) are antibiotics that are manufactured in combination because they are more effective when used together. Ormetoprim is similar to trimethoprim (see *Tribrissen*), and both combinations have similar abilities to kill bacteria. These combination drugs are called potentiated sulfas. They are effective against most strains of staphylococci, streptococci, and many gram-negative bacteria, such as *E. coli* and *Salmonella*, but not *Pseudomonas*. Some protozoa such as *Pneumocystis carinii*, *Coccidia* and *Toxoplasma* are also susceptible to the potentiated sulfas. See *Sulfadimethoxine* for more information.

Cautions and Warnings

■ Primor is FDA approved for use in dogs only. It should not be used in cats.

■ Sulfadimethoxine may cause keratoconjunctivitis sicca (dry eye, or KCS) in dogs. KCS may be irreversible, especially if the dog is older or has been treated long-term. Schirmer tear tests should be used weekly or monthly to monitor for decreased tear production if the dog is being treated with sulfonamides long-term.

■ The sulfonamides cause sulfa crystals to form in the urine, so make sure that the animal drinks a lot of water during treatment.

■ This drug should be avoided or used with caution in animals with liver or kidney disease.

■ Do not use Primor in dogs with blood or bone marrow disorders.

■ The sulfa drugs may cause decreased thyroid function with long-term use (see "Special Information").

■ Contact your veterinarian if you think your dog or cat may be having an adverse reaction to Primor.

■ U.S. federal law restricts the use of this drug by or on the lawful written or oral order of a licensed veterinarian within the context of a valid veterinarian-client-patient relationship.

Possible Side Effects

▼ Common: sulfa crystals in the urine (in dehydrated animals) and decreased thyroid function (with long-term use).

▼ Rare: KCS; bone marrow depression; allergic reactions such as skin rashes and facial swelling; focal retinitis; fever; non-septic polyarthritis; hemolytic anemia; diarrhea; and neurologic side effects such as behavior changes, unsteady gait, seizures, aggression, and hyperexcitability.

Drug Interactions

• Sulfadimethoxine may enhance the effects of methotrexate, warfarin, phenylbutazone, thiazide diuretics, salicylates, probenecid, and phenytoin.

• Antacids may decrease the effectiveness of sulfadimethoxine and should be given 2 to 3 hours before or after the dose of sulfadimethoxine.

Food Interactions

None known.

Usual Dose

Dogs: starting dose—25 mg/lb orally, on the first day. Maintenance dose—12.5 mg/lb once a day for at least 2 days after symptoms are gone. Not approved for treatment longer than 21 days.

Cats: not recommended for cats.

Drug Form: 120-, 240-, 600-, and 1200-mg tablets.

Overdosage

Overdose of Primor may cause tremors, excitement, decreased appetite, depression, and seizures. In case of accidental ingestion or overdose, contact your veterinarian or the National Animal Poison Control Center. ALWAYS bring the prescription bottle or container with you if you go for treatment.

Special Information

Decreased thyroid function is a common side effect of long-term Primor use. After 6 weeks of treatment, 16 of 20 dogs had markedly decreased thyroid function. Thyroid function may remain decreased for 3 months or longer after the drug is stopped. Dogs treated for four weeks had no apparent change in thyroid function.

Special Populations

Pregnancy/Lactation

Sulfadimethoxine may cause damage to the fetus in high doses, so Primor should be avoided in pregnant or lactating animals unless the benefits outweigh the risks.

Puppies/Kittens

Primor should be safe to use in puppies that are well hydrated.

Senior Animals

Primor should be safe to use in older animals but should be avoided or used with caution in those with liver or kidney disease (see "Cautions and Warnings").

Type of Drug

Progestins (proe-JES-tins)

Brand Names

Generic Ingredient: Megestrol Acetate [G]
Ovaban [V]   Megace [H]

Generic Ingredient: Medroxyprogesterone Acetate [G]
Amen [H]   Depo-Provera [H]
Curretab [H]   Provera [H]
Cycrin [H]

Prescribed for

Estrus suppression and termination of false pregnancy, other conditions associated with reproduction and the associated organs, sex hormone associated behavioral problems, and some inflammatory conditions in dogs and cats.

General Information

Progesterone and other natural progestins are steroid hormones produced by the ovary in females and by the placenta in pregnant females. They interact with many other hormones to regulate all aspects of reproduction. They stimulate the lining of the uterus to develop and accept the recently fertilized egg, help support the growing fetus and maintain pregnancy, and stimulate mammary gland development. In general, their role is to oppose the effects of estrogen, the other major female sex hormone.

Megestrol Acetate (MA) and Medroxyprogesterone Acetate (MPA) are synthetic progestins that have been used to treat a wide range of conditions. Like natural progestins, they oppose the effects of estrogen. In this context, they are used to prevent estrus (heat) and signs of false pregnancy in females. This use in dogs is the only FDA approved use of MA. MPA is not approved for use in animals in the U.S.

Progestins also oppose the effects of testosterone, the major male sex hormone, and are used to suppress male sexual behavior, including fighting, roaming, urine marking, and inappropriate mounting in males. Success depends on using behavior modification at the same time as the progestins. The behavioral effect is thought to be the result of a calming or tranquilizing effect in addition to the reduction in testosterone-mediated sex drive. Because of the potential side effects (see "Possible Side Effects"), surgical neutering, behavior modification, and/or antianxiety drugs are preferred first choice treatments.

Progestins may be used to maintain pregnancy in animals with a history of abortion caused by decreased production of progesterone. Progesterone in oil is the preferred drug for this if available, but MA and MPA have been used.

MA and MPA have powerful anti-inflammatory effects similar to the corticosteroids (see *Corticosteroids*). This property has been used to treat immune-mediated and inflammatory conditions of the skin, eyes, urinary tract, and genital tract. The tranquilizing effect may also contribute to the improvement in these cases. Corticosteroids or other anti-inflammatory drugs are safer first choice therapy for these problems.

The risk of serious side effects with the synthetic progestins reduces the clinical usefulness of these drugs. The stimulatory effect on the uterus results in thickening of the uterine lining and increases the risk of pyometra (infection of the uterus). Stimulation of mammary development increases the risk of breast cancer. MA and MPA suppress adrenal function, which is potentially fatal. Animals that must undergo surgery or are otherwise subject to increased stress may need to be treated with corticosteroids to counteract the progestin-induced adrenal suppression.

MA and MPA have been used to treat many conditions that were difficult to treat with the drugs available several years ago; the benefits of using progestins may have been worth the risk at that time. More specific and safer drugs are currently available and should be used when possible.

Cautions and Warnings

■ Do not use in animals that are pregnant or have uterine disease, diabetes mellitus, or mammary cancer.

■ Do not use in dogs before their first estrus or when the estrus cycles are not normal. Do not allow dogs to mate within 1 month of stopping MA or MPA.

■ Always give the entire dose prescribed to prevent estrus and do not use for more than 2 consecutive cycles, because this increases the risk of pyometra.

■ Contact your veterinarian if you think your dog or cat may be having an adverse reaction to MA or MPA.

■ MA is FDA approved to postpone estrus and alleviate false pregnancy in dogs. Use for all other condition in dogs, all use in cats, and all use of MPA in dogs and cats are extralabel in the U.S. They are not recommended unless other available options have failed and only after considering the potential for serious side effects.

■ U.S. federal law restricts the use of these drugs by or on the lawful written or oral order of a licensed veterinarian within the context of a valid veterinarian-client-patient relationship.

Possible Side Effects

▼ Common: increased appetite and thirst, obesity, increased urination, mammary enlargement, reduced activity, temperament changes, cystic hyperplasia of the uterus and infertility; hair loss and depigmentation at the injection site may occur with MPA.

▼ Rare: adrenal suppression, mammary tumors, pyometra (0.6% estimated by manufacturer), and diabetes mellitus.

Drug Interactions

• Rifampin may decrease the activity of progestins.
• Corticosteroids used at the same time as progestins may result in increased adrenal suppression.
• Progestins increase the dose of insulin needed to control diabetes mellitus.

Food Interactions

None known.

Usual Dose

Dogs
  MA: to prevent estrus—0.25 mg/lb once a day for 32 days if started before estrus starts or 1 mg/lb once a day for 8 days if started during proestrus (period before standing heat). To alleviate false pregnancy—1 mg/lb once a day for 8 days. The dose used for other conditions treated with MA range from 0.25–1 mg/lb for 1–4 weeks.

Injectable MPA—5–10 mg/lb. Repeat in 4–6 months as needed.

Cats

MA: to stop estrus—5 mg/cat once a day until estrus stops, generally 3–5 days, then 2.5 mg once a week for up to 10 weeks. To prevent estrus—2.5 mg once a week for up to 18 months. The dose used for other conditions treated with MA ranges from 2.5–5 mg once every 1–2 days, then 2.5 mg 1–2 times a week as needed to control signs.

Oral MPA: 2.5–5 mg/cat once a day for 5 days, then once a week. *Injectable MPA:* 25–100 mg every 1–6 months, depending on the condition being treated and response. For recurrent abortion due to progesterone-deficiency—0.5–1 mg/lb once a week. Stop 7–10 days before delivery.

Drug Form

MA: 5-, 20-, and 40-mg tablets.

MPA: 2.5-, 5-, and 10-mg tablets and 100 and 400 mg/ml injectable.

Overdosage

No specific information on overdosage in dogs and cats is available. In case of accidental ingestion or overdose, contact your veterinarian or the National Animal Poison Control Center. ALWAYS bring the prescription bottle or container with you if you go for treatment.

Special Populations

Pregnancy/Lactation

MA and MPA should not be used in pregnant or lactating animals. Pregnant dogs treated during the second half of pregnancy had an increased risk of small litters and dead puppies.

Puppies/Kittens

MA and MPA are not recommended for use in puppies or kittens.

Senior Animals

There are no specific contraindications in senior animals. MA and MPA should not be used in diabetics or animals being treated with corticosteroids.

Generic Name

Propionibacterium acnes

Brand Name

Immunoregulin [V]

Type of Drug

Immunostimulant/immunomodulatory bacterin.

Prescribed for

Chronic pyoderma (bacterial skin infection) in dogs, feline leukemia virus (FeLV), feline immunodeficiency virus (FIV), and feline viral rhinotracheitis infections, and cancer.

General Information

Immunoregulin is an injectable solution containing the killed bacteria *Propionibacterium acnes*. It is a nonspecific stimulant of the immune system. Immunostimulants allow treated animals to fight off infections more effectively, especially if the disease process is causing immune suppression. Viral infections with FeLV and FIV, certain chronic infections like canine pyoderma, as well as a variety of cancers, are associated with immune suppression. Immunoregulin may be an important adjunct to therapy of these and other diseases that are associated with immune suppression.

Cautions and Warnings

■ Immunoregulin is only FDA approved for use in dogs with chronic bacterial skin infections as an adjunct to antibiotic therapy. It is used to treat cats with viral infections, and both dogs and cats with cancer, and is considered accepted practice.

■ Use with caution or avoid in animals with heart disease.

■ Do not use in animals with autoimmune or immune-mediated diseases.

■ Contact your veterinarian if you think your dog or cat may be having an adverse reaction to Immunoregulin.

■ U.S. federal law restricts the use of this drug by or on the lawful written or oral order of a licensed veterinarian within the context of a valid veterinarian-client-patient relationship.

Possible Side Effects

▼ Rare: allergic or anaphylactic (severe systemic allergic) reactions, lethargy, fever, chills, decreased appetite (within hours of injection), and local tissue irritation (if the solution leaks outside of the vein).

Drug Interactions

• Corticosteroids blunt or negate the effects of Immunoregulin. Corticosteroids or other immunosuppressive drugs should be discontinued at least 7 days before starting treatment.

Food Interactions

None known.

Usual Dose

Dogs: up to 15 lbs—0.25–0.5 ml; 15–45 lbs—0.25–1 ml; 45–75 lbs—1–1.5 ml; over 75 lbs—1.5–2 ml (0.015–0.035 ml/lb) once or twice a week by injection into a vein (IV injection). Maintenance doses once a month may be required.

Cats: 0.25–0.5 ml once or twice a week by IV injection. Maintenance doses once a month may be required.

Drug Form: an injectable liquid suspension of *P. acnes* in ethanol and saline.

Overdosage

Long-term overdoses may cause vomiting, decreased appetite, acidosis (excess acid in the blood), increased water consumption and liver damage. In case of accidental ingestion or overdose, contact your veterinarian or the National Animal Poison Control Center. ALWAYS bring the prescription bottle or container with you if you go for treatment.

Special Information

Recurrent pyoderma in dogs is usually a lifelong disease that is unlikely to be cured and usually requires lifelong treatment. Young dogs may rarely grow out of the disease at 1 to 1.5 years of age. Older dogs who acquire the disease usually have some other problem, such as cancer or Cushing's disease as the underlying cause. About 30% to 50% of dogs with recurrent pyoderma respond to adjunct treatment with Immunoregulin. About 70% of dogs with recurrent pyoderma will respond to another licensed bacterin, Staphylococcus Phage Lysate (SPL) (see *Staphylococcal Bacterins*). If a dog is going to respond to the bacterins, it will usually do so within 3 months.

Immunoregulin is one of the promising new treatments for FeLV, FIV and feline rhinotracheitis virus infections. There are other promising treatments for FeLV/FIV infected cats as well. Acemannan, an immunostimulant derived from aloe, has prolonged the survival and improved the quality of life of infected cats, and seems to work as well orally as by injection. Acemannan is also effective against a variety of cancers when injected into the tumor and is licensed by the FDA for this use in dogs and cats (see *Acemannan*). Staphylococcal protein A (SPA), SPL, and interferon (see *Interferon* and *Staphylococcal Bacterins*) may also be effective as immunostimulants. Immunoregulin given with interferon was able to prolong survival and temporarily suppress symptoms in cats with feline infectious peritonitis (FIP).

Special Populations

Pregnancy/Lactation
There are no safety studies of Immunoregulin in pregnant dogs or cats, and it should be avoided unless the benefits outweigh the risks.

Puppies/Kittens
There are no safety studies of Immunoregulin in puppies or kittens, and it should be avoided unless the benefits outweigh the risks.

Senior Animals
Immunoregulin should be safe to use in older animals, but it should be avoided or used with caution in those with heart disease.

Type of Drug

Prostaglandins (PROS-tuh-GLAN-dinz)

Brand Name

Generic Ingredient: Prostaglandin F2 alpha (Dinoprost Tromethamine)
Lutalyse [V]

Generic Ingredient: Cloprostenol
Estrumate [V]

Prescribed for

Termination of pregnancy and pyometra (infection of the uterus).

General Information

In the vast majority of dogs and cats with unwanted pregnancy or with pyometra, the recommended treatment is ovariohysterectomy (OVH), or spaying. However, there may be a desire to preserve breeding potential in valuable breeding animals.

In the past, estradiol cypionate—ECP (see *Estrogens*) has been used to end unwanted pregnancies. The side effects with this treatment are common and severe enough that ECP is no longer recommended. There are no FDA approved drugs to end pregnancy in dogs or cats. There are experimental protocols for dogs using prostaglandin F2 alpha (PGF) and cloprostenol sodium, and a protocol for cats using PGF. These prostaglandins destroy the corpus luteum, which is the source of progesterone in the ovary; progesterone is the hormone required to maintain pregnancy. They also cause contraction of the muscles of the uterus, which adds to their ability to end pregnancy. In dogs, treatment usually requires hospitalization with repeated doses of PGF for 4 days or until abortion is complete. There is an experimental protocol for termination of pregnancy in cats after 40 days gestation. Two doses of PGF, 24 hours apart, are injected under the skin. Abortion usually occurs in 8 to 24 hours.

The treatment of choice for pyometra, after stabilization with fluids and antibiotics, is OVH. Antibiotic treatment alone is not effective. In some animals it may be possible to treat pyometra medically to preserve the breeding potential of valuable breeding animals. Medical treatment of pyometra is only recommended if the cervix is open (vaginal discharge present), and the animal is not seriously ill. In these animals, PGF may be used to treat pyometra, along with antibiotics and fluids. Treatment usually requires hospitalization, but some animals may be treated as outpatients. Treated dogs and cats should be bred on the following estrus to avoid recurrence of pyometra.

Because prostaglandins affect many body systems, side effects are common and expected. They may be quite dramatic but usually are not life-threatening. Side effects usually diminish in 30 to 60 minutes and decrease in severity over the course of treatment. Side effects may be minimized in dogs by walking them for 20 to 30 minutes after the injection.

Cautions and Warnings

For Owners/Handlers

■ Prostaglandins should ONLY be used by veterinarians. Pregnant women, asthmatics or other persons with bronchial disease should handle this product with extreme caution. Any accidental exposure to skin should be washed off immediately.

For Animals

■ Prostaglandins are not FDA approved for use in dogs or cats for treatment of pyometra or termination of pregnancy. Their use is considered experimental but accepted practice.

■ PGF should NOT be used to treat closed-cervix pyometra, or those that have sepsis, peritonitis, or are otherwise ill or have mummified fetal remains. In closed-cervix pyometra or severely ill animals, prostaglandins may cause rupture of the uterus, peritonitis, and death.

■ Prostaglandins should be avoided in animals with allergic lung disease or asthma, heart, kidney, or liver disease.

■ Contact your veterinarian if you think your dog or cat may be having an adverse reaction to prostaglandins.

■ U.S. federal law restricts the use of this drug by or on the lawful written or oral order of a licensed veterinarian within the context of a valid veterinarian-client-patient relationship.

Possible Side Effects

▼ Common: restlessness, salivation, panting, high heart rate, vomiting, diarrhea, urination, and defecation.

▼ Rare: at higher doses, incoordination, mild central nervous system signs, and death.

Drug Interactions

• None known. Anticholinergics such as atropine may reduce side effects.

Food Interactions

Withholding food before drug administration may reduce side effects.

Usual Dose

PGF

Dogs: for pregnancy termination—175 mcg/lb, by injection under the skin, twice a day for 4 days, or until abortion is complete. For pyometra—10–175 mcg/lb, by injection under the skin, once a day for 3–5 days.

Cats: for pregnancy termination after day 40 of gestation—0.25-0.5 mg/lb, by injection under the skin once, and repeat in 24 hours. For pyometra—10–175 mcg/lb, by injection under the skin, once a day for 3–5 days.

Drug Form: 5 mg/ml injectable.

Cloprostenol

Dogs: for pregnancy termination—1.75 mcg/lb, by injection under the skin 3 times at 48-hour intervals.

Drug Form: 250 mcg/ml injectable.

Overdosage

Signs of overdose include exaggerated side effects (see "Potential Side Effects"). In case of accidental ingestion or overdose, contact your veterinarian or the National Animal Poison Control Center. ALWAYS bring the prescription bottle or container with you if you go for treatment.

Special Information

There are other unapproved drugs for termination of unwanted pregnancy in dogs. Epostane, mifepristone (RU 486), and dexamethasone are successful when given orally or by injection. Discuss the risks and benefits of pregnancy termination versus OVH with your veterinarian to determine the best solution for your animal.

Special Populations

Pregnancy/Lactation
Prostaglandins should not be given to pregnant animals—unless abortion is the desired result—or lactating animals.

Puppies/Kittens
Prostaglandins should not be used in puppies or kittens.

Senior Animals
Prostaglandins should not be used in older animals, especially those over age 8.

Generic Name

Psyllium (SIL-ee-um) [G]

Brand Names

First Priority Equine Psyllium [V]   Metamucil [H]
Vetasyl [V]   Perdiem Fiber [H]

Type of Drug

Bulk laxative.

Prescribed for

Constipation, megacolon, and large bowel diarrhea.

General Information

Laxatives are used to prevent or relieve constipation. They are classified by their action as lubricant, emollient (stool softeners), bulk-forming, osmotic, or stimulant. The choice of laxative, dose, and frequency of administration must be adjusted for each individual to obtain the desired stool consistency and frequency of defecation. Vomiting, straining, and other signs of constipation may be caused by serious problems. Consult your veterinarian before administering laxatives or any medication to your pet.

Psyllium is a bulk-forming laxative obtained from the fibrous coating of a plant seed. It is high in nondigestible fiber that is not absorbed from the intestines. The fiber absorbs water and swells, making the feces softer and adding bulk to the intestinal contents. Fermentation in the colon produces substances that exert an osmotic effect further increasing the water content. The increased bulk stimulates intestinal contractions and improves transit through the intestines. This type of laxative takes up to 72 hours to see an effect.

Psyllium is useful in long-term control of megacolon. Megacolon is a disorder seen most frequently in cats. An enlarged colon with decreased muscle function results in the accumulation of huge amounts of fecal material, making it painful and ultimately impossible to defecate. There is no cure, but the constipation may be managed with individually tailored treatment plans based on the use of various types of laxatives. The softer, bulkier stool makes defecation easier and long-term use of psyllium is safe.

Psyllium is also used to treat some cases of large bowel diarrhea, such as inflammatory colitis and irritable bowel syndrome (spastic colitis). The bulk normalizes motility of the colon and absorbs free water, which improves the consistency of the feces.

Cautions and Warnings

■ Do not use if prompt defecation is required, or if fecal impaction, constipation, or intestinal obstruction is possible. Be sure the animal has constant access to fresh water.

■ Contact your veterinarian if you think your dog or cat may be having an adverse reaction to psyllium.

■ FDA approved for over-the-counter (OTC) use in dogs and cats.

Possible Side Effects

▼ Common: increased flatulence.
▼ Rare: bowel obstruction, particularly if access to drinking water is restricted.

Drug Interactions

• Psyllium may bind to digoxin, salicylates and nitrofurantoin and reduce their absorption. Administer these drugs at least 3 hours before or after psyllium.

Food Interactions

Administer with water.

Usual Dose

Dogs: 2–10 g 1–2 times a day or as needed mixed with wet food.

Cats: 1–4 g 1–2 times a day or as needed mixed with food.

Drug Form: 500-mg capsules; 3.4 g/tsp powder; and 500- and 700-mg wafers.

Storage: Store in tightly closed containers and protect from moisture.

Overdosage

Fluid stool is the primary effect of an overdose provided it is administered with sufficient liquid. It may cause obstruction of the intestines in animals that do not have free access to water. In case of accidental ingestion or overdose, contact your veterinarian or the National Animal Poison Control Center. ALWAYS bring the prescription bottle or container with you if you go for treatment.

Special Information

There are a number of sources of poorly digestible fiber that are useful as bulk laxatives. These include prunes, bran, pumpkin, and other fruit. The taste of canned pumpkin is often well accepted by dogs and cats. There are also several high-fiber prescription diets available that may be used when increased fiber is indicated.

Special Populations

Pregnancy/Lactation
Psyllium is considered safe to use in pregnant and lactating dogs and cats.

Puppies/Kittens
No specific information was found, but young animals seldom have the type of problem for which psyllium would be indicated. Use only if the potential benefits clearly outweigh the risks.

Senior Animals

Psyllium is considered safe to use in senior dogs and cats.

Generic Name

Pyrantel (pih-RAN-tul) [G]

Brand Names

Nemex [V]   Strongid T [V]

Pyratabs [V]

Combination Products

Generic Ingredients: Ivermectin + Pyrantel Pamoate
Heartgard-30 Plus [V]

Generic Ingredients: Praziquantel + Pyrantel Pamoate
Drontal for Cats and Kittens [V]

Generic Ingredients: Praziquantel + Pyrantel Pamoate + Febantel
Drontal Plus for Dogs [V]

Type of Drug

Anthelmintic (dewormer).

Prescribed for

Removal of gastrointestinal (GI) parasites (roundworms and hookworms) in dogs and cats.

General Information

Pyrantel pamoate is a pyrimidine-derived anthelmintic. Pyrantel is effective against two of the most common families of worms that infect cats and dogs, hookworms and roundworms, but is not effective against whipworms or tapeworms. It kills the susceptible parasites by paralyzing them. Pyrantel pamoate is poorly absorbed from the GI tract of dogs and cats, thereby allowing it to reach the lower GI tract. The portion of the drug that is absorbed is rapidly metabolized and excreted in urine and feces.

Cautions and Warnings

■ All of the brands of pyrantel listed above are FDA

approved for use in dogs. Only Drontal is FDA approved for use in cats. Pyrantel is considered safe and effective in cats; it is commonly used and considered accepted practice. This drug is considered very safe but it should probably not be used in severely debilitated animals.

■ U.S. federal law restricts the use of this drug by or on the lawful written or oral order of a licensed veterinarian within the context of a valid veterinarian-client-patient relationship.

Possible Side Effects

▼ Rare: vomiting.

Drug Interactions

• Because of similar mechanisms of action (and toxicity), pyrantel should not be used concurrently with morantel or levamisole (two other dewormers).

• There is an increased likelihood of adverse drug reactions if pyrantel is used concurrently with organophosphates or diethylcarbamazine.

Food Interactions

Fasting is not recommended before giving pyrantel, and it may be given with food.

Usual Dose

Pyrantel
  Dogs: 2.3 mg/lb once, then repeat in 7–10 days.
  Puppies and Kittens and Their Mothers: 2.3 mg/lb at weeks 2, 4, 6, and 8.
  Cats: 9 mg/lb once, then repeat in 7–10 days.
  Drug Form: Tablets (Nemex and Pyratabs) come in two sizes; for large dogs, 113.5-mg tablet, and for small dogs, 22.7 mg tablet. Liquid suspension—(Nemex 2) 4.54 mg/ml; Strongid: 50 mg/ml. Shake before using.

Drontal for Cats and Kittens
  Cats: 1.5–2 lbs—¼ tablet; 2–3 lbs—½ tablet; 4–8 lbs—1 tablet; 9–12 lbs—1½ tablets; 13–16 lbs—2 tablets.
  Drug Form: Tablets containing 18.2 mg praziquantel + 72.6 mg pyrantel pamoate.

Drontal Plus for Dogs
   See *Febantel* for usual dose.

Heartgard-30 Plus
   See *Ivermectin* for usual dose.

Overdosage

Pyrantel has a moderate margin of safety. Doses up to approximately 7 times the recommended dose generally have not resulted in toxic reactions. Signs of overdose could include panting, staggering, or loss of balance. In cases of accidental overdose, contact your veterinarian or the National Animal Poison Control Center. ALWAYS bring the prescription bottle or container with you if you go for treatment.

Special Information

Control of roundworms and hookworms in your pet is of particular importance because both of these groups of worms can infect and cause disease in humans. Human ingestion of the eggs of *Toxocara canis*, a common roundworm in dogs, results in infection with migrating worm larvae. The larvae can cause damage to the eyes and other organs. These diseases, known as ocular larva migrans, visceral larva migrans, and neurologic larva migrans, are serious and occur commonly in children in North America (see *Zoonotic Diseases of Dogs and Cats*). The larvae of all canine hookworms are able to penetrate intact human skin, causing a skin disease known as cutaneous larva migrans.

Special Populations

Pregnancy/Lactation
Pyrantel can be safely used during pregnancy and lactation (Drontal and Drontal Plus should not be used in pregnant animals). It is important to use pyrantel during lactation because kittens and puppies are infected with roundworms and hookworms during gestation (puppies), and when nursing (puppies and kittens). During pregnancy and lactation, encysted (dormant) larvae in the mother become active and migrate from the mother's tissues, across the placenta and into the babies, or directly into the milk. Most if not all puppies and kittens have roundworms or hookworms, and they should be dewormed at 2, 4, 6, and 8 weeks of age. At 6 to 8 weeks, puppies should

then start a monthly heartworm preventive, either Heartgard-30 Plus or Interceptor, because these medications also control and eliminate roundworms and hookworms. The encysted larvae are resistant to anthelmintics because they are walled off from the drugs, and they are dormant, so female dogs or cats who were dewormed before they became pregnant may still pass worms to their babies.

Puppies/Kittens
Pyrantel is considered safe to use in puppies and kittens as young as 2 weeks of age.

Senior Animals
Pyrantel is considered safe to use in senior animals.

Generic Name

Pyrethrins (pye-RETH-rinz)

Most Common Brand Names

Adams 14 Day Flea Dip/Ear Mite Lotion/Dust/Shampoo [V]
Cerumite [V]
C-Ten Flea Foam [V]
Defend Just-for-Cats Foam/Spray [V]
Defend Just-for-Dogs [V]
Defend Just-for-Homes [V]
Defend Pyrethrin Shampoo [V]
DuoCide L.A. Spray [V]
DuraKyl Pet Dip/Spray [V]
Ecto-Soothe Shampoo/3X Shampoo [V]
Interrupt Total Release Fogger [V]
KC 14-Day Flea & Tick Mist with Aloe [V]
Mita-Clear [V]
Mycodex Environmental Control Aerosol Fogger [V]
Mycodex FastAct IGR Flea & Tick Spray [V]
Mycodex Pet Shampoo with 3X Pyrethrins [V]
Nolvacide Insecticide Shampoo/Mist II [V]
Nolvamite [V]
Ovitrol Plus Spray/Flea & Tick Dip/Mousse [V]

Siphotrol Premise Spray [V]
VIP Fogger [V]

The information in this monograph also applies to the following drugs:

Generic Ingredient: Allethrin [G]
Defend Premise Spray [V]
DuoCide Shampoo [V]
Escort Flea and Tick Home and Carpet Spray [V]
Mycodex SensiCare Flea & Tick Shampoo [V]

Generic Ingredient: Permethrin [G]
Adam's 14 Day Flea Dip/Tick Killer [V]
Bio Spot [V] (Permethrin + Biolar IGR)
Breakthru! Inverted Aerosol Carpet Spray/Total Release Fogger [V]
Breakthru! With Nylar Spot-On for Dogs [V]
Defend EXspot Insecticide for Dogs [V]
Defend Flea & Tick Cream Rinse/Shampoo/House and Carpet Spray [V]
Defend Just-for-Dogs/Just-for-Homes [V]
Defend Permethrin Dip for Dogs [V]
DuoCide L.A. Spray [V]
EctoKyl IGR Total Release Fogger [V]
Escort P Flea & Tick Collar for Dogs and Cats [V]
Interrupt Total Release Fogger with Nylar [V]
Mycodex SensiCare LA Flea Spray/Environmental Control Aerosol Fogger/Environmental Lawn and Kennel Spray [V]
Nolvacide Mist II [V]
Proticall [V]
Happy Jack Repel-A-Cide Dip [V]
Siphotrol Plus II House Treatment [V]
SynerKyl Pet Spray/Creme Rinse/Pet Shampoo/Total Release Indoor Fogger [V]
Vet-Kem Vet Fog [V]
Virbac Knockout Room and Area Fogger [V]

Generic Ingredient: Resmethrin [G]
DuraKyl Pet Shampoo [V]

Type of Drug

Insecticide.

Prescribed for

Flea and tick control on dogs and cats and in the environment.

General Information

Pyrethrins are derived from the flower of the pyrethrum plant, *Chrysanthemum cinerariaefolium*. They kill fleas, ticks, mites, and other insects and are popular among people who prefer to use all-natural products. Many synthetic pyrethroids that are more stable and last longer than the natural pyrethrins have been developed. Allethrin, permethrin, and resmethrin are the most commonly used pyrethroids in products for small animals, including collars, dips, sprays, shampoos, and spot treatments. They are also used in products for home and premise treatment. Both the natural and synthetic compounds work by interfering with the normal function of nerves, which paralyzes and kills the parasite.

Pyrethrins have very low toxicity for dogs and cats. Most pyrethroids are safe, but it is important to check the label. Products labeled for use in dogs should not be used in cats, kittens, or puppies. The label should say it is safe for cats before using in cats and should say it is safe for puppies and/or kittens before using in young animals. Several products with permethrin are very toxic for cats and are labeled for use in dogs only. They have been associated with fatalities when used on cats and even after being used on dogs that live in close contact with cats.

Except for resmethrin, pyrethrin and pyrethroid activity is enhanced when combined with synergists such as piperonyl butoxide and N-octyl-bicycloheptene dicarboximide (MGK264). These increase the activity of the insecticide by inhibiting the flea's enzymes that normally degrade the insecticide. Their use also reduces the amount of insecticide that must be used to be effective. In general, the toxicity of synergists is low. However, caution is indicated when using products containing piperonyl butoxide on cats. It may increase the risk of neurologic side effects such as tremors, incoordination, and lethargy even at the concentration found in many commercial products.

Many products also have insect growth regulators (IGRs); (see *Insect Growth Regulator*) added. These compounds prevent flea eggs from hatching and greatly improve the overall level of flea control.

Flea control requires that the problem be attacked on several levels. Adult fleas on the animal must be killed. Flea shampoos, powders, sprays, and dips work at this level. Mechanical removal by frequent grooming and keeping your pet away from other animals and places where new fleas may be acquired also helps. However, addressing the infestation on the animal is rarely enough because fleas remaining in the environment continue to reproduce very rapidly. Environmental treatment with bombs or sprays kills many fleas. A major limitation is that bombs and sprays do not reach all of the flea's hiding places, which leaves live fleas to continue the infestation. Residual action products help extend the action, but still fall short of giving good control and may result in increased levels of toxic insecticides in the home and environment. In addition, most insecticides do not kill flea eggs, which hatch into new adult fleas within a few days. The use of IGRs, which prevent eggs from hatching, dramatically increases the effectiveness of flea control on animals and in the environment. Very good flea control is possible by combining insecticides and IGRs in a multilevel approach. The drawback is that it demands a great deal of motivation on the part of the owner.

Because of the potential for affecting the environment, insecticide use is primarily regulated by the Environmental Protection Agency (EPA). Label instructions should be carefully read and followed.

Cautions and Warnings

■ Some products containing permethrin are toxic and may be fatal if used on cats or cats that live in close contact with treated dogs. Read the label carefully before using any insecticide on your pet.

■ Do not contaminate streams, ponds, or other waterways. Pyrethroids are toxic for aquatic life.

■ Contact your veterinarian if you think your dog or cat may be having an adverse reaction to pyrethrins or pyrethroids.

■ It is a violation of federal law to use these products in a manner inconsistent with their labeling.

Possible Side Effects

▼ Common: salivation.
▼ Rare: vomiting, diarrhea, loss of coordination, hyper-excitability, seizures, and changes in temperature.

Food and Drug Interactions

None known.

Usual Dose

Dogs and Cats: Read and follow label directions.
Drug Form: shampoos, powders, sprays, dips, spot treatments, collars, and premise bombs and sprays.

Overdosage

It usually takes about 1,000 times the insecticidal dose of pyrethrins to produce toxicity in dogs and cats (see "Cautions and Warnings"). The pyrethroids, particularly permethrin in cats, may be toxic at lower doses. Signs include excessive salivation, vomiting, diarrhea, loss of coordination, hyperexcitability, seizures, and increased or decreased temperature depending on the stage of intoxication. In case of accidental ingestion or overdose, contact your veterinarian or the National Animal Poison Control Center. ALWAYS bring the prescription bottle or container with you if you go for treatment.

Special Information

See *Fipronil* for more information on fleas and ticks.

Special Populations

Pregnancy/Lactation
These insecticides are generally considered safe to use during pregnancy and lactation. Do not use directly on mammary glands or surrounding skin.

Puppies/Kittens
Read label instructions. In general, these products should not be used on nursing puppies and kittens unless the benefits outweigh the risks.

Senior Animals
These products are generally considered safe to use on senior animals.

Generic Name

Quinidine (QUIN-ih-dene) G

Most Common Brand Names

Generic Ingredient: Quinidine Gluconate
Quinaglute Dura-Tabs H

Generic Ingredient: Quinidine Polygalacturonate
Cardioquin H

Generic Ingredient: Quinidine Sulfate
Quinidex Extentabs H

Type of Drug

Antiarrhythmic.

Prescribed for

Abnormal heart rhythms.

General Information

Quinidine is related to the antimalarial drug quinine and is derived from the bark of the cinchona tree. It decreases the excitability of muscle cells and conduction fibers in the heart, so it tends to slow the heart rate and allows normal rhythms to take over. Quinidine may be used to treat abnormal fast rhythms arising from the ventricles, high heart rates that do not respond to other treatments, and a condition called atrial fibrillation. Treatment of arrhythmias that are not life-threatening is associated with increased mortality in people. It is not known whether this is true in dogs or cats. Discuss the risks and benefits of treating arrhythmias with your veterinarian or veterinary cardiologist.

Cautions and Warnings

■ Quinidine is not FDA approved for use in dogs or cats. It is used occasionally and is considered accepted practice.

■ Quinidine should not be used in animals with heart (AV) block, digoxin toxicity, or myasthenia gravis.

■ Quinidine should not be used in animals with abnormal blood electrolytes or acid-base balance.

■ Quinidine should be used with caution and with reduced doses in animals with decreased liver or kidney function. It may be best to measure blood quinidine levels to ensure that the dose is correct.

■ Contact your veterinarian if you think your dog or cat may be having an adverse reaction to quinidine.

■ U.S. federal law restricts the use of this drug by or on the lawful written or oral order of a licensed veterinarian within the context of a valid veterinarian-client-patient relationship.

Possible Side Effects

▼ Common: decreased appetite, vomiting, diarrhea, and weakness with low blood pressure.

▼ Rare: abnormal heart rhythms, allergic reactions, reversible aplastic anemia.

Drug Interactions

• Digoxin levels may be increased significantly by quinidine. The dose of digoxin should probably be reduced by half during quinidine treatment.

• Quinidine may increase the effects of warfarin anti-coagulants, and neuromuscular blocking agents like succinyl choline.

• Quinidine may decrease the effectiveness of pyridostigmine or neostigmine in animals with myasthenia gravis.

• Cimetidine, carbonic anhydrase inhibitors, thiazide diuretics, sodium bicarbonate, and antacids may increase the effects of quinidine.

• Methionine, ammonium chloride, phenobarbital, phenytoin, and rifampin may decrease the effects of quinidine.

• Additive depression of heart function may occur if quinidine is used with other antiarrhythmics like procainamide, or with phenothiazines.

• Quinidine may enhance the effect of other antihypertensive agents like ACE inhibitors, beta-blockers, or calcium channel blockers.

Food Interactions

Giving with food may reduce gastrointestinal side effects.

Usual Dose

Dogs: 3–10 mg/lb orally 3–4 times a day. The sustained-release preparations are recommended for the 3 times a day dosing.

Cats: 2–5 mg/lb orally 3 times a day.

Drug Form: Cardioquin—275-mg tablet; Quinaglute Dura-Tabs—sustained-release 324-mg tablet; Quinidex Extentabs—sustained-release 300-mg tablet; quinidine sulfate—200- and 300-mg tablets available generically.

Overdosage

Signs of overdose may include depression, weakness, lethargy, confusion, seizures, vomiting, diarrhea, and decreased urine output. In case of accidental ingestion or overdose, contact your veterinarian or the National Animal Poison Control Center. ALWAYS bring the prescription bottle or container with you if you go for treatment.

Special Populations

Pregnancy/Lactation

Quinidine causes damage to the fetus and is excreted in milk. It should be avoided in pregnant or lactating animals unless the benefits outweigh the risks.

Puppies/Kittens

Quinidine should be avoided in puppies and kittens unless under the supervision of a veterinary cardiologist.

Senior Animals

Quinidine should be safe to use in senior animals with normal kidney and liver function (see "Cautions and Warnings"), and with attention paid to possible drug interactions. Ideally, quinidine should be used under the supervision of a veterinary cardiologist.

Type of Drug

Quinolone (Fluoroquinolone) Antibiotics (KWIN-oe-lone)

Most Common Brand Names

Generic Ingredient: Difloxacin
Dicural [V]

Generic Ingredient: Enrofloxacin
Baytril [V]

Generic Ingredient: Orbifloxacin
Orbax [V]

Prescribed for

Susceptible bacterial infections.

General Information

The fluoroquinolone or quinolone antibiotics are a relatively new class of antibiotics able to kill many kinds of bacteria. The three quinolones that are approved for use by the FDA in animals are enrofloxacin (Baytril), difloxacin (Dicural), and orbifloxacin (Orbax). The quinolones are well absorbed from the gastrointestinal tract after oral administration. They are considered very safe antibiotics, and because they are concentrated in urine and a variety of tissues, they are very useful for treating bacterial infections of the urinary tract, prostate, lungs, gastrointestinal tract, and liver. The quinolones also reach reasonable levels in skin, ears, bone, central nervous system (CNS), and other tissues.

Cautions and Warnings

For Owners/Handlers
■ Keep out of reach of children. Not for human use.
■ Avoid contact with eyes, and flush eyes with water for 15 minutes if exposure occurs.
■ Wash skin with soap and water after contact.
■ Consult a physician in case of accidental ingestion by humans or if irritation persists after skin or eye contact.
■ Avoid sunlight after accidental ingestion.

For Animals

■ The main problem with the quinolone antibiotics is that they may cause damage to the joint cartilage in some young animals. Dogs seem to be the animals most susceptible to this adverse reaction. This is true for all of the quinolones. This adverse reaction was seen in some young dogs, but only at higher than recommended doses. Because of this potential adverse reaction in the joints of growing animals, the quinolones should probably be avoided in dogs between the ages of 2 and 8 months, in large breeds until 12 months, and in giant breeds until 18 months. Kittens at 8 to 10 weeks of age tolerated high doses of enrofloxacin with no adverse effects, so it may be safe to use in young cats.

■ Orbifloxacin should be used with caution in animals with known or suspected CNS disorders. In these animals, quinolones have, in rare instances, been associated with CNS stimulation, which may lead to seizures.

■ Enrofloxacin and orbifloxacin are FDA approved for use in dogs and cats. Difloxacin is FDA approved for use in dogs only; its safety in cats has not been documented.

■ Contact your veterinarian if you think your dog or cat may be having an adverse reaction to these antibiotics.

■ To report suspected adverse reactions of your animal to Orbax (orbifloxacin), call 1-800-932-0473.

■ U.S. federal law restricts the use of this drug by or on the lawful written or oral order of a licensed veterinarian within the context of a valid veterinarian-client-patient relationship.

Possible Side Effects

▼ Rare: decreased appetite, vomiting, and diarrhea; CNS excitement in animals with CNS disease; allergic reactions; crystals in the urine with dehydration; and dizziness.

Drug Interactions

• Antacids and sucralfate will inhibit absorption of the quinolones and should be given separately, at least 2 hours apart.

• The quinolones may increase theophylline blood levels.

• Probenicid blocks kidney excretion of the quinolones and may increase blood levels of the antibiotic.

Food Interactions

Food and multivitamin/mineral supplements may prevent absorption of the quinolones into the bloodstream, so they should not be given with the quinolones. It is probably best to give the dose of quinolone 2 hours or more before or after feeding.

Usual Dose

Difloxacin (Dicural)
  Dogs: 2.5–5 mg/lb orally once a day.
  Drug Form: 11.4-, 45.4-, and 136-mg tablets.

Enrofloxacin (Baytril)
  Dogs and Cats: 1.75–2.5 mg/lb orally twice a day; or 2.5 mg/lb once a day. Some sources suggest up to 7.5 mg/lb twice a day in dogs.
  Drug Form: 5.7-, 22.7-, and 68-mg tablets and "Taste Tabs." The liquid form for injection contains 22.7 mg/ml, and although it is only recommended for use as a single injection in a muscle, it is considered accepted practice to use it for repeated injections under the skin, in a muscle, or in a vein.

Orbifloxacin (Orbax)
  Dogs and Cats: 1.75–3.75 mg/lb orally once a day.
  Drug Form: 5.7-, 22.7-, and 68-mg tablets.

Overdosage

Overdoses of the quinolones are likely to produce decreased appetite, vomiting, and diarrhea. In case of accidental ingestion or overdose, contact your veterinarian or the National Animal Poison Control Center. ALWAYS bring the prescription bottle or container with you if you go for treatment.

Special Information

The quinolone antibiotics are newer drugs that kill many different kinds of bacteria, are very safe to use, except in young animals, and are therefore being used extensively. Older antibiotics may be ineffective because resistant bacterial strains have emerged, or they may have more dangerous potential side effects. Because of the extensive use of enrofloxacin in the past few years, resistant bacteria are now emerging. Orbifloxacin and difloxacin are less likely to have this problem, because they have only recently become available. Some veterinarians use ciprofloxacin in animals. This quinolone should probably be reserved for human use, unless the bacteria being treated are resistant to enrofloxacin, difloxacin, and orbifloxacin.

Because bacteria are developing resistance to many of the antibiotics in common use, especially antibiotics such as gentamicin, the approved topical medications for ear infections may not be effective. Many veterinarians use enrofloxacin injectable, combining it with ear medications like Synotic, in order to effectively treat resistant bacteria. This type of extra-label use of enrofloxacin is becoming widespread, and is considered accepted practice.

Special Populations

Pregnancy/Lactation
Enrofloxacin, orbifloxacin, and difloxacin have not been tested in pregnant or lactating animals and should probably be avoided because of the potential risks to the joints of young animals.

Puppies/Kittens
Because of the potential for damage to the joints of young animals, quinolones should probably be avoided in young or growing animals, especially dogs. Use in young animals only when the benefits outweigh the potential risks.

Senior Animals
There are no studies to confirm the safety of the quinolones in older animals, but they should be safe to use.

Generic Name

Rotenone (ROE-tuh-none) G

Brand Names

Duradip V
DuraKyl Pet Dip/Pet Spray V
Ear Miticide V

Goodwinol Ointment V
KC Ear Mite Drops V

Type of Drug

Botanical insecticide.

Prescribed for

Control of fleas, ticks, lice, and mites on dogs and cats.

General Information

Rotenone is an extract of *Derris elliptica* and some other plants in this family. It is commonly known as derris root, tuba root, and aker tuba. It works by interfering with the parasite's respiratory system. Rotenone is more toxic than the other botanical insecticides, pyrethrins and limonene, but is generally considered safe in dogs and cats. It is very toxic in pigs, snakes, and fish and should not be used if these species are in the household.

Flea control requires that the problem be attacked on several levels. Adult fleas on the animal must be killed. Flea shampoos, powders, sprays, and dips work at this level. Mechanical removal by frequent grooming and keeping your pet away from other animals and places where new fleas may be acquired also helps. However, addressing the infestation on the animal is rarely enough because fleas remaining in the environment continue to reproduce very rapidly. Environmental treatment with bombs or sprays kills many fleas. A major limitation is that bombs and sprays do not reach all of the flea's hiding places, which leaves live fleas to continue the infestation. Residual action products help extend the action but still fall short of giving good control and may result in increased levels of toxic insecticides in the home and environment. In addition, most insecticides do not kill flea eggs, which hatch into new adult fleas within a few days. The use of insect growth regulators (IGRs), which prevent eggs from hatching, dramatically increases the effectiveness of flea control on animals and in the environment. Very good flea control is possible by combining insecticides and IGRs in a multilevel approach. The drawback is that it demands a great deal of motivation on the part of the owner.

Because of the potential for affecting the environment, insecticide use is primarily regulated by the Environmental Protection Agency (EPA). Label instructions should be carefully read and followed.

Cautions and Warnings

For Owners/Handlers
   ■ Harmful if swallowed or absorbed through the skin. Avoid inhaling vapors or spray mist. Avoid contact with skin and eyes.

For Animals

■ Do not use on puppies less than 4 weeks old. Toxic to fish. Do not contaminate waterways.

■ Contact your veterinarian if you think your dog or cat may be having an adverse reaction to rotenone.

■ It is a violation of federal law to use these products in a manner inconsistent with their labeling.

■ Some products are veterinary prescription products and U.S. federal law restricts their use by or on the lawful written or oral order of a licensed veterinarian in the context of a valid veterinarian-client-patient relationship.

Possible Side Effects

▼ Rare: skin irritation and irritation to the airways if inhaled.

Food and Drug Interactions

None known.

Usual Dose

Dogs and Cats: Read and follow label directions.

Drug Form: sprays, dips, and topical ear and skin preparations.

Storage: Store in original container away from heat or light and in a secured location.

Overdosage

Signs of overdose include vomiting, diarrhea, and increased respiratory rate followed by depressed respiration, seizures, coma, and death. In case of accidental ingestion or overdose, contact your veterinarian or the National Animal Poison Control Center. ALWAYS bring the prescription bottle or container with you if you go for treatment.

Special Information

See *Fipronil* for more information on fleas and ticks.

Special Populations

Pregnancy/Lactation

Rotenone is generally considered safe to use in pregnant ani-

mals. Do not use this drug in lactating animals if nursing pup-
pies/kittens might be exposed.

Puppies/Kittens
Rotenone is generally considered safe to use in puppies and
kittens but should not be used while still nursing.

Senior Animals
Rotenone is considered safe when used as recommended in
senior animals.

Generic Name
Selegiline (seh-LEJ-uh-lene)

Most Common Brand Names

Anipryl [V]   Eldepryl [H]

Type of Drug

Monoamine oxidase inhibitor (MAOI).

Prescribed for

Cushing's disease caused by tumors of the pituitary gland,
canine cognitive dysfunction, and senile dementia.

General Information

Selegiline hydrochloride, formerly known as deprenyl, is a
monoamine oxidase inhibitor (MAOI). Selegiline works by
increasing available dopamine in the brain. Selegiline has been
used in humans for the treatment of Parkinson's disease and
has been recently approved by the FDA for treatment of a specific form of Cushing's disease in the dog caused by a pituitary
tumor. In this specific type of Cushing's disease, increased
available dopamine allows better brain regulation of the abnormal pituitary gland. The manufacturer claims that 80% to 88%
of these dogs improved on selegiline.

Selegiline is also used for canine cognitive dysfunction
(CD). CD is a form of senile dementia in dogs. The drug is not
FDA approved for treatment of CD, but results so far have been
promising.

Cautions and Warnings

■ Selegiline is FDA approved for use in dogs.

■ Selegiline should not be used in dogs whose Cushing's disease is caused by adrenal tumors or administration of corticosteroids. Endocrine function testing to confirm the diagnosis of pituitary Cushing's should be done before selegiline therapy is begun. Approximately 20% of dogs with pituitary Cushing's will not respond to selegiline.

■ U.S. federal law restricts the use of this drug by or on the lawful written or oral order of a licensed veterinarian within the context of a valid veterinarian-client-patient relationship.

Possible Side Effects

▼ Common: diarrhea, vomiting, and lethargy.

▼ Rare: disorientation, repetitive behaviors, increased salivation, loss of appetite, diminished hearing, itching, and trembling.

Drug Interactions

• Selegiline should not be given with antidepressants or selective serotonin reuptake inhibitors (SSRIs) such as fluoxetine (Prozac). There is no information on this drug interaction in dogs, but it can be fatal in humans. In humans, 2 to 5 weeks should elapse between the antidepressant and the start of selegiline therapy.

• Selegiline should not be given with meperidine or other narcotics.

• Selegiline should not be used with ephedrine, or MAOIs such as amitraz.

Food Interactions

None known.

Usual Dose

Dogs: 0.5 mg/lb once a day for 2 months. If the dog has not improved after 2 months, the dose may be increased to 1 mg/lb.

Drug Form: Anipryl: 2-, 5-, 10-, 15-, and 30-mg tablets. Eldepryl: 5-mg tablets.

Overdosage

Limited information is available on overdoses because this is such a new drug. In people, signs associated with overdoses of MAOIs may not appear immediately. Clinical signs may not occur for up to 12 hours after ingestion of the drug. Peak intensity of clinical signs may not be seen until a day after the overdose. In humans, death has resulted from overdoses of MAOIs. If you suspect an overdose of selegiline, contact your veterinarian immediately, even before the onset of any signs. Clinical signs may include salivation, decreased pupillary response, panting, dehydration, and unusual or repetitive behaviors. In case of accidental ingestion or overdose, contact your veterinarian or the National Animal Poison Control Center. ALWAYS bring the prescription bottle or container with you if you go for treatment.

Special Information

Response to selegiline may take 1 to 2 months. If your dog has not responded after 2 months, your veterinarian may increase the dose (see "Usual Dose"), but not above 1 mg/lb. Duration of response to selegiline is also variable. Some dogs show a good response for over 1 year, and others have a good initial response followed by recurrence of clinical signs several months later.

Selegiline is a newly approved drug, and studies where side effects were determined involved relatively few dogs—132 dogs were treated for 18 months. In these studies, side effects were not severe, but severe enough in 5% of the dogs for them to be removed from the study or their dose decreased. Dogs with Cushing's disease are usually older animals and frequently have other medical problems. It is sometimes difficult to separate mild drug-induced side effects from other underlying medical problems. You will need to stay in close contact with your veterinarian while arriving at a proper dose for your dog. Approximately 20% of dogs will not respond to selegiline.

Special Population

Pregnancy/Lactation
The effect of selegiline on pregnant or lactating dogs has not been determined.

Puppies

The effect of selegiline on puppies is not known.

Senior Animals

This drug is used primarily in senior animals, so all the information here is based on that population.

Generic Name

Silver Sulfadiazine

(SIL-ver sul-fuh-DYE-uh-zene) Ⓖ

Brand Names

Silvadene Ⓗ

Type of Drug

Antimicrobial.

Prescribed for

Wounds and burns.

General Information

Silver sulfadiazine is used for the prevention and treatment of infections and sepsis (blood infection) from extensive skin wounds or burns. It kills many gram-positive bacteria, such as streptococcus and staphylococcus, and gram-negative bacteria, such as *E. coli* and *Salmonella*, and is also effective against yeast. It is not known exactly how silver sulfadiazine works, but it is effective against bacteria that are resistant to other antimicrobial agents, and it works better than sulfadiazine. The cream base spreads easily and can be washed off readily with water.

Cautions and Warnings

■ Silver sulfadiazine is not FDA approved for use in dogs or cats. It is commonly used on dogs and cats and is considered accepted practice.

■ In extensive wounds or burns, enough sulfadiazine may be absorbed to reach therapeutic blood levels.

■ Sulfadiazine, like other sulfonamide antibiotics, may cause keratoconjunctivitis sicca (dry eye or KCS) in dogs. KCS may be irreversible, especially if the dog has been treated long-term or is older. Tear production should be monitored weekly or monthly with Schirmer tear tests, if the dog is being treated with sulfonamides long-term.

■ The sulfonamides cause sulfa crystals to form in the urine. It is important that the animal drink a lot of water during treatment.

■ Sulfa drugs should be avoided or used with caution in animals with liver or kidney disease.

■ Contact your veterinarian if you think your dog or cat may be having an adverse reaction to silver sulfadiazine.

■ U.S. federal law restricts the use of this drug by or on the lawful written or oral order of a licensed veterinarian within the context of a valid veterinarian-client-patient relationship.

Possible Side Effects

▼ Rare: allergic reactions, fungal infections, and KCS in dogs if used extensively and systemic levels of sulfadiazine occur; in people, transient low white blood cell count, skin damage, burning sensation, rash, and kidney damage.

Food and Drug Interactions

None known.

Usual Dose

Dogs and Cats: apply to wounds once or twice a day after cleaning to remove exudate (pus and other debris) and crusts. Dressings may be used but are not required.

Drug Form: cream for external use.

Overdosage

Silver sulfadiazine is considered a very safe drug. In one study of massive single doses of oral sulfonamides in dogs, diarrhea was the only adverse effect seen. Vomiting, bone marrow depression, allergic reactions, focal retinitis (damage to the back of the eye), fever, nonseptic polyarthritis (joint inflammation), and excitement are possible with oral overdoses of sulfonamides. In case of accidental ingestion or overdose, contact your veterinarian or the National Animal Poison Control Center. ALWAYS bring the prescription bottle or container with you if you go for treatment.

Special Populations

Pregnancy/Lactation
There are no safety studies of silver sulfadiazine in pregnant dogs or cats. It seems to be safe in pregnant laboratory animals, but it should probably be avoided in dogs and cats unless the benefits outweigh the risks.

Puppies/Kittens
Silver sulfadiazine should be safe to use in puppies and kittens, but there are no studies to confirm its safety.

Senior Animals
Silver sulfadiazine should be safe to use in older animals, but there are no studies to confirm its safety. It should be used with caution in animals with kidney or liver disease.

Generic Name

Stanozolol (STAN-oe-zoe-LOL)

Brand Name
Winstrol H V

Type of Drug
Anabolic steroid.

Prescribed for
Appetite stimulation and chronic anemia.

General Information
Anabolic steroids, such as stanozolol, are synthetic derivatives of the male hormone testosterone. They may be used in debilitated or weakened animals to stimulate appetite, increase weight gain, strength, and vigor. Stanozolol may be prescribed for the treatment of chronic anemia although it is not always effective for this purpose (see *Erythropoietin*).

Stanozolol has a pronounced anabolic effect with less masculinizing side effects than some other anabolic steroids. Anabolic steroids should only be used as a part of an overall program with other supportive and nutritional therapies.

Cautions and Warnings

■ Stanozolol is FDA approved for use in cats and dogs. It is classified as a controlled substance under the Anabolic Steroid Control Act (Schedule III).

■ Stanozolol should be used with caution in animals with heart or kidney problems.

■ Stanozolol should not be used in animals with breast cancer or prostate cancer.

■ Contact your veterinarian if you think your dog or cat may be having an adverse reaction to stanozolol.

■ U.S. federal law restricts the use of this drug by or on the lawful written or oral order of a licensed veterinarian within the context of a valid veterinarian-client-patient relationship.

Possible Side Effects

▼ Common: masculine behavior and appearance and impairment of fertility.
▼ Rare: liver failure (reported in people).

Drug Interactions

• Anabolic steroids increase the effects of warfarin and other anticoagulants.

Food Interactions

None known.

Usual Dose

Dogs: 1–4 mg orally twice a day; or 25–50 mg injected into a muscle (IM) weekly.
Cats: 0.5–2 mg orally twice a day; or 10–25 mg IM weekly.
Drug Form: 2-mg tablets and 50 mg/ml injectable.

Overdosage

There is no specific information available on overdose of stanozolol in animals. In humans, sodium and water retention may occur after anabolic steroid overdose. In case of accidental ingestion or overdose, contact your veterinarian or the National Animal Poison Control Center. ALWAYS bring the prescription bottle or container with you if you go for treatment.

Special Information

Stanozolol is sometimes used to treat anemia and improve immune function in animals with chronic kidney failure. The results in animals are variable. In humans with anemia from chronic kidney failure, male hormones are more effective if given by injection, and they must be administered for several months before a beneficial effect is seen. Erythropoietin has replaced anabolic steroids in the treatment of people with anemia from chronic kidney failure.

Stanozolol and other anabolic steroids are controlled drugs because of the abuse potential by human athletes seeking to increase muscle mass and strength.

Special Populations

Pregnancy/Lactation

Stanozolol should not be used in pregnant animals because of masculinization of the fetuses. It is not known if stanozolol is excreted in milk and should not be used during lactation unless the benefits clearly outweigh the risks.

Puppies/Kittens

Anabolic steroids should be not be used in young animals because it can cause serious disturbances in bone growth and sexual development.

Senior Animals

Stanozolol should be safe to use in older animals without heart or kidney problems. Older men have an increased risk of prostatic enlargement with stanozolol use, and this may be true for older intact male dogs as well.

Generic Name

Staphylococcal Bacterins

(STAF-uh-loe-KOK-ul BAK-ter-inz)

Brand Names

Staphage Lysate [V] [H]   Staphylococcus Protein A [H]

Type of Drug

Immunostimulant, immunomodulatory bacterin.

Prescribed for

Chronic pyoderma (bacterial skin infection) in dogs, feline leukemia virus (FeLV), feline immunodeficiency virus (FIV) and feline infectious peritonitis (FIP) infections, and cancer.

General Information

Staphylococcal phage lysate (SPL) and Staphylococcus Protein A (SPA) are both derived from the bacteria *Staphylococcus aureus*. They contain no live bacteria so they are not able to cause infections, but they are able to stimulate the immune system so that it is more effective. They are used to treat some chronic diseases and conditions associated with immune suppression. They also increase the ability of immune cells to kill or inactivate staphylococci, which makes them helpful in the majority of cases of chronic pyoderma in dogs. They are used in addition to antibiotic therapy and may help cure and prevent recurrence of this chronic disease. Staphylococcal bacterins are effective in about 70% of dogs with chronic pyoderma (see "Special Information"). Staphylococcal bacterins may also be useful in those dogs with allergies to their own skin staphylococci. These products have also shown promise in the treatment of immune suppression that occurs in FeLV, FIV, and FIP infected cats. They do not cure these diseases but may prolong and improve the quality of life.

Cautions and Warnings

■ Staphylococcal bacterins may cause general vaccine-type reactions, such as fever, chills, decreased appetite, and lethargy.

■ Transient redness, itching, and swelling may occur at the injection site 2 to 3 hours after injection and may last up to 3 days.

■ All highly allergic patients should be skin-tested initially to assess their sensitivity to staphylococcal bacterins. Patients should be observed for 45 to 60 minutes after injection for immediate allergic reactions, and up to 48 hours for delayed allergic reactions.

■ Avoid previous injection sites with repeated injections under the skin.

■ Contact your veterinarian if you think your dog or cat may be having an adverse reaction to staphylococcal bacterins.

■ U.S. federal law restricts the use of this drug by or on the lawful written or oral order of a licensed veterinarian within the context of a valid veterinarian-client-patient relationship.

Possible Side Effects

▼ Common: mild fever, lethargy, and inflammation at the site of injection.

▼ Rare: allergic or anaphylactic (serious systemic allergic) reactions with possible weakness, vomiting, diarrhea, severe itching, rapid breathing, and increased heart rate.

Drug Interactions

• Corticosteroids may blunt or negate the effects of staphylococcal bacterins. Corticosteroids or other immunosuppressive drugs should be discontinued at least 7 days before starting treatment. In some situations, such as severe allergies or FeLV infection with hemolysis and bone marrow suppression, it may be advisable to give corticosteroids along with the staphylococcal bacterin.

Food Interactions

None known.

Usual Dose

SPL

Allergic Dogs: skin test—0.05–0.1 ml injected into the skin; therapy—0.2 ml injected under the skin, then incremental doses under the skin once a week to 1.0 ml (a total of 5 injections).

Nonallergic Dogs: starting dose—0.5 ml injected under the skin twice a week for 10–12 weeks, then 0.5–1.0 ml (maximum 1.5 ml in large dogs) every 1–2 weeks. Maintenance dose—0.5–1.0 ml at a gradually lengthened interval that still maintains adequate control.

Drug Form: liquid for injection; keep refrigerated.

SPA

Cats: 3.5 mcg/lb injected in the abdomen twice a week for 10 weeks.

Dogs: 30–300 mcg/lb injected in a vein once a week for several weeks for cancer.

Drug Form: liquid for injection; keep refrigerated.

Overdosage

In case of accidental ingestion or overdose, contact your veterinarian or the National Animal Poison Control Center. ALWAYS bring the prescription bottle or container with you if you go for treatment.

Special Information

Recurrent pyoderma in dogs is usually a lifelong disease that is unlikely to be cured and usually requires lifelong treatment. Young dogs may rarely grow out of the disease at 1 to 1.5 years of age. Older dogs who acquire the disease usually have some other problem, such as cancer or Cushing's disease, as the underlying cause. About 70% of dogs with recurrent pyoderma respond to SPL. If a dog is going to respond to the bacterins, it will usually do so within 3 months.

There are a number of other immunostimulants that may be useful in treating the diseases associated with immune suppression (see *Interferon, Mycobacterium bovis/Bacillus Calmette-Guérin, Propionibacterium acnes* (Immunoregulin), *Acemannan,* and *Piroxicam*).

Special Populations

Pregnancy/Lactation
There are no safety studies in pregnant or lactating dogs or cats. Staphylococcal bacterins seem to be safe to use in pregnant rats and rabbits, but they should be avoided unless the benefits outweigh the risks.

Puppies/Kittens
There are no safety studies in puppies or kittens, and staphylococcal bacterins should be avoided unless the benefits outweigh the risks.

Senior Animals
Staphylococcal bacterins should be safe to use in older animals. Dogs that are hypothyroid should be treated before starting therapy. Owners should be aware of the risks of possible allergic or anaphylactic reactions. These reactions may have more serious consequences in older or debilitated animals.

Generic Name

Sucralfate (suc-KRAL-fate)

Brand Name

Carafate [H]

Type of Drug

Antiulcer.

Prescribed for

Reflux esophagitis, stomach ulcers and irritation, and duodenal ulcers.

General Information

Sucralfate is an aluminum salt that selectively binds to and forms a protective coating over injured mucosa (lining) of the throat, esophagus, stomach, and duodenum. Sucralfate neutralizes stomach acid, inactivates pepsin, adsorbs bile acids and pancreatic enzymes, and stimulates local prostaglandins that protect the mucosa. The drug acts locally and very little is absorbed into the bloodstream. Sucralfate is also used for the prevention of ulcers and irritation in those at high risk for ulcers, such as those on nonsteroidal anti-inflammatory drugs (NSAIDs) or high-dose steroids (corticosteroids) or those in kidney failure or under significant stress.

Cautions and Warnings

■ Sucralfate is not FDA approved for use in dogs or cats. It is commonly used, however, and is considered accepted practice.

■ Sucralfate may bind to other drugs given orally at the same time, which could prevent the other drugs from being absorbed properly and could reduce their effectiveness (see "Drug Interactions").

■ U.S. federal law restricts the use of this drug by or on the lawful written or oral order of a licensed veterinarian within the context of a valid veterinarian-client-patient relationship.

Possible Side Effects

▼ Rare: in humans, constipation, diarrhea, nausea, upset stomach, indigestion, dry mouth, rash, itching, back pain, dizziness and sleepiness. These side effects probably do not occur in animals; however, sucralfate has not been studied extensively in animals so side effects are not known.

Drug Interactions

• Other oral drugs given at the same time as sucralfate may not be absorbed properly because they may bind to sucralfate. Sucralfate may reduce the effectiveness of phenytoin, tetracycline, and fluoroquinolone/quinolone antibiotics, and these drugs should be given at least 2 hours before or after sucralfate. Sucralfate has no effect on the absorption of digoxin, quinidine, propranolol, aminophylline, diazepam, imipramine, or chlorpromazine. Sucralfate has only a minor effect on cimetidine absorption, which is not significant at higher doses of cimetidine.

• Antacids interfere with the binding of sucralfate to injured mucosa, so they should be given 30 minutes or more after sucralfate.

• Long-term use of sucralfate in animals that have kidney failure, or are being given aluminum-containing antacids, may be a problem because of aluminum accumulation, which can cause weakening of the bones and adverse effects on the brain.

Food Interactions

Sucralfate works best on an empty stomach, so give 1 hour before or 2 hours after a meal.

Usual Dose

Dosing interval varies and depends on the severity of the problem. Four times a day is ideal, 2–3 times a day may be adequate. A slurry of sucralfate (mix of sucralfate and water) should be used for ulcers in the throat or esophagus.

Large Dogs: 1000 mg orally 2–4 times a day.
Small Dogs: 500 mg orally 2–4 times a day.

Cats: 250 mg orally 2–4 times a day.
Drug Form: 1000-mg caplet.

Overdosage

There have been no reports of sucralfate overdose. Animals given up to 5.5 g/lb had no ill effects. The risk associated with sucralfate overdose is thought to be minimal.

Special Information

For the initial treatment of stomach ulcers, a histamine H_2 blocker (such as cimetidine) to control acid production, is usually given in combination with sucralfate.

Special Populations

Pregnancy/Lactation

There are no studies on sucralfate in this group, but it is probably safe to use in pregnant or lactating animals, because so little of the drug gets into the bloodstream.

Puppies/Kittens

There are no studies on sucralfate in puppies or kittens, but it is probably safe to use.

Senior Animals

Sucralfate is safe to use in older animals and is one of the best ways to prevent and treat stomach ulcers in dogs with chronic kidney failure or other diseases of senior animals. The accumulation of aluminum with long-term use of sucralfate in animals with chronic kidney failure, or in those being given aluminum-containing antacids, is a potential problem but probably not a serious concern in most cases. Aluminum toxicity can cause weakening of bones and adverse effects on the brain but is unlikely to be a problem in dogs or cats, unless sucralfate or aluminum-containing antacids are used for many months or years.

Generic Name

Sulfadimethoxine

(sul-fuh-dye-muh-THOK-sene) G

Brand Names

Albon V   Bactrovet V

Type of Drug

Antibiotic and antiprotozoal.

Prescribed for

Susceptible bacterial infections and coccidial infection.

General Information

Sulfadimethoxine is a sulfonamide antibiotic, effective against
a variety of bacteria and also coccidia (a form of parasite). It
stops susceptible bacteria and coccidia from growing. Many
bacteria that were susceptible to the sulfonamides have now
developed resistance. Sulfadimethoxine stops coccidia from
growing and treats the bacterial enteritis often associated with
coccidiosis. However, it is the host that actually eliminates the
coccidial infection.

Cautions and Warnings

■ Sulfadimethoxine is FDA approved for treatment of bacterial infections, but it is not approved for treatment of coccidial
infections. It is commonly used to treat coccidia, however, and
is considered accepted practice.

■ Sulfadimethoxine may cause keratoconjunctivitis sicca
(dry eye, or KCS) in dogs. KCS may be irreversible, especially
if the dog has been treated long-term or is older. It is best to
monitor weekly or monthly for decreased tear production with
Schirmer tear tests if the dog is being treated with sulfonamides long-term.

■ The sulfonamides cause sulfa crystals to form in the urine,
so make sure that the animal drinks a lot of water during treatment. If the animal becomes dehydrated during therapy, kidney
damage may occur during crystal deposition.

■ The sulfa drugs should be avoided or used with caution in animals with liver or kidney disease.

■ Contact your veterinarian if you think your dog or cat may be having an adverse reaction to sulfadimethoxine.

■ U.S. federal law restricts the use of this drug by or on the lawful written or oral order of a licensed veterinarian within the context of a valid veterinarian-client-patient relationship.

Possible Side Effects

▼ Common: sulfa crystals in the urine (not a problem in well-hydrated animals).

▼ Rare: KCS, bone marrow depression, allergic reactions, focal retinitis (damage to the back of the eye), fever, nonseptic polyarthritis (joint inflammation), diarrhea as a result of altered populations of bacteria in the gastrointestinal tract, and kidney damage from crystal deposition in dehydrated animals.

Drug Interactions

• Sulfadimethoxine may enhance the effects of methotrexate, warfarin, phenylbutazone, thiazide diuretics, salicylates, probenecid, and phenytoin.

• Antacids may decrease the effectiveness of sulfadimethoxine and should be given 2 to 3 hours before or after the dose of sulfadimethoxine.

Food Interactions

None known.

Usual Dose

Dogs and Cats: starting dose—25 mg/lb (1 tsp liquid/10 lbs) orally once a day. Maintenance dose—12.5 mg/lb (0.5 tsp liquid/10 lbs) once a day for 9–20 days or until the animal has no symptoms for 2 days.

Drug Form: 125-, 250- and 500-mg tablets and 5% oral liquid suspension.

Overdosage

Sulfadimethoxine is considered a very safe drug. With massive single doses in dogs, diarrhea was the only adverse effect.

Vomiting, bone marrow depression, allergic reactions, focal retinitis, fever, nonseptic polyarthritis, and excitement are possible signs of overdose. In case of accidental ingestion or overdose, contact your veterinarian or the National Animal Poison Control Center. ALWAYS bring the prescription bottle or container with you if you go for treatment.

Special Information

Albon liquid is an especially effective, easily administered, and palatable treatment for diarrhea or bacterial enteritis/coccidiosis in puppies and kittens.

Special Populations

Pregnancy/Lactation
Sulfadimethoxine may cause damage to the fetus in high doses, so it should be avoided in pregnant or lactating animals unless the benefits outweigh the risks.

Puppies/Kittens
Sulfadimethoxine is safe to use in puppies and kittens that are well hydrated.

Senior Animals
Sulfadimethoxine is probably safe to use in older animals but should be avoided or used with caution in those with liver or kidney disease (see "Cautions and Warnings").

Generic Name

Sulfasalazine (sul-fuh-SAL-uh-zene)

Most Common Brand Names

Azulfidine [H]   Azulfidine EN-Tabs [H]

Type of Drug

Antibiotic (sulfa drug), nonsteroidal anti-inflammatory drug (NSAID), and immunosuppressant.

Prescribed for

Inflammatory bowel disease, colitis, irritable bowel syndrome, and immune-mediated joint disease/arthritis.

General Information

It is not known exactly how sulfasalazine works. The drug molecule is a sulfa antibiotic joined to salicylate (aspirin). It is broken down into its two halves by bacteria in the colon, where the sulfa portion kills susceptible bacteria, and the salicylate decreases inflammation in the bowel and elsewhere in the body. It also has immunosuppressive effects. It may be effective treatment for all of the large bowel diseases of unknown cause (see "Prescribed For"), but known to be immune-mediated. It may also help relieve the pain and inflammation of the immune-mediated joint diseases. It may be helpful in both the rheumatoid or erosive type of arthritis, as well as the nonerosive types.

Cautions and Warnings

■ Sulfasalazine may cause keratoconjunctivitis sicca (dry eye, or KCS) in dogs, as other sulfa antibiotics can. Sulfasalazine may cause vomiting, hemolytic anemia, stomatitis (gum disease), jaundice (yellow gums and eyes), allergic skin disease, and low white blood cell counts.

■ Sulfasalazine should be used with caution or avoided in those with liver, kidney, or blood disorders.

■ Sulfasalazine should be used with caution or avoided in cats, due to their slow metabolism of salicylates and increased risk of side effects.

■ Contact your veterinarian if you think your dog or cat may be having an adverse reaction to sulfasalazine.

■ U.S. federal law restricts the use of this drug by or on the lawful written or oral order of a licensed veterinarian within the context of a valid veterinarian-client-patient relationship.

Possible Side Effects

▼ Rare: KCS, vomiting, hemolytic anemia, stomatitis, jaundice, allergic skin disease, and low white blood cell counts.

Drug Interactions

• Sulfasalazine may enhance the effects of methotrexate, warfarin, phenylbutazone, thiazide diuretics, salicylates, probenecid, and phenytoin.

• Salicylate toxicity is possible if sulfasalazine is used with other salicylates such as aspirin or bismuth subsalicylate (Pepto-Bismol).

• Antacids may decrease the effectiveness of sulfasalazine, and should be given 2 to 3 hours before or after the dose of sulfasalazine.

• Sulfasalazine may decrease the effects of digoxin.

Food Interactions

It may be necessary to give the B vitamin, folic acid, as a supplement during long-term sulfasalazine therapy.

Usual Dose

Dogs: 10–15 mg/lb orally twice a day for 2–4 months for arthritis and for 3–6 weeks for inflammatory bowel disease, then taper the dose.

Cats: 5–10 mg/lb orally once or twice a day for a maximum of 10 days.

Drug Form: plain or enteric-coated 500-mg tablets and 50 mg/ml oral suspension.

Overdosage

There is little information about overdoses of sulfasalazine. It may cause salicylate or sulfonamide toxicity in massive doses. Sulfa overdose may cause sulfa crystals in the urine and kidney damage, KCS, bone marrow suppression, retinal damage, fever, vomiting, diarrhea, nonseptic arthritis, central nervous system stimulation, and nerve damage. Salicylate overdose may cause blood electrolyte and acid-base disturbances, fever, bleeding, liver and kidney damage, and convulsions. In case of accidental ingestion or overdose, contact your veterinarian or the National Animal Poison Control Center. ALWAYS bring the prescription bottle or container with you if you go for treatment.

Special Information

Asacol, olsalazine, and balsalazide are all newer drugs that are similar to sulfasalazine and used in human medicine to treat inflammatory bowel disease. These may be used to treat animals, but there is very little information on their use in dogs and cats at this time.

KCS caused by sulfasalazine may be irreversible, and most experts recommend that a Schirmer tear test be done before therapy begins and then at weekly to monthly intervals to monitor for onset of decreased tear production. This is especially important for dogs treated with sulfasalazine long-term.

Special Populations

Pregnancy/Lactation
Sulfasalazine may cause damage to the fetus and should probably be avoided in pregnant or lactating animals.

Puppies/Kittens
There are no safety studies in young animals and sulfasalazine should probably be avoided in puppies and kittens.

Senior Animals
Sulfasalazine should be used with caution in older animals, especially those with liver, kidney, or blood disorders.

Generic Name

Taurine (TAW-rene) G

Brand Names

Dyna-Taurine V   Felo-Form V

Type of Drug

Amino acid and nutritional supplement.

Prescribed for

Dilated cardiomyopathy, retinal degeneration, and other syndromes caused by deficiency.

General Information

Taurine is an amino acid that is important in maintaining normal function of many systems including vision, blood platelets, and the heart. Taurine deficiency causes retinal (back of the eye) degeneration, blindness, reproductive failure, growth retardation, abnormally increased clot formation, and dilated cardiomyopathy (heart muscle disease).

Most species including dogs are able to make taurine from

other amino acids. Cats are not able to do this and require a dietary source. Taurine is found only in animal tissue; it is not present in grains, vegetables, or from any plant source. Cats, as strict carnivores, would normally get enough taurine in the diet. The problem occurs when they are fed diets that contain mainly plant source proteins, such as commercial dog food, generic commercial cat food, or vegetarian diets.

During the 1980s heart failure was diagnosed with increasing frequency in well cared for cats. The heart failure was caused by a heart (cardio-) muscle (-myo-) disease (-pathy) that causes the muscle to stretch and the heart chambers to enlarge (dilate)—dilated cardiomyopathy. The affected cats were generally kept indoors and fed quality cat food. Taurine deficiency was proven to be the cause, even though the diets contained levels at or above those recommended at that time. Administering extra taurine reversed the signs of disease in most cats and prevented the development of heart failure in cats not as severely affected. The reason that the taurine in the diet was not available or was insufficient is not known; however, taurine levels in commercial diets have since been increased and the problem is now rare in cats fed commercial diets.

Low taurine levels have been reported in some dogs with dilated cardiomyopathy. Most of the deficient dogs have been either American cocker spaniels or golden retrievers. This may indicate that some breeds of dogs have an increased risk of heart failure resulting from taurine deficiency (see "Special Information").

Cautions and Warnings

■ Dilated cardiomyopathy is a serious disease. If you think your cat or dog may have signs of heart disease or other nutritional deficiency, see your veterinarian so the problem may be diagnosed. Treating with supplements may delay proper treatment and put your pet's health and life in danger.

■ Contact your veterinarian if you think your dog or cat may be having an adverse reaction to taurine.

Possible Side Effects

Side effects are rarely seen with taurine supplementation.

Food and Drug Interactions

None known.

Usual Dose

Dogs: 500 mg/dog twice a day.
Cats: 250–500 mg/cat twice a day.
Drug Form: 60- and 250-mg tablets and 75 mg/ml paste.

Overdosage

No information is available on overdosage. In case of accidental ingestion or overdose, contact your veterinarian or the National Animal Poison Control Center. ALWAYS bring the prescription bottle or container with you if you go for treatment.

Special Information

A recent study on American cocker spaniels with dilated cardiomyopathy found decreased taurine blood levels and normal carnitine blood levels. Heart muscle levels of carnitine (see *Carnitine*), which is a much better indication of deficiency, were not measured in this study. The majority of these dogs improved significantly with a combination of taurine and carnitine supplementation. Although none improved enough to stop treatment with cardiac drugs, the doses needed were reduced. This study suggests that taurine deficiency may be a factor in heart failure in some breeds of dogs.

Special Populations

Pregnancy/Lactation

Taurine is known to be required for normal pregnancy. Although supplementation is probably safe, it should not be required provided a high-quality meat-based diet is fed.

Puppies/Kittens

Dietary taurine is needed for normal growth and development, particularly in kittens. Although supplementation is probably safe, it should not be required provided a high-quality meat-based diet is fed.

Senior Animals

Dietary taurine is needed for normal health in senior animals. Although supplementation is probably safe, it should not be required provided a high-quality meat-based diet is fed.

Generic Name

Terbutaline (ter-BUE-tuh-lene)

Most Common Brand Names

Brethine Ⓗ   Bricanyl Ⓗ

Type of Drug

Bronchodilator.

Prescribed for

Asthma, collapsing trachea, chronic allergic bronchitis, and chronic obstructive pulmonary disease.

General Information

Terbutaline opens airways in the lungs that are closed because of smooth muscle contraction. It decreases allergic inflammation in the lung, increases clearance of material up out of the airways, and stops leaking of fluid out of small vessels in the lung. Terbutaline may be helpful in the management of allergic airway disease in dogs and cats. It is also used to help diagnose asthma and treat acute asthma attacks in cats.

Cautions and Warnings

■ Terbutaline is not FDA approved for use in dogs or cats. It is commonly used to treat asthma and is considered accepted practice. Terbutaline should be used with caution in animals with diabetes, hyperthyroidism, high blood pressure, seizures, heart disease, or abnormal heart rhythms.

■ Contact your veterinarian if you think your dog or cat may be having an adverse reaction to terbutaline.

■ U.S. federal law restricts the use of this drug by or on the lawful written or oral order of a licensed veterinarian within the context of a valid veterinarian-client-patient relationship.

Possible Side Effects

▼ Rare: increased heart rate, low blood pressure, gastrointestinal upset, weakness, general inactivity, and depression.

Drug Interactions

• Terbutaline should not be given with theophylline; the combination may cause heart damage.

• Other adrenergic agonists should not be given at the same time as terbutaline.

• Beta-adrenergic blockers, such as propranolol, may decrease the effectiveness of terbutaline.

• Avoid using terbutaline with tricyclic antidepressants, monoamine oxidase inhibitors (MAOIs), digoxin, and the inhaled anesthetics.

Food Interactions

None known.

Usual Dose

Dogs: 0.005 mg/lb by injection under the skin every 4 hours; 1.25–5 mg orally 2–3 times a day.

Cats: 0.005 mg/lb by injection under the skin every 4 hours; 0.625 mg orally 2–3 times a day.

Drug Form: 2.5- and 5-mg tablets and 1 mg/ml injectable in 1-ml ampules.

Overdosage

Overdose may cause abnormal heart rhythms, high blood pressure, fever, vomiting, constricted pupils, and excitement. In case of accidental ingestion or overdose, contact your veterinarian or the National Animal Poison Control Center. ALWAYS bring the prescription bottle or container with you if you go for treatment.

Special Information

Injection of terbutaline under the skin relieves asthma attacks within minutes in about 75% of cats with an acute asthma attack and severe respiratory distress. Your veterinarian may teach you how to give your cat terbutaline by injection at home for occasional severe asthma attacks.

Special Populations

Pregnancy/Lactation

Terbutaline has not been studied thoroughly in cats and dogs. It should probably be avoided in pregnant or lactating animals unless the benefits outweigh the risks.

Puppies/Kittens
Terbutaline should be avoided in puppies and kittens.

Senior Animals
Terbutaline should be safe to use in older animals, as long as it is avoided or used with caution in those with diabetes, hyperthyroidism, high blood pressure, seizures, heart disease, or abnormal heart rhythms, or on medications that may interact with terbutaline (see "Drug Interactions").

Type of Drug

Tetracycline Antibiotics

(TEH-truh-SIKE-lene)

Most Common Brand Names

Generic Ingredient: Doxycycline Hydrochloride [G]
Monodex [H]   Vibra-Tabs [H]
Vibramycin [H]

Generic Ingredient: Minocycline Hydrochloride [G]
Dynacin [H]   Vectrin [H]
Minocin [H]

Generic Ingredient: Oxytetracycline [G]
Terramycin [V] [H]

Generic Ingredient: Tetracycline Hydrochloride [G]
Achromycin (eye ointment/drops) [H]
Achromycin-V [H]
Panmycin Aquadrops [V]

Combination Products

Generic Ingredients: Tetracycline Hydrochloride + Novobiocin Sodium
Albaplex [V]

Generic Ingredients: Tetracycline Hydrochloride + Novobiocin Sodium + Prednisolone
Delta Albaplex [V]

Prescribed for

Infections caused by susceptible microorganisms (see below).

General Information

Tetracycline antibiotics are effective against a variety of bacterial infections. It is frequently the first choice antibiotic for diseases caused by *Rickettsia* species including Rocky Mountain spotted fever, salmon poisoning, *Haemobartonella* in cats, *Ehrlichia* in cats and dogs, and coxiellosis in cats. Tetracyclines are also the primary antibiotics used to treat Lyme disease, *Brucella* infection in dogs, mycobacterial skin infections in dogs and cats, gum disease in dogs and cats, bacterial overgrowth due to feline pancreatic insufficiency, genital mycoplasmas in dogs, kidney infections, and immune-mediated claw disease.

The tetracycline antibiotics work by interfering with the normal growth cycle of the invading bacteria, thus preventing them from reproducing (bacteriostatic). This allows the body's defenses to fight off the infection. Tetracycline and oxytetracycline are excreted primarily in the urine, while doxycycline and minocycline are primarily excreted in the feces. Doxycycline and minocycline are safer drugs to use in patients that have questionable or poor kidney function.

Cautions and Warnings

■ Tetracycline and oxytetracycline are FDA approved for use in dogs and cats. Doxycycline and minocycline are not FDA approved for veterinary use, but it is accepted practice to use them in cats and dogs.

■ Tetracycline antibiotics should be used with care in animals with liver or kidney disease.

■ Tetracycline antibiotics cross the placenta and are present in milk. They affect bone and tooth development and their use should be avoided in pregnant animals, lactating animals, and young puppies or kittens.

■ U.S. federal law restricts the use of these drugs by or on the lawful written or oral order of a licensed veterinarian within the context of a valid veterinarian-client-patient relationship.

Possible Side Effects

▼ Common: symptoms relating to the gastrointestinal tract, nausea, vomiting, diarrhea, and loss of interest in

Possible Side Effects *(continued)*

food. Cats may have more difficulty tolerating tetracyclines. They may exhibit stomach pain, fever, hair loss, and depression.

▼ Rare: photosensitivity, liver damage, and changes in blood cells.

Drug Interactions

• Tetracycline antibiotics, which are bacteriostatic, may interfere with the action of bactericidal (bacteria-killing) antibiotics such as penicillin. Do not give your animal more than one antibiotic without specific instructions from your veterinarian.

• Antacids, sodium bicarbonate powder, mineral supplements, and multivitamins containing bismuth, calcium, zinc, magnesium, and iron can reduce the effectiveness of tetracycline antibiotics by interfering with their absorption into the bloodstream. Doxycycline and minocycline are less affected. Doses of antacid, mineral and vitamin supplements, or sodium bicarbonate should be separated from the antibiotic by at least 2 hours.

• Tetracycline antibiotics may increase the effect of anticoagulant drugs such as warfarin. Your animal's warfarin dose may need to be decreased.

• Barbiturates and some other antiseizure medications may increase the rate at which doxycycline is broken down by the liver, reducing its effectiveness. The dose of the antibiotic may need to be increased.

• Cimetidine, ranitidine, and other H_2 blockers may reduce the amount of tetracyclines absorbed in the bloodstream, decreasing their effectiveness.

• Tetracycline antibiotics may reduce insulin requirements in some human diabetics. If your animal is diabetic, you may be advised to monitor blood sugar levels during tetracycline treatment.

• Tetracycline has been shown to increase blood levels of digoxin in some people.

Food Interactions

Tetracycline and oxytetracycline are better absorbed on an empty stomach. Food will reduce absorption by as much as

50%. Doxycycline is well absorbed even with food in the stomach.

Usual Dose

Doxycycline
   Dogs: starting dose—2.5–10 mg/lb orally once a day. Maintenance dose—5 mg/lb once a day.
   Cats: 1.4–8.25 mg/lb orally twice a day.
   Drug Form: 50- and 100-mg tablets and capsules, 5 mg/ml oral suspension, and 10 mg/ml oral syrup.

Minocycline
   Dogs: 14 mg/lb orally 2–3 times a day.
   Drug Form: 50- and 100-mg capsules and 50 mg/tsp (5 ml) oral suspension.

Oxytetracycline
   Dogs: 12 mg/lb orally 3 times a day.
   Cats: 8.25 mg/lb orally 3 times a day.
   Drug Form: 250-mg capsules.

Tetracycline
   Dogs: 12–22 mg/lb orally 3 times a day.
   Cats: 5.5–14.0 mg/lb orally 2–3 times a day.
   Drug Form: 100-, 250-, and 500-mg capsules and tablets and 25 and 100 mg/ml oral suspension.

Tetracycline + Novobiocin (Albaplex)
   Dogs: 10 mg/lb orally twice a day.
   Drug Form: tablets containing 60-mg tetracycline and 60-mg novobiocin sodium.

Tetracycline + Novobiocin + Prednisolone (Delta-Albaplex)
   Dogs: 10 mg/lb of each antibiotic with 0.25 mg/lb prednisolone orally twice a day for 2 days.
   Drug Form: tablets containing 60-mg tetracycline + 60-mg novobiocin + 1.5-mg prednisolone or 180-mg tetracycline + 180-mg novobiocin sodium + 4.5-mg prednisolone.

Overdosage

Tetracyclines are generally well tolerated after acute oral overdoses. Oral overdoses may cause vomiting, loss of appetite, and diarrhea. Chronic overdoses may result in kidney damage. In case of accidental ingestion or overdose, contact your veterinarian or the National Animal Poison Control Center. ALWAYS bring the prescription bottle or container with you if you go for treatment.

Special Information

Tetracycline and niacinamide may be used to treat refractory autoimmune diseases, such as onychomadeses (claw diseases), discoid lupus, pemphigus, and interdigital cysts (skin diseases). It is not known how this combination works, but it seems to be unrelated to the antibiotic action of tetracycline. The two medications are given 3 times a day for 3 months, twice a day for 2 months, then once a day for 1 month. If the disease recurs, indefinite maintenance therapy may be needed.

Special Populations

Pregnancy/Lactation
Tetracycline antibiotics should not be used in pregnant animals as it can retard bone growth in the fetus and discolor teeth. Tetracyclines will cross into the milk of lactating animals and should be avoided for the same reasons.

Puppies/Kittens
Tetracycline can retard bone growth and discolor teeth. If possible, it should not be used in the young puppy or kitten.

Senior Animals
Tetracyclines can be used with care in older patients with normal kidney and liver function.

Generic Name

Theophylline (thee-AH-fih-lin) [G]

Most Common Brand Names

Elixophyllin [H]	Theo-Dur [H]
Slo-bid [H]	Uniphyl [H]
Slo-Phyllin [H]	

The information in this profile also applies to the following drug:

Generic Ingredient: Aminophylline
Available as a generic in liquid form.

Type of Drug

Bronchodilator.

Prescribed for

Relief of bronchial asthma and chronic obstructive pulmonary disease (COPD).

General Information

Theophylline and aminophylline are from a group of drugs called xanthine bronchodilators. They work primarily by relaxing bronchial smooth muscle and opening constricted airways in the lungs. They also improve clearance of secretions from the lungs, and increase the diaphragm's ability to contract. Theophylline comes in oral immediate release, oral slow release, and injectable form. Theophylline is the parent compound of aminophylline. These drugs are metabolized by the liver and are rapidly absorbed orally.

Theophylline is used primarily in the management of feline asthma, and occasionally in the management of canine chronic bronchitis. The primary cause of chronic bronchitis in humans is inhaled tobacco smoke. Inhalation of secondary smoke may be important in dogs and cats as well. It is thought that chronic bronchitis/asthma in cats is caused by allergies to cat litter and household dust, smoke, kapok (a material used as mattress filling and in insulation), talc, and other inhaled allergens. Canine chronic bronchitis may be caused by many different factors, including environmental, inherited, and infectious causes. Bronchodilators are frequently used with corticosteroids and may permit lower doses of the corticosteroids. Cats with feline asthma will sometimes present as an emergency in respiratory distress. Because theophylline is so well absorbed orally, it is frequently given orally even in these circumstances to minimize stress.

Theophylline is also used as a bronchodilator in some heart problems, aspiration pneumonia, and in some trauma patients.

Cautions and Warnings

■ Theophylline is not FDA approved for use in dogs or cats.

It is commonly used in dogs and cats and is considered accepted practice.

■ Theophylline should not be used in patients hypersensitive to any of the xanthines, including theobromine and caffeine.

■ Theophylline should be used with caution in animals with severe heart disease, stomach ulcers, hyperthyroidism, kidney or liver disease, high blood pressure, or low blood oxygen.

■ Theophylline may cause or worsen abnormal heart rhythms. It should be used with caution and careful monitoring in patients prone to cardiac arrhythmias.

■ Contact your veterinarian if you think your dog or cat may be having an adverse reaction to theophylline.

■ U.S. federal law restricts the use of this drug by or on the lawful written or oral order of a licensed veterinarian within the context of a valid veterinarian-client-patient relationship.

Possible Side Effects

Most side effects are dose related, and each animal may need some dose adjustments.

▼ Common: central nervous system excitement, insomnia, gastrointestinal upset, including nausea, vomiting, diarrhea, and increased stomach acid secretion, and increased hunger or thirst.

Drug Interactions

• Phenobarbital and phenytoin decrease the effect of theophylline.
• Cimetidine, erythromycin, allopurinol, thiabendazole, clindamycin, and lincomycin increase the effect of theophylline.
• Theophylline and beta-adrenergic blockers may antagonize each other's effects.
• Theophylline should not be used with ephedrine, isoproterenol, or halothane because of cardiac (heart) side effects.
• Theophylline should not be given with ketamine because of an increased likelihood of seizures.

Food Interactions

Theophylline absorption is affected by food in humans. To obtain a consistent effect from the medication, it should be given at the same time every day and preferably on an empty stomach. If the theophylline upsets your animal's stomach, it may be given with a small meal.

Usual Dose

The drug absorption varies between brands of sustained release theophylline. Your veterinarian may prescribe a different dose based on the brand used.

Dogs: aminophylline—3–6 mg/lb 2–3 times a day. Theophylline immediate release—5 mg/lb orally 3–4 times a day. Theophylline sustained release—10 mg/lb twice a day (Theo-Dur).

Cats: aminophylline—2–3 mg/lb 2–3 times a day. Theophylline—2 mg/lb orally 2–3 times a day. Theophylline sustained release—12 mg/lb once a day (Theo-Dur and Slo-bid).

Drug Form: aminophylline: 105 mg/5 ml oral solution. Theophylline: 50-, 100-, 125-, 130-, 200-, 250-, 260-, and 300-mg timed release tablets and capsules.

Overdosage

Overdoses cause central nervous system disturbances, including seizures and fever, and life-threatening rapid heart rate and abnormal heart rhythms. In case of accidental ingestion or overdose, contact your veterinarian or the National Animal Poison Control Center. ALWAYS bring the prescription bottle or container with you if you go for treatment.

Special Information

In humans, there is a great deal of variability in the absorption and blood levels of theophylline between individuals. Theophylline levels are frequently monitored after the first week or 10 days of therapy to try to establish the appropriate dose. Most side effects may be minimized by dose adjustments and monitoring. Because of the way theophylline is metabolized, the dose for an animal should be calculated on ideal, or lean, body weight, even if the animal is overweight.

It is very important not to let your animal chew the timed release or slow release capsules or tablets. This may result in a sudden large burst of medication, which may cause serious side effects. Do not change brands of medication without discussing the change with your veterinarian. Different brands may be absorbed differently.

Special Populations

Pregnancy/Lactation
Theophylline crosses the placenta and is excreted in milk. It should only be used when the benefits outweigh the risks.

Puppies/Kittens
Very young animals may have decreased clearance of theophylline, and are more susceptible to toxic side effects.

Senior Animals
Geriatric animals may have decreased clearance of theophylline and are more susceptible to toxic side effects.

Generic Name

Thiacetarsamide (thye-ah-set-AR-suh-mide)

Brand Name
Caparsolate V

Type of Drug
Antiheartworm/anthelmintic.

Prescribed for
Removal of adult heartworms.

General Information
Thiacetarsamide sodium is an arsenic compound used to kill adult heartworms *Dirofilaria immitis* in dogs. Heartworm disease is serious and potentially fatal. Thiacetarsamide is recommended for treatment of dogs with stabilized Class 1 or 2 heartworm disease. Class 1 is mild or asymptomatic disease. Class 2 is moderate disease with anemia, heart enlargement and abnormal lungs on x-ray, exercise intolerance, poor condition, and occasional cough. Class 3 is severe disease with right heart failure, constant fatigue and cough, difficulty breathing, anemia, and signs of lung clots (pulmonary thromboembolism) on x-rays, or many worms with few if any signs of disease. The prognosis for dogs with Class 3 heartworm disease treated with thiacetarsamide is guarded to poor. These dogs should be stabilized prior to treatment, and should proba-

bly be given the graded dose of melarsomine (see *Melarsomine*).

Class 4 heartworm disease (Caval Syndrome) is very severe, with heartworms in the vena cava (veins supplying the heart) and right atrium. Dogs with Class 4 disease should not be treated with thiacetarsamide unless worms are surgically removed from the vena cava before treatment.

Cautions and Warnings

For Owners/Handlers
- Avoid human exposure.
- Wash hands thoroughly after use or wear gloves.
- May cause eye irritation. Flush eyes with copious amounts of water if exposed.
- Consult a physician in case of accidental exposure by any route: ingestion, exposure to skin or eyes, or injection.

For Animals
- Thiacetarsamide is FDA approved for use in dogs only.
- It should not be used in dogs with Class 4 heartworm disease, unless heartworms are surgically removed from the vena cava and right atrium.
- All dogs with heartworm disease are at risk for pulmonary thromboembolism, as dead and dying worms pass from the right heart and pulmonary arteries into the lungs. Death of worms may cause fever, weakness, and cough.
- Dogs with severe damage to pulmonary arteries from heartworm disease may have difficulty breathing, coughing up blood, right heart failure, and death after treatment with thiacetarsamide.
- Dogs should be monitored carefully during treatment and restricted from exercise.
- Class 3 dogs should be hospitalized during and after treatment with severe exercise restriction. They should probably be given a graded dose of melarsomine instead of thiacetarsamide to improve chances of survival. Expect 10% to 20% of Class 3 dogs to die even after the safer melarsomine treatment.
- Severe injection site reactions are likely if even tiny amounts of thiacetarsamide leak outside of the vein.
- Thiacetarsamide may cause severe liver damage even at recommended doses. Treatment should be discontinued if there is bilirubin in the urine after the second or third injection.

■ Thiacetarsamide should be avoided or used with extreme caution in dogs with any significant impairment of kidney, liver, heart, or lung function.

■ Dogs should be kept quiet and confined for 4 to 6 weeks after treatment.

■ Heartworm preventives should not be given for 1 month after treatment.

■ Recommended treatment with thiacetarsamide kills all adult heartworms less than half the time. Follow-up heartworm antigen testing at 4 months is advised to determine if treatment was completely successful.

■ Contact your veterinarian if you think your dog may be having an adverse reaction to thiacetarsamide.

■ U.S. federal law restricts the use of this drug by or on the lawful written or oral order of a licensed veterinarian within the context of a valid veterinarian-client-patient relationship.

Possible Side Effects

▼ Common: severe inflammation at the injection site with pain, swelling, and sloughing of skin if the drug leaks outside of the vein during or after the injection; coughing, gagging, depression, lethargy, decreased appetite, fever, lung congestion, low platelet counts, vomiting, and in 20% of dogs, liver damage.

▼ Rare: severe liver damage, severe pulmonary thromboembolism, and death.

Drug Interactions

• Corticosteroids have a protective effect on adult heartworms and should not be given at the same time as thiacetarsamide.

Food Interactions

None known.

Usual Dose

Dogs: 1.1 mg/lb by injection into a vein twice a day 6–8 hours apart, on 2 successive days.
Drug Form: injectable.

Overdosage

Thiacetarsamide has a low margin of safety. A single dose of three times the recommended amount may cause lung damage and death. Prolonged overdose causes kidney damage. Tremors, lethargy, restlessness, unsteady gait, panting, difficulty breathing, severe drooling, and vomiting may progress to collapse, coma, and death. In case of accidental ingestion or overdose, contact your veterinarian or the National Animal Poison Control Center. ALWAYS bring the prescription bottle or container with you if you go for treatment.

Special Information

There are only two treatments for removal of adult heartworms: thiacetarsamide and melarsomine. Thiacetarsemide is the older of the two arsenic compounds used. It is more difficult to administer than melarsomine because it must be given intravenously, and it causes severe local reactions if even the tiniest amount goes outside of the vein. It is not as effective as melarsomine and kills all worms less than half the time. It may cause severe liver damage at the recommended dose. It cannot be given as a graded dose to dogs with severe heartworm disease, as melarsomine can. Because of these factors, melarsomine is usually the preferred treatment.

Dogs with Class 4 heartworm disease should have worms surgically removed from the vena cava and right atrium before treatment. Treatment with melarsomine is probably safer, because a graded dose can be given. The prognosis for these dogs is guarded to poor.

Special Populations

Cats

Cats with heartworms may be treated with thiacetarsamide, but they are more likely to have fatal reactions and it is usually not recommended. The life span of heartworms is shorter in cats and there are usually fewer worms, so cats are often treated with corticosteroids to alleviate symptoms, as the disease is allowed to run its course.

Pregnancy/Lactation

The safety of thiacetarsamide has not been established in

pregnant or lactating dogs, and it should not be used in this group unless the benefits outweigh the risks.

Senior Animals

Older dogs are more likely to have problems with thiacetarsamide. Thiacetarsamide should be avoided or used with extreme caution in dogs with diabetes mellitus; gastrointestinal, kidney, or liver disease; or Cushing's disease. Light heartworm infections (few worms) may cause few if any symptoms. In some older animals the risks of treatment may outweigh the benefits. In older dogs with mild infections it may be best to treat with milbemycin or ivermectin to kill microfilaria and prevent reinfection, and allow the adult worms to eventually die on their own.

Type of Drug

Thiazide Diuretics

(THYE-uh-zide dye-ue-RET-iks)

Most Common Brand Names

Generic Ingredient: Hydrochlorothiazide [G]
HydroDIURIL [H]   Oretic [H]

Generic Ingredient: Chlorothiazide [G]
Diuril [H] [V]

Prescribed for

Congestive heart failure, nephrogenic and central diabetes insipidus, systemic high blood pressure (hypertension), and to prevent the recurrence of calcium oxalate urinary stones.

General Information

Chlorothiazide and hydrochlorothiazide are two of the thiazide diuretics. Thiazides are older drugs that have been largely replaced in veterinary medicine by other medications such as furosemide, enalapril, and others.

Diuretics are the foundation of therapy for congestive heart failure. In heart failure the kidney retains fluid to compensate for the failing heart. This attempt to compensate goes too far and ultimately causes too much fluid to be retained. Diuretics reverse this process by promoting sodium and water loss through the kidneys. Thiazides are useful in mild to moderate, but not severe, congestive heart failure or severe pulmonary edema. Furosemide is a more potent diuretic and is the drug of choice for these conditions. Hydrochlorothiazide may be useful combined with furosemide to treat refractory right-sided congestive heart failure in cats.

Thiazides may be helpful in the management of both central and nephrogenic diabetes insipidus (see *Desmopressin*).

Essential hypertension is a relatively rare disorder in dogs and cats. Hypertension is common in dogs and cats with kidney failure. The mechanism by which the thiazides reduce blood pressure is not known, but hydrochlorothiazide may be useful in treatment of this disorder. Other adjunct treatments might include low salt diet, and atenolol, prazosin, or enalapril for those resistant to diuretic and dietary therapy.

Chlorothiazide has very unpredictable effects on calcium excretion in the dog kidney and therefore is no longer recommended for prevention of calcium oxalate stones. Hydrochlorothiazide is effective at lowering calcium excretion and may be worth using to prevent calcium oxalate stone recurrence in some dogs, along with other preventive measures such as low dietary calcium.

Cautions and Warnings

■ Chlorothiazide is FDA approved for use in dogs, but not cats. There is no veterinary product currently on the market except one for use in cattle. Hydrochlorothiazide is not FDA approved for use in dogs or cats. Both medications are occasionally used in both species, and are considered accepted practice.

■ Chronic use of thiazides can cause dehydration, low blood potassium, and high blood calcium, so patients should be monitored carefully.

■ Thiazides should not be used in patients with significant kidney or liver disease, preexisting electrolyte abnormalities, dehydration, lupus, diabetes, increased urine uric acid, or urate urinary stones.

■ Contact your veterinarian if you think your dog or cat may be having an adverse reaction to thiazides.

■ U.S. federal law restricts the use of these drugs by or on the lawful written or oral order of a licensed veterinarian within the context of a valid veterinarian-client-patient relationship.

Possible Side Effects

▼ Common: low blood potassium, dehydration, and high blood calcium.

▼ Rare: in people, allergy, vomiting, diarrhea, blood toxicity, high blood sugar, and low blood pressure.

Drug Interactions

• There is a greater risk of low blood potassium when thiazides are given with corticosteroids or amphotericin B.

• There is a greater risk of high blood calcium when thiazides are given with vitamin D or calcium.

• Thiazides may alter the requirement for insulin in diabetics.

• The dose of thiazide may need to be reduced in animals given sulfonamides.

• Digitalis toxicity is more likely in animals with low blood potassium from thiazides.

• Quinidine and neuromuscular blocking agents may be altered by the use of thiazides.

Food Interactions

None known.

Usual Dose

Dogs and Cats
   Chlorothiazide: 5–20 mg/lb orally twice a day.
   Hydrochlorothiazide: 1 mg/lb twice a day, to prevent recurrence of calcium oxalate stones in dogs; 5–10 mg/cat once or twice a day for refractory right-sided heart failure in cats (with furosemide); 1–2 mg/lb for hypertension.

Drug Form
   Chlorothiazide: 250- and 500-mg tablets, 50 mg/ml oral suspension, and powder for reconstitution injection.
   Hydrochlorothiazide: 25-, 50- and 100-mg tablets.

Overdosage

Overdose may cause electrolyte imbalances and dehydration,

lethargy, coma, seizures, and gastrointestinal distress. In case of accidental ingestion or overdose, contact your veterinarian or the National Animal Poison Control Center. ALWAYS bring the prescription bottle or container with you if you go for treatment.

Special Populations

Pregnancy/Lactation
Thiazides should be avoided in pregnant and lactating animals.

Puppies/Kittens
Thiazides should be avoided in puppies and kittens.

Senior Animals
Thiazides should be safe to use in older animals as long as kidney and liver function are not severely impaired (see "Cautions and Warnings").

Generic Name

Thyroxine

Most Common Brand Names

Levotabs V	Thyro-Form V
Levothroid H	Thyro-L V
Levoxine H	Thyrosyn V
NutriVed T-4 Chewables V	Thyro-Tabs V
Soloxine V	Thyroxin-L Tablets V
Synthroid H	Thyrozine V

Type of Drug

Synthetic thyroid hormone.

Prescribed for

Hypothyroidism.

General Information

Thyroxine, also known as levothyroxine sodium (L-thyroxin), is manufactured thyroid hormone. Hypothyroidism is a common disease of middle-aged to older dogs in which the thyroid gland stops making thyroid hormone. About 90% of hypothyroid dogs have decreased function of the thyroid gland because of thyroid gland damage of unknown cause. Less than 10% of hypothyroid dogs have secondary hypothyroidism, or a lack of thyroid stimulating hormone (TSH) from the pituitary gland (base of the brain). Thyroxine provides thyroid replacement therapy for all forms of inadequate production of thyroid hormone. Signs of hypothyroidism include lethargy, lack of endurance, increased sleeping, slow heart rate, preference for warmth, weight gain, thickened skin, and dry, coarse, sparse haircoat. Hypothyroidism is extremely rare in cats, except as a result of methimazole overtreatment of hyperthyroidism.

Cautions and Warnings

■ Thyroxine should be used with caution in dogs with significant heart disease or high blood pressure or other complications in which a sharply increased metabolic rate may be hazardous.

■ Contact your veterinarian if you think your dog or cat may be having an adverse reaction to thyroxine.

■ U.S. federal law restricts the use of this drug by or on the lawful written or oral order of a licensed veterinarian within the context of a valid veterinarian-client-patient relationship.

Possible Side Effects

When given at an appropriate dose to dogs requiring thyroid replacement or supplement, there should be no side effects (see "Overdosage").

Drug Interactions

• Thyroxine increases the effects of epinephrine, norepinephrine, and warfarin.

• Thyroxine may decrease the effects of digoxin.

• Thyroxine may increase insulin requirements in diabetic patients.

• Estrogens may increase the requirement for thyroxine.

• Ketamine may cause increased heart rate and high blood pressure in animals on thyroxine.

Food Interactions

None known.

Usual Dose

Dogs: starting dose—0.1 mg/10 lb body weight. Maintenance dose is then adjusted according to your dog's response by checking T4 blood levels every 2–4 weeks.

Drug Form: 0.1-, 0.2-, 0.3-, 0.4-, 0.5-, 0.6-, 0.7- and 0.8-mg tablets and chewables.

Overdosage

Chronic overdoses will cause hyperthyroidism or thyrotoxicosis (excess thyroid hormone). Signs include increased water intake and urination, increased appetite, heat intolerance, hyperactivity, or personality change. To avoid overdosing, have T4 blood levels checked routinely (see "Special Information"). Acute massive overdose is a medical emergency requiring immediate veterinary intensive care. In case of accidental ingestion or overdose, contact your veterinarian or the National Animal Poison Control Center. ALWAYS bring the prescription bottle or container with you if you go for treatment.

Special Information

There are differences in potency between brands of thyroxine, so it is recommended that you stay with one brand if possible. Changing brands may require retesting and adjusting the dose. Dogs on thyroxine should have their T4 rechecked every 6 months after the maintenance dose has been established. The amount of thyroxine needed may change over time, and rechecks are necessary to avoid over- or underdosing.

Special Populations

Giant/Larger Breeds
Hypothyroidism usually occurs in middle-aged to older dogs, but it may occur in younger dogs of the larger breeds.

Pregnancy/Lactation
It is probably safe to use thyroxine during pregnancy and lactation, but there have been no safety studies to confirm this.

Puppies/Kittens
Hypothyroidism is not a disease of puppies or kittens; safety in this group is unknown.

Senior Animals
Thyroxine is safe to use in older animals, but it should be started cautiously in those with heart disease, high blood pressure, or other complications where a sudden increase in metabolic rate may be harmful.

Generic Name

Timolol (TIM-oe-lol)

Most Common Brand Names

Timoptic [H]   Timoptic–XE [H]

Timoptic Ocudose [H]

Type of Drug

Beta-adrenergic blocker and eyedrop.

Prescribed for

Glaucoma.

General Information

Timolol maleate is a beta-adrenergic blocking drug. It interferes with the action of a specific part of the nervous system. In the eye, it reduces the production of intraocular fluid and decreases intraocular pressure. Intraocular fluid fills the globe of the eye and maintains the normal shape and pressure. In glaucoma, the amount of fluid and pressure increases. This damages the delicate structures of the eye causing redness, clouding of the cornea, pain, and eventually blindness. The pupil is characteristically dilated and the globe enlarged in chronic cases. Timolol is used along with other systemic and topical eye medications in both the affected eye and the unaffected one to prevent glaucoma from developing.

Cautions and Warnings

■ Do not use timolol or use with caution in animals with asthma, other allergic respiratory disease, or congestive heart failure.

■ Contact your veterinarian if you think your dog or cat may be having an adverse reaction to timolol.

■ Timolol is not FDA approved for use in dogs or cats but its use is considered accepted practice.

■ U.S. federal law restricts the use of this drug by or on the lawful written or oral order of a licensed veterinarian within the context of a valid veterinarian-client-patient relationship.

Possible Side Effects

Side effects are rare in dogs and cats because timolol is
only used as an eye drop in very small amounts.

Drug Interactions

• A small amount of timolol is absorbed into the body after
using timolol eye drops, but the quantity is so low that drug
interactions are very unlikely. If you are administering other eye
medicines, separate them by at least five minutes so they have
time to work and do not mix.

Food Interactions

None known.

Usual Dose

Dogs and Cats: one drop twice a day of the 0.5% solution.
The 0.25% solution is not effective in dogs and cats. Wait at
least 5 minutes between applications of eye medications.

Drug Form: 0.25% (not recommended) and 0.5% solution.

Storage: Protect from light and freezing. Keep in protective
overwrap and use within 1 month of opening.

Overdosage

Overdosage of eye drops is extremely unlikely. Signs of oral
overdose include changes in heartbeat, difficulty breathing,
blue or gray colored gums, and seizures. In case of accidental
ingestion or overdose, contact your veterinarian or the National
Animal Poison Control Center. ALWAYS bring the prescription
bottle or container with you if you go for treatment.

Special Information

Glaucoma is a common cause of blindness in dogs. It also
occurs in cats, but is less common. Acute glaucoma is considered a medical emergency. Rapid, effective treatment is
required to save vision and control pain. It is treated using a
number of different types of drugs and each must be administered based on the individual animal's response. Even in the
best of circumstances, medical treatment is complicated and
frequently not successful at preserving vision or controlling the

pain. Surgery is the best option in most cases both to preserve vision if possible and deal with the pain. For more information on glaucoma in dogs and cats, call your veterinarian or a veterinary ophthalmologist.

Special Populations

Pregnancy/Lactation
Eye drops should be safe to use in pregnant and lactating animals because the amount absorbed is very small.

Puppies/Kittens
No studies were found, but eye drops should be safe in puppies and kittens because only very small amounts are absorbed.

Senior Animals
Timolol is considered safe to use in senior dogs and cats.

Brand Name

Tresaderm (TREZ-uh-derm) Ⓥ

Generic Ingredients

Dexamethasone + Neomycin Sulfate + Thiabendazole

Type of Drug

Topical corticosteroid, antibiotic, antifungal, mitacide combination.

Prescribed for

Superficial bacterial or fungal infections, ear mites, and/or itching of ears and skin.

General Information

Tresaderm is effective in a variety of conditions because it is a combination of dexamethasone (see *Corticosteroids, Topical*) to control inflammation and itching, neomycin (see *Aminoglycoside Antibiotics* and *NeoSporin*) as a powerful topical antibiotic, and thiabendazole to kill ear mites (*Otodectes cynotis*) and control fungal infections. Thiabendazole is classified as a benzimidazole (see *Fenbendazole*). This group of drugs is widely used to treat intestinal parasites. Thiabendazole is also effective against mites and many ear and skin fungal infections.

Tresaderm is an excellent first-line drug for minor skin infections, ear infections, and/or ear mites. If the condition being treated is not cured within the recommended treatment period, further diagnostic testing may be indicated to determine the exact cause of the problem.

Topical preparations may be difficult to use effectively on large areas of skin because the haircoat prevents easy application without first shaving the area and the solution may make the haircoat feel sticky. Another drawback is that dogs and cats lick themselves and will ingest most or all of topically applied products. Although rare, side effects after accidental ingestion are possible.

Tresaderm works best if the ears or skin are cleaned first to remove excessive exudate (pus and other debris). Exudate prevents the drug from contacting the lining of the ear canal or skin and prevents it from working. Thickened skin or ear canal lining caused by long-standing irritation also reduces the effectiveness of Tresaderm.

Cautions and Warnings

■ Contact your veterinarian if you think your dog or cat may be having an adverse reaction to Tresaderm.

■ FDA approved for use in dogs and cats.

■ U.S. federal law restricts the use of this drug by or on the lawful written or oral order of a licensed veterinarian within the context of a valid veterinarian-client-patient relationship.

Possible Side Effects

▼ Common: burning or pain for a short time after application to irritated skin or ears.

▼ Rare: allergic reaction to neomycin.

Drug Interactions

None known.

Usual Dose

Dogs and Cats: ears—5–15 drops twice a day for 7–10

days. Skin—surface should be well moistened using 2–4 drops/square inch twice a day. For ear mites, repeat treatment in 7–10 days.

Drug Form: Solution contains per ml—4-mg thiabendazole, 1-mg dexamethasone, and 3.2 mg neomycin.

Storage: Refrigerate at 36–46°F.

Overdosage

Overdosage is generally due to treatment of large areas of irritated skin for prolonged periods. The most common signs are due to corticosteroids and include increased thirst, increased urination, increased appetite, and weight gain (see *Corticosteroids*). Diarrhea, deafness, and/or kidney damage are not likely, but possible due to the neomycin. In case of accidental ingestion or overdose, contact your veterinarian or the National Animal Poison Control Center. ALWAYS bring the prescription bottle or container with you if you go for treatment.

Special Populations

Pregnancy/Lactation
Tresaderm is generally considered safe to use during pregnancy and lactation. Care should be taken to avoid long-term use or application to the mammary glands and surrounding area.

Puppies/Kittens
Tresaderm is generally considered safe to use in puppies and kittens. The smallest quantity possible should be used to avoid side effects.

Senior Animals
Tresaderm is generally considered safe to use in senior animals.

Brand Names

Tribrissen (trye-BRIS-en) Ⓥ

Generic Ingredients

Trimethoprim + Sulfadiazine

Other Brand Names
Di-Trim Ⓥ

The information in this profile also applies to the following drugs:

Generic Ingredients: Trimethoprim + Sulfamethoxazole G

Bactrim H   Septra H
Cotrim H   Sulfatrim H

Type of Drug

Antibiotic combination.

Prescribed for

Susceptible bacterial infections, and coccidial infection.

General Information

Trimethoprim and sulfadiazine or sulfamethoxazole (trimethoprim-sulfa) are antibiotics that are manufactured as combination drugs because they are more effective when used together. Trimethoprim is similar to ormetoprim (see *Primor*), and both combinations have similar abilities to kill bacteria. These combination drugs are called potentiated sulfas. They are effective against most strains of staphylococci, streptococci, many gram-negative bacteria (such as *E. coli* and *Salmonella*, but not *Pseudomonas*), and some protozoa such as *Pneumocystis carinii, Coccidia,* and *Toxoplasma.* See *Sulfadimethoxine* for more information. Tribrissen is recommended for treatment of pyoderma (bacterial skin infections) and urinary tract infections. It may also be useful for a variety of other soft-tissue infections.

Cautions and Warnings

■ Tribrissen and Di-Trim are FDA approved for use in dogs only. However, they are used in cats and it is considered accepted practice.

■ Sulfonamides may cause keratoconjunctivitis sicca (dry eye, or KCS) in dogs. KCS may be irreversible, especially if the dog has been treated long-term or is older. Schirmer tear tests should be performed weekly or monthly to monitor tear production if the dog is being treated with sulfonamides long-term.

■ The sulfonamides cause sulfa crystals to form in the urine, so make sure that the animal drinks a lot of water during treatment.

■ The sulfa drugs should be avoided or used with caution in animals with liver or kidney disease.

■ Do not use these medications in dogs with blood or bone marrow disorders.

■ The sulfa drugs may cause decreased thyroid function with long-term use (see "Special Information").

■ Tribrissen is not recommended for treatment longer than 14 days. If treatment does last longer, routine complete blood counts are recommended.

■ Contact your veterinarian if you think your dog or cat may be having an adverse reaction to Tribrissen.

■ U.S. federal law restricts the use of these drugs by or on the lawful written or oral order of a licensed veterinarian within the context of a valid veterinarian-client-patient relationship.

Possible Side Effects

▼ Common: sulfa crystals in the urine (not a problem in well-hydrated animals) and decreased thyroid function (with long-term use).

▼ Rare: KCS; bone marrow depression; allergic reactions (skin rashes and facial swelling); focal retinitis (damage to the back of the eye); fever; nonseptic polyarthritis (joint inflammation); hemolytic anemia; diarrhea; and neurologic side effects such as behavior changes, unsteady gait, seizures, aggression, and hyperexcitability.

Drug Interactions

• Sulfa drugs may enhance the effects of methotrexate, warfarin, phenylbutazone, thiazide diuretics, salicylates, probenecid, and phenytoin.

• Antacids may decrease the effectiveness of sulfa drugs, and should be given 2–3 hours before or after the dose of trimethoprim-sulfa.

Food Interactions

None known.

Usual Dose

Dogs and Cats: 8–15 mg/lb orally or by injection under the skin or in a muscle once or twice a day.

Drug Form: Tribrissen and Di-Trim—30-, 120-, 480-, and 960-mg tablets and 24% solution for injection. Bactrim and Septra—480- and 960-mg tablets; 240 mg/ml oral suspension; and 96 mg/ml injectable.

Overdosage

These drugs have a wide margin of safety in dogs. Doses of 10 times the recommended dose produced no signs of overdose in dogs. Doses 100 times the recommended dose for 20 days caused slight changes in blood values. In case of accidental ingestion or overdose, contact your veterinarian or the National Animal Poison Control Center. ALWAYS bring the prescription bottle or container with you if you go for treatment.

Special Information

Decreased thyroid function is a common side effect of long-term use. After 6 weeks of treatment, 16 of 20 dogs had markedly decreased thyroid function. Thyroid function may remain decreased for 3 months or longer after the drug is stopped. Dogs treated for 4 weeks had no apparent change in thyroid function.

Special Populations

Pregnancy/Lactation

Tribrissen was studied in a small group of pregnant dogs and was apparently safe at recommended doses. Sulfa drugs may cause damage to the fetus in high doses, so these medications should be avoided in pregnant or lactating animals unless the benefits outweigh the risks.

Puppies/Kittens

There are no safety studies in puppies or kittens. Trimethoprim-sulfa medications are not recommended in children less than age 2 months. They should be safe to use in puppies and kittens that are well hydrated but should probably be avoided unless the benefits outweigh the risks.

Senior Animals

Trimethoprim-sulfa medications should be safe to use in older animals, but should be avoided or used with caution in those with liver or kidney disease (see "Cautions and Warnings").

Generic Name

Tylosin (TYE-loe-sin) [G]

Brand Name

Tylan [V]
The generic is available in injectable form only.

Type of Drug

Antibiotic.

Prescribed for

Clostridium perfringens enterotoxicosis in dogs, chronic colitis, canine genital mycoplasma infections, and other susceptible bacterial infections.

General Information

Tylosin is a macrolide antibiotic similar to erythromycin. It has been recommended for years in the treatment of chronic diarrhea in dogs and cats. Tylosin causes minimal bacterial antibiotic resistance, does not alter the normal bacterial populations in the gastrointestinal tract, and has no systemic side effects or toxicity.

Clostridium perfringens is a bacterium that can be a normal inhabitant of the gastrointestinal tract and may cause no disease. However, when it forms spores, it produces a toxin (enterotoxin) that damages the intestines and causes diarrhea. *C. perfringens* enterotoxin causes one of the most common forms of food poisoning in people. Animals with *C. perfringens* enterotoxemia usually respond to treatment with amoxicillin, ampicillin, or metronidazole within 3 to 4 days, and do not have a recurrence after a 7-day course of treatment. Animals with chronic intermittent diarrhea are more difficult to treat. Some *C. perfringens* strains are resistant to the penicillins and to metronidazole, but so far none have been resistant to tylosin. Animals with chronic intermittent disease generally require long-term treatment, and some may require lifelong treatment. Some of these animals may do better on high-fiber diets. It is important to make sure there is no other disease present, besides the *C. perfringens* enterotoxemia.

Tylosin is the antibiotic of choice for *Mycoplasma* infections

of the genital tract of male and female dogs, as it is the only
antibiotic to which all mycoplasmas tested have been susceptible. These infections may cause decreased fertility.

Cautions and Warnings

◼ Tylosin should be avoided in animals allergic to erythromycin or other macrolide antibiotics.

◼ Contact your veterinarian if you think your dog or cat may
be having an adverse reaction to tylosin.

◼ U.S. federal law restricts the use of this drug by or on the
lawful written or oral order of a licensed veterinarian within the
context of a valid veterinarian-client-patient relationship.

Possible Side Effects

▼ Rare: allergic reactions, mild decreased appetite and
diarrhea, and pain and swelling at muscle injection sites.

Drug Interactions

• Drug interactions with tylosin are not well documented.
They may be similar to interactions of erythromycin (see *Erythromycin*).

• Tylosin may cause increased digoxin blood levels and
increase the risk of digoxin toxicity.

Food Interactions

None known.

Usual Dose

Dogs: for colitis—10–20 mg/lb orally, mixed with food, twice
a day; or 2.5–12 mg/lb 2–4 times a day orally or by injection
into a muscle (IM) or vein (IV).

Cats: for colitis—2.5–5 mg/lb orally, mixed with food, twice a
day; or 2.5–7 mg/lb 2–4 times a day orally or by IM or IV injection.

Drug Form: Tylan soluble (tylosin tartrate) for chickens and
turkeys, each teaspoon containing 2.27-g tylosin; ¹⁄₁₆ tsp in
dogs under 25 lbs, ⅛ tsp in dogs under 50 lbs, and ¼ tsp in
dogs over 50 lbs are the recommended doses of this form. This
is the only available oral form at present. Contact your veterinarian for advice on how to dilute Tylan soluble to make a

proper dose for cats. Also available as a generic 50 and 200 mg/ml injectable.

Overdosage

Signs of oral overdose of tylosin are very unlikely. Tylosin caused no signs of adverse side effects in dogs given 200 times the recommended dose, or when given 100 times the recommended dose for 2 years. In case of accidental ingestion or overdose, contact your veterinarian or the National Animal Poison Control Center. ALWAYS bring the prescription bottle or container with you if you go for treatment.

Special Information

Tylosin powder has a bitter taste, and if it is not well tolerated when mixed with food, it may be mixed with a palatable vitamin-mineral paste or some other food that your pet will eat readily, like liverwurst, peanut butter, or cream cheese.

Special Populations

Pregnancy/Lactation
There are no safety studies of tylosin in pregnant or lactating dogs or cats. Tylosin is excreted in the milk. It is probably safe to use but may be best to avoid unless the benefits outweigh the risks.

Puppies/Kittens
There are no safety studies of tylosin in puppies or kittens. It is probably safe to use but may be best to avoid unless the benefits outweigh the risks.

Senior Animals
Tylosin is safe to use in senior animals.

Type of Drug

Vitamin A

Most Common Brand Names*

Generic Ingredient: Acitretin
Soriatane

Generic Ingredient: Etretinate
Tegison

Generic Ingredient: Isotretinoin
Accutane

Generic Ingredient: Tretinoin
Avita Cream [H]   Retin-A [H]
Renova Cream [H]

Generic Ingredient: Vitamin A
Retinol

There are many brand names of oral and injectable vitamins. See Calorie-Vitamin-Mineral Supplements for a list of some of the dietary supplements available for animals.

Prescribed for

Supplementation of the diet when animals are not eating adequately, antioxidant or other support during illness, vitamin deficiency, cancer prevention and treatment, and a variety of skin disorders.

General Information

Good quality commercial dog and cat foods are carefully formulated to be complete feeds. They contain all of the vitamins, minerals, energy, and protein required for your dog or cat. Dogs and cats do have different nutritional requirements. It is not good for dogs to eat cat food, or for cats to eat dog food on a regular basis, or as a significant part of their diet.

In certain conditions or diseases, dietary supplements may be an important and even critical part of therapy. Many diseases may cause a decrease in appetite at just the time when an animal is most in need of nutritional support and even extra vitamins. Consult your veterinarian for advice on the best vitamin supplement for your dog or cat.

Vitamin A is a fat-soluble vitamin that is either absorbed from the diet or made from its precursor, beta-carotene. Vitamin A is required for normal growth, vision, reproduction, skin and epithelial function, and immune function. It is also an important antioxidant and possible cancer preventive.

Of all the vitamins, vitamin A is the one most likely to cause problems from oversupplementation. Overdoses cause problems with the other fat-soluble vitamins, D, E, and K, which leads to problems with bone, blood clotting, and antioxidant functions. Chronic overdoses cause bone malformations, fractures, reduced growth (dwarfism), weight loss, skin diseases, anemia, and abnormal gastrointestinal tract function (diarrhea, etc.).

The synthetic retinoid drugs are derivatives of vitamin A. They are less toxic than vitamin A and are more effective therapy for a variety of diseases. It is not known exactly how the retinoids work, but they do seem to be anti-inflammatory, as well as able to correct some underlying skin disorders. The retinoids have been used in veterinary medicine for the last 15 years to treat a variety of skin diseases. These include keratinization disorders (primary seborrhea) in dogs, sebaceous adenitis, hair follicle dysplasia, skin damage caused by the sun (actinic keratosis, squamous cell carcinoma), mycosis fungoides/skin lymphoma, benign skin tumors (multiple sebaceous adenomas), epidermal cysts, and acanthomas. The synthetic retinoids have been used less in cats than dogs, but they may be useful for precancerous skin damage caused by the sun, and for treatment of inoperable solar-induced squamous cell carcinoma. They are also used to treat skin lymphoma and feline acne that does not respond to conventional treatment. Consult your veterinarian or veterinary dermatologist for the latest information on the use of retinoids in dogs and cats.

Cautions and Warnings

For Owners/Handlers

■ Synthetic retinoids, especially etretinate, are serious teratogens (cause abnormal development of sperm, eggs, and fetus) and should not be used by people unless under the direction of a physician. They should NOT be handled by pregnant women.

For Animals

■ Synthetic retinoids, especially etretinate, are serious teratogens and should not be used in unspayed females or breeding males.

■ Retinoids should be used with caution in those animals with a history of pancreatitis, liver disease, or diabetes mellitus. Monthly blood chemistry tests are advised.

■ Dogs on retinoid therapy should be monitored carefully for decreased tear production (see "Possible Side Effects").

■ Contact your veterinarian if you think your dog or cat may be having an adverse reaction to vitamin A or the synthetic retinoids.

■ U.S. federal law restricts the use of these drugs by or on the lawful written or oral order of a licensed veterinarian within the context of a valid veterinarian-client-patient relationship.

Possible Side Effects

▼ Rare: in dogs, decreased appetite, vomiting, diarrhea, increased thirst, itching, conjunctivitis, keratoconjunctivitis sicca (dry eye, or KCS), inflammation and cracking of the lips, stiffness, and hyperactivity. The most common side effect in cats is decreased appetite with resulting weight loss. Increased liver enzymes, blood triglycerides, and cholesterol have also been seen in dogs and cats; these blood abnormalities were mild and not associated with any adverse effects.

Drug Interactions

• Synthetic retinoids should not be given with each other, with vitamin A, or with other drugs that may cause liver damage, such as anabolic steroids (stanozolol), erythromycin, cancer drugs, estrogens, griseofulvin, ketoconazole, fluconazole, or sulfonamides.

• Use of tetracyclines with retinoids may cause damage to the brain.

Food Interactions

Retinoids should be given with a fatty meal.

Usual Dose

Dogs
 Etretinate: 0.5–1 mg/lb orally once a day.
 Isotretinoin: 0.5–1 mg/lb orally twice a day. After 1 month decrease to once a day, then every other day.

Cats
 Isotretinoin and Etretinate: 10 mg/cat orally once a day.

Tretinoin: 0.025% applied to the affected area every 24–48 hours; topical therapy for feline acne should be used *very* sparingly, or it will produce severe skin irritation. Follow the advice of your veterinarian or veterinary dermatologist.

Drug Form
  Acitretin: 10- and 25-mg capsules.
  Etretinate: 10- and 25-mg capsules.
  Isotretinoin: 10-, 20- and 40-mg capsules.
  Tretinoin: 0.025%, 0.05%, and 0.1% cream; 0.01% and 0.025% gel; and 0.05% liquid.

Overdosage

In case of accidental ingestion or overdose, contact your veterinarian or the National Animal Poison Control Center. See "General Information" and "Possible Side Effects" for signs of overdose. ALWAYS bring the prescription bottle or container with you if you go for treatment.

Special Information

The incidence of side effects in dogs and cats with synthetic retinoids is less than in people. Most animals show no side effects. Side effects are due to the vitamin A activity of retinoids and are similar to those seen with vitamin A overdose (see "General Information"). Etretinate causes fewer side effects and is the retinoid recommended for diseases requiring long-term therapy. Long-term adverse effects are not known yet in people or animals as they have not been in use long enough.

Side effects resolve when the dose is lowered or discontinued. Dogs should be monitored carefully for signs of KCS with monthly Schirmer tear tests to check for early decreased tear production. Dogs with retinoid-induced KCS respond to cyclosporine or stopping the retinoid therapy.

Special Populations

Breeding Animals
Do not use retinoids in unspayed females or breeding males (see "Cautions and Warnings").

Pregnancy/Lactation
Do not use retinoids in pregnant or lactating dogs or cats.

Puppies/Kittens

Do not use retinoids in puppies or kittens. Do not give vitamin A supplements to puppies or kittens unless under the advice of your veterinarian. As little as 4 times the recommended amount of vitamin A may cause toxicity and severe adverse reactions (see "General Information").

Senior Animals

Any healthy senior dog or cat may be treated with retinoids with little likelihood of side effects. Careful monitoring is recommended (see "Cautions and Warnings" and "Possible Side Effects").

Type of Drug

Vitamin B Complex

Generic Ingredients

Vitamin B_1 (thiamine) + Vitamin B_2 (riboflavin) + Vitamin B_3 (niacin/niacinamide) + Vitamin B_6 (pyridoxine) + Pantothenic acid/panthenol + Biotin + Folic Acid + Vitamin B_{12} (cyanocobalamin)

Brand Names

There are many brand names of oral and injectable vitamins. See Calorie-Vitamin-Mineral Supplements for a list of some of the dietary supplements available for animals.

Prescribed for

Supplementation of the diet when animals are not eating adequately, antioxidant or other support during illness, vitamin deficiencies, specific disease therapy.

General Information

The B complex vitamins are a group of water-soluble vitamins that are required for cell functions throughout the body. They cannot be stored by the body and are required daily. Stress and illness may greatly increase the requirements for B vitamins. B vitamins may be an important part of supportive treatment for animals that are ill, and your veterinarian may give B complex vitamins by injection to those patients that are unable or unwilling to eat. They may help stimulate appetite and greatly enhance the ability to fight off infections, heal, or recover from illness. Animals in kidney failure, cats especially, are at risk for deficiencies of B vitamins. This deficiency may partly cause the decreased appetite of kidney failure patients. The daily B vitamin requirement of normal cats is estimated to be 6 to 8 times greater than that of dogs. Use B vitamin supplements instead of multivitamins, to avoid overdosing with the fat-soluble vitamins. Individual B vitamins may be used in certain conditions. Niacin may be used with tetracycline to treat certain immune-mediated skin and nail problems (see *Tetracycline Antibiotics*). Riboflavin may be prescribed as part of therapy for a rare inherited disorder of dogs called lipid storage myopathy.

All of the B vitamins are relatively nontoxic even at high doses and excess amounts are excreted by the kidneys. High doses of niacin may cause vasodilation, itching, heat sensations, vomiting, headaches, and skin lesions in people. In dogs, 2 g/day for 2 days caused bloody feces, convulsions, and death. The upper safe limit of nicotinamide is 175 mg/lb/day, which may be as much as 1,000 times the nutritional requirement. For more information about vitamins, see *Calorie-Vitamin-Mineral Supplements.*

Cautions and Warnings

■ Avoid massive vitamin overdoses, especially niacin and pyridoxine.

■ Use B complex supplements when trying to treat B vitamin deficiencies. Multivitamins may cause overdose of fat-soluble vitamins.

■ Do not give vitamin supplements without the advice of your veterinarian.

■ Contact your veterinarian if you think your dog or cat may be having an adverse reaction to B vitamins.

■ Use of these drugs should be by or on the lawful written or oral order of a licensed veterinarian within the context of a valid veterinarian-client-patient relationship.

Possible Side Effects

▼ Rare: allergic reactions to injectable vitamins.

Drug Interactions

- Large doses of thiamine may decrease the effectiveness of amprolium.
- Folic acid supplements may be needed during long-term sulfasalazine treatment.

Food Interactions

Vitamin supplements are best given with food.

Usual Dose

Dogs: Thiamine—10–100 mg/day orally. Riboflavin—10–20 mg/day orally. Vitamin B_{12}—100–200 mcg/day orally.

Cats: Thiamine—5–30 mg/day orally (maximum dose 50 mg/day). Riboflavin—5–10 mg/day orally. Vitamin B_{12}—50–100 mcg/day orally.

Drug Form: tablets, paste, chewables, liquids, and injectables. Consult your veterinarian for advice on the best form of B vitamins for your pet.

Overdosage

Overdoses of B vitamins are unlikely to cause symptoms, except for massive doses of niacin (see "General Information") or vitamin B_6 (pyridoxine). Very high B_6 doses in dogs cause nervous system damage similar to B_6 deficiency. In case of accidental ingestion or overdose, contact your veterinarian or the National Animal Poison Control Center. ALWAYS bring the prescription bottle or container with you if you go for treatment.

Special Populations

Pregnancy/Lactation

Vitamin needs increase during pregnancy and lactation, but supplementation should not be necessary for animals on good quality commercial diets. B vitamins are unlikely to be harmful, but overdoses of minerals and fat-soluble vitamins may cause serious problems (see *Calorie-Vitamin-Mineral Supplements* and *Vitamin A*).

Puppies/Kittens

Puppies and kittens on good quality commercial milk replacer or puppy/kitten chow should not need vitamin B supplements. Vitamin B supplements may be given to sick animals but only under the direction of your veterinarian.

Senior Animals

B vitamins should be safe to use in older animals and may be especially helpful in those that are sick or have chronic illnesses, such as kidney failure.

Generic Name

Vitamin C (Ascorbic Acid)

Brand Names

There are many brand names of oral and injectable vitamins. See *Calorie-Vitamin-Mineral Supplements* for a list of some of the dietary supplements available for animals.

Type of Drug

Vitamin.

Prescribed for

Supplementation of the diet when animals are not eating adequately, antioxidant or other support during illness, vitamin deficiencies.

General Information

Unlike people and guinea pigs who cannot make vitamin C, dogs and cats are able to synthesize the vitamin and do not rely on diet as a source. Vitamin C is an antioxidant that may be needed in greater amounts during stress or illness. Aside from nonspecific supplementation of severely ill animals, there is little if any indication for its use in dogs or cats. It has been used in the past as a urine acidifier (see *Ammonium Chloride* and *Methionine*) but is not recommended. It is not very effective and may increase the risk of oxalate, urate, or cystine stone formation in susceptible animals. Some dog breeders advocate the use of vitamin C. There is no evidence that it is helpful, and it may even worsen the bone diseases of young, rapidly growing dogs. For more information about vitamins, see *Calorie-Vitamin-Mineral Supplements*.

Cautions and Warnings

■ Contact your veterinarian if you think your dog or cat may be having an adverse reaction to ascorbic acid.

■ Use of this drug should be by or on the lawful written or oral order of a licensed veterinarian within the context of a valid veterinarian-client-patient relationship.

Possible Side Effects

▼ Common: large doses of vitamin C may cause diarrhea and urinary stone formation in susceptible animals.

Drug Interactions

• Vitamin C may increase the excretion of quinidine and make it less effective.

• Large doses of vitamin C will reduce the effectiveness of the aminoglycosides and erythromycin if used for urinary tract infections.

Food Interactions

None known.

Usual Dose

Dogs and Cats: 100–500 mg/day.

Drug Form: A variety of tablets and oral solutions are available over-the-counter for use in people.

Overdosage

See "Possible Side Effects" for signs of overdose. In case of accidental ingestion or overdose, contact your veterinarian or the National Animal Poison Control Center. ALWAYS bring the prescription bottle or container with you if you go for treatment.

Special Populations

Pregnancy/Lactation

Vitamin C is probably safe to use in pregnancy and lactation, but it is not recommended, especially in large doses.

Puppies/Kittens

Vitamin C should be avoided in puppies and kittens.

Senior Animals

Vitamin C is probably safe to use in senior animals and may be helpful in illness or chronic disease, but it should not be used in high doses (see "Possible Side Effects").

Generic Name

Vitamin D/Calcitriol

Most Common Brand Name*

Rocaltrol [H]

*There are many brand names of oral and injectable vitamins. See Calorie-Vitamin-Mineral Supplements for a list of some of the dietary supplements available for animals. Rocaltrol is a brand name of calcitriol.

Type of Drug

Vitamin.

Prescribed for

Supplementation of the diet when animals are not eating adequately, antioxidant or other support during illness, vitamin deficiencies, hypocalcemia following thyroid surgery, and chronic kidney failure.

General Information

Vitamin D is a fat soluble vitamin that is made in the skin with exposure to sunlight and is also absorbed from the diet. Vitamin D is involved in calcium and phosphate regulation and is needed for normal bone growth, absorption of calcium and phosphate from the gastrointestinal tract, and excretion by the kidneys. It is also involved in immune regulation and blood formation. Vitamin D deficiency causes abnormal bone development (rickets), primarily in those with abnormal calcium and phosphate intake and lack of exposure to sunlight.

There are many forms of vitamin D. Calcitriol (Rocaltrol) is the form of vitamin D that is most active and easy to regulate when vitamin D is used as a treatment. Calcitriol is used with oral calcium supplements to treat low blood calcium that may occur following thyroid surgery, or as a result of chronic kidney failure. These treatments are experimental and require a significant commitment on the part of owners to monitor blood tests of calcium and parathyroid hormone (PTH) during treatment, as well as follow many other management and treatment recommendations. Not all animals with chronic kidney failure need calcitriol treatment, and not all those that are treated respond.

Following vitamin A, vitamin D is the next most likely to cause toxic effects when oversupplemented. Too much vitamin D interferes with calcium and phosphate metabolism, and causes harm indirectly by interfering with the other fat-soluble vitamins A, E, and K. Signs of excess vitamin D include loss of mineral from bone, excess mineral in soft tissues, high blood calcium, high blood pressure, increased drinking and urination, lethargy, vomiting, abnormal heart rhythms, and neurologic signs. For more information about vitamins, see *Calorie-Vitamin-Mineral Supplements*.

Cautions and Warnings

■ Use vitamin D supplements only on the recommendation of your veterinarian.

■ Do not give vitamin D to animals with high blood phosphate.

■ Frequent measurements of blood calcium and PTH are required during calcitriol treatment of chronic kidney failure.

■ Contact your veterinarian if you think your dog or cat may be having an adverse reaction to vitamin D.

■ Use of this vitamin should be by or on the lawful written or oral order of a licensed veterinarian within the context of a valid veterinarian-client-patient relationship.

■ U.S. federal law restricts the use of calcitriol by or on the lawful written or oral order of a licensed veterinarian within the context of a valid veterinarian-client-patient relationship.

Possible Side Effects

▼ Common: high blood calcium and phosphate.

Drug Interactions

• Vitamin D should not be given at the same time as phosphate binders containing calcium (see *Antacids/Phosphate Binders*).

• Calcitriol should not be given with any other forms of vitamin D.

Food Interactions

None known for vitamin supplements. Calcitriol should be given several hours before a meal.

Usual Dose

Calcitriol

 Dogs and Cats: 0.0012–0.005 mcg/lb/day (1.2–5 ng/lb) orally once a day. Adjust the dose as needed based on blood calcium and PTH measurements.

 Drug Form:—0.25- and 0.5-mcg capsules (calcitriol). Vitamin supplements containing vitamin D are available as tablets, paste, chewables, liquid, and injectables (see *Calorie-Vitamin-Mineral Supplements*). Consult your veterinarian for the best form of vitamin D to give your dog or cat.

Overdosage

Toxic doses are only about 10 times the recommended dose when given chronically. See "General Information" for signs of overdose. In case of accidental ingestion or overdose, contact your veterinarian or the National Animal Poison Control Center. ALWAYS bring the prescription bottle or container with you if you go for treatment.

Special Populations

Pregnancy/Lactation

Vitamin D supplements should not be necessary for dogs and cats on good quality commercial diets. Supplement pregnant or lactating animals only on the recommendation of your veterinarian.

Puppies/Kittens

Vitamin D supplements should not be necessary for puppies and kittens on good quality commercial diets. Supplement young animals only on the recommendation of your veterinarian.

Senior Animals

Vitamin D supplements should not be necessary in older animals on good quality commercial diets, unless as treatment for chronic kidney failure or other disorders of low blood calcium.

Generic Name

Vitamin E/Alpha-Tocopherol

(AL-fuh toe-KOF-ur-ole)

Brand Names

Vitamin E is available over-the-counter, and in a variety of multivitamin and fatty acid supplements for dogs and cats (see *Fatty Acids* and *Calorie-Vitamin-Mineral Supplements*).

Type of Drug

Vitamin and antioxidant.

Prescribed for

Supplementation of the diet when animals are not eating adequately, antioxidant or other support during illness, vitamin deficiency, and treatment of discoid lupus (autoimmune skin disease).

General Information

Vitamin E is a fat-soluble vitamin that functions in the body as an antioxidant. It is required for maintenance of cell membrane structure, prostaglandin synthesis, blood coagulation, reproduction, and immune function. For more information about vitamins, see *Calorie-Vitamin-Mineral Supplements*.

Vitamin E is recommended for dogs with exocrine pancreatic insufficiency (see *Pancreatic Enzymes*). These dogs are likely to have deficiencies of all the fat soluble vitamins, and severe deficiencies of vitamin E and vitamin B_{12}. High doses should be given initially to correct the deficiency. Vitamin E should be given orally, 500 units, once a day for the first month.

Vitamin E is also part of the treatment for one of the autoimmune diseases called discoid lupus erythematosus. Vitamin E is given orally along with corticosteroids. It may take 1 to 2 months for the effect of vitamin E to be apparent. It is continued for the life of the patient along with topical corticosteroids and sunscreens for the affected skin on the top of the nose.

Cautions and Warnings

■ Contact your veterinarian if you think your dog or cat may be having an adverse reaction to vitamin E.

■ Use of this drug should be by or on the lawful written or oral order of a licensed veterinarian within the context of a valid veterinarian-client-patient relationship.

Possible Side Effects

None known.

Drug Interactions

- Mineral oil may prevent the absorption of vitamin E.
- Vitamin E may enhance the absorption of vitamin A.
- Large doses of vitamin E may delay the response to iron therapy in iron-deficiency anemia.

Food Interactions

Give vitamin E 2 hours before or after meals.

Usual Dose

Dogs: for discoid lupus—400–600 units twice a day. For dietary supplementation or antioxidant therapy—100–500 units once a day.

Cats: 100–400 units orally once a day.

Drug Form: Vitamin E capsules are available over-the-counter.

Overdosage

Vitamin E is relatively nontoxic compared to vitamins A and D. Upper safe limits are approximately 100 times the nutritional requirement. Very high doses cause defects in clotting, probably because of interference with vitamin K. In case of accidental ingestion or overdose, contact your veterinarian or the National Animal Poison Control Center. ALWAYS bring the prescription bottle or container with you if you go for treatment.

Special Populations

Pregnancy/Lactation

Vitamin E supplementation should not be necessary for dogs and cats on good quality commercial diets. Supplement pregnant or lactating animals only on the recommendation of your veterinarian.

Puppies/Kittens

Vitamin E supplementation should not be necessary for puppies and kittens on good quality commercial diets. Supplement young animals only on the recommendation of your veterinarian.

Senior Animals

Vitamin E supplements should not be necessary in older animals on good quality commercial diets, unless as treatment for exocrine pancreatic insufficiency or discoid lupus. Vitamin E may be helpful in preventing cancer and delaying aging because of its antioxidant properties.

Generic Name

Vitamin K₁ G

Brand Names

AquaMEPHYTON H   Mephyton H

Type of Drug

Vitamin and antidote for warfarin poisoning or overdose.

Prescribed for

Poisoning with warfarin/anticoagulant rodenticides and warfarin/oral anticoagulant overdose.

General Information

Vitamin K₁ (phytonadione) is required for the synthesis of 4 of the 12 clotting factors in the clotting pathway, and 2 of the clotting proteins (C and S). Warfarin interferes with the function of vitamin K₁ and makes the animal essentially vitamin K deficient. When warfarin is ingested, clotting factors decrease in the blood over a few days and clotting is inhibited. This is how warfarin works when it is used as an anticoagulant and also as rat or mouse poison. Overdoses or poisonings with warfarin cause uncontrolled bleeding.

Poisoning with anticoagulant rat or mouse poison is very common in dogs and occasionally happens in cats. The anticoagulant rat and mouse poisons are all derivatives of warfarin. Warfarin is short-acting and seldom used as rat or mouse poison. The newer rat and mouse poisons, such as brodifacoum and diphacinone, are 40 to 200 times as toxic as warfarin, and last for weeks instead of hours to days. Dogs and cats who eat rat or mouse poison commonly have rapid or labored breathing, decreased appetite, lethargy, and signs of bleeding, such as black or bloody stool, nose bleeds, blood in the urine, and bleeding from vein puncture sites. Bleeding into the lungs, around the lungs, and into the abdomen are common. Animals may die from rat or mouse poison without any signs of external bleeding. The diagnosis of anticoagulant rat or mouse poisoning is based on symptoms, a history of exposure or possible exposure, and abnormal blood clotting tests—prolonged prothrombin time (PT) and partial thromboplastin time (PTT). Vitamin K$_1$ is the specific antidote for anticoagulant rat or mouse poison. The dose and duration of treatment depend on the type of anticoagulant rat or mouse poison ingested (see "Usual Dose"). Always bring the poison container with you if possible when you go for treatment.

It may take 6 to12 hours after the start of vitamin K$_1$ treatment for new clotting factors to be made. Whole blood transfusions or fresh frozen plasma may be needed during this time to replace clotting factors and prevent fatal bleeding.

Vitamin K$_1$ is also the treatment for warfarin overdose when it is used as an anticoagulant (see *Warfarin*).

Cautions and Warnings

■ Injections of vitamin K$_1$ into a vein or into the muscle should be avoided (see "Possible Side Effects"). Very fine needles should be used for injections under the skin to avoid bleeding.

■ Vitamin K$_3$ is not effective for treatment of anticoagulant rodenticide poisoning.

■ It may take 6 to 12 hours after the start of vitamin K$_1$ treatment for clotting factors to increase.

■ Contact your veterinarian if you think your dog or cat may be having an adverse reaction to vitamin K$_1$.

■ U.S. federal law restricts the use of this drug by or on the lawful written or oral order of a licensed veterinarian within the context of a valid veterinarian-client-patient relationship.

Possible Side Effects

Allergic or anaphylactic reactions may occur when vitamin K$_1$ is given by injection into a vein. Injections into a muscle may cause bleeding during the early stages of treatment and should be avoided.

Drug Interactions

- Phenylbutazone, aspirin, chloramphenicol, sulfonamides (trimethoprim-sulfa), diazoxide, allopurinol, cimetidine, metronidazole, anabolic steroids (stanozolol), erythromycin, ketoconazole, propranolol, and thyroxin may all enhance the effects of anticoagulants and inhibit the effects of vitamin K$_1$.
- Mineral oil may reduce the oral absorption of vitamin K$_1$.

Food Interactions

Always give with food, preferably a fatty meal.

Usual Dose

Dogs and Cats: For warfarin, fumarin, pindone, and valone overdose or poisoning—0.5 mg/lb orally once a day for 4–6 days. For diphacinone, chlorophacinone, and brodifacoum poisoning—1.2–2.5 mg/lb orally once a day for 2–4 weeks. PT and PTT should be checked 2–5 days after vitamin K$_1$ is discontinued. If the results are abnormal, vitamin K$_1$ should be restarted.

Vitamin K$_1$ may be given by injection under the skin if the animal is vomiting.

Drug Form: 25-mg veterinary generic vitamin K$_1$ capsules and veterinary generic injectable 25 mg/ml. Mephyton—5-mg tablets. AquaMEPHYTON—2 and 10 mg/ml injectable.

Storage: Protect from light.

Overdosage

There is no specific information available on vitamin K$_1$ overdoses. Vitamin K$_1$ is relatively nontoxic and single oral overdoses should not be a problem. The lethal dose in mice is 5 times the recommended dose in dogs and cats. In case of accidental ingestion or overdose, contact your veterinarian or the National Animal Poison Control Center. ALWAYS bring the prescription bottle or container with you if you go for treatment.

Special Information

Vitamin K₁ is best absorbed after it is given orally; therefore, injections are no longer recommended for initial vitamin K₁ therapy. Injections are only recommended if the animal is vomiting or there is some other reason that oral medication will not be absorbed. Injection under the skin is the only recommended injection route.

Some anticoagulant mouse and rat poisons remain in the liver for weeks after recovery. Animals re-exposed within weeks to months of initial recovery may be sensitive to much smaller amounts of poison.

The veterinary vitamin K₁ products are far less expensive than the human products.

Special Populations

Pregnancy/Lactation

Pregnant bitches with anticoagulant poisoning should be treated with vitamin K₁ until whelping and then the puppies should be started on vitamin K₁ immediately and treated for at least 1 week. Lactating bitches that have been poisoned should have their puppies removed and treated with vitamin K₁ for 2 to 3 weeks. Another alternative is to leave the puppies with the mother, treat the mother and the puppies with vitamin K₁ and stop treatment in the puppies 1 week after treatment is stopped in the mother.

Puppies/Kittens

Puppies and kittens are more sensitive to the effects of anticoagulant rat and mouse poison, and should be treated with vitamin K₁ and monitored carefully (see "Pregnancy/Lactation"). Vitamin K₁ is safe to use in puppies and kittens at the recommended dose.

Senior Animals

Vitamin K₁ is safe to use in older animals at the recommended dose.

Generic Name

Warfarin (WOR-far-in) Ⓖ

Most Common Brand Name

Coumadin Ⓗ

Type of Drug

Anticoagulant.

Prescribed for

Diseases and conditions where there is excessive clotting or
increased risk of clotting, such as thromboembolism secondary
to cardiomyopathy in cats, pulmonary thromboembolism,
chronic kidney failure, and antithrombin III deficiency.

General Information

Warfarin decreases the blood's ability to clot by interfering with
the actions of vitamin K. Vitamin K is required for the synthesis
of 4 of the 12 clotting factors in the clotting pathway, and 2 of
the clotting proteins (C and S). When warfarin is ingested,
these clotting factors decrease in the blood over a few days
and clotting is inhibited. This is how warfarin works when it is
used as an anticoagulant and also as rat/mouse poison (see
Vitamin K₁). Overdoses or poisonings cause uncontrolled
bleeding.

Chronic kidney failure with severe protein loss in the urine
may cause deficiency of one of the clotting proteins called
antithrombin III. This puts the animal at risk for clotting and
especially pulmonary thromboembolism (clotting of the lungs).
Other conditions such as pancreatitis, burns, and heart disease
may also put animals at risk for clotting (see "Special Information"). Anticoagulants may be needed in all of these conditions.

Warfarin may be used to treat or prevent clotting in a number
of diseases where excessive clotting has already occurred and
is likely to spread, or where there is an increased risk of clotting. Heparin is usually used to treat patients initially (see
Heparin). Oral warfarin may then be used for longer-term anticoagulation. Warfarin is the treatment of choice for antithrombin III deficiency. Heparin is not effective, as it requires the
presence of antithrombin III to work.

Cautions and Warnings

■ Warfarin should not be used in patients with preexisting bleeding tendencies or diseases such as hemophilia (von Willebrand's disease) or in those with active bleeding from the gastrointestinal, respiratory, genital, or urinary tracts.

■ Warfarin should not be used in animals undergoing surgery.

■ Warfarin should not be used in animals with acute kidney disease, bleeding in the brain (stroke), uncontrolled high blood pressure, liver disease, or cancer in the abdomen or chest.

■ Monitor prothrombin time (PT), a clotting function test, frequently to determine effectiveness of anticoagulant therapy and avoid overdosing. Improper dose regulation may cause bleeding (see "Possible Side Effects")

■ Do not use warfarin in animals with low platelet counts.

■ Contact your veterinarian if you think your dog or cat may be having an adverse reaction to warfarin.

■ U.S. federal law restricts the use of this drug by or on the lawful written or oral order of a licensed veterinarian within the context of a valid veterinarian-client-patient relationship.

Possible Side Effects

Bleeding from any part of the body may occur with overzealous use of anticoagulants or with a change in the animal's own clotting functions during warfarin therapy. Nosebleeds, bruising, bloody vomit, black or bloody stool, bleeding into a joint, or into the abdomen, chest, or brain are all possible. This bleeding may cause anemia, low platelet counts, and death.

Drug Interactions

• Warfarin should be used with caution when other anticoagulants such as aspirin, heparin, dipyridamole, or phenylbutazone are given. Increased monitoring is recommended.

• All of the following drugs may increase the anticoagulant effects of warfarin: allopurinol, anabolic steroids (Winstrol/stanozolol), chloramphenicol, cimetidine, omeprazole, erythromycin, trimethoprim-sulfa drugs, danazol, NSAIDs, metronidazole, miconazole, fluconazole, ketoconazole, tetracycline, thyroxine, oral neomycin, and quinidine.

• Barbiturates (phenobarbital), corticosteroids, griseofulvin, estrogens, rifampin, spironolactone, sucralfate, and vitamin K decrease the anticoagulant effect of warfarin.

Food Interactions

None known.

Usual Dose

Dogs: starting dose—0.05–0.1 mg/lb orally once a day. Maintenance dose—0.025–0.05 mg/lb orally once a day or as indicated by response to therapy. Start measuring PT 3–4 days after the start of therapy, and adjust the dose based on the results of the PT. Heparin may be stopped once the appropriate warfarin dose is achieved. Anticoagulant therapy may be continued for several months and PT should be measured once a month after the initial dose adjustments.

Cats: starting dose for thromboembolism—0.5 mg/cat orally once a day. A daily blood sample to determine PT measurements are recommended for about a week, then weekly or monthly as the target dose is found. Heparin is given 50 units/lb by injection under the skin 3 times a day for the first 3–4 days of warfarin treatment. Maintenance dose is based on the results of the PT tests.

Drug Form: 1-, 2-, 2.5-, 3-, 4-, 5-, 6-, 7.5-, and 10-mg tablets and 2 mg/ml injectable.

Overdosage

Overdose of anticoagulants may cause bleeding into the urine, body cavities, or gastrointestinal tract, from the gums, or respiratory tract, or excessive bruising/bleeding at sites of trauma. In case of accidental overdose, contact your veterinarian or the National Animal Poison Control Center. ALWAYS bring the prescription bottle or container with you if you go for treatment.

Special Information

Some experts believe that aspirin is ineffective in preventing recurrent thromboembolism in cats with heart disease. They strongly recommend the use of warfarin in these cats. The disadvantages of warfarin include the dangers of inadvertent overdosing and risks of bleeding, as well as the expense of monitoring PT during therapy.

Pulmonary thromboembolism is a serious, potentially life-threatening, and underdiagnosed problem in animals, as it is in people. It may occur as a result of heartworm disease (see *Melarsomine* and *Thiacetarsamide*), hypothyroidism, pancreatitis, kidney disease, DIC, antithrombin III deficiency, hyperadrenocorticism/Cushing's disease, and immune-mediated hemolytic anemia (AIHA). The most common sign is sudden onset of rapid or difficult breathing. Some experts recommend heparin for all cases of AHIA, and severe cases of pancreatitis. Clinical studies are needed to determine which animals will benefit from anticoagulant therapy.

Special Populations

Pregnancy/Lactation
Warfarin causes damage to the fetus and should not be used during pregnancy. If warfarin is necessary during lactation, puppies or kittens should be removed from the mother and hand-raised.

Puppies/Kittens
Warfarin should not be used in puppies or kittens. Their small size usually makes monitoring of clotting function difficult or impossible.

Senior Animals
Warfarin should be safe to use in older animals with proper monitoring. It should be used with extreme caution or avoided in older animals with liver disease or those on other medications (see "Cautions and Warnings" and "Drug Interactions").

Resources for Pet Owners

- American Holistic Veterinary Medical Association (AHVMA)
  2214 Old Emmorton Road
  Bel Air, MD 21015
  Phone: 410-569-0795
  Fax: 410-569-2346

- American Veterinary Chiropractic Association (AVCA)
  623 Main
  Hillsdale, IL 61257
  Phone: 309-658-2920
  Fax: 309-658-2622

- American Veterinary Medical Association (AVMA)
  1931 North Meacham Road
  Suite 100
  Schaumberg, IL 60173
  Phone: 847-925-8070
  Fax: 847-925-1329
  (See Internet listing on next page)

- Dr Louis J. Camuti Memorial Feline Consultation and
  Diagnostic Service
  Sponsored by the Cornell Feline Health Center, a source of
  information on feline diseases and management
  phone: 800-KITTY-DR (800-548-8937)

- International Veterinary Acupuncture Society (IVAS)
  P.O. Box 1478
  Longmont, CO 80502-1478
  Phone: 303-682-1167
  Fax: 303-682-1168
  Email: ivasoffice@aol.com
  (For a directory of certified veterinarians)

- Internet sites
  The best source for veterinary and health care information is
  on the Internet. Through the Internet you can access the
  AVMA, NetVet, and the Electronic Zoo, among other sites.
  These sites have links to hundreds of other sites. Some use-
  ful site addresses are as follows:

AltVetMed (Complementary and Alternative Veterinary
   Medicine): http://www.altvetmed.com

AVMA: http://www.avma.org/default.htm

Electronic Zoo: http://www.avma.org/netvet/e-zoo.htm

NetVet: http://www.avma.org/netvet/vet.htm

- National Animal Poison Control Center
  (University of Illinois College of Veterinary Medicine)
  Phone: 900-680-0000 ($20 for the first 5 minutes, $2.95 for
  each additional minute; calls average 10 minutes)
  or
  phone: 800-548-2423 ($30/case, credit cards only)

- Pet Loss Support Hotlines (grief counseling)
  A list of phone numbers is available through the AVMA web-
  site at http://www.avma.org/care4pets/losshotl.htm

- The Veterinary Institute for Therapeutic Alternatives (VITA)
  15 Sunset Terrace
  Sherman, CT 06784
  phone: 860-354-2287

Index of Generic and Brand-Name Drugs

The entries listed in boldface refer to brand-name products.